THE BEST RECIPE

GRILLING & BARBECUE

THE BEST RECIPE

Grilling & Barbecue

BY THE EDITORS OF

COOK'S ILLUSTRATED

ILLUSTRATIONS BY JOHN BURGOYNE

PHOTOGRAPHY BY CARL TREMBLAY

BOSTON COMMON PRESS

BROOKLINE, MASSACHUSETTS

Boston Common Press
17 Station Street
Brookline, Massachusetts 02445

ISBN 0-936184-51-5
Library of Congress Cataloging-in-Publication Data
The Editors of *Cook's Illustrated*
The Best Recipe: Grilling & Barbecue—We lit more than 5,000 fires to find the absolute best way to grill
favorite foods. Here are 400 exhaustively tested recipes plus no-nonsense kitchen tests and tastings.
1st edition

ISBN 0-936184-51-5 (hardback): $29.95
I. Cooking. I. Title
2001

Manufactured in the United States of America

Distributed by Boston Common Press, 17 Station Street, Brookline, MA 02445.

Designed by Amy Klee
Edited by Jack Bishop

CONTENTS

PREFACE

THERE ARE PLENTY OF TOP-NOTCH GRILLING and barbecue books on the market these days, and they sell not only because many of them are good cookbooks, but because outdoor cooking suits our needs. Grilling is fast, cleanup is easy, and the process adds lots of flavor. So the first question we had to address before beginning this project was, "Can *Cook's Illustrated* offer a useful, unique book on grilling and barbecue?"

We quickly decided that this sort of cooking lends itself admirably to our methodical, almost plodding, method of developing recipes. Expensive pieces of meat or fish can be incinerated in just seconds. Delicate foods, especially seafood, often stick to the grill grates. Most people would also agree that many recipes published in magazines and cookbooks are maddeningly vague. Just because grilling feels casual doesn't mean that recipes on grilling must be written with an easygoing, often imprecise style. Sure, outdoor cooking is fun, but there is a science to it. If you know the secrets of great pulled pork, it will be just as good as the barbecue you remember from your favorite barbecue shack in North Carolina. If you just throw a pork butt on the grill, odds are that you will end up with a hunk of tough, dry meat.

So we set out to learn what makes great grilled foods and barbecue, paying attention to detail and having an appetite for the rules and techniques that separate the great from the mediocre. We tested gas grills, starters, wood chips, types of charcoal—even fish baskets—and we tasted barbecue sauces and different cuts of steaks and chops. We have an opinion about 90 percent lean hamburger versus 80 percent, we tested every possible method for building fires, and we investigated short ribs, baby back ribs, country ribs, and flanken-style ribs to find out what they were and how to cook them.

Of course, we lit thousands of fires and spent thousands of hours testing and developing methods and recipes. The point was not to write an academic tome on the subject but to do the testing so you won't have to. We tried a dozen different methods of cooking pork ribs so that you can simply follow the recipe and know that it is going to work. The next time you want to grill corn, you can use our recipe with confidence, knowing that we tried it with the husk on, soaked in water, bare-naked, and partially husked to find the best method. (Silked and partially husked was the winner.)

Is this the only grilling and barbecue book you will ever need? No. But if you want to understand how these particular methods of cooking work and if you want a book full of well-tested recipes, we think you will find your money well spent. With *Grilling & Barbecue* at the ready, you can start up the grill, pop open a beer, and appear the very model of the easygoing barbecue chef. Let us worry about technique—you can sit back and enjoy the food and the company.

Chris Kimball
Editor and Publisher
Cook's Illustrated

ACKNOWLEDGMENTS

ALL OF THE PROJECTS UNDERTAKEN AT *COOK'S Illustrated* are collective efforts, and this book is no exception.

Editor Jack Bishop spearheaded this project. Anne Yamanaka spent a year developing recipes for it. Art director Amy Klee and graphic designer Nina Madjid transformed computer files and digital scans into a book you can hold in your hands. Bridget Lancaster, Kay Rentschler, and Julia Collin organized photography shoots; Carl Tremblay captured the black-and-white images that appear at the beginning of each chapter; and John Burgoyne drew the illustrations. Thanks as well to the following individuals: Barbara Bourassa, Rich Cassidy, Mary Connelly, Barry Estabrook, Daniel Frey, India Koopman, Jessica Lindheimer, Jim McCormack, and Marcia Palmater.

Some of the recipes and techniques in this book are based on work that has been in *Cook's Illustrated* magazine. Thanks to the following authors for their contributions: Pam Anderson, Jack Bishop, Mark Bittman, Lauren Chattman, Maryellen Driscoll, Steve Johnson, Bridget Lancaster, Stephanie Lyness, Adam Ried, Chris Schlesinger, A. Cort Sinnes, John Willoughby, and Anne Yamanaka.

How to Use This Book

MOST COOKS USE THE TERM *GRILLING* TO describe all cooking that takes place outdoors. However, this book recognizes two basic cooking methods possible on a charcoal or gas grill. Within each cooking method, there are several variations in technique, which are discussed in chapters 2 and 14. Each one of these technique chapters is followed by recipe chapters, which illustrate how the cooking technique works.

Grilling refers to cooking foods completely or partially over direct heat. Thin cuts such as steaks, as well as delicate foods like seafood and vegetables, are grilled. Once the food is seared on both sides, it's probably done. This simplest outdoor cooking technique, the kind most cooks are familiar with, is covered in chapters 2 through 13.

A thick pork roast or turkey cannot be grilled—the exterior would be charred and ashen well before the interior of such a large piece of meat could cook through. The solution is indirect cooking. With indirect cooking the lid of the grill is down (not up, as in grilling). This traps heat and creates a regulated cooking environment much like that of an oven. While grilling calls for filling the grill with charcoal or lighting all the gas burners, indirect cooking involves a smaller fire. The lit coals are banked on one side of the grill, or one of the gas burners is turned off. Foods cooked by indirect heat are placed over the "cool" part of the grill. Since there is no direct heat, the food cooks evenly, without flare-ups.

Indirect cooking is generally divided into two categories: *grill-roasting,* in which food is cooked relatively quickly at a fairly high heat, and *barbecuing,* in which food is cooked quite slowly at low temperatures. Grill-roasting and barbecuing are covered in chapters 14 through 18.

Grill-roasting is best for foods that are already tender and don't require prolonged cooking. Birds are especially well suited to grill-roasting (at lower temperatures the skin remains soft and flabby), as are tender cuts of meat (like beef tenderloin) that need to develop a crisp crust during their relatively short cooking time. Grill-roasting occurs between 300 and 400 degrees. (It's hard to sustain higher temperatures with indirect cooking; in comparison, grilling occurs at temperatures in excess of 500 degrees.)

Barbecuing is the traditional low and slow cooking method used with ribs, pulled pork (shredded Boston butt), and brisket. The goal is to impart as much smoke flavor as possible—hence a long cooking time over a fairly low fire. Barbecuing also provides ample time for fatty, tough cuts to give up (or render) their fat and become tender. Although there is much debate among barbecue experts as to the proper cooking temperature, we believe that barbecuing should take place between 250 and 300 degrees. While some chefs and pit masters argue that ribs are best barbecued at 180 degrees, we find it very difficult to maintain such a low fire. Also, such low temperatures increase the risk of food-borne illnesses.

PART I

GEARING UP

1

BUYING GUIDE TO OUTDOOR EQUIPMENT

YOU CAN'T GRILL WITHOUT THE RIGHT gear. When our fathers manned the grill, the equipment choices were fairly limited. Not so today. You can spend thousands of dollars on a grill and buy dozens of tools and gadgets designed for use with outdoor equipment. We have tested hundreds of pieces of grilling equipment over the years. Here are our findings about what works, what doesn't, and what you really need to cook outdoors. Thankfully, the list ends up being pretty short.

There are three areas of equipment to consider—the grill itself, the fuel (propane, charcoal, wood chips, wood chunks), and the gadgets (tongs, baskets, thermometers).

THE GRILL

THE FIRST CHOICE YOU HAVE TO MAKE IS charcoal or gas. We have tested all the recipes in this book on both charcoal and gas grills and made plenty of general observations in the process.

You can't beat a gas grill for convenience. You can grill in poor weather—even in the rain. It's hard to imagine spending the time outdoors to light a charcoal fire during a New England winter, but a 30-second dash through the snow to light a gas grill is not unthinkable. While you need to keep an eye on the gas gauge to make sure you don't run out of fuel, a gas grill is predictable and nearly foolproof. The fire will always light.

In addition to being convenient, a gas grill is consistent. Given constant weather conditions, a grill with both burners set to medium will always be about the same temperature. There's a learning curve with a gas grill. But with some practice, you will realize that a particular corner runs a bit hotter and is ideal for searing steaks, or that the middle area between the burners is the best spot to cook delicate vegetables. These quirks vary from grill to grill, so they are hard to detail. The point is that the experienced griller can depend on a gas grill to deliver the same results day in, day out, for better or for worse.

The one variable here is weather. All grills (gas and charcoal) will be more fickle in windy or cold weather. Fires may die out in extremely windy conditions. Wind and cold will lower the internal temperature of the grill, and food will take longer to cook. Under such adverse conditions, however, a gas grill is far more reliable than a charcoal grill.

Of course, there are some trade-offs you must make for all this convenience and consistency. We have found that even the best gas grills don't brown and sear as well as a charcoal fire. That's because a charcoal fire, built with a lot of charcoal, gets hotter than a gas fire. However, more heat isn't always a good thing. Vegetables cook up just fine on gas because they require only a moderate flame. But if you think steak or meat when you think grilling, charcoal delivers better results. More browning means more flavor, and while gas grills can do a good job with a strip steak or lamb chop, a charcoal grill (when properly used) will put a better crust on these kinds of foods.

Besides searing, charcoal has another distinct advantage over gas—smoke flavor. If you are grilling a couple of zucchini, they don't spend enough time on the grill (whether gas or charcoal) to pick up much flavor. With longer-cooking items, however, charcoal imparts more smoke and wood flavor. A charcoal fire also does a better job of burning wood chunks and chips. Gas adds no flavor on its own, and gas burners don't burn chips especially well. Also, it's nearly impossible to add more wood to a gas grill as the food cooks. For authentic, smoky-tasting ribs or brisket, you must use a charcoal grill.

ADDING MORE COALS TO A LIT CHARCOAL FIRE

We recommend that you buy a charcoal grill with a hinged cooking grate. This feature allows you to lift up the edge of the grate and add more unlit charcoal as needed. If your grill doesn't have this feature, you must transfer foods to a tray, lift up the grate with fireproof gloves, then add coals. A hinged cooking grate allows foods to stay in place as you add coals.

Another consideration is cost. For about $125 you can get a large kettle grill. We find that a good gas grill will cost three times as much.

Finally, we like the challenge and fun of cooking over a live fire. Charcoal is unpredictable, but that's part of its charm. Charcoal grilling is an art, and there's something satisfying about mastering this art.

CHARCOAL GRILLS

THERE ARE TWO MAIN CHOICES FOR CHARCOAL grilling. The rectangular hibachi is cheap but limited in function. The surface area is usually quite small and the charcoal area so shallow that the fire rarely gets superhot. Perhaps the greatest drawback to the hibachi is its lack of a cover. You can grill quick-cooking foods over direct heat, but forget about grill-roasting a whole chicken or barbecuing brisket on a hibachi. (See page xiii for the definitions of grilling, grill-roasting, and barbecuing used in this book.)

For these reasons, it's no surprise that the covered kettle grill is the most popular with home cooks. Weber popularized this design, which has changed little over the past decades. Inside the deep, bowl-shaped grill are two separate racks (or grates)—one for holding the lit charcoal, the other for cooking the food. There's plenty of room between these two racks (at least six inches) so you can build a hot fire with a lot of charcoal.

In some instances, it would be nice if the bottom rack for the charcoal was adjustable so the coals could be moved closer to the food. Simple grilling tasks such as cooking vegetables or toasting bread would then require much less charcoal. But this is a minor quibble.

The bowl-shaped grill is covered with a domed lid, which is tall enough to accommodate a large roast or turkey. Both the grill and lid have adjustable air vents that let you control the rate at which the fuel burns. Open the vents to feed the fire with oxygen. It will burn hotter at first but then die out more quickly. For a slower, more controlled fire, keep the vents partially open. Don't close the vents unless you want to kill the fire.

Some charcoal grill racks have hinged sections that make it much easier to add coals during cooking. If you have a choice, buy a grill with this feature (see illustration on page 4).

We use the Weber kettle grill, which is the most common (and often the only) charcoal option in hardware stores. We recommend that you buy the 22-inch grill, which is large enough to hold a couple of racks of ribs, 8 or 10 steaks, or a dozen or more chicken parts. On smaller grills, the "cool" part of the grill will be too cramped to accommodate a large brisket or two slabs of ribs when barbecuing.

There is one drawback to this grill. Over time, soot and resinous compounds can build up on the inside of the grill cover. For this reason, we don't use the cover when grilling since we find that it often imparts a slightly "off" flavor to the food that can best be described as resembling the odor of stale smoke. We prefer to use a disposable aluminum roasting or pie pan to cover foods that require some buildup of heat to cook them through.

When barbecuing or grill-roasting, however, the lid must be used to trap heat. We find that the smoky flavor the food absorbs from wood chips or chunks, which are used in all recipes that call for indirect cooking, masks any off flavor the lid may impart.

GAS GRILLS

GAS GRILLS NOW ACCOUNT FOR 6 OUT OF 10 grills sold in this country. The reason for their increasing popularity is clear: the fire is easy to light and control. While there are few options when buying a charcoal grill, there are dozens and dozens of gas grills on the market. We tested six from the leading manufacturers and came to the following conclusions.

In general, we found that you get what you pay for. Inexpensive gas grills, priced at $200 or under, are generally inferior. If you are willing to spend more money (about $400), you can buy a gas grill that works extremely well, with results that can compete with the charcoal grill.

Several features and design elements separate a good gas grill from a poor one. A built-in thermometer that registers real numbers (not just low, medium, and hot) is essential. A gauge that tells you how much gas is left in the tank is also a plus. As you might expect, a large grill offers the cook more possibilities. Unless the cooking surface has an area of at least 400 square inches, you will need to cook one slab of ribs at a time. (If the grill comes with a warming rack, you may cook a second slab there.) In addition to size, the number of burners is critical. It's not possible to cook by indirect heat on a grill with only one burner because the burner is usually positioned in the center of the grill and the "cool" parts of the grill are too small to accommodate most foods. Indirect cooking requires a grill with at least two burners. With one burner on and one burner off, at least half of the grill will be cool enough for slow cooking.

The heat should be evenly distributed across the entire surface of the grill. We found that most gas grills are plenty hot. A bigger problem is that gas grills are often unable to sustain temperatures low enough for barbecuing. Many of the cheaper grills we tested were unable to barbecue a brisket without burning the exterior before the meat was tender. A good grill will heat up to 600 degrees and maintain a temperature of 250 degrees when the lid is down and just one burner is lit and turned to low.

Perhaps the most shocking conclusion we came to during our testing of gas grills concerned flare-ups. We found that lava rocks soak up dripping fat and will catch fire as soon as there is some sort of flare-up. Several times we moved flaming chicken parts to the cool side of the grill (without a lit burner), and they still flamed from below for several minutes. It wasn't the chicken that was on fire; it was the lava rocks, which had caught fire even though the burner underneath them was cool.

Lava rocks are not the sole reason for flare-ups. Poor design that traps grease on the bottom of the grill doesn't help either. We consider a drainage system mandatory. The bottom of the cooking chamber should be sloped so that fat runs through an opening in the center and into a drip pan below.

Weber grills do not have lava rocks. Bars, made from steel coated with porcelain-enamel and shaped like an upside-down V, channel fat down into the bottom of the grill and eventually into a drip pan attached to the underside of the cooking chamber. We find this drainage system to be far superior to other options. For all of these reasons, our favorite grills are the Weber Genesis and the Weber Spirit. If you entertain a lot, you will want the bigger and more expensive Weber Genesis, which has three burners. If your needs (or budget) are more modest,

the two-burner Weber Spirit is an excellent choice.

Most gas grills come with two temperature controls, each regulating a separate burner. You can use the dials to change the heat level on the entire grill, turning it from high to medium once food has been seared. The dials can also be manipulated to create two heat levels simultaneously on the cooking surface. For instance, you can set one burner at high for searing and the other at medium for cooking foods through or to subdue the fire on foods that have ignited.

The recipe instructions in this book give the proper heat level, which is determined by the length of time you can hold your hand five inches above the cooking grate (see illustration on page 19). With a gas grill, you need only adjust the dials as necessary to produce the correct temperature.

One final note about gas grills. Unlike charcoal grills, the inside of the cover stays fairly clean. Since there is no buildup of resinous smoke, the grill cover (rather than a disposable aluminum pan) can be used for recipes such as grilled chicken breasts, in which a cover is needed to cook foods through.

EQUIPMENT: Luxury Gas Grills

We admit that the notion of spending thousands of dollars on a gas grill strikes us as odd. We've seen grills that retail for as much as a small car. Can a luxury grill really work all that much better than a regular grill that costs $500?

To see what all the fuss was about, we cooked on a Weber Summit (with a suggested retail price of nearly $3,000) for a couple of months. This huge stainless steel grill comes with four burners, a side burner (where you can simmer a pot of beans or make rice), and tons of storage cabinets and trays. The cooking area, however, is no bigger than that of the Weber Genesis, the company's three-burner grill that we like so much and that costs just $500.

So how did the Summit perform? It heats to a blistering 725 degrees and thus sears steaks beautifully. Four-burner controls making grill-roasting a turkey or barbecuing ribs a breeze since there are so many ways to manipulate the heat.

Is this grill worth $3,000? It doesn't work six times better than the $500 Genesis. But it does look six times better. So if money is no object and design really matters to you, this might be the grill for you.

THE FUEL

YOU'VE GOT A GRILL, SO NOW YOU NEED to light a fire. This section considers the kinds of fuel available for charcoal fires, the best way to light a charcoal fire and a gas fire, and the wood chunks and chips that can be used to flavor foods as they cook.

UNDERSTANDING CHARCOAL

CHARCOAL IS MADE BY BURNING PIECES of wood in a controlled environment without oxygen. The wood burns and smokes so that most of the water and resins evaporate. However, because the wood is charred without oxygen present, it is not completely consumed by fire. The remaining portion of combustible material, what we call charcoal, is much easier to light than just-cut wood. It burns hotter than just-cut wood and is much lighter and thus easier to transport.

Traditional charcoal has come back into vogue in the past decade. Irregularly shaped lumps of charred wood burn hotter and faster than the neat briquettes that became popular in the United States after World War II. Lump hardwood charcoal, also known as charwood, is more expensive that the ubiquitous briquettes but is our preferred product for most direct grilling chores because it puts out so much heat. We also like the fact that this product is 100 percent hardwood and contains no additives. Look for it in hardware stores, although it occasionally shows up in supermarkets.

Square, pillow-shaped briquettes deliver even, moderate heat and are relatively easy to light. However, most brands contain a petroleum-based binder that helps the briquettes to ignite. The problem is that when these binders burn they can give delicate foods like fish or vegetables an off flavor. (For the same reason, we don't use chemical lighter fluids.) If you can find something called natural briquettes, this product is the better option. Like regular briquettes, natural briquettes contain wood scraps and sawdust (not chunks of real wood), but they are made without any petroleum-based binders.

For direct grilling, we prefer lump hardwood charcoal; that is what we have used in our recipe testing. Because it burns hotter and faster than briquettes, lump hardwood charcoal does a better job of

CHARCOAL FUELS

A charcoal fire can be made with the following fuels and flavoring agents (clockwise from the top right): charcoal briquettes, lump hardwood charcoal, wood chips, and hardwood logs. We prefer lump hardwood charcoal for direct grilling because it burns hotter and faster than briquettes. However, for covered grilling, we prefer the slow, even heat of briquettes.

browning foods. It also imparts a bit of smoky flavor to foods as they grill. (You can, of course, use briquettes for direct grilling; see page 8 for details.)

For indirect cooking in a covered grill (grill-roasting or barbecuing), we prefer briquettes because they burn more evenly and slowly. Hardwood charcoal runs very hot and then dies out relatively quickly, two traits that make slow, low cooking more difficult.

While we do prefer natural briquettes to regular briquettes for grill-roasting or barbecuing, for the

MEASURING CHARCOAL

Many recipes call for a particular volume of charcoal, such as four quarts. An easy way to measure it is to use an empty half-gallon carton of milk or juice. Just wash the carton thoroughly and store it with the charcoal. Each full carton equals roughly two quarts.

reasons described above, regular briquettes don't seem to impart an off flavor to slow-cooked foods, as they do in direct grilling. First of all, fish and vegetables, which are most likely to pick up these off flavors, are generally not slow-cooked. However, even when salmon is barbecued, we have noticed that the smoke flavor from slow cooking seems to hide any unwanted flavors that may be imparted by regular briquettes. The wood chips or chunks, which are a part of every slow-cooked grill recipe, overpower and disguise these undesirable flavors.

LIGHTING A CHARCOAL FIRE

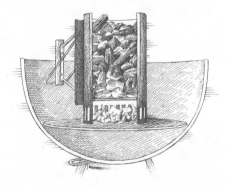

Our favorite way to start a charcoal fire is with a chimney starter, also known as a flue starter. To use this simple device, fill the bottom section with crumpled newspaper, set the starter on the grill grate, and fill the top with charcoal. When you light the newspaper, flames will shoot up through the charcoal, igniting it. When the coals are well-lit and covered with a layer of gray ash, dump them onto the charcoal grate. (If you need more than five quarts of charcoal, add some unlit charcoal. Continue heating until all the coals are gray.)

Some grill aficionados like to add a small hardwood log to a grill fire, which gives foods a delicious flavor. The wood must be seasoned, or aged, however, and most cooks don't have access to seasoned logs. Even if they do, logs can be tricky to light. If you have fire-ready logs, we suggest adding them once the charcoal has been lit. Use only hardwoods, such as hickory, oak, or mesquite. Softwoods, such as pine, can impart an unpleasant resinous flavor.

Wood chunks and chips are bits of hardwood logs that have been cut into more manageable pieces. (For more information, see page 7). Because of their relatively small size and high cost, we consider chunks and chips more as flavoring agents than fuel.

CHIMNEY STARTER

MOST COOKS USE LIGHTER FLUID TO START a charcoal fire. Not only is this method messy and possibly dangerous, but chemical starters can impart an off flavor to grilled foods. In our tests, we found that vegetables, seafood, and chicken are particularly susceptible to picking up harsh, acrid flavors from lighter fluid. Even if your food remains unscathed, who wants a backyard that smells like diesel fumes?

We find that a chimney starter (also called a flue starter) is the best way to light charcoal. (See the illustration at left.) A chimney starter is foolproof, and it eliminates the need for lighter fluid. We strongly recommend that you visit a hardware store (or other shop that sells grilling equipment) and purchase this indispensable device.

Comparing Hardwood Lump Charcoal and Briquettes

Ounce for ounce, hardwood lump charcoal burns much hotter than briquettes. However, because of its regular shape, the differences are less dramatic when the charcoals are measured by volume. (The briquette shape compacts more easily so you can fit more coals into a contained space.) For all practical purposes, a heaping chimney of charcoal briquettes will make a fire that is as hot as a level chimney of hardwood lump charcoal. So if you need to substitute briquettes for hardwood, use slightly more briquettes to achieve the same heat level. The following chart is based on a five-quart chimney. Because of its irregular shape, lump charcoal should be measured by volume or weight, not the number of pieces.

HOW FULL IS THE CHIMNEY?	VOLUME	LUMP CHARCOAL	BRIQUETTES
Half	2½ qts	1¼ lbs	2¾ lbs (45 pieces)
Two-thirds	generous 3 qts	1¾ lbs	3¾ lbs (60 pieces)
Three-quarters	4 qts	2 lbs	4 lbs (65 to 70 pieces)
Full	5 qts	2½ lbs	5½ lbs (90 pieces)

Chimney starters are cylindrical, with an attached heatproof handle. They resemble huge beer mugs. Inside the cylinder, just a few inches up from the bottom, a perforated metal plate separates the large upper chamber from the small lower chamber. To use a chimney starter, place several sheets of crumpled newspaper in the lower chamber and set the starter on the bottom rack of a kettle grill (where the charcoal will eventually go); the top cooking grate should not be in place. Fill the upper chamber with as much charcoal as directed. Light the newspaper through the holes in the side of the chimney starter and wait until the coals at the top of the pile are covered with light gray ash. (This will take about 20 minutes.) Dump the lit charcoal in the bottom of the grill and arrange as directed. (For additional firepower, add more unlit charcoal and wait until it has caught fire before grilling.) You can then set the cooking grate in place, allow it to heat up, and then clean it. After that, you are ready to grill.

Note that once you empty the lit charcoal into the grill, the starter will be very hot. Don't put it down on the lawn—it will burn the grass. Instead, set the starter on a concrete or stone surface away from any flammable objects and allow it to cool off for at least half an hour. Make sure you choose a spot away from children and pets.

Different models of chimney starters show very little variation. Some have wooden handles, some have plastic handles, but all do just about the same thing. One thing to keep in mind when buying a chimney is the charcoal capacity. We like a large chimney (one that holds about 5 quarts of charcoal briquettes and measures 7½ inches across by 12 inches high) because it holds just the right amount for grilling most foods at a medium-hot heat in a large kettle grill. Smaller chimneys necessitate extra heating time for the coals that cannot fit into the chimney.

ELECTRIC STARTER

IF YOU KEEP YOUR GRILL ON A DECK OR patio with a nearby source of electricity, you might consider using an electric starter to ignite charcoal. Most models have an oval heating coil that you nestle in a pile of coals. The starter is plugged in and after about half an hour the coals will be covered with light gray ash.

As with the chimney starter, there is no need to use any lighter fluid, which is why we like this gad-

---

MAKING YOUR OWN CHIMNEY STARTER

Although a chimney starter is relatively inexpensive (about $15 to $20), you may want to save money and improvise with an empty 39-ounce coffee can that has had both ends removed with a can opener. Note that there are two drawbacks to this method. Because the improvised starter has no handles, you must maneuver it with long-handled tongs. Also, because of its size, this improvised starter can't light enough charcoal for most grilling jobs; you will need to add unlit coals once the lit coals have been dumped onto the charcoal grate.

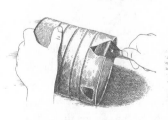

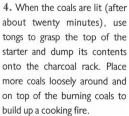

1. Using a church-key can opener, punch six holes along the lower circumference of the can.

2. Set the can on the grill's charcoal rack with the triangular holes at the bottom. Load the can about one-half to two-thirds full with crumpled newspaper, and top it off with charcoal.

3. Insert a long match through one of the triangular holes at the bottom to set the crumpled paper on fire.

4. When the coals are lit (after about twenty minutes), use tongs to grasp the top of the starter and dump its contents onto the charcoal rack. Place more coals loosely around and on top of the burning coals to build up a cooking fire.

LIGHTING A FIRE WITHOUT A STARTER

If you don't have access to a chimney starter and don't have an empty coffee can around, use this method as a last resort.

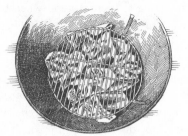

1. Place eight crumpled sheets of newspaper beneath the rack on which the charcoal sits.

2. With the bottom air vents open, pile the charcoal on the rack and light the paper. After about twenty minutes, the coals should be covered with light gray ash and ready for cooking.

get. There is one minor drawback. We find that an electric starter takes longer to heat up coals than a chimney, especially if you are trying to ignite a large pile of coals. However, there's no need to find old newspaper or matches and the wind can never blow out the flames, which can happen on rare occasions with a chimney.

As with the chimney, an electric starter should be removed from the coals when they are covered with light gray ash. It will be glowing red and extremely hot. Set it down on a fireproof surface away from foot traffic.

LIGHTING A GAS GRILL

LIGHTING A GAS GRILL IS REMARKABLY easy. Make sure to read all instructions in your owner's manual thoroughly and to follow directions regarding the order in which the burners must be lit. In most instances, an electric igniter will light the burners. We have found that electric igniters can fail occasionally, though, especially in windy conditions. Most models have a hole for lighting the burners with a match. Read all directions carefully and make sure to wait several minutes (or as directed) between attempts at lighting the grill. This waiting time allows excess gas to dissipate and is an important safety measure.

WOOD CHIPS AND CHUNKS

ONE OF THE BEST REASONS TO BARBECUE or grill-roast is to flavor foods with smoke. (Grilled foods, like steaks or chops, spend so little time on the grill that we don't think there's much point in using wood chips or chunks.) Charcoal itself adds some flavor (gas adds none), but the real smoky flavor of good ribs or brisket comes from wood chunks or chips. Chips will work on either a charcoal or gas grill, but chunks are suited to charcoal fires only, since they must rest in a pile of lit coals to work. (For more details on chips and chunks, see chapter 14.)

THE GADGETS

A GRILL AND SOME SORT OF FUEL ARE essential. Gadgets are accessories—all are nice to have, but it is possible to do without them in a pinch. Here's a list of what we've found to be the most useful gadgets for grilling.

WIRE GRILL BRUSH

A GRILL BRUSH KEEPS THE GRILL CLEAN between uses, removing old food particles and burnt remnants from the cooking grate. The bristles are usually made of thick wire, and the arm of the brush is usually made of plastic or wood. Use the grill brush after the grill has been heated up but before loading it with food. It is also a good idea to scrape the cooking rack clean five minutes after removing the food from the grill (assuming that the fire is still going). Any food left on the grill will easily be swept away.

We recommend grill brushes with strong, stiff wire bristles and wooden handles. Plastic-handled brushes tend to melt and lose their bristles, lasting through only a few cleanings. In our tests, we preferred brushes that had flat metal blades on their ends that allow you to scrape away any stubborn bits of food that cling to the cooking grate.

TONGS

A PAIR OF TONGS IS THE IDEAL TOOL FOR turning foods as they cook. A large fork pierces foods and causes some loss of fluids. A spatula is fine for small, flat foods, especially those prone to sticking, but it is useless with flank steak or chicken parts. A pair of tongs is the most useful and versatile turner of the lot, capable of flipping something as delicate as thin asparagus spears or as heavy as a rack of ribs. There are three basic choices.

Standard barbecue tongs are operated by pushing the arms of the tongs together. The pincers have either rounded or serrated teeth that are designed to grab onto foods. These tongs are similar to ones you might use indoors, except that the handles have wood panels (which keep cool near the fire) and most have rawhide loops for hanging the tongs from the grill. In addition, these tongs are bigger than the tongs you would use in the kitchen.

Multipurpose tongs are designed for grill use. One tong is a spatula, the other a standard tong with a serrated pincer. They are not spring-loaded—you must push the arms together to close them.

Stainless steel locking tongs are spring-loaded. They have scalloped pincers and are usually lightweight. Although not specifically designed for outdoor cooking, many professionals swear by them for grill use.

We tested nine different sets of tongs—a mixture of models designed especially for the grill and others useful indoors or outside. We grilled asparagus spears to see how the tongs handled thin, delicate foods; chicken drumsticks to see how they handled slippery, oddly shaped foods; and three-pound racks of ribs to see how they performed with oversized, heavy items.

The standard tongs varied greatly in blade type but not in performance. They tended to be either exceedingly stiff and hard to squeeze or so weak as to bend from the weight of heavy foods. Either way, we needed two hands to turn the ribs. They also did a better job with asparagus and chicken, although models with serrated teeth sometimes bruised and nicked the tender flesh of the asparagus and a couple of times the serrated teeth caught on the chicken skin, separating and tearing it from the meat.

The multipurpose tongs were useful in some regards but not perfect. While the angled spatula end was helpful in performing many tasks, the opposing pincer tong was so small in comparison that it felt quite unsteady and unreliable. Moreover, the handles were awkward and stiff. It was easy to slide or push meat around the grill, but turning the meat was no easy task. Similarly, the fact that these were not spring-loaded meant that the mouth opened only so wide; when trying to grip anything wider, it tore the skin or was simply impossible.

The stainless steel locking tongs outperformed the other models in all regards. We found that

CHECKING GAS LEVEL IN A TANK

There's nothing worse than running out of fuel halfway through grilling. If your grill doesn't have a gas gauge, use this technique to estimate how much gas is left in the tank.

1. Bring a cup or so of water to a boil in a small saucepan or glass measuring cup (if using the microwave). Pour the water over the side of the tank.

2. Feel the metal with your hand. Where the water has succeeded in warming the tank, it is empty; where the tank remains cool to the touch, there is still propane inside.

16-inch tongs were the perfect length. These tongs could handle single asparagus spears or several in a bunch, without a single one twisting, turning, or falling. Similarly, slippery and delicate chicken drumsticks could be perfectly cradled without tearing or separating the skin. These tongs were by far the best with heavy ribs, requiring just one hand to turn a whole rack.

The spring-loaded feature was great, handling pieces of meat of just about any size, and, when locked, could efficiently handle small, delicate pieces as well. The fact that these tongs are all metal made no difference—they were long enough to keep hands far away from the heat and stayed quite cool, mostly because they allowed efficient and quick turning.

The bottom line is simple: Don't bother with specially designed grill tongs, and certainly don't waste $50 on a set of grill tools just to get some tongs. Inexpensive stainless steel locking tongs—the kind used by restaurant chefs—are the best choice when cooking on the grill or the stovetop. Best of all, they cost about $10.

SPATULA

CERTAIN FOODS, ESPECIALLY THOSE PRONE to sticking such as burgers and fish, are best turned with a spatula. Since grill heat is intense, a long-handled metal spatula is a must.

We tested a variety of grill spatulas against our favorite indoor spatula—called a dogleg, or offset, spatula. These names refer to the angle of the blade, which is on a plane that is different from that of the handle. Our favorite offset spatula has a blade that is three inches wide and six inches long.

In our testing of spatulas, size and strength turned out to be the most important variables. Larger spatulas did a better job turning burgers and fish fillets and made breakage far less likely. A stiff but thin blade got under foods easily and separated them from the grill grate. None of these long-handled grill spatulas, however, could outperform our offset spatula. Yes, the extra handle length was nice, but you can flip burgers so easily and quickly with a large offset spatula that your hands don't spend enough time near the coals to get hot. In addition, most of the grill spatulas were flimsy and

much too flexible. Also, when turning large fish fillets, we really appreciated the large surface area of the offset spatula. Most grill spatulas are not even half as large, so foods hang off the edges of the turning blade and can break apart.

GRILLING GRID

GRILLING GRIDS, ALSO CALLED VEGETABLE grids, are useful for cooking small pieces of food that might fall into the fire if placed on the cooking grate that comes with most grills. A grilling grid goes on top of the grill's cooking grate, is allowed to heat up, and is then used as the cooking surface for the food. The grid is usually made out of wire, which is cross-hatched to prevent small pieces of food from falling through the holes; it can also be made out of any metal sheet perforated with holes to allow smoke and heat to directly hit the surface of the food.

While both designs work well for small, cut-up vegetables, we found that the perforated grilling grids are more versatile. On these flat grids, you can cook delicate foods such as fish fillets and fish burgers and thus avoid the problems of sticking and tearing. In contrast, the wire grids have an uneven surface that makes it difficult to turn and move these delicate items. It's hard to slip these spatulas under burgers on a grid because part of the meat actually drops into the squares of cross-hatched wire.

Perforated grilling grids are available at cookware shops and many hardware stores. They range in price from about $11 to $25. We found the optimum size to be about half the size of a kettle grill or gas grill (depending on what you have), so that you can cook vegetables at the same time that you cook your main dish (steaks, chicken, etc.).

We also found that the type of material the grill grid is made out of makes a difference. We tried three grids made from three different materials: stainless steel, porcelain-coated steel, and nonstick-coated steel. While all grilling grids did fine when cooking vegetables, when cooking delicate fish burgers the type of material made a difference. Of the three types of grilling grids, the porcelain-coated grid performed the best. When using the nonstick and stainless steel grids, the tuna burger did not brown well (the stainless steel grid was worst of all). The porcelain-coated grilling grid browned fish burgers the best, without any sticking.

Surprisingly, the nonstick coated steel grid wasn't any better than the other two grids when it came to turning or moving the burgers; none gave us any problems. The stainless steel grid buckled because of the high heat. We liked the sturdiness and the dark color of the porcelain-coated grill grid, which not only kept its shape but also held more heat (or got hotter) than the other two grids.

In addition to these grids, we tried out a cast-iron grilling grid, which has a parallel series of slats, just like the grill's cooking grate. While this is a nice gadget for those who like to grill steaks and chops with the heat of a cast-iron surface for better marking and searing, it really doesn't work well with vegetables and delicate items; it is not designed for cooking these foods.

SKEWERS

SKEWERS ARE GREAT TO HAVE FOR GRILLING button mushrooms or sliced onions (the other option is a grill grid) and are essential when grilling kebabs. You basically have two choices: metal or wood. We prefer metal skewers, which can be used over and over again and do not burn on the grill. Wood skewers often do burn on the grill, even when soaked.

We have also seen some metal skewers at grilling stores with wood or plastic handles, supposedly for easy turning. These handles are not meant for use right above the fire but are supposed to hang over the side of the grill. Because of this design, all the food on the skewer will not have direct contact with the cooking grates, making even cooking impossible. For this reason, we do not recommend these types of skewers. Just use tongs to turn metal skewers on the grill.

A better option still is a double metal skewer shaped like a giant U. Foods are threaded through the two prongs, which are joined by a loop of metal at one end. The advantage is that kebabs won't spin around the skewer when you try to turn them. You can achieve the same effect by threading foods through two separate skewers, held parallel to each other, at the same time (see the illustration on page 69). For more information on skewers, see chapter 5.

FISH BASKET

WE FOUND FISH BASKETS TO BE UNNECESSARY for the grill. Grilling both whole fish and fillets can be done easily if your grill is clean, hot, and well oiled. When testing fish baskets, we found that unless the basket is well oiled, it too will stick to the fish, making it hard to remove the fish from the basket. If you prefer to use a fish basket on the grill, make sure to oil the basket very well to prevent sticking. For more information on our tests with fish baskets, see chapter 11.

SPRAYER/MISTER

NOTHING IS WORSE WHEN GRILLING THAN an uncontrolled fire that chars food. We recommend that you keep a plant mister or spray bottle filled with water on hand to keep a grease fire from ruining your meal. At the first sign of flames, try to pull foods to a cool part of the grill and douse the flames with water.

THERMOMETERS

WE RELY ON TWO KINDS OF THERMOMETERS when grilling. A grill thermometer will tell you what the temperature is inside a covered grill. Most gas grills come with this gauge. If you have a charcoal grill, you will need to buy a grill thermometer at a hardware store. This kind of thermometer has a dial face with numbers and a long stem. To use this device on a charcoal grill, simply insert it into the vents on the lid (see the illustration on page 232).

An instant-read thermometer is the best (and we would say, the only) way to determine when foods are properly cooked. If you want steaks cooked to medium-rare (not medium or rare) or a chicken that is cooked through but not dry, use an instant-read thermometer.

Unlike traditional meat thermometers, instant-read thermometers are not designed to be left in the foods as they cook. Prolonged exposure of the whole unit to heat will destroy the measuring mechanism. When you think foods might be done, simply insert the probe deep into the food (away from any bones) and wait 10 seconds for the temperature to register.

There are two types of instant-read thermometers on the market: dial-face and digital. Though pocket-sized dial-face thermometers are less expensive than digitals, they are also less precise, and most read temperatures in a narrower range. Although this is not an issue when grilling, it can be a problem when chilling custards for ice cream or making caramel sauce. Our favorite digital thermometer registers temperatures from below 0 to 500 degrees.

Another important difference between digital and dial-face thermometers is the location of the temperature sensor. On a dial-face thermometer, the sensor is roughly 1½ inches from the tip of the stem. The sensor on a digital thermometer is usually located at the very tip of the stem. What this means is that the stem of the dial-face thermometer must be stuck deep into the meat or other food. A digital thermometer will deliver a more accurate reading in thin cutlets or chops.

There is one last factor to consider when buying an instant-read thermometer. In our testing of nine models, we found that some responded in just 10 seconds while others took as long as 30 seconds to report the correct temperature. There is no point in keeping the grill lid open longer than is necessary, so choose a fast-responding model such as the Owen Instruments Thermapen or Taylor Digital Pocket.

SCIENCE: Food Safety

We find that most cuts of beef, pork, lamb, and fish are more flavorful and juicy when cooked to rare, medium-rare, or medium, depending on the food in question. As the internal temperature of all meats and fish rise, juices are expelled. Tough cuts such as brisket are best fully cooked so they will become tender. They might lose juices but at least they won't be tough. However, the majority of steaks, chops, and fillets start out tender. Cooking them past medium has no benefit; it just makes them dry.

Of course, these culinary judgments don't take into account the possible dangers of eating food contaminated with bacteria. If safety is your primary concern, you should cook all foods (especially hamburgers) to an internal temperature of 160 degrees, or until well-done.

Luckily, palatability and safety come together when it comes to cooking poultry. We find that birds are best cooked to an internal temperature of at least 160 degrees (and often higher) so that meat near the bone is no longer bloody. Any temperature above 160 degrees ensures that all bacteria have been killed.

SMALL BRUSHES

YOU WILL NEED A VARIETY OF PASTRY-TYPE or paint brushes to coat foods with barbecue sauce and to perform other, similar tasks. Choose brushes with soft bristles and make sure to wash brushes well after each use to prolong their usefulness.

FOIL PANS, HEAVY-DUTY FOIL, BROWN PAPER BAGS, AND PAPER TOWELS

IT MAY SEEM UNNECESSARY TO WRITE ABOUT this kind of equipment, but often a foil pan or a paper bag makes the difference between good food from the grill and great food from the grill. Here are some notes on these essential, if mundane, items.

Keep disposable aluminum pans in a variety of sizes on hand. You may want to use these pans to transfer foods from the kitchen to the grill. (Make sure to wash them before putting cooked foods back in them.) When grilling, we like to use these pans to cover certain foods to heat them through more quickly so the exterior doesn't burn. For instance, an aluminum pan helps to heat up pizza toppings before the bottom crust has a chance to burn. Likewise, a pan placed over bone-in chicken breasts on the cool part of the grill captures the available heat and cooks the meat through to the bone with little further browning of the skin.

Heavy-duty aluminum foil is the best material in which to wrap wood chips. Don't use regular foil. It's not nearly as thick, and chips will ignite more quickly. We found that wrapping barbecued foods such as brisket and ribs in foil when they come off the grill helps trap moisture and allows the juices in the meat to be redistributed as the meat rests. We place the wrapped meat in a brown paper bag (the kind you get at the supermarket), which helps trap heat and keeps the food from cooling off too much as it rests.

Paper towels serve several functions at the grill. We often dip a wad of towels in vegetable oil, grasp the oiled towels with tongs, and rub the oil over the cooking grate. This both cleans the grate and greases it, so that fish and other delicate foods won't stick. We also use wads of paper towels to turn whole birds on the grill.

PART 2

GRILLING

2

BASIC PRINCIPLES OF GRILLING

GRILLING IS THE QUICK-COOKING (OR searing) of foods over an open fire. Relatively thin cuts such as steaks as well as delicate foods like seafood and vegetables are grilled. Once the food is seared on both sides, it's probably done. True grilling (as opposed to grill-roasting or barbecuing with the cover on) is hot and fast. (See page xiii for the definitions of grilling, grill-roasting, and barbecuing used in this book.)

To put a good crust on foods, especially grilled meats, you must use enough charcoal. Because heat is so important, we prefer lump hardwood charcoal (see page 7) when grilling. It burns hotter than briquettes and is well suited to this kind of outdoor cooking.

Once the coals are lit, there are several ways to arrange them in the grill. They can be spread out in a single layer across the bottom of the grill (see first illustration below). A single-level fire delivers even heat across the cooking grate, usually at a moderate temperature, because the coals are fairly distant from the cooking grate. We often use this kind of single-level fire to cook vegetables and fish. (You can make a more intense single-level fire by adding unlit coals to the grill once the lit coals have been turned out of the chimney starter. Wait about 10 minutes for these new coals to catch fire. For instance, a large, super-hot fire is best for grilling a lot of steaks at one time.)

A second option, one that we often employ when grilling meat, is to build a two-level fire (see second illustration below). Once the coals are lit, some of them are spread out in a single layer over half of the grill. The remaining coals are piled up on the other side of the grill so they are closer to the cooking grate. In effect, this arrangement creates two levels of heat intensity on the grill. The part of the cooking grate above the taller pile of coals is quite hot, perfect for searing foods. The heat above the single level of coals is less intense, making this an ideal spot to cook thicker foods through once they have been browned.

THREE TYPES OF CHARCOAL FIRES

BUILDING A SINGLE-LEVEL FIRE
Once the lit charcoal is in the grill, the coals can be arranged in an even layer to create a single-level fire. This kind of fire delivers even heat and is best for quick searing at a moderate temperature.

BUILDING A TWO-LEVEL FIRE
Another option is to build a two-level fire, which permits searing over very hot coals and slower cooking over medium-hot coals to cook through thicker cuts. To build a two-level fire, spread some of the lit coals in a single layer over half of the grill. Leave the remaining coals in a pile that rises to within 2 or 2 1/2 inches of the cooking grate. If necessary, you may add some unlit charcoal on the hot side of the grill. Wait 10 minutes or so for these coals to become hot.

BUILDING A MODIFIED TWO-LEVEL FIRE
When we build a two-level fire, we generally follow the method outlined in the drawing above. With foods that are susceptible to burning but require a long cooking time (such as chicken breasts), we sometimes build a modified two-level fire. All the lit coals are piled into half the grill to create a hot place for searing. The remaining portion of the grill is left empty. Some heat from the coals will still cook foods placed over the empty part of the grill, but the heat is very gentle and little browning will occur here. We often cover foods on the cool part of the grill with a disposable aluminum pan to trap heat and create an oven-like cooking environment (see page 106).

TAKING THE TEMPERATURE OF THE FIRE

Use the chart below to determine the intensity of the fire. The terms hot fire, medium-hot fire, medium fire, and medium-low fire are used throughout this book. When using a gas grill, ignore dial readings such as medium or medium-low in favor of actual measurements of the temperature, as described here.

INTENSITY OF FIRE	TIME YOU CAN HOLD YOUR HAND 5 INCHES ABOVE GRATE
Hot fire	2 seconds
Medium-hot fire	3 to 4 seconds
Medium fire	5 to 6 seconds
Medium-low fire	7 seconds

Once the coals have been spread out in the bottom of the grill, put the cooking grate in place and put the cover on for five minutes to heat up the grate. (On gas, preheat with the lid down and all burners on high for 15 minutes.) Scrape the cooking grate clean and then take the temperature of the fire by holding your hand five inches above the cooking grate and seeing how long you can comfortably leave it in place.

This cooler fire also comes in handy if flames engulf the food. Simply drag the food to the cooler part of the grill, and the flames should subside.

We use a two-level fire for grilling thick steaks and chops. A standard single-level fire is not quite hot enough to sear meats properly. You could bulk up the fire with more coals, but then the exterior tends to burn before the meat is cooked through. The two-level fire is the best of both worlds—a hot fire that will sear foods and a cooler spot that will allow slow, thorough cooking.

In a few instances, we prefer to use a modified two-level fire (see third illustration, page 18). We pile up all of the lit coals in half of the grill and leave the other half empty. This arrangement works for bone-in chicken breasts and other delicate foods that can dry out easily. We sear them over the hot coals then let them cook through by means of gentle, indirect heat.

No matter how we build a charcoal fire for grilling, we always leave the cover off. As mentioned in chapter 1, over time, soot and resinous compounds can build up on the inside of a kettle grill lid, which can then impart an "off" flavor, reminiscent of stale smoke, to the food. This effect is most noticeable in fish, poultry, and chicken. When we want to trap heat on an open charcoal grill to make sure the food cooks through, we prefer to cover it with a disposable aluminum roasting pan or pie plate. (Note that for grill-roasting and barbecuing, the grill cover

FOUR TIPS FOR BETTER CHARCOAL GRILLING

Here are four key points to keep in mind when working with a charcoal grill:

1. Use enough charcoal. Many cooks skimp on fuel when grilling and never get the temperature high enough. There's no use spending $30 on steaks and then steaming them over an inadequate fire. The size of your grill, the amount of food being cooked, and the desired intensity of the fire are all factors in deciding how much charcoal to use. In the end, you want a fire that is slightly larger than the space on the cooking grate occupied by the food. The higher you pile the charcoal (and thus the closer it is to the cooking grate), the more intense the fire will be.

2. Make sure the coals are covered with light gray ash before you start to grill. Light gray ash is a sign that the coals are fully lit and hot.

3. Once the coals are ready, set the cooking rack in place and let it heat up for 5 minutes. Scrape the hot rack with a wire-bristle brush to remove any bits of food.

4. Don't use the cover when grilling. It can impart an off flavor to foods, especially fish, vegetables, and chicken. If you need to trap heat to cook something through, cover the food with a disposable aluminum roasting pan.

must be kept on to trap heat. However, the use of wood chips and chunks overpowers the off flavor the lid can impart.)

Grilling on gas requires slightly different (but similar) procedures. You can create a single-level fire by adjusting all burners—keeping them at high for the hottest fire or turning all burners to medium for a moderate fire once the grill has been preheated. For a two-level fire, simply leave one burner on high or medium-high and turn the other burners to medium or medium-low. The idea is the same here as with charcoal. Sear foods over the more intense burner, then slide foods to the cooler part of the grill to cook them through.

We find that gas grills work best with the lid down in all instances. They put out a lot less heat than a charcoal fire and foods won't brown properly if the lid is left open. Because gas burns cleanly, there's no build-up of soot on the inside of the lid and thus no danger that foods cooked in a covered gas grill will pick up an off flavor.

With both charcoal and gas, it's imperative to use the right level of heat. To make our recipes easy to follow, we have devised a system that quantifies the heat level by measuring the amount of time you can comfortably hold your hand above the cooking grate (see page 19 for details). If you use this system, the cooking times in our recipes will be excellent guidelines. However, we always recommend that you test foods often on the grill.

Grilling over a live fire is not like cooking in a precisely calibrated oven. Be prepared to adjust the timing, especially if grilling in cool or windy weather. An instant-read thermometer is the best way to gauge the progress of most foods on the grill. The other option is remove a test piece and peek into the food with the tip of a knife.

THREE TIPS FOR BETTER GAS GRILLING

Here are three key points to keep in mind when working with a gas grill:

1. Remove the warming rack before lighting the grill unless you know you are going to need it. On most grills, the rack is very close to the cooking surface, and it can be hard to reach foods on the back of the grill without burning your hands on the hot metal.

2. Preheat the grill with all burners turned to high (even if you plan on cooking over low heat) and the lid down for at least 15 minutes. Once the grill is blazing hot, scrape the grate clean with a wire-bristle brush, then adjust the burners as desired.

3. Whether cooking by direct or indirect heat, keep the lid down. With charcoal grills, residue from the briquettes can build up on the inside of the lid and give quickly cooked foods an off flavor, but this isn't a problem with gas grills because gas burns cleanly. Keeping the lid down concentrates the heat when searing and keeps the temperature steady when slow-cooking.

3

STEAKS

GRILLED STEAKS ARE AN AMERICAN CLASSIC. There are two main areas that separate great steaks from mediocre ones. First, you have to buy the right cuts of meat. We find that some steaks, no matter how they are seasoned or grilled, are always disappointing. This chapter offers a selection of expensive and inexpensive steaks that we think are best suited to outdoor cooking. Second, you need to use a grilling technique that is right for a particular cut. Thicker steaks must be grilled differently from thin ones. Likewise, the presence of a bone can necessitate some adjustments in technique, as can the fat content. We started our work on steaks at the supermarket, and then focused on grilling techniques.

Steaks generally come from six places on the cow (discussed on page 23). For all cuts of steak, look for meat that has a bright, lively color. Beef normally ranges in color from pink to red. A dark color is often an indication that the meat came from an older animal and will be tough.

The external fat as well as the fat that runs through the meat (called intramuscular fat) should be as white as possible. As a general rule, the more intramuscular fat (called marbling), the more flavorful and juicy the steak will be (see box below for more information). The marbling should be smooth and fine, running all through the meat rather than showing up in clumps; smooth marbling melts into the meat during cooking, contributing to flavor and tenderness, while clumps of fat simply remain clumps of fat.

Stay away from packaged steaks that show a lot of red juice (known as purge). The purge may indicate a bad job of freezing; your steak will be dry and cottony.

Steaks sport different names in different parts of the United States. We've used industry names that we feel best describe where the steaks lie on the cow. In some cases, we have listed a few other common names.

INGREDIENTS: Prime, Choice, and Select Beef

There are eight USDA (U.S. Department of Agriculture) beef grades, but most everything available to consumers falls into the top three: Prime, Choice, and Select. The grades classify meat according to fat marbling and age, which are relatively accurate predictors of palatability; they have nothing to do with freshness or purity. Grading is voluntary on the part of the meat packer. If the meat is graded, it should bear a USDA stamp indicating the grade, but it may not be visible. Ask the butcher when in doubt. We grilled rib-eye steaks from all three grades and then conducted a blind tasting. Prime ranked first for its tender, buttery texture and rich beefy flavor; it was discernibly fattier. Choice came in second, with solid flavor and a little more chew. The Select steak was tough and stringy, with flavor that was only "acceptable." The lesson here is that you get what you pay for. Prime steaks are worth the extra money, but Choice steaks with a moderate amount of marbling are a fine and more affordable option. (Most Prime steaks end up in restaurant kitchens. If you want to buy Prime meat, visit a butcher shop. Most supermarkets carry only Choice and Select cuts.)

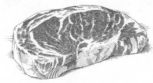

PRIME
Prime meat is heavily marbled with intramuscular fat, which makes for a tender, flavorful steak. A very small percentage (about 2 percent) of graded beef is graded Prime. Prime meat is most often served in restaurants or sold in high-end grocery stores and butcher shops. It is more expensive than meat graded either Choice or Select.

CHOICE
The majority of beef receives the grade called Choice. Choice beef is moderately marbled with intramuscular fat, but within this category there are varying levels of marbling. For best flavor, look for steaks with lots of white lines throughout—a sign that the steaks are well marbled.

SELECT
Select beef has little marbling, and its small amount of intramuscular fat can make it drier, tougher, and less flavorful than the two higher grades.

INGREDIENTS: Common Steaks

SHOULDER/CHUCK STEAKS Often (mis)labeled as London broil (which is really a technique for preparing steak and not a true cut of steak; see "London Broil" on page 35), steaks from the shoulder of the cow, often called chuck, are boneless and consist of a single muscle. Buy a shoulder steak that is 1½ to 2 pounds and slice it thin on the bias after cooking. We find that shoulder steaks offer the best value for cost-conscious shoppers.

RIB STEAKS Steaks cut from the rib are very tender and smooth-textured, with a distinctive, robust, beefy taste. They are very rich, with good-sized pockets of fat. The rib steak is cut from the rib roast (or prime rib) and comes with the curved bone attached. More often, you will see boneless steaks from the rib, called rib-eye steaks. The rib eye has an oval shape with a narrow strip of meat that curves around one end. Rib eye is also known as Delmonico steak in New York and as Spencer steak in the West.

SHORT LOIN STEAKS Our favorite steak, the strip, is cut from the short loin. The strip (also called shell, Kansas City strip, New York strip, or top loin) has a noticeable grain and a moderate amount of chew. The flavor is excellent, and the meat is a bit less fatty than in rib steaks. These steaks are slightly more expensive than rib steaks.

The tenderloin and the filet mignon are also from the short loin. Actually, filet mignon is the name for individual steaks cut from the tenderloin, a narrow strip of muscle known more for its tenderness than its flavor. Because these steaks are not as flavorful as other premium steaks, they are not our favorites. Many people, however, love their buttery, smooth texture.

The T-bone and porterhouse contain a nice balance of chewy strip and buttery tenderloin and are a better bet than filet mignon. The porterhouse, cut from farther back in the animal, has a larger piece of tenderloin than the T-bone, while the grain of the strip piece on a porterhouse is rougher than that on a T-bone. The T-bone cut combines an oblong piece of strip with a small piece of tenderloin that measures less than 1½ inches across. Because the grain of the strip piece on the T-bone is finer, it is often considered more desirable than that of porterhouse.

SIRLOIN STEAKS These steaks, like shoulder/chuck steaks, are sometimes labeled London broil. They are often tough and overpriced. Your best bet for a sirloin steak is a round-bone or shell sirloin, although we usually prefer a shoulder steak. Shell sirloin is simply the round-bone sirloin with the small piece of tenderloin removed. This cut is commonly found in the Northeast, where it is often called New York sirloin. Do not confuse sirloin steaks with New York strip steaks, which, cut from the short loin, are far superior in all regards.

ROUND STEAKS Steaks cut from the round are most often called London broil. They are boneless and quite lean. We find them dry and chewy and do not recommend them.

FLANK STEAKS The tender, boneless, single-muscle steak from the flank is fairly thin (no more than an inch thick) and weighs 2 to 2½ pounds. Like shoulder/chuck steaks, flank is less expensive than rib or short loin steak and is quite good when sliced thin on the bias before serving. It has a distinct longitudinal grain. To minimize the stringy, chewy nature of flank steak, do not grill it past medium-rare. Flank steak is sometimes called jiffy steak.

SHOULDER STEAK

RIB STEAK

RIB-EYE STEAK

STRIP STEAK
(also known as top loin steak)

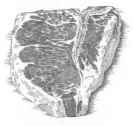

T-BONE STEAK

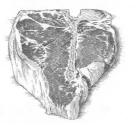

PORTERHOUSE STEAK

FILET MIGNON
(also known as tenderloin steak)

ROUND-BONE SIRLOIN STEAK

FLANK STEAK

Premium Steaks

WE FOUND THAT PREMIUM STEAKS FROM the rib and short loin can be cooked and seasoned pretty much the same way, although filet mignon needs a slightly different treatment. (Tougher London broil [from the shoulder] and flank steaks require different cooking regimens; see pages 35 and 36 for instructions for London broil, and pages 31 to 34 for details on cooking flank steak.)

Grilled premium steaks have many attractive qualities: rich, beefy flavor; a thick, caramelized crust; and almost no prep or cleanup for the cook. But sometimes a small bonfire fueled by steak fat can leave expensive steaks charred and tasting of resinous smoke. Other times the coals burn down so low that the steaks end up with pale, wimpy grill marks and almost no flavor at all. In these cases, you probably tried to leave the steaks on the grill long enough to develop flavor, but they just overcooked.

So we went to work, promising ourselves we'd figure out how to use the grill to cook the entire steak perfectly: meat seared evenly on both sides so that the juices are concentrated into a powerfully flavored, dark brown, brittle coating of crust; the juicy inside cooked a little past rare; and the outside strip of rich, soft fat crisped and browned slightly on the edges.

We decided to focus on the steaks from the short loin and rib sections of the animal that we think are the best the cow has to offer—the T-bone and porterhouse as well as the strip and filet mignon (all

from the short loin) and the rib eye (a rib steak without the bone, which is the most common way this cut is sold). We figured these steaks were bound to cook pretty much the same because they were all cut from the same general part of the cow.

Early on in our testing, we determined that we needed a very hot fire to get the crust we wanted without overcooking the steak. We could get that kind of heat by building the charcoal up to within 2 or 2½ inches of the grilling grate. But with this arrangement, we ran into problems with the fat dripping down onto the charcoal and flaming. We had already decided that a thick steak—at least 1½ inches thick, to be precise—was optimum, because at that thickness we got a tasty contrast between the charcoal flavoring on the outside of the steak and the beefy flavor on the inside. The problem was that we couldn't cook a thick steak over consistently high heat without burning it.

After considerable experimentation, we found the answer to this dilemma: We had to build a fire with two levels of heat. Once we realized that we needed a fire with a lot of coals on one side and far fewer coals on the other, we could sear the steak properly at the beginning of cooking, then pull it onto the cooler half of the grill to finish cooking at a lower temperature. We could also use the dual heat levels to cook thin steaks as well as thick ones properly, and the system provided insurance against bonfires as well—if a steak flared up, we simply moved it off the high heat.

We gauged the level of heat on both sides of the fire by holding a hand about five inches over the cooking grate (as explained on page 19). When the medium-hot side of the grill was hot enough for searing, we could stand to hold a hand over the grill only for three or four seconds. For the cooler side of the grill, we could count seven seconds. (This is how we adapted our recipes for a gas grill, using burners set to high and medium.)

A two-level fire is also good for cooking porterhouse and T-bone, two of our favorite cuts, which are especially tricky to cook properly. Both consist of two muscles (strip and tenderloin) with a T-shaped bone in between. When grilled long enough to cook the strip section perfectly, the lean tenderloin is inevitably overcooked, dry, and flavorless. We found

THE EIGHT PRIMAL CUTS OF BEEF

that if we grilled the steak with the tenderloin toward the cooler side of the fire, it cooked more slowly and reached proper doneness at the same time as the strip.

Common cooking wisdom suggests that bringing meat to room temperature before grilling will cause it to cook more evenly and that letting it rest for five minutes after taking it off the grill will both preserve the juices and provide a more even color. We tested the first of these theories by simultaneously grilling two similar steaks, one straight from the refrigerator and a second that had stood at room temperature for one hour. We noticed no difference in the cooked steaks except that the room temperature steak cooked a couple of minutes faster than the other. The second test was more conclusive. Letting a cooked steak rest for five minutes does indeed help the meat retain more juices when sliced and promotes a more even color throughout the meat.

We tried lightly oiling steaks before grilling to see if they browned better that way, and tried brushing with butter halfway through grilling to see if the flavor improved. Although the oiled steaks browned a tiny bit better, the difference wasn't significant enough to merit the added ingredient. (The filet mignon steaks were an exception; oiling improved browning in these leaner steaks). As for the butter, we couldn't taste any difference.

INGREDIENT: Salt

There are several kinds of salt available to home cooks. Regular table salt comes from underground mines around the world. It has fine crystals and contains an anticaking agent so that it pours easily. Some cooks can detect an off flavor from this anticaking agent when they taste table salt straight from the box. Once you cook with table salt, it becomes considerably more difficult to notice any off flavors.

Kosher salt is made without any anticaking agents. Our preference in the test kitchen is for kosher salt. We keep a small ramekin near the stove and sprinkle it on foods as needed. Its large crystals are easy to pick up, and we like its clean, pure flavor.

Another option is sea salt, which comes in a variety of grinds from fine to coarse. Sea salt is made from dried seawater and often contains other minerals found in the sea. Again, while it is possible to detect subtle (and delicious) nuances in many sea salts, these nuances mostly disappear once you cook.

For this book, we have tested recipes with regular table salt since that's the kind of salt most home cooks have on hand. When we find that a coarser texture is desirable (for instance, in a salt-and-pepper rub for steaks), we have specifically called for kosher or coarse sea salt. You can get away with table salt in these recipes, as long as you use less. Because of their larger crystals, kosher and coarse sea salt are about half as salty as table salt. Therefore, if using table salt in a recipe that calls for kosher salt, use about half as much.

JUDGING WHEN STEAKS ARE DONE

There are two ways to tell when a steak is properly cooked. (You can also cut into the meat, but this causes some loss of juices.)

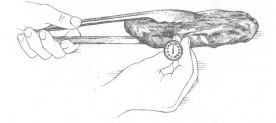

1. To judge doneness by texture, pick up the steak with a pair of tongs and compare its texture with that of your hand. A rare steak will approximate the soft, squishy feel of the skin between your thumb and forefinger. Make a fist and touch the same area to approximate the springy feel of medium. A well-done steak will approximate the firmness of the tip of your nose.

2. While chefs rely on the "touch" method, most home cooks will want to use an instant-read thermometer to judge when a steak is done. Hold the steak with a pair of tongs and push the tip of the thermometer through the edge of steak until most of the shaft is embedded in the meat and not touching any bone. Pull the steak off the grill when it registers 120 degrees for rare; 125 to 130 degrees for medium-rare; and 135 to 140 degrees for medium. Note that the internal temperature will rise another 5 degrees or so as the steak rests.

We did find that proper seasoning with salt and pepper before grilling is essential. Seasonings added after cooking sit on the surface and don't penetrate as well as salt and pepper added before cooking. Be liberal with the salt and pepper. A fair amount falls off during the cooking process. Finally, consider using coarse sea salt or kosher salt. In our tests, tasters consistently preferred steaks sprinkled with coarse salt before grilling compared with those sprinkled with table salt. The larger crystals are more easily absorbed by the meat and sprinkle more evenly. (See page 25 for more information.)

Charcoal-Grilled Strip or Rib Steaks

SERVES 4

A steak that's from 1¼ to 1½ inches thick gives you a solid meat flavor as well as a little taste of the grill; cut any thicker, the steak becomes too thick for one person to eat. If your guests are more likely to eat only an 8-ounce steak, grill two 1-pounders, slice them, and serve each person a half steak. The most accurate way to judge doneness is to stick an instant-read thermometer through the side of the steak deep into the meat, so that most of the shaft is embedded in the steak.

    4   strip or rib steaks with or without bone, 1¼ to
           1½ inches thick (12 to 16 ounces each),
           patted dry
           Salt and ground black pepper

1. Light a large chimney starter filled with hardwood charcoal (about 2½ pounds) and allow to burn until all the charcoal is covered with a layer of fine gray ash. Build a two-level fire by stacking most of the coals on one side of the grill, arranging the remaining coals in a single layer on the other side of the grill. Set the cooking rack in place, cover the grill with the lid, and let the rack heat up, about 5 minutes. Use a wire brush to scrape clean the cooking rack. The grill is ready when the pile of coals is medium-hot and the single layer is medium-low (see how to gauge heat level on page 19).

2. Meanwhile, sprinkle both sides of the steaks with salt and pepper to taste. Grill the steaks, uncovered, over the hotter part of the fire until well browned on one side, 2 to 3 minutes. Turn the steaks; grill until well browned on the other side, 2 to 3 minutes. (If the steaks start to flame, pull them to the cooler part of the grill and/or extinguish flames with a squirt bottle.)

3. Once the steaks are well browned on both sides, slide them to the cooler part of grill. Continue grilling, uncovered, to the desired doneness, 5 to 6 minutes more for rare (120 degrees on instant-read thermometer), 6 to 7 minutes for medium-rare on the rare side (125 degrees), 7 to 8 minutes for medium-rare on the medium side (130 degrees), or 8 to 9 minutes for medium (135 to 140 degrees).

4. Remove the steaks from the grill and let rest for 5 minutes. Serve immediately.

Gas-Grilled Strip or Rib Steaks

SERVES 4

Steaks cut thick, as recommended in this recipe, first need to be seared over medium-high heat, then moved to a cooler fire to finish cooking. To judge doneness, stick an instant-read thermometer through the side of the steak, deep into the meat.

    4   strip or rib steaks with or without bone, 1¼ to
           1½ inches thick (12 to 16 ounces each),
           patted dry
           Salt and ground black pepper

1. Preheat the grill with all burners set to high and the lid down until the grill is very hot, about 15 minutes. Use a wire brush to scrape clean the cooking grate. Leave one burner on high and turn the other burner(s) down to medium.

2. Meanwhile, sprinkle both sides of the steaks with salt and pepper to taste. Grill the steaks, covered, over the hotter part of the grill until well browned on one side, 3 minutes. Turn the steaks; grill until well browned on the other side, 3 minutes. (If the steaks start to flame, pull them to the cooler part of the grill and/or extinguish flames with a squirt bottle.)

3. Once the steaks are well browned on both sides, slide them to the cooler part of grill. Continue grilling, covered, to the desired doneness, 7 to 8 minutes more for rare (120 degrees on instant-read thermometer), 9 to 10 minutes for medium-rare on the rare side (125 degrees), 11 to 12 minutes for

medium-rare on the medium side (130 degrees), or 12 to 13 minutes for medium (135 to 140 degrees).

4. Remove the steaks from the grill and let rest for 5 minutes. Serve immediately.

Charcoal-Grilled Porterhouse or T-Bone Steaks

SERVES 4

How can you argue with a steak that gives you two different tastes and textures—from the strip and the tenderloin—in one cut, plus the bone? Since T-bone and porterhouse steaks are so large, it's best to have the butcher cut them thick (1½ inches) and let one steak serve two people. The key to keeping the delicate tenderloin from overcooking is to sear the steaks with the strip portions over the hottest coals and the tenderloin portions facing the cooler part of the fire.

2   porterhouse or T-bone steaks, each 1½ inches
     thick (about 3½ pounds total), patted dry
     Salt and ground black pepper

1. Light a large chimney starter filled with hardwood charcoal (about 2½ pounds) and allow to burn until all the charcoal is covered with a layer of fine gray ash. Build a two-level fire by stacking most of the coals on one side of the grill and arranging the remaining coals in a single layer on the other side of the grill. Set the cooking rack in place, cover the grill

GRILLING T-BONE AND PORTERHOUSE STEAKS

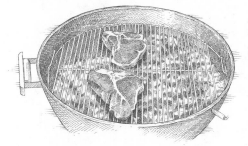

The delicate, buttery tenderloin portion must be protected when grilling porterhouse and T-bone steaks. Keep the tenderloin (the smaller portion on the left side of the bone on these steaks) over the cooler part of the fire.

with the lid, and let the rack heat up, about 5 minutes. Use a wire brush to scrape clean the cooking rack. The grill is ready when the pile of coals is medium-hot and the single layer of coals is medium-low (see page 19 to gauge heat level).

2. Meanwhile, sprinkle both sides of the steaks with salt and pepper to taste. Position the steaks on the grill so the tenderloin pieces are over the cooler part of the fire but the strip pieces are over the hotter part of the fire (see illustration, below left). Grill the steaks, uncovered, until well browned on one side, 2 to 3 minutes. Turn the steaks; grill until well browned on the other side, 2 to 3 minutes. (If the steaks start to flame, pull them to cooler part of the grill and/or extinguish flames with a squirt bottle.)

3. Once the steaks are well browned on both sides, slide them completely to the cooler part of grill. Continue grilling, uncovered, to the desired doneness, 5 to 6 minutes more for rare (120 degrees on instant-read thermometer), 6 to 7 minutes for medium-rare on the rare side (125 degrees), 7 to 8 minutes for medium-rare on the medium side (130 degrees), or 8 to 9 minutes for medium (135 to 140 degrees).

4. Remove the steaks from the grill and let rest for 5 minutes. Cut the strip and filet pieces off the bones and slice them each crosswise about ⅓ inch thick (see illustrations, page 28). Serve immediately.

Gas-Grilled Porterhouse or T-Bone Steaks

SERVES 4

The key to keeping the delicate tenderloin portions of the steaks from overcooking is to sear the steaks with the strip portions over the burner turned to high and the tenderloin facing the burner turned to medium.

2   porterhouse or T-bone steaks, each 1½ inches
     thick (about 3½ pounds total), patted dry
     Salt and ground black pepper

1. Preheat the grill with all burners set to high and the lid down until the grill is very hot, about 15 minutes. Use a wire brush to scrape clean the cooking grate. Leave one burner on high and turn the other burner(s) down to medium.

2. Meanwhile, sprinkle both sides of the steaks with salt and pepper to taste. Position the steaks on the grill so the tenderloin pieces are over the cooler part of the fire but the strip pieces are over the hotter part of the fire. Grill the steaks, covered, until well browned on one side, about 3 minutes. Turn the steaks; grill until well browned on the other side, about 3 minutes.

3. Once the steaks are well browned on both sides, slide them to the cooler part of the grill. Continue grilling, covered, to the desired doneness, 7 to 8 minutes more for rare (120 degrees on instant-read thermometer), 9 to 10 minutes for medium-rare on the rare side (125 degrees), 11 to 12 minutes for medium-rare on the medium side (130 degrees), or 12 to 13 minutes for medium (135 to 140 degrees).

4. Remove the steaks from the grill and let rest for 5 minutes. Cut the strip and filet pieces off the bones and slice them each crosswise about ⅓ inch thick (see illustrations below). Serve immediately.

➤ VARIATION

Tuscan Steak with Lemon and Olive Oil

Called bistecca Fiorentina, this dish is traditionally made with T-bone steaks.

Follow recipe for Charcoal-Grilled or Gas-Grilled Porterhouse or T-Bone Steaks, rubbing each steak with 2 tablespoons extra-virgin olive oil and then sprinkling with salt and pepper at the start of step 2. Grill as directed. Serve steaks with 2 lemons, cut into wedges.

Charcoal-Grilled Filet Mignon

SERVES 4

Filet mignon steaks are cut from the tenderloin, which is, as the name indicates, an extremely tender portion of meat. Though tender, the steaks are not extremely flavorful and not very fatty. We suggest using either the Cracked Peppercorn Rub or Rosemary Garlic Paste on page 29; since this cut of meat is not as beefy as other premium steaks, these rubs help to make the steak more full-flavored.

4   filet mignon steaks, about 2 inches thick
     (8 ounces each), patted dry
1 ½   tablespoons extra-virgin olive oil
     Salt and ground black pepper

1. Light a large chimney starter filled with hardwood charcoal (about 2½ pounds) and allow to burn until all the charcoal is covered with a layer of fine gray ash. Build a two-level fire by stacking most of the coals on one side of the grill and arranging the remaining coals in a single layer on the other side of the grill. Set the cooking rack in place, cover the grill with the lid, and let the rack heat up, about 5 minutes. Use a wire brush to scrape clean the cooking rack. The grill is ready when the pile of coals is medium-hot and the single layer of coals is medium-low (see how to gauge heat level on page 19).

CARVING T-BONE AND PORTERHOUSE STEAKS

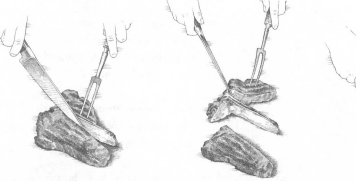

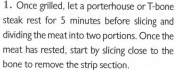

1. Once grilled, let a porterhouse or T-bone steak rest for 5 minutes before slicing and dividing the meat into two portions. Once the meat has rested, start by slicing close to the bone to remove the strip section.

2. Turn the steak around and cut the tenderloin section off the bone.

3. Slice each piece crosswise into portions ⅓ inch thick and serve immediately.

SEASONING PREMIUM STEAKS

We generally leave premium steak (strip, rib, porterhouse, and T-bone) as is. Yes, they must be seasoned generously with salt and pepper, but we don't quite understand why you would want to coat a T-bone with a complex spice rub. You are paying a lot of money for beefy flavor, so there's little sense in masking it.

Like the other premium steaks, filet mignon is tender (actually, even more so) but also a bit mild tasting or even bland, depending on your personal taste and the quality of the steaks. We think filet mignon benefits from a pepper or herb rub. Keep the rub simple and don't use any overpowering spices.

These simple rubs can be used with the other premium steaks as well. The flavors are straightforward and complement (rather than overwhelm) the beefy flavor of expensive steaks. However, unlike filet mignon, other premium steaks are fine with just salt and pepper, and no rub.

Cracked Peppercorn Rub

MAKES ABOUT 4 TABLESPOONS,
ENOUGH FOR 4 SMALL OR 2 LARGE STEAKS

To coarsely grind the black peppercorns, use a spice grinder, or crush manually with a mortar and pestle. You can improvise with a coffee mug and glass spice bottle as directed below.

2   tablespoons coarsely ground black pepper
1   tablespoon kosher or coarse sea salt

Mix the pepper and salt together in a small bowl. Rub this mixture onto steaks before grilling, omitting the salt and pepper in the recipe.

AN IMPROVISED MORTAR AND PESTLE

Stone, marble, wood, or porcelain mortars (bowls) and pestles (dowel-shaped grinding tools) are great for grinding peppercorns and other whole spices. Many modern kitchens may not have this tool. If you do not, you can improvise with a shallow, diner-style coffee cup and a heavy glass spice bottle. Place the peppercorns or other spices to be ground in the cup and then grind them to the desired consistency with the bottom of the spice bottle.

Rosemary Garlic Paste

MAKES ABOUT 4 TABLESPOONS,
ENOUGH FOR 4 SMALL OR 2 LARGE STEAKS

This paste is best when left on the steak for at least 2 hours prior to grilling. If you don't have time to let the steaks sit, however, you will still get a good, though less pronounced, garlic and herb flavor.

4   medium garlic cloves, minced with a pinch
       of kosher or coarse sea salt into a fine paste
       (see illustrations on page 137)
1½   teaspoons chopped fresh rosemary leaves
2   tablespoons extra-virgin olive oil

Mix all of the ingredients together in a small bowl. Rub the paste onto steaks, cover, and refrigerate steaks for at least 2 hours and up to 1 day. Season the steaks with salt and pepper to taste as directed in the appropriate recipe. Grill as directed.

COMPOUND BUTTERS

While we generally season premium steaks with just salt and pepper before cooking, we often serve them with a dollop of seasoned butter, called a compound butter.

Compound Butters for Grilled Steaks

ENOUGH FOR 4 SERVINGS

You can double or triple any of these recipes and store extra butter in the freezer. If making a large batch of compound butter, use a standing mixer to combine the ingredients evenly. The butter moistens the meat and improves its mouthfeel, especially if grilling steaks that are not well marbled.

PARSLEY BUTTER

4	tablespoons unsalted butter, softened
2	tablespoons minced fresh parsley leaves
2	tablespoons minced shallot, optional
1/8	teaspoon salt
	Pinch ground black pepper

PARSLEY-CAPER BUTTER

4	tablespoons unsalted butter, softened
2	tablespoons minced fresh parsley leaves
2	teaspoons minced capers
1/8	teaspoon salt
	Pinch ground black pepper

PARSLEY-LEMON BUTTER

4	tablespoons unsalted butter, softened
2	tablespoons minced fresh parsley leaves
2	teaspoons grated lemon zest
1/8	teaspoon salt
	Pinch ground black pepper

ROQUEFORT BUTTER

4	tablespoons unsalted butter, softened
3	tablespoons crumbled Roquefort cheese
2	teaspoons minced fresh sage leaves
1	teaspoon minced fresh parsley leaves
1	medium shallot, minced
2	teaspoons port
1/8	teaspoon salt
	Pinch ground black pepper

ROSEMARY-PARMESAN BUTTER

4	tablespoons unsalted butter, softened
3	tablespoons grated Parmesan cheese
2	teaspoons chopped fresh rosemary
1	small garlic clove, minced
1/8	teaspoon hot red pepper flakes
1/8	teaspoon salt

TAPENADE BUTTER

4	tablespoons unsalted butter, softened
1	teaspoon minced fresh thyme leaves
1	small garlic clove, minced (about 1 teaspoon)
1/8	teaspoon finely grated orange zest
1/2	anchovy fillet, minced
10	pitted and finely chopped oil-cured black olives (about 2 tablespoons)
1 1/2	teaspoons brandy
1/8	teaspoon salt
	Pinch ground black pepper

TARRAGON-LIME BUTTER

4	tablespoons unsalted butter, softened
1	tablespoon minced fresh tarragon leaves
2	tablespoons minced scallion (green and white parts)
2	teaspoons lime juice
1/8	teaspoon salt
	Pinch ground black pepper

1. Beat the butter with a large fork in a medium bowl until light and fluffy. Add the remaining ingredients and mix to combine.

2. Following illustration 1 on page 31, roll the butter into a log about 3 inches long and 1½ inches in diameter. Refrigerate until firm, at least 2 hours and up to 3 days. (Butter can be frozen for 2 months. When ready to use, let soften just until butter can be cut, about 15 minutes.)

3. When ready to use, remove the butter from the refrigerator and slice into 4 pieces just before grilling steaks. After grilling, place one piece of butter on each serving (see illustration 2 on page 31). Let rest for 2 minutes before serving.

2. Meanwhile, lightly rub the steaks with the oil, then sprinkle both sides with salt and pepper to taste. Grill the steaks, uncovered, over the hotter part of the fire until well browned on one side, 2 to 3 minutes. Turn the steaks; grill until well browned on the other side, 2 to 3 minutes.

3. Once steaks are well browned on both sides, slide them to the cooler part of the grill. Continue grilling, uncovered, to the desired doneness, 7 to 8 minutes more for rare (120 degrees on instant-read thermometer), 8 to 9 minutes for medium-rare on the rare side (125 degrees), 10 to 11 minutes for medium-rare on the medium side (130 degrees), or 11 to 12 minutes for medium (135 to 140 degrees).

4. Remove the steaks from the grill and let rest for 5 minutes. Serve immediately.

COMPOUND BUTTERS

1. Compound butters are a great way to add flavor to cooked steak. Once the ingredients have been combined, place the butter mixture in the center of a piece of plastic wrap. Fold one edge of the plastic wrap over the butter. Glide your hands back and forth over the butter to shape it into a 3-inch cylinder. Twist the ends of the plastic wrap shut and refrigerate until firm.

2. When ready to use, unwrap the butter and cut it into 4 equal pieces. Place each piece on top of a just-cooked steak.

Gas-Grilled Filet Mignon
SERVES 4

We recommend using either the Cracked Peppercorn Rub or Rosemary Garlic Paste on page 29 with this relatively mild-tasting steak. Do not cook these steaks past medium or they will be dry.

4	filet mignon steaks, about 2 inches thick (8 ounces each), patted dry
1½	tablespoons extra-virgin olive oil
	Salt and ground black pepper

1. Preheat the grill with all burners set to high and the lid down until the grill is very hot, about 15 minutes. Use a wire brush to scrape clean the cooking grate. Leave one burner on high and turn the other burner(s) down to medium.

2. Meanwhile, lightly rub the steaks with the oil, then sprinkle both sides with salt and pepper to taste. Grill the steaks, covered, over the hotter part of the fire until well browned on one side, about 3 minutes. Turn the steaks; grill, covered, until well browned on the other side, about 3 minutes.

3. Once the steaks are well browned on both sides, slide them to cooler part of grill. Continue grilling, covered, to the desired doneness, 8 to 9 minutes for rare (120 degrees on instant-read thermometer), 10 to 11 minutes for medium-rare on the rare side (125 degrees), 12 to 13 minutes for medium-rare on medium side (130 degrees), or 13 to 14 minutes for medium (135 to 140 degrees).

4. Remove the steaks from the grill and let rest for 5 minutes. Serve immediately.

FLANK STEAK

THANKS TO FAJITAS, FLANK STEAK HAS BECOME the darling of Tex-Mex fans from New York to California and everywhere in between. But there are good reasons for the popularity of flank steak in addition to mere culinary fashion. Like other steaks cut from the chest and side of the cow, flank has a rich, full, beefy flavor. Also, because it is very thin, it cooks quite quickly. Flank steak is too large to fit in a pan, so grilling makes the most sense for this cut.

Although grilling flank steak appeared to be a pretty straightforward proposition, we still had some questions about what was exactly the best way to go about it. All of these questions concerned the achievement of two very simple goals: getting a good sear on the outside of this thin cut of meat before overcooking on the inside, and keeping it tender. We wondered whether the meat should be marinated or rubbed with spices, how hot the fire should be, and how long the meat should be cooked.

Virtually every recipe we found for flank steak called for marinating. Most sources championed the marinade as a means of tenderizing the meat as well as adding flavor. We found that marinades with a lot of acid eventually made this thin cut mushy and unappealing. If we left out the acid, we could flavor the meat, but this took at least 12 hours. As for tenderness, when the cooked steaks were sliced thin against the grain, there was virtually no difference between those that were marinated and those that were not.

With marinades out, we turned to spice rubs. We rubbed one steak with a spice rub eight hours before cooking, one an hour before, and one just before we put it over the flames. One steak was cooked just like the others, but with no spice rub at all. The three spice-rubbed steaks all had about the same amount of flavor, and all developed almost identical dark brown, very flavorful crusts. The plain steak did not develop nearly as nice a crust but cooked in approximately the same amount of time. We noticed no differences in tenderness among the steaks.

Since spice rubs create an excellent crust with plenty of intense flavor, they are our first choice for flank steaks. They are not good, however, for folks who like their steak medium, because if you leave the steak on long enough to get it that done, the spices burn. You even have to be a bit careful to keep them from burning if you like your steak medium-rare. But if you don't mind exercising that small degree of care, we highly recommend using spice rubs for flank steak. If you want to cook flank steak further, try adding flavor by passing a sauce separately at the table.

Every source we checked was in the same camp when it came to cooking flank steak, and it is the right camp. These steaks should be cooked over high heat for a short period of time. We tried lower heat

and longer times, but inevitably the meat ended up being tough. Because flank steak is too thin to be checked with a meat thermometer, you must resort to a very primitive method of checking for doneness: Cut into the meat and see if it is done to your liking. Remember that carryover heat will continue to cook the steak after it comes off the grill. So if you want the steak medium-rare, take it off the heat when it looks rare, and so on.

Most sources were also in the same camp when it came to letting the steak rest after cooking. During cooking, the heat drives the juices to the center of the meat. This phenomenon is particularly noticeable with high-heat cooking. If you cut the meat right after it comes off the heat, much more of the juice spills out than if you allow the meat to rest, during which time the blood becomes evenly distributed throughout the meat once again. This is common wisdom among cooks, but to be sure it was correct, we cooked two more flank steaks, sliced one up immediately after it came off the fire, and allowed the second to rest for five minutes before slicing it. Not only did the first steak exude almost twice as much juice when sliced as the second, it also looked grayer and was not as tender. So in this case, it is crucial to follow conventional wisdom: Give your steak a rest.

Charcoal-Grilled Flank Steak

SERVES 4 TO 6

For this recipe, the coals are banked on one side of the grill to create an especially hot fire. Because flank steak is so thin, there's no need to use the cooler part of the grill for cooking the meat through. To keep juices in the meat, it is very important for the steak to rest after it comes off the grill.

1 flank steak (about 2½ pounds)
 Salt and ground black pepper

1. Light a large chimney starter filled with hardwood charcoal (about 2½ pounds) and allow to burn until all the charcoal is covered with a layer of fine gray ash. Build a modified two-level fire by stacking all of the coals on one side of the grill. Set the cooking rack in place, cover the grill with the lid, and let the rack heat up, about 5 minutes. Use a wire brush

to scrape clean the cooking grate. The grill is ready when you have a hot fire (see how to gauge heat level on page 19).

2. Generously sprinkle both sides of the steak with salt and pepper to taste. Grill the steak over the coals until well seared and dark brown on one side, 5 to 7 minutes. Flip the steak using tongs; continue grilling on the other side until the interior of the meat is slightly less done than you want it to be when you eat it, 2 to 5 minutes more for rare or medium-rare (depending on the heat of the fire and thickness of the steak).

3. Transfer the meat to a cutting board; cover it loosely with foil and let rest for 5 minutes. Slice the steak very thinly on the bias against the grain; adjust the seasonings with additional salt and pepper and serve immediately.

Gas-Grilled Flank Steak

SERVES 4 TO 6

With the cover down, flank steak cooks very quickly on a gas grill.

I   flank steak (about 2½ pounds)
     Salt and ground black pepper

1. Preheat the grill with all burners set to high and the lid down until the grill is very hot, about 15 minutes. Use a wire brush to scrape clean the cooking grate. Leave both burners on high.

2. Generously sprinkle both sides of the steak with salt and pepper to taste. Grill the steak, covered, until well seared and dark brown on one side, 4 to 6 minutes. Flip the steak using tongs; continue grilling on the other side until the interior of the meat is slightly less done than you want it to be when you eat it, 2 to 5 minutes more for rare or medium-rare (depending on the heat of the fire and thickness of the steak).

3. Transfer the meat to a cutting board; cover it loosely with foil and let rest for 5 minutes. Slice the steak very thinly on the bias against the grain; adjust the seasonings with additional salt and pepper and serve immediately.

➤ VARIATIONS

Grilled Flank Steak Rubbed with Latin Spices

Watch the meat carefully as it cooks to ensure that the spice rub darkens but does not burn. If necessary, slide the steak to the cooler part of the grill to keep the steak from charring. Flank steak can also be rubbed with Simple Spice Rub for Beef or Lamb on page 293.

2   tablespoons ground cumin
2   tablespoons chili powder
I   tablespoon ground coriander
I½   teaspoons salt
2   teaspoons ground black pepper
½   teaspoon ground cinnamon
½   teaspoon hot red pepper flakes
I   recipe Charcoal-Grilled or Gas-Grilled Flank
       Steak (page 32 and at left)

1. Combine the spices in a small bowl.

2. Follow the steak recipe, omitting the salt and pepper and rubbing the steak with the spice mixture instead.

Grilled Flank Steak with Sweet and Sour Chipotle Sauce

If you can't find chipotles, substitute a mixture of ½ teaspoon liquid smoke, 2 minced jalapeño chiles, and 3 tablespoons ketchup.

¼   cup honey
2   tablespoons vegetable oil
3   chipotle chiles packed in adobo sauce
2   tablespoons balsamic vinegar
2   tablespoons grainy mustard
½   cup lime juice
2   medium garlic cloves, minced
I   teaspoon ground cumin
2   tablespoons chopped fresh cilantro leaves
½   teaspoon salt
       Ground black pepper
I   recipe Charcoal-Grilled or Gas-Grilled Flank
       Steak (page 32 and at left)

1. Combine honey, oil, chipotles, vinegar, mustard, lime juice, garlic, and cumin in a blender jar or workbowl of food processor fitted with steel blade; puree or

process until smooth. Transfer to a small bowl and stir in the cilantro, salt, and pepper to taste; set aside. (Sauce can be covered and refrigerated for up to 3 days.)

2. Generously brush both sides of the meat with the sauce after grilling but before resting. Pass remaining sauce separately with the sliced steak.

Grilled Flank Steak with Spicy Parsley Sauce

This simple, thick, almost spreadable sauce lets the flavor of the flank steak come through.

I	cup minced fresh parsley leaves
3	medium garlic cloves, minced
I	medium jalapeño chile, minced
½	cup extra-virgin olive oil
3	tablespoons red wine vinegar
	Salt and ground black pepper
I	recipe Charcoal-Grilled or Gas-Grilled Flank Steak (pages 32 and 33)

1. Mix the parsley, garlic, chile, olive oil, vinegar, and salt and pepper to taste in a small bowl. (Sauce can be covered and refrigerated up to 3 days.)

2. Serve sauce, passing separately, with the sliced steak.

Classic Fajitas
SERVES 8

Although it was originally made with skirt steak (a fattier cut with more flavor; see box below), this combination of flank steak and vegetables grilled and then wrapped in warm tortillas is the dish that put flank steak on the culinary map in the United States. The ingredients go on the grill in order as the fire dies down: steak over a hot fire, vegetables over a medium fire, and tortillas around the edge of the medium to low fire just to warm them. Alternately, the tortillas can be wrapped together in a clean, damp dish towel and warmed in a microwave oven for about 3 minutes at full power; keep them wrapped until you're ready to use them. Make sure to cover the grilled but unsliced flank steak with foil; it will take you at least 10 minutes to cook the vegetables and warm the tortillas.

I	recipe Charcoal-Grilled or Gas-Grilled Flank Steak; steak sprinkled with ¼ cup lime juice and salt and pepper to taste before cooking
I	very large onion, peeled and cut into ½-inch rounds
2	very large red or green bell peppers, cored, seeded, and cut into large wedges
16	flour tortillas (10-inch)
I	recipe Classic Red Table Salsa (page 299)
I	recipe Chunky Guacamole (page 300)

INGREDIENTS: Three Flat Steaks

Like flank steak, the other two cuts most similar to it—skirt steak and hanger steak—have become fashionable. These now-popular steaks share the distinction of coming from the chest and side of the animal. Hanger and flank both come from the rear side, while skirt comes from the area between the abdomen and the chest cavity. In addition to location, these steaks share certain other basic qualities: all are long, relatively thin, quite tough, and grainy, but with rich, deep, beefy flavor.

Of course, there are also differences among these flavorful steaks. Hanger, a thick muscle that is attached to the diaphragm, derives its name from the fact that when a cow is butchered, this steak hangs down into the center of the carcass. Because it is a classic French bistro dish, this cut is highly prized in restaurants and therefore difficult to find in butcher shops. We don't think this is a great loss since the hangers we sampled had the toughest texture and least rich flavor of these three cuts.

Fortunately, flank steak is easy to find in any supermarket. It has great beef flavor and is quite tender if cooked rare or medium-rare and sliced thin against the grain. Because of the popularity of fajitas, flank steak has become somewhat expensive, often retailing for $7 a pound.

The skirt steak, the cut originally used for fajitas, can be hard to locate in supermarkets and even butcher shops. This is a real pity because the skirt steak has more fat than the flank steak, which makes it juicier and richer-tasting. At the same time, it has a deep, beefy flavor that outdoes either hanger or flank steak. If you see skirt steak, buy it, and cook it like flank.

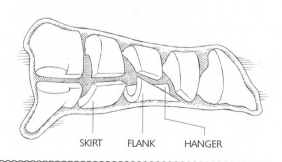

SKIRT   FLANK   HANGER

1. Follow recipe for either Charcoal-Grilled or Gas-Grilled Flank Steak, sprinkling the steak with the lime juice and salt and pepper to taste before cooking.

2. While the meat rests and the charcoal fire has died down to medium or gas grill burners have been adjusted to medium, grill the onions and peppers, turning occasionally, until the onions are lightly charred, about 6 minutes, and the peppers are streaked with dark grill marks, about 10 minutes. Remove the vegetables from the grill and cut into long, thin strips; set aside. Arrange the tortillas around the edge of the grill; heat until just warmed, about 20 seconds per side. (Take care not to dry out tortillas or they will become brittle; wrap the tortillas in a towel to keep warm and then place them in a basket.)

3. Slice the meat. Arrange the sliced meat and vegetables on a large platter; serve immediately with the tortillas, salsa, and guacamole passed separately.

LONDON BROIL

LONDON BROIL IS A RECIPE, NOT A PARTICULAR cut of meat. It involves taking a thick steak (steaks labeled London broil are usually taken from the shoulder or round and sometimes the sirloin); grilling, broiling, or pan-grilling it; then slicing it thin on the bias across the grain. This process makes the most of these often inexpensive cuts of beef.

It was for thinner flank steak that the tradition of preparing steak this way originated. Since flank steak has some marbling and is not a supertough cut, it is ideal for this purpose. (See pages 31 to 32 for more details on cooking flank steak.) However, now that flank steak costs $7 a pound, it's not such an inexpensive cut anymore, especially since cuts from the round or shoulder can cost just $2 or $3 a pound. We wanted to figure out how to cook these cheap cuts, which are quite lean and pose numerous challenges for the cook.

Before figuring out which of the cheaper cuts would work best for London broil, we wanted to decide on the cooking technique. We were looking for a London broil with a nice crisp crust and rare-to-medium-rare interior. (Because they are so lean, London broil cuts will become intolerably dry and tough if cooked to medium or beyond. If you don't like a pink steak, try a cut with more fat, such as rib-eye steak.) A two-level fire, which allowed the meat to be seared and then cooked through over moderate heat, worked best.

To work as London broil, a cut must be made up of one muscle; otherwise it simply falls apart when you slice it. There are only a few cuts of beef that meet this criterion. We eliminated one of them, the tri-tip cut, because it is too difficult for most consumers to find. We put top sirloin out of the running along with the flank because they are too expensive. Eye of round has the wrong shape for steaks, while bottom round is almost always used for roasts.

That left us two cuts—the top round and the shoulder. When we began investigating them, we quickly made an important discovery. Although supermarkets tend to sell top round and shoulder the same way (as thick steaks labeled London Broil), the cuts are very different.

If you treat a 1- or 1½-inch-thick shoulder steak like flank steak, you get good results—a chewy, flavorful steak. Not only is shoulder the least expensive steak you can buy, it also has a little bit of fat, which you want. If, however, you cook a thick cut of top round like a flank steak, you will be disappointed. The round is lean and tight-grained, with a liverlike flavor that is almost disgusting in quickly cooked muscle meat. Shoulder has a robust beef flavor and a reasonably tender texture that are far superior.

London broil can be seasoned with just salt and pepper but also works well with the spice rubs and sauces in the preceding section on flank steak. Because London broil is relatively lean, it is especially good when served with any of the compound butters on page 30.

Charcoal-Grilled London Broil
SERVES 4

Because the shoulder steak is so thick, it must be grilled over a two-level fire. Do not cook past medium-rare or this lean cut will be unpalatably dry.

1   boneless shoulder steak, 1½ inches thick
     (1½ to 2 pounds)
     Salt and ground black pepper

1. Light a large chimney starter filled with hardwood charcoal (about 2½ pounds) and allow to burn until all the charcoal is covered with a layer of fine gray ash. Build a two-level fire by stacking most of the coals on one side of the grill and arranging the remaining coals in a single layer on the other side of the grill. Set the cooking rack in place, cover the grill with the lid, and let the rack heat up, about 5 minutes. Use a wire brush to scrape clean the cooking rack. The grill is ready when the pile of coals is medium-hot and the single layer is medium-low (see how to gauge heat level on page 19).

2. Meanwhile, sprinkle both sides of the steak with salt and pepper to taste. Grill the steak, uncovered, over the hotter part of the fire until well browned on one side, 2 to 3 minutes. Turn the steak; grill until well browned on the other side, 2 to 3 minutes.

3. Once steak is well browned on both sides, slide it to the cooler part of the grill. Continue grilling, uncovered, to the desired doneness, 5 to 6 minutes more for rare (120 degrees on instant-read thermometer), 6 to 7 minutes for medium-rare on the rare side (125 degrees), or 7 to 8 minutes for medium-rare on the medium side (130 degrees).

4. Remove the steak from the grill and let rest for 5 minutes. Slice the steak very thinly on the bias against the grain; adjust the seasonings with additional salt and pepper and serve immediately.

Gas-Grilled London Broil

SERVES 4

As in charcoal grilling, gas-grilled London broil should be cooked over a two-level fire.

I	boneless shoulder steak, 1½ inches thick
	(1½ to 2 pounds)
	Salt and ground black pepper

1. Preheat the grill with all burners set to high and the lid down until the grill is very hot, about 15 minutes. Use a wire brush to scrape clean the cooking grate. Leave one burner on high and turn the other burner(s) down to medium.

2. Meanwhile, sprinkle both sides of the steak with salt and pepper to taste. Grill the steak, covered, over the hotter part of the fire until well browned on one side, 2 to 3 minutes. Turn the steak; grill until well browned on the other side, 2 to 3 minutes.

3. Once steak is well browned on both sides, slide it to cooler part of grill. Continue grilling, covered, to the desired doneness, 7 to 8 minutes more for rare (120 degrees on instant-read thermometer), 8 to 9 minutes for medium-rare on the rare side (125 degrees), or 10 to 11 minutes for medium-rare on the medium side (130 degrees).

4. Remove the steak from the grill and let rest for 5 minutes. Slice the steak very thinly on the bias against the grain; adjust the seasonings with additional salt and pepper and serve immediately.

4
BURGERS AND SAUSAGES

BURGERS AND SAUSAGES BOTH START WITH ground meat and are favorites for grilling, in part because they are so easy to cook. Burgers need only to be shaped into patties, while sausage links are grill-ready—they don't even need to be seasoned. Although seemingly easy to grill, burgers and sausages can go wrong. Everyone has incinerated sausage on the grill or had burgers stick to it. We set out to perfect our cooking methods for both of these summertime favorites.

Beef burgers (aka hamburgers) are the classic American grilled sandwich. However, burgers made from ground turkey as well as fresh salmon and tuna have become popular in recent years. Each kind of burger presents its own challenges, all of which are detailed in the sections that follow. They do, however, have at least one thing in common: Ground meats and finely chopped fish tend to stick to the grill. To prevent sticking, make sure your grill is superhot and completely clean. Oiling the grill also helps.

A hot grill ensures that burgers will develop that signature crusty exterior that does so much for flavor and texture. To promote the development of a thick crust, avoid the temptation to continually flip the burger during cooking. Follow the cooking times in the recipes, setting a timer if you like. When the buzzer goes off, flip the burger. When the buzzer goes off again, pull that burger confidently from the heat.

Like burgers, sausages begin with ground meat, but the cooking issues are different. Sticking is never really a problem. Traditional sausages contain so much fat that flare-ups are the greatest challenge for the cook. It's easier to prevent flare-ups when cooking low-fat poultry or pork sausages, but these lean links can dry out and come off the grill with a poor texture.

HAMBURGERS

LOTS OF HAMBURGERS SEEM MERELY TO satisfy hunger rather than give pleasure. Too bad, because making an exceptional hamburger isn't that hard or time-consuming. Fast-food chains no doubt had good reasons when they decided against selling hand-formed, 100 percent ground-chuck burgers; home cooks, however, do not. If you have the right ground beef, the perfect hamburger can

be ready in fewer than 15 minutes, assuming you season, form, and cook it properly. The biggest difficulty for many cooks, though, may be finding the right beef.

To test which cut or cuts of beef cook up into the best burger, we called a butcher and ordered chuck, round, rump, sirloin, and hanging tenderloin, all ground to order with 20 percent fat. (Although we would question fat percentages in later testing, we needed a standard for these early tests. Based on experience, this percentage seemed right.) After a side-by-side taste test, we quickly concluded that most cuts of ground beef are pleasant but bland when compared with the robust, beefy flavored ground chuck. Pricier ground sirloin, for example, cooked up into a particularly boring burger.

So pure ground chuck—the cut of beef that starts where the ribs end and travels up to the shoulder and neck, ending at the foreshank—was the clear winner. We were ready to race ahead to seasonings, but before moving on we stopped to ask ourselves, "Will cooks buying ground chuck from the grocery store agree with our choice?" Our efforts to determine whether grocery-store ground chuck and ground-to-order chuck were even remotely similar took us along a culinary blue highway from kitchen to packing plant, butcher shop, and science lab.

According to the National Livestock and Meat Board, the percentage of fat in beef is checked and enforced at the retail level. If a package of beef is labeled 90 percent lean, then it must contain no more than 10 percent fat, give or take a point. Retail stores are required to test each batch of ground beef, make the necessary adjustments, and keep a log of the results. Local inspectors routinely pull ground beef from a store's meat case for a fat check. If the fat content is not within 1 percent of the package sticker, the store is fined.

Whether a package labeled ground chuck is, in fact, 100 percent ground chuck is a different story. First, we surveyed a number of grocery store meat department managers, who said that what was written on the label did match what was in the package. For instance, a package labeled "ground chuck" would have been made only from chuck trimmings. Same for sirloin and round. Only "ground beef" would be made from mixed beef trimmings.

We got a little closer to the truth, however, by interviewing a respected butcher in the Chicago area. At the several grocery stores and butcher shops where he had worked over the years, he had never known a store to segregate meat trimmings. In fact, in his present butcher shop, he sells only two kinds of ground beef: sirloin and chuck. He defines ground sirloin as ground beef (mostly but not exclusively sirloin) that's labeled 90 percent lean, and chuck as ground beef (including a lot of chuck trimmings) that's labeled 85 percent lean.

Only meat ground at federally inspected plants is guaranteed to match its label. At these plants, an inspector checks to make sure that labeled ground beef actually comes from the cut of beef named on the label and that the fat percentage is correct. Most retailers, though, cannot guarantee that their ground beef has been made from a specific cut; they can only guarantee fat percentages.

Because the labeling of retail ground beef can be deceptive, we suggest that you buy a chuck roast and have the butcher grind it for you. Even at a local grocery store, we found that the butcher was willing to grind to order. Some meat always gets lost in the grinder, so count on losing a bit (2 to 3 percent).

Because commercially ground beef is at risk for contamination with the bacteria E. coli, we thought it made theoretical sense for home cooks to grind their beef at home, thereby reducing their odds of eating tainted beef. It doesn't make much practical sense, though. Not all cooks own a grinder. And even if they did, we thought home grinding demanded far too much setup, cleanup, and effort for a dish meant to be so simple.

To see if there was an easier way, we tried chopping by hand and grinding in the food processor. The hibachi-style hand-chopping method was just as time-consuming and even more messy than the traditional grinder. In this method, you must slice the meat thin and then cut it into cubes before going at it with two chef's knives. The fat doesn't distribute evenly, meat flies everywhere, and, unless your knives are razor sharp, it's difficult to chop through the meat. What's worse, you can't efficiently chop more than two burgers at a time. In the end, the cooked burgers can be mistaken for chopped steak.

The food processor did a surprisingly good job of grinding meat. We thought the steel blade would raggedly chew the meat, but the hamburger turned out evenly chopped and fluffy. (For more information, see "Food Processor as Grinder," page 41.)

We figured the average chuck roast to be about 80 percent lean. To check its leanness, we bought a chuck roast—not too fatty, not too lean—and ground it in the food processor. We then took our ground chuck back to the grocery store and asked the butcher to check its fat content in the Univex Fat Analyzer, a machine the store uses to check each batch of beef it grinds. A plug of our ground beef scored an almost perfect 21 percent fat when tested.

SCIENCE: Puffy Burgers

All too often, burgers come off the grill with a domed, puffy shape that makes it impossible to keep condiments from sliding off. Fast-food restaurants produce burgers that are even, but they are also extremely thin. We wondered if we could find a way to produce a meatier burger that would have the same thickness from edge to edge, giving the condiments a nice, flat top to sit on.

We shaped six-ounce portions of ground beef into patties that were one inch, three-quarters inch, and one-half inch thick. Once cooked, all of these burgers looked like tennis balls, and it was nearly impossible to anchor ketchup and other goodies on top. After talking to several food scientists, we understood why this happens.

The culprit behind puffy burgers is the connective tissue, or collagen, that is ground up along with the meat. When the connective tissue in a patty heats up to roughly 130 degrees, it shrinks. This happens first on the flat top and bottom surfaces of the burger and then on the sides, where the tightening acts like a belt. When the sides tighten, the interior meat volume is forced up and down, so the burger puffs.

One of the cooks in the test kitchen suggested a trick she had picked up when working in a restaurant. We shaped patties three-quarters inch thick but then formed a slight depression in the center of each patty so that the edges were thicker than the center. On the grill, the center puffed up to the point where it was the same height as the edges. Finally, a level burger that could hold onto toppings.

Up to this point, all of our beef had been ground with approximately 20 percent fat. A quick test of burgers with less and more fat helped us to decide that 20 percent fat, give or take a few percentage points, was good for burgers. Any more fat and the burgers are just too greasy. Any less and you start compromising the beef's juicy, moist texture.

When to season the meat with salt and pepper may seem like an insignificant detail, but when making a dish as simple as a hamburger, little things matter. We tried seasoning the meat at four different times during the process. Our first burger was seasoned before the meat was shaped, the second burger was seasoned right before cooking, the third after each side was seared, and the fourth after the burger had been fully cooked.

SHAPING HAMBURGERS

1. With cupped hands, toss one portion of meat back and forth from hand to hand to shape it into a loose ball.

2. Pat lightly to flatten the meat into a three-quarter-inch-thick burger that measures about 4½ inches across. Press the center of the patty down with your fingertips until it is about one-half inch thick, thus creating a well in the center. Repeat with the remaining portions of ground meat.

Predictably, the burger that had been seasoned throughout was our preference. All the surface-seasoned burgers were the same. You got a hit of salt up front, then the burger went bland. The thin surface area was well seasoned while the rest was not.

Working with fresh-ground chuck seasoned with salt and pepper, we now moved on to shaping and cooking. To defy the overpacking and overhandling warning you see in many recipes, we thoroughly worked a portion of ground beef before cooking it. The well-done burger exterior was nearly as dense as a meat pâté, and the less well-done interior was compact and pasty.

It's pretty hard to overhandle a beef patty, though, especially if you're trying not to. Once the meat has been divided into portions, we found that tossing each portion from one hand to the other helped bring the meat together into a ball without overworking it. We made one of our most interesting discoveries when we tested various shaping techniques for the patties. A well in the center of each burger ensures that they come off the grill with an even thickness instead of puffed up like a tennis ball. (For more on shaping burgers, see illustration at left.)

To our taste, a four-ounce burger seemed a little skimpy. A six-ounce portion of meat patted into a nicely sized burger fit perfectly in a bun.

Now nearly done with our testing, we needed only to perfect our grilling method. Burgers require a real blast of heat if they are to form a crunchy, flavorful crust before the interior overcooks. While many of the recipes we looked at advise the cook to grill burgers over a hot fire, we suspected we'd have to adjust the heat because our patties were quite thin in the middle. Sure enough, a superhot fire made it too easy to overcook the burgers. We found a medium-hot fire formed a crust quickly, while also providing a wider margin of error for properly cooking the center.

Nonetheless, burgers cook quickly—needing only 2½ to 3½ minutes per side. Don't walk away from the grill when cooking burgers.

To keep the burgers from sticking to the grill, we coated it with oil. All you need to do is dip a wad of paper towels in some vegetable oil, hold the wad with long-handled tongs, and rub the oil on the hot grate just before adding the burgers.

One last finding from our testing: Don't ever press down on burgers as they cook. Rather than speeding their cooking, pressing on the patties serves only to squeeze out their juices and make the burgers dry.

Even though we have a meat grinder in our test kitchen, we don't regularly grind meat ourselves. The setup, breakdown, and cleanup required for a two-pound chuck roast is just not worth the effort. Besides, hamburgers are supposed to be impromptu, fast, fun food.

To our surprise, though, the food processor does a respectable grinding job, and it's much easier to use than a grinder. The key is to make sure the roast is cold, that it is cut into small chunks, and that it is processed in small batches. For a two-pound roast, cut the meat into one-inch chunks. Divide the chunks into four equal portions. Place one portion of meat in the workbowl of a food processor fitted with a steel blade. Pulse the cubes until the meat is ground, 15 to 20 one-second pulses. Repeat with the remaining portions of beef. Then shape the ground meat as directed.

Charcoal-Grilled Hamburgers

SERVES 4

For those who like their burgers well-done, we found that poking a small indentation in the center of the patty before cooking helped the burger cook through to the center before the edges dried out. See box on page 39 and illustrations on page 40 for tips on shaping burgers.

1½	pounds 100 percent ground chuck
1	teaspoon salt
½	teaspoon ground black pepper
	Vegetable oil for grill rack
	Buns and desired toppings

1. Light a large chimney starter filled with hardwood charcoal (about 2½ pounds) and allow to burn until all the charcoal is covered with a layer of fine gray ash. Build a single-level fire by spreading the coals evenly out over the bottom of the grill. Set the cooking rack in place, cover the grill with the lid, and let the rack heat up, about 5 minutes. Use a wire

brush to scrape clean the cooking grate. The grill is ready when the coals are medium-hot. (See how to gauge heat level on page 19.)

2. Meanwhile, break up the chuck to increase the surface area for seasoning. Sprinkle the salt and pepper over the meat; toss lightly with hands to distribute the seasonings. Divide the meat into four equal portions (6 ounces each); with cupped hands, toss one portion of meat back and forth to form a loose ball. Pat lightly to flatten the meat into a ¾-inch-thick burger that measures about 4½ inches across. Press the center of the patty down with your fingertips until about ½ inch thick, thus creating a well in the center of the patty. Repeat with the remaining portions of meat.

3. Lightly dip a small wad of paper towels in vegetable oil; holding wad with tongs, wipe grill rack. Grill the burgers, uncovered and without pressing down on them, until well seared on the first side, about 2½ minutes. Flip the burgers with a wide metal spatula. Continue grilling to the desired doneness, about 2 minutes for rare, 2½ minutes for medium-rare, 3 minutes for medium, or 4 minutes for well-done. Serve immediately.

Gas-Grilled Hamburgers

SERVES 4

See the illustrations on page 40 for tips on shaping burgers.

1½	pounds 100 percent ground chuck
1	teaspoon salt
½	teaspoon ground black pepper
	Vegetable oil for grill rack
	Buns and desired toppings

1. Preheat the grill with all burners set to high and the lid down until the grill is very hot, about 15 minutes. Use a wire brush to scrape clean the cooking grate. Leave both burners on high.

2. Meanwhile, break up the chuck to increase the surface area for seasoning. Sprinkle the salt and pepper over the meat; toss lightly with hands to distribute the seasonings. Divide the meat into four equal portions (6 ounces each); with cupped hands, toss one portion of meat back and forth to form a loose ball. Pat lightly to flatten the meat into a ¾-inch-thick

burger that measures about 4½ inches across. Press the center of the patty down with your fingertips until about ½ inch thick, thus creating a well in the center. Repeat with the remaining portions of meat.

3. Lightly dip a small wad of paper towels in vegetable oil; holding wad with tongs, wipe grill rack. Grill the burgers, covered and without pressing down on them, until well seared on the first side, about 3 minutes. Flip burgers with a wide metal spatula. Continue grilling, covered, to the desired doneness, about 3 minutes for rare, 3½ minutes for medium-rare, 4 minutes for medium, or 5 minutes for well-done. Serve immediately.

DRESSING UP HAMBURGERS

There are countless ways to dress up basic burgers. We find that about ¼ cup of a chunky salsa or sauce (such as the Black Bean and Mango Salsa or the Chunky Guacamole on page 300) is right for each burger. If using a thinner salsa (such as the Classic Red Table Salsa on page 299), use about 3 tablespoons per burger and use a slotted spoon to drain off any excess liquid before spooning the salsa over the burgers.

➤ VARIATIONS

Grilled Cheeseburgers

For those who love cheese, we suggest grating it into the raw beef as opposed to melting it on top. Because the cheese is more evenly distributed, a little goes much farther than a big chunk on top. Also, there's no danger of overcooking the burgers while you wait for the cheese to melt.

Follow recipe for Charcoal-Grilled Burgers or Gas-Grilled Burgers, mixing 3½ ounces cheddar, Swiss, Jack, or blue cheese, shredded or crumbled as necessary, into the ground chuck along with the salt and pepper. Shape and cook burgers as directed.

Grilled Hamburgers with Garlic, Chipotles, and Scallions

Toast 3 medium unpeeled garlic cloves in a small dry skillet over medium heat, shaking pan occasionally, until fragrant and color deepens slightly, about 8 minutes. When cool enough to handle, skin and mince the garlic. Follow recipe for Charcoal-Grilled Burgers or Gas-Grilled Burgers, mixing garlic, 1 tablespoon minced chipotle chile in adobo sauce, and 2 tablespoons minced scallions into the meat along with the salt and pepper.

Grilled Hamburgers with Cognac, Mustard, and Chives

Mix 1½ tablespoons cognac, 2 teaspoons Dijon mustard, and 1 tablespoon minced fresh chives in a small bowl. Follow recipe for Charcoal-Grilled Burgers or Gas-Grilled Burgers, mixing cognac mixture into the meat along with the salt and pepper.

Grilled Hamburgers with Porcini Mushrooms and Thyme

Cover ½ ounce dried porcini mushroom pieces with ½ cup hot tap water in a small microwave-safe bowl; cover with plastic wrap, cut several steam vents with a paring knife, and microwave on high power for 30 seconds. Let stand until the mushrooms soften, about 5 minutes. Lift the mushrooms from the liquid with a fork and mince, using a chef's knife (you should have about 2 tablespoons). Follow recipe for Charcoal-Grilled Burgers or Gas-Grilled Burgers, mixing the porcini mushrooms and 1 teaspoon minced fresh thyme leaves into the meat along with the salt and pepper.

EQUIPMENT: Hamburger Presses

We have formed plenty of hamburgers in our test kitchen. While we don't consider patting a burger out by hand to be a problem, we wondered about all the gadgets specifically designed for this task. Could they make a simple task even simpler?

We rounded up four models and began testing. All of the presses easily accommodated six-ounce portions of ground meat. That said, the only general advantage these gadgets seemed to offer was that they kept your hands from becoming very greasy by limiting contact with the meat. As advantages go, this was pretty thin. You still have to touch the meat and thus wash your hands well. Save the money and cabinet space for something more useful.

INGREDIENTS: Ketchup

For many people, a burger isn't done until it has been coated liberally with ketchup. This condiment originated in Asia as a salty, fermented medium for pickling or preserving ingredients, primarily fish. Early versions were made with anchovies and generally were highly spiced.

Tomato-based ketchup has its origins in nineteenth-century America. We now consume more than 600 million pints of ketchup every year, much of it landing on top of burgers. But as any ketchup connoisseur knows, not all brands are created equal. To find out which is the best, we tasted 13 different samples, including several fancy mail-order ketchups and one we made in our test kitchen.

It wasn't much of a surprise that the winner was Heinz. For all tasters but one, Heinz ranked first or second, and they described it with words like "classic" and "perfect." A tiny bit sweeter than Heinz, Del Monte took second place, while Hunt's (the other leading national brand, along with Heinz and Del Monte) rated third.

What about the mail-order, organic, fruit-sweetened, and homemade ketchups? Most tasters felt these samples were overly thick and not smooth enough. Some were too spicy, others too vinegary. Our homemade ketchup was too chunky, more like "tomato jam" than ketchup. In color, consistency, and flavor, none of these interlopers could match the archetypal ketchup, Heinz.

TURKEY BURGERS

A LEAN, FULLY COOKED TURKEY BURGER, seasoned with salt and pepper, is a weak stand-in for an all-beef burger. Simply put, it is dry, tasteless, and colorless. We wanted a turkey burger with beef burger qualities—dark and crusty on the outside and full-flavored and juicy with every bite.

Finding the right meat was crucial to developing the best turkey burger. According to the National Turkey Federation, there are three options: white meat (with 1 to 2 percent fat), dark meat (more than 15 percent fat), and a blend of the two (ranging from 7 to 15 percent fat).

At the grocery store, we found multiple variations on the white meat/dark meat theme, including preformed lean patties, higher-fat ground fresh turkey on Styrofoam trays or frozen in tubes like bulk sausage, and lower-fat ground turkey breasts; then there were the individual turkey parts we could grind up ourselves. We bought them all, took them back to the test kitchen, and fired up the grill.

We first tested the preformed lean patties—refrigerated and frozen—and found them mediocre. To varying degrees, the frozen ones had a week-old-roast-turkey taste. A few bites from one of the refrigerated varieties turned up significant turkey debris: tendon, ground-up gristle, and bonelike chips. We moved on to bulk ground turkey.

The higher-fat (15 percent) ground turkey turned out to be flavorful and reasonably juicy, with a decent, burgerlike crust. Frankly, these burgers didn't need too much help. On the other hand, we didn't see much point in eating them, either. Given that a great beef burger contains only 20 percent fat, a mere 5 percent fat savings didn't seem worth it.

At the other extreme, with only 1 or 2 percent fat, was ground turkey breast. As we were mixing and forming these patties, we knew we had about as much chance of making them look, taste, and feel like real burgers as we did of making vanilla wafers taste like chocolate chip cookies. They needed a binder to keep them from falling apart. They needed extra fat to keep them from parching and sticking to the grill. And they needed flavor to save them from blandness.

With 7 percent fat, lean ground turkey was the most popular variety at all the grocery stores we checked. Burgers made from this mix were dry, rubbery textured, and mild flavored. With a little help, however, these leaner patties were meaty enough to have real burger potential.

Most flavorful of all were the boned and skinless turkey thighs we ground ourselves in the food processor. We first tried grinding the skin with the meat but found that it ground inconsistently, and we had to pick it out. In the next batch we left it out and found the result to be equally flavorful and much lower in calories. As a matter of fact, our butcher declared our home-ground skinless turkey almost 90 percent lean when he tested it in his Univex Fat Analyzer.

For all the obvious reasons, we had sworn that even if we liked the outcome we weren't going to make grind-your-own-turkey part of the recipe, but these burgers—meaty flavored with a beeflike chew—were far superior to any we made with the commercially ground turkey. Of course, we had suspected as much, given our liking for grind-your-own-chuck beef burgers (see page 39). If you are willing to take the time, turkey thighs ground up in the food processor cook up into low-fat turkey burgers with great flavor and texture.

For those not inclined to grind their own meat, we decided to see what we could do to improve the lean commercially ground turkey (with 7 percent fat). To improve texture and juiciness, we started with milk-soaked bread. For comparison, we also made burgers with buttermilk- and yogurt-soaked bread. All these additions made the burgers feel too much like meat loaf and destroyed whatever meaty flavor there had been, since turkey is mild to start with. The bread and milk lightened the meat's color unpleasantly, while the sugar in both ingredients caused the burgers to burn easily and made it impossible to develop a good thick crust.

We tried other fillers to improve the texture, including cornmeal mush, mashed pinto beans, and minced tempeh, but their flavors were too distinct. Minced, rehydrated, dried mushrooms added a moist, chewy texture that the burgers desperately needed. They also offered an earthy, meaty, yet not overly distinct flavor. However, the real winner—for flavor, texture, and easy availability—was ricotta cheese. Moist and chewy, it gave the burger the texture boost it needed and required very little effort.

Finally, we decided to experiment a bit with added flavorings. We wanted only those that would enhance the flavor of the burger without drawing attention to themselves. We tried more than 25 different flavorings—from fermented black beans to olive paste to teriyaki marinade—and found only two that we liked: Worcestershire sauce and Dijon mustard.

Next we turned to the cooking method. Since turkey burgers must be well-done for safety reasons, cooking them can be a bit tricky. If the heat is too high, they burn before they're done; too low, and they look pale and steamed. A two-level fire proved to be the right solution. The burgers are seared over high heat and then moved to the cooler part of the grill where they can cook through. With charcoal grilling, we recommend that you place an aluminum roasting pan over the burgers to contain the heat and ensure even cooking.

Although our generous cooking times should ensure a fully cooked burger, as an extra precaution you may want to test for doneness by sticking an instant-read thermometer through the side and into the center of one of them. The burgers are done at 160 degrees.

A final note about shaping turkey burgers. Unlike beef, ground turkey does not contain a high percentage of collagen. You can make evenly shaped patties and they won't puff up on the grill.

Charcoal-Grilled Turkey Burgers

SERVES 4

Ricotta cheese keeps ground turkey moist as it cooks. Unlike other kinds of burgers, turkey burgers must be thoroughly cooked for the sake of safety and flavor.

1¼	pounds 93 percent lean ground turkey
½	cup ricotta cheese
½	teaspoon salt
½	teaspoon ground black pepper
2	teaspoons Worcestershire sauce
2	teaspoons Dijon mustard
	Vegetable oil for grill rack
	Disposable aluminum roasting pan

1. Light a large chimney starter filled with hardwood charcoal (about 2½ pounds) and allow to burn until all the charcoal is covered with a layer of fine gray ash. Build a two-level fire by stacking most of the coals on one side of the grill and arranging the remaining coals in a single layer on the other side of the grill. Set the cooking rack in place, cover the grill with the lid, and let the rack heat up, about 5 minutes. Use a wire brush to scrape clean the cooking rack. The grill is ready when the temperature of the stacked coals is medium-hot and the remaining coals medium-low. (See how to gauge heat level on page 19.)

2. Meanwhile, combine the ground turkey, cheese, salt, pepper, Worcestershire sauce, and mustard in a medium bowl until blended. Divide the meat into 4 portions. Lightly toss one portion from hand to hand to form a ball, then lightly flatten ball with fingertips into a 1-inch-thick patty. Repeat with the remaining portions of meat.

3. Lightly dip a small wad of paper towels in vegetable oil; holding wad with tongs, wipe grill rack. Grill the burgers, uncovered, over the hotter part of the grill, turning once, until well browned on both sides, 6 to 8 minutes. Slide the burgers to the cooler part of the grill, cover them with a disposable aluminum roasting pan, and continue grilling until cooked through, another 5 to 7 minutes. To test for doneness, either peek into the thickest part of the burgers with the tip of a small knife (you should see no redness at the center) or insert an instant-read thermometer from the side of the burger into the center (it should register 160 degrees). Serve immediately.

Gas-Grilled Turkey Burgers

SERVES 4

To ensure that your burgers are cooked through, use an instant-read thermometer inserted through the side of the burger toward the center; it should read 160 degrees.

1¼	pounds 93 percent lean ground turkey
½	cup ricotta cheese
½	teaspoon salt
½	teaspoon ground black pepper
2	teaspoons Worcestershire sauce
2	teaspoons Dijon mustard
	Vegetable oil for grill rack

1. Preheat the grill with all burners set to high and the lid down until the grill is very hot, about 15 minutes. Use a wire brush to scrape clean the cooking grate. Leave one burner on high and turn the other burner(s) down to medium-low.

2. Meanwhile, combine the ground turkey, cheese, salt, pepper, Worcestershire sauce, and mustard in a medium bowl until blended. Divide the meat into 4 portions. Lightly toss one portion from hand to hand to form a ball, then lightly flatten ball with fingertips into a 1-inch-thick patty. Repeat with the remaining portions of meat.

3. Lightly dip a small wad of paper towels in vegetable oil; holding wad with tongs, wipe the grill rack. Grill the burgers, covered, over the hotter part of the grill, turning once, until well browned on both sides, 8 to 10 minutes. Slide the burgers to the cooler part of the grill and continue grilling, cov-

ered, until cooked through, another 5 to 7 minutes. To test for doneness, either peek into the thickest part of the burgers with the tip of a small knife (you should see no redness at the center) or insert an instant-read thermometer from the side of the burger into the center (it should register 160 degrees). Serve immediately.

✒ VARIATIONS

Turkey Burgers with Porcini Mushrooms

Reconstituted dried porcini mushrooms give turkey burgers a particularly meaty flavor. Dried shiitakes also work well.

Follow recipe for Charcoal-Grilled or Gas-Grilled Turkey Burgers, replacing the Worcestershire sauce and mustard with 1 ounce dried porcini mushrooms that have been rehydrated in 1 cup hot water for 15 minutes, squeezed dry, and minced fine.

Turkey Burgers with Miso

Miso is a fermented soybean paste with a pungent, robust flavor. It is sold in Asian markets as well as natural food stores. It comes in several colors, any of which can be used in this recipe.

Follow recipe for Charcoal-Grilled or Gas-Grilled Turkey Burgers, replacing the Worcestershire sauce and mustard with 2 teaspoons miso thinned with 2 teaspoons water.

OILING THE GRILL RACK

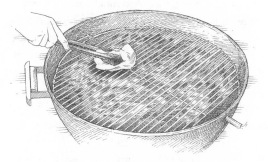

We find it helpful to oil the grill grate just before cooking foods such as burgers and fish, which are prone to sticking. Dip a large wad of paper towels in vegetable oil, grab the wad with tongs, and wipe the grill rack thoroughly to lubricate it and prevent sticking. Wiping the grill rack also cleans off any residue your wire brush may have missed. An impeccably clean grill is especially important when cooking fish, which can very easily pick up off flavors.

Ultimate Turkey Burgers

We found that the extra step of grinding fresh turkey thighs ourselves made the most flavorful, best-textured burgers. If you can, buy boneless turkey thighs.

Cut 1½ pounds skinless, boneless thighs into 1-inch chunks and arrange in a single layer on a baking sheet. Freeze until somewhat firm, about 30 minutes. Working in three batches, place the semi-frozen turkey chunks in the workbowl of a food processor fitted with its steel blade; pulse until the largest pieces are no bigger than ⅛ inch, 12 to 14 one-second pulses. Follow recipe for Charcoal-Grilled or Gas-Grilled Turkey Burgers, using homemade ground turkey and omitting the ricotta cheese.

SALMON AND TUNA BURGERS

THE ANTI–RED MEAT CRAZE HAS SPAWNED some worthy culinary inventions. Restaurant chefs know that their patrons love burgers. Since beef is taboo in certain circles, trendy restaurants have turned fresh salmon and tuna into burgers. When you just gotta have a burger but don't want beef, these burgers can be delicious alternatives.

Like turkey burgers, salmon and tuna burgers can be dry. They don't have a lot of fat and can taste awful if overcooked. After some initial tests, we concluded that burgers made with fresh fish must be undercooked. Tuna burgers should be medium-rare (pink in the center). If cooked much further, the texture resembles canned tuna. Given the high price of tuna, this is an expensive mistake. Salmon has more fat than tuna so it is a tad more forgiving. However, salmon burgers cooked until the flesh is completely opaque will be dry and disappointing.

While undercooking helped, we wondered if there was an additional way to ensure moistness. We quickly realized that salmon and tuna are fundamentally different from ground turkey. Turkey is bland, so adding miso, porcini mushrooms, or ricotta cheese gives the meat a flavor boost as well as more moisture. However, salmon and tuna are delicious on their own. We needed something subtler in flavor than ricotta cheese to help keep these burgers moist. We tried adding melted butter and vegetable oil, but

these burgers were greasy. Egg yolks worked better, but tasters felt the egg flavor was too noticeable. We hit upon the right solution when we added some mayonnaise to salmon burgers. Just two tablespoons for four burgers added some creaminess and moisture. When we tried adding more mayonnaise, the burgers became greasy.

The subtle tang of mayonnaise worked well in salmon burgers, but tasters did not like the flavor of the mayonnaise in tuna burgers. In the end, we decided to leave the tuna burgers alone. Tuna has a more delicate flavor than salmon, and we didn't want to overwhelm it with mayonnaise or any other moisture-rich ingredient. We did find that the tuna burgers benefited from the addition of some garlic and ginger. However, to keep these burgers moist you simply must cook them right.

Most sources we consulted suggest chopping skinless salmon or tuna with a knife until finely ground. We wondered if the food processor could save some time here. After several attempts, we concluded that the knife is essential. There's no margin

MAKING SALMON BURGERS

1. Rub your fingers over the surface of the fillet to feel for pin bones. Remove them using tweezers or needle-nose pliers.

2. Place the fillet skin-side down on a cutting board. Holding a sharp knife parallel to the board, slice just above the skin to separate it from the flesh.

for error with a food processor. More often than not, we ended up with fish pureed to a mousselike texture. For the best results, salmon and tuna should be chopped to resemble the texture of ground meat. Pieces that measure about ⅛ inch are ideal.

Our tests also revealed another problem when making salmon and tuna burgers—sticking. We lost many burgers in our early tests. Heating the grill thoroughly and then rubbing the surface with an oil-soaked paper towel helped, but these steps did not guarantee that the burgers could be flipped or removed from the grill. In the end, we turned to a grill grid, which we coated with oil for added protection. Coating the spatula with nonstick cooking spray also helps loosen the burger from the grill grid.

Charcoal-Grilled Salmon Burgers

SERVES 4

Be sure that your salmon burgers are refrigerated for at least 15 minutes before being grilled. Chilled burgers are more likely to hold their shape when grilled. Use a grill grid (see page 12) to prevent the burgers from falling apart and into the coals, and coat a metal spatula with nonstick cooking spray to help loosen the burger from the grill grid.

1¼	pounds salmon fillets
2	tablespoons mayonnaise
2	tablespoons finely grated onion
¼	cup chopped fresh parsley leaves
1	tablespoon lemon juice
½	teaspoon salt
	Ground black pepper
	Vegetable oil for grill grid

1. Remove any pin bones from salmon flesh using tweezers or needle-nose pliers; separate flesh from skin, discarding skin (see illustrations on page 46). Chop salmon into ¼-inch pieces. Using a rocking motion with the knife, continue to chop salmon until it is coarsely ground into pieces roughly ⅛ inch each.

2. Place the salmon in a bowl and mix with the mayonnaise, onion, parsley, lemon juice, salt, and pepper to taste. Divide the mixture into 4 equal portions (about 5 ounces each), and use your hands to press into compact patties, about 1 inch thick. Place pat-

ties on a parchment-lined baking sheet and refrigerate for at least 15 minutes.

3. Meanwhile, light a large chimney starter filled with hardwood charcoal (about 2½ pounds) and allow to burn until all the charcoal is covered with a layer of fine gray ash. Build a single-level fire by spreading the coals out evenly over the bottom of the grill. Set the cooking rack in place, place the grill grid on top of the cooking rack, cover the grill with the lid, and let the rack heat up, about 5 minutes. The grill is ready when the coals are medium-hot. (See how to gauge heat level on page 19.)

4. Lightly dip a small wad of paper towels in vegetable oil; holding wad with tongs, wipe the grill grid. Grill the salmon burgers, uncovered, until well browned on one side, 3 to 4 minutes. Flip the burgers with a greased spatula. Continue grilling, uncovered, until the other side is well browned and the burgers are barely translucent at the center, about 3 minutes. Serve immediately.

Gas-Grilled Salmon Burgers

SERVES 4

Be sure that your salmon burgers are refrigerated for at least 15 minutes before being grilled. Chilled burgers are more likely to hold their shape when grilled. Use a grill grid (see page 12) to prevent the burgers from falling apart and into the coals, and coat a metal spatula with nonstick cooking spray to help loosen the burger from the grill grid.

1¼	pounds salmon fillets
2	tablespoons mayonnaise
2	tablespoons finely grated onion
¼	cup chopped fresh parsley leaves
1	tablespoon lemon juice
½	teaspoon salt
	Ground black pepper
	Vegetable oil for grill grid

1. Remove any pin bones from salmon flesh using tweezers or needle-nose pliers; separate flesh from skin, discarding skin (see illustrations on page 46). Chop salmon into ¼-inch pieces. Using a rocking motion with the knife, continue to chop salmon until it is coarsely ground into pieces roughly ⅛ inch each.

2. Place the salmon in a bowl and mix with the

mayonnaise, onion, parsley, lemon juice, salt, and pepper to taste. Divide the mixture into 4 equal portions (about 5 ounces each) and use your hands to press into compact patties, about 1 inch thick. Place patties on a parchment-lined baking sheet and refrigerate for at least 15 minutes.

3. Place the grill grid on top of the cooking grate of the grill. Preheat the grill with all burners set to high and the lid down until very hot, about 15 minutes. Leave the burners on high.

4. Lightly dip a small wad of paper towels in vegetable oil; holding wad with tongs, wipe the grill grid. Grill the salmon burgers, covered, until well browned on one side, 4 to 5 minutes. Flip the burgers with a greased spatula. Continue grilling, covered, until the other side is well browned and the burgers are barely translucent at the center, about 4 minutes. Serve immediately.

Charcoal-Grilled Tuna Burgers
SERVES 4

Do not let these burgers overcook; tuna tends to get very dry when cooked for too long. Because we recommend that you serve the burgers medium-rare to medium, we suggest that you use the highest quality tuna you can find. We use a grill grid (see page 12), which prevents the tuna from falling through the cooking grate during grilling. The garlic and ginger are subtle additions that we strongly recommend, although they can be omitted if you prefer. These lean burgers are greatly enhanced by one of the sauces on page 49. We particularly like the tuna paired with the Wasabi Mayonnaise.

1¼	pounds high-quality tuna steaks
1	teaspoon minced garlic
1	teaspoon minced fresh ginger
½	teaspoon salt
	Ground black pepper
	Vegetable oil for grill grid

1. Chop the tuna into ¼- to ⅓-inch pieces. Using a rocking motion with the knife, continue to chop the tuna until it is coarsely ground into pieces roughly ⅛ inch each. Mix with the garlic, ginger, salt, and pepper to taste. Divide the mixture into 4 equal portions (about 5 ounces each) and use your hands to press into compact patties, about 1 inch thick. Place

the patties on a parchment-lined baking sheet and refrigerate for at least 15 minutes.

2. Meanwhile, light a large chimney starter filled with hardwood charcoal (about 2½ pounds) and allow to burn until all the charcoal is covered with a layer of fine gray ash. Build a single-level fire by spreading the coals evenly out over the bottom of the grill. Set the cooking rack in place, place the grill grid on top of the cooking rack, cover the grill with the lid, and let the rack heat up, about 5 minutes. The grill is ready when the coals are medium-hot. (See how to gauge heat level on page 19.)

3. Lightly dip a small wad of paper towels in vegetable oil; holding wad with tongs, wipe the grill grid. Grill the tuna burgers, uncovered, until well browned on one side, about 3 minutes. Flip the burgers with a greased spatula. Continue grilling, uncovered, to the desired doneness, about 2 minutes for medium-rare or 3 minutes for medium. Serve immediately.

Gas-Grilled Tuna Burgers
SERVES 4

Set the grill grid (page 12) onto the grill before lighting it. Cook the burgers with the lid down over the highest possible heat.

1¼	pounds high-quality tuna steaks
1	teaspoon minced garlic
1	teaspoon minced fresh ginger
½	teaspoon salt
	Ground black pepper
	Vegetable oil for grill grid

1. Chop the tuna into ¼- to ⅓-inch pieces. Using a rocking motion with the knife, continue to chop the tuna until it is coarsely ground into pieces roughly ⅛ inch each. Mix with the garlic, ginger, salt, and pepper to taste. Divide the mixture into 4 equal portions (about 5 ounces each) and use your hands to press into compact patties, about 1 inch thick. Place the patties on a parchment-lined baking sheet and refrigerate for at least 15 minutes.

2. Place the grill grid on top of the cooking grate of the grill. Preheat the grill with all burners set to high and the lid down until very hot, about 15 minutes. Leave all burners on high.

SAUCES FOR FISH BURGERS

Salsas are good with fish burgers. We especially like Black Bean and Mango Salsa (page 300) with Salmon Burgers. In general, any sauce that would taste good with a piece of grilled salmon or tuna will work with grilled salmon or tuna burgers. We often omit the bun and serve fish burgers over lightly dressed greens.

If you want to slide these burgers onto buns, you need some sort of sauce. Salmon and tuna burgers call for something other than the usual ketchup. The following sauces are designed to spread on buns and will work with tuna or salmon. Each recipe yields enough sauce for four fish burgers.

Creamy Lemon Herb Sauce

MAKES ABOUT ⅓ CUP

Other fresh herbs, such as basil, cilantro, mint, or tarragon, can be used in place of the parsley and thyme if you like.

¼	cup mayonnaise
1	tablespoon lemon juice
1½	teaspoons minced fresh parsley leaves
1½	teaspoons minced fresh thyme leaves
1	small scallion, white and green parts, minced (about 1½ tablespoons)
¼	teaspoon salt
	Ground black pepper

Mix all ingredients together in a small bowl, including pepper to taste. Cover with plastic wrap and chill until flavors blend, at least 30 minutes.

Wasabi Mayonnaise

MAKES ABOUT ¼ CUP

This mayonnaise is particularly delicious with the tuna burgers.

¼	cup mayonnaise
1	teaspoon soy sauce
1	teaspoon wasabi powder

Mix all ingredients together in a small bowl. Cover with plastic wrap and chill until flavors blend, at least 10 minutes.

Creamy Chipotle Lime Sauce

MAKES ABOUT ⅓ CUP

This sauce lends a southwestern flair to burgers. Serve with sliced avocados and tomatoes.

2	small garlic cloves, unpeeled
¼	cup mayonnaise
½	chipotle chile in adobo sauce, minced (about 1 teaspoon), with ½ teaspoon adobo sauce
1½	teaspoons lime juice

1. Place the garlic cloves in a small, heavy-bottomed skillet over medium heat. Toast, turning the cloves occasionally, until they are fragrant and the skins have browned, 10 to 12 minutes. Cool, peel, and mince. (You should have about 1½ teaspoons.)

2. Mix the garlic, mayonnaise, chile, and lime juice together in a small bowl. Cover with plastic wrap and chill until flavors blend, at least 30 minutes.

3. Lightly dip a small wad of paper towels in vegetable oil; holding wad with tongs, wipe the grill grid. Grill the tuna burgers, covered, until well browned on one side, about 3 minutes. Flip the burgers with a greased spatula. Continue grilling, covered, to the desired doneness, about 3 minutes for medium-rare or 4 minutes for medium. Serve immediately.

TRADITIONAL PORK SAUSAGES

FRESH LINK SAUSAGES ARE NOTHING MORE than ground meat (usually pork) with seasonings and fat added for lubrication. Traditional Italian sausages—the kind sold in supermarkets in sweet and hot versions—contain a lot of fat, making flare-ups the biggest cooking challenge. We wanted the links to cook through in the center while developing a crisp exterior that was nicely browned but not charred.

We started our testing by cooking the links over a medium-hot fire. By the time the center had cooked through, the sausages were too dark. A medium fire proved easier to work with. The sausages were evenly browned and had a moist, juicy interior that was cooked through. Over a cooler fire, the links simply took longer to brown and dried out a bit in the center.

Although we had fewer problems with flare-ups when cooking the links over a medium fire, we still recommend that you keep a spray bottle filled with water ready to douse any flames. Building a modified two-level fire, with half the grill free of coals, is also

a good idea. If flames become too intense, just roll the links to this cool spot on the grill and wait until the fire is back under control to continue grilling.

Several sources we consulted suggested precooking the links, either by poaching or microwaving. We poached links for five minutes and then grilled them over a medium fire. The links were slightly waterlogged and less caramelized. Tasters deemed the results acceptable but by no means better than the sausages cooked directly over a medium fire without any precooking. Microwaving—we cooked the links in a covered dish filled with half an inch of water for two minutes—caused the sausages to be slightly shrunken and a bit tough when grilled, although browning was better than with links that had been poached. Here, too, the results were acceptable but no better than just throwing the sausages on the grill from the start.

We had noticed during our testing that the casing would occasionally burst or split open on the grill. Poking the sausages as they cooked prevented this but also caused the loss of juices and fat, which encouraged flare-ups and made the links a bit dry. In the end, we decided to live with the occasional link that split open. We did notice that links that were overstuffed tended to burst more often than links with a little headspace at the knotted end, so try to shop accordingly.

INGREDIENTS: Coiled Sausage

Some markets fill a single casing that is several feet long and then shape the filled sausage into a coil. We find that this type of sausage is harder to cook than links for several reasons. First of all, it's harder to get the casing nicely browned, especially on the inner rings of the coil. Second, the outer rings of the coil tend to cook faster than the inner rings. If you have a choice, buy link sausage, which browns better and cooks more evenly. If you do cook coiled fresh pork sausage, we suggest that you try the following technique. It will promote (but cannot guarantee) more even cooking.

Lay the coiled sausage on a baking sheet and pull apart the rings so that there is a space of 1/2 inch between each ring. Insert a metal skewer, parallel to the tray, through the center of all the rings. Use another large metal skewer inserted perpendicularly through all the rings so that the skewers are at right angles to one another. Grill as directed, turning only once, and increasing the cooking time on charcoal or gas by several minutes.

PEPPERS AND ONIONS

For many cooks, grilled onions and peppers are a non-negotiable accompaniment to grilled sausages. Onions and peppers are best cooked over a medium-hot fire (see the onion recipe on page 194 and the pepper recipe on page 196.) Therefore, you should start the vegetables as soon as the grill rack is hot. By the time the vegetables are done (this takes about 10 minutes), the coals will have cooled down enough to cook the sausage. To keep the grilled vegetables warm, simply cover them with foil or throw them back on the grill for a minute or two once the sausage is nearly done.

Charcoal-Grilled Italian Sausages

SERVES 4

Flare-ups are common when grilling high-fat links. Don't walk away when grilling these sausages, and keep a spray bottle filled with water on hand to douse flames. We tested this recipe using supermarket Italian sausage links that measured about 1 inch thick. If your sausages are thicker, simply leave them on the grill a few minutes longer.

2   pounds fresh pork sausage (8 links)

1. Light a large chimney filled halfway with hardwood charcoal (about 1¼ pounds) and allow to burn until all the charcoal is covered in a layer of fine gray ash. Build a modified two-level fire by spreading the coals out over half of the grill bottom. Set the cooking rack in place. Cover the grill with the lid and let the rack heat up, about 5 minutes. Use a wire brush to scrape clean the grill. The grill is ready when you have a medium fire. (See how to gauge heat level on page 19.)

2. Grill the sausages, uncovered, directly over the coals, turning them every minute or two so that all sides are evenly browned, until the casings are richly caramelized and the centers are cooked through, 9 to 11 minutes. (To check for doneness, cut one of the sausages down the center with a knife; the interior should no longer be pink. Alternatively, insert an instant-read thermometer through one end of the link; the center of the link should register at least 170 degrees.) Serve immediately.

Gas-Grilled Italian Sausages

SERVES 4

Be sure to stay near the grill as you cook these sausages. They are very high in fat, so flare-ups are common. Be ready to move the sausages around the grill to prevent them from scorching.

2   pounds fresh pork sausage (8 links)

1. Preheat the grill with all burners set to high and the lid down until very hot, about 15 minutes.

Use a wire brush to scrape clean the cooking grate. Turn all burners to medium.

2. Grill the sausages, covered, turning them every minute or two so that all sides are evenly browned, until the casings are richly caramelized and the centers are cooked through, 10 to 12 minutes. (To check for doneness, cut one of the sausages down the center with a knife; the interior should no longer be pink. Alternatively, insert an instant-read thermometer through one end of the link; the center of the link should register at least 170 degrees.) Serve immediately.

INGREDIENTS: Smoked Sausages

Italian sausages start with fresh (uncooked) pork. Pork is also used to make smoked, fully cooked sausages, such as kielbasa. The packaging on these sausages usually indicates that they are fully cooked. Grilling these sausages requires only that you brown them and heat them through.

As with fresh pork sausages, we found that smoked links are best cooked over a medium fire. Since you don't need to worry about bringing the center of the links up to temperature, simply grill smoked sausages until nicely browned. Follow the recipes on this page, shaving a minute or two off the cooking times.

POULTRY SAUSAGE

OUR GOALS FOR GRILLING LOWER-FAT poultry sausages were essentially the same as for the traditional higher-fat pork sausages. We wanted sausage with a moist interior (although we knew they would be drier than the higher-fat sausages), with nicely caramelized casings. Of course, we also wanted to ensure that the sausages were thoroughly cooked.

Because of their lower fat content, poultry sausages have a tendency to dry out on the grill. We figured that the best way to grill them would be quickly, to better retain the juices. We began by using direct heat but found the sausages a bit dry. We tried various heat levels, cooking them as quickly as possible over a hot fire and more gently over a moderate fire. In every case, the sausages were acceptable but not great.

At this point, we turned our attention to precooking the links. By shortening the grilling time, we hoped to reduce moisture loss. We microwaved the links in a glass pie plate filled with ½ inch of water and covered tightly with plastic wrap for 1½ minutes. As with pork sausage, we found that microwaved poultry links looked shrunken after grilling and were slightly tough. We noticed that the sausages also seemed to have released a lot of juices and fat into the steaming water in the pie plate.

We next tried poaching the sausages in simmering water for five minutes and then grilling. This method resulted in the best poultry sausages, more moist and juicy than links cooked over direct heat and much better than links that were microwaved before grilling. (As an aside, the sausages released minimal amounts of fat and juices into the poaching water.) Once grilled, these links were slightly less caramelized than those simply grilled over direct heat. Overall, though, we felt that they had as good a flavor and a far better mouthfeel and texture than links grilled without any precooking.

Charcoal-Grilled Poultry Sausages

SERVES 4

The recipe was developed for 1-inch-thick links; make adjustments as necessary when cooking thinner or thicker links.

2 pounds lean poultry sausage (8 links)

1. Light a large chimney filled halfway with hardwood charcoal (about 1¼ pounds) and allow to burn until all the charcoal is covered in a layer of fine gray ash. Build a modified two-level fire by spreading the coals out over half of the grill bottom. Set the cooking rack in place. Cover the grill with the lid and let the rack heat up, about 5 minutes. Use a wire brush to scrape clean the grill. The grill is ready when you have a medium fire. (See how to gauge heat level on page 19.)

2. Meanwhile, fill a large saucepan with approximately 2 inches of water; bring to a boil over high heat. Add the sausages, reduce the heat to low, and cover. Simmer the sausages for 4 minutes. Transfer the sausages to a plate.

3. Grill the sausages, uncovered, directly over the coals, turning them every minute or two so that all sides are evenly browned, until the casings are richly caramelized and the centers are cooked through, 6 to 7 minutes. (To check for doneness, cut one of the sausages down the center with a knife; the interior should no longer be pink. Alternatively, insert an instant-read thermometer through one end of the link; the center of the link should register at least 170 degrees.) Serve immediately.

Gas-Grilled Poultry Sausages

SERVES 4

Make sure to turn the sausages frequently to promote even browning, but work quickly so that too much heat doesn't escape when the lid is opened.

2 pounds lean poultry sausage (8 links)

1. Preheat grill with all burners set to high and the lid down until very hot, about 15 minutes. Use a wire brush to scrape clean the cooking grate. Turn all burners to medium.

2. Meanwhile, fill a large saucepan with approximately 2 inches of water; bring to a boil over high heat. Add the sausages, reduce the heat to low, and cover. Simmer the sausages for 4 minutes. Transfer the sausages to a plate.

3. Grill the sausages, covered, turning them every minute or two so that all sides are evenly browned, until the casings are richly caramelized and the centers are cooked through, 7 to 8 minutes. (To check for doneness, cut one of the sausages down the center with a knife; the interior should no longer be pink. Alternatively, insert an instant-read thermometer through one end of the link; the center of the link should register at least 170 degrees.) Serve immediately.

5

KEBABS

THERE'S SOMETHING UNIVERSALLY APPEALING about grilled meat, chicken, or fish on a stick. Almost every culture has some version of this dish. In many places, kebabs are street foods, eaten as snacks between meals. In this country, we generally think of kebabs as more substantial fare, appropriate for dinner. Because kebabs combine meat and vegetables, they are nearly complete meals; just add some rice, potatoes, or bread.

As stated in chapter 1, we prefer metal skewers to wooden ones. Even when soaked, wooden skewers burn. Buy metal skewers once and you will own them for life. If possible, choose skewers with sharp ends (which make threading meat and vegetables much easier). Also, thinner skewers are less likely to cause delicate foods to fall apart. On occasion, we've worked with very thick skewers that can tear chick-en or fish and cause them to break in half. Some metal skewers have wood or plastic handles. Because the handles are supposed to hang over the side of the grill, the food near the handle end of the skewer doesn't have direct contact with the cooking grate, making even cooking impossible. For this reason, we do not recommend skewers with handles. Just use tongs to turn metal skewers on the grill.

This chapter considers skewers made with five kinds of protein: beef, lamb, pork, chicken, and swordfish. Beef, lamb, and pork have similar (although slightly different) cooking challenges. Chicken and swordfish have far less fat than meat, so the issues are different.

BEST CUTS FOR BEEF KEBABS

TOP BLADE STEAK
These small steaks are cut from the shoulder area of the cow and make the best kebabs. Top blade steaks are tender, but each has a line of gristle running down the center, which should be removed. Top blade steak is often called flatiron steak or blade steak.

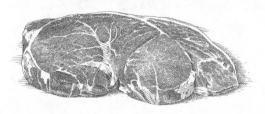

TOP SIRLOIN
This steak is merely a boneless shell sirloin steak. It is sometimes sold as boneless sirloin butt steak or top sirloin butt center cut steak. Do not confuse this steak with top loin steak, which is sometimes called sirloin strip steak. It is our second choice for kebabs.

BEEF KEBABS

OUR GOALS WHEN DEVELOPING A RECIPE for beef kebabs seemed simple. We wanted meat that was nicely seared but not overcooked and vegetables that were tender but not mushy. We also wanted to cook the meat and vegetables on the same skewer so that their flavors could meld. Finally, we didn't want to spend a fortune on meat. It makes little sense to buy a premium steak and then cut it up into chunks for kebabs.

The concept behind grilled beef and vegetable kebabs is ingenious. Cut beef into small pieces, skewer along with flavorful, aromatic vegetables, and grill over a live fire—the juices emitted during cooking flavor the vegetables, and the vegetables in turn add flavor to the pieces of beef, while both are seared by the intense heat and infused with the smoke of the grill. Unfortunately, the idea of a kebab is often more appealing than the kebab itself; the pitfalls of grilling on skewers are many. To begin with, it's very easy to pick the wrong cut of beef. There are dozens of choices. It's also not very hard to overcook the meat when it's cut into smaller pieces. Or you can grill the skewers over a heat that's too intense and end up with meat that's charred on the outside and raw on the inside and vegetables that are just plain raw. When not seasoned carefully, kebabs can taste dull and bland.

We were looking for a straightforward, easy recipe that highlights the juiciness and flavor of beef, that lets the vegetables cook through without getting mushy, and that allows the meat to become richly caramelized on the outside but to cook from medium-rare to medium at the center. To reach this goal, we had to answer a number of questions: How can you prepare and grill the beef to get a decently caramelized surface without overcooking the meat? How can you ensure that the vegetables cook through so that they aren't still raw when the beef is cooked to the right temperature? And what are the cuts of beef that will give tender, flavorful kebab meat without breaking the bank?

We knew that choosing the right cut of beef was the most important of these factors. Given that we didn't want to pay top price for a premium cut, we considered which cheaper cuts of meat would be tender enough to use for kebabs. We also wanted a cut of meat that wasn't too hard to cut into little pieces. In some cuts of meat, fat and sinew are abundant, making it extremely hard to prepare evenly sized pieces for the skewer. We weren't about to spend hours trimming and cutting intermuscular fat and connective tissue to make kebabs. It had to be a simple, quick process.

So we began skewering and grilling different cuts of meat from the less expensive parts of the steer. From the chuck we tried the mock tender steak, clod steak, and top blade steak; from the round we tested steaks cut from the top, bottom, and eye of round muscles; from the plate came the skirt and flank steak; and from the sirloin portion we tried a top sirloin steak.

The cuts from the round portion of the cow were quite dry and chewy, with a weak, livery beef flavor. The skirt and flank steak were both flavorful and juicy, but their flat configuration and loose grain made them almost impossible to grill along with vegetables and even harder to cook to medium or medium-rare. They are much more fit for satay, in which long, thin strips of meat are skewered by themselves.

Not surprisingly, all but one of the nonpremium cuts from the chuck were also too tough. We say it is not surprising because this part of the steer—the neck, arm, and shoulder—is known to be flavorful but quite tough, best suited for stewing and braising. This was definitely true of the clod steak and mock tender steak. But the top blade steak was a different matter entirely—well marbled, intensely beefy, and

surprisingly tender and suitable for grilling. It was our first choice for skewers.

Our second choice was the top sirloin. This steak comes from the sirloin portion of the cow, just behind the short loin, which is the source of premium steaks such as porterhouse, filet mignon, and New York strip. The sirloin is made up of several muscles, the most tender of which is the top sirloin, from which this particular steak is cut.

So at the end of this first round of testing, we had two steaks that offered a reasonable texture and great beefy flavor at a reasonable price: top blade steak ($3.28/pound), and top sirloin steak ($4.99/pound). Both were also were quite easy to cut into even-sized, skewerable pieces of meat.

Though the top sirloin and top blade steaks were relatively flavorful and tender on their own, we hoped that marinating the steaks would not only flavor the kebabs but also add some moisture. Thus far, we had approached the kebabs as we would a steak, seasoning with salt and pepper only. While the results were decent, the meat was a touch dry and bland. Most kebab recipes call for marinating the meat in an acidic marinade, which supposedly tenderizes it, before grilling. We tried both an acidic and a nonacidic (oil-based) marinade and left pieces of meat in both, for one hour, two hours, and four hours.

In all three cases the acidic marinade produced meat that was mushier on the surface but not noticeably more tender than the meat in the oil-based marinade. (For more information, see "Do Marinades Work?" on page 56.) The oil-based marinade didn't really change the texture of the meat, but the olive oil in it kept the meat from drying out on the grill and served as a great flavor vehicle for garlic, salt, and pepper. The lime juice in the acidic marinade, however, did contribute a nice flavor. We decided that instead of marinating the meat in the acid, we would marinate the meat in an oil-based marinade and squirt a little lime or lemon juice onto the kebabs after they came off the grill. We liked the results. The meat was tender yet still firm, and the lime or lemon juice tasted fresher when added to the meat just before serving.

The next step was to figure out how best to cut the steaks for skewering. As many meat connoisseurs know, beef cooked past medium becomes dry and tough. We wanted the kebabs to be cooked to medium-rare or, at most, to medium. This meant that the cubes of beef would have to be relatively large. After a few rounds of grilling, we noticed that any beef cut into pieces smaller than an inch was very hard to keep from overcooking. On the other hand, pieces of beef cut this large took quite a bit of time to marinate fully. We tried marinating overnight, and the meat still tasted a little bland because the seasoning didn't penetrate the surface very much.

After researching a number of kebab recipes, we came upon one from Paula Wolfert's *The Cooking of the Eastern Mediterranean* (HarperCollins, 1994), in which cubes of lamb are butterflied (cut open and flattened) before being skewered for kebabs. This, we thought, might produce a more flavorful kebab. Because the pieces of meat would have more surface area, more marinade might penetrate the surface in a shorter period of time. We tested this theory out and were pleased to find the meat more flavorful; it was also easier to eat and less chewy. Unfortunately, since the meat was also thinner after being butterflied, it was getting cooked to the well-done stage. To combat this problem, we simply butterflied the meat, marinated it, and then put it on the skewer as if it were still a cube. This technique worked perfectly. Now the meat was easier to eat and packed with flavor all the way through to the center, and it

was also nicely caramelized without being overcooked at the interior.

The final problem that most of us encounter when making meat and vegetable kebabs is getting both components to cook at the same rate. We noticed that if we cut the vegetables too thick, they ended up raw at the center. Our first thought was to skewer the meat and vegetables separately, but after trying a few batches of kebabs this way, we realized that both the meat and vegetables tasted much better when cooked together on the skewer.

The logical solution to the problem was to precook the vegetables. We ruled out both parboiling and presteaming because each meant dirtying another pan and making something complicated out of a dish that should be simple. The only precooking idea that made any sense was to microwave the vegetables before grilling.

After figuring out the appropriate timing in the microwave for each vegetable, we began cooking and skewering. We found this process to be extremely labor intensive; not only did we have to cut and microwave the vegetables, but the onions and peppers were slightly soft and wet, which made it hard to skewer them neatly. The kebabs already required a good deal of preparation—cutting and butterflying the meat, cutting the vegetables, and skewering both.

SCIENCE: Do Marinades Work?

Can tough cuts of beef, lamb, and pork yield tender results if marinated long enough? Many cookbooks suggest tenderizing meat in acidic marinades, often for several days. The science here is pretty straightforward. Acids, such as lemon juice, vinegar, and wine, break protein strands apart and cause the structure of meats to soften over time. What actually happens in the refrigerator under real-life conditions is another question. We went into the test kitchen to find out.

We took London broil from the round (a particularly lean cut and therefore prone to being tough when cooked), cut it into two-inch cubes, and then marinated the cubes in various solutions for 24 hours. Marinades with little or no acid had no effect on the texture of the meat. When we used more acid, the outer layer of the meat turned gray and dry—it had "cooked." While some might call the texture tender, we found the meat to be mushy and the flavor of the acid to be overpowering. Our conclusion was simple—if you want tender meat, you must pay attention to the cut you purchase and the cooking method and forget about tenderizing with marinades.

Although marinades may not tenderize meat, they can give it a delicious flavor, as long as you soak the food for an appropriate amount of time. We marinated cubes of beef, lamb, and pork, as well as chicken parts, flounder, and tuna, in low-acid marinades for varying amounts of time. As might be expected, fish picked up flavor rather quickly, in as little as 15 minutes for flounder and 30 minutes for the firmer tuna. Chicken was somewhat slower to become fully flavored, with skinless pieces taking about 3 hours and skin-on pieces taking at least 8 hours. Denser meats take even more time to absorb marinades. It took 8 hours for the flavor to penetrate beyond the surface of beef, lamb, and pork, and meat marinated for 24 hours absorbed even more flavor. After a day, we found that meat gained little extra flavor. Although you can leave meat in a low-acid marinade for days, we don't really see the point.

Adding another step made it just too complicated.

Surprisingly, even though the precooked vegetables were softer at the center after grilling, we didn't necessarily find them more appealing than those grilled from the raw stage. In fact, some of the vegetables, including the onions and bell peppers, maintained a pleasant tender-crisp texture (like that of a stir-fry) when skewered raw, and we found this to be a nice contrast with the texture of the meat. In the case of the onions and peppers, the trick is to cut them to the right dimensions (see page 58) so that they don't come off the grill undercooked.

Mushrooms and zucchini were deemed too soft to grill with beef, although we later found that they are good with firmer and drier chicken and fish chunks. To add variety to meat skewers, we added chunks of pineapple; they grill well and add a nice sweetness and fruitiness to the kebabs.

There were two options when it came to grilling the kebabs: cooking over a single-level fire or over a two-level fire. Thinking that simpler is better, we started cooking the kebabs over a single-level fire. Because we wanted the kebabs to cook quickly, so that the exterior would become nicely browned while the interior retained as much juice as possible, we started with a medium-hot fire. While meat cooked this way came out relatively well browned, we thought it might be even better if cooked over a hotter fire. Instead of covering the entire grill with the hot charcoal, we used the same amount and covered only three-quarters of the grill bottom. This produced a more intense fire when cooking directly over the charcoal, searing the outside of the kebabs more successfully. The meat was richly caramelized, with a perfectly cooked, juicy interior.

Charcoal-Grilled Beef Kebabs
SERVES 4 TO 6

Our favorite cut of beef for kebabs is top blade steak (known sometimes as blade or flatiron steak), but you can also use top sirloin. If you do, ask the butcher to cut the top sirloin steak between 1 and 1¼ inches thick (most packaged sirloin steaks are thinner). If desired, add 2 teaspoons minced fresh rosemary, thyme, basil, or oregano to the garlic and oil mixture for this marinade. For maximum efficiency, prepare the fruit and vegetables while the meat is marinating.

MARINADE

- ¼ cup extra-virgin olive oil
- 3 medium garlic cloves, minced
- ¾ teaspoon salt
- ½ teaspoon ground black pepper

MEAT

- 2 pounds top blade steaks (about 4 to 5 steaks), trimmed of fat and prepared according to illustrations 1 to 3, below

FRUIT AND VEGETABLES

- 1 pineapple (about 3½ pounds), prepared according to chart on page 58
- 1 medium red bell pepper (about 5½ ounces), prepared according to chart on page 58
- 1 medium yellow bell pepper (about 5½ ounces), prepared according to chart on page 58

PREPARING BEEF FOR KEBABS
Steps 1 and 2 are necessary if using top blade steaks. If using top sirloin, trim away gristle and cut into cubes as in step 3.

1. Halve each blade steak lengthwise, leaving gristle on one half.

2. Cut away the gristle from the half to which it is still attached.

3. Cut the meat into 1¼-inch cubes, then cut each cube almost through at the center to butterfly the cube.

2 tablespoons extra-virgin olive oil
Salt and ground black pepper

1 large red onion (about 10 ounces), prepared according to chart below
Lemon or lime wedges for serving (optional)

1. FOR THE MARINADE: Combine the oil, garlic, salt, and pepper in a large bowl. Add the steak cubes and toss to coat evenly. Cover and refrigerate until fully seasoned, at least 1 hour or up to 24 hours.

2. Light a large chimney starter filled with hardwood charcoal (about 2½ pounds) and allow to burn until all the charcoal is covered with a layer of fine gray ash. Build a single-level fire, but spread the coals over just three-quarters of the grill bottom. Set the cooking rack in place, cover the grill with the lid, and let the rack heat up, about 5 minutes. Use a wire brush to scrape clean the cooking rack. The grill is ready when you have a hot fire. (See how to gauge heat level on page 19.)

3. FOR THE FRUIT AND VEGETABLES: Meanwhile, toss the pineapple and peppers with 1½ tablespoons olive oil in a medium bowl and season with salt and pepper to taste. Brush the onion with remaining 1½ teaspoons oil and season with salt and pepper to taste. Using 8 twelve-inch metal skewers, thread each skewer with a pineapple piece, an onion

wedge, a cube of meat (skewering as if it were an uncut cube), and one piece of each kind of pepper, and then repeat this sequence two more times. Brush any oil remaining in the bowl over the skewers.

4. Grill the kebabs directly over the coals, uncovered, turning each kebab one-quarter turn every 1¾ minutes, until the meat is well browned, grill marked, and cooked to medium-rare, about 7 minutes (or about 8 minutes for medium). Transfer the kebabs to a serving platter and squeeze the lemon or lime wedges over the kebabs, if desired. Serve immediately.

Gas-Grilled Beef Kebabs

SERVES 4 TO 6

If desired, add 2 teaspoons minced fresh rosemary, thyme, basil, or oregano to the garlic and oil mixture for this marinade. For maximum efficiency, prepare the fruit and vegetables while the meat is marinating. Work quickly when opening the lid to turn the kebabs; you don't want too much heat to escape.

Perfect recipe

MARINADE

¼ cup extra-virgin olive oil

3 medium garlic cloves, minced

¾ teaspoon salt

½ teaspoon ground black pepper

Preparing Vegetables and Fruits for Skewering

If prepared according to these directions, the following vegetables and fruits will cook through at the same rate as the meat or chicken chunks. We found that the tendency of chicken to be bland and dry permits a wider range of vegetable and fruit selections than meat. See recipes for specific recommendations. Use ripe fruit that is still fairly firm. Mushy fruit will fall apart on the grill. We have suggested marinades for the chicken (page 68) that work well with each vegetable, keeping in mind cultural traditions as well as the flavor and texture of the vegetable or fruit.

VEGETABLE OR FRUIT	PREPARATION	MARINADE FOR CHICKEN
Mushrooms, button (small)	Slice off stems and wipe clean	Garlic and Herb, Southwestern, Asian
Onions	Peel and cut into ½-inch-thick wedges	Any marinade
Peppers, bell	Core, seed, and cut into 1-inch-wide wedges	Any marinade
Shallots (small)	Peel and skewer whole	Any marinade
Zucchini	Remove ends; slice into ½-inch-thick rounds	Garlic and Herb, Middle Eastern, Curry, Asian
Apples	Core and cut into 1-inch cubes	Garlic and Herb, Middle Eastern, Curry, Asian
Peaches	Halve, pit, and cut each half in thirds	Garlic and Herb, Curry, Caribbean
Pears	Core and cut into 1-inch cubes	Garlic and Herb, Middle Eastern, Curry, Asian
Pineapples	Peel, core, and cut into 1-inch cubes	Southwestern, Curry, Caribbean

MEAT

Used Sirloin

2 pounds top blade steaks (about 4 to 5 steaks), trimmed of fat and prepared according to illustrations on page 57

FRUIT AND VEGETABLES

I pineapple (about 3½ pounds), prepared according to chart on page 58

I medium red bell pepper (about 5½ ounces), prepared according to chart on page 58

I medium yellow bell pepper (about 5½ ounces), prepared according to chart on page 58

2 tablespoons extra-virgin olive oil
Salt and ground black pepper

I large red onion (about 10 ounces), prepared according to chart on page 58
Lemon or lime wedges for serving (optional)

1. FOR THE MARINADE: Combine the oil, garlic, salt, and pepper in a large bowl. Add the steak cubes and toss to coat evenly. Cover and refrigerate until fully seasoned, at least 1 hour or up to 24 hours.

2. Preheat the grill with all burners set to high and the lid down until the grill is very hot, about 15 minutes. Use a wire brush to scrape clean the cooking grate. Leave all burners on high.

3. FOR THE FRUIT AND VEGETABLES: Meanwhile, toss the pineapple and peppers with 1½ tablespoons olive oil in a medium bowl and season with salt and pepper to taste. Brush the onion with remaining 1½ teaspoons oil and season with salt and pepper to taste. Using 8 twelve-inch metal skewers, thread each skewer with a pineapple piece, an onion wedge, a cube of meat (skewering as if it were an uncut cube), and one piece of each kind of pepper, and then repeat this sequence two more times. Brush any oil remaining in the bowl over the skewers.

4. Grill the kebabs, covered, turning each kebab one-quarter turn every 2 minutes, until the meat is well browned, grill marked, and cooked to medium-rare, about 8 minutes (or about 9 minutes for medium). Transfer the kebabs to serving platter and squeeze the lemon or lime wedges over kebabs, if desired. Serve immediately.

perfect

➤ VARIATIONS

Beef Kebabs with Asian Flavors
Follow recipe for Charcoal-Grilled or Gas-Grilled Beef Kebabs, substituting 3 tablespoons vegetable oil and 1 tablespoon Asian sesame oil for the olive oil in the garlic marinade and adding 1½ teaspoons minced fresh ginger, 2 tablespoons soy sauce, 1 teaspoon sugar, ½ teaspoon hot red pepper flakes, and 2 minced scallions. Continue with the recipe, substituting an equal amount of vegetable oil for the olive oil for coating the fruit and vegetables.

Southwestern Beef Kebabs
Follow recipe for Charcoal-Grilled or Gas-Grilled Beef Kebabs, adding ½ teaspoon ground cumin, ½ teaspoon chili powder, 1 minced chipotle chile in adobo sauce, and 2 tablespoons minced fresh cilantro leaves to the oil and garlic marinade.

LAMB KEBABS

THERE ARE MANY QUESTIONS TO ASK WHEN grilling lamb kebabs. To begin, what affordable cuts respond best to grilling on a skewer? How do you get the meat and vegetables to cook at the same rate? How do you get the pieces to be full flavored and moist throughout?

We began by searching for the best cut of lamb to use for the skewers, ruling out expensive cuts like loin chops. At $13.99 per pound, these chops are too pricey to cut up for kebabs. Rib chops were also far too expensive, with little meat to offer.

We had better luck with meatier sirloin chops ($4.99/pound), shoulder chops ($4.99/pound), and, best of all, boned leg of lamb. We found that one-half of a boned leg of lamb (shank portion) had just the right amount of meat, once trimmed of sinew and fat, to feed four (about 1½ pounds of meat, trimmed). The large sirloin half can also be used (the meat is slightly more tender here), but you will have more meat than you need. We suggest that you buy the half-leg of lamb boned, or ask your butcher to bone the leg for you, since removing the bones can be a time-consuming and tricky project. Though kebabs made from leg meat were tastier and juicier than those made from the sirloin and shoulder chops, these cuts of meat are excellent alternatives to the leg meat.

Once the meat is trimmed, it should be cut into 1¼-inch chunks. Because the thickness of meat varies on the leg, you cannot always cut precise cubes. If you have a piece that is thinner than the rest, you can cut a slightly larger piece of meat and fold it back over itself to have a double layer of meat on the skewer; this imitates the desired 1¼-inch thickness of meat. Areas on the boned leg of lamb that are thick enough to cut into a 1¼-inch chunk can be cut into partway, but not all the way through, and skewered as if an intact cube. As with beef kebabs, cutting the meat this way allows the marinade to penetrate to the center of the meat, making for a fuller flavored kebab. On the grill, the meat gets caramelized on the outside, while the piece of meat is large enough to cook just to medium-rare at the center.

We found that a direct, single-level fire is optimum for cooking lamb kebabs. As with beef kebabs, we found it best to cover only three-quarters of the bot-

tom of the grill with coals to produce a hot fire that will quickly mark and brown the kebabs, without allowing the center of the meat to overcook. The kebabs should be cooked, at most, to medium; lamb meat becomes less tender and juicy when cooked beyond this stage.

Lamb is extremely flavorful on its own and can be enjoyed with a simple garlic marinade. However, lamb also responds extremely well to strong, spicy, and tangy flavors.

PREPARING LAMB FOR KEBABS

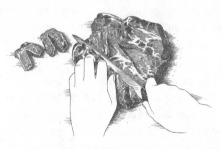

1. Cut the meat into 1¼-inch cubes, then cut each cube almost through at the center to butterfly the cube.

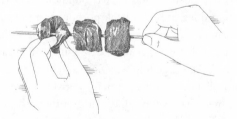

2. For areas of the boned leg of lamb that are thinner than 1¼ inches, cut the lamb into pieces that are approximately 2½ by 1¼-inch rectangles. Skewer thinner pieces of meat by folding the pieces in half and skewering them through the center to imitate a 1¼-inch cube.

Charcoal-Grilled Lamb Kebabs
SERVES 4 TO 6

If you wish, add 2 teaspoons chopped fresh rosemary, basil, or thyme to the marinade. Look for a half leg cut from the shank end (see page 59); once boned, the meat should weigh about 2 pounds. (The sirloin end is delicious but too large if just feeding four.) By the time you trim fat and sinew, you'll probably have 1½ pounds of trimmed meat. Although we recommend meat from the leg, shoulder chops (see page 59) and sirloin chops are acceptable alternatives. Have the butcher cut these chops 1¼ inches thick. You can then easily cut the meat away from the bone and into 1¼-inch cubes.

MARINADE
¼   cup extra-virgin olive oil
3   medium garlic cloves, minced
¾   teaspoon salt
½   teaspoon ground black pepper

MEAT
2   pounds boned meat from leg of lamb, trimmed of fat and prepared according to illustrations at left

VEGETABLES
1   medium red bell pepper (about 5½ ounces), prepared according to chart on page 58
1   medium yellow bell pepper (about 5½ ounces), prepared according to chart on page 58
1   medium orange bell pepper (about 5½ ounces), prepared according to chart on page 58
2   tablespoons extra-virgin olive oil
    Salt and ground black pepper
1   large red onion (about 10 ounces), prepared according to chart on page 58
    Lemon or lime wedges for serving (optional)

1. **FOR THE MARINADE:** Combine the oil, garlic, salt, and pepper in a large bowl. Add the lamb cubes and toss to coat evenly. Cover and refrigerate until fully seasoned, at least 1 hour or up to 24 hours.

2. Light a large chimney starter filled with hardwood charcoal (about 2½ pounds) and allow to burn until all the charcoal is covered with a layer of fine gray ash. Build a single-level fire, but spread the coals over just three-quarters of the grill bottom. Set the cooking rack in place, cover the grill with the lid, and let the rack heat up, about 5 minutes. Use a wire brush to scrape clean the cooking rack. The grill is ready when you have a hot fire. (See how to gauge heat level on page 19.)

3. **FOR THE VEGETABLES:** Meanwhile, toss the peppers with 1½ tablespoons olive oil in a medium bowl and season with salt and pepper to taste. Brush the onion with remaining 1½ teaspoons oil and season with salt and pepper to taste. Using 8 twelve-inch metal skewers, thread each skewer with an onion wedge, a cube of meat (skewering as if it were an uncut cube), and one piece of each kind of pepper, and then repeat this sequence two more times. Brush any oil remaining in the bowl over the skewers.

4. Grill the kebabs directly over the coals, uncovered, turning each kebab one-quarter turn every 1¾ minutes, until the meat is well browned, grill marked, and cooked to medium-rare, about 7 minutes (or about 8 minutes for medium). Transfer the kebabs to a serving platter and squeeze the lemon or lime wedges over the kebabs, if desired. Serve immediately.

~≈

Gas-Grilled Lamb Kebabs

SERVES 4 TO 6

If you wish, add 2 teaspoons chopped fresh rosemary, basil, or thyme to the marinade. Look for a half leg cut from the shank end (see page 59); once boned, the meat should weigh about 2 pounds. (The sirloin end is delicious but too large if just feeding four.) By the time you trim fat and sinew, you'll probably have 1½ pounds of trimmed meat. Although we recommend meat from the leg, shoulder chops (see page 59) and sirloin chops are acceptable alternatives. Have the butcher cut these chops 1¼ inches thick. You can then easily cut the meat away from the bone and into 1¼ inch-cubes. Work quickly when opening the lid to turn the kebabs; you don't want too much heat to escape.

MARINADE

¼	cup extra-virgin olive oil
3	medium garlic cloves, minced
¾	teaspoon salt
½	teaspoon ground black pepper

MEAT

2	pounds boned meat from leg of lamb, trimmed of fat and prepared according to illustrations on page 60

VEGETABLES

1	medium red bell pepper (about 5½ ounces), prepared according to chart on page 58
1	medium yellow bell pepper (about 5½ ounces), prepared according to chart on page 58
1	medium orange bell pepper (about 5½ ounces), prepared according to chart on page 58
2	tablespoons extra-virgin olive oil
	Salt and ground black pepper
1	large red onion (about 10 ounces), prepared according to chart on page 58
	Lemon or lime wedges for serving (optional)

1. **FOR THE MARINADE:** Combine the oil, garlic, salt, and pepper in a large bowl. Add the lamb cubes and toss to coat evenly. Cover and refrigerate until fully seasoned, at least 1 hour or up to 24 hours.

2. Preheat the grill with all burners set to high and the lid down until the grill is very hot, about 15 minutes. Use a wire brush to scrape clean the cooking grate. Leave all burners on high.

3. **FOR THE VEGETABLES:** Meanwhile, toss the peppers with 1½ tablespoons olive oil in a medium bowl and season with salt and pepper to taste. Brush the onion with remaining 1½ teaspoons oil and season with salt and pepper to taste. Using 8 twelve-inch metal skewers, thread each skewer with an onion wedge, a cube of meat (skewering as if it were an uncut cube), and one piece of each kind of pepper, and then repeat this sequence two more times. Brush any oil remaining in the bowl over the skewers.

4. Grill the kebabs, covered, turning each kebab one-quarter turn every 2 minutes, until the meat is well browned, grill marked, and cooked to medium-rare, about 8 minutes (or about 9 minutes

for medium). Transfer the kebabs to a serving platter and squeeze the lemon or lime wedges over the kebabs, if desired. Serve immediately.

➤ VARIATIONS

Lamb Kebabs with Middle Eastern Marinade

Follow recipe for Charcoal-Grilled or Gas-Grilled Lamb Kebabs, replacing the garlic in the marinade with ¼ cup grated onion, 2 teaspoons lemon juice, 1 teaspoon sweet paprika, ½ teaspoon sugar, and ¼ teaspoon ground cinnamon. Proceed as directed.

Lamb Kebabs with Indian Yogurt Marinade

Serve these kebabs with rice, preferably basmati rice.

2	medium garlic cloves, coarsely chopped
I	tablespoon roughly chopped fresh ginger
½	medium onion, coarsely chopped
½	medium jalapeño chile, stemmed, seeded, and coarsely chopped
2	tablespoons lemon juice
¾	teaspoon ground cumin
¼	teaspoon ground cinnamon
¼	teaspoon ground cardamom
¼	teaspoon ground coriander
	Pinch ground cloves
¾	cup plain yogurt
I	teaspoon salt
I	recipe Charcoal-Grilled or Gas-Grilled Lamb Kebabs (without marinade)

1. Place the garlic, ginger, onion, chile, lemon juice, and spices in the workbowl of a food processor and pulse to mince finely. Add the yogurt and salt and process until smooth.

2. Place the lamb and yogurt mixture in a large bowl and toss to coat evenly. Cover and refrigerate until fully seasoned, at least 3 hours or up to 24 hours. Proceed as directed.

PORK KEBABS

THE MAJOR ISSUE THAT MUST BE DEALT WITH when making kebabs with pork is its tendency to dry out on the grill. We wanted to develop a method that delivers moist, tender meat. The other major issue was flavor. Unlike beef and lamb, pork can be fairly bland—especially the tender cuts from the loin, which, because they cook quickly, we expected would work best for kebabs. We needed to figure out a way to boost flavor.

We focused on two tender cuts—the loin and the tenderloin. As its name indicates, the tenderloin is plenty tender, but tasters felt it cooked up a bit mushy. We found the pork loin more appealing. It has a slightly fuller flavor, and, while still tender, it has an appealing resistance when you bite into it. A moderate degree of chew is pleasing and works well on a kebab.

Unfortunately, as expected, the loin meat dried out easily. As we often recommend when cooking meat or poultry that tends to dry out, we tried brining the loin. (For a complete discussion of how and why to brine meat and poultry, see page 102). In addition to brining, we tested marinating the meat in an oil-based marinade to see if it would combat dryness. Side-by-side tastings showed that the marinated kebabs were tastier and just as moist and juicy as the brined meat. The marinade not only moistened the meat but also added richness of flavor that was lacking in the lean pork loin. The oil in the

PREPARING PORK FOR KEBABS

Cut the boneless pork chops into 1¼-inch cubes, then cut each cube almost through at the center to butterfly.

marinade lubricated the meat and improved its texture. The marinade also made a great vehicle for adding other flavors to the meat.

Whether marinated or not, pork that is overcooked will be dry. We found that pork kebabs should be cooked until barely pink at the center—an internal temperature of 145 degrees is ideal. (See page 73 for more information about cooking pork and safety issues.)

To cook the pork through at the center and get a good caramelization on the outside without singeing, we found that we needed to use a more moderate level of heat than with beef or lamb. A medium-hot fire worked like a charm. The outside of the pork was well marked, and the meat cooked through to the center. The meat also cooked through quickly, giving the moisture little time to escape from the meat and resulting in a tasty, moist kebab.

Because pork loin is neutral-tasting (some would say bland), with little fat, we wanted to infuse as much flavor and seasoning as possible into the meat before grilling. We decided to cube and then butterfly each cube, as we had done with the lamb and beef, to expose the most surface area possible to the marinade.

Charcoal-Grilled Pork Kebabs

SERVES 4 TO 6

If the prepackaged pork chops at your market are too thin, have your butcher cut 4 to 5 boneless, center-cut pork chops, 1¼ inches thick. Be sure not to overcook the pork, since this meat is prone to drying out. To make sure that pork is done, you can peek into the cut that was made into the meat before skewering. It should appear opaque and just barely pink.

MARINADE

- ¼ cup extra-virgin olive oil
- 3 medium garlic cloves, minced
- ¾ teaspoon salt
- ½ teaspoon ground black pepper

MEAT

- 1¾ pounds boneless center-cut pork chops, 1¼ inches thick (about 4 to 5 chops), cut into 1¼-inch cubes and butterflied (see illustration on page 62)

FRUIT AND VEGETABLES

- 1 pineapple (about 3½ pounds), prepared according to chart on page 58
- 1 medium red bell pepper (about 5½ ounces), prepared according to chart on page 58
- 1 medium yellow bell pepper (about 5½ ounces), prepared according to chart on page 58
- 2 tablespoons extra-virgin olive oil
  Salt and ground black pepper
- 1 large red onion (about 10 ounces), prepared according to chart on page 58
  Lemon or lime wedges for serving (optional)

1. FOR THE MARINADE: Combine the oil, garlic, salt, and pepper in a large bowl. Add the pork cubes and toss to coat evenly. Cover and refrigerate until fully seasoned, at least 1 hour or up to 24 hours.

2. Light a large chimney starter filled with hardwood charcoal (about 2½ pounds) and allow to burn until all the charcoal is covered with a layer of fine gray ash. Build a single-level fire by spreading the coals over the grill bottom. Set the cooking rack in place, cover the grill with the lid, and let the rack heat up, about 5 minutes. Use a wire brush to scrape clean the cooking rack. The grill is ready when you have a medium-hot fire. (See how to gauge heat level on page 19.)

3. FOR THE FRUIT AND VEGETABLES: Meanwhile, toss the pineapple and peppers with 1½ tablespoons olive oil in a medium bowl and season with salt and pepper to taste. Brush the onion with remaining 1½ teaspoons oil and season with salt and pepper to taste. Using eight 12-inch metal skewers, thread each skewer with a pineapple piece, an onion wedge, a cube of meat (skewering as if it were an uncut cube), and one piece of each kind of pepper, and then repeat this sequence two more times. Brush any oil remaining in the bowl over the skewers.

4. Grill the kebabs, uncovered, turning each kebab one-quarter turn every 2½ minutes, until the meat is well browned, grill marked, and cooked to medium-rare, 9 to 10 minutes. Transfer the kebabs to a serving platter and squeeze the lemon or lime wedges over the kebabs, if desired. Serve immediately.

Gas-Grilled Pork Kebabs

SERVES 4 TO 6

If the prepackaged pork chops at your market are too thin, have your butcher cut 4 to 5 boneless, center-cut pork chops, 1¼ inches thick. Be sure not to overcook the pork, since this meat is prone to drying out. To make sure that pork is done, you can peek into the cut that was made into the meat before skewering. It should appear opaque and just barely pink. Work quickly when opening the lid to turn the kebabs; you don't want too much heat to escape.

MARINADE

¼	cup extra-virgin olive oil
3	medium garlic cloves, minced
¾	teaspoon salt
½	teaspoon ground black pepper

MEAT

1¾	pounds boneless center-cut pork chops, 1¼ inches thick (about 4 to 5 chops), cut into 1¼-inch cubes and butterflied (see illustration on page 62)

FRUIT AND VEGETABLES

1	pineapple (about 3½ pounds), prepared according to chart on page 58
1	medium red bell pepper (about 5½ ounces), prepared according to chart on page 58
1	medium yellow bell pepper (about 5½ ounces), prepared according to chart on page 58
2	tablespoons extra-virgin olive oil
	Salt and ground black pepper
1	large red onion (about 10 ounces), prepared according to chart on page 58
	Lemon or lime wedges for serving (optional)

1. FOR THE MARINADE: Combine the oil, garlic, salt, and pepper in a large bowl. Add the pork cubes and toss to coat evenly. Cover and refrigerate until fully seasoned, at least 1 hour or up to 24 hours.

2. Preheat the grill with all burners set to high and the lid down until the grill is very hot, about 15 minutes. Use a wire brush to scrape clean the cooking grate. Turn all burners to medium-high.

3. FOR THE FRUIT AND VEGETABLES: Meanwhile, toss the pineapple and peppers with 1½

tablespoons olive oil in a medium bowl and season with salt and pepper to taste. Brush the onion with remaining 1½ teaspoons oil and season with salt and pepper to taste. Using 8 twelve-inch metal skewers, thread each skewer with a pineapple piece, an onion wedge, a cube of meat (skewering as if it were an uncut cube), and one piece of each kind of pepper, and then repeat this sequence two more times. Brush any oil remaining in the bowl over the skewers.

4. Grill the kebabs, covered, turning each kebab one-quarter turn every 2½ to 3 minutes, until the meat is well browned, grill marked, and cooked to medium-rare, 10 to 12 minutes. Transfer the kebabs to serving platter and squeeze the lemon or lime wedges over kebabs, if desired. Serve immediately.

➤ VARIATIONS

Grilled Pork Kebabs with West Indian Flavors

Be extremely careful handling the habanero chile pepper: Wash your hands immediately after chopping, and keep your hands away from your eyes. You may want to use disposable gloves when working with these explosively hot peppers.

3	medium scallions, sliced thin
3	medium garlic cloves, roughly chopped
½	medium habanero chile, stemmed, seeded, and roughly chopped
4½	tablespoons lime juice
¼	cup vegetable oil
1	tablespoon plus 2 teaspoons brown sugar
1	teaspoon minced fresh thyme leaves
	Pinch ground allspice
1	teaspoon salt
1	recipe Charcoal-Grilled or Gas-Grilled Pork Kebabs (without marinade)

1. Place the scallions, garlic, chile, lime juice, oil, sugar, thyme, allspice, and salt in the workbowl of a food processor and process until smooth.

2. Place the pork and lime juice mixture in a large bowl and toss to coat evenly. Cover and refrigerate until fully seasoned, at least 3 hours or up to 24 hours. Proceed as directed, tossing the fruit and vegetables with vegetable oil instead of olive oil.

Grilled Pork Kebabs with Southeast Asian Flavors

Thai fish sauce has a more authentic flavor, but, if unavailable, soy sauce may be used in its place.

¼	cup fish sauce or soy sauce
¼	cup sugar
¼	cup vegetable oil
¼	cup lime juice
3	medium garlic cloves, minced
2	teaspoons minced fresh ginger
2	medium scallions, thinly sliced
2	tablespoons minced fresh cilantro leaves
1	recipe Charcoal-Grilled or Gas-Grilled Pork Kebabs (without marinade)

1. Combine the fish sauce, sugar, oil, lime juice, garlic, ginger, scallions, and cilantro in a large bowl, stirring to dissolve the sugar.

2. Add the pork to the bowl and toss to coat evenly. Cover and refrigerate until fully seasoned, at least 1 hour or up to 8 hours. Proceed as directed, tossing the fruit and vegetables with vegetable oil instead of olive oil.

CHICKEN KEBABS

CHICKEN AND FRESH VEGETABLE KEBABS grilled to juicy perfection make great summer fare, either as appetizers eaten right off the skewers or as the main course. The best grilled chicken kebabs are succulent, well-seasoned, and really taste like they've been cooked over an open fire. They are complemented by fruits and vegetables that are equally satisfying—grill-marked but juicy, cooked all the way through but neither shrunken nor incinerated.

When we started our testing, we figured it would be simple. After all, skewered chicken is simple food, a standby of every street-corner grill cook from here to China. But in our early attempts, we ran into a few difficulties. When we simply threaded the chicken and veggies on skewers, brushed them with a little oil, and sprinkled them with salt and pepper, we were always disappointed. Sometimes the components cooked at different rates, resulting in dry meat and undercooked vegetables. Even when nicely grilled, quick-cooking kebabs didn't absorb much flavor from the fire and were bland. White meat seemed to lose moisture as it cooked, so that by the time it had reached a temperature zone that made it safe to eat, it was also too dry to enjoy. With its extra fat, dark meat was invariably juicier than white meat, but still needed a considerable flavor boost before it could be called perfect. Sticking with dark meat, we decided to attack the flavor problem first, reasoning that once we could produce well-seasoned, juicy chicken chunks, we'd work out the kinks of cooking fruits and vegetables at the same time.

Always thinking that simpler is better, we decided to start with the simplest solution, a spice rub. We'd had success with rubs on grilled chicken parts, and we saw no reason why rubs wouldn't lend flavor to kebabs as well. Intrigued by a suggestion in a recent cookbook that the rub might be sprinkled on the cooked meat immediately after grilling rather than worked into it beforehand, we decided to try this, too. The spice rub was disappointing all around. The chicken pieces looked and tasted dry. Because chicken chunks consist mostly of surface area, the flavors of the rub became much more prominent than with chicken parts, obscuring any grilled flavor. Furthermore, because the chunks are skinless, there was no fat to dissolve the spices and help form a crispy crust. The surface of the chunks looked and tasted dry, and the spices were a little powdery and raw-tasting, especially when sprinkled on after cooking.

Wanting to add a little moisture, we turned to "wet" preparations, or marinades. We mixed together a simple marinade of lemon juice, olive oil, garlic, and herbs and soaked the chicken in it for three hours, the recommended time for skin-on chicken parts. We liked the glossy, slightly moist grilled crust that the marinade produced and the way the garlic and herb flavors had penetrated the meat. But we found the flavor of the lemon juice to be overpowering on these small chunks. More of a problem, however, was the way the acid-based marinade "tenderized" the chicken. When chicken parts are bathed in this solution, the skin protects the meat, which grills up juicy and firm. Even with shorter marinating times (we tried one hour and half an hour), the skinless chunks were mushy after cooking.

Was there a way to season the chicken all the way

through and keep it moist on the grill without the acid? We ruled out brining because it would make the small skinless chicken chunks much too salty. But we wanted to get the juiciness and flavor that brining imparts. Figuring that soaking the chicken in a lightly salted marinade (rather than the large quantities of water and salt called for in brining) might work, we prepared two batches of acid-free olive oil marinade, one with salt and one without, and let the chunks sit in the marinade for three hours before grilling. The results were what we hoped for. The salted marinade produced plump, well-seasoned kebabs. The chicken marinated without salt was drier and seemed to have absorbed less flavor from the garlic and herbs.

One small problem remained. What if we wanted a little bit of lemon flavor on our chicken without sacrificing texture? We made up a batch of our marinade and added just a teaspoon of lemon juice to see what would happen. After just half an hour with such a small amount of juice, the chicken chunks had turned white, indicating that they had been partially cooked by the acid. When cooked, they exhibited the same softening as chicken marinated for a longer time in a much more acidic solution. Our suggestion for people who like their chicken kebabs lemony, then, is to squirt the kebabs with a wedge of lemon after they come off the grill instead of adding lemon juice to the marinade (just as we suggest for beef kebabs).

After fine-tuning the method, we settled on 1 teaspoon salt (this quantity seasons the chicken without making it overly salty) for 1½ pounds of chicken and a marinating time of at least three hours (during testing, chicken marinated for less time did not absorb enough flavor). Because there is no acid in the marinade and thus no danger of it breaking down the texture of the meat, it can be combined with the chicken up to 24 hours before cooking.

It was clear early on that cooking chicken and vegetables together enhances the flavor of both. Therefore, we needed to figure out how to prepare the vegetables so that they would cook at the same rate as the chicken. Precooking seemed like a hassle, so we eliminated items like potatoes and yams, which always take more time to cook through on the grill than chicken. Because the chicken was so

highly flavored from the marinade, and because we did not like the way some vegetables and fruits began to lose their characteristic flavor after just a short dip, we decided against marinating them. We found that simply tossing the fruits and vegetables with a little olive oil, salt, and pepper produced the best-textured and -flavored chunks.

In general, resilient (but not rock-hard) vegetables fared well. When cut into proper sizes, zucchini, mushrooms, and bell peppers cook thoroughly but stay moist and lend good flavor and crunch to chicken skewers. Cherry tomatoes, on the other hand, cook too quickly and tend to disintegrate by the time the chicken is done. Firm-textured fruits like apples, pears, and pineapples grill beautifully, holding their shape while cooking all the way through. Fruits that tend toward softness when overripe, like peaches and nectarines, work fine if still firm. Softer fruits like mangoes or grapes turn to mush after 10 minutes over the fire, no matter what size you cut them. Certain fruits and vegetables are obvious matches for certain marinades. With curry-marinated chicken, we like pineapple cubes and slices of onion. With middle eastern flavors, zucchini is a good choice. See the chart on page 58 for information on preparing individual fruits and vegetables for chicken skewers and matching them with marinades.

As for the fire, we found medium-high to be best. A hotter fire chars the outside before the inside is done; a cooler fire won't give you those appetizing grill marks and may dry out the chicken as it cooks it. For the juiciest chicken with the strongest grilled flavor, skewers should be cooked for 8 to 10 minutes. Check for doneness by cutting into one of the pieces with a small knife as soon as the chicken looks opaque on all sides. Remove it from the grill as soon as there is no sign of pink at the center.

After experimenting with various sizes and shapes, we chose 1½-inch chunks, small enough for easy eating but big enough to get some good grilled flavor before they have to come off the grill. With smaller chunks and thin strips, there's no margin for error; a few seconds too long on the grill and you'll wind up with a dry-as-dust dinner.

A final note on skewering itself. Chicken simply skewered through the center may spin around when you lift it from the grill, inhibiting even cooking.

(For some reason, this is less of a problem with meat, probably because chicken is just slippery by nature.) We tried out some heavy-gauge twisted metal skewers designed to prevent this problem, but in the end found that threading the ingredients through two thinner skewers at once (see illustration on page 69) was more effective. We prefer thin but sturdy metal skewers that can fit two at a time through the kebabs but won't bend under the weight of the food.

Charcoal-Grilled Chicken Kebabs

SERVES 4 AS A MAIN COURSE OR 8 AS AN APPETIZER

Although white breast meat can be used, we prefer the juicier, more flavorful dark thigh meat for these kebabs. Whichever you choose, do not mix white and dark meat on the same skewer, since they cook at slightly different rates.

I	recipe marinade of choice (see page 68)
I ½	pounds skinless boneless chicken thighs or breasts, cut into I ½-inch chunks
3	cups vegetables and/or fruit, prepared according to chart on page 58
2	tablespoons extra-virgin olive oil
	Salt and ground black pepper
	Lemon wedges for serving (optional)

1. Mix the marinade and the chicken in a gallon-sized zipper-lock plastic bag; seal the bag and refrigerate, turning once or twice, until the chicken has marinated fully, at least 3 and up to 24 hours.

2. Light a large chimney starter filled with hardwood charcoal (about 2½ pounds) and allow to burn until all the charcoal is covered with a layer of fine gray ash. Build a single-level fire by spreading the coals evenly out over the bottom of the grill. Set the cooking grate in place, cover the grill with the lid, and let the grate heat up, about 5 minutes. Use a wire brush to scrape clean the cooking grate. The grill is ready when you have a medium-hot fire. (See how to gauge heat level on page 19.)

3. Meanwhile, lightly coat the vegetables and/or fruit by tossing them in a medium bowl with the oil and salt and pepper to taste.

4. Remove the chicken chunks from the bag; dis-
card the marinade. Use one hand to hold two skewers about ½ inch apart, then thread a portion of the chicken and vegetables on both skewers at once for easy turning on the grill (see illustration on page 69). Repeat with the remaining chicken and vegetables to make 8 sets of double skewers.

5. Grill the kebabs, uncovered, turning each kebab one-quarter turn every 2 minutes, until the chicken and vegetables and/or fruit are lightly browned and meat is fully cooked, about 8 minutes for white meat and 9 minutes for dark meat. (Check for doneness by cutting into one piece when it looks opaque on all sides. Remove the kebabs from the grill when there is no pink at the center.) Serve immediately.

Gas-Grilled Chicken Kebabs

SERVES 4 AS A MAIN COURSE OR 8 AS AN APPETIZER

Preheat the grill until very hot to burn off any residue from your last meal, but then turn the burners down to medium-high to avoid singeing the kebabs.

I	recipe marinade of choice (see page 68)
I ½	pounds skinless boneless chicken thighs or breasts, cut into I ½-inch chunks
3	cups vegetables and/or fruit, prepared according to chart on page 58
2	tablespoons extra-virgin olive oil
	Salt and ground black pepper
	Lemon wedges for serving (optional)

1. Mix the marinade and the chicken in a gallon-sized zipper-lock plastic bag; seal the bag and refrigerate, turning once or twice, until the chicken has marinated fully, at least 3 and up to 24 hours.

2. Preheat the grill with all burners set to high and the lid down until the grill is very hot, about 15 minutes. Use a wire brush to scrape clean the cooking grate. Turn all burners to medium-high.

3. Meanwhile, lightly coat the vegetables and/or fruit by tossing them in a medium bowl with the oil and salt and pepper to taste.

4. Remove the chicken chunks from the bag; discard the marinade. Use one hand to hold two skewers about ½ inch apart, then thread a portion of the chicken and vegetables on both skewers at once for

MARINADES FOR CHICKEN KEBABS

Master Recipe for Garlic and Herb Marinade

MAKES SCANT 3/4 CUP, ENOUGH TO COAT
1 1/2 POUNDS CHICKEN CHUNKS

1/2	cup extra-virgin olive oil
2	tablespoons minced garlic
1/4	cup minced fresh basil, parsley, tarragon, oregano, mint, cilantro, or snipped chives, or 2 tablespoons minced fresh thyme or rosemary
1	teaspoon salt
	Ground black pepper

Whisk the ingredients, including pepper to taste, together in a small bowl.

➤ VARIATIONS

Middle Eastern Marinade

Follow master recipe, using 1/4 cup minced fresh mint or parsley leaves, alone or in combination, and adding 1/2 teaspoon ground cinnamon, 1/2 teaspoon ground allspice, and 1/4 teaspoon cayenne.

Southwestern Marinade

Follow master recipe, using 1/4 cup minced fresh cilantro, decreasing salt to 1/2 teaspoon, and adding 1 teaspoon ground cumin, 1 teaspoon chili powder, 1 teaspoon ground turmeric, and 1 seeded and minced small fresh chile, such as a jalapeño.

Curry Marinade

Follow master recipe, using 1/4 cup minced fresh mint or cilantro leaves and adding 1 teaspoon curry powder.

Caribbean Marinade

Follow master recipe, using 1/4 cup minced fresh parsley leaves and adding 1 teaspoon ground cumin, 1 teaspoon chili powder, 1/2 teaspoon ground allspice, 1/2 teaspoon pepper, and 1/4 teaspoon ground cinnamon.

Asian Marinade

MAKES 3/4 CUP, ENOUGH TO COAT
1 1/2 POUNDS CHICKEN CHUNKS

6	tablespoons vegetable oil
2	tablespoons Asian sesame oil
1/4	cup soy sauce
2	tablespoons minced garlic
1	tablespoon minced fresh ginger
1/4	cup minced fresh cilantro leaves
2	medium scallions, white and green parts, thinly sliced
	Ground black pepper

Whisk the ingredients, including pepper to taste, together in a small bowl.

easy turning on the grill (see illustration on page 69). Repeat with the remaining chicken and vegetables to make 8 sets of double skewers.

5. Grill the skewers, covered, turning each kebab one-quarter turn every 2 minutes, until the chicken and vegetables and/or fruit are lightly browned and meat is fully cooked, about 8 minutes for white meat and 9 minutes for dark meat. (Check for doneness by cutting into one piece when it looks opaque on all sides. Remove the kebabs from the grill when there is no pink at the center.) Serve immediately.

➤ VARIATIONS

Grilled Caribbean Chicken Skewers with Black Bean and Mango Salsa

The bright, sweet flavor of mango salsa works especially well with Caribbean flavors.

Follow recipe for Charcoal-Grilled or Gas-Grilled Chicken Skewers, using Caribbean Marinade and 2 medium onions, peeled and cut into 1/2-inch-thick wedges (about 3 cups), for the vegetable. Serve with Black Bean and Mango Salsa (page 300).

Thai Chicken Satay with Spicy Peanut Sauce

Grilled chicken skewers are paired with peanut sauce for a Thai-influenced satay. For more authentic Thai flavor, substitute fish sauce for soy sauce in the Asian Marinade recipe. Serve as an appetizer.

Follow recipe for Charcoal-Grilled or Gas-Grilled Chicken Skewers, using Asian Marinade and 2 medium red bell peppers, cored, seeded, and cut into 1-inch-wide wedges (about 3 cups), for the vegetable. Toss peppers with peanut oil in place of olive oil. Serve with Spicy Peanut Dipping Sauce (page 111).

Curried Chicken Skewers and Cucumber Salad with Yogurt and Mint

The flavor of this cucumber salad is similar to that of raita, a yogurt-based condiment from India that tames the heat of spicy food. Here it serves the same purpose, a cool foil to the complex flavor of curried chicken. Serve with a pilaf, made from aromatic rice such as basmati, to complete the meal.

Follow recipe for Charcoal-Grilled or Gas-Grilled Chicken Skewers, using Curry Marinade and 1 small pineapple, peeled, cored, and cut into 1-inch cubes (about 3 cups), for the fruit. Serve with Cucumber Salad with Yogurt and Mint (page 303).

Southwestern Skewers with Red Pepper–Jicama Slaw

A sweet, crunchy slaw is an excellent foil to the spicy kebabs.

Follow recipe for Charcoal-Grilled or Gas-Grilled Chicken Skewers, using Southwestern Marinade and 1 medium onion, cut into ½-inch-thick wedges, and 1 medium green bell pepper, cored, seeded, and cut into 1½-inch chunks (about 3 cups total), for the vegetable. Serve with Red Pepper–Jicama Slaw (page 301).

SWORDFISH KEBABS

SWORDFISH IS IDEAL FOR KEBABS BECAUSE the flesh is firm and has a steaklike quality. Because the fish is cut into small pieces, it cooks very quickly and does not dry out. (Coating the fish with some olive oil helps keep it moist, too.) In fact, we almost like the kebabs better than the steaks because there is more surface area for caramelization. Because swordfish kebabs cook so quickly, we found that vegetables must be cooked on separate skewers, giving them the extra time they need to cook through. While thick swordfish steaks are best grilled over a two-level fire (see page 18), we found that kebabs can be cooked over a medium-hot, single level fire. For more information on swordfish, including what to look for when you buy it, see page 163.

Charcoal-Grilled Swordfish Kebabs

SERVES 4

You should grill vegetable kebabs alongside the swordfish on separate skewers, since the vegetables take a few minutes longer to cook through. See the chart on page 58 for directions on preparing the vegetables for skewers, tossing vegetables with some oil and seasoning with salt and pepper before cooking. Grill the vegetable skewers until tender and nicely browned, 8 to 10 minutes.

2	swordfish steaks, 1 inch thick (about 2 pounds total), skin removed and cut into 1-inch cubes
3	tablespoons extra-virgin olive oil
	Salt and ground black pepper
	Vegetable oil for grill rack
	Lemon or lime wedges (optional)

1. Toss the swordfish cubes and oil in a large bowl. Season with salt and pepper to taste.

THREADING CHICKEN ON DOUBLE SKEWERS

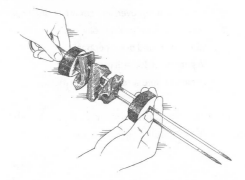

Pieces of chicken tend to spin around on a single skewer. To prevent this problem, we like to thread chicken kebabs onto double skewers. Use one hand to hold two skewers about ½ inch apart, then thread the chicken and vegetables onto the skewers simultaneously.

2. Light a large chimney starter filled with hardwood charcoal (about 2½ pounds) and allow to burn until all the charcoal is covered with a layer of fine gray ash. Build a single-level fire by spreading the coals out evenly over the bottom of the grill. Set the cooking rack in place, cover the grill with the lid, and let the rack heat up, about 5 minutes. Use a wire brush to scrape clean the cooking rack. The grill is ready when you have a medium-hot fire. (See how to gauge heat level on page 19.)

3. Thread the swordfish cubes onto skewers. Lightly dip a small wad of paper towels in vegetable oil; holding wad with tongs, wipe the grill rack.

4. Grill the kebabs, uncovered, giving each one-quarter turn every 1¾ minutes, until the center of swordfish is no longer translucent, about 7 minutes. Transfer the kebabs to serving platter and squeeze the lemon or lime wedges over kebabs, if desired. Serve immediately.

Gas-Grilled Swordfish Kebabs

SERVES 4

You should grill vegetable kebabs alongside the swordfish on separate skewers, since the vegetables take a few minutes longer to cook through. See the chart on page 58 for directions on preparing the vegetables for skewers, tossing vegetables with some oil and seasoning with salt and pepper before cooking. Grill the vegetable skewers until tender and nicely browned, 8 to 10 minutes. Work quickly when you open the lid to turn the kebabs to keep the heat from dissipating.

2   swordfish steaks, 1 inch thick (about 2 pounds total), skin removed and cut into 1-inch cubes

3   tablespoons extra virgin olive oil

     Salt and ground black pepper

     Vegetable oil for grill rack

     Lemon or lime wedges (optional)

1. Toss the swordfish cubes and oil in a large bowl. Season with salt and pepper to taste.

2. Preheat the grill with all burners set to high and the lid down until very hot, about 15 minutes. Use a wire brush to scrape clean the cooking grate. Leave all burners on high.

3. Thread the swordfish cubes onto skewers. Lightly dip a small wad of paper towels in vegetable oil; holding wad with tongs, wipe the grill rack.

4. Grill the kebabs, covered, giving each one-quarter turn every 2 minutes, until the center of swordfish is no longer translucent, about 8 minutes. Transfer the kebabs to serving platter and squeeze the lemon or lime wedges over kebabs, if desired. Serve immediately.

Southeast Asian–Style Swordfish Kebabs

SERVES 4 AS A MAIN COURSE,
8 AS AN APPETIZER

The sugar in the marinade creates a wonderful deep caramelization on the grilled swordfish. If you wish, you can serve these with the Spicy Peanut Dipping Sauce on page 111.

4   tablespoons fish sauce or soy sauce

4   tablespoons vegetable oil

2   tablespoons lime juice

4   teaspoons sugar

3   medium garlic cloves, minced

2   swordfish steaks, 1 inch thick (about 2 pounds total), skin removed and cut into 1-inch cubes

     Lime wedges

1. Mix together fish sauce, vegetable oil, lime juice, sugar, and garlic in a small bowl. Place swordfish cubes in a gallon-sized zipper-lock plastic bag. Pour fish sauce mixture over fish and seal. Toss gently to coat fish with marinade. Refrigerate until swordfish is well seasoned, 15 to 30 minutes to 2 hours.

2. Grill the kebabs as directed in the previous charcoal or gas recipe, serving them with lime wedges.

6

CHOPS AND PORK TENDERLOIN

THIS CHAPTER COVERS THREE KINDS OF chops—pork, lamb, and veal—as well as the pork tenderloin, which can be seasoned much like pork chops.

As this chapter demonstrates, chops can be cut from various animals and from various locations on the same animal. Chops can come from the shoulder, rib, loin, or even sirloin areas. In general, a chop is about the size of an adult hand and contains meat and bone. (Some chops are sold boneless, but we find that cooking meat on the bone improves its flavor and so prefer to buy bone-in chops.)

Chops can vary in thickness from one-half inch to as much as two inches. We find that thick (but not gargantuan) chops are the easiest to grill. Thin chops tend to overcook by the time the exterior is seared. Really thick chops have the opposite problem—the exterior can char before the meat near the bone is done. For best results, follow the recommendations in the recipes about the thickness of the chops.

Because we prefer moderately thick chops (usually between 1 and 1½ inches), we find that they are best cooked over a two-level fire. We sear the chops over the hotter part of the grill and then drag them to the cooler part of the grill to finish cooking. Most chops are a bit fatty. This is part of their charm and what makes them so delicious. However, all that fat can cause flare-ups. The two-level fire gives you a place to drag the chops if a flare-up does occur. We also suggest keeping a spray bottle filled with water near the grill when cooking chops.

As with steaks, we like to let chops rest for about 5 minutes once they come off the grill. This resting time allows the juices to redistribute themselves evenly throughout the meat. Note that the internal temperature of the chop will rise by at least 5 degrees as it rests. For this reason, we often pull the chops from the grill at temperatures that may seem a bit low. By the time the meat reaches the table, it should be cooked to the desired doneness.

One note about pork tenderloin. While this long, lean cut has little in common with pork, lamb, and veal chops, we included it in this chapter because we like to use the same rubs and salsas with pork chops and pork tenderloin. Including both in the same chapter thus makes for easy cross-referencing of the rubs and salsas.

PORK CHOPS

WHEN WAS THE LAST TIME YOU HAD A really juicy, really tender pork chop? These days it is likely to be something you remember, not something you recently enjoyed. In response to American demands for low-fat meat, the pork industry has systematically trimmed down the hefty fat-producing hogs of the past to create today's new pig, sleek of silhouette and lean of flesh. (See "Pork Cuts" on page 73 for more information.) Healthy? Yes. Tasty? We're not so sure.

All of this notwithstanding, we love grilled pork chops and wanted to figure out a way to get them as juicy and flavorful as possible. After settling on rib loin chops (see "Which Pork Chop Is Best?" on page 76), we started testing grilling methods.

Over direct heat, the chops tended to burn on the exterior before they were cooked through to the bone. This was especially a problem when cooking thick-cut chops. After encountering the same problem over hot and medium fires, we decided to test cooking the chops over a two-level fire.

First we seared the meat over the hotter part of the grill, then we moved it to more moderate heat. Although the chops looked good, they were taking a long time to come up to temperature. We found that covering the chops with a disposable aluminum roasting pan as they grilled over the cooler fire speeded up the final cooking process. The chops cooked quickly (but without burning, as did chops

THE FOUR PRIMAL CUTS OF PORK

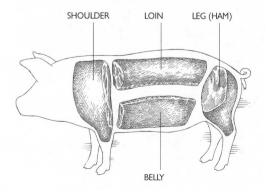

SHOULDER   LOIN   LEG (HAM)

BELLY

SCIENCE: Pork Cuts

Up until World War II, pigs were raised as much for their fat as for their meat. A pig with four to five inches of exterior fat (equivalent to about 60 pounds of lard) at slaughter was the norm. After the war, vegetable sources of fat (oil, shortening, margarine) became preferred over animal choices, and lard was no longer an asset. This trend, coupled with concerns over the past two or three decades for healthy eating that generally discouraged intake of animal fat, caused the industry to "lean up" its pork, largely through genetic engineering. Today, many processors penalize producers for pigs that carry an exterior layer of fat of more than ⅘ inch (or more than eight pounds). All told, today's pork has about 30 percent less fat than it did 20 years ago.

The industry's success at eliminating the pig's surface fat, however, has resulted in the loss of intramuscular fat as well. Known as marbling, this fat traps and retains juices during cooking and gives the meat flavor and body. This reduction in fat poses the greatest challenge for the cook in the loin, the area that extends from the back of the shoulder down to the hip and is home to chops as well as the tenderloin and crown roast of pork. Because they are so lean, these cuts require special treatment to prevent them from becoming tough and chewy.

Although health experts recommend cooking all meat (including pork) to an internal temperature of 160 degrees, we find that most pork cuts cooked to this temperature are dry and tough. An internal temperature of 145 to 150 degrees is our preference. At this temperature the meat, when cut, is ivory in color and reveals a distinct grain, but the juices still run pale pink.

Fear of trichinosis should not prompt anyone to overcook pork: the trichinae parasite is killed at 137 degrees, when pork is still medium-rare. (As an aside, trichinosis is very uncommon in the United States. Only 230 cases were reported nationwide between 1991 and 1996, and the source of contamination in some 40 percent of these cases was wild game.) If you are unalterably opposed to pinkish pork juices (or are concerned about salmonella from cross-contamination), you should cook pork to 160 degrees, but the meat will be quite dry.

Cuts from the shoulder, belly, and leg are less prone to drying out. Meat from these areas tends to be much fattier and also tough, requiring long, slow cooking if they are to become fork-tender. The shoulder is divided into two cuts, the picnic roast and Boston butt. The leg is sold as ham, and the belly is where bacon and spareribs come from.

---

cooked solely over direct heat), so there was less time for them to dry out.

We had found the best cooking method, but the chops were still lacking in flavor and moistness. Owing to their relative absence of fat, these chops were clearly perfect candidates for brining. (See page 102 for more information on this technique of soaking foods in saltwater or in a solution of salt and sugar. Soaking in a salt solution helps the food, usually meat or poultry, to retain its juices while cooking. Sugar is often added to brines for pork to give the meat a touch of sweetness and to increase caramelization on the grill.)

Most of the recipes we looked at involved fairly long immersion in brines with rather low concentrations of sugar and salt, about ½ cup of each per 2 quarts of water. After trying a number of time periods, from several hours to two days, we found that the resulting cooked chops, while indeed more moist, had become almost watery, with a webby, hamlike texture. Unfortunately, shorter soaks in this mild brine did little for the flavor and texture.

We next increased the proportions of sugar and salt to compensate for a shorter brining time. Bingo. The chops tasted great after just one hour in this concentrated brine. We also found that brown sugar adds slightly more flavor than regular sugar and encourages more caramelization on the grill. Adding garlic, herbs, and spices to the brine added flavor to the somewhat bland-tasting pork as well. If serving the chops plain (without a spice rub or salsa), we recommend adding these aromatic elements to the brine.

BUYING PORK CHOPS

Supermarket chops are often cut thick at the bone and thinner at the outer edge, like the one on the left. With such chops, the thinner periphery will overcook before the thicker meat near the bone is finished. Make sure to buy chops that are of even thickness, like the one at the right.

Our final step in the testing process was to determine the exact relationship between flavor and the internal temperature of the meat. Pork chops taken off the grill at 145 degrees were dry after a five-minute rest. After fiddling with various options, we found that pork chops should be taken off the grill when the internal temperature registers 130 degrees, then covered with a foil pan for five minutes to allow the temperature to rise to 145 degrees. (See "Pork Cuts" on page 73 for information on safe internal temperatures for pork.) Cooked this way, chops relinquish a minimum of juice on the plate and retain the barest whisper of pink on the interior. They are downright succulent.

This method works because the gentle residual heat in the chops finishes the cooking process. However, you must use an accurate instant-read thermometer. Time estimates will be just that—estimates—and no amount of prodding or poking with your finger or a knife can tell you precisely when it's time to take the chops off the grill.

Because the flavor of pork is so mild, we like to rub the chops with spices after brining but before grilling. In this case, though, a simple salt-and-sugar brine is fine, although you can add the garlic, herbs, and spices for more flavor. For both flavor and a bit of moisture, serve salsa along with the chops. We find that salsas that have a sweet edge to them are especially nice with the flavor of pork.

Charcoal-Grilled Pork Chops

SERVES 4

You may opt to use only sugar and salt in the brine and omit the other flavorings if you are using a spice rub (see page 77) or serving salsa (see page 75) with the chops. Use the disposable aluminum pan to cover the chops on the grill and then again immediately after grilling so that they reach an internal temperature of 145 degrees after resting for 5 minutes.

¾	cup lightly packed dark brown sugar
½	cup kosher salt (or ¼ cup table salt)
10	medium garlic cloves, crushed
4	bay leaves, crumbled
8	whole cloves
3	tablespoons whole black peppercorns, crushed
4	bone-in rib loin pork chops, each 1 inch thick (about 2 pounds total)
2	tablespoons extra-virgin olive oil
	Ground black pepper
	Disposable aluminum roasting pan

1. Dissolve the sugar and salt in 2 cups hot water in a gallon-sized zipper-lock plastic bag. Add the garlic, bay leaves, cloves, peppercorns, and 4 cups cold water; cool the mixture to room temperature. Add the pork chops, then seal bag, pressing out as much air as possible. Refrigerate, turning bag once,

CUTTING UP A PINEAPPLE

1. Start by trimming the ends of the pineapple so it will sit flat on a work surface. Cut the pineapple through the ends into four quarters.

2. Lay each quarter, cut side up, on a work surface, and slide a knife between the skin and flesh to remove the skin.

3. Stand each peeled quarter on end and slice off the tough, light-colored core attached to the inside of the piece. The peeled and cored pineapple can be sliced as desired.

SALSAS AND RELISHES FOR PORK CHOPS

Sweet salsas complement the flavor of grilled pork. Moist, juicy salsas also keep pork from tasting dry. You might also try the Black Bean and Mango Salsa (page 300) with pork.

Pineapple Salsa

MAKES ABOUT 2 1/2 CUPS

See page 74 for information on cutting up a pineapple.

- 1/4 small pineapple, peeled, cored, and cut into 3/8-inch dice (about 1 1/4 cups)
- 1 small barely ripe banana, peeled and cut into 3/8-inch dice
- 1/2 cup seedless green grapes, halved or quartered
- 1/2 firm avocado, peeled and cut into 3/8-inch dice
- 4 teaspoons lime juice
- 1 jalapeño chile, stemmed, seeded, and minced
- 1 teaspoon minced fresh oregano leaves
  Salt

Combine all ingredients, including salt to taste, in a medium bowl. Let stand at room temperature for 30 minutes. (Banana and avocado will darken if salsa is prepared much further in advance.) Serve alongside chops or grilled pork tenderloin.

Peach Salsa

MAKES ABOUT 2 1/2 CUPS

Mangoes or nectarines can be substituted for peaches if desired.

- 2 ripe but firm peaches, pitted and chopped coarse
- 1 small red bell pepper, cored, seeded, and diced
- 1 small red onion, diced
- 1/4 cup chopped fresh parsley leaves
- 1 medium garlic clove, minced
- 1/4 cup pineapple juice
- 6 tablespoons lime juice

- 1 jalapeño or other fresh chile, stemmed, seeded, and minced
  Salt

Combine all ingredients, including salt to taste, in a medium bowl. Cover and refrigerate to blend flavors, at least 1 hour or up to 4 days. Serve alongside chops or grilled pork tenderloin.

Cranberry-Onion Relish

MAKES 1 1/2 CUPS

This sweet-sour condiment goes very well with pork, although a little goes a long way.

- 3 tablespoons unsalted butter
- 2 large onions (1 1/4 pounds), halved and thinly sliced
- 1/4 cup sugar
- 1 cup whole cranberries, picked through
- 1/2 cup red wine
- 2 tablespoons red wine vinegar
- 1 1/2 tablespoons grenadine (optional)
- 1/2 teaspoon salt

1. Melt the butter in a large sauté pan. Add the onions and cook over medium-low heat until the they are very soft, about 25 minutes. Increase the heat to medium-high and add sugar; cook, stirring frequently, until the onions are golden brown and caramelized, 10 to 12 minutes longer.

2. Add the remaining ingredients and bring the mixture to a boil. Reduce the heat and simmer, partially covered, until most of liquid has evaporated and the mixture has a jamlike consistency, about 20 minutes. Serve warm or at room temperature. (Relish can be refrigerated in an airtight container for up to 1 week. Bring to room temperature before serving.)

until the chops are fully seasoned, about 1 hour. Remove the chops from the brine, rinse briefly, and dry thoroughly with paper towels.

2. Light a large chimney starter filled with hardwood charcoal (about 2½ pounds) and allow to burn until all the charcoal is covered with a layer of fine gray ash. Build a two-level fire by stacking most of the coals on one side of the grill and arranging the remaining coals in a single layer on the other side of

MEASURING THE INTERNAL TEMPERATURE OF A CHOP

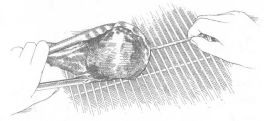

When you think a chop might be done, use a pair of tongs to hold the chop and then slide an instant-read thermometer through the edge of the chop and deep into the meat, making sure to avoid the bone.

the grill. Set the cooking rack in place, cover the grill with the lid, and let the rack heat up, about 5 minutes. Use a wire brush to scrape clean the cooking rack. The grill is ready when the temperature of the stacked coals is medium-hot and that of the remaining coals is medium-low. (See how to gauge heat level on page 19.)

3. Rub the chops with oil and sprinkle with pepper to taste.

4. Cook the chops, uncovered, over the hotter part of the grill until browned, about 3 minutes on each side. Move the chops to the cooler part of the grill and cover with a disposable aluminum roasting pan. Continue grilling, turning once, until an instant-read thermometer inserted through the side of a chop and away from the bone (see the illustration at left) registers 130 degrees, 4 to 6 minutes longer. Transfer the chops to a platter; cover with the foil pan and let rest about 5 minutes. (The internal temperature should rise to 145 degrees while resting). Serve immediately.

INGREDIENTS: Which Pork Chop Is Best?

In many supermarkets, all pork chops from the loin are simply labeled "loin chops." However, there are significant differences in the four types of chops that come from the loin. Two—the blade chop and the sirloin chop—are less common and more likely to be labeled correctly. The two chops labeled "loin chops" that you are most likely to run into are the center-cut chop and the rib chop.

As the name implies, center-cut chops are cut right out of the center of the loin. You can pick them out by the bone that divides them into two sections, giving them a close resemblance to a T-bone steak. Like a T-bone, they have meat from the loin on one side of the bone and a small portion of the tenderloin muscle on the other side. Some people prefer these center-cut chops because the tenderloin portion in particular is extremely tender. These chops work fine on the grill. Our top choice, though, is the rib chop, cut from the rib section of the loin, which is slightly closer to the shoulder. It has a somewhat higher fat content, which makes it both more flavorsome and less likely to dry out during cooking. The rib pork chop can be distinguished by the section of rib bone along one side. Sometimes rib and center-cut chops are

sold boneless, making it much more difficult to tell them apart. But since we find bone-in meat juicier when cooked, we suggest you look for bone-in chops.

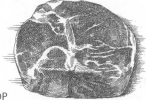

CENTER-CUT CHOP
A bone runs through the middle of the center-cut chop with meat on either side. The meat on the left side of the bone is from the tenderloin.

RIB CHOP
The bone on a rib chop runs along one edge of the chop with all the meat on just one side of the bone.

DRY SPICE RUBS FOR PORK

Pork benefits from assertive seasonings, especially when it will be grilled and there is no opportunity to make a pan sauce. These four rubs are especially well suited to chops and tenderloins.

Fragrant Spice Rub for Pork

ENOUGH FOR 4 CHOPS OR 2 TENDERLOINS

Because this rub contains sugar, make sure to mind the grill and turn the pork often to keep the sugar from burning.

1	tablespoon fennel seeds
1	tablespoon cumin seeds
1	tablespoon coriander seeds
¾	teaspoon ground cinnamon
1½	teaspoons dry mustard
1½	teaspoons brown sugar

Toast the seeds in a small skillet over medium heat, shaking the pan occasionally to prevent burning, until the first wisps of smoke appear, 3 to 5 minutes. Cool to room temperature. Mix with the remaining ingredients and grind to a powder in a spice grinder. Rub the mixture over oiled and seasoned pork before grilling.

Herb Rub for Pork

ENOUGH FOR 4 CHOPS OR 2 TENDERLOINS

The salt is added directly to this rub to help break down the spices into a powder when ground.

1½	teaspoons dried thyme
1½	teaspoons dried rosemary
1½	teaspoons black peppercorns
2	bay leaves, crumbled
2	whole cloves or allspice berries
½	teaspoon salt

Grind the ingredients to a powder in a spice grinder. Rub the mixture over oiled but unseasoned pork (do not sprinkle pork with pepper) before grilling.

Chipotle and Ancho Chile Rub for Pork

ENOUGH FOR 4 CHOPS OR 2 TENDERLOINS

This rub contains brown sugar and can burn on the grill. Be sure to turn the pork often and watch for flare-ups to prevent charring. The flavor of the chiles is strong, so a little of this rub goes a long way.

1	dried chipotle chile (not in adobo sauce), stemmed, seeded, and broken into 1-inch pieces
½	medium ancho chile, stemmed, seeded, and broken into 1-inch pieces
1	teaspoon dried oregano
¼	teaspoon garlic powder
¼	teaspoon salt
2	teaspoons brown sugar

Place the chipotle and ancho chiles in a spice grinder and process into a powder. Transfer ground chiles to a small bowl and mix in the oregano, garlic powder, salt, and brown sugar. Rub the mixture over oiled but unseasoned pork (do not sprinkle pork with pepper) before grilling.

Curry Rub for Pork

ENOUGH FOR 4 CHOPS OR 2 TENDERLOINS

This rub works especially well with the Pineapple Salsa.

4	teaspoons curry powder
¼	teaspoon garlic powder
¼	teaspoon ground ginger
2	teaspoons brown sugar
½	teaspoon salt
¼	teaspoon ground black pepper

Mix all ingredients together in a small bowl. Rub the mixture over oiled but unseasoned pork (do not sprinkle pork with pepper) before grilling.

Gas-Grilled Pork Chops

SERVES 4

You may opt to use only sugar and salt in the brine and omit the other flavorings if you are using a spice rub (see page 77) or serving salsa (see page 75) with the chops. With the lid down on a gas grill, there's no need to use a disposable roasting pan. Just cover the chops with foil once they come off the grill to bring them up to temperature.

³⁄₄	cup lightly packed dark brown sugar
¹⁄₂	cup kosher salt (or ¹⁄₄ cup table salt)
10	medium garlic cloves, crushed
4	bay leaves, crumbled
8	whole cloves
3	tablespoons whole black peppercorns, crushed
4	bone-in rib loin pork chops, each 1 inch thick (about 2 pounds total)
2	tablespoons extra-virgin olive oil
	Ground black pepper
	Aluminum foil

1. Dissolve the sugar and salt in 2 cups hot water in a gallon-sized zipper-lock plastic bag. Add the garlic, bay leaves, cloves, peppercorns, and 4 cups cold water; cool the mixture to room temperature. Add the pork chops, then seal bag, pressing out as much air as possible. Refrigerate, turning bag once, until the chops are fully seasoned, about 1 hour. Remove the chops from the brine, rinse briefly, and dry thoroughly with paper towels.

2. Preheat the grill with all burners set to high and the lid down until the grill is very hot, about 15 minutes. Use a wire brush to scrape clean the cooking grate. Leave one burner on high and turn the other burner(s) down to medium-low.

3. Rub the chops with oil and sprinkle with pepper to taste.

4. Cook the chops, covered, over the hotter part of the grill until browned, about 3 minutes on each side. Move the chops to the cooler part of the grill. Continue grilling, covered, turning once, until an instant-read thermometer inserted through the side of a chop and away from the bone (see the illustration on page 76) registers 130 degrees, 5 to 7 minutes longer. Transfer the chops to a platter; cover loosely with foil (do not wrap foil tightly around

meat), and let rest about 5 minutes. (The internal temperature should rise to 145 degrees while resting). Serve immediately.

➤ VARIATION

Grilled Thick-Cut Pork Chops

Thick-cut chops require slightly more cooking.

Follow recipe for Charcoal-Grilled or Gas-Grilled Pork Chops, using 4 bone-in rib loin pork chops, each about 1¹⁄₂ inches thick (about 3 pounds total). Sear over the hotter part of the grill as directed and then move the chops to the cooler part of the grill. Increase the cooking on the cooler part of the grill to 6 to 8 minutes whether cooking on charcoal or gas.

LAMB CHOPS

LAMB CHOPS DON'T HAVE TO BE A RARE (and expensive) treat. True, loin and rib chops (together, the eight rib chops form the cut known as rack of lamb) can cost upward of $12 a pound. But we love the meaty flavor and chewy (but not tough) texture of shoulder chops (see page 79 for more information). We also like the fact that they cost only about $4 per pound.

In a side-by-side taste test, we grilled loin, rib, and

LOIN AND RIB LAMB CHOPS

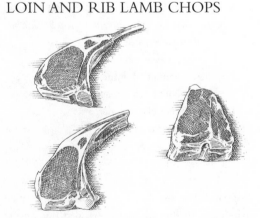

A rib chop (bottom left) often contains a lot of fat on the bone. Have your butcher "french" the chop (top left) by scraping away this fat. Like a T-bone steak, a loin chop (right) has meat on either side of the bone. The small piece on the right side of the bone on this chop is very tender and fine-grained. The larger piece of meat on the other side of the bone is chewier.

shoulder chops to medium-rare and let them stand about 5 minutes before tasting. The rib chop was the most refined of the three, with a mild, almost sweet flavor and tender texture. The loin chop had a slightly stronger flavor, and the texture was a bit firmer (but not chewier) than the rib chop. The shoulder chop had a distinctly gutsier flavor than the other two. While it was not at all tough, it was chewier. If you like the flavor of lamb (and we do) and are trying to keep within a budget, then try shoulder chops.

We also tried a second test in which we grilled the chops to medium, a stage at which many people prefer lamb. Both the rib and loin chops were dry and less flavorful and juicy than they were at medium-rare. The shoulder chop held its own, in both taste and texture, displaying another advantage besides price.

Shoulder chops can range in thickness from half an inch to an inch. We prefer the thicker chops; you should ask your butcher to cut them for you if necessary. Loin and rib chops are usually thicker, often close to 1½ inches.

In our testing, we found that all of these chops should be cooked over a two-level fire to bring the inside up to temperature without charring the exterior. A two-level fire also makes sense because lamb tends to flame; the cooler part of the grill is the perfect place to let flames die down. Even when cooking thinner chops, we found that the flames often became too intense on a single-level fire. When

BLADE CHOP AND ROUND-BONE CHOP

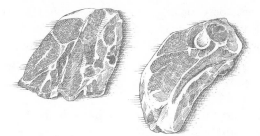

There are two kinds of shoulder chops. The blade chop (left) is roughly rectangular in shape and contains a piece of the chine bone and a thin piece of the blade bone. The arm, or round-bone, chop (right) is leaner and contains a round cross-section of the arm bone. The extra fat in blade chops melts on the grill, flavoring and moistening the meat. The arm bone chop has a tiny line of riblets on the side of each chop, which are delicious. Either chop takes well to grilling.

cooking lamb, it is a good idea to have somewhere to drag the meat if flames become too intense. A squirt bottle filled with water is also a handy item to have near the grill.

Charcoal-Grilled Shoulder Lamb Chops

SERVES 4

Try to get shoulder lamb chops that are at least ¾ inch thick, since they are less likely to overcook. If you can only find chops that are ½ inch thick, reduce the cooking time over the medium-low fire by about 30 seconds on each side. For information about the different kinds of shoulder chops, see box on this page and on page 81.

4	shoulder lamb chops (blade or round bone), ¾ to 1 inch thick
2	tablespoons extra-virgin olive oil
	Salt and ground black pepper

1. Light a large chimney starter filled with hardwood charcoal (about 2½ pounds) and allow to burn until all the charcoal is covered with a layer of fine gray ash. Build a two-level fire by stacking most of the coals on one side of the grill and arranging the remaining coals in a single layer on the other side of the grill. Set the cooking rack in place, cover the grill with the lid, and let the rack heat up, about 5 minutes. Use a wire brush to scrape clean the cooking rack. The grill is ready when the temperature of the stacked coals is medium-hot and that of the remaining coals is medium-low. (See how to gauge heat level on page 19.)

2. Rub the chops with oil and sprinkle with salt and pepper to taste.

3. Grill the chops, uncovered, over the hotter part of the grill, turning them once, until well browned, about 4 minutes. (If the chops start to flame, drag them to the cooler part of the grill and/or extinguish flames with a squirt bottle.) Move the chops to the cooler part of the grill and continue grilling, turning once, to the desired doneness, about 5 minutes for rare (about 120 degrees on an instant-read thermometer), about 7 minutes for medium (about 130 degrees), or about 9 minutes for well-done (140 to 150 degrees).

4. Remove the chops from the grill and let rest for 5 minutes. Serve immediately.

Gas-Grilled Shoulder Lamb Chops

SERVES 4

To make sure the lamb chops aren't flaming up under the grill cover, watch for any substantial amount of smoke coming through the vents. This indicates that flare-ups are occurring and need to be extinguished. For information about the different kinds of shoulder chops, see boxes on pages 79 and 81.

4	shoulder lamb chops (blade or round bone), ¾ to 1 inch thick
2	tablespoons extra-virgin olive oil
	Salt and ground black pepper

1. Preheat the grill with all burners set to high and the lid down until the grill is very hot, about 15 minutes. Use a wire brush to scrape clean the cooking grate. Leave one burner on high and turn the other burner(s) down to medium.

2. Rub the chops with oil and sprinkle with salt and pepper to taste.

3. Grill the chops, covered, over the hotter part of the grill, turning them once, until well browned, about 4 minutes. (If the chops start to flame, drag them to the cooler part of the grill for a moment and/or extinguish the flames with a squirt bottle.) Move the chops to the cooler part of the grill. Continue grilling, covered and turning once, to the desired doneness, about 6 minutes for rare (about 120 degrees on an instant-read thermometer), about 8 minutes for medium (about 130 degrees), or about 10 minutes for well-done (140 to 150 degrees).

4. Remove the chops from the grill and let rest for 5 minutes. Serve immediately.

➤ VARIATIONS

Grilled Shoulder Lamb Chops with Near East Red Pepper Paste

Sweet and spicy, this paste both encourages browning and lends an interesting flavor to the lamb chops

3	tablespoons extra-virgin olive oil
½	medium red bell pepper, cored, seeded, and roughly chopped
½	medium serrano or jalapeño chile, stemmed, seeded, and roughly chopped
1	medium garlic clove, minced
½	teaspoon ground cumin
½	teaspoon dried summer savory
¼	teaspoon ground cinnamon
½	teaspoon dried mint or 1½ teaspoons chopped fresh mint leaves
2	teaspoons lemon juice
1	recipe Charcoal-Grilled or Gas-Grilled Shoulder Lamb Chops

1. Heat 1 tablespoon oil in a small skillet over medium-high heat until shimmering. Add red bell pepper and chile and sauté until they start to soften, about 2 minutes. Reduce heat to medium-low and continue to cook until softened, about 5 minutes.

2. Transfer the contents of the skillet to a food processor. Add the garlic, cumin, summer savory, cinnamon, mint, lemon juice, and remaining 2 tablespoons oil and process until almost smooth (there will still be some chunky pieces of pepper).

3. Proceed with the lamb recipe, rubbing the chops with the paste instead of oil and marinating them for at least 20 minutes or up to 1 day in the refrigerator. Sprinkle the chops with salt and pepper and grill as directed.

Grilled Shoulder Lamb Chops with Garlic-Rosemary Marinade

Garlic and rosemary are classic accompaniments for lamb.

Combine 2 tablespoons extra-virgin olive oil, 2 large garlic cloves, minced very fine or put through a press, 1 tablespoon minced fresh rosemary leaves, and a pinch of cayenne pepper in a small bowl. Follow recipe for Charcoal-Grilled or Gas-Grilled Lamb Chops, rubbing chops with garlic-rosemary mixture instead of plain olive oil. Marinate in the refrigerator for at least 20 minutes or up to 1 day. Sprinkle the chops with salt and pepper and grill as directed.

Grilled Shoulder Lamb Chops with Soy-Shallot Marinade

Soy sauce works well with the gutsy flavor of shoulder chops.

Combine 2 tablespoons canola oil, ¼ cup minced shallot or scallion, 2 tablespoons each minced fresh thyme and parsley leaves, 3 tablespoons lemon juice, 2 tablespoons soy sauce, and ground black pepper to taste in a shallow dish. Follow recipe for Charcoal-Grilled or Gas-Grilled Lamb Chops, marinating chops in soy mixture for at least 20 minutes or up to 1 hour in the refrigerator. (Do not marinate longer.) Do not rub the chops with oil or sprinkle with salt and pepper. Grill as directed.

Spiced Grilled Shoulder Lamb Chops with Quick Onion and Parsley Relish

The relish provides a cool and refreshing foil for the savory lamb chops. You can make the onion and parsley relish a day ahead of time if you like and store it in the refrigerator.

Follow recipe for Charcoal-Grilled or Gas-Grilled Lamb Chops, rubbing each with oil as directed and then with 1½ teaspoons Simple Spice Rub for Beef or Lamb (page 293). Sprinkle with salt but not pepper. Grill as directed and serve with Quick Onion and Parsley Relish (page 303).

INGREDIENTS: Shoulder Lamb Chops

Lamb shoulder is sliced into two different cuts, blade and round-bone chops. You'll find them sold in a range of thicknesses (from about one-half inch to more than one inch thick), depending on who's doing the butchering. (In our experience, supermarkets tend to cut them thinner, while independent butchers cut them thicker.) Blade chops are roughly rectangular in shape, and some are thickly striated with fat. Each blade chop includes a piece of the chine bone (the backbone of the animal) and a thin piece of the blade bone (the shoulder blade of the animal).

Round-bone chops, also called arm chops, are more oval in shape and as a rule are substantially leaner than blade chops. Each contains a round cross-section of the arm bone so that the chop looks a bit like a small ham steak. In addition to the arm bone, there's also a tiny line of riblets on the side of each chop.

As to which chop is better, we didn't find any difference in taste or texture between the two types except that the blade chops generally have more fat. We grill both blade and round-bone chops. We like the way the fat in the blade chop melts on the grill, flavoring and moistening the meat, and we love the grilled riblets from the round bone chop. For braising, though, we always prefer round-bone chops because they add less fat to the sauce. That said, blade chops vary quite a bit in fat content; those with little intramuscular fat will work fine if well trimmed.

Charcoal-Grilled Loin or Rib Lamb Chops
SERVES 4

While loin and rib chops are especially tender cuts of lamb, they tend to dry out if cooked past medium since they have less intramuscular fat than shoulder chops. To make these chops worth their high price, keep an eye on the grill to make sure the meat does not overcook. These chops are smaller than shoulder chops, so you will need two for each serving. Their flavor is more delicate and refined, so season lightly with just salt and pepper, or perhaps herbs (as in the variation on page 82). Aggressive spices don't make sense with these rarefied chops.

8   loin or rib lamb chops, 1¼ to 1½ inches thick
2   tablespoons extra-virgin olive oil
    Salt and ground black pepper

1. Light a large chimney starter filled with hardwood charcoal (about 2½ pounds) and allow to burn until all the charcoal is covered with a layer of fine gray ash. Build a two-level fire by stacking most of the coals on one side of the grill and arranging the remaining coals in a single layer on the other side of the grill. Set the cooking rack in place, cover the grill with the lid, and let the rack heat up, about 5 minutes. Use a wire brush to scrape clean the cooking rack. The grill is ready when the temperature of the stacked coals is medium-hot and that of the remaining coals is medium-low. (See how to gauge heat level on page 19.)

2. Rub the chops with oil and sprinkle with salt and pepper to taste.

3. Grill the chops, uncovered, over the hotter part of the grill, turning them once, until well browned, about 4 minutes. (If the chops start to flame, drag them to the cooler part of the grill for a moment and/or extinguish the flames with a squirt bottle.) Move the chops to the cooler part of the grill and continue grilling, turning once, to the desired doneness, about 6 minutes for rare (about 120 degrees on an instant-read thermometer) or about 8 minutes for medium (about 130 degrees).

4. Remove the chops from the grill and let rest for 5 minutes. Serve immediately.

Gas-Grilled Loin or Rib Lamb Chops

SERVES 4

With the cover down, it can be hard to detect any flames. Watch for excessive smoking and extinguish flames with a squirt bottle as soon as they erupt.

8   loin or rib lamb chops, 1¼ to 1½ inches thick
2   tablespoons extra-virgin olive oil
     Salt and ground black pepper

1. Preheat the grill with all burners set to high and the lid down until the grill is very hot, about 15 minutes. Use a wire brush to scrape clean the cooking grate. Leave one burner on high and turn the other burner(s) down to medium-low.

2. Rub the chops with oil and sprinkle with salt and pepper to taste.

3. Grill the chops, covered, over the hotter part of the grill, turning them once, until well browned, about 4 minutes. (If the chops start to flame, drag them to the cooler part of the grill for a moment and/or extinguish the flames with a squirt bottle.) Move the chops to the cooler part of the grill. Continue grilling, covered and turning once, to the desired doneness, about 7 minutes for rare (about 120 degrees on an instant-read thermometer) or about 9 minutes for medium (about 130 degrees).

4. Remove the chops from the grill and let rest for 5 minutes. Serve immediately.

> VARIATIONS

Grilled Loin or Rib Lamb Chops with Mediterranean Herb and Garlic Paste

The more delicate lamb flavor of the rib and loin chop are enhanced but not overwhelmed by the flavors of herbs and garlic.

Follow recipe for Charcoal-Grilled or Gas-Grilled Loin or Rib Lamb Chops, rubbing chops with Mediterranean Herb and Garlic Paste (page 295) instead of oil. Marinate for at least 20 minutes or up to 1 day in the refrigerator. Sprinkle with salt and pepper and grill as directed.

VEAL CHOPS

VEAL CHOPS ARE NOT AS POPULAR AS PORK chops or even lamb chops. One reason is certainly price. Another reason may be flavor. Veal chops can be a bit bland, especially if you try to broil or sauté them. At upwards of $13 per pound, bland veal chops can be an expensive disappointment. Yet another reason is the way in which some of the calves used for veal are raised (see "Milk-Fed versus Natural Veal" on page 83).

We think that if you're going to spend the money for veal chops, you must grill them. The combination of smoky flavor and intense browning does these expensive chops justice. That said, you need the right grilling technique. Should the chops be cooked over direct heat, or do they need a two-level fire? And what about the various choices at the market? There are chops from the shoulder, loin, and rib, as well as milk-fed and natural veal.

We began by testing various types of veal chops on the grill. We quickly dismissed inexpensive shoulder chops. They were tough and chewy and seemed better suited to braising or cutting up for stews.

Both the loin and rib chops were exceptionally tender and expensive—$13 to $14 in our local markets. The rib chops were a touch juicier and richer in flavor than the loin chops, so they are our first choice. However, if your market carries only loin chops, don't worry. These chops are quite good and can be grilled just like rib chops.

RIB VERSUS LOIN CHOPS

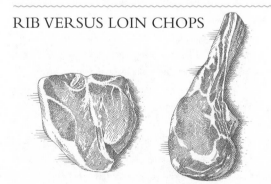

The best veal chops come from the rib area and the loin. (We find that shoulder chops can be tough and are best braised or cut off the bone and used in stews.) A loin chop (left) looks like a T-bone steak, with the bone running down the center and meat on either side. Rib chops (right) are juicier and more flavorful than loin chops. The bone runs along the edge of a rib chop, with all the meat on one side.

With our type of chops chosen, we focused on size. We found that thin chops are hard to cook correctly because they dry out before you can get any color on the exterior. Likewise, super-thick chops can over-brown by the time the meat near the bone is done. We had the best luck with chops about 1¼ inches thick. Slightly thicker chops (up to 1½ inches) are fine, and will take just an extra minute or so to grill.

It was then time to perfect our grilling technique. It quickly became clear that veal chops did not fare well when cooked solely over hot coals. The exterior burned before the center was done. Cooking over a two-level fire produced chops that were evenly cooked and nicely caramelized on the exterior. Our tasters preferred chops pulled off the grill when the internal temperature reached 130 degrees. At this stage, the chops have just a tinge of pink in the center. Do not cook veal chops past this point or they will be tough and dry.

We did have problems with flare-ups. When we trimmed away excess fat, flare-ups were reduced but not eliminated. We decided not to oil these chops to further reduce the risk of flare-ups. Keep the spray bottle close at hand while grilling to tame any flare-ups that might occur.

Grilled veal chops are delicious with a simple seasoning of salt and pepper. If you choose to add more flavor, we suggest herbs or something fairly mild. There's no sense masking the delicate veal flavor with too many spices or chiles.

Charcoal-Grilled Rib Veal Chops

SERVES 4

Be sure to trim the veal chops of any excess fat to prevent flare-ups. Keep a squirt bottle on hand filled with water to spray on flare-ups that may still occur. Veal chops need to be cooked over a two-level fire to ensure a nicely caramelized crust and a center perfectly cooked to medium. Use an instant-read thermometer to ensure that the chops don't get overcooked.

4   bone-in rib veal chops, about 1¼ inches thick,
     excess fat trimmed
     Salt and ground black pepper

1. Light a large chimney starter filled with hardwood charcoal (about 2½ pounds) and allow to burn

INGREDIENTS: Milk-Fed versus Natural Veal

Many people are opposed to milk-fed veal because the calves are confined to small stalls before being butchered. *Natural* is the term used to inform the consumer that the calves are allowed to move freely, without the confines of stalls. Natural veal is generally raised on grass (the calves can forage) and without hormones or antibiotics.

Moral issues aside, the differences in how the calves are raised create differences in the texture and flavor of the veal. Natural veal is darker, meatier, and more like beef. Milk-fed is paler in color, more tender, and milder in flavor. When we grilled both types of veal chops in the test kitchen, each had its supporters.

Several tasters preferred the meatier, more intense flavor of the natural veal. They thought the milk-fed veal seemed bland in comparison. Other tasters preferred the softer texture and milder flavor of the milk-fed veal. They felt that the natural veal tasted like "wimpy" beef and that the milk-fed chops had the mild, sweet flavor they expected from veal.

Both natural and milk-fed veal chops grill well, so the choice is really a personal one. Milk-fed veal is sold in most grocery stores, while natural veal is available at butcher shops, specialty markets, and natural food markets.

until all the charcoal is covered with a layer of fine gray ash. Build a two-level fire by stacking most of the coals on one side of the grill and arranging the remaining coals in a single layer on the other side of the grill. Set the cooking rack in place, cover the grill with the lid, and let the rack heat up, about 5 minutes. Use a wire brush to scrape clean the cooking rack. The grill is ready when the temperature of the stacked coals is medium-hot and that of the remaining coals is medium-low. (See how to gauge heat level on page 19.)

2. Sprinkle the chops with salt and pepper to taste.

3. Grill the chops, uncovered, over the hotter part of the grill until browned, about 2 minutes on each side. (If the chops start to flame, drag them to the cooler part of the grill for a moment and/or extinguish the flames with a squirt bottle.) Move the chops to the cooler part of the grill. Continue grilling, turning once, until the meat is still rosy pink at the center and an instant-read thermometer inserted through the side of the chop and away from

the bone (see illustration on page 76) registers 130 degrees, 10 to 11 minutes.

4. Remove the chops from the grill and let rest for 5 minutes. Serve immediately.

❧

Gas-Grilled Rib Veal Chops

SERVES 4

Be sure to trim the veal chops of any excess fat to prevent flare-ups. Keep a squirt bottle on hand filled with water to spray on flare-ups that may still occur. Use an instant-read thermometer to ensure that the chops don't get overcooked.

4	bone-in rib veal chops, about 1¼ inches, excess fat trimmed
	Salt and ground black pepper

1. Preheat the grill with all the burners turned to high and the lid down until very hot, about 15 minutes. Use a wire brush to scrape clean the cooking rack. Leave one burner on high and turn the other burner(s) down to medium.

2. Sprinkle the chops with salt and pepper to taste.

3. Grill the chops, covered, over the hotter part of the grill until browned, about 2 minutes on each side. (If the chops start to flame, drag them to the cooler part of the grill for a moment and/or extinguish the flames with a squirt bottle.) Move the chops to the cooler part of the grill. Continue grilling, covered and turning once, until meat is still rosy pink at the center and an instant-read thermometer inserted through side of chop and away from bone (see illustration on page 76) registers 130 degrees, about 11 minutes.

4. Remove the chops from the grill and let rest for 5 minutes. Serve immediately.

➤ VARIATIONS

Grilled Veal Chops with Mediterranean Herb Paste

These herb- and garlic-infused chops go very well with mashed potatoes. Because of the oil in the herb paste, these chops are prone to flare-ups, so be vigilant.

Follow recipe for Charcoal-Grilled or Gas-Grilled Rib Veal Chops, rubbing the chops with Mediterranean Herb and Garlic Paste (page 295) and then sprinkling with salt and pepper to taste. Grill as directed and serve with lemon wedges.

Porcini-Rubbed Grilled Veal Chops

Dried porcini mushrooms can be ground to a powder and then moistened with oil to form a thick paste. When spread on veal chops, the mushroom paste gives veal chops an especially meaty flavor. If you don't have a spice grinder, use a blender to grind the mushrooms into a fine powder. You can substitute other dried mushrooms, such as shiitakes or oysters, for the porcini.

Grind ½ ounce dried porcini to a powder in a spice grinder. Mix the ground mushrooms in a small bowl with 2 minced garlic cloves, 6 tablespoons extra-virgin olive oil, 1 teaspoon salt, and ¼ teaspoon ground black pepper. Follow the recipe for Charcoal-Grilled or Gas-Grilled Rib Veal Chops, rubbing the chops with the mushroom paste. Do not sprinkle with salt and pepper. Grill as directed.

Grilled Veal Chops on a Bed of Arugula

The balsamic vinegar not only dresses the arugula in this recipe, it also offsets the meaty richness of the veal. The heat of the chops wilts the arugula slightly and softens its texture.

1	recipe Charcoal-Grilled or Gas-Grilled Rib Veal Chops
1½	tablespoons balsamic vinegar
1	small garlic clove, minced very fine or pressed
5	tablespoons extra-virgin olive oil
	Salt and ground black pepper
8	cups lightly packed stemmed arugula, washed and thoroughly dried

1. Grill the chops as directed.

2. While the chops are cooking, whisk together the vinegar, garlic, and oil in a small bowl. Season with salt and pepper to taste. Toss the arugula and dressing in a large bowl. Transfer the arugula to a platter or divide it among individual plates.

3. As soon as the chops are done, transfer them to the platter or plates. Let the chops rest for 5 minutes on the platter. Serve immediately.

PORK TENDERLOIN

GRILLING IS A TERRIFIC WAY TO COOK pork tenderloin, a sublimely tender cut that benefits especially from the flavor boost provided by fire. But grilling a tenderloin does have its challenges. The chief problem is how to achieve a rich, golden, caramelized crust without destroying the delicate texture of the meat by overcooking it. What level of heat is best, and exactly how long should a tenderloin cook? Will grilling alone adequately flavor the meat, or should you pull another flavor-building trick from your culinary magic hat?

As the name suggests, tenderness is the tenderloin's main appeal. Anatomically speaking, the tenderloin is a small, cylindrical muscle located against the inside of the pig's ribcage. (In a human being, the equivalent muscle is in the midback area.) Because this muscle doesn't get much use, it remains very tender. Also, because the tenderloin is small, usually weighing about 12 to 16 ounces, it cooks very quickly. So it is great for fast, easy weeknight dinners.

Another reason for the tenderloin's popularity is its natural leanness. Though this is good news for diners concerned about fat intake, it can cause problems for the cook. The cut has almost no marbling, the threads of intramuscular fat that contribute a great deal of flavor to meat. Marbling also helps ensure juiciness, since the fat between the muscle fibers melts during cooking. Without that extra measure of protection, the long, slender, quick-cooking tenderloin can overcook and dry out much faster than fattier cuts.

To guard against this problem, the tenderloin should be cooked to medium so it will retain a slightly rosy hue in the center. The internal temperature should be 145 to 150 degrees, which is just short of the 160 degrees recommended by the U.S. Department of Agriculture. In the time it takes this cut to reach 160 degrees, the meat becomes dry, chewy, grayish white, and unappetizing. (For information on safe internal temperatures when cooking pork, see "Pork Cuts" on page 73.)

Before setting match to charcoal, we reviewed numerous grilled tenderloin recipes and found most to be more confusing than enlightening. Many recipes were vague, offering ambiguous directions such as "grill the tenderloins for 10 to 12 minutes, turning." Those which did provide detail disagreed on almost every point, from method (direct or indirect heat, open or covered grill) to heat level (hot, medium-hot, medium, or medium-low), timing (anywhere from 12 to 60 minutes), and internal temperature (from 145 to 160 degrees).

Direct grilling over hot, medium-hot, medium, and medium-low fires constituted our first series of tests. While the meat certainly cooked over all of these fires, it didn't cook perfectly over any of them. The medium-low fire failed to produce the essential crust. Each of the other fires produced more of a crust than we wanted by the time the internal temperature of the tenderloins had reached 145 degrees. Even the medium fire, which took 16 minutes to cook the tenderloin to 145 degrees, charred the crust a little too much by the time the meat had cooked through. The more intense medium-hot and hot fires cooked the meat a little faster, which meant less time on the grill, but the crust was still overly blackened in some spots.

It was clear at this point that building a two-level fire and some indirect cooking on a cooler area of the grill would be necessary to allow the tenderloin to cook through without getting charred. Cooking over a hot fire seared the meat steadily and evenly in 2½ minutes on each of four sides, but the internal temperature at this point usually hovered around 125 degrees. To finish cooking, we moved the tenderloin to the cooler part of the grill and waited for the internal temperature to climb. And we waited, and waited some more. About 10 seemingly endless minutes and countless temperature checks later, the meat arrived at 145 degrees. Since this took so long, we tried speeding up the process by covering the tenderloin with a disposable aluminum roasting pan. In just 2½ minutes under the pan, the tenderloin reached an internal temperature of 145 degrees without picking up additional char on the crust.

The well-developed crust did the tenderloin a world of good, but we knew there were other flavor development methods to try, including marinating, using dry and wet flavor rubs, and brining. Marinating, which required at least 2 to 3 hours and often up to 24 hours, simply took too long, especially for an impromptu weeknight meal. Next we tried using both dry and wet flavor rubs. Our favorite dry spice rubs for pork (see page 77) were a snap to put together and gave the tenderloin a fantastic crust. We also had good luck with wet rubs (see page 87). They are also easy to make, have strong flavors, and give the pork a lovely, crusty, glazed effect.

As good as these methods are, though, the meat still lacked seasoning at its center. So we tried brining. Since it takes close to an hour to make a rub and any side dishes, prepare the fire, and heat the grill rack, we reasoned that the tenderloins could spend that time—but no more—sitting in a brine. We started out with a simple saltwater brine, which seasoned the meat nicely throughout. Then, picking up on the subtle sweetness we liked in the dry and wet rubs, we added some sugar to the brine. The results were spectacular. The sweetness enhanced the flavor of the pork, and the brine ensured robust flavor in every bite of every slice of meat.

Grilled pork tenderloin, then, can be more than just a tender, lean cut of meat that cooks up quickly. With a combination of brining to season the interior of the meat, using a rub to season the exterior, and careful grilling to produce a glistening, caramelized crust without overcooking, it is a real treat to eat, too.

INGREDIENTS: Preflavored Pork Tenderloin

The fact that today's leaner pork is less flavorful is recognized by the industry as well as by consumers. This development, coupled with sheer convenience, may be why some distributors now offer various superlean cuts, including the tenderloin and the center cut loin filet, vacuum packed in their own "flavoring solutions." The flavoring choices in our local market were peppercorn and teriyaki for tenderloins and lemon-garlic and honey-mustard for center-cut loin filets.

Curious, we bought one of each and grilled them carefully for a test kitchen tasting. The results fell far short of the mark. Sitting in the flavoring solutions for who knows how long obliterated the texture of the meat, making it soft, wet, and spongy. In addition, these flavorings tasted genuinely awful; none allowed the taste of the pork itself to come through.

Charcoal-Grilled Pork Tenderloin
SERVES 6 TO 8

Pork tenderloins are often sold two to a package, each piece usually weighing 12 to 16 ounces. The cooking times below are for two average 12-ounce tenderloins; if necessary, adjust the cooking times to suit the size of the cuts you are cooking. For maximum efficiency, make the flavor rub and then light the fire while the pork is brining. If you opt not to brine, bypass step 1 in the recipe below and sprinkle the tenderloins generously with salt before grilling. Use a spice rub whether or not the pork has been brined—it adds extra flavor and forms a nice crust on the meat. If rubbing tenderloins with dry spices, consider serving with a salsa (see page 75) for added moisture and flavor.

3	tablespoons kosher salt (or 1½ tablespoons table salt)
¾	cup sugar
2	pork tenderloins, 1½ to 2 pounds total, trimmed of silver skin (see illustration on page 88)
1	recipe wet spice rub (page 87) or 2 tablespoons olive oil and 1 recipe dry spice rub (see page 77)
	Disposable aluminum roasting pan

1. Dissolve the salt and sugar in 2 cups hot water in a medium bowl. Stir in 2 cups cold water; cool the mixture to room temperature. Add the tenderloins, cover the bowl with plastic wrap, and refrigerate until fully seasoned, about 1 hour. Remove the tenderloins from the brine, rinse well, and dry thoroughly with paper towels. Set aside.

2. Light a large chimney starter filled with hardwood charcoal (about 2½ pounds) and allow to burn until all the charcoal is covered with a layer of fine gray ash. Build a modified two-level fire by spreading the coals evenly over half the grill bottom. Set the cooking rack in place, cover the grill with the lid, and let the rack heat up, about 5 minutes. Use a wire brush to scrape clean the cooking rack. The grill is ready when the coals are hot. (See how to gauge heat level on page 19.)

3. If using a wet spice rub, rub the tenderloins with the mixture. If using a dry spice rub, coat the

WET SPICE RUBS FOR PORK TENDERLOIN

A spice rub helps develop the crust on a pork tenderloin and adds some much-needed flavor. If using a wet rub (with spices and liquid ingredients), simply massage the mixture into the meat. If using a dry rub (with spices only), massage the meat with olive oil and then coat with the rub. See page 77 for dry rub recipes.

Orange, Sage, and Garlic Wet Rub

MAKES ABOUT 1/3 CUP, ENOUGH FOR
2 TENDERLOINS

If you have no orange marmalade, substitute an equal amount of honey.

2	large garlic cloves, minced
1	tablespoon grated orange zest
1	tablespoon chopped fresh sage leaves
1/2	teaspoon ground black pepper
1/4	teaspoon salt
1	tablespoon orange marmalade
1	tablespoon extra-virgin olive oil

Mix all ingredients together in a small bowl.

Caribbean Wet Rub

MAKES ABOUT 1/3 CUP, ENOUGH FOR
2 TENDERLOINS

Scotch bonnet chiles are extremely hot, so be certain to wash your hands thoroughly with soap and hot water right after handling or, better yet, wear rubber gloves.

1/2	medium Scotch Bonnet or habanero chile, stemmed, seeded, and minced (about 1 teaspoon)
1	tablespoon chopped fresh thyme leaves
2	medium scallions, white and green parts, minced
1	large garlic clove, minced
1	tablespoon grated lime zest
	Pinch ground allspice
1	tablespoon light brown sugar
1	teaspoon dry mustard powder
1	tablespoon extra-virgin olive oil

Mix all ingredients together in a small bowl.

Asian Wet Rub

MAKES ABOUT 1/3 CUP, ENOUGH FOR
2 TENDERLOINS

If you don't have hoisin sauce on hand, you can substitute an equal amount of soy sauce in its place.

2	large garlic cloves, minced
2	tablespoons minced fresh ginger
2	medium scallions, white and green parts, minced
2	tablespoons light brown sugar
1/2	teaspoon hot red pepper flakes
1/4	teaspoon five-spice powder
1/4	teaspoon salt
1	tablespoon hoisin sauce
1	tablespoon Asian sesame oil

Mix all ingredients together in a small bowl.

Mustard, Garlic, and Honey Wet Rub

MAKES ABOUT 1/3 CUP, ENOUGH FOR
2 TENDERLOINS

You can substitute 1 teaspoon dried rosemary for the fresh herb if desired.

2	large garlic cloves, minced
2	teaspoons honey
2	teaspoons Dijon mustard
2	teaspoons chopped fresh rosemary leaves
1	teaspoon grated lemon zest
1/2	teaspoon ground black pepper
1/4	teaspoon salt
1	tablespoon extra-virgin olive oil

Mix all ingredients together in a small bowl.

tenderloins with oil and then rub with the spice mixture.

4. Cook the tenderloins, uncovered, over the hotter part of the grill until browned on all four sides, about 2½ minutes on each side. Move the tenderloins to the cooler part of the grill and cover with a disposable aluminum roasting pan. Grill, turning once, until an instant-read thermometer inserted into the thickest part of the tenderloin registers 145 degrees or until the meat is slightly pink at the center when cut with a paring knife, 2 to 3 minutes longer. Transfer the tenderloins to a cutting board, cover with the disposable aluminum pan, and let rest about 5 minutes. Slice crosswise into 1-inch-thick pieces and serve.

Gas-Grilled Pork Tenderloin

SERVES 6 TO 8

If you opt not to brine, bypass step 1 in the recipe below and sprinkle the tenderloins generously with salt before grilling. Use a spice rub whether or not the pork has been brined— it adds extra flavor and forms a nice crust on the meat. If rubbing tenderloins with dry spices, consider serving with a salsa (see page 75) for added moisture and flavor. A gas grill runs slightly cooler than a charcoal fire so the tenderloins can be cooked over direct heat for the entire time.

3	tablespoons kosher salt (or 1½ tablespoons table salt)
¾	cup sugar
2	pork tenderloins, 1½ to 2 pounds total, trimmed of silver skin (see illustration at right)
1	recipe wet spice rub (page 87) or 2 tablespoons olive oil and 1 recipe dry spice rub (see page 77) **Aluminum foil**

1. Dissolve the salt and sugar in 2 cups hot water in a medium bowl. Stir in 2 cups cold water; cool the mixture to room temperature. Add the tenderloins, cover the bowl with plastic wrap, and refrigerate until fully seasoned, about 1 hour. Remove the tenderloins from the brine, rinse well, and dry thoroughly with paper towels. Set aside.

2. Preheat the grill with all burners set to high and the lid down until the grill is very hot, about 15 minutes. Use a wire brush to scrape clean the cooking grate. Leave all burners on high.

3. If using a wet spice rub, rub the tenderloins with the mixture. If using a dry spice rub, coat tenderloins with oil and then rub with the spice mixture.

4. Cook the tenderloins, covered, until well browned on three sides, about 3½ minutes on each side. Grill on the fourth and final side until well browned and an instant-read thermometer inserted into the thickest part of the tenderloin registers 145 degrees or until the meat is slightly pink at the center when cut with a paring knife, about 2½ minutes longer. Transfer the tenderloins to a cutting board, cover with a piece of foil, and let rest about 5 minutes. Slice crosswise into 1-inch-thick pieces and serve.

REMOVING THE SILVER SKIN

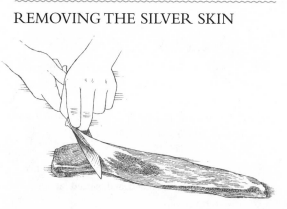

The tenderloin is covered with a thin, pearlescent membrane called the silver skin. If left on the meat, the silver skin shrinks and can cause the tenderloin to bow and thus cook unevenly. To remove the silver skin before cooking, slip a paring knife between the silver skin and the muscle fibers, angle the knife slightly upward, and use a gentle back-and-forth sawing action.

7

RACK OF LAMB AND BUTTERFLIED LEG

LIKE BEEF, LAMB HAS A RICH RED COLOR, but the meat is generally stronger tasting. This is because the muscle itself is quite tasty and because lamb fat has a particularly strong flavor. In fact, lamb fat can be overpowering, which is why lamb cuts are generally well trimmed before cooking.

Most lamb sold in the supermarket has been slaughtered when 6 to 12 months old. (When the animal is slaughtered past the first year, the meat must be labeled mutton.) Generally, younger lamb has a milder flavor that most people prefer. The only indication of slaughter age at the supermarket is size. A whole leg of lamb weighing nine pounds is likely to have come from an older animal than a whole leg weighing just six pounds.

Lamb is initially divided into five primal (or major) cuts. The shoulder area extends from the neck through the fourth rib. Meat from this area is flavorful, although it contains a fair amount of connective tissue and can be tough. Chops, roasts, and boneless stew meat all come from the shoulder.

The rib area is directly behind the shoulder and extends from the fifth to the twelfth rib. The rack (all eight ribs from this section) is cut from the rib. When cut into individual chops, the meat is called rib chops (see page 78). Meat from this area has a fine, tender grain and a mild flavor.

The loin extends from the last rib down to the hip area. Several roasts popular with restaurant chefs, such as the saddle, come from this region. For consumers, the loin chop (see page 78) is the most familiar cut from this part of the sheep. Like the rib chop, it is ten-der and has a mild, sometimes sweet lamb flavor.

The leg area runs from the hip down to the hoof. It may be sold whole or broken into smaller roasts and shanks (one comes from each hind leg). These roasts may be sold with the bones in, or they may be butterflied and sold boneless.

The final primal cut is from the underside of the animal and is called the foreshank and breast. This area includes the two front legs (each yields a shank) as well as the breast, which is rarely sold in super-markets.

THE FIVE PRIMAL CUTS OF LAMB

SHOULDER   RIB (RACK)   LOIN   LEG

FORESHANK AND BREAST

RACK OF LAMB

THE WORD MOUTHWATERING MUST HAVE been invented to describe rack of lamb. The meat is ultratender and luscious tasting, more refined in flavor than almost any other cut of lamb, but no less satisfying. But, at $17 to $18 a pound, there's hardly a cut of meat more expensive. And like other simple but fabulous dishes (roast chicken comes to mind), there's nothing to cooking it except that there's no disguising imperfection. You want the meat to be perfectly pink and juicy, the outside to be intensely browned to boost flavor and provide contrasting texture, and the fat to be well enough rendered to encase the meat in a thin, crisp, brittle shell.

With all of this in mind, we set out to find a fool-proof way to grill this extravagant cut. We started our tests by focusing on trimming the racks. Rack of lamb has a lot of excess fat, and we wondered how much would have to be removed before grilling. We found that racks sold at butcher shops and higher-end grocery stores tend to be frenched—that is, the butcher has removed the fat and gristle between each chop to expose the ends of the bones. The chine bone had been removed from most racks that we purchased at butcher shops. At many supermarkets, we found racks that were not frenched and still had the chine bone attached. If the chine bone is left on, it is very hard to separate the grilled rack into individual chops. Since it is quite difficult to remove the chine bone at home, ask the butcher to do this. (Also, why pay $17 a pound for useless bone?) We found that most frenched racks with the chine bone removed weigh in at about 1½ pounds or so, and that racks weighing

2 pounds or more usually need more butchering. If you are about to purchase a rack that is this heavy, ask the butcher to make sure that the chine bone has been removed.

Even if you buy a frenched rack with the chine bone removed, you will still have some work to do. A typical rack is thicker at one end. At the thicker end, there is a layer of fat covering a thin layer of meat, called the cap. Another thin layer of fat rests underneath the cap. Trying to save as much meat as we could on the rack, we trimmed off only the first layer of fat. Unfortunately, however, the thin layer of meat was not really worth saving—the extra layer of fat underneath caused flare-ups on the grill, and we found the meat hard to eat because there was just too much fat surrounding it. We also found that leaving on the extra layer of meat and fat made the rack cook unevenly—the small end was overdone by the time the thicker end cooked to medium-rare. So we trimmed the cap and all the fat underneath it, leaving only a minimal amount of fat at the top of the rack and covering the bones to give the cut its characteristic rounded shape.

With our trimming tests completed, we turned to grilling. Our research uncovered three options: grilling the racks directly over the coals, searing the racks over hot coals and then sliding them to a cooler part of the grill to cook by indirect heat, or cooking the racks completely over indirect heat.

Direct heat was unsuccessful when cooking the racks over a medium-hot fire as well as over a medium fire. We found that the racks charred on the outside, while the inside was still raw. Grilling over direct heat using a cooler fire just doesn't make sense; there are too few coals, which will burn out too quickly.

A combination of direct and indirect heat worked better. First, we seared the racks directly over a hot fire and then moved the meat to indirect heat on the other side of the grill. The racks were satisfactorily cooked to medium-rare at the center. However, the outer layers of meat were a tad overdone.

We were surprised to find that cooking completely by indirect heat worked best. The racks slowly developed a rich crust, and the interior was more evenly cooked to medium-rare than by the direct/indirect method. On charcoal, we had to use disposable aluminum pie plates to cover each of the racks to prevent the meat from drying out (as total grill time is 17 to 18 minutes) and to speed up grilling time. The racks must also be placed quite close to but not directly over the pile of coals. To ensure even cooking, the racks must be turned 180 degrees on each side in addition to being flipped over. Some sources suggest covering the protruding bones with foil to keep them from charring. We didn't have a problem with bones burning, so we feel that this extra step is not necessary.

Our final tests concerned flavoring. Rack of lamb is so tasty (that's why we are willing to pay so dearly for it) that it doesn't need much help, just a little salt and pepper to heighten its natural flavor. For variety, though, we found that both dry rubs and pastes work equally well to flavor the exterior of the meat. Rack of lamb has a tendency to be soft and mushy, and we found that marinades only exacerbated this problem.

One final note. We strongly recommend using an instant-read thermometer when grilling the rack of lamb. There is no other reliable way to tell if the rack is properly cooked. No one wants to ruin $50 worth

PREPARING A RACK OF LAMB

1. Using a boning or paring knife, scrape the ribs clean of any scraps of meat or fat.

2. Trim off the outer layer of fat, the flap of meat underneath it, and the fat underneath that flap.

3. Remove the silver skin by sliding the boning knife between the silver skin and the flesh.

of meat because they overcooked it. Simply slide an instant-read thermometer through the end of the meat, toward the center but away from any bones, to gauge the temperature at the center of the rack.

We found that cooking the meat to 125 degrees is perfect for medium-rare, as long as the meat is allowed to rest, tented with foil, after coming off the grill. Carry-over cooking brings the temperature of the meat up to between 135 and 140 degrees after 10 minutes. For those who like their rack cooked further, 130 degrees is right for medium. After resting, the meat will reach 140 to 145 degrees. Keep in mind that the chops closer to the ends of the rack will cook somewhat ahead of the chops at the center. For example, when the chops are medium-rare at the center, you can expect those toward the ends to be cooked to medium, and for racks where the center chop is medium, the chops at the end will be medium-well to well-done.

Charcoal-Grilled Rack of Lamb

SERVES 4

Have your butcher french the racks of lamb for you (this means that part of the rib bones is exposed). If the racks are available already frenched, chances are there is still a good deal of fat on one side. Be sure to trim this excess fat away (according to illustrations on page 91) to prevent flare-ups on the grill. Also, make sure that the chine bone (the bone running along the bottom of the rack) has been removed to ensure that it will be easy to cut between the ribs after cooking. Ask the butcher to do it; it's very hard to cut off at home.

2   racks of lamb (about 1½ pounds each), trimmed according to illustrations on page 91
     Salt and ground black pepper
2   nine-inch disposable pie plates
     Aluminum foil

1. Light a large chimney ¾ full with hardwood charcoal (about 2 pounds) and allow to burn until all the charcoal is covered with a layer of fine gray ash. Build a modified two-level fire by spreading the coals over half the grill bottom. Set the cooking rack in place, cover the grill with the lid, and let the rack heat up, about 5 minutes. Use a wire brush to scrape clean

the cooking rack. The grill is ready when the coals are medium-hot. (See how to gauge heat level on page 19.)

2. Meanwhile, sprinkle the trimmed racks with a generous amount of salt and pepper on both sides.

3. Place the racks of lamb, bone-side up, on the grill, with the meaty side of the racks very close to, but not quite over, the hot coals. Cover with pie plates and grill until a deeply colored crust develops, about 8½ minutes, rotating the racks halfway through the cooking time so that the protruding bones are closer to the coals. Turn the racks over, bone-side down, and cover with pie plates. Grill, rotating the racks halfway through for even cooking, until an instant-read thermometer inserted from the side of the rack through to the center, but away from any bone, reads 125 degrees for medium-rare or 130 degrees for medium, another 8½ to 10 minutes.

4. Remove the lamb from the grill and allow to rest, tented with foil, for 10 minutes (the racks will continue to cook while resting). Cut between each rib to separate chops and serve immediately.

Gas-Grilled Rack of Lamb

SERVES 4

Have your butcher french the racks of lamb for you (this means that part of the rib bones is exposed). If the racks are available already frenched, chances are there is still a good deal of fat on one side. Be sure to trim this excess fat away (according to illustrations on page 91) to prevent flare-ups on the grill. Also, make sure that the chine bone (the bone running along the bottom of the rack) has been removed to ensure that it will be easy to cut between the ribs after cooking. Ask the butcher to do it; it's very hard to cut off at home. Because the lid on the gas grill is down during cooking, there is no need to cover the racks with a pie plate, as in charcoal grilling.

2   racks of lamb (about 1½ pounds each), trimmed according to illustrations on page 91
     Salt and ground black pepper
     Aluminum foil

1. Preheat the grill with all burners set to high and the lid down until very hot, about 15 minutes. Use a wire brush to scrape clean the cooking rack.

Leave one burner on high and turn the other burner(s) to medium-low.

2. Meanwhile, sprinkle the trimmed racks with a generous amount of salt and pepper on both sides.

3. Place the racks of lamb, bone-side up, on the cooler part of the grill, with the meaty side of the racks facing the hotter burner. Cook, covered, rotating the racks after 5 minutes so that the protruding bones are closer to the hotter burner, until a deeply colored crust develops, 10 minutes. Turn the racks over, bone-side down, cover, and grill, rotating the racks halfway through for even cooking, until an instant-read thermometer inserted from the side of the rack through to the center, but away from any bone, reads 125 degrees for medium-rare or 130 degrees for medium, another 10 to 12 minutes.

4. Remove the lamb from the grill and allow to rest, tented with foil, for 10 minutes (the racks will continue to cook while resting). Cut between each rib to separate chops and serve immediately.

➤ VARIATIONS

Grilled Rack of Lamb with Garlic and Herbs

In a small bowl, mix together 4 teaspoons chopped fresh rosemary, 2 teaspoons chopped fresh thyme, 2 minced garlic cloves, and 4 teaspoons extra-virgin olive oil. Follow recipe for Charcoal-Grilled or Gas-Grilled Rack of Lamb, rubbing herb/garlic mixture over lamb after seasoning with salt and pepper.

Grilled Rack of Lamb with Turkish Spice Rub

Pickling spice is a spice blend sold in many supermarkets.

Grind 1 tablespoon pickling spice in a spice grinder. In a small bowl, mix the ground pickling spice, 1 teaspoon dried summer savory, ½ teaspoon ground black pepper, ½ teaspoon ground cumin, ¼ teaspoon ground nutmeg, ¼ teaspoon ground cinnamon, and ¾ teaspoon salt. Follow recipe for Charcoal-Grilled or Gas-Grilled Rack of Lamb, rubbing with spices instead of sprinkling with salt and pepper.

Grilled Rack of Lamb with Mustard, Parsley, and Breadcrumbs

Mix together 3 tablespoons softened unsalted butter, 1 minced garlic clove, 3 tablespoons chopped fresh parsley leaves, ½ cup fresh breadcrumbs, and salt and pepper to taste. Season and grill lamb, bone-side up, as directed in the recipe for Charcoal-Grilled or Gas-Grilled Rack of Lamb. Remove the lamb from the grill and place it bone-side down onto a plate or tray. Spread 1½ tablespoons Dijon mustard onto each rack, then carefully press half of breadcrumb mixture onto each rack. Place racks, bone-side down, back onto the grill and continue with recipe (allowing to cook without pie plates if using a charcoal grill) for the last 4 minutes of cooking. Allow the racks to rest uncovered to prevent the breadcrumbs from becoming soggy. Carve as directed.

BUTTERFLIED LEG OF LAMB

A LEG OF LAMB CAN BE GRILLED IF THE LEG is boned and then butterflied, a technique in which several cuts are made in the boned flesh to open and flatten the leg so that its uneven topography is smoothed to an even thickness. A butterflied leg of lamb is a large, unwieldy piece of meat, about ¾-inch thick and covered with a thin layer of fat. You can butterfly a leg of lamb yourself or buy a butterflied leg of lamb at the supermarket (see page 97 for more detailed information on both of these options).

For our first test, we used a kettle grill and our preferred fuel—hardwood charcoal—to build a two-level fire. We seasoned the butterflied meat with salt and pepper and, wary of flaming, used no oil. We placed the meat fat-side down over the coals, intending to brown it quickly over direct heat and then finish it over indirect heat.

The results dismayed us. The leg flamed and blackened. It was difficult to maneuver on the grill because of its size. The connective tissue in the shank retracted and curled so badly that eventually we had to cut it off and cook it longer. The rest of the leg cooked unevenly and tasted oily as well as scorched from the flame. Because it was so thin, it was difficult to carve into attractive slices.

We made up our minds to start from scratch and find out the best way to grill a leg of lamb. We had several questions: First, what's the best way to butterfly a leg of lamb? Is there a way to grill the shank attached to the leg, or must we always cut it off? Direct heat chars the leg more than we like, but how else can we grill it? Do we need to cover the grill to control the flaming? And is it necessary to carve a leg of lamb against the grain for the sake of tenderness?

Our goal was to come up with a butchering technique that would yield an easy-to-manage piece of meat, thick enough to carve into attractive slices. And, as always when grilling, we wanted a crust that was caramelized but not blackened and a moist, tender interior.

To start, it helps to understand the structure of the leg, which consists of six different muscles: the meaty, dome-shaped top and smaller bottom rounds; the small cylindrical eye of round; the flat trapezoidal hip; the round knuckle; and the oblong shank. Restaurant chefs sometimes separate the muscles from one another (they pull apart very easily) and then cook and carve each separately because that allows each muscle to be cooked perfectly and carved against the grain into large slices for optimum tenderness. (After the meat is butterflied, the grain runs every which way, so it's impossible to carve against the grain.)

Cooking the muscles separately doesn't make sense for a home cook, particularly since people tend to turn to this cut when planning for a crowd. But we tried to adapt this technique by boning the leg and cooking it as is—with all the muscles intact and unbutterflied—planning to cut the muscles apart after cooking and carve each one separately. This

time, to solve the flaming problem, we cooked the lamb entirely over indirect heat. It browned beautifully and didn't flame, but after 40 minutes it was clear that there wasn't enough heat to cook through the larger muscles (the top round and knuckle). We then turned our thoughts to butchering the leg to allow for more even cooking.

We were familiar with two methods of butterflying. One calls for cutting straight down into the meat and then spreading the meat open on either side of the cut. The second technique is to cut into the meat horizontally and then open it out like a book. We tried both and found that a combination of the two techniques worked best (see page 97). What we were after was a single piece of meat about three-quarter-inch thick. Traditional butterflying, as done by most butchers, produces a flat piece of meat, but it can be uneven in thickness. The butterflying method we adopted produces the evenness we wanted.

The butterflied leg was very large, however, so we cut it in half along a natural separation between the muscles. This enabled us to turn each piece with a single pair of tongs rather than struggle with a pair of tongs in each hand. This also made it more practical to buy, since you can freeze half if you are cooking for only four.

Satisfied with our butchering technique, we returned to the cooking. Working again over indirect heat, we grilled the butterflied leg pieces, cut-side up, for five minutes. Then we turned them 180 degrees and cooked them five more minutes to ensure that the meat cooked evenly all around. After

BUYING LEG OF LAMB

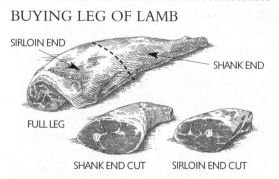

When you go to the supermarket, you will probably be able to buy either a whole leg or a half leg. When buying a half, you can get either the sirloin (the upper half) or the shank (the lower half). Of the two, we prefer the sirloin end because it is slightly more tender.

LEG OF LAMB: THE BONES

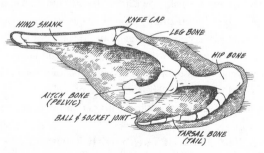

When butterflying a leg of lamb (see step-by-step illustrations on page 97), it is helpful to know the inner skeletal structure. In particular, note where all the bones come together in the center of the leg at the large ball and socket joint.

10 minutes the leg was well browned on the skin side, so we turned the pieces over and repeated the procedure, cooking the meat another 10 minutes, until it registered 130 degrees on a meat thermometer. We let the meat rest 10 minutes and then sliced into it. The outside crust was perfect, but inside we still had problems. While the meat in the center was a beautiful medium-rare, the perimeter of the leg was still pale because it needed more time to rest. And the shank meat was still undercooked.

The problem with the shank was easy enough to solve; we decided to cut it off and save it for another use. (Some supermarkets also sell the leg without the shank.) Then we tested resting times, letting the meat rest 15, 20, and 25 minutes, and found that 20 minutes was ample time for the juices to be redistributed throughout the leg. Finally, we experimented with carving to test for tenderness. We carved the meat into thin slices on an angle (to produce slices as large as possible) and disregarded the grain. As it

BONING A LEG OF LAMB

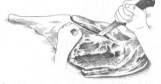

1. Using the tip of a boning knife, make the first cut at the top of the shank, cutting around the knee cap, and continuing down one side of the leg bone.

2. Cut straight down to the leg bone with the tip of the knife, and, using the bone as a guide, cut until you reach the hipbone and must stop. Repeat on the other side.

3. Cut under and around the knee cap and along the side of the leg bone, loosening the meat from the bone as you go.

4. Cut around the hipbone to loosen the meat from the bone.

5. Using the tip of the knife, cut the meat away from the aitchbone (or pelvic bone).

6. At this point, the meat should be free from the leg bone (center), the aitchbone (lower left center), and the hip bone (lower right). The ball and socket joint is in the center.

7. Cut beneath the tarsal bone, keeping the knife right along the bone.

8. Lift the tarsal bone and continue scraping the meat away from the bone until you reach the ball and socket joint.

9. With the tip of the knife, scrape along and beneath the ball and socket joint to loosen it from the meat, and cut between the ball and socket to loosen.

10. Snap the ball and socket apart and pull the tail-, hip-, and aitchbones away from the leg bone (save this piece for stock or discard).

11. Continue to cut beneath the leg bone, lifting it from the meat as you cut.

12. Lift the leg bone and cartilage around the knee cap to totally separate the leg from the shank portion (if the leg came shank attached) and remove shank (save for stock or discard).

turned out, this was a good decision. Although the different muscles varied in taste and texture, they were all plenty tender. (Anyone who would rather not bone and/or butterfly a leg of lamb at home should see "Simplified Butterflied Leg of Lamb" on page 97. We don't think that the results will be quite as good, but the effort is greatly reduced.)

Charcoal-Grilled Butterflied Leg of Lamb

SERVES 8 TO 10

Watch out for flare-ups on the grill. Be sure to have a spray bottle filled with water ready to dampen the flames, if necessary. On those occasions when we want to cook only half a leg of lamb, we prefer the sirloin (see page 94). This recipe is quite plain; see page 98 for some interesting marinades.

1	seven-pound leg of lamb, boned, butterflied, and halved between the eye and the bottom round (see illustrations on pages 95 and 97)
1½	tablespoons extra-virgin olive oil
	Salt and ground black pepper
	Aluminum foil

1. Light a large chimney generously filled with hardwood charcoal (about 2½ pounds) and allow to burn until it is completely covered with a thin layer of gray ash. Build a modified two-level fire by spreading the coals over half the grill bottom. Set the cooking rack in place, cover the grill with the lid, and let the rack heat up, about 5 minutes. Use a wire brush to scrape clean the cooking rack. The grill is ready when the coals are hot. (See how to gauge heat level on page 19.)

2. Rub both sides of the lamb pieces with oil and sprinkle generously with salt and pepper to taste.

3. Place the lamb pieces, fat-side down, on the side of the rack that is not directly over the coals but close to the fire. Grill the lamb, uncovered, for 5 minutes. Rotate the meat so that the outside edges are now closest to the fire. Grill, uncovered, until the fat side of the lamb is a rich dark brown, 5 minutes longer. With tongs or a large meat fork, turn both pieces over. Cook, fat-side up, for 5 minutes, then move meat directly over the coals (they will have partially burned out by this point, putting out less

heat), and cook until an instant-read thermometer inserted into the thickest part of each piece registers 125 to 130 degrees for medium-rare or 135 degrees for medium, 5 to 7 minutes longer.

4. Transfer the meat to a large platter or cutting board, tent with foil, and let rest 20 minutes. Slice thinly on an angle and serve.

Gas-Grilled Butterflied Leg of Lamb

SERVES 8 TO 10

Watch the grill for signs of excess smoke. Be sure to have a spray bottle filled with water ready to dampen the flames, if necessary. On those occasions when we want to cook only half a leg of lamb, we prefer the sirloin (see page 94). This recipe is quite plain; see page 98 for some interesting marinades.

1	seven-pound leg of lamb, boned, butterflied, and halved between the eye and the bottom round (see illustrations on pages 95 and 97)
1½	tablespoons extra-virgin olive oil
	Salt and ground black pepper
	Aluminum foil

1. Preheat the grill with all burners set to high and the lid down, until very hot, about 15 minutes. Scrape clean the cooking grate with a wire brush. Leave one burner on high and turn the other burner(s) down to medium.

2. Rub both sides of the lamb pieces with oil and sprinkle generously with salt and pepper to taste.

3. Place the lamb pieces, fat-side down, over the burner(s) set to medium. Grill the lamb, covered, for 5 minutes. Rotate the meat so that the outside edges are now facing the hotter burner. Grill, covered, until the fat side of the lamb is a rich dark brown, 5 minutes longer. With tongs or a large meat fork, turn both pieces over. Cook, fat-side up, for 5 minutes, then rotate the meat 180 degrees to ensure even cooking. Continue grilling, covered, until an instant-read thermometer inserted into the thickest part of each piece registers 125 to 130 degrees for medium-rare or 135 degrees for medium, 10 to 12 minutes longer.

4. Transfer the meat to a large platter or cutting board, tent with foil, and let rest 20 minutes. Slice thinly on an angle and serve.

BUTTERFLYING A BONED LEG OF LAMB

1. To butterfly, lay a large chef's knife flat on the center of the meat, at the thinnest part, parallel to the top round.

2. Keeping the knife blade parallel to the board, begin slicing through the muscle. Cut horizontally about 1 inch.

3. Begin to unroll the meat (it's like unrolling a carpet) with your other hand as you continue to cut into the muscle, always keeping the knife blade parallel to the board, cutting about 1 inch at a time, and unrolling as you cut.

4. Stopping about 1 inch from the end, unfold the edge of the meat and flatten it.

5. The butterflied muscle should be even in thickness.

6. Turn the board around and cut the knuckle muscle on the other side using the same method as in steps 1 through 4.

7. Near the center of the bottom round locate a hard thick section of fat. Using the tip of the boning knife, cut into the fat to locate the lymph node (a ½-inch round, grayish flat nodule). Carefully remove and discard.

8. Divide the butterflied meat in half by cutting between the eye and the bottom round.

9. Turn the pieces of meat over and use a boning knife to cut away the thick pieces of fat, leaving about ⅛-inch thickness for self-basting during grilling.

SIMPLIFIED BUTTERFLIED LEG OF LAMB

So you don't want to bone and butterfly a leg of lamb on your own and just want to buy something straight from the meat case that can be seasoned and grilled? Here's how to adapt our recipe. The cooking times are the same, but note that you will probably have more gradations in the meat, with some parts more well-done and other parts rarer since a leg of lamb that is butterflied according to the traditional method usually has an uneven thickness.

Buy a 4½- to 5-pound boned and butterflied leg of lamb that has been divided into two equal pieces (this makes turning the lamb easier). The lamb should be about 1 inch thick throughout. If you cannot find this at your supermarket, we suggest that you buy a bone-in whole leg of lamb that weighs between 6½ and 7 pounds and ask to have it boned and butterflied. Be sure to indicate that you want the meat to be about 1 inch thick throughout, and ask the butcher to divide the lamb into two pieces after butterflying. You may also find a boneless whole leg of lamb roast that has been rolled and tied. This roast simply needs to be butterflied. Again, you can ask your butcher to do this for you.

Because this recipe feeds a crowd (between 8 and 10 people), you may want to grill only half a leg of lamb. Supermarkets usually sell half legs of lamb, either the shank end or the sirloin end. Once again, you can purchase this cut of meat with the bone in and have it boned and butterflied by your butcher, again 1 inch thick throughout. Also remember to cut the ingredients in the marinade by half.

MARINADES FOR GRILLED LEG OF LAMB

Leg of lamb has a rich flavor that stands up well to a variety of marinades. To use any of these marinades, butcher the lamb as directed, place the lamb in a large shallow pan or baking dish, and rub the marinade into all parts of the meat with your hands. Cover the pan with plastic wrap and refrigerate it for at least 8 hours and up to 24 hours. Except for the Soy-Honey Marinade with Thyme, which is salty on its own, season the marinated lamb with salt and pepper just before grilling, but do not oil the lamb. If grilling just half a leg, cut the marinade ingredients in half.

Tandoori Marinade

ENOUGH FOR I BUTTERFLIED LEG OF LAMB

The yogurt forms an especially thick, browned crust when the lamb is grilled.

$^1/_3$	cup plain yogurt
5 to 6	medium garlic cloves, minced (about 4 teaspoons)
I	tablespoon grated fresh ginger
2	tablespoons lemon juice
2	teaspoons ground cumin
2	teaspoons ground coriander
I	teaspoon ground turmeric
I	teaspoon cayenne pepper
$^1/_2$	teaspoon ground cinnamon

Mix the ingredients together in a small bowl.

Lemon Marinade with Greek Flavorings

ENOUGH FOR I BUTTERFLIED LEG OF LAMB

If you like, use fresh oregano and thyme, doubling their amounts, in this marinade.

$^1/_4$	cup extra-virgin olive oil
2	tablespoons lemon juice
3 to 4	medium garlic cloves, minced (about I tablespoon)
I	tablespoon dried oregano
I	tablespoon dried thyme
	Pinch sweet paprika

Mix the ingredients together in a small bowl.

Garlic and Rosemary Marinade

ENOUGH FOR I BUTTERFLIED LEG OF LAMB

A leg of lamb will be nicely flavored after just three hours in this marinade, but can be marinated longer if you like.

6 to 8	medium garlic cloves, minced (about 2 tablespoons)
I$^1/_2$	tablespoons minced fresh rosemary
$^1/_4$	cup extra-virgin olive oil

Mix the ingredients together in a small bowl.

Soy-Honey Marinade with Thyme

ENOUGH FOR I BUTTERFLIED LEG OF LAMB

Minced fresh chile or hot red pepper flakes make a good addition to this marinade.

$^1/_3$	cup soy sauce
$^1/_3$	cup honey
2 to 3	medium garlic cloves, minced (about 2 teaspoons)
I	tablespoon grated fresh ginger
I	teaspoon minced fresh thyme leaves
	Pinch cayenne pepper

Mix the ingredients together in a small bowl.

8

CHICKEN PARTS AND BUTTERFLIED CHICKEN

CHICKEN IS ONE OF THE MOST POPULAR items for grilling—and for good reason. Because it takes well to numerous seasonings, it need never taste or appear to be quite the same from one meal to another. The fact that chicken takes so many forms—parts, whole birds, and cutlets—adds to its appeal.

This chapter examines four forms of chicken that can all be grilled. (Whole birds, which require the special treatment of grill-roasting, are discussed in chapter 16.) We start with an overview of chicken parts—legs, thighs, and breasts. Chicken wings are technically chicken parts, but because they are usually served as an appetizer (rather than as a main course) and have special cooking challenges, they are considered separately in the second section of this chapter. Boneless, skinless chicken parts (both breasts and thighs) are covered next, followed by an examination of butterflied chicken (a whole chicken with the backbone removed so the bird can be opened up to form a flat shape suitable for grilling).

Before getting into the grilling methods for these various chicken products, we would like to address the products themselves—what's available to the consumer at the supermarket and how to pick and choose. Mass-market chickens, such as Tyson and Perdue, aim to produce a good chicken at a low cost. Kosher chickens, always popular in urban areas with large Jewish populations, have become increasingly available at supermarkets because of consumer concerns about cleanliness in chicken processing. In accordance with religious law, kosher chickens are bathed in a saltwater bath to remove blood and impurities. In effect, the chickens are brined, albeit briefly, before being packaged. (For more on brining, see "How Brining Works," page 102.) All kosher chickens must be raised and processed according to a standardized protocol and are clearly labeled as such. Many small chicken farms have returned to the animal-raising practices of the past to produce free-range chickens. Although there is no one clear definition of this term, most chicken operations that use this term allow their birds access to the outdoors. Many free-range chickens are also labeled organic or natural. Again, definitions can be hazy, but most farmers who use one or both of these terms rely on organic feed and reject the use of antibiotics to treat disease in their flock.

To make some sense of the vast array of choices, we conducted a blind tasting in which we pitted four of the leading supermarket chickens (all mass-market brands) against five specialty or premium chickens. The latter group included kosher, free-range, and organic chickens, all of which had one thing in common: they cost more than the mass-market brands. We purchased one bird from each company and then roasted it plain, without seasonings, until the internal temperature was 160 degrees. Half of each bird was carved; the rest of the meat was left on the carcass so panelists could judge the bird's overall appearance. The results of our tasting were quite clear. The mass-market brands received uniformly negative marks. Several panelists said they would rather swear off chicken than eat these tasteless, mushy birds. In comparison, most of the premium chickens were thoroughly enjoyed. The flavor of these birds was stronger and sometimes even a bit gamy. The texture was also firmer, but not tough. We talked to industry experts to find out why premium or specialty chickens taste so much better, and they offered several explanations.

First, many small companies have invested heavily in livestock gene pool development. Some specialty companies are using French birds; others use old-fashioned American varieties known for their superior flavor. (Larger companies may be more concerned with the size of the breast or other breeding characteristics that involve keeping costs down or appealing to perceived consumer interests, such as skin color.)

Second, some of the premium chickens have access to the outdoors, or at least the freedom to wander in a fairly large indoor area. Exercise is directly linked to flavor development and any hint of gaminess. The more a bird exercises, the leaner it becomes and the more flavorful (and darker) the muscles, especially in the legs, become.

Third, many small outfits take extra steps in processing (also a reason for their higher cost). Bell & Evans, an East Coast brand that came out on top in our ratings, ships chickens loose on ice so that they can weep fluids and blood as they make their way from processing plant to supermarket. The net weight of each bird is reduced, so the company actually earns less for every chicken. In contrast, mass-market

CUTTING UP A WHOLE CHICKEN

Many of the best-tasting birds available in supermarkets are only sold whole. Parts come from mass-market brands and are rarely your best option. For this reason, every cook should know how to cut a whole chicken into eight parts—two wings, two thighs, two drumsticks, and two breasts.

Cutting up a whole chicken takes less than five minutes but does require a sharp chef's knife. We like to use poultry scissors to separate the back from the breast, but you can complete this step with a knife. The cook who takes the time to butcher a chicken at home is rewarded with backs that can be frozen and used to make stock.

1. With a sharp chef's knife, cut through the skin around the leg where it attaches to the breast.

2. Using both hands, pop the leg out of its socket.

3. Use your chef's knife to cut through the flesh and skin to detach the leg from the body.

4. A line of fat separates the thigh and drumstick. Cut through the joint at this point. Repeat steps 2, 3, and 4 with the other leg.

5. Bend the wing out from the breast and cut to remove the wing. Repeat with the other wing.

6. Using poultry shears, cut down along the ribs between the back and the breast to totally separate the back from the breast.

7. Place a chef's knife directly on the breastbone, then apply pressure to cut through the bone and separate the breast into two halves.

brands are usually shrink-wrapped at the plant and then frozen to keep moisture from accumulating in the packages. But many experts believe that a chicken must lose these fluids if a stronger, meatier flavor is to be developed.

Fourth, many smaller companies "grow out" their birds for eight or nine weeks instead of slaughtering them at six or seven weeks, as the industry giants do. Generally, the older the bird, the more flavorful the muscles.

In sum, we think it's worth spending a little extra money to get a chicken that tastes great. In addition to Bell & Evans chickens, our panel gave high ratings to kosher chickens from Empire (which are sold nationwide), free-range, natural chickens from

D'Artagnan (available in some markets, mostly in the East, and by mail), and free-range chickens from La Belle Rouge, which are raised without growth stimulants or antibiotics and are available in select locations around the country. These premium chickens range in price from $1.59 to $3 per pound, but we have found that you get what you pay for when it comes to chicken.

Whether buying a premium or mass-market brand, make sure the chicken you buy is fresh. If you detect off odors—strong enough to permeate plastic wrap—or see excess liquid in the package, walk away. Since poultry is shrink-wrapped, you must rely mostly on "sell-by" dates rather than your senses. Many supermarkets label birds with a sell-by date that is a week or more away from the day on which the birds were delivered. You don't want to buy a bird that has been sitting in the supermarket for a week. Therefore, always look at the sell-by date and try to get a chicken that still has plenty of shelf life left.

GRILLED CHICKEN PARTS (LEGS, THIGHS, AND BREASTS)

GRILLED CHICKEN PARTS SHOULD HAVE richly caramelized, golden brown (not burnt) skin and moist, juicy meat. As soon as our testing started, we realized we needed to develop slightly different methods for dark and white meat parts. The higher fat content in thighs and legs makes flare-ups a greater problem, while the breasts have a tendency to dry out. (Wings are different from both dark meat and breasts because they have so much skin and fat

and relatively little meat. They require a completely different cooking method. For more information, see page 109).

We started with dark meat since we feel it has more inherent flavor and because its extra fat makes it better suited to grilling. We divided our tests into three parts. The first involved partial cooking off the grill; the second involved particular ways of moving the chicken around on the grill surface, as well as using the grill cover for part of the cooking time; and the third involved various ways of treating the chicken before cooking it, both to add flavor and to improve texture.

We had thought that some of the methods of partially cooking the chicken off the grill would work pretty well, but we were wrong. Poaching the chicken before grilling resulted in dry chicken with a cottony texture. Microwaving prior to grilling was even worse: The chicken ended up not only dry but rubbery, and the skin failed to crisp despite its post-microwave time on the grill.

SCIENCE: How Brining Works

We find that soaking chicken, Cornish hens, and turkey in a saltwater solution before cooking best protects delicate white meat. Whether we are roasting a turkey or grilling chicken parts, we have consistently found that brining keeps the meat juicier. Brining also gives delicate (and sometimes mushy) poultry a meatier, firmer consistency and seasons the meat down to the bone. (We also find that brining adds moisture to pork and shrimp and improves their texture and flavor when grilled.)

To explain these sensory perceptions, we ran some tests. We started by weighing several 11-pound turkeys after they had been brined for 12 hours and found an average weight gain of almost ¾ pound (12 ounces). Even more impressive, we found that brined birds weighed six to eight ounces more after roasting than a same-sized bird that had not been brined. Our taste buds were right: brined birds are juicier.

So how does brining work? Brining actually promotes a change in the structure of the proteins in the muscle. The salt causes protein strands to become denatured, or unwound. This is the same process that occurs when proteins are exposed to heat, acid, or alcohol. When protein strands unwind, they get tangled in one another and trap water in the matrix that forms. Salt is commonly used to give processed meats a better texture. For example, hot dogs made without salt would be limp.

Depending on the size of the bird, it is necessary to vary the amount of salt in the solution and the brining time. In general, bigger birds require a longer soaking time in a less concentrated solution. A less salty solution seasons the meat evenly and prevents the skin and outside layers of meat from becoming too salty in the time it takes to season the meat near the bone. In contrast, chicken parts can be brined in a much saltier solution for less time. Follow the specific directions in the recipes that follow with regard to the proportion of salt to water and the optimum brining time.

In some cases, we have added sugar to a brine. The sugar does not affect the texture of the meat, but it does add flavor. For instance, we find that brining chicken parts in a sugar-salt solution enhances the caramelization that occurs when the parts are grilled.

Note that we listed kosher or regular table salt in recipes that call for brining. Because the crystals of table salt are quite a bit smaller and therefore more compact than those of kosher salt, cup for cup, table salt is about twice as strong as kosher salt.

SCIENCE: Chicken Safety

Given the prevalence of bacteria in the poultry supply in this country, it's probably best to assume that the bird you buy is contaminated. That means you need to follow some simple rules to minimize the danger to you and your family:

➤ Keep poultry refrigerated until just before cooking. Bacteria thrive at temperatures between 40 and 140 degrees. This also means that leftovers should be promptly refrigerated.

➤ When handling poultry, make sure to wash hands, knives, cutting boards, and counters (or anything else that has come into contact with the raw bird, its juices, or your hands) with hot, soapy water. Be especially careful not to let the chicken, its juices, or your hands touch foods that will be eaten raw, such as salad ingredients.

➤ Cook poultry to an internal temperature of 160 degrees or higher to ensure that any bacteria has been killed.

Our next approach was to sear the thighs and legs on the grill first, then finish the cooking off the grill. Using the microwave to finish cooking after a two-minute sear on the grill wasn't bad and would be acceptable for those times when you're in a hurry to get food on the table. Unlike the chicken that was microwaved before grilling, these pieces had crispy skin, and the meat was evenly cooked throughout. But this chicken was slightly less juicy than that cooked only on the grill.

Our final attempt at combined cooking methods came even closer to the goal. Again we seared the thighs and legs on the grill but this time finished cooking them in a 350-degree oven. The meat was evenly cooked and remained juicy, with none of the toughness experienced with other combined cooking methods; the skin, which had crisped up nicely during its time on the grill, remained quite crisp after its sojourn in the oven.

The differences between this method and our final favorite were differences of degree: The meat was just slightly less tender, the skin a bit less crispy. More important, this oven method used two different appliances and required you to do part of the cooking outside on the grill and the rest in the kitchen. Not only was this needlessly cumbersome, it was also less fun, given that part of the appeal of grilling is standing around the fire sipping your favorite beverage and passing the time of day as you cook. So we consigned this method to the reject pile along with the other less successful combination cooking techniques.

We next moved on to test methods that involved cooking on the grill alone. Each method involved some variation on the two-level fire—that is, a fire in which one area is hotter than the other. The idea in every case was to get the sear from the hotter fire and cook the chicken evenly all the way through over the cooler fire.

The first of these methods seemed illogical, but a friend had insisted that it worked, so we gave it a try. In this method, the chicken was to be cooked on a low fire first, then finished up on a hot fire. Like microwaving, however, this backward approach resulted in dry meat—a lame result for a method that saved no time or energy.

Next we tried the method that intuitively seemed most likely to succeed: searing the chicken over a medium-hot fire and then moving it to a medium-low fire to finish cooking. This approach proved to be a winner. The interior was evenly cooked, moist, and tender, and the skin dark and crisp. We found that we could use this method to cook whole legs with thighs attached or just the thighs alone with only one difference—timing. With thighs alone, you take about four to eight minutes off the cooking time.

It was then time to consider ways of adding flavor to the chicken. Options included marinades, spice rubs and pastes, barbecue sauces, salsas, and brines.

The results of marinating the chicken were disappointing. Even several hours in a classic oil-and-acid marinade added only a small amount of flavor to the finished chicken, and oil dripping off the marinated chicken caused constant flare-ups during the initial searing period.

Rubbing the chicken with a spice rub prior to grilling proved far more satisfactory. Because the rubs and pastes are composed almost entirely of spices, they have enough flavor intensity to stand up to the smoky grilled flavor and, as a result, come through much more clearly than marinades. Wet pastes and barbecue sauces often contain some sweetener and can burn if brushed on the chicken before cooking. We found it best to brush them on just before taking the chicken off the grill and then to serve extra sauce at the table.

If serving salsa or chutney at the table with the chicken, you don't need to add special flavors to the chicken before or during cooking. You should, however, still season the raw chicken with salt and pepper.

As a final test, we tried brining the chicken before grilling it. Admittedly, we didn't approach this test with a lot of enthusiasm—it seemed like too much bother for what should be a simple cooking process. That just goes to show how preconceptions can be faulty, though, because it turned out to be an excellent idea.

We tried brining for various amounts of time and found that by using a brine with a high concentration of salt and sugar we could achieve the result we wanted in only about 1½ hours. The brine penetrated the chicken, seasoning it and slightly firming up its texture before it was grilled. On a molecular level, what actually happened was that the salt caused the strands of protein in the chicken meat to unwind and get tangled up with one another, forming a matrix that then served to trap water. When the chicken was grilled, this matrix formed a sort of barrier that kept liquids from leaking out of the bird. As a result, the finished brined chicken was juicier and more tender than the unbrined chicken. (For more information, see "How Brining Works," page 102.)

The sugar in the brine had one very good effect that carried with it the potential for a minor problem. The traces of sugar left on the exterior of the chicken, while not enough to affect the flavor, did cause the chicken to brown more quickly and thoroughly. Since browning adds rich, deep flavor to any food, this was a decided advantage. However, since the browning took place more quickly than with nonbrined chicken, on our first try we managed to burn the skin of some pieces. So, when grilling brined chicken, be sure to watch it very carefully during the initial browning period to prevent charring.

If you don't have time to brine your chicken, you can still get excellent results with the two-level fire method by adding deep flavor with a spice rub or paste. Also make sure to sprinkle the chicken with salt before heading to the grill to compensate for not brining.

Having conducted all of the above tests with legs, we then turned to breasts, which proved even more challenging. Bone-in chicken breasts can be especially tricky to grill because they're thick and unevenly shaped. Grilling thighs, legs, or boneless breasts is much easier. But when properly grilled, bone-in, skin-on breasts can be particularly tasty. As with dark meat parts, we found partial cooking of the breasts before grilling (by poaching, roasting, or microwaving) to be unsatisfactory. Likewise, starting the chicken on the grill and finishing indoors was ruled out. We wanted to figure out how to cook the parts completely on the grill.

Like legs, breasts are best started over a medium-hot fire and then moved to a cooler part of the grill. Because bone-in breasts are thicker than thighs or legs, cooking times were significantly longer. The breasts refused to cook through to the bone in less than half an hour. By this time the skin had burned and the outer layers of meat were dry. We tried using the grill cover, but again detected some off flavors from the burned-on ashes on the inside of the cover. (See chapter 1, page 5, for more information on the effects of charcoal grilling with the grill cover down.)

We did notice, however, that cooking with the cover cut the grilling time back to 20 minutes, about the same amount of time needed for legs and thighs. And this shorter cooking time translated into skin that was not black and meat that was still juicy. We decided to improvise a cover, using an old restaurant trick—a disposable aluminum roasting pan—to build up heat around the breasts and help speed the cooking along. After searing for five minutes, we moved the breasts to a cooler part of the fire, covered them with a disposable pan, and continued grilling for another 15 minutes or so. This allowed the breasts to cook through without burning.

Like legs and thighs, breasts respond well to brining before grilling. The same collection of rubs, pastes, sauces, and salsas works as well with breasts as with legs. You can grill dark and white meat parts together, if you like. Set up a three-level fire with most of the coals on one side of the grill, some coals in the middle, and no coals on the opposite side. Sear all the chicken parts over the hottest part of the fire, then finish cooking the legs and thighs over the medium-low heat in the middle, and move the seared breasts to the coolest part of the grill and cover with a disposable pan. It sounds complicated, but it makes perfect sense once you try it and taste the results.

Charcoal-Grilled Bone-In Chicken Thighs or Legs

SERVES 4

Brining improves the chicken's flavor, but if you're short on time, skip step 1 and season the chicken generously with salt and pepper before cooking. Add flavorings before or during cooking: Rub the chicken parts with a spice rub or paste before putting them on the grill, or brush them with barbecue sauce during the final 2 minutes of cooking (see pages 107, 108, and 109 for details). If the fire flares because of dripping fat or a gust of wind, move the chicken to the area without coals until the flames die down.

8	chicken thighs or 4 whole legs
¾	cup kosher salt or 6 tablespoons table salt
¾	cup sugar
	Ground black pepper

1. To prevent burning, trim overhanging fat and skin from the chicken pieces. Dissolve the salt and sugar in 1 quart of cold water in a gallon-sized zipper-lock plastic bag. Add the chicken; press out as much air as possible from the bag and seal; refrigerate until fully seasoned, about 1½ hours.

2. Light a large chimney starter filled with hardwood charcoal (about 2½ pounds) and allow to burn until all the charcoal is covered with a layer of fine gray ash. Build a two-level fire by stacking most of the coals on one side of the grill and arranging the remaining coals in a single layer on the other side of the grill. Set the cooking rack in place, cover the grill with the lid, and let the rack heat up, about 5 minutes. Use a wire brush to scrape clean the cooking rack. The grill is ready when the temperature of the stacked coals is medium-hot and that of the remaining coals is medium-low. (See how to gauge heat level on page 19.)

3. Meanwhile, remove the chicken from the brine, rinse well, dry thoroughly with paper towels, and season with pepper to taste or one of the spice rubs or pastes on pages 108 and 109.

4. Cook the chicken, uncovered, over the hotter part of the grill until seared, about 1 to 2 minutes on each side. Move the chicken to the cooler part of the grill; continue to grill, uncovered, turning occasionally, until dark and fully cooked, 12 to 16 minutes for thighs, 16

to 20 minutes for whole legs. To test for doneness, either peek into the thickest part of the chicken with the tip of a small knife (you should see no redness near the bone) or check the internal temperature at the thickest part with an instant-read thermometer, which should register 165 degrees. Transfer to a serving platter. Serve warm or at room temperature.

Gas-Grilled Bone-In Chicken Thighs or Legs

SERVES 4

Brining improves the chicken's flavor, but if you're short on time, skip step 1 and season the chicken generously with salt and pepper before cooking. Add flavorings before or during cooking: Rub the chicken parts with a spice rub or paste before putting them on the grill, or brush them with barbecue sauce during the final 2 minutes of cooking (see pages 107, 108, and 109 for details). Initial high heat is crucial in order to produce crisp skin. The heat is then reduced to medium-low to cook the chicken through.

8	chicken thighs or 4 whole legs
¾	cup kosher salt or 6 tablespoons table salt
¾	cup sugar
	Ground black pepper

1. To prevent burning, trim overhanging fat and skin from the chicken pieces. Dissolve the salt and sugar in 1 quart of cold water in a gallon-sized zipper-lock plastic bag. Add the chicken; press out as much air as possible from the bag and seal; refrigerate until fully seasoned, about 1½ hours.

2. Preheat the grill with all burners set to high and the lid down until the grill is very hot, about 15 minutes. Use a wire brush to scrape clean the cooking grate. Leave one burner on high and turn the other burner(s) down to medium-low.

3. Meanwhile, remove the chicken from the brine, rinse well, dry thoroughly with paper towels, and season with pepper to taste or one of the spice rubs or pastes on pages 108 and 109.

4. Cook the chicken, covered, over the hotter part of the grill until seared, about 1 to 2 minutes on each side. Move the chicken to the cooler part of the grill; continue to grill, covered, turning occasionally, until dark and fully cooked, 12 to 16 minutes for thighs,

16 to 20 minutes for whole legs. To test for doneness, either peek into the thickest part of the chicken with the tip of a small knife (you should see no redness near the bone) or check the internal temperature at the thickest part with an instant-read thermometer, which should register 165 degrees. Transfer to a serving platter. Serve warm or at room temperature.

Charcoal-Grilled Bone-In Chicken Breasts

SERVES 4

Brining improves the chicken's flavor, but if you're short on time, skip step 1 and season the chicken generously with salt and pepper before cooking. Add flavorings before or during cooking: Rub the chicken parts with a spice rub or paste before they go on the grill, or brush them with barbecue sauce during the final 2 minutes of cooking (see pages 107, 108, and 109 for details). If the fire flares because of dripping fat or a gust of wind, move the chicken to the area without coals until the flames die down.

    ¾   cup kosher salt or 6 tablespoons table salt
    ¾   cup sugar
    4   split chicken breasts (bone-in, skin-on),
        10 to 12 ounces each
        Ground black pepper
        Disposable aluminum roasting pan

1. Dissolve the salt and sugar in 1 quart of cold water in a gallon-sized zipper-lock plastic bag. Add the chicken; press out as much air as possible from the bag and seal; refrigerate until fully seasoned, about 1½ hours.

2. Light a large chimney starter filled with hardwood charcoal (about 2½ pounds) and allow to burn until all the charcoal is covered with a layer of fine gray ash. Build a modified two-level fire by stacking all of the coals on one side of the grill. Set the cooking rack in place, cover the grill with the lid, and let the rack heat up, about 5 minutes. The grill is ready when the temperature of the coals is hot. (See how to gauge heat level on page 19.) Use a wire brush to scrape clean the cooking rack.

3. Meanwhile, remove the chicken from the brine, rinse well, dry thoroughly with paper towels, and season with pepper to taste or one of the spice rubs or pastes on pages 108 and 109.

4. Cook the chicken, uncovered, over the hotter part of the grill until well browned, 2 to 3 minutes per side. Move the chicken to the cooler part of the grill and cover with a disposable aluminum roasting pan; continue to cook, skin-side up, for 10 minutes. Turn and cook for 5 minutes more or until done. To test for doneness, either peek into the thickest part of the chicken with the tip of a small knife (you should see no redness near the bone) or check the internal temperature at the thickest part with an instant-read thermometer, which should register 160 degrees. Transfer to a serving platter. Serve warm or at room temperature.

Gas-Grilled Bone-In Chicken Breasts

SERVES 4

Brining improves the chicken's flavor, but if you're short on time, skip step 1 and season the chicken generously with salt and pepper before cooking. Add flavorings before or during cooking: Rub chicken with a spice rub or paste before placing on the grill, or brush with barbecue sauce during the final 2 minutes of cooking (see pages 107, 108, and 109 for details). With the lid down on a gas grill, there's no need to cook the chicken under a disposable roasting pan, as in charcoal grilling.

    ¾   cup kosher salt or 6 tablespoons table salt
    ¾   cup sugar
    4   split chicken breasts (bone-in, skin-on),
        10 to 12 ounces each
        Ground black pepper

GRILLING BONE-IN CHICKEN BREASTS

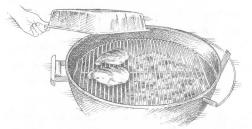

Covering chicken breasts with a disposable aluminum roasting pan while they cook on a charcoal grill creates an ovenlike effect that speeds up grilling but still allows air to circulate. Do not use the grill cover; built-up soot on the inside of the cover can give the chicken an off flavor.

1. Dissolve the salt and sugar in 1 quart of cold water in a gallon-sized zipper-lock plastic bag. Add the chicken; press out as much air as possible from the bag and seal; refrigerate until fully seasoned, about 1½ hours.

2. Preheat the grill with all burners set to high and the lid down until the grill is very hot, about 15 minutes. Use a wire brush to scrape clean the cooking grate. Leave one burner on high and turn the other burner(s) down to medium-low.

3. Meanwhile, remove the chicken from the brine, rinse well, dry thoroughly with paper towels, and season with pepper to taste or one of the spice rubs or pastes on pages 108 and 109.

4. Cook the chicken, covered, over the hotter part of the grill until well browned, 2 to 3 minutes per side. Move the chicken to the cooler part of the grill; continue to cook, covered, skin-side up, for 10 minutes. Turn and cook for 5 minutes more or until done. To test for doneness, either peek into the thickest part of the chicken with the tip of a small knife (you should see no redness near the bone) or check the internal temperature at the thickest part with an instant-read thermometer, which should register 160 degrees. Transfer to a serving platter. Serve warm or at room temperature.

Charcoal-Grilled Mixed Chicken Parts

SERVES 8

Although dark meat and white meat require different grilling techniques, you can cook legs, thighs, and breasts together if you follow this method. Basically, you need to build a three-level fire, with most of the coals on one side of the grill, some coals in the middle, and no coals on the opposite side. Sear all the chicken parts over the hottest part of the fire, finish cooking the legs and thighs in the middle of the grill, and moved the seared breasts to the coolest part of the grill and cover with a disposable pan. As always, brining improves the chicken's flavor, but if you're short on time, skip step 1 and season the chicken generously with salt and pepper before cooking. Add flavorings before or during cooking: Rub the chicken parts with a spice rub or paste before they go on the grill or brush them with barbecue sauce during the final 2 minutes of cooking (see pages 108 and 109 and box at right for details).

1½	cups kosher salt or ¾ cup table salt
1½	cups sugar
8	chicken thighs or 4 whole legs
4	split chicken breasts (bone-in, skin-on), 10 to 12 ounces each
	Ground black pepper

1. Dissolve half the salt and sugar in 1 quart of cold water in a gallon-sized zipper-lock plastic bag. Add the chicken thighs or legs; press out as much air as possible from the bag and seal. Repeat the process in a second bag with the remaining salt, sugar, 1 quart of cold water, and chicken breasts. Refrigerate both bags until the chicken is fully seasoned, about 1½ hours.

2. Light a large chimney starter filled with hardwood charcoal (about 2½ pounds) and allow to burn until all the charcoal is covered with a layer of fine gray ash. Build a three-level fire by stacking most of the coals on one side of the grill, arranging the remaining coals in a single layer in the middle of the grill, and leaving the remaining side empty of coals. Set the cooking rack in place, cover the grill with the lid, and let the rack heat up, about 5 minutes. Use a wire brush to scrape clean the cooking rack. The grill is ready when the temperature of the stacked coals is medium-hot and that of the single layer of coals is medium-low. (See how to gauge heat level on page 19.)

3. Meanwhile, remove the chicken from the brine, rinse well, dry thoroughly with paper towels, and season with pepper to taste or one of the spice rubs or pastes on pages 108 and 109.

CHICKEN PARTS WITH BARBECUE SAUCE

Any of the tomato-based barbecue sauces in chapter 19 will taste great on grilled chicken. To use barbecue sauce, grill the chicken following the instructions in the appropriate recipe. During the last 2 minutes of cooking, brush with some of the sauce, cook about 1 minute, turn over, brush again, and cook 1 minute more. Transfer the chicken to a serving platter, brush with additional sauce to taste, and serve, with more sauce passed at the table if desired. Plan on using about ½ cup of barbecue sauce for a single chicken recipe, more if you serve barbecue sauce at the table.

4. Cook the chicken, uncovered, over the hotter part of the grill until well browned, 2 to 3 minutes per side. Move the chicken thighs or legs to the middle part of the grill and move the chicken breasts to the area with no fire and cover with a disposable aluminum roasting pan. Continue to grill the legs, uncovered, turning occasionally, until dark and fully cooked, 12 to 16 minutes for thighs, 16 to 20 minutes for whole legs. Continue to grill the breasts, skin-side up, for 10 minutes. Turn and cook for 5 minutes more or until done. To test for doneness, either peek into the thickest part of the chicken with the tip of a small knife (you should see no redness near the bone) or check the internal temperature at the thickest part with an instant-read thermometer, which should register 165 degrees for dark meat and 160 degrees for breasts. Transfer to a serving platter. Serve warm or at room temperature.

> VARIATION

Gas-Grilled Mixed Chicken Parts

Since the grilling technique for light and dark meat parts is basically the same on gas, there's not much need to adapt your cooking technique. Simply brine the breasts in one bag, the thighs or legs in another, and then proceed as directed, setting the burners to high and medium-low once the grill has been preheated. Sear all parts over high heat and then cook through over medium-low heat. For dark meat, follow the cooking times listed in the recipe for Gas-Grilled Bone-In Chicken Thighs or Legs. For white meat, follow the cooking times listed in the recipe for Gas-Grilled Bone-In Chicken Breasts. As always, brining improves the chicken's flavor, but if you're short on time, skip step 1 and season the chicken generously with salt and pepper before cooking. Add flavorings before or during cooking: Rub the chicken parts with a spice rub or paste before they go on the grill or brush them with barbecue sauce during the final 2 minutes of cooking (see page 107, this page, and page 109 for details).

RUBS AND PASTES FOR GRILLED CHICKEN PARTS

RUBS ARE MADE WITH GROUND DRY SPICES and are best applied with your fingers. Pastes contain some sort of liquid and can be applied with your fingers or a brush. If you have decided to skip brining, make sure to season the parts with salt.

~

Pantry Spice Rub for Chicken

MAKES ABOUT ½ CUP, ENOUGH TO COAT A SINGLE RECIPE OF EITHER DARK OR WHITE MEAT PARTS

- 2 tablespoons ground cumin
- 2 tablespoons curry powder
- 2 tablespoons chili powder
- I tablespoon ground allspice
- I tablespoon ground black pepper
- I teaspoon ground cinnamon

Combine all ingredients in a small bowl. Rub the mixture over brined and dried chicken parts before grilling.

~

Garam Masala Spice Rub for Chicken

MAKES ABOUT ½ CUP, ENOUGH TO COAT A SINGLE RECIPE OF EITHER DARK OR WHITE MEAT PARTS

- 2 tablespoons fennel seeds
- 2 tablespoons anise seeds
- 2 tablespoons cardamom pods
- 2 tablespoons black peppercorns
- I teaspoon whole cloves
- I cinnamon stick, broken into several pieces

Toast the ingredients in a dry skillet until fragrant, about 2 minutes. Grind to a powder in a spice grinder. Rub the mixture over brined and dried chicken parts before grilling.

Asian Spice Paste for Chicken

MAKES ABOUT 1/3 CUP, ENOUGH TO
SEASON A SINGLE RECIPE OF EITHER
DARK OR WHITE MEAT PARTS

2   tablespoons soy sauce
2   tablespoons peanut oil
1   tablespoon minced jalapeño or other fresh
    chile, stemmed and seeded
1   tablespoon chopped fresh ginger
1   garlic clove, peeled
2   tablespoons fresh cilantro leaves

Puree all ingredients in a food processor or blender until smooth. Rub the paste over brined and dried chicken parts before grilling.

Mediterranean Spice Paste for Chicken

MAKES ABOUT 1/2 CUP, ENOUGH TO
SEASON A SINGLE RECIPE OF EITHER
DARK OR WHITE MEAT PARTS

4   medium garlic cloves, peeled
2   tablespoons grated lemon zest
1/4 cup packed fresh parsley leaves
1/4 cup extra-virgin olive oil
1   tablespoon fresh thyme leaves
1   tablespoon fresh rosemary leaves
1   tablespoon fresh sage leaves
1/2 teaspoon salt

Puree all ingredients in a food processor or blender until smooth. Rub the paste over brined and dried chicken parts before grilling.

Citrus and Cilantro Spice Paste for Chicken

MAKES ABOUT 1/3 CUP, ENOUGH TO
SEASON A SINGLE RECIPE OF EITHER
DARK OR WHITE MEAT PARTS

1   teaspoon ground cumin
1   teaspoon chili powder
1   teaspoon sweet paprika
1   teaspoon ground coriander
2   tablespoons orange juice
1   tablespoon lime juice
1   tablespoon olive oil
1   garlic clove, peeled
2   tablespoons fresh cilantro leaves

Puree all ingredients in a food processor or blender until smooth. Rub the paste over brined and dried chicken parts before grilling.

CHICKEN WINGS

CHICKEN WINGS ARE BEST COOKED ON the grill so that their fat is rendered and falls away onto the coals. Cooked in the oven, the wings rest in their own fat and turn out flabby. But grill wings incorrectly and you get greasy meat, surrounded by a charred, rubbery, thick coating of skin that is hardly appealing. We wanted to develop a grilling technique that was foolproof, that would produce wings with crisp, thin, caramelized skin, tender and moist meat, and smoky grilled flavor that was well seasoned throughout. Furthermore, we wanted wings to be eater-friendly; eating them should not be a chore.

Wings are made up of three parts: the meaty, drumsticklike portion that is closest to the breast section of the bird; the two-boned center portion that is surrounded by a band of meat and skin; and the small, almost meatless wingtip. After cutting and grilling wings several different ways, we concluded that wingtips are not worth grilling. They offer almost no meat and char long before the other two parts are even close to being cooked through.

Wingtips discarded, we pushed the meat up the bones of the remaining, meatier parts to replicate the lollipop-shaped wings favored by traditional chefs. This took too much time and effort. We then decided that the best method for preparing wings is to separate the usable two portions at the joint. The pieces are small enough to be eaten as finger food and are less awkward to eat than a whole wing.

Our first round of tests was disappointing. Grilling the wings directly over the coals at temperatures ranging from high heat to low heat produced wings that were mediocre at best. Those cooked over medium-high and high heat charred quickly, and the skin remained thick and tough. Grilling the wings over medium and medium-low heat produced better wings; the skin was crispier and thinner, but the wings still lacked the great caramelized crust that we desired.

It was at this point that we tried a modified two-level fire, banking all of the coals on one side of the grill and leaving the other side empty. We then cooked the wings, covered, over the empty side of the grill, until cooked through. The result was a nicely moist interior, but the skin was flaccid and had a very unappealing grayish tint.

Gathering information from these initial tests, we concluded that a more sophisticated grilling technique was necessary and that perhaps even a second method of cooking was in order. We tried blanching the wings for various amounts of time before throwing them on the grill for crisping and browning, but this technique, while producing thinner, crispier skin, yielded wings with less flavor and drier meat. It was also time-consuming and added extra clean-up.

So far, the best wings were those cooked directly over the coals at a medium-low heat level (a single layer of charcoal). Although they were acceptable, we felt that the texture and flavor would be greatly improved with a crispier, darker exterior. At this point we decided to try a two-level fire (not modified), in which the coals are stacked on one side of the grill (for a medium-hot fire) and placed in a single layer on the other side (for a medium-low fire). We grilled the chicken wings using two different methods. One batch was browned over medium-high heat and then moved to the cooler side of the grill to continue cooking slowly, while the other was started on medium-low heat to cook low and slow and then moved to medium-high heat to get a final quick crisping and browning. While both methods worked well, the wings cooked first over medium-low heat and then moved to medium-high heat were superior, rendering more fat from the skin and thereby producing a thin, delicate crust.

Prompted by past experience, we felt that brining might improve the flavor as well as the texture of our chicken wings. We used a brining solution in which equal amounts of sugar and kosher salt are added to water. Tasting the wings as they came off the grill, we happily discovered that the brined chicken wings were not only tasty and well seasoned throughout but that brining had produced several unexpected bonuses. The brined chicken meat was noticeably plumper before grilling and more tender after, and the wings developed a crispier, more caramelized skin than those which had not been brined.

Charcoal-Grilled Chicken Wings

SERVES 4 TO 6 AS AN APPETIZER

Make sure your grill is large enough to hold all the wings over roughly one-half of the rack surface. To save time, brine the wings while the grill heats up. Serve the wings as is, with a squeeze of lemon or lime, or with one of the sauce recipes on page 111.

¾	cup kosher salt or 6 tablespoons table salt
¾	cup sugar
12	whole chicken wings (about 2½ pounds), separated into sections following illustrations on page 112, wingtips discarded
	Ground black pepper

1. Dissolve the salt and sugar in 1 quart of cold water in a gallon-sized zipper-lock plastic bag. Add the chicken, press out as much air as possible from the bag and seal, then refrigerate until fully seasoned, 30 minutes.

2. Light a large chimney starter filled with hardwood charcoal (about 2½ pounds) and allow to burn until all the charcoal is covered with a layer of fine gray ash. Build a two-level fire by stacking most of the coals on one side of the grill and arranging the remaining coals in a single layer on the other side. Set the cooking rack in place, cover the grill with the lid, and let the rack heat up, about 5 minutes. Use a wire brush to scrape clean the cooking rack. The grill is ready when the temperature of the stacked coals is medium-hot and that of the remaining coals is medium-low. (See how to gauge heat level on page 19.)

3. Meanwhile, remove the chicken from the brine, rinse well, dry thoroughly with paper towels, and season with pepper to taste.

4. Cook the chicken, uncovered, over the cooler part of the grill, turning once, until the color is light spotty

SAUCES FOR CHICKEN WINGS

Serve grilled wings with one of the following sauces or with store-bought or homemade barbecue sauce (any of the tomato-based sauces in chapter 19). A few of these sauces (as indicated) can be brushed on just before the wings come off the grill for a light glaze. All can be served at the table as dipping sauces.

Hoisin-Sesame Sauce

MAKES ENOUGH FOR 12 WINGS

Use as a light glaze while the wings are still on the grill or at the table as a dipping sauce.

2	tablespoons hoisin sauce
1	tablespoon rice vinegar
1	tablespoon soy sauce
1	teaspoon Asian sesame oil
1	tablespoon vegetable oil
2	tablespoons minced fresh ginger
2	medium garlic cloves, minced
2	tablespoons minced fresh cilantro leaves

1. Mix together the hoisin sauce, vinegar, soy sauce, sesame oil, and 2 tablespoons water.

2. Heat the vegetable oil in a small saucepan over medium heat. Add the ginger and garlic and sauté until fragrant but not browned, about 30 seconds. Add the hoisin mixture and cook until thickened, 1 to 2 minutes. Off heat, stir in the cilantro.

Spicy Peanut Dipping Sauce

MAKES ENOUGH FOR 12 WINGS

This Southeast Asian–style sauce is rich and smooth. Use this sauce at the table.

5	tablespoons creamy peanut butter
2	tablespoons fish sauce
2	tablespoons lime juice
1/4	cup unsweetened coconut milk
1	tablespoon honey
1	tablespoon minced fresh ginger
2	medium garlic cloves, minced
1/2	teaspoon hot red pepper flakes
1	teaspoon curry powder (optional)

Puree all ingredients in a blender until smooth.

Spicy Sauce for Buffalo Wings

MAKES ENOUGH FOR 12 WINGS

This is the classic spicy sauce for wings. Serve with blue cheese dressing.

1 1/2	tablespoons unsalted butter, melted
1 1/2	tablespoons Tabasco sauce

Mix the butter and Tabasco sauce together in a large bowl. When chicken wings are cooked through, immediately toss them in the bowl with the Tabasco mixture. Serve with blue cheese dressing if desired.

Blue Cheese Dressing

MAKES ENOUGH FOR 12 WINGS

This is the classic accompaniment to buffalo wings. Serve as a dipping sauce at the table.

2 1/2	ounces crumbled blue cheese (about 1/2 cup)
3	tablespoons buttermilk
3	tablespoons sour cream
2	tablespoons mayonnaise
2	teaspoons white wine vinegar
1/4	teaspoon sugar
1/8	teaspoon garlic powder
	Salt and ground black pepper

Mash the blue cheese and buttermilk in a small bowl with fork until mixture resembles cottage cheese with small curds. Stir in the sour cream, mayonnaise, vinegar, sugar, and garlic powder. Taste and adjust seasonings with salt and pepper. (The dressing can be refrigerated in an airtight container up to 1 week.)

brown, the skin has thinned, and the fat has rendered, 8 to 10 minutes. Move the chicken pieces to the hotter part of the grill; continue to grill, turning often to prevent charring, until the wings are dark spotty brown and the skin has crisped, 2 to 3 minutes longer. Transfer to a serving platter and serve immediately.

Gas-Grilled Chicken Wings

SERVES 4 TO 6 AS AN APPETIZER

Chicken wings require a lot of space on the grill. Rather than regulating the burners to create two heat levels, both burners are turned to medium heat for the initial phase of cooking and then turned to high to finish the process. Serve the wings as is, with a squeeze of lemon or lime, or with one of the sauce recipes on page 111.

- ¾ cup kosher salt or 6 tablespoons table salt
- ¾ cup sugar
- 12 whole chicken wings (about 2½ pounds), separated into sections following illustrations below, wingtips discarded
  Ground black pepper

1. Dissolve the salt and sugar in 1 quart of cold water in a gallon-sized zipper-lock plastic bag. Add the chicken, press out as much air as possible from the bag and seal, then refrigerate until fully seasoned, 30 minutes.

2. Preheat the grill with all burners set to high and the lid down until the grill is very hot, about 15 minutes. Use a wire brush to scrape clean the cooking grate. Turn the burners down to medium.

3. Meanwhile, remove the chicken from the brine, rinse well, dry thoroughly with paper towels, and season with pepper to taste.

4. Cook the chicken, larger drummettes toward the back of the grill (where the heat is usually more intense), covered, turning once, until the color is light spotty brown, the skin has thinned, and the fat has rendered, 12 to 14 minutes. Turn burners up to high heat; continue to grill, covered, turning often to prevent charring, until the wings are dark spotty brown and the skin has crisped, 3 to 4 minutes longer. Transfer to a serving platter and serve immediately.

BONELESS CHICKEN BREASTS AND THIGHS

WITHOUT SKIN, BONELESS BREASTS AND thighs are especially prone to burning and drying out on the grill. They are more difficult to cook than chicken parts with skin (which keeps moisture in) and bones (which add flavor).

However, many people don't eat chicken skin and would rather not bother with bones. If that's the case, it seems pointless to rub spices into bone-in, skin-on parts and then throw out the skin after cooking. If you don't eat skin, we think you might as well start with boneless, skinless parts and apply the seasonings where they can be enjoyed.

Our goal was clear: develop a technique for cooking boneless, skinless breasts and thighs that would keep these delicate parts as moist as possible. We started with breasts and figured we could refine our final technique for thighs, which contain more fat and are generally more forgiving when cooked.

Boneless, skinless breasts have almost no fat and can dry out easily with any cooking method. From

PREPARING CHICKEN WINGS

1. With a chef's knife, cut into the skin between the two larger sections of the wing until you hit the joint.

2. Bend back the two sections to pop and break the joint.

3. Cut through the skin and flesh to completely separate the two meaty portions.

4. Hack off the wingtip and discard.

our initial tests, it was clear that we needed to get them on and off the grill as quickly as possible. Cooking them over high heat and turning them just once was the best method we tested.

To make the fire quite intense, we spread a full chimney of lit charcoal out over just two-thirds of the grill. The concentrated fire shortened the cooking time by a minute or two. On gas, we just kept the burners on high the whole time and lifted the lid as infrequently as possible.

Although this super-fast cooking method was delivering good results, we still had some tweaking to do. The part between the tenderloin and breast wasn't cooking through. The meat is so thick here that cooking takes a few minutes longer. You have two options: remove the tenderloin, or leave it on and overcook most of the breast just to get the meat underneath the tenderloin cooked through. We opted to remove the tenderloins. Save them for a stir-fry or grill them with the breasts, reducing their cooking time by more than half.

We found it imperative to brush the breasts with a bit of oil to keep them from sticking to the grill. The oil also helped to keep the outer layer of meat from becoming dry and tough.

We had one last test to run: brining. In our initial tests, we used the same brine we had developed for bone-in, skin-on parts. It was much too salty, especially if these skinless parts were left in for 1½ hours, the time that works· for skin-on breasts. After much tinkering, we found that a brine with just one-half cup each of kosher salt and sugar (as opposed to three-quarters cup each for skin-on parts) was plenty strong. As for brining time, boneless parts are fully seasoned in just 20 minutes. This means you can brine the breasts while waiting for the coals to heat up.

While brined breasts were juicy and well seasoned, they clearly needed a flavor boost. We found that sticky glazes and pastes (such as barbecue sauce) are best applied when the breasts are almost cooked through. If applied earlier, they will burn. The other option is to moisten grilled chicken breasts after cooking with some sort of dipping sauce. See pages 116 and 117 for glazes and pastes and page 115 for details on dipping sauces.

At this point in our testing, we turned our attention to boneless, skinless thighs. We found that thighs, which have more internal fat than breasts, don't need to be brushed with oil before cooking. They exude enough fat to prevent sticking to the grill. Because of the higher fat content, we found that thighs can be cooked over an even hotter fire than breasts. On charcoal, this means piling a chimney full of lit charcoal over just half the grill, not two-thirds, as we recommend when cooking breasts.

One final point when cooking either boneless, skinless breasts or thighs: Be wary of overcooking, especially if your grill runs hot. To check for doneness, insert a knife into the thickest part of the meat; there should be no pinkness or blood. You can try to use an instant-read thermometer (an internal temperature of 160 degrees is just right for breasts; let thighs go to 165 degrees), but this can be tricky on such thin cuts. If you use a thermometer, slide it into the thickest part of the meat on an angle, and make sure it does not go entirely through and out the bottom of the meat, in which case the reading will be off.

Charcoal-Grilled Boneless, Skinless Chicken Breasts

SERVES 4

It's imperative to coat the breasts with a little oil so they don't stick to the grill. Note the short brining time here; the chicken will be finished brining by the time the charcoal is ready.

½	cup kosher salt or ¼ cup table salt
½	cup sugar
4	boneless, skinless chicken breasts (1½ to 1¾ pounds), tenderloins removed and reserved for another use
1	tablespoon extra-virgin olive oil
	Ground black pepper

1. Dissolve the salt and sugar in 1 quart of cold water in a gallon-sized zipper-lock plastic bag. Add the chicken breasts; press out as much air as possible from the bag and seal. Refrigerate until fully seasoned, about 20 minutes.

2. Light a large chimney starter filled with charcoal (about 2½ pounds) and allow to burn until all the charcoal is covered with a layer of fine gray ash. Build a modified two-level fire by spreading all the coals over two-thirds of the grill. Set the cooking rack

in place, cover the grill with the lid, and let the rack heat up, about 5 minutes. Use a wire brush to scrape clean the cooking grate. The grill is ready when the coals are hot. (See how to gauge heat level on page 19.)

3. Meanwhile, remove the chicken from the brine, rinse well under cold, running water, and dry thoroughly with paper towels. Toss chicken in a medium bowl with oil to coat. Season with pepper to taste.

4. Cook the chicken, uncovered, smooth-side down, directly over the hot coals until the chicken is opaque about two-thirds up the sides and rich brown grill marks appear, 4 to 5 minutes. Turn and continue grilling until the chicken is fully cooked, about 4 minutes. (If using a glaze or paste [pages 116–117], cook for 3 minutes after turning the chicken, brush the glaze or paste on both sides, and cook another minute or so, turning once.) To test for doneness, peek into the thickest part of the chicken with the tip of a small knife (it should be opaque at the center), or check the internal temperature with an instant-read thermometer, which should register 160 degrees.

5. Transfer the chicken to a serving platter. Serve hot or at room temperature, with a dipping sauce (page 115) if desired.

Gas-Grilled Boneless, Skinless Chicken Breasts

SERVES 4

On a gas grill, cook boneless breasts over high heat as quickly as possible to keep them moist and juicy.

½	cup kosher salt or ¼ cup table salt
½	cup sugar
4	boneless, skinless chicken breasts (1½ to 1¾ pounds), tenderloins removed and reserved for another use
1	tablespoon extra-virgin olive oil Ground black pepper

1. Dissolve the salt and sugar in 1 quart of cold water in a gallon-sized zipper-lock plastic bag. Add the chicken breasts; press out as much air as possible from the bag and seal. Refrigerate until fully seasoned, about 20 minutes.

2. Preheat the grill with all burners set to high and the lid down until the grill is very hot, about 15

minutes. Use a wire brush to scrape clean the cooking grate. Leave the burners on high.

3. Meanwhile, remove the chicken from the brine, rinse well under cold, running water, and dry thoroughly with paper towels. Toss the chicken in a medium bowl with oil to coat. Season with pepper to taste.

4. Cook the chicken, covered, smooth-side down, until dark brown grill marks appear, about 5 minutes. Turn and continue grilling, covered, until the chicken is fully cooked, 4 to 5 minutes. (If using a glaze or paste [pages 116–117], cook for 3 minutes after turning the chicken, brush the glaze or paste on both sides, and cook another minute or two, turning once.) To test for doneness, peek into the thickest part of the chicken with the tip of a small knife (it should be opaque at the center), or check the internal temperature with an instant-read thermometer, which should register 160 degrees.

5. Transfer the chicken to a serving platter. Serve hot or at room temperature, with a dipping sauce (page 115) if desired.

Charcoal-Grilled Boneless, Skinless Chicken Thighs

SERVES 4

Thighs can withstand more heat than breasts, so spread the charcoal out over just half the grill to concentrate the fire. There's no need to oil thighs before grilling—they have more internal fat than breasts and won't stick or burn.

½	cup kosher salt or ¼ cup table salt
½	cup sugar
6	boneless, skinless chicken thighs (1¼ to 1½ pounds) Ground black pepper

1. Dissolve the salt and sugar in 1 quart of cold water in a gallon-sized zipper-lock plastic bag. Add the chicken thighs; press out as much air as possible from the bag and seal. Refrigerate until fully seasoned, about 20 minutes.

2. Light a large chimney starter filled with hardwood charcoal (about 2½ pounds) and allow to burn until all the charcoal is covered with a layer of fine gray ash. Build a modified two-level fire by spreading all the

Grilled boneless breasts and thighs can be cooked with just salt and pepper and then served at the table with a highly seasoned sauce.

Moroccan-Style Sauce

MAKES ABOUT ½ CUP SAUCE,
ENOUGH FOR 4 CHICKEN BREASTS
OR 6 CHICKEN THIGHS

This sauce is modeled after charmoula sauce, which usually includes herbs, spices, garlic, and lemon juice. For more flavor, double this recipe, place half of the sauce in a wide, shallow dish (such as a pie plate), and dip the chicken in the sauce just before grilling.

2   tablespoons lemon juice
I   medium garlic clove, minced
¼   teaspoon ground cumin
¼   teaspoon sweet paprika
    Pinch cayenne pepper (more if desired)
¼   teaspoon salt
⅓   cup extra-virgin olive oil
2   tablespoons minced fresh cilantro leaves

Whisk the lemon juice, garlic, cumin, paprika, cayenne, and salt together in a small bowl. Gradually whisk in the oil; stir in the cilantro. Serve as a dipping sauce or drizzle over sliced, grilled chicken.

Lemon-Parsley Sauce with Capers

MAKES GENEROUS ⅓ CUP,
ENOUGH FOR 4 CHICKEN BREASTS
OR 6 CHICKEN THIGHS

Fresh and tangy, this sauce lends a wonderful acidity to grilled chicken. It is especially good on chicken breasts, which are leaner than thighs, allowing the clean flavor of lemon, parsley, and olive oil to come through more readily.

¼   cup chopped fresh parsley leaves
I   medium clove garlic, minced
2   teaspoons drained capers, chopped

I   tablespoon lemon juice
¼   cup extra-virgin olive oil
    Salt and ground black pepper

Mix all ingredients together in a small bowl. Serve as a dipping sauce or drizzle over sliced, grilled chicken.

Korean-Style Dipping Sauce

MAKES ABOUT ¾ CUP,
ENOUGH FOR 4 CHICKEN BREASTS
OR 6 CHICKEN THIGHS

For a Korean-style barbecue, simply divide this sauce in two and dip the chicken into the sauce before grilling. Serve the chicken, sliced, with extra sauce on the side, along with steamed plain short-grain rice and hot Korean pickles known as kimchee. Be sure to use light soy sauce, as the chicken is already well seasoned from the brine. This sauce lends itself best to boneless chicken thighs, as the strong soy flavor is balanced by the richer dark meat.

½   cup light soy sauce
2   tablespoons sugar
2   tablespoons minced fresh ginger
2   medium garlic cloves, minced
I   teaspoon hot red pepper flakes
4   scallions, whites and green parts, sliced into
    thin rounds
2   tablespoons toasted sesame seeds
2   teaspoons Asian sesame oil

Mix all ingredients together in a small bowl. Serve as a dipping sauce with sliced, grilled chicken.

coals over half of the grill. Set the cooking rack in place, cover the grill with the lid, and let the rack heat up, about 5 minutes. Use a wire brush to scrape clean the cooking grate. The grill is ready when you have a hot fire. (See how to gauge heat levels on page 19.)

3. Meanwhile, remove the chicken from the brine, rinse well under cold, running water, and dry thoroughly with paper towels. Season with pepper to taste.

4. Cook the chicken, uncovered, smooth-side down, directly over the hot coals until the chicken is opaque about two-thirds up the sides and rich brown grill marks appear, about 4 minutes. Turn and continue grilling until the chicken is fully cooked, another 4 minutes. (If using a glaze or paste [see this page and next], cook for 3 minutes after turning the chicken, brush the glaze or paste on both sides, and cook another minute or so, turning once). To test for doneness, peek into the thickest part of the chicken with the tip of a small knife (it should be opaque at the center), or check the internal temperature with an instant-read thermometer, which should register 165 degrees.

5. Transfer the chicken to a serving platter. Serve hot or at room temperature, with a dipping sauce (page 115) if desired.

Gas-Grilled Boneless, Skinless Chicken Thighs

SERVES 4

To produce the hot fire needed to cook the chicken quickly, keep the grill at the highest possible setting.

½   cup kosher salt or ¼ cup table salt

½   cup sugar

6   boneless, skinless chicken thighs
     (1¼ to 1½ pounds)
     Ground black pepper

1. Dissolve the salt and sugar in 1 quart of cold water in a gallon-sized zipper-lock plastic bag. Add the chicken thighs; press out as much air as possible from the bag and seal. Refrigerate until fully seasoned, about 20 minutes.

2. Preheat the grill with all burners set to high and the lid down until the grill is very hot, about 15 minutes. Use a wire brush to scrape clean the cooking grate. Leave the burners on high.

3. Meanwhile, remove the chicken from the brine, rinse well under cold, running water, and dry thoroughly with paper towels. Season with pepper to taste.

4. Cook the chicken, covered, smooth-side down, until dark brown grill marks appear, about 5 minutes. Turn and continue grilling, covered, until the chicken is fully cooked, about 5 minutes. (If using a glaze or paste [see this page and next], cook for 3 minutes after turning the chicken, brush the glaze or paste on both sides, and cook another minute or so, turning once). To test for doneness, peek into the thickest part of the chicken with the tip of a small knife (it should be opaque at the center), or check the internal temperature with an instant-read thermometer, which should register 165 degrees.

5. Transfer the chicken to a serving platter. Serve hot or at room temperature, with a dipping sauce (page 115) if desired.

GLAZES AND PASTES FOR BONELESS CHICKEN

THICK GLAZES AND SPICE PASTES ARE APPLIED while the chicken breasts or thighs are still on the grill. About two minutes before chicken is cooked through, brush the glaze or paste on both sides of the meat and allow to cook another minute or so, turning once.

Prepared or homemade barbecue sauce (use any of the tomato-based sauces in chapter 19) can be used in the same manner. One recipe of grilled boneless, skinless chicken breasts or thighs will require about one-half cup of barbecue sauce.

Smoky Orange Chile Glaze

MAKES ½ CUP, ENOUGH FOR
4 CHICKEN BREASTS OR 6 CHICKEN THIGHS

Chipotle peppers add a smoky, hot flavor to plain chicken breasts or thighs. Orange zest and juice, cilantro, molasses, and a touch of lime add sweet and sour notes that balance the heat and smoke of the peppers.

4   chipotle chiles in adobo sauce, roughly
     chopped (about 2½ tablespoons) with
     2 tablespoons adobo sauce

I	teaspoon grated orange zest
2	tablespoons orange juice
1/4	cup lightly packed cilantro leaves
2	teaspoons molasses
3	tablespoons vegetable oil
I	lime, cut into 8 wedges

1. Place the chipotle chiles, adobo sauce, zest, juice, cilantro, and molasses into the workbowl of a food processor and puree until smooth. Slowly add the oil in a thin stream until incorporated.

2. Apply the glaze as directed in one of the recipes for boneless chicken. Serve the grilled chicken with lime wedges.

Sweet Onion, Balsamic, and Rosemary Glaze

MAKES 1/2 CUP, ENOUGH FOR
4 CHICKEN BREASTS OR 6 CHICKEN THIGHS

Balsamic vinegar makes a lovely glaze when combined with rosemary, onions, and garlic. As with all other glazes, it should be applied to the chicken during the last few minutes of cooking—just long enough for the glaze to caramelize slightly. This glaze is also good on grilled vegetables, such as zucchini, peppers, and eggplant; make extra glaze and cook the vegetables alongside the chicken to serve as a side dish.

I	tablespoon extra-virgin olive oil
I	medium onion, finely chopped
I	teaspoon sugar
I	medium garlic clove, minced
2	teaspoons minced fresh rosemary
1/4	cup balsamic vinegar
1/2	cup canned low-sodium chicken broth
I	teaspoon honey

1. Heat the oil in a medium skillet over medium-high heat until shimmering. Add the onion and cook until brown around the edges, 4 to 5 minutes. Reduce the heat to medium-low, add the sugar, and cook until the onions are a deep golden color and caramelized, 4 to 5 minutes longer. Add the garlic and rosemary and cook until fragrant, about 1 minute.

2. Return the heat to medium-high; add the vinegar, broth, and honey and bring to a boil. Reduce to medium heat and simmer until the mix-

ture reduces to a syrupy consistency, another 4 to 5 minutes. Remove the pan from the heat and cool to room temperature.

3. Apply the glaze as directed in one of the recipes for boneless chicken.

Maple Mustard Glaze

MAKES 1/2 CUP, ENOUGH FOR
4 CHICKEN BREASTS OR 6 CHICKEN THIGHS

Sharp and sweet, the combination of real maple syrup and whole grain mustard makes a delicious sweet and sour glaze that can be quickly made while the chicken is cooking on the grill. Because of the high level of sugar in this glaze, make sure to watch the chicken very carefully once the glaze has been applied. This glaze is also delicious with pork.

1/4	cup maple syrup
1/3	cup whole grain mustard
I	teaspoon balsamic vinegar

Mix all ingredients together in a small bowl. Apply the glaze as directed in one of the recipes for boneless chicken.

Simple Spice Paste

MAKES 1/4 CUP, ENOUGH FOR 4 CHICKEN
BREASTS OR 6 CHICKEN THIGHS

2	teaspoons ground cumin
I	teaspoon chili powder
1/2	teaspoon brown sugar
1/2	teaspoon dried oregano
1/2	teaspoon ground black pepper
1/2	teaspoon ground cinnamon
	Pinch cayenne pepper, or more if desired
	2 tablespoons vegetable oil
	I teaspoon lime juice

Mix all ingredients together in a small bowl. Apply the glaze as directed in one of the recipes for boneless chicken.

Butterflied Chicken

REMOVING THE BACKBONE FROM A WHOLE chicken—a process known as butterflying—may seem like an unnecessary and time-consuming process. But we have found that this relatively quick and simple procedure provides many benefits, because it leaves the bird with a more even thickness. Basically, butterflying lets you grill a whole chicken in much the same way that you grill parts.

A flattened three-pound chicken cooks in half an hour or less, whereas a whole grill-roasted bird requires 1½ hours of cooking. (Grill-roasting is a slower method of cooking using indirect heat. To grill-roast a chicken, see chapter 16.) In addition, because the breast isn't sticking out exposed to the heat while the legs are tucked under and away from the heat, all the parts of a flattened bird get done at the same time. Finally, unlike a whole roasted chicken, butterflied chicken is a breeze to separate into sections when carving. One cut down the breast with the kitchen shears, a quick snip of the skin holding the legs, and the job is done (see page 120).

Most recipes for butterflied chicken call for weighting the bird on the grill to promote fast, even cooking. The chicken is covered with a jelly roll pan and weighted down with heavy cans or bricks. We grilled butterflied chicken with and without weights and found that the weighted bird cooked more quickly and looked more attractive.

We still had a number of questions about the butterflying and cooking. Was it necessary to cut slits on either side of the breast so that we could tuck in each leg? And did we really need to pound the chicken after we butterflied it, or was it enough to just flatten it with our hands? Finally, we wanted to know if we could season the chicken with herbs and garlic without having the seasonings burn on the grill.

We quickly discovered that tucking the chicken legs under was worth the effort, if only for visual appeal. Chickens cooked with untucked legs tended to bow and warp.

We thought pounding the chicken might decrease cooking time, but it made no noticeable difference. However, it was easier to weight a chicken that had been pounded to a uniform thickness. We also liked the look of the really flattened chicken.

We used a mallet with a flat side for this purpose, but whatever tool you use, make sure it has a smooth face. A rough-textured mallet will tear the chicken and give it a pockmarked appearance.

Seasoning the outside of the chicken with herbs and garlic proved to be pointless; the herbs charred and the garlic burned. But butterflied chickens are especially easy to season under the skin. Since the backs are removed, access to the legs and thighs is easy. Barbecue sauces and glazes can be brushed onto the skin once the chicken is nearly done. After just two or three minutes on the grill, the glaze will caramelize nicely and give the skin excellent flavor.

Many recipes call for turning the chicken several times on the grill. Since it is weighted, this is cumbersome. If possible, we wanted to turn the bird just once. We found that one turn was fine as long as the chicken was started skin-side up on a charcoal grill. Every time we started the chicken skin-side down, the skin burned because the grill was a bit too hot. The opposite was true on a gas grill. We found it worked better to start the chicken skin-side down for the best coloring. If we started the bird skin-side up, the grill surface had cooled by the time the bird was flipped and the skin on the cooked chicken looked a bit anemic.

INGREDIENTS: Big Chickens Not Advised

We tested a variety of chicken sizes and found that small chickens (3 to 3½ pounds) work best for butterflying. Larger chickens take longer to cook through to the bone, so that the skin is exposed to the heat that much longer. We found that burning was a real problem with larger chickens.

While larger chickens are best cooked by other methods, Cornish game hens are excellent candidates for butterflying, especially when there are only two people for dinner. The cooked hen can be cut along the breast into two pieces, each sufficient as a main course serving, especially if side dishes are plentiful.

Use a 1½ pound Cornish game hen in any of the recipes in this section, halving the herb paste and adjusting the cooking time as follows: On charcoal, grill for 12 minutes with the skin-side up, followed by 10 minutes with the skin-side down; on gas, grill for 12 minutes with the skin-side down, followed by 10 to 12 minutes with the skin-side up.

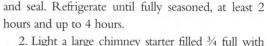

Charcoal-Grilled Butterflied Chicken

SERVES 4

We tested this recipe several times with a 3-pound chicken. Although grilling conditions vary, each time we cooked the chicken, it was done in less than 30 minutes—12 minutes on one side and 12 to 15 minutes on the other. For chickens that weigh closer to 3½ pounds, plan on the full 15 minutes once the chicken has been turned.

¾	cup kosher salt or 6 tablespoons table salt
¾	cup sugar
1	whole chicken (3 to 3½ pounds), butterflied (see illustrations below)
	Ground black pepper

1. Dissolve the salt and sugar in 1 quart of cold water in a gallon-sized zipper-lock plastic bag. Add the chicken; press out as much air as possible from the bag and seal. Refrigerate until fully seasoned, at least 2 hours and up to 4 hours.

2. Light a large chimney starter filled ¾ full with hardwood charcoal (about 2 pounds); let burn until all charcoal is covered with a layer of fine gray ash. Build a single-level fire by spreading the coals evenly over the bottom of the grill. Set the cooking rack in place, cover the grill with the lid, and let the rack heat up, about 5 minutes. Use a wire brush to scrape clean the cooking grate. The grill is ready when the coals are medium-hot. (See how to gauge heat level on page 19.)

3. Meanwhile, remove the chicken from the brine, rinse well, dry thoroughly with paper towels, and season with pepper to taste. Reposition chicken parts if necessary.

4. Place the chicken, bone-side down, on the grill rack. Set a jelly roll or other flat pan on top of chicken; put 2 bricks in the jelly roll pan (see illustration on page 121). Grill until the chicken is deep brown, about 12 minutes. Turn the chicken with tongs.

BUTTERFLYING A CHICKEN

1. With the breast-side down and the tail of the chicken facing you, use poultry shears to cut along one side of the backbone down its entire length.

2. With the breast side still down, turn the neck end to face you and cut along the other side of the backbone and remove it.

3. Turn the chicken breast-side up; open the chicken out on the work surface. Use the palm of your hand to flatten it.

4. Make ½-inch slits on either side of each breast about 1 inch from the tip; tuck the legs into these openings.

5. Use the smooth face of a mallet to pound the chicken to a fairly even thickness.

Replace the jelly roll pan and bricks, and continue cooking until the chicken juices run clear and an instant-read thermometer inserted deep into the thigh registers 165 degrees, 12 to 15 minutes more.

5. Remove the chicken from the grill, then cover with foil and let rest for 10 to 15 minutes. Carve (see below) and serve.

Gas-Grilled Butterflied Chicken

SERVES 4

Because the heat is less intense on a gas grill, the chicken can be started skin-side down. Since the grill surface is a bit hotter when the chicken first hits it, we found that the skin browns better when compared with birds started skin-side up.

¾ **cup kosher salt or 6 tablespoons table salt**

¾ **cup sugar**

I **whole chicken (3 to 3½ pounds), butterflied (see illustrations on page II9)**
    Ground black pepper

1. Dissolve the salt and sugar in 1 quart of cold water in a gallon-sized zipper-lock plastic bag. Add the chicken; press out as much air as possible from the bag and seal. Refrigerate until fully seasoned, at least 2 hours and up to 4 hours.

2. Preheat the grill with all burners set to high and the lid down until the grill is very hot, about 15 minutes. Use a wire brush to scrape clean the cooking grate. Turn all burners down to medium.

3. Meanwhile, remove the chicken from the brine, rinse well, dry thoroughly with paper towels, and season with pepper to taste. Reposition chicken parts if necessary.

4. Place the chicken, skin-side down, on the grill rack. Set a jelly roll or other flat pan on top of chicken; put 2 bricks in the jelly roll pan (see illustration on page 121). Cover and grill until the chicken skin is deep browned and shows grill marks, 12 to 15 minutes. Turn the chicken with tongs. Replace the jelly roll pan, bricks, and grill lid, and continue cooking until the chicken juices run clear and an instant-read thermometer inserted deep into the thigh registers 165 degrees, about 15 minutes more.

5. Remove the chicken from the grill, then cover with foil and let rest for 10 to 15 minutes. Carve (see below) and serve.

➤ VARIATIONS

Butterflied Chicken with Chipotle, Honey, and Lime

A spicy paste (made with smoky chipotle chiles) is rubbed under the chicken skin before cooking, and a sweet-and-sour honey/lime juice glaze is applied once the chicken is almost done.

Mix 3 minced chipotle chiles in adobo sauce, 2 teaspoons minced cilantro leaves, and ½ teaspoon grated lime zest together in a small bowl. Whisk 3 tablespoons lime juice and 2 tablespoons honey together in another small bowl. Follow the recipe for Charcoal-Grilled or Gas-Grilled Butterflied Chicken, brining, rinsing, and drying the chicken as direct-

CARVING A BUTTERFLIED CHICKEN

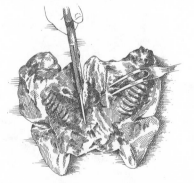

1. Place chicken skin-side down and use kitchen shears to cut through the breastbone. (Since the breastbone is broken and the meat is flattened during pounding, this should be easy.)

2. Once the breast has been split, only the skin holds the portions together. Separate each leg and thigh from each breast and wing.

ed. Rub the chile mixture under the skin of the breasts, thighs, and legs. Reposition chicken parts and season with ground black pepper. Grill as directed, brushing both sides of the chicken with the honey/lime juice glaze during the last 2 minutes of cooking time.

Butterflied Chicken with Pesto

Classic basil pesto is delicious, but feel free to use almost any herb paste, including pesto made with cilantro, arugula, or mint. Store-bought pesto works well in this recipe.

Follow the recipe for Charcoal-Grilled or Gas-Grilled Butterflied Chicken, brining, rinsing, and drying the chicken as directed. Rub ½ cup Classic Pesto (page 294) under the skin of the breasts, thighs, and legs. Reposition chicken parts and season with pepper. Grill as directed.

Butterflied Chicken with Barbecue Sauce

Use one of the tomato-based barbecue sauces in chapter 19 or store-bought sauce if you like.

Follow the recipe for Charcoal-Grilled or Gas-Grilled Butterflied Chicken, brushing both sides of the chicken with ⅓ cup barbecue sauce during the last 2 minutes of the cooking time.

WEIGHTING A BUTTERFLIED CHICKEN

To weight a butterflied chicken while it grills, find an old jelly roll pan or cookie sheet and set it on top of the chicken. Put 2 bricks in the pan.

Butterflied Chicken with Green Olive Tapenade

The tapenade is pretty salty, so make sure to rinse the chicken very thoroughly after brining.

Pulse 10 large pitted Spanish green olives, 1 chopped garlic clove, 2 anchovy fillets, 1 teaspoon drained capers, and 3 tablespoons extra-virgin olive oil in a food processor until the mixture becomes a slightly chunky paste (do not overprocess). Follow the recipe for Charcoal-Grilled or Gas-Grilled Butterflied Chicken, brining, rinsing, and drying the chicken as directed. Rub the olive mixture under the skin of the breasts, thighs, and legs. Reposition chicken parts and season with pepper. Grill as directed.

Butterflied Chicken with Lemon and Rosemary

An Italian classic. Try other herbs, including oregano, sage, thyme, or marjoram, in place of the rosemary.

Mix 2 teaspoons minced lemon zest, 2 minced garlic cloves, and 1 teaspoon minced fresh rosemary together in a small bowl. Whisk 3 tablespoons lemon juice and 3 tablespoons extra-virgin olive oil together in another small bowl. Follow recipe for Charcoal-Grilled or Gas-Grilled Butterflied Chicken, brining, rinsing, and drying the bird as directed. Rub the lemon zest, garlic, and rosemary mixture under the skin of the breasts, thighs, and legs. Reposition chicken parts and season with pepper. Grill as directed, brushing both sides of the chicken with the lemon-oil mixture during the last 2 minutes of cooking time.

9
DUCK BREASTS, QUAIL, AND SQUAB

THERE'S A REASON WHY CHICKEN IS SO popular. The combination of crisp, well-browned skin and tender, juicy meat holds plenty of attraction. But there are occasions when you may not want to serve "plain old chicken." The birds covered in this chapter offer a nice alternative.

Whole quail and squab are small enough that they can be grilled. (Other whole birds are too large to cook through by means of direct cooking, so they must be cooked by the slower, lower-level heat of grill-roasting. See page xiii for definitions of grilling and grill-roasting. Grill-roasting larger whole birds is covered in chapter 16.) While a whole duck is an ideal candidate for grill-roasting, boneless breasts— an item made popular by restaurant chefs but increasingly available at butcher shops—are thin enough to grill much as you would chicken breasts.

A note about the recipes in this chapter. The basic recipes call for very simple seasoning. The variations, however, are more complex (and sophisticated) than most of the other recipes in this book, reflecting the way we think people will want to prepare these fancy birds.

Duck, quail, and squab are prone to flare-ups, so stick close by the grill and be ready to slide foods to a cool part of the grill or douse flames with water from a spray bottle.

Although some supermarkets carry these birds, you are more likely to find them at a butcher shop.

DUCK BREASTS

THE DEMAND FOR DUCK BREASTS HAS BEEN fueled by their popularity with chefs. In response to restaurant patrons who want to re-create these dishes at home, boneless duck breasts have become a standard item in a number of supermarkets and most butcher shops. Unfortunately, restaurant recipes rarely work for home cooks (professional equipment for cooking meat, such as an indoor grill or a salamander [a high-powered broiler], is completely different from home options), and few duck breast recipes have been published in cookbooks. With little good information to begin with, we wanted to figure out how to grill this special cut.

Depending on the variety of duck, an entire breast can weigh anywhere from 12 to 20 ounces. The most commonly available size is 12 ounces, which splits neatly into two breast halves, each weighing about 6 ounces—an ideal serving for one person.

Duck breast meat is firm and flavorful and tastes best when cooked to medium-rare, 140 degrees measured on an instant-read thermometer. Although health experts recommend cooking all poultry, including duck, to at least 160 degrees, we find that duck breast cooked to this stage is akin to a well-done steak. If you are concerned about eating medium-rare duck breast, roast a whole duck, which should be cooked to an internal temperature well above 160 degrees in order to render the fat.

Speaking of fat, the skin on a duck breast adds flavor and a pleasantly crisp texture when prepared correctly. However, when we prepared many recipes in the past, the skin has been flabby or chewy and there has been way too much of it. We knew the skin was going to be a central theme in our testing.

At first, we simply seasoned a duck breast with a little salt and pepper and grilled it. As might be expected, the flare-ups were soon out of control. We tried to rescue the meat, but by the time we contained the inferno the duck breasts were charred. This failure clearly illustrated the need to remove some of the fat.

When we removed the excess fat (bits hanging off the meat itself), the results were better. The skin that remained became fairly crisp and there were no flare-ups. Several sources suggest scoring the skin with a sharp knife to help render more fat. When we tried this, we found that the skin cooked up crisper and with very little chewiness. Some of our testers, though, still thought the skin was overpowering the meat; it was delicious, but the meat seemed like an afterthought. When we removed all but a two-inch-wide strip of skin at the center of the duck breast, everyone reacted positively. The balance between skin and meat was just right.

With the skin issue settled, we next focused on the heat level. We wondered if duck breasts would respond best to high heat or if indirect or medium heat might render more fat and cook the breasts more evenly. Indirect heat did not work because the skin did not crisp up. The same thing happened over a medium-low fire. Clearly, we needed a fairly hot (but not scorching) fire to crisp the skin and cook the breasts quickly before they had time to dry out. A medium-hot fire crisped up the skin and cooked the meat perfectly.

With our testing almost done, we stumbled upon one last trick. We let one batch go skin-side down too long. Thinking that we had ruined the breasts, we turned them back over and finished cooking for a few minutes. To our surprise, the meat was perfectly cooked and the skin was even crisper than before. Upon reflection, we realized that it makes sense to cook the duck breast longer on the skin side. The extra cooking time renders more fat, and, because the skin protects the meat from the heat, the meat is less likely to dry out.

A final set of tests revolved around flavoring the duck before grilling. We tried several marinades but were unimpressed. Unlike chicken, duck has so much intrinsic flavor that it does not need a big boost. Salt and pepper are adequate, although a spice rub or simple paste (such as the tapenade on page 126) is certainly appropriate as well.

It's best to let cooked duck breast rest several minutes under foil before carving. As with beef, the meat redistributes and holds onto its juices better if allowed to rest. As for carving, we like to cut the breast on the diagonal into half-inch slices and then fan the slices out over a plate. Of course, you can serve the duck breast halves whole (like chicken cutlets) and let diners cut their own meat, but the sliced presentation is attractive and works especially well with sauces or chutneys.

Charcoal-Grilled Duck Breasts

SERVES 4

Trimmed and scored duck breasts may be rubbed with a mixture of spices (see the curry variation) or simply sprinkled with salt and pepper before being placed on the grill.

> 2   whole boneless duck breasts (about 12 ounces each), split and trimmed of excess skin and fat; remaining skin scored 3 or 4 times diagonally (see illustrations on page 127)
> Salt and ground black pepper

1. Light a large chimney starter filled with hardwood charcoal (about 2½ pounds) and allow to burn until all the charcoal is covered with a layer of fine gray ash. Build a single-level fire by spreading the coals evenly over the bottom of the grill. Set the cooking rack in place, cover the grill with the lid, and let the rack heat up, about 5 minutes. Use a wire brush to scrape clean the cooking rack. The grill is ready when the coals are medium-hot. (See how to gauge heat level on page 19.)

2. Sprinkle the duck breasts with salt and pepper to taste. Place the duck breasts, skin-side down, on the grill. Grill the duck breasts, uncovered, until the skin is nicely browned, about 8 minutes. Turn the duck breasts and continue grilling until medium-rare (an instant-read thermometer inserted into the thickest part of the breast will read 140 degrees), 3 to 4 minutes more.

3. Remove the breasts from the grill, tent with foil, and let rest for 5 minutes. Slice the breasts diagonally into eight slices, ½ inch thick, and fan a sliced breast half on each dinner plate. Serve immediately.

Gas-Grilled Duck Breasts

SERVES 4

Trimmed and scored duck breasts may be rubbed with a mixture of spices (see the curry variation) or simply sprinkled with salt and pepper before being placed on the grill. Duck breasts tend to cause flare-ups on a gas grill. Be ready to move duck breasts to a cooler spot on the grill if flare-ups occur in the first half of the cooking time.

> 2   whole boneless duck breasts (about 12 ounces each), split and trimmed of excess skin and fat; remaining skin scored 3 or 4 times diagonally (see illustrations on page 127)
> Salt and ground black pepper

1. Preheat the grill with all the burners set to high and the lid down until the grill is very hot, about 15 minutes. Use a wire brush to scrape clean the cooking rack. Turn the burners down to medium-high.

2. Sprinkle the duck breasts with salt and pepper to taste. Place the duck breasts, skin-side down, on the grill. Grill the duck breasts, covered, until the skin is nicely browned, about 8 minutes. Turn the duck breasts and continue grilling, covered, until medium-rare (an instant-read thermometer inserted into the thickest part of the breast will read 140 degrees), 3 to 4 minutes more.

3. Remove the breasts from the grill, tent with foil, and let rest for 5 minutes. Slice the breasts diagonally

into eight slices, ½ inch thick, and fan a sliced breast half on each dinner plate. Serve immediately.

➤ VARIATIONS

Curried Grilled Duck Breasts

Serve with Cucumber Salad with Yogurt and Mint (page 303) or Fresh Mango Salsa (page 302).

Combine 2 tablespoons curry powder, ½ teaspoon salt, and ¼ teaspoon ground black pepper in a small bowl. Follow recipe for Charcoal-Grilled or Gas-Grilled Duck Breasts, rubbing breasts with curry mixture instead of salt and pepper. Proceed as directed.

Grilled Duck Breasts with Peach-Habanero Chutney

An extremely spicy habanero chile provides the heat in this fruit chutney. Be very careful when working with this pepper. We recommend using thin plastic gloves when coring, seeding, and mincing it. If you cannot find a habanero, substitute one whole serrano or jalapeño chile. Leave the seeds in if you like it spicy; omit them for a milder sauce.

1½	tablespoons vegetable oil
1	medium red onion, chopped fine
2	medium ripe but firm peaches, halved, pitted, and chopped
½	medium habanero chile, stemmed, seeded, and finely minced
¼	teaspoon ground ginger
	Pinch ground allspice
	Pinch ground cloves
¼	cup light brown sugar
¼	cup red wine vinegar
1	tablespoon thinly slivered fresh mint leaves
1	recipe Charcoal-Grilled or Gas-Grilled Duck Breasts

1. Heat the oil in a medium saucepan over medium heat until shimmering. Add the onion and cook until soft, about 7 minutes. Add the peaches and cook until they are soft but still intact, about 4 minutes longer. Add the chile and spices and cook until fragrant, about 1 minute longer. Stir in the brown sugar and vinegar and bring to a simmer. Reduce the heat to low and simmer until liquid is very thick and syrupy, about 9 minutes. Transfer the mixture to a heatproof bowl and cool to room temperature. Stir in the mint and set the chutney aside. (The chutney can be refrigerated in an airtight container for several days.)

2. Grill and slice the duck breasts as directed. Serve with chutney on the side.

Grilled Duck Breasts with Pickled Ginger Relish

Simple, fresh-tasting pickled ginger relish offsets the richness of duck breast. You can usually find Japanese pickled ginger in the Asian section of the supermarket or at Asian specialty food stores. Serve with steamed rice.

4	tablespoons finely chopped pickled ginger
2	medium scallions, sliced thin
1	tablespoon minced fresh cilantro leaves
¼	cup rice vinegar
2	tablespoons sugar
2	teaspoons Asian sesame oil
¼	cup vegetable oil
1	recipe Charcoal-Grilled or Gas-Grilled Duck Breasts

1. Mix together the ginger, scallions, cilantro, vinegar, sugar, sesame oil, and vegetable oil in a medium bowl.

2. Grill and slice the duck breasts as directed. Drizzle some ginger relish over the duck slices and serve immediately.

Grilled Duck Breasts with Tapenade

Tapenade is a Provençal spread, or condiment, consisting of olives, capers, garlic, and anchovies. Here, half of the tapenade is rubbed onto the duck breast before it is grilled (do not be alarmed if some of it sticks to the cooking grate; its flavor will still infuse the meat), and the other half can be eaten alongside the sliced meat. Grilled bread is a great accompaniment to the duck. (Try Bruschetta with Fresh Herbs on page 223.) The tapenade can be spread atop the bread as well.

1	cup kalamata olives, pitted
2	small garlic cloves, peeled and chopped
4	anchovy fillets, chopped
2	teaspoons drained capers
¼	cup extra-virgin olive oil
1	recipe Charcoal-Grilled or Gas-Grilled Duck Breasts (without salt and pepper)

1. Place the olives, garlic, anchovies, and capers into the workbowl of a food processor and pulse one

or two times. With the motor running, drizzle the oil into the olive mixture and process until oil is incorporated. (The mixture should still be slightly chunky.) Transfer the tapenade to a small bowl and cover.

2. Follow recipe for Charcoal-Grilled or Gas-Grilled Duck Breasts, rubbing each breast with a little tapenade before grilling. Proceed as directed, serving extra tapenade at the table with the sliced duck.

QUAIL

QUAIL HAVE A RICH, MEATY FLAVOR THAT IS well suited to grilling. Grilling also crisps the skin on these small birds.

Quail meat is uniformly dark, both on the breasts and legs. Although bobwhite quail are native to this country (it is what hunters shoot), most commercial operations raise an Asian variety called Corturnix. These quail range in size from four to six ounces each, depending on where they were raised and their age at slaughter. We prefer larger quail, at least five ounces, since they are less bony and easier to eat.

Once you get quail home, you may need to remove the feet and pluck out a few remaining feathers. A thorough rinsing and drying with paper towels is also required. We tried boning quail and found that they are too small to survive this procedure. Be pre-

pared to gnaw on tiny bones when serving it.

We found it best to split the quail along the backbone in a procedure called butterflying that lets the birds lie flat on the grill. Butterflying the quail also reduces grilling time, which keeps them from drying out. A medium-hot fire gets the skin as crisp as possible.

We found that cooking the meat just until it is no longer pink is best; it will be juicier and more flavorful than when cooked further. Although it is hard to measure the temperature in the tiny thighs and breasts of these birds, we found that an internal temperature of 160 to 165 degrees was ideal. Higher temperatures will produce meat that is dry and tough.

Charcoal-Grilled Quail

SERVES 4

Cook the quail over a medium-hot fire, taking care to douse any flames with a squirt bottle and/or move the quail to a cooler part of the grill if flare-ups occur.

8   quail (about 5 ounces each), rinsed and patted dry, and prepared according to the illustrations on page 128
2   tablespoons extra-virgin olive oil
    Salt and ground black pepper

1. Light a large chimney starter filled with hardwood charcoal (about 2½ pounds) and allow to burn

PREPARING DUCK BREASTS

1. To prepare a whole boneless duck breast for grilling, first split the breast into two halves.

2. With a sharp chef's knife, trim any overhanging skin and fat from around each half. Slide fingers under the remaining skin along the length of the breast half to loosen. Turn the breast half on its side and slice off some of the skin and fat so that only a strip of skin (1½ to 2 inches) remains in the center of each breast half.

3. Using a paring knife, score the skin on each breast half diagonally 3 or 4 times to allow the fat to melt during cooking.

until all the charcoal is covered with a layer of fine gray ash. Build a single-level fire by spreading the coals evenly over the bottom of the grill. Set the cooking rack in place, cover the grill with the lid, and let the rack heat up, about 5 minutes. Use a wire brush to scrape clean the cooking grate. The grill is ready when the coals are medium-hot. (See how to gauge heat level on page 19.)

2. Meanwhile, brush the quail with oil and sprinkle with salt and pepper to taste.

3. Place the quail, skin-side down, on the grill. Grill the quail, uncovered, until well browned, 5 to 6 minutes. Turn and cook the quail until the juices run clear when the thighs are pierced with a fork, about 5 minutes, or check the internal temperature with an instant-read thermometer, which should register 160 to 165 degrees. Serve immediately.

Gas-Grilled Quail

SERVES 4

Quail is small enough to grill over a hot gas fire. Just watch the birds carefully to make sure they are not burning, and keep an eye out for flare-ups.

- 8   quail (about 5 ounces each), rinsed and patted dry, and prepared according to the illustrations below
- 2   tablespoons extra-virgin olive oil
       Salt and ground black pepper

1. Preheat the grill with all burners set to high and the lid down until the grill is very hot, about 15 minutes. Use a wire brush to scrape clean the cooking grate. Leave the burners on high.

2. Meanwhile, brush the quail with oil and sprinkle with salt and pepper to taste.

3. Place the quail, skin-side down, on the grill. Grill the quail, covered, until well browned, 6 to 7 minutes. Turn and cook the quail, covered, until the juices run clear when the thighs are pierced with a fork, about 5 minutes, or check the internal temperature with an instant-read thermometer, which should register 160 to 165 degrees. Serve immediately.

➤ VARIATIONS

Grilled Quail with Sage, Mustard, and Honey

A whole leaf of sage is tucked under the skin of each side of the breast. The quail is grilled, then glazed with mustard and honey.

Mix 3 tablespoons Dijon mustard and 3 tablespoons honey together in a bowl. Follow the recipe for Charcoal-Grilled or Gas-Grilled Quail, using your fingertip to separate the skin from the breast meat and then inserting a flat sage leaf under the skin of each side of the breastbone. (You will need a total of 16 sage leaves for 8 quail.) Oil and season the quail as directed. Grill, brushing the mustard-honey mixture over the birds during the last 2 minutes of cooking time.

PREPARING QUAIL

1. The tiny wingtips will singe on the grill. Use poultry scissors or a chef's knife to remove the tip from each wing.

2. Butterflied quail will cook more evenly on the grill. To butterfly, insert poultry or kitchen shears into the cavity and cut along one side of the backbone. The backbone is so small that there is no need to cut along the other side of the bone to remove it, as is necessary when butterflying a chicken.

3. Turn the butterflied bird skin-side up and flatten it by pressing down with your hands.

Grilled Quail with Chili-Lime Glaze

This sweet, spicy glaze is delicious with quail.

½	cup lime juice
3	tablespoons brown sugar
I	tablespoon chili powder
I	teaspoon ground cumin
2	medium garlic cloves, minced
I	recipe Charcoal-Grilled or Gas-Grilled Quail

1. Mix the lime juice, brown sugar, spices, and garlic together in a small bowl.

2. Oil, season, and grill the birds as directed, brushing the chili-lime glaze over the birds during the last 2 minutes of cooking time.

Grilled Quail with Cherry-Port Sauce

Savory grilled quail goes well with a sweet-and-sour pan sauce made with port and dried cherries. Other dried fruit, such as figs (cut into slices), raisins, or cranberries can be substituted for the cherries. Do not buy expensive port for this dish; less costly bottles will work fine. The sauce is made ahead and then finished at the last minute with the addition of butter, which enriches and binds the ingredients, and some fresh thyme.

I ½	cups ruby port
½	cup dry red wine
2	tablespoons red wine vinegar
4	medium shallots, chopped fine (½ cup)
½	cup dried tart cherries
I	recipe Charcoal-Grilled or Gas-Grilled Quail
2	tablespoons chilled unsalted butter, cut into ¼ -inch cubes
2	teaspoons minced fresh thyme leaves
	Salt and ground black pepper

1. Bring the port, red wine, vinegar, shallots, and cherries to a boil in a large skillet. Simmer over medium-high heat until syrupy, 12 to 15 minutes. Remove the pan from the heat.

2. Oil, season, and grill the birds as directed in recipe. Transfer the grilled quail to a serving platter and cover with foil.

3. Bring the port sauce back up to a simmer over medium-high heat. Reduce the heat to low and add the butter and thyme. Swirl the pan to incorporate the butter into the sauce. Remove the pan from the heat and season the sauce with salt and pepper to taste. Remove the foil from the platter and spoon the sauce over and around quail. Serve immediately.

SQUAB

A SQUAB IS A YOUNG PIGEON THAT CANNOT fly because its feathers have not developed fully. It bears little resemblance to other birds. The flesh is rich and gamy, more like venison or beef than chicken. Squab are meatier than quail, weighing about a pound each.

Given the strong flavor of squab, it's no surprise that we found strong seasonings—such as chiles and garlic—work best with this bird. Unlike other whole birds, squab are best cooked to medium-rare. The meat will be pink, and an instant-read thermometer will register about 145 degrees. If you can't stand the notion of pink poultry, you can cook squab a few minutes longer to an internal temperature of 160 degrees. The meat will be far less juicy and will resemble well-done beef in texture.

We tested grilling whole squab and found that they are difficult to cook properly. When grilled over direct heat, the skin burned before the meat was cooked. A two-level fire worked better, but we discovered an option that is easier in terms of both cooking and eating.

Semiboneless squab are available at most butcher shops and they cook much more evenly. (The wings and legs still contain bones, but the bird has been freed from the back, breast, and thigh bones.) Without these major bones, squab are much thinner and can be cooked over direct heat. Needless to say, squab with fewer bones are also easier to eat.

In our initial tests, boneless squab cooked fairly evenly, except for the back portion of the breast. The wings were preventing the breasts from lying flat against the grill. Since there's no meat on the wings, we decided to clip them before cooking. With the wings gone, the breasts cooked flat against the grill.

Charcoal-Grilled Squab

SERVES 4 AS A MAIN COURSE
OR 8 AS AN APPETIZER

We find that boneless squab (the leg and wing bones are still in place) are essential when grilling. You could bone the squab yourself, but we strongly recommend buying squab that have been boned during processing. Squab is pretty fatty, so keep a close eye on the grill and be ready to douse any flames with a squirt bottle filled with water. We feel that squab is best eaten medium-rare; cooked to a higher temperature, it becomes tough and dry. For eight appetizer portions, use kitchen shears to split the squab in half lengthwise after grilling. Serve with a fruit salsa (see chapter 19) or Curried Fruit Chutney with Lime and Ginger (page 304).

4   boneless squab (about 10 ounces each), rinsed
      and patted dry; wings removed (see illustration
      on page 131)
1   tablespoon extra-virgin olive oil
      Salt and ground black pepper

1. Light a large chimney starter filled with hardwood charcoal (about 2½ pounds) and allow to burn until all the charcoal is covered with a layer of fine gray ash. Build a single-level fire by spreading the coals evenly over the bottom of the grill. Set the cooking rack in place, cover the grill with the lid, and let the rack heat up, about 5 minutes. Use a wire brush to scrape clean the cooking grate. The grill is ready when the coals are medium-hot. (See how to gauge heat level on page 19.)

2. Meanwhile, brush the squab with oil and sprinkle liberally with salt and pepper to taste.

3. Place the squab, breast-side down, on the grill. Grill the squab, uncovered, until well browned, 5 to 7 minutes. Turn and cook the squab until medium-rare, about 4 minutes, or until an instant-read thermometer reads 145 degrees at the thickest part of the breast. (To test for doneness, peek into the thickest part of the breast with the tip of a small knife; it should be a dark rosy red color toward the center.)

4. Transfer the squab to a serving platter and serve immediately.

Gas-Grilled Squab

SERVES 4 AS A MAIN COURSE
OR 8 AS AN APPETIZER

We find that boneless squab (the leg and wing bones are still in place) are essential when grilling. You could bone the squab yourself, but we recommend buying squab that have been boned during processing. Squab is pretty fatty, so keep a close eye on the grill and be ready to douse any flames with a squirt bottle filled with water. We feel that squab is best eaten medium-rare; cooked to a higher temperature, it becomes tough and dry. For eight appetizer portions, use kitchen shears to split the squab in half lengthwise after grilling. Serve with a fruit salsa (see chapter 19) or Curried Fruit Chutney with Lime and Ginger (page 304).

4   boneless squab (about 10 ounces each), rinsed
      and patted dry; wings removed (see illustration
      on page 131)
1   tablespoon extra-virgin olive oil
      Salt and ground black pepper

1. Preheat the grill with all burners set to high and the lid down until the grill is very hot, about 15 minutes. Use a wire brush to scrape clean the cooking grate. Leave all burners on high.

2. Meanwhile, brush the squab with oil and sprinkle liberally with salt and pepper to taste.

3. Place the squab, breast-side down, on the grill. Grill the squab, covered, until well browned, 6 to 7 minutes. Turn and cook the squab until medium-rare, about 4 minutes, or until an instant-read thermometer reads 145 degrees at the thickest part of the breast. (To test for doneness, peek into the thickest part of the breast with the tip of a small knife; it should be a dark rosy red color toward the center.)

4. Transfer the squab to a serving platter and serve immediately.

➤ VARIATIONS

Asian-Style Grilled Squab on Salad with Grilled Shiitake Mushrooms

Gamy and full-flavored, squab takes well to strong flavors. Here it is paired with a soy sauce, ginger, garlic, and scallion marinade and balanced with a light green salad and grilled mushrooms. If you cut the grilled squab in half, this salad can be eaten as a light meal or as first course salad for a special occasion. For a more refined presentation, slice the squab meat off the remaining bones and then fan the slices out over the salad.

½	cup soy sauce
6	tablespoons rice vinegar
2½	tablespoons honey
1½	tablespoons minced fresh ginger
3	medium garlic cloves, minced
4	small scallions, thinly sliced (about ½ cup)
4	boneless squab (about 10 ounces each), rinsed and patted dry; wings removed (see illustration below)
8	ounces shiitake mushrooms, stems discarded, caps washed
1	small carrot
¼	cup peanut oil
4	red radishes, ends trimmed and cut into thin circles
8	cups lightly packed mesclun or other tender salad greens, washed and thoroughly dried

PREPARING SQUAB

The wings of a squab are not very meaty and can prevent the nearby breast meat from cooking properly. Use a chef's knife or poultry scissors to remove the wings before grilling squab.

1. Whisk together soy sauce, vinegar, honey, ginger, garlic, and scallions in a medium bowl; measure out ⅓ cup of this mixture and set it aside. Place the squab and mushroom caps in a gallon-sized zipper-lock plastic bag and pour the remaining soy sauce marinade over the top. Press out as much air as possible and seal the bag. Marinate the squab and mushrooms in the refrigerator for 1 hour.

2. Ready grill according to instructions in recipe for Charcoal-Grilled or Gas-Grilled Squab.

3. Meanwhile, place the carrot in the bowl of a food processor fitted with the steel blade. Pulse until chopped fine, scraping down the sides of the bowl if necessary. Add the reserved soy mixture and process until blended, about 10 seconds. With the motor running, drizzle in the oil until smooth. Transfer the dressing to a clean bowl.

4. Remove the squab and mushrooms from the marinade. Place the mushrooms and the squab, breast-side down, on the grill. Grill the squab, uncovered, until well browned, 5 to 7 minutes. Turn and cook the squab until medium-rare, about 4 minutes, or until an instant-read thermometer reads 145 degrees at the thickest part of the breast. (To test for doneness, peek into the thickest part of the breast with the tip of a small knife; it should be a dark rosy red color toward the center.) At the same time, grill the mushrooms, turning them once, until streaked with dark grill marks, about 6 minutes total. Transfer the squab to a platter when done; cover with foil. Transfer the mushrooms to a cutting board when done.

5. Cut the grilled mushrooms in half. Toss the mushrooms, radishes, mesclun, and carrot dressing in a large bowl. Divide the salad among 4 dinner plates or 8 salad plates. Place one squab (or a half, if serving as an appetizer) on each plate and serve immediately.

Grilled Squab with Greek Flavors

For this recipe, squab is marinated in a mixture of lemon juice, oregano, garlic, and olive oil, grilled, then served over slices of tomato that have been sprinkled with feta cheese. The acidity of the lemon juice balances the rich meaty flavor of the squab. To prevent major flare-ups, be sure to shake off any excess marinade before grilling. Be ready to move the bird to another part of the grill if flare-ups occur. If fresh oregano is unavailable, substitute 1¼ teaspoons dried oregano.

6 tablespoons lemon juice

3 medium garlic cloves, minced

2 tablespoons chopped fresh oregano leaves

1½ teaspoons salt

Ground black pepper

¾ cup extra-virgin olive oil

4 boneless squab (about 10 ounces each),
rinsed and patted dry; wings removed
(see illustration on page 131)

4 large tomatoes, cored and cut crosswise into
¼-inch-thick slices

4 ounces feta cheese, crumbled

1. Whisk together the lemon juice, garlic, oregano, salt, and pepper to taste in a small bowl. Whisk in the oil. Measure out ½ cup of the mixture; cover and refrigerate the remaining dressing.

2. Place the squab in a gallon-sized zipper-lock plastic bag and pour the ½ cup lemon marinade over the top. Press out as much air as possible and seal the bag. Marinate the squab in the refrigerator for 30 to 60 minutes.

3. Ready grill according to instructions in recipe for Charcoal-Grilled or Gas-Grilled Squab.

4. Remove the squab from the marinade, making sure to shake off excess marinade. Place the squab, breast-side down, on the grill. Grill the squab, uncovered, until well browned, 5 to 7 minutes. Turn and cook the squab until medium-rare, about 4 minutes, or until an instant-read thermometer reads 145 degrees at the thickest part of the breast. (To test for doneness, peek into the thickest part of the breast with the tip of a small knife; it should be a dark rosy red color toward the center.)

5. While the squab are on the grill, fan the tomato slices out on a large serving platter or on individual plates. Sprinkle with crumbled feta cheese.

6. Place the grilled squab on top of the tomatoes and drizzle with the reserved dressing. Serve immediately.

10

SHELLFISH

THIS CHAPTER COVERS THE MOST COMMONLY available shellfish, all of which are suitable for grilling. This includes shrimp, scallops, clams, mussels, oysters, lobsters, crabs, and squid. Even though shellfish cooks in a matter of minutes on the grill, it does pick up some smoky flavor that nicely complements the inherent richness and briny character of most shellfish.

It goes without saying that shellfish must be purchased from a trusted source. Many shellfish are sold alive. This means lobsters should be moving around in the tank, and oysters, clams, and mussels should be tightly shut. If the shellfish doesn't smell fresh or look fresh, it probably isn't. Given the perishability of shellfish, we suggest shopping and cooking on the same day.

SHRIMP

IT'S SAFE TO SAY THAT ANY SHRIMP YOU BUY have been frozen (and usually thawed by the retailer), but not all shrimp are the same—far from it. The Gulf of Mexico supplies about 200 million pounds of shrimp annually to the rest of the country, but three times that amount is imported, mostly from Asia and Central and South America.

After tasting all of the commonly available varieties of shrimp several times, we had little trouble declaring two favorites. Mexican whites *(Panaeus vannamei)*, from the Pacific coast, are usually the best. A close second, and often just as good, are Gulf whites *(Panaeus setiferus)*. Either of these may be wild or farm-raised. Unfortunately, these are rarely the shrimp you're offered in supermarkets. The shrimp most commonly found in supermarkets is Black Tiger, a farmed shrimp from Asia. Its quality is inconsistent, but it can be quite flavorful and firm. And even if you go to a fishmonger and ask for white shrimp, you may get farm-raised shrimp from China—a less expensive and decidedly inferior species *(Panaeus chinensis)*. (There are more than 300 species of shrimp in the world but not nearly that many have common names.)

All you can do is try to buy the best shrimp available, and buy it right. Beyond choosing the best species you can find, you should also consider some of the other factors affecting quality, described below.

Buy still-frozen shrimp rather than thawed. Because almost all shrimp are frozen at sea immediately after being caught, and because thawed shrimp start losing their flavor in just a couple of days, buying thawed shrimp gives you neither the flavor of fresh nor the flexibility of frozen. We found that shrimp stored in the freezer retain peak quality for several weeks, deteriorating very slowly after that until about the three-month point, at which point we detected a noticeable deterioration in quality. If you do buy thawed shrimp, they should smell of salt water and little else, and they should be firm and fill their shells fully.

Avoid prepeeled and deveined shrimp; cleaning before freezing unquestionably deprives shrimp of some of their flavor and texture. Everyone we asked to sample precleaned shrimp found them to be nearly tasteless. In addition, precleaned shrimp may have added tripolyphosphate, a chemical that aids in water retention and can give shrimp an off flavor.

Shrimp should have on their shells no black spots, or melanosis, which indicate that a breakdown of the meat has begun. Be equally suspicious of shrimp with yellowing shells or those that feel gritty. Either of these conditions may indicate the overuse of sodium bisulfite, a bleaching agent sometimes used to retard melanosis.

Despite the popularity of shrimp, there are no standards for size. Small, medium, large, extralarge, jumbo, and other size classifications are subjective and relative. Small shrimp of 70 or so to the pound are frequently labeled "medium," as are those twice that size and even larger. It pays, then, to judge shrimp size by the number of shrimp per pound, as retailers do. Shrimp labeled "16/20," for example, require 16 to 20 (usually closer to 20) individual specimens to make a pound. Those labeled "U-20" require fewer than 20 to make a pound. For grilling, large shrimp of 21 to 25 per pound usually yield the best combination of flavor, ease of preparation (threading a lot of shrimp is a pain), and value (really big shrimp usually cost more than $10 per pound).

Once shrimp are purchased, they need to be prepared before being cooked. Should they be peeled? Should the vein that runs down the back of each shrimp be removed?

After some initial tests, we concluded that shrimp

destined for the grill should not be peeled. The shell shields the meat from the intense heat and helps to keep the shrimp moist and tender. Try as we might, we found it impossible to grill peeled shrimp without overcooking them and making the meat dry and tough, especially the exterior layers. The only method for peeled shrimp that worked was to intentionally undercook them, but that left the inside a little gooey, something that almost no one enjoyed.

To make it easier to eat grilled shrimp, we found it useful to slit open the shells with a pair of manicure scissors. The shells still protect the meat as the shrimp cook, but they come right off at the table.

In addition to peeling, the issue of deveining generates much controversy, even among experts. Although some people won't eat shrimp that have not been deveined, others believe that the "vein"—actually the animal's intestinal tract—contributes flavor and insist on leaving it in. In our tests, we could not detect an effect on flavor (either positive or negative) when we left the vein in. The vein is generally so tiny in most medium-sized shrimp that it virtually disappears after cooking. Out of laziness, we leave it in. In very large shrimp, the vein is usually larger as well. Very large veins are unsightly and can detract from the overall texture of the shrimp, so they are best removed before cooking.

Once you've bought and prepared your shrimp, the hard part is over. Grilling is simple; as soon as the shrimp turn pink, they are done. That said, we did find it advisable to add one more step to preparation

to keep the shrimp from drying out, as they tend to do over intense dry heat. We discovered that brining—soaking the shrimp in a salt solution before cooking—which works so well with poultry (see page 102 for details) also works with shrimp. Brining causes shrimp to become especially firm and plump (we found that they may gain as much as 10 percent in water weight).

The science is fairly simple. The salt causes protein strands in the shrimp to unwind, allowing them to trap and hold onto more moisture when cooked. At its most successful, brining gives mushy shrimp

---

INGREDIENTS: Frozen Shrimp

Because most shrimp sold as "fresh" at the retail level are actually frozen shrimp that have been thawed, uncooked frozen shrimp offer the best quality to consumers. One drawback for the home cook, however, is that frozen shrimp are generally sold in five-pound blocks, which can be difficult to handle. Rather than trying to saw through a block of ice, we recommend placing the frozen block of shrimp under cold running water and pulling off individual shrimp as they become free. When you have the desired amount of shrimp separated, place what remains of the block back in the freezer and proceed with brining the partially thawed shrimp.

If you want to use frozen shrimp in any of the following recipes, place them in the brine while still frozen, adding 3½ cups cold water rather than ice water to the room-temperature salt solution. Proceed as directed in the recipe.

PREPARING SHRIMP

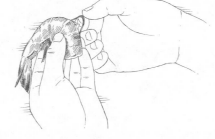

1. When grilling shrimp, we find it best to keep them in their shells. The shells hold in moisture as well as flavor as the shrimp cook. However, eating shrimp cooked in its shell can be a challenge. As a compromise, we found it helpful to slit the back of the shell with a manicure or other small scissors with a fine point. When ready to eat, each person can quickly and easily peel away the shell.

2. Slitting the back of the shell makes it easy to devein the shrimp as well. Except in cases where the vein was especially dark and thick, we found no benefit from deveining in our testing. If you choose to devein shrimp, slit open the back of the shell as in step 1. Invariably you will cut a little into the meat and expose the vein as you do this. Use the tip of the scissors to lift up the vein and then grab it with your fingers and discard.

the firm yet tender texture of a lobster tail. Even top-quality shrimp are improved by this process. We tested various concentrations of salt and brining times and in the end settled on soaking shrimp in a strong salt solution (3 cups kosher salt dissolved in 5½ cups water) for 20 to 25 minutes.

Once the shrimp have been brined, they can be threaded onto skewers and grilled. We found that shrimp should be cooked quickly to prevent them from toughening. This means using a very hot fire.

When grilling, we like to coat shrimp with a paste or marinade before cooking. The flavorings adhere to the shell beautifully. When you peel the shrimp at the table, the seasonings stick to your fingers and are in turn transferred directly to the meat as you eat it. Licking your fingers also helps.

Charcoal-Grilled Shrimp
SERVES 4 TO 6

We recommend brining the shrimp before grilling to make them especially plump and juicy. To keep the shrimp from dropping through the grill rack onto the hot coals, thread them onto skewers. You can also cook shrimp loose on a perforated grilling grid (see page 12) that rests right on the cooking grate. The problem with this method is that each shrimp must be turned individually with tongs. The shrimp are more likely to cook unevenly on a grid because it takes so long to turn them all.

3   **cups kosher salt or 1½ cups table salt**
2   **pounds large shrimp (21 to 25 count per pound)**
2   **tablespoons extra-virgin olive oil**
     Lemon wedges

1. Pour 2 cups hot water into a gallon-sized zipper-lock bag. Add the salt, stirring to dissolve, and cool to room temperature. Add 3½ cups ice water along with the shrimp and let stand 20 to 25 minutes. Drain and rinse thoroughly under cold running water. Open the back of the shells with a manicure scissors, and devein if desired (see illustrations on page 135). Toss the shrimp and oil in a medium bowl to coat.

2. Meanwhile, light a large chimney starter filled with hardwood charcoal (about 2½ pounds) and allow to burn until all the charcoal is covered with a layer of fine gray ash. Build a single-level fire by spreading the coals evenly over the bottom of the grill. Set the cooking rack in place, cover the grill with the lid, and let the rack heat up, about 5 minutes. Use a wire brush to scrape clean the cooking grate. The grill is ready when the coals are medium-hot. (See how to gauge heat level on page 19.)

3. Thread the shrimp onto skewers, then grill the shrimp, uncovered, turning the skewers once (see illustrations below), until the shells are barely charred and bright pink, 4 to 6 minutes. Serve shrimp hot or at room temperature with lemon wedges.

SKEWERING SHRIMP

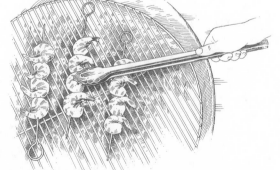

1. Thread shrimp onto a skewer by passing the skewer through the body near the tail, folding the shrimp over, and passing the skewer through the body again near the head. Threading each shrimp twice keeps it in place (it won't spin around) so it makes it easier to cook the shrimp on both sides, turning the skewer just once.

2. Long-handled tongs make it easy to turn hot skewers on the grill. Lightly grab onto a single shrimp to turn the entire skewer.

Gas-Grilled Shrimp

SERVES 4 TO 6

We recommend that you brine the shrimp before grilling to make them especially plump and juicy. To keep the shrimp from dropping through the grill rack, thread them onto skewers.

    3   **cups kosher salt or 1½ cups table salt**
    2   **pounds large shrimp (21 to 25 count per pound)**
    2   **tablespoons extra-virgin olive oil**
        Lemon wedges

1. Pour 2 cups hot water into a gallon-sized zipper-lock bag. Add the salt, stirring to dissolve, and cool to room temperature. Add 3½ cups ice water along with the shrimp and let stand 20 to 25 minutes. Drain and rinse thoroughly under cold running water. Open the back of the shells with a manicure scissors, and devein if desired (see illustrations on page 135). Toss the shrimp and oil in a medium bowl to coat.

2. Preheat the grill with all burners set to high and the lid down until the grill is very hot, about 15 minutes. Use a wire brush to scrape clean the cooking grate. Leave the burners on high.

3. Thread the shrimp onto skewers, then grill the shrimp, covered, turning the skewers once (see illustrations on page 136), until the shells are barely charred and bright pink, 5 to 6 minutes. Serve shrimp hot or at room temperature with lemon wedges.

➤ VARIATIONS

Grilled Shrimp with Spicy Garlic Paste

The garlic paste adheres perfectly to the shells and will coat your fingers as you peel and eat the grilled shrimp.

Mince 1 large garlic clove with 1 teaspoon salt to form a smooth paste (see illustration at right). Combine the garlic paste with ½ teaspoon cayenne pepper, 1 teaspoon sweet paprika, 2 tablespoons extra-virgin olive oil, and 2 teaspoons lemon juice in a medium bowl. Follow the recipe for Charcoal-Grilled or Gas-Grilled Shrimp, tossing the brined and drained shrimp with the garlic mixture instead of the oil to coat well. Thread the shrimp on skewers and grill as directed.

Grilled Shrimp with Lemon, Garlic, and Oregano Paste

The fresh oregano in this recipe can be replaced with other fresh herbs, including chives, tarragon, parsley, or basil.

Mince 1 large garlic clove with 1 teaspoon salt to form a smooth paste (see illustration below). Combine the garlic paste with 2 tablespoons extra-virgin olive oil, 2 teaspoons lemon juice, and 2 teaspoons chopped fresh oregano leaves in a medium bowl. Follow the recipe for Charcoal-Grilled or Gas-Grilled Shrimp, tossing the brined and drained shrimp with the garlic mixture instead of the oil to coat well. Thread the shrimp on skewers and grill as directed.

Grilled Shrimp with Southwestern Flavors

Serve these shrimp with warm cornbread.

Heat 2 tablespoons extra-virgin olive oil in a small skillet over medium heat. Add 2 minced garlic cloves, 2 teaspoons chili powder, and ¾ teaspoon ground cumin and sauté until the garlic is fragrant, 30 to 45 seconds. Scrape the mixture into a heatproof bowl and cool to room temperature. Mix in 2½ tablespoons lime juice and 2 tablespoons minced fresh cilantro leaves. Follow the recipe for Charcoal-Grilled or Gas-Grilled Shrimp, tossing the brined and drained shrimp with the garlic mixture instead of the oil to coat well. Thread the shrimp on skewers and grill as directed. Serve with lime wedges instead of lemon wedges.

MINCING GARLIC INTO A PASTE

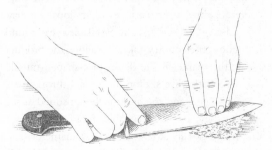

Mince garlic as you normally would on a cutting board with a chef's knife. Sprinkle the minced garlic with salt and then drag the side of the chef's knife over the garlic-salt mixture to form a fine puree. Continue to mince and drag the knife as necessary until the puree is smooth. If possible, use kosher or coarse salt; the larger crystals do a better job of breaking down garlic than fine table salt.

New Orleans-Style Grilled Shrimp

Shrimp are tossed with a spicy paste, grilled, and drizzled with a rich butter-garlic mixture.

1	teaspoon dried thyme
1	teaspoon dried oregano
1	teaspoon sweet paprika
1	teaspoon garlic powder
	Pinch cayenne pepper
½	teaspoon salt
4	tablespoons unsalted butter
2	medium garlic cloves, minced
1	recipe Charcoal-Grilled or Gas-Grilled Shrimp (omit olive oil)
1½	tablespoons vegetable oil

1. Mix thyme, oregano, paprika, garlic powder, cayenne, and salt together in a small bowl.

2. Melt butter in a small saucepan over medium heat. When the butter begins to sizzle, add the garlic and cook for 30 seconds. Remove the pan from the heat, cover, and keep warm.

3. Prepare the shrimp as directed, tossing them with vegetable oil and the spice mixture instead of olive oil. Grill shrimp, then arrange skewers on a platter. Drizzle with the butter mixture and serve with lemon wedges.

SCALLOPS

SCALLOPS OFFER SEVERAL CHOICES FOR THE cook, both when shopping and when cooking. There are three main varieties of scallops: sea, bay, and calico. Sea scallops are available year-round throughout the country. Like all scallops, the product sold at the market is the dense, disk-shaped muscle that propels the live scallop in its shell through the water. The guts and roe are usually jettisoned at sea because they are so perishable. Ivory-colored sea scallops are usually at least an inch in diameter (and often much bigger) and look like squat marshmallows. Sometimes they are sold cut up, but we found that they can lose moisture when handled this way and are best purchased whole.

Small, cork-shaped bay scallops (about one-half inch in diameter) are harvested in a small area from Cape Cod to Long Island. Bay scallops are seasonal—available from late fall through midwinter—and are very expensive, up to $20 a pound. They are delicious but nearly impossible to find outside of top restaurants.

Calico scallops are a small species (less than one-half inch across and taller than they are wide) harvested in the southern United States and around the world. They are inexpensive (often priced at just a few dollars per pound) but generally not terribly good. Unlike sea and bay scallops, which are harvested by hand, calicos are shucked by machine steaming. This steaming partially cooks the scallops and gives them an opaque look. Calicos are often sold as "bays," but they are not the same thing. In our kitchen tests, we found that calicos are easy to overcook and often end up with a rubbery, eraser-like texture.

We tested all three kinds of scallops on the grill. Sea scallops were the hands-down winner. Because they are much larger than bay or calico scallops, sea scallops can remain on the grill long enough to pick up some smoky flavor and caramelization. Smaller scallops overcook before they pick up any grill flavor and won't brown in the minute or two it takes for them to cook through.

In addition to choosing the right species, you should inquire about processing when purchasing scallops. Most scallops (by some estimates up to 90 percent of the retail supply) are dipped in a phosphate and water mixture that may also contain citric and sorbic acids. Processing extends shelf life but harms the flavor and texture of scallops. Their naturally delicate, sweet flavor can be masked by the bitter-tasting chemicals. Even worse, during processing scallops absorb water. Besides the obvious objections (why pay for water weight or processing that detracts from their natural flavor?), processed scallops are more difficult to cook. They contain so much water that they "steam" on the grill, so it's nearly impossible to get them to brown well. A caramelized exterior greatly enhances the natural sweetness of the scallop and provides a nice crisp contrast with the tender interior. It is a must.

By law, processed scallops must be identified as such at the wholesale level, so ask your fishmonger. Also, look at the scallops. Scallops are naturally ivory or pinkish tan; processing turns them bright white.

Processed scallops are slippery and swollen and are usually sitting in milky white liquid at the store. Unprocessed scallops (also called dry scallops) are sticky and flabby. If they are surrounded by any liquid (and often they are not), the juices are clear, not white.

To preserve the creamy texture of the flesh, we like to cook scallops to medium-rare, which means the scallop is hot all the way through but the center still retains some translucence. As a scallop cooks, the soft flesh firms and you can see an opaqueness that starts at the bottom of the scallop, where it touches the grill, and slowly creeps up toward the center. The scallop is medium-rare when the sides have firmed up and all but the middle third of the scallop has turned opaque.

We tried grilling plain scallops, scallops that had been blanched (a technique advocated by several sources), scallops tossed with melted butter, and scallops tossed with oil. The blanched scallops did not caramelize at all and were terrible. The plain scallops browned a bit but were dry around the edges. The scallops tossed with melted butter or oil before being cooked browned better and tasted better than plain scallops. The edges were crisp but not dry, as was the case with plain scallops.

In most cases (and in all of the recipes that follow), we prefer the sweet, nutty flavor of butter with scallops. However, oil makes sense with certain seasonings, especially Asian ingredients. Despite being coated with fat, scallops can still stick to the grill. Make sure the grill is extremely hot (a hot grill will pro-mote fast browning, too) and perfectly clean. As an added precaution, rub an oil-soaked paper towel over the grill just before placing the scallops on the grate.

Charcoal-Grilled Scallops
SERVES 4

Ask for "dry" scallops, which haven't been treated with chemicals to extend shelf life. "Dry" scallops are far sweeter and less watery, so they caramelize better on the grill. To ensure that the scallops do not stick to the cooking grate, be sure to oil the grate before starting to cook.

1 ½	pounds large sea scallops, tough tendon removed (see illustration, below left)
1 ½	tablespoons unsalted butter, melted and cooled
	Salt and ground black pepper
	Vegetable oil for grill rack
	Lemon wedges

1. Light a large chimney starter filled with hard-wood charcoal (about 2½ pounds) and allow to burn until all the charcoal is covered with a layer of fine gray ash. Build a single-level fire by spreading the coals evenly over the bottom of the grill. Set the cooking rack in place, cover the grill with the lid, and let the rack heat up, about 5 minutes. Use a wire brush to scrape clean the cooking grate.

2. Meanwhile, toss the scallops and butter together in a medium bowl. Season with salt and pepper to taste. Thread the scallops onto doubled skewers (see

PREPARING SCALLOPS

1. The small, rough-textured, crescent-shaped tendon that attaches the scallop to the shell is not always removed during processing. You can readily remove any tendons that are still attached. If you don't, they will toughen slightly during cooking and are not very appealing to eat.

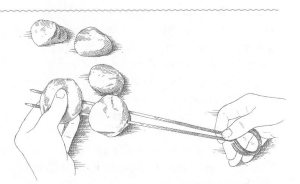

2. Thread scallops onto doubled skewers so that the flat sides of each scallop will directly touch the cooking grate. This promotes better browning on each scallop. To turn the skewers, gently hold one scallop with a pair of tongs and flip. (This method is the same as the one used for shrimp. See illustration on page 136.)

illustration on page 139) so that the flat sides of the scallops will directly touch the cooking grate. The grill is ready when the coals are medium-hot. (See how to gauge heat level on page 19.)

3. Lightly dip a small wad of paper towels in vegetable oil; holding wad with tongs, wipe grill rack (see page 45). Grill the scallops, uncovered, turning skewers once (see illustration on page 136), until richly caramelized on each side and medium-rare (sides of scallops will be firm and all but middle third of each scallop will be opaque), 5 to 7 minutes. Serve hot or at room temperature with lemon wedges.

Gas-Grilled Scallops

SERVES 4

Get the gas grill as hot as possible so the scallops will brown. Also be sure to oil the grill rack before starting to cook, to make sure the scallops do not stick to the rack.

1½	pounds large sea scallops, tough tendon removed (see illustration on page 139)
1½	tablespoons unsalted butter, melted and cooled
	Salt and ground black pepper
	Vegetable oil for grill rack
	Lemon wedges

1. Preheat the grill with all burners set to high and the lid down until the grill is very hot, about 15 minutes. Use a wire brush to scrape clean the cooking grate. Leave all burners on high.

2. Meanwhile, toss the scallops and butter together in a medium bowl. Season with salt and pepper to taste. Thread the scallops onto doubled skewers (see illustration on page 139) so that the flat sides of the scallops will directly touch the cooking grate.

3. Lightly dip a small wad of paper towels in vegetable oil; holding wad with tongs, wipe grill rack (see page 45). Grill the scallops, covered, turning skewers once (see illustration on page 136), until richly caramelized on each side and medium-rare (sides of scallops will be firm and all but middle third of each scallop will be opaque), 6 to 8 minutes. Serve hot or at room temperature with lemon wedges.

➤ VARIATIONS

Grilled Scallops with Mustard, Sherry, and Cream

A rich sherry cream sauce provides the perfect backdrop for sweet, grilled scallops. Whole-grain mustard and sherry vinegar add texture and brightness to the sauce.

1	recipe Charcoal-Grilled or Gas-Grilled Scallops
2	medium shallots, minced (about ¼ cup)
½	cup dry sherry
½	cup heavy cream
1	tablespoon whole-grain mustard
	Salt and ground black pepper
1	teaspoon sherry vinegar

1. Follow recipe for Charcoal-Grilled or Gas-Grilled Scallops through step 1, heating grill as directed.

2. While waiting for the grill to heat up, place the shallots and sherry in a small saucepan and bring to a boil over high heat. Lower the heat to medium-high and simmer until the sherry has almost evaporated, about 7 minutes. Add the cream and mustard and simmer until slightly thickened, about 2 minutes. Season with salt and pepper to taste. Remove the pan from the heat and cover to keep warm.

3. Toss the scallops with butter, salt, and pepper, thread on skewers, and grill as directed. Place the skewers with the grilled scallops on a platter.

4. Whisk the vinegar into the sauce, then drizzle the sauce over the grilled scallops. Serve immediately with lemon wedges.

Grilled Scallops with Orange-Chile Vinaigrette

For a complete meal, serve the scallops as part of a composed salad of mixed greens, crumbled bacon, diced hard-boiled eggs, and thinly sliced red onion. Make twice as much vinaigrette, using half for the scallops and half to toss with the salad greens.

1	recipe Charcoal-Grilled or Gas-Grilled Scallops
2	medium shallots, minced (about ¼ cup)
¾	cup orange juice
½	teaspoon chili powder
1	teaspoon honey
1	tablespoon red wine vinegar

⅓ cup vegetable oil
2 tablespoons minced fresh cilantro leaves
Salt and ground black pepper

1. Follow recipe for Charcoal-Grilled or Gas-Grilled Scallops through Step 1, heating grill as directed.

2. While waiting for the grill to heat, combine the shallots, orange juice, and chili powder in a small saucepan and bring to a boil over high heat. Lower the heat to medium-high and simmer until thick and syrupy, about 8 minutes. Transfer the mixture to a heatproof mixing bowl and cool to room temperature. Whisk in the honey and vinegar. Slowly whisk in the oil until the dressing is smooth. Stir in the cilantro and salt and pepper to taste.

3. Toss scallops with butter, salt, and pepper, thread on skewers, and grill as directed. Place the skewers with the grilled scallops on a platter.

4. Drizzle the dressing over the grilled scallops. Serve immediately with lemon wedges.

CLAMS, MUSSELS, AND OYSTERS

CLAMS, MUSSELS, AND OYSTERS BELONG to the group of shellfish known as bivalves (scallops are also bivalves), and they can all be grilled in the same fashion. These two-shelled creatures are easy to cook; when they open, they are done. One of the biggest challenges when cooking bivalves is making sure they are clean. Even perfectly cooked clams and mussels can be made inedible by lingering sand. (Sand is not much of an issue with oysters as long as you scrub the shells well before cooking.)

After much trial and error in the test kitchen, we concluded that it is impossible to remove all the sand from dirty clams and mussels before cooking. We tried various soaking regimens—such as soaking in cold water for two hours, soaking in water with flour, soaking in water with cornmeal, and scrubbing and rinsing in five changes of water. None of these techniques worked.

During the course of this testing, we noticed that some varieties of clams and mussels were extremely clean and free of grit. A quick scrub of the shell exterior and these bivalves were ready for the pot. After

talking to seafood experts around the country, we came to this conclusion: If you want to minimize your kitchen work and ensure that your clams and mussels are free of grit, you must shop carefully.

Clams can be divided into two categories: hard-shell varieties (such as littlenecks and cherrystones) and soft-shell varieties (such as steamers and razor clams). Hard-shells grow along sandy beaches and bays; soft-shells in muddy tidal flats. A modest shift in location makes all the difference in the kitchen.

When harvested, hard-shells remain tightly closed. In our tests, we found that the meat inside was always free of sand. The exterior of each clam should be scrubbed under cold running water to remove any caked-on mud, but otherwise these clams can be cooked without further worry about gritty broths.

Soft-shell clams gape when they are alive. We found that they almost always contain a lot of sand. While it's worthwhile to soak them in several batches of cold water to remove some of the sand, you can never get rid of it all. In the end, you must strain the cooking liquid. And sometimes you must rinse the cooked clams after shucking as well.

We ultimately concluded that hard-shell clams (that is, littlenecks or cherrystones) are worth the extra money at the market. Gritty clams, no matter how cheap, are inedible. Buying either littlenecks or cherrystones ensures that the clams will be clean.

A similar distinction can be made with mussels based on how and where they are grown. Most mussels are now farmed, either on ropes or along seabeds. (You may also see "wild" mussels at the market. These mussels are caught the old-fashioned way—by dredging along the sea floor. In our tests, we found them extremely muddy and practically inedible.) Rope-cultured mussels can cost up to twice as much as wild or bottom-cultured mussels, but we found them to be free of grit. Since mussels are relatively inexpensive (no more than a few dollars per pound), we think clean mussels are worth the extra money. Look for tags, usually attached to bags of mussels, indicating how and where the mussels were grown.

Sand is not an issue when buying oysters, but careful shopping is still very important. In general, we prefer oysters from cold northern waters, which tend to be briny and have a flavor that's more crisp than that of oysters from warmer southern waters.

When shopping, look for tightly closed clams, mussels, and oysters (avoid any that are gaping, which may be dying or dead). Clams need only be scrubbed. Mussels may need scrubbing as well as debearding. Simply grab onto the weedy protrusion and pull it out from between the shells and discard. Don't debeard mussels until you are ready to cook them, as debearding can cause mussels to die. Mussels or clams kept in sealed plastic bags or under water will also die. Keep them in a bowl in the refrigerator and use them within a day or two for best results.

While steaming is the easiest way to cook clams and mussels (oysters are often eaten raw on the half shell), grilling these bivalves is an interesting option, especially for summer entertaining. If you are cooking outside and want to throw a few clams or mussels on the grill to serve as an appetizer, we think you will be pleased with the results.

We found that it is important not to move the shellfish around on the grill and to handle them carefully once they open. You want to preserve the natural juices, so when the clams or mussels open, transfer them with tongs to a platter, holding them steady so as not to spill any of the liquid.

SERVING CLAMS, MUSSELS, AND OYSTERS

The easiest way to serve grilled clams, mussels, or oysters is to divide them among small plates and give each person a small fork. However, if you want guests to eat them while milling about the grill, try the following method.

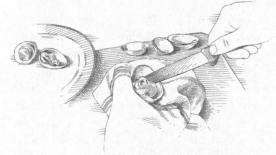

Holding each clam, mussel, or oyster in a kitchen towel as it comes off the grill, pull off and discard the top shell, then slide a paring knife under the meat to detach it from the bottom shell. By the time you have done this to each clam, oyster, or mussel, the shells should have cooled enough to permit everyone to pick them up and slurp the meat directly from the shells.

Charcoal-Grilled Clams, Mussels, or Oysters

SERVES 4 TO 6 AS AN APPETIZER

We often like to throw clams or mussels on the grill and cook them just until they open. Don't move the shellfish around too much or you risk spilling the liquor out of the shells. This cooking method delivers pure clam, oyster, or mussel flavor. If you like, serve with lemon wedges, a bottle of Tabasco or other hot sauce, and some fresh tomato salsa (see Classic Red Table Salsa on page 299).

24	clams or oysters, or 30 to 35 mussels (about 2 pounds), scrubbed and debearded if cooking mussels
	Lemon wedges, hot sauce, and/or salsa

1. Light a large chimney starter filled with hardwood charcoal (about 2½ pounds) and allow to burn until all the charcoal is covered with a layer of fine gray ash. Build a single-level fire by spreading the coals evenly over the bottom of the grill. Set the cooking rack in place, cover the grill with the lid, and let the rack heat up, about 5 minutes. Use a wire brush to scrape clean the cooking grate. The grill is ready when the coals are medium-hot. (See how to gauge heat level on page 19.)

2. Place the shellfish directly on the cooking grate. Grill, uncovered and without turning, until the shellfish open, 3 to 5 minutes for mussels and oysters or 6 to 10 minutes for clams.

3. With tongs, carefully transfer the opened shellfish to a flat serving platter, trying to preserve the juices. Discard the top shells and loosen the meat in the bottom shells before serving, if desired (see illustration at left). Serve with lemon wedges, hot sauce, and/or salsa passed separately.

Gas-Grilled Clams, Mussels, or Oysters

SERVES 4 TO 6 AS AN APPETIZER

Don't move the shellfish around too much or you risk spilling the liquor out of the shells. This cooking method delivers pure clam, oyster, or mussel flavor. If you like, serve with lemon wedges, a bottle of Tabasco or other hot sauce, and some fresh tomato salsa (see Classic Red Table Salsa on page 299).

24   clams or oysters, or 30 to 35 mussels (about 2 pounds), scrubbed and debearded if cooking mussels
Lemon wedges, hot sauce, and/or salsa

1. Preheat the grill with all burners set to high and the lid down until the grill is very hot, about 15 minutes. Use a wire brush to scrape clean the cooking grate. Leave the burners on high.

2. Place the shellfish directly on the cooking grate. Cover and grill, without turning, until the shellfish open, 4 to 6 minutes for mussels and oysters or 7 to 10 minutes for clams.

3. With tongs, carefully transfer the opened shellfish to a flat serving platter, trying to preserve the juices. Discard the top shells and loosen the meat in the bottom shells before serving, if desired (see illustration, page 142). Serve with lemon wedges, hot sauce, and/or salsa passed separately.

➤ VARIATIONS

Grilled Clams, Mussels, or Oysters with Lemon-Tabasco Butter

Have your guests remove the meat of the shellfish with small forks and dip it into this tangy, spicy butter.

4   tablespoons unsalted butter
1/4   teaspoon salt
I   tablespoon Tabasco sauce
I   teaspoon lemon juice
I   recipe Charcoal-Grilled or Gas-Grilled Clams, Mussels, or Oysters
    Lemon wedges

1. Melt the butter in a small saucepan over medium-low heat. Remove the pan from the heat and add the salt, Tabasco sauce, and lemon juice. Keep the sauce warm.

2. Grill the shellfish as directed, discarding the top shells when cooking is done. Pour the warm lemon-Tabasco butter into a small serving bowl. Serve the shellfish with the lemon-Tabasco butter for dipping, as well as with lemon wedges.

Grilled Clams, Mussels, or Oysters with Tangy Soy-Citrus Sauce

A combination of lemon and lime juices is added to light soy sauce to make a fresh, straightforward sauce for shellfish. This sauce is based on a traditional ponzu sauce from Japan, which is a simple combination of soy sauce and citron juice. Because of its clean, clear flavors, ponzu sauce is often paired with seafood.

1/2   cup light soy sauce
I   teaspoon grated fresh ginger
I   tablespoon lemon juice
I   tablespoon lime juice
I   scallion, thinly sliced into rounds
I   recipe Charcoal-Grilled or Gas-Grilled Clams, Mussels, or Oysters (without lemon wedges, hot sauce, or salsa)

1. Combine the soy sauce, ginger, citrus juices, and scallion in a small bowl. Set the sauce aside.

2. Grill the shellfish as directed, discarding the top shells when cooking is done. Drizzle the sauce over the shellfish and serve immediately.

Grilled Clams, Mussels, or Oysters with Mignonette Sauce

Bright and clean, mignonette sauce brings out the best in briny, fresh shellfish. One warning: Use this tangy sauce sparingly. A little goes a long way.

2   medium shallots, chopped fine, or 1/4 cup minced red onion
1/2   cup red wine vinegar
1 1/2   tablespoons minced fresh parsley leaves
2   tablespoons lemon juice
I   recipe Charcoal-Grilled or Gas-Grilled Clams, Mussels, or Oysters (without lemon wedges, hot sauce, or salsa)

1. Mix together the shallots, vinegar, parsley, and lemon juice in a small serving bowl.

2. Grill the shellfish as directed, discarding the top shells when cooking is done. Serve with mignonette sauce for dipping.

LOBSTER

THE IDEA OF GRILLING LOBSTERS IS CERTAINLY appealing. Smoke is an ideal complement to sweet, rich lobster meat. The problem is keeping the lobster on the grill long enough for the meat to pick up some grill flavor without drying out.

Lobsters must be split in half lengthwise before being grilled. If grilled whole, the shell will char a bit but the meat will steam and ultimately taste no different from a lobster cooked in a pot. The issue of splitting aside, we had many questions on the best way to grill a lobster. What size lobster is best for grilling? Should it be grilled plain or basted with butter or oil? Will the claws (which are not open) cook at the same rate as the exposed meat, or do they need some help?

Our initial tests clearly demonstrated the advantages of working with medium-large lobsters. Small lobsters spent so little time on the grill that they picked up almost no smoke flavor. Large lobsters were hard to position on the grill. In fact, two split three-pounders were hanging off the sides of our gas grill. The ideal lobster for grilling weighs between 1½ and 2 pounds—big enough to spend a decent amount of time on the grill but still small enough to fit on most grills.

We always remove the stomach sac and intestinal tract when cooking split lobsters. Grilling is no exception. We wondered if we should do something with the tomalley. When roasting lobsters, we often enrich the tomalley with breadcrumbs and butter. The same idea worked beautifully on the grill, as long as we waited to add the tomalley mixture until the lobster had been flipped cut-side up.

As might be expected, we found that lobsters grilled without butter were dry. A liberal basting with butter helped keep the meat tender and added a delicious flavor.

The various recipes we consulted were split on the issue of turning the lobsters. Some said it was best to cook the lobsters cut side down for maximum browning. Some said it was best to cook the lobsters cut side up for maximum juice retention.

PREPARING LOBSTER FOR GRILLING

1. With the blade of a chef's knife facing the head, kill the lobster by plunging the knife into the body at the point where the shell forms a "T." Move the blade down straight through the head.

2. Holding the upper body with one hand and positioning the knife blade so it faces the tail end, cut through the body toward the tail, making sure to cut all the way through the shell. You should have two halves now.

3. Use a spoon to remove and discard the stomach sac.

4. Remove and discard the intestinal tract.

5. Scoop out the green tomalley and transfer to medium bowl.

6. To accelerate cooking of the claws, which cook more slowly than the rest of the lobster, use the back of a chef's knife to whack one side of each claw to make a small opening.

Other sources argued for a middle ground.

We grilled lobsters cut-side up for the entire cooking time as well as cut-side down for the entire cooking time and found both methods to be problematic. The meat needs some browning for flavor, but cooking the lobsters cut-side down does promote the loss of juices and toughens the tail meat. As a compromise, we started the lobsters cut-side down, cooked them for just two minutes to keep moisture loss to a minimum, then flipped the lobsters cut-side up and continued grilling. This method also afforded us an opportunity to add the tomalley mixture and give it plenty of time to heat through.

This regimen worked fine for the tomalley, body, and tail, but the claws were a problem. Because they were not cut in half, as was the rest of the lobster, they took longer to cook. Several times we removed lobsters from the grill thinking they were perfectly cooked only to find that the claws were almost raw. Lobster sushi is an expensive mistake.

Jasper White, a consulting editor for *Cook's Illustrated* magazine and the author of *Lobster at Home* (Scribner, 1998), the definitive book on lobster cookery, suggested cracking one side of each claw to speed their cooking. (Cracking just one side of the claws minimizes the loss of juices.) He also suggested covering the claws with a disposable aluminum pie plate or roasting pan to ensure that they get cooked through. We found that both tips worked beautifully.

Our final experiment revolved around the heat level of the grill. We wondered if there was any advantage to a medium or low fire. We found that there was not. We discovered that grilling over a medium-hot fire cooks the lobsters quickly, which lets them retain more moisture than when cooked over cooler fires. A split 1½-pound lobster can be done in as little as six minutes over a blazing fire.

Charcoal-Grilled Lobsters

SERVES 4 AS AN APPETIZER,
2 AS A MAIN COURSE

Be sure not to overcook the lobster; like other shellfish, lobster meat gets tough when cooked for too long. The lobsters are done when the tomalley mixture is bubbling and the tail meat has turned a creamy opaque white. Have all garlic and parsley minced and the breadcrumbs ready before you start the grill. For the breadcrumbs, use bread that is a few days old, cut it into ½-inch cubes, and pulse the cubes in a food processor until they turn into fine crumbs. Don't halve the lobsters until the charcoal has been lit.

6	tablespoons unsalted butter, melted
2	medium garlic cloves, minced
2	live lobsters (each 1½ to 2 pounds)
2	tablespoons minced fresh parsley leaves
¼	cup fresh breadcrumbs
	Salt and ground black pepper
	Vegetable oil for grill rack
2	disposable aluminum pie plates or small roasting pans
	Lemon wedges

1. Light a large chimney starter filled with hardwood charcoal (about 2½ pounds) and allow to burn until all the charcoal is covered with a layer of fine gray ash. Build a single-level fire by spreading the coals evenly over the bottom of the grill. Set the cooking rack in place, cover the grill with the lid, and let the rack heat up, about 5 minutes. Use a wire brush to scrape clean the cooking grate. The grill is ready when the coals are medium-hot. (See how to gauge the heat level on page 19.)

2. Meanwhile, mix together the butter and garlic in a small bowl. Split the lobsters in half lengthwise, according to the illustrations on page 144, removing the stomach sac and intestinal tract. Scoop out the green tomalley and place it in a medium bowl. Using the back of a knife, whack one side of each claw, just to make an opening (this will help accelerate cooking). Add the parsley, breadcrumbs, and 2 tablespoons of the melted butter/garlic mixture to the bowl with the tomalley. Use a fork to mix together, breaking up the tomalley at the same time. Season lightly with salt and pepper to taste.

3. Season the tail meat with salt and pepper to taste. Brush the lobster halves with some of the remaining garlic butter. Take the lobsters to the grill on a large tray. Lightly dip a small wad of paper towels in vegetable oil; holding wad with tongs, wipe grill rack.

4. Place the lobsters on the grill shell-side up. Grill, uncovered, for 2 minutes. Transfer the lobsters to the tray, turning them shell-side down. Spoon the

tomalley mixture evenly into the open cavities of all four lobster halves. Place the lobsters back onto the grill, shell-side down. Baste the lobsters with the remaining garlic butter and cover the claws with disposable aluminum pie plates or roasting pans. Grill until the tail meat turns an opaque creamy white color and the tomalley mixture is bubbly and has begun to brown on top, 4 to 6 minutes.

5. Serve the lobsters immediately with lemon wedges. Use lobster picks to get meat from inside the claws and knuckles.

Gas-Grilled Lobsters

SERVES 4 AS AN APPETIZER, 2 AS A MAIN COURSE

Be sure not to overcook the lobster; like other shellfish, lobster meat gets tough when cooked for too long. The lobsters are done when the tomalley mixture is bubbling and the tail meat has turned a creamy opaque white. Have all garlic and parsley minced and the breadcrumbs ready before you start the grill. For the breadcrumbs, use bread that is a few days old, cut it into ½-inch cubes, and pulse the cubes in a food processor until they turn into fine crumbs. Even though the grill cover is down, you should still use two disposable aluminum pie plates or roasting pans to cover the claws as they cook.

6	tablespoons unsalted butter, melted
2	medium garlic cloves, minced
2	live lobsters (each 1½ to 2 pounds)
2	tablespoons minced fresh parsley leaves
¼	cup fresh breadcrumbs
	Salt and ground black pepper
	Vegetable oil for grill rack
2	disposable aluminum pie plates or small roasting pans
	Lemon wedges

1. Preheat the grill with all burners set to high and the lid down until very hot, about 15 minutes. Use a wire brush to scrape clean the cooking grate. Leave the burners on high.

2. Meanwhile, mix together the butter and garlic in a small bowl. Split the lobsters in half lengthwise, according to the illustrations on page 144, removing the stomach sac and intestinal tract. Scoop out the green tomalley and place it in a medium bowl. Using

the back of a knife, whack one side of each claw, just to make an opening (this will help accelerate cooking). Add the parsley, breadcrumbs, and 2 tablespoons of the melted butter/garlic mixture to the bowl with the tomalley. Use a fork to mix together, breaking up the tomalley at the same time. Season lightly with salt and pepper to taste.

3. Season the tail meat with salt and pepper to taste. Brush the lobster halves with some of the remaining garlic butter. Take the lobsters to the grill on a large tray. Lightly dip a small wad of paper towels in vegetable oil; holding wad with tongs, wipe grill rack.

4. Place the lobsters on the grill shell-side up. Cover and grill for 2 minutes. Transfer the lobsters to the tray, turning them shell-side down. Spoon the tomalley mixture evenly into the open cavities of all four lobster halves. Place the lobsters back onto the grill, shell-side down. Baste the lobsters with the remaining garlic butter and cover the claws with disposable aluminum pie plates or roasting pans. Close grill lid and grill until the tail meat turns an opaque creamy white color and the tomalley mixture is bubbly and has begun to brown on top, 5 to 7 minutes.

5. Serve the lobsters immediately with lemon wedges. Use lobster picks to get meat from inside the claws and knuckles.

> VARIATIONS

Grilled Lobsters with Tarragon-Chive Butter

Other fresh herbs, including chervil or cilantro, can be used to flavor the garlic butter.

Follow the recipe for Charcoal-Grilled or Gas-Grilled Lobsters, adding 2 teaspoons minced fresh chives and 1 teaspoon minced fresh tarragon to the garlic butter. Replace the parsley in the breadcrumb mixture with 2 tablespoons minced fresh chives and 2 teaspoons minced fresh tarragon leaves.

Grilled Lobsters with Chili Butter

Serve with lime wedges instead of lemon.

Follow the recipe for Charcoal-Grilled or Gas-Grilled Lobsters, adding 1½ teaspoons chili powder and ¼ to ½ teaspoon cayenne pepper to the garlic butter. Serve lobsters with lime wedges.

SOFT-SHELL CRABS

THERE ARE DOZENS OF SPECIES OF CRABS, but the blue crab, which is found in waters along the East Coast, is the most common variety. A soft-shell crab is a blue crab that has been taken out of the water just after shedding its shell. At this brief stage of its life, the whole crab, with its new, soft, gray skin, is almost completely edible and fabulously delicious.

For the cook, soft-shells are a wonderfully immediate experience; once cleaned, they demand to be cooked and eaten on the spot, so they offer a very direct taste of the sea. Because they must be cooked so quickly after they are killed and cleaned, home cooks have an advantage over restaurants. We're convinced that the best way to enjoy soft-shells is to cook them at home, where you can be sure to eat them within minutes of cleaning them.

The goal in preparing soft-shells is to get them crisp. The legs should crunch delicately, while the body should provide a contrast between its thin, crisp outer skin and the soft, rich interior that explodes juicily in the mouth. Frying delivers these results, but it is better suited to restaurants. Air pockets and water in the crab cause a lot of dangerous splattering. Grilling is a better choice for home cooks because it is safe and clean.

Grilling crabs is fairly straightforward. Since the crabs should be crisp, it's no surprise that we found high heat delivers the best results. We grilled plain crabs as well as crabs basted with melted butter and oil. The plain crabs did not crisp up as well as those basted with fat. In addition, the plain crabs stuck a bit to the grill. We felt that the flavor of melted butter tasted better with the crabs than oil. However, oil is fine for an Asian variation with a ginger and garlic sauce.

We tried soaking the crabs in milk before grilling (a tip advocated by some experts) and found that the crabs browned slightly better but that the difference was too slight to warrant the soaking time.

If you're serving crabs as a main course, count on two crabs per person. Serve one crab per person as an appetizer.

Charcoal-Grilled Soft-Shell Crabs

SERVES 4 AS A MAIN COURSE,
8 AS AN APPETIZER

Grilling is a great way to prepare crab at home, highlighting the sweetness and freshness of the crab without the fuss or mess of frying. The secret to great soft-shells is to make sure that the thin shells become crisp and appealing. In this recipe, butter and cooking over a hot fire crisp the thin shell beautifully. If you like the flavor of garlic, add 1 clove, very finely minced, to the melted butter.

8   medium-to-large soft-shell crabs, cleaned
    (see illustrations below)
4   tablespoons unsalted butter, melted
    Salt
    Lemon wedges

CLEANING SOFT-SHELL CRAB

1. Don't clean crabs until you are ready to cook. Start by cutting off the crab's mouth with kitchen scissors; the mouth is the first part of the shell to harden. You can also cut off the eyes at the same time.

2. Next, lift the pointed side of the crab and cut out the spongy off-white gills underneath; the gills are fibrous, watery, and unpleasant to eat.

3. Finally, turn the crab on its back and cut off the triangular, or T-shaped, "apron flap."

1. Light a large chimney starter filled with hardwood charcoal (about 2½ pounds) and allow to burn until all the charcoal is covered with a layer of fine gray ash. Build a single-level fire by spreading the coals evenly over the bottom of the grill. Set the cooking rack in place, cover the grill with the lid, and let the rack heat up, about 5 minutes. Use a wire brush to scrape clean the cooking grate. The grill is ready when the coals are medium-hot. (To gauge heat level see page 19.)

2. Brush both sides of the crabs with butter and season with salt to taste. Grill the crabs, uncovered, turning them every few minutes and brushing often with butter, until the shells turn orange and spotty brown and the crabs are cooked through, about 6 minutes for medium crabs, and up to 9 minutes for larger crabs. Serve immediately with lemon wedges.

Gas-Grilled Soft-Shell Crabs

SERVES 4 AS A MAIN COURSE, 8 AS AN APPETIZER

If you like the flavor of garlic, add 1 clove, very finely minced, to the melted butter. When lifting the lid to turn and baste the crabs, work quickly so the grill does not cool down too much.

8	medium-to-large soft-shell crabs, cleaned (see illustrations on page 147)
4	tablespoons unsalted butter, melted
	Salt
	Lemon wedges

1. Preheat the grill with all burners set to high and the lid down until very hot, about 15 minutes. Use a wire brush to scrape clean the cooking grate. Leave the burners on high.

2. Brush both sides of the crabs with butter and season with salt to taste. Grill the crabs, covered, turning them every few minutes and brushing often with butter, until the shells turn orange and spotty brown and the crabs are cooked through, about 7 minutes for medium crabs, and up to 10 minutes for larger crabs. Serve immediately with lemon wedges.

➤ VARIATIONS

Grilled Soft-Shell Crabs with Tabasco Butter

Tabasco sauce lends a spicy and tangy twist to soft-shell crabs.

Follow recipe for Charcoal-Grilled or Gas-Grilled Soft-Shell Crabs, stirring 1 tablespoon Tabasco sauce into the melted butter.

Grilled Soft-Shell Crabs with Tartar Sauce

Cornichons are tiny, intensely flavored pickles available jarred in most supermarkets and sold by the pound in delis. If you like, add 1 tablespoon minced fresh tarragon to give the tartar sauce a bright, anise flavor.

¾	cup mayonnaise
1½	tablespoons minced cornichons (about 3 large), plus 1 teaspoon cornichon juice
1	tablespoon minced scallion
1	tablespoon minced red onion
1	tablespoons drained capers, minced
1	recipe Charcoal-Grilled or Gas-Grilled Soft-Shell Crabs

1. Mix together the mayonnaise, cornichons and juice, scallion, red onion, and capers in a medium bowl. Cover and refrigerate the tartar sauce until the flavors blend, at least 30 minutes or up to 2 days.

2. Prepare crabs as directed. Serve the grilled crabs with tartar sauce on the side.

SQUID

"COOK IT A MINUTE OR COOK IT AN HOUR, but not in between." Chefs like to repeat this adage about squid to young cooks, and with good reason. We find that if lightly cooked, squid remains chewy but tender. However, if cooked for more than a few minutes, squid becomes tough and rubbery. Squid cooked 10 or 15 minutes is so tough it is nearly inedible. Yet, if braised in a tomato sauce or other liquid for a long time, squid will become tender again. This process may not take a full hour (a half hour will usually do), but the general sentiment behind this culinary adage is certainly true.

Since grilling squid for half an hour is not an option (it would be reduced to ashes), we knew that quick cooking was a must. After much testing, we found that squid cooks in as little as three minutes over a hot fire. In our tests, tasters consistently preferred smaller squid (no more than four inches long). These squid were more tender than larger specimens.

To promote maximum browning and even cooking, we found it best to slit the squid bodies lengthwise and then open the bodies to create a single rectangular piece of squid. These squid "steaks" lie flat on the grill, so there's no need to worry about the inside cooking more slowly than the exterior.

Small tentacles are delicious grilled. However, they tend to fall through the grill grate. Skewering them solved this problem. The tentacles taste best when quite crisp. Since they don't seem to toughen as quickly as the bodies, we found that they can be grilled for an extra minute or two without danger.

Most markets sell cleaned squid that can be ready to grill in just a few minutes. If you want to take the time, you can buy uncleaned squid. However, the cleaning process is tedious and time-consuming. While uncleaned squid may seem like a bargain at the market, there's a tremendous amount of waste (almost 50 percent), so by the time you have cleaned it, the difference in cost between cleaned and uncleaned squid is negligible.

Charcoal-Grilled Squid

SERVES 4

Be sure to use small squid (with bodies 3 to 4 inches in length), which cook more quickly and are more tender than large squid. We suggest using cleaned squid if you can find it. It saves a great deal of time. If not, follow the illustrations below, which show how to clean squid. It takes about 2¾ pounds of uncleaned squid to yield 1½ pounds of cleaned squid.

1½   **pounds cleaned squid (see illustrations below), bodies approximately 3 to 4 inches in length, prepared according to illustration on page 150**

2   **tablespoons extra-virgin olive oil**
      Salt and ground black pepper
      Lemon wedges

1. Light a large chimney starter full of hardwood charcoal (about 2½ pounds) and allow to burn until

CLEANING SQUID

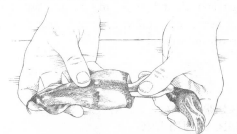

1. Reach into the body with your fingers and grasp as much of the innards as you can. Gently pull out the heart and innards.

2. You may have to make a second attempt to remove the hard, plasticlike quill; it will come out easily once you find it.

3. Cut the tentacles just above the squid's eye. Be careful of the black ink, which does stain. Discard innards.

4. Check tentacles for a beak. Squeeze out and discard beak if necessary. Reserve tentacles.

5. The thin, membranelike skin on the squid body is edible but can be easily peeled off for a white appearance.

all the charcoal is covered with a layer of fine gray ash. Build a single-level fire by spreading the coals evenly over about ⅔ of the grill bottom (confining the coals to a smaller space makes for a hotter fire). Set the cooking rack in place, cover the grill with the lid, and let the rack heat up, about 5 minutes. Use a wire brush to scrape clean the cooking grate. The grill is ready when the coals are hot. (See how to gauge heat level on page 19.)

2. Place the tentacles and bodies into a large bowl and toss with oil. Season with salt and pepper to taste. Thread the tentacles onto skewers.

3. Grill the squid bodies and tentacles, uncovered, directly over the hot coals. The bodies should be turned once during cooking; grill until curled, opaque, and lightly browned on edges, about 3 minutes. Do not overcook. The tentacles should be turned several times as they cook and are done when ends are brown and crisp, 4 to 5 minutes. Transfer the bodies to a cutting board and cut them into thin strips. The tentacles should be left whole. Serve immediately with lemon wedges.

Gas-Grilled Squid

SERVES 4

We suggest using cleaned squid if you can find it. It saves a great deal of time. If not, follow the illustrations on page 149, which show how to clean squid. It takes about 2¾ pounds of uncleaned squid to yield 1½ pounds of cleaned squid. Make sure the grill is as hot as possible so the squid will brown before it becomes tough.

1½   pounds cleaned squid, bodies approximately 3 to 4 inches in length, prepared according to illustration at right

2   tablespoons extra-virgin olive oil
     Salt and ground black pepper
     Lemon wedges

1. Preheat the grill with both burners set to high and the lid down until very hot, about 15 minutes. Use a wire brush to scrape clean the cooking grate. Leave the burners on high.

2. Place the tentacles and bodies into a large bowl and toss with oil. Season with salt and pepper to taste. Thread the tentacles onto skewers.

3. Grill the squid bodies and tentacles, covered. The bodies should be turned once during cooking; grill until curled, opaque, and lightly browned on edges, about 4 minutes. Do not overcook. The tentacles should be turned several times as they cook and are done when ends are brown and crisp, about 5 minutes. Transfer the bodies to a cutting board and cut them into thin strips. The tentacles should be left whole. Serve immediately with lemon wedges.

➤ VARIATION
Chilled Grilled Squid Salad with Lime, Red Onion, and Cilantro

This recipe is perfect for a hot summer day. It combines the smoke of the grill with the freshness of lime juice, cilantro, and red onion. Be sure to serve this salad cold.

1   recipe Charcoal-Grilled or Gas-Grilled Squid (without lemon wedges)
½   cup lime juice
2   teaspoons hot sauce, such as Tabasco
½   small red onion, sliced very thin
½   teaspoon sugar
     Salt and ground black pepper
2   tablespoons roughly chopped fresh cilantro leaves

Toss the squid, lime juice, hot sauce, red onion, sugar, and salt and pepper to taste in a large bowl. Refrigerate until chilled, about 2 hours. Stir in the cilantro and serve chilled.

PREPARING CLEANED SQUID FOR GRILLING

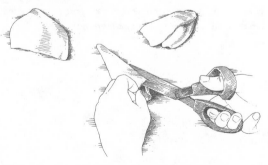

Use a pair of kitchen shears to cut lengthwise down one side of the squid body. Open the squid and flatten into a single piece for easy grilling. Wash and pat dry with paper towels.

11
FISH

FISH IS IN SOME WAYS EASY TO COOK. THE actual cooking time for most of the recipes in this chapter is under 10 minutes. That said, keeping seafood moist is a constant challenge. The most important thing you can do to ensure good results is not to overcook fish. While we like most fish cooked through (salmon and tuna are exceptions), fish that is overcooked becomes dry and overly flaky.

A few general points about fish. You must buy from a trusted source, preferably one with a high volume that ensures freshness. While cooking can hide imperfections in meat and poultry, there is little the cook can do to salvage a tired piece of salmon or tuna.

So what should you look for at the seafood shop? Fish should smell like the sea, not fishy or sour. The flesh should look bright, shiny, and firm, not dull or mushy. When possible, try to get your fishmonger to slice steaks and fillets to order, rather than buying pre-cut pieces that may have been sitting for some time and thereby lost some fluids. Avoid fish that is shrink-wrapped, since the packaging makes it difficult to examine and smell the fish. No matter how you buy fish, make sure it has been kept chilled until the minute you buy it; get fish home and into the refrigerator quickly.

This chapter is divided into two sections: the first on cooking fillets and steaks, the second on cooking whole fish. We have included only those fish you are likely to see in most fish shops and that are good candidates for grilling. Thin, flaky fish, such as flounder, are better cooked indoors. Meaty, dense, thicker fish, especially those that are a bit oily, are better suited to grilling.

FISH FILLETS AND STEAKS

FILLETS ARE PIECES OF BONELESS FISH CUT along the length of the fish from head to tail. They may be sold with or without the skin attached. Steaks usually come from larger fish and are cut across the belly of the fish. Some steaks (such as salmon steaks) have bones. However, many are not an entire cross-section of the fish but just a portion of a cross-section; these are sold off the bone.

Cooking fish fillets and steaks is easy. Because the pieces are generally thin (between ½ and 1½ inches thick), the fish is done by the time it is seared. The biggest issue is sticking. Many times we've put perfect, gleaming fillets on the grill only to have them stick and tear when we tried to turn them; this ruins the presentation of the fish, making it look like something the cat dragged in.

In developing recipes for this section, we found it useful to rub the heated grill grate with a wad of paper towels dipped lightly in vegetable oil and held by long-handled tongs. (The paper doesn't catch fire.) This extra step not only lubricates the grate but cleans off lingering residue as well, which is important given the delicate flavor and light color of most fish fillets.

We conducted several tests cooking fillets in a fish basket. A fish basket is a long-handled wire contraption that's shaped something like a sandwich press. The two rectangular halves (each half is a wire grid) sandwich the food between them. The fish is cooked in the basket on top of the grill grate. Our first attempt was a bust; the fillets browned well but stuck to the basket. We oiled the basket for the next test; this method worked better. On the downside, we found that fillets cooked in a basket did not develop as nice a crust as fillets cooked right on the grill. Also, the basket does not allow the cook to compensate for thinner or thicker fillets, or for hotter or cooler spots on the grill, since everything must be turned at the same time. We prefer to move fish around gently with a metal spatula (see illustration on page 153). If you decide to use a fish basket, remove the fish immediately from the basket once it is cooked. The skin will stick to the wire as it cools.

The other key to keeping fish from sticking is the use of a moderately hot fire. Fish grilled over a superhot fire will burn. However, if the fire is too cool, the fish will stick. In most cases, a medium-hot fire works best.

BLUEFISH FILLETS

BLUEFISH IS IN SEASON ON THE EASTERN seaboard from late spring until early fall. The fillets are gray-brown in color with a bluish tinge. Some fillets may contain a darker brown streak, which is the bloodline running down the center of the fillet.

Bluefish has a reputation for tasting fishy and oily. While this reputation is deserved, we find the flavor delicious, especially when the fish has been seasoned aggressively. In our testing, we found that lemon and a bit of mustard combat the oiliness of the bluefish. That said, bluefish will always taste somewhat oily, but we like to think of this as an asset. Bluefish doesn't dry out on the grill as easily as leaner fish such as tuna or swordfish.

Cooking bluefish is easy. We didn't have any problems with it sticking as long as the grill was hot, scraped clean, and well oiled. We tried cooking the fish in a basket but found that a basket just made the process harder. The fish actually stuck to the basket, and it didn't develop as nice a crust as it did when placed directly onto the cooking grate.

Like other thinner fish fillets, bluefish will flake, so exercise caution when turning it on the grill. Slide a metal spatula under the fillets to turn them.

Bluefish does not keep well; that "fishy" flavor becomes pronounced the longer the fish sits on ice. Make sure to buy from a reputable fishmonger with access to fresh bluefish.

Charcoal-Grilled Bluefish Fillets

SERVES 4

Acidic ingredients marry very well with oily, strong-flavored bluefish. Be sure to get bluefish as close to the catch as possible and store it over ice; this fish quickly loses its freshness. The gray-brown flesh turns white once it is cooked through.

3	tablespoons extra-virgin olive oil
1	medium garlic clove, minced
1½	tablespoons lemon juice
1	teaspoon Dijon mustard
¼	teaspoon salt
	Ground black pepper
4	skinless bluefish fillets (6½ to 7 ounces each)
	Vegetable oil for grill rack
	Lemon wedges

1. Mix the olive oil, garlic, lemon juice, mustard, salt, and pepper to taste together in a small bowl. Place the bluefish in a single layer in a large baking dish and pour the lemon-oil mixture over the fillets. Rub the mixture all over the fillets to coat evenly. Cover and refrigerate for 30 minutes.

2. Light a large chimney filled with hardwood charcoal (about 2½ pounds) and allow to burn until all the charcoal is covered with a layer of fine gray ash. Build a single-level fire by spreading the coals evenly over the bottom of the grill. Set the cooking rack in place, cover the grill with the lid, and let the rack heat up, about 5 minutes. Use a wire brush to scrape clean the cooking rack. The grill is ready when the coals are medium-hot. (See how to gauge heat level on page 19.)

3. Lightly dip a small wad of paper towels in vegetable oil; holding wad with tongs, wipe grill rack (see page 45). Remove the bluefish fillets from the marinade and place them on the grill. Grill, uncovered, turning once (using a metal spatula), until the fish is no longer gray-brown in the center, about 7 minutes. Serve immediately with lemon wedges.

Gas-Grilled Bluefish Fillets

SERVES 4

Acidic ingredients marry very well with oily, strong-flavored bluefish. Be sure to get bluefish as close to the catch as possible and store it over ice; this fish quickly loses its freshness. The gray-brown flesh turns white once it is cooked through.

3	tablespoons extra-virgin olive oil
1	medium garlic clove, minced
1½	tablespoons lemon juice
1	teaspoon Dijon mustard
¼	teaspoon salt
	Ground black pepper
4	skinless bluefish fillets (6½ to 7 ounces each)
	Vegetable oil for grill rack
	Lemon wedges

TURNING FISH FILLETS AND STEAKS

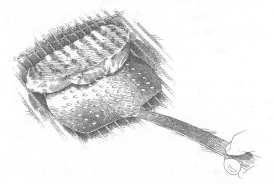

Use a metal spatula (pancake turner) for flipping fish. Always slide the spatula under the fish parallel to the bars of the cooking grate.

1. Mix the olive oil, garlic, lemon juice, mustard, salt, and pepper to taste together in a small bowl. Place the bluefish in a single layer in a large baking dish and pour the lemon-oil mixture over the fillets. Rub the mixture all over the fillets to coat evenly. Cover and refrigerate for 30 minutes.

2. Preheat the grill with all burners set to high and the lid down until very hot, about 15 minutes. Use a wire brush to scrape clean the cooking rack. Leave all burners on high.

3. Lightly dip a small wad of paper towels in vegetable oil; holding wad with tongs, wipe grill rack (see page 45). Remove the bluefish fillets from the marinade and place them on the grill. Grill, covered, turning once (using a metal spatula), until the fish is no longer gray-brown in the center, about 8 minutes. Serve immediately, with lemon wedges.

➤ VARIATION

Cumin-Crusted Bluefish with Avocado-Corn Relish

Bluefish stands up nicely to the strong flavors of spice rubs. Here we have paired the fish with cumin, cayenne, and chili powder. This fish would also taste great if coated with the Simple Spice Rub for Fish (page 293). If you like, pass warmed corn tortillas with the fish and relish and let everyone make their own fish tacos.

4	teaspoons ground cumin
1	teaspoon chili powder
¼	teaspoon cayenne pepper
¼	teaspoon salt
¼	teaspoon ground black pepper
4	skinless bluefish fillets (6½ to 7 ounces each)
3	tablespoons extra-virgin olive oil
	Vegetable oil for grill rack
	Lime wedges
2	cups Avocado-Corn Relish (page 299)

1. Mix the cumin, chili powder, cayenne, salt, and pepper together in a small bowl. Rub the bluefish fillets with olive oil, then rub the spice mixture onto the fillets until evenly coated. Cover and refrigerate for 30 minutes.

2. Prepare charcoal grill or gas grill according to directions in the preceding recipes. Use a wire brush to scrape clean the cooking grate. Rub an oil-soaked wad of paper towels over the cooking grate to prevent sticking.

3. Grill the fillets according to the directions in the recipes for charcoal-grilled or gas-grilled bluefish. Remove the fish from the grill and serve immediately, with lime wedges and relish passed separately at the table.

HALIBUT STEAKS

HALIBUT IS A MILD-FLAVORED, LEAN, WHITE fish with firm flesh, making it a perfect choice for those who also like mild-flavored, steak-like fish such as swordfish or tuna. It is an easy fish to grill as long as you don't get a steak that is too thin and you don't allow it to overcook on the grill.

Halibut can dry out if overcooked, so remove steaks from the grill once the center is just barely translucent.

We found halibut steaks in various forms at markets around town. Some were boneless, others had two sections of flesh separated by a bone, and others had four sections of meat separated by bone and membrane. Because you are most likely to see boneless steaks, we have written our halibut recipes for this cut. (In case you can find only bone-in steaks at the market, we provide instructions for boning below.)

Halibut is best simply prepared. No marinades are necessary, just a brush of oil, which keeps it from sticking to the grill, and some salt and pepper. Like swordfish, however (and like beef steak), halibut takes well to flavorings such as butters and sauces.

PREPARING HALIBUT STEAKS

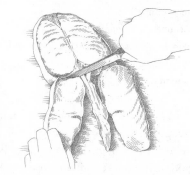

Whole, bone-in halibut steaks come with four sections of flesh divided by a long bone that runs down the center, crossed by a thin membrane. To remove the bone and separate the four boneless steaks, simply run a knife along the sides of the bone, then follow the line of the thin membrane with the knife to separate it from the flesh.

Charcoal-Grilled Halibut Steaks

SERVES 4

In this recipe we use boneless, skin-on halibut steaks. If the only kind of halibut steak you can find still has a bone running down the center, see page 154 for instructions on boning. If your market carries only half steaks, which consist of two sections of flesh separated by a thin, long bone, you will need two steaks, each about 1 pound and 1 inch thick, for this recipe. If your market carries only whole halibut steaks (they have four sections of flesh divided by bone and membrane), you will need only one 2-pound steak, about 1 inch thick.

4	skin-on boneless halibut steaks, I inch thick (7 to 8 ounces each)
2	tablespoons extra-virgin olive oil
	Salt and ground black pepper
	Vegetable oil for grill rack
	Lemon wedges

1. Light a large chimney filled with hardwood charcoal (about 2½ pounds) and allow to burn until all the charcoal is covered with a layer of fine gray ash. Build a single-level fire by spreading the coals evenly over the bottom of the grill. Set the cooking rack in place, cover the grill with the lid, and let the rack heat up, about 5 minutes. Use a wire brush to scrape clean the cooking rack. The grill is ready when the coals are medium-hot. (See how to gauge heat level on page 19.)

2. Brush the halibut with olive oil and season well with salt and pepper to taste.

3. Lightly dip a small wad of paper towels in vegetable oil; holding wad with tongs, wipe grill rack (see page 45). Grill the halibut, uncovered, turning once (using a metal spatula), until barely translucent at the very center of the steak, 7 to 8 minutes. Serve immediately with lemon wedges.

Gas-Grilled Halibut Steaks

SERVES 4

In this recipe we use boneless, skin-on halibut steaks. If the only kind of halibut steak you can find still has a bone running down the center, see page 154 for instructions on boning. If your market carries only half steaks, which consist of two sections of flesh separated by a thin, long bone, you will need two steaks, each about 1 pound and 1 inch thick, for this recipe. If your market carries only whole halibut steaks (they have four sections of flesh divided by bone and membrane), you will need only one 2-pound steak, about 1 inch thick.

4	skin-on boneless halibut steaks, I inch thick (7 to 8 ounces each)
2	tablespoons extra-virgin olive oil
	Salt and ground black pepper
	Vegetable oil for grill rack
	Lemon wedges

1. Preheat grill with all burners set to high and the lid down until very hot, about 15 minutes. Use a wire brush to scrape clean the cooking rack. Leave all burners on high.

2. Brush the halibut with olive oil and season well with salt and pepper to taste.

3. Lightly dip a small wad of paper towels in vegetable oil; holding wad with tongs, wipe grill rack (see page 45). Grill the halibut, covered, turning once (using a metal spatula), until barely translucent at the very center of the steak, 8 to 9 minutes. Serve immediately with lemon wedges.

➤ VARIATION

Grilled Halibut Steaks with Chipotle-Lime Butter

Chipotles are actually dried, smoked jalapeño chiles. Small amounts of chipotle add gentle heat to the butter in this recipe. Here, we've used a chipotle chile in adobo sauce (a dark red sauce made with herbs, vinegar, and ground chiles), available in small cans in the ethnic food aisle of most supermarkets. Refrigerate or freeze any leftover peppers and sauce for future use. If you like, you can substitute Tarragon-Lime Butter or Tapenade Butter (see page 30).

4	tablespoons unsalted butter, softened
2	teaspoons lime juice
I	chipotle chile packed in adobo sauce, chopped fine
I	medium garlic clove, minced
¼	teaspoon salt
I	tablespoon roughly chopped fresh cilantro leaves
I	recipe Charcoal-Grilled or Gas-Grilled Halibut Steaks (without lemon wedges)

1. Beat the butter with a large fork in a medium bowl until light and fluffy. Add lime juice, chile, garlic, salt, and cilantro and mix to combine. Following the illustrations on page 31, roll butter into a log about 3 inches long and 1½ inches in diameter. Refrigerate until firm, at least 2 hours and up to 3 days. (Butter can be frozen for 2 months. When ready to use, let soften just until butter can be cut, about 15 minutes).

2. Prepare the fish as directed. Transfer the steaks to individual plates and set a slice of chipotle butter on top of each hot steak. Serve immediately.

MAHI-MAHI FILLETS

MAHI-MAHI WAS A LITTLE MORE DIFFICULT to grill than we had imagined. Its texture is similar to swordfish, but the flesh is actually a little oilier and fishier tasting. Despite the extra oil, we found that mahi-mahi still has a tendency to dry out on the grill.

We asked the fishmonger to cut a side of mahi-mahi (also known as dolphinfish—not to be confused with the mammal) into eight-ounce portions, just as you would cut a side of salmon into fillets. The fillets cut from the center of the side are thicker and more desirable than thinner fillets cut from the ends. Buy mahi-mahi fillets that have a bright coral pink tinge and a slightly darker line running through the middle. This indicates freshness. Do not buy fillets that are streaked with a very dark (brown) line through the middle—they are probably past their prime. When cooked, mahi-mahi turns the color of swordfish.

Our mahi-mahi steaks were quite thick, so they needed to be cooked over a two-level fire. Mahi-mahi needs to be cooked to between medium and medium-well, with no translucence left in the center of the meat. Even when cooked over a two-level fire and to medium, however, the fish was still a little dry and sawdusty, just as tuna becomes when it's cooked that far. We tried presoaking it in extra-virgin olive oil, which helped keep thinner cuts of tuna from drying out, but this didn't help all that much on such thick, large fillets.

Next, we tried brining the fish in a salt and sugar water solution. The fish was much, much better, both more juicy and more tasty. Since mahi-mahi can be a little fishy, the sugar and salt in the brine helped to balance out the flavors. The sugar also encouraged the formation of a caramelized crust on the fillet.

Charcoal-Grilled Mahi-Mahi Fillets
SERVES 4

We brine the mahi-mahi because, much like chicken breasts, mahi-mahi fillets tend to dry out quickly when grilled. Brining seasons the fish beautifully, adding a balance of saltiness and sweetness.

- ¾ cup kosher salt or 6 tablespoons table salt
- ¾ cup sugar
- 4 skinless mahi-mahi fillets, center cut, if possible (7 to 8 ounces each)
- 3 tablespoons extra-virgin olive oil
- Ground black pepper
- Vegetable oil for grill rack
- Lemon wedges

1. Dissolve the salt and sugar in 1 quart of cold water in a gallon-sized zipper-lock plastic bag. Add the fish; press out as much air as possible from the bag and seal. Refrigerate until fully seasoned, about 40 minutes.

2. Meanwhile, light a large chimney starter filled with hardwood charcoal (about 2½ pounds) and allow to burn until all the charcoal is covered with a layer of fine gray ash. Build a two-level fire by stacking most of the coals on one side of the grill and arranging the remaining coals in a single layer on the other side of the grill. Set the cooking rack in place, cover the grill with the lid, and let the rack heat up, about 5 minutes. Use a wire brush to scrape clean the cooking rack. The grill is ready when the temperature of the stacked coals is medium-hot and that of the remaining coals is medium-low. (See how to gauge heat level on page 19.)

3. Remove the fish from the brine and rinse well. Pat dry the fillets with paper towels. Brush the fish fillets with olive oil and season to taste with pepper.

4. Lightly dip a small wad of paper towels in vegetable oil; holding wad with tongs, wipe grill rack (see page 45). Grill the mahi-mahi, uncovered, turning once (using a metal spatula), over the hotter part of the grill until dark grill marks appear, about 5 minutes total. Move the fillets to the cooler part of

the grill and cook, turning once, until the fish is no longer translucent at the center, 3 to 4 minutes. Serve immediately with lemon wedges.

Gas-Grilled Mahi-Mahi Fillets
SERVES 4

To cook the mahi-mahi over a gas fire, grill with all burners set to high for several minutes, then turn the burners down to medium to cook the fish through and prevent it from browning too much.

¾	cup kosher salt or 6 tablespoons table salt
¾	cup sugar
4	skinless mahi-mahi fillets, center cut, if possible (7 to 8 ounces each)
3	tablespoons extra-virgin olive oil
	Ground black pepper
	Vegetable oil for grill rack
	Lemon wedges

1. Dissolve the salt and sugar in 1 quart of cold water in a gallon-sized zipper-lock plastic bag. Add the fish; press out as much air as possible from the bag and seal. Refrigerate until fully seasoned, about 40 minutes.

2. Preheat the grill with all burners set to high and the lid down until very hot, about 15 minutes. Use a wire brush to scrape clean the cooking rack. Leave all burners on high.

3. Remove the fish from the brine and rinse well. Pat dry the fillets with paper towels. Brush the fish fillets with olive oil and season to taste with pepper.

4. Lightly dip a small wad of paper towels in vegetable oil; holding wad with tongs, wipe grill rack (see page 45). Grill the mahi-mahi, covered, turning once (using a metal spatula), until dark grill marks appear, about 6 minutes total. Turn all burners down to medium. Cover and continue grilling, turning once, until the fish is no longer translucent at the center, about 4 minutes. Serve immediately with lemon wedges.

➤ VARIATION

Grilled Mahi-Mahi with Shallots, Lime, and Cilantro

Mahi-mahi goes very well with assertive flavors such as acidic lime juice, cooling cilantro, and pungent shallots, ginger, and garlic. If shallots are unavailable, use ⅓ cup minced red onion instead.

1	recipe Charcoal-Grilled or Gas-Grilled Mahi-Mahi (without olive oil, pepper, and lemon wedges)
4	tablespoons extra-virgin olive oil
4	medium shallots, finely chopped (about ½ cup)
2	teaspoons minced fresh ginger
4	medium garlic cloves, minced
1½	teaspoons ground cumin
2	teaspoons brown sugar
3	tablespoons lime juice
¼	teaspoon salt
2	teaspoons hot sauce, plus more to pass at the table
2	tablespoons chopped fresh cilantro leaves
	Ground black pepper
	Lime wedges

1. Brine the fish as directed.

2. Meanwhile, heat the olive oil in a large skillet over medium-high heat until shimmering. Reduce the heat to medium and add the shallots; cook until soft, about 4 minutes. Add the ginger, garlic, cumin, and brown sugar and cook until fragrant, about 1 minute longer. Remove the pan from the heat and stir in the lime juice, salt, hot sauce, and cilantro. Transfer the mixture to a heatproof bowl and refrigerate until cool.

3. Prepare the charcoal grill or gas grill according to the directions in the preceding recipes.

4. Meanwhile, rinse and dry the fillets as directed. Place them in a large dish or pie plate and pour the cooled shallot-lime mixture over them. Season the fish with ground black pepper. Cover the dish and marinate in the refrigerator for 20 minutes.

5. Rub an oil-soaked wad of paper towels over the cooking grate to prevent sticking. Remove the fish from the marinade and grill as directed. Serve with lime wedges and hot sauce.

RED SNAPPER FILLETS

RED SNAPPER IS EASY TO GRILL. THE FILLETS are pretty thin—one-half to three-quarters inch at the thickest part—so they cook through in about five minutes. Red snapper is less dense and more flaky than steaklike fish such as tuna or mahi-mahi, so it cooks more quickly than you might think. The main challenge for the cook is to prevent the delicate fillets from falling apart. We found it wise to oil both the grill and the fish. When turning, slide a metal spatula under the fish and flip carefully.

We like the flavor of red snapper, so we took a purist approach to seasoning the fillets—salt and pepper before cooking, lemon wedges at the table. We found that spices and marinades detract from the delicate, almost sweet flavor of this fish, but you might add a salsa for more flavor and moisture.

When buying red snapper, look for fillets with gleaming reddish-pink flesh that smells fresh and doesn't look dried out.

Charcoal-Grilled
Red Snapper Fillets

SERVES 4

Skinless red snapper fillets are quick and easy to grill, but they do require a gentle hand. Carefully turn these fillets over with a spatula and be sure that both the fish and the grill are well oiled. Because these fillets are so thin, they only take about 5 minutes to cook through.

> 4   skinless red snapper fillets (7 to 8 ounces each)
> 2   tablespoons extra-virgin olive oil
>   Salt and ground black pepper
>   Vegetable oil for grill rack
>   Lemon wedges

1. Light a large chimney filled with hardwood charcoal (about 2½ pounds) and allow to burn until all the charcoal is covered with a layer of fine gray ash. Build a single-level fire by spreading the coals evenly over the bottom of the grill. Set the cooking rack in place, cover the grill with the lid, and let the rack heat up, about 5 minutes. Use a wire brush to scrape clean the cooking rack. The grill is ready when the coals are medium-hot. (See how to gauge heat level on page 19.)

2. Brush the red snapper fillets with olive oil and season with salt and pepper to taste.

3. Lightly dip a small wad of paper towels in vegetable oil; holding wad with tongs, wipe grill rack (see page 45). Grill the fillets, uncovered, turning once (using a metal spatula), until the snapper flakes at the center but is still moist, 5 to 5½ minutes total. Serve immediately with lemon wedges.

Gas-Grilled
Red Snapper Fillets

SERVES 4

Red snapper fillets require a gentle hand. Carefully turn the fillets over with a spatula. To prevent sticking, make sure that both the fish and the grill are well oiled. A perfectly clean grill is essential.

> 4   skinless red snapper fillets (7 to 8 ounces each)
> 2   tablespoons extra-virgin olive oil
>   Salt and ground black pepper
>   Vegetable oil for grill rack
>   Lemon wedges

1. Preheat the grill with all burners set to high and the lid down until very hot, about 15 minutes. Use a wire brush to scrape clean the cooking rack. Leave all burners on high.

2. Brush the red snapper fillets with olive oil and season with salt and pepper to taste.

3. Lightly dip a small wad of paper towels in vegetable oil; holding wad with tongs, wipe grill rack (see page 45). Grill the fillets, covered, turning once (using a metal spatula), until the snapper flakes at the center but is still moist, 6 to 6½ minutes total. Serve immediately with lemon wedges.

➤ VARIATION

Grilled Red Snapper Fillets with Spicy Yellow Pepper and Tomato Salsa

Follow the recipe for Charcoal-Grilled or Gas-Grilled Red Snapper, serving the grilled fish with 2 cups Spicy Yellow Pepper and Tomato Salsa (page 301) and lime wedges instead of lemon wedges.

SALMON FILLETS

SALMON IS OUR FAVORITE FISH TO GRILL. Not only does it taste great, but it's firm enough to hold together better than many other fish. With its abundant natural fats and oils, salmon is also less prone to drying out than most other fish. While leaner fish like tuna, swordfish, and halibut benefit from a brush with oil before being grilled to help retain moisture, salmon needs no such treatment.

The cut of salmon we used for our tests was boneless, individual-portion farmed salmon fillets, skin on, weighing about six ounces each. Salmon can be purchased as boneless fillets or as steaks. We prefer fillets over steaks because fillets are boneless and thus easier to eat. Whenever possible, we buy center-cut fillets because in farmed salmon (see page 161 for more information) the center cut is often almost exactly 1½ inches thick and thus cooks consistently from one piece to the next. Cuts from the tail are thinner and thus easier to overcook, while cuts from the head end are thicker and tend to take too long to cook through. Several tests proved that a medium-hot fire browned the salmon fillets without burning them and conveniently created a crust that made for fairly easy turning on the grill after some initial prodding with long-handled tongs or a spatula. (We thus also found that oiling the salmon for purposes of easier turning was unnecessary.)

While the center cut cooked well over the direct heat of a single-level fire, we thought we would try a two-level fire, browning the fillets over the higher heat and then letting them cook through over the lower heat. We found no difference in taste or texture between the fillets grilled entirely over direct heat and those finished over indirect heat. Because direct heat cooks faster, we opted for that. That said, we found the direct/indirect method to be an excellent way to cook thin tail pieces; by the time the flesh had seared enough to turn, the fish was almost cooked through and needed just a minute or so of gentle heat to finish it without overcooking.

As we grilled the salmon, we remained alert for clues to tell us when it was properly cooked. We like salmon that is medium-rare in the center, or still slightly translucent. Mostly we found that by the time 1½-inch-thick fillets were well browned on both sides, the center was perfect—slightly undercooked, but close enough to finish cooking the last little bit on the plate. We also developed a tactile test. As the salmon cooks, we pull it off the grill every now and then and squeeze the sides of the fillet gently between our fingertips. Raw salmon feels squishy; medium-rare salmon is firm but not hard. Of course, if you're stumped and want to be really sure, just cut into the fillet with a paring knife and take a look.

TURNING A SALMON FILLET INTO A STEAK

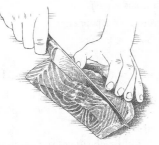

1. Because they are thinner at the edges, salmon fillets do not cook through evenly. We like the gradation from well-done at the edges to rare in the center, but not everyone does. Steaks, which have an even thickness throughout, cook more evenly, but they are bony. However, it is possible to turn a fillet into a steak. Start by cutting through a 3-inch-wide fillet lengthwise down to, but not through, the skin.

2. Fold the two pieces of flesh out, with the skin acting as a hinge.

3. A 3-inch-wide fillet will now look like a steak, but without any bones, and have an even thickness of 1½ inches. The one drawback is that the skin won't crisp, since it is sandwiched in the middle of the steak. If you like to eat the skin, cook the fillets as they are. The cooking time for mock steaks is the same as for regular fillets.

Charcoal-Grilled Salmon Fillets

SERVES 4

If your fillets are less than 1½ inches thick, decrease the grilling time by roughly 30 seconds per side. To test fillets for doneness, either peek into the salmon with the tip of a small knife or remove the salmon from the grill and squeeze both sides of the fillet gently with your fingertips (raw salmon is squishy; medium-rare salmon is firm, but not hard).

> 4   center-cut salmon fillets, each 6 to 7 ounces
>   and 1½ inches thick, pin bones removed
>   (see illustrations below)
>   Salt and ground black pepper
>   Vegetable oil for grill rack

1. Light a large chimney starter filled with hardwood charcoal (about 2½ pounds) and allow to burn until all the charcoal is covered with a layer of fine gray ash. Build a single-level fire by spreading the coals evenly over the bottom of the grill. Set the cooking rack in place, cover the grill with the lid, and let the rack heat up, about 5 minutes. Use a wire brush to scrape clean the cooking rack. The grill is ready when the coals are medium-hot. (See how to gauge heat level on page 19.)

2. Generously sprinkle each side of the salmon fillets with salt and pepper.

3. Lightly dip a small wad of paper towels in vegetable oil; holding wad with tongs, wipe grill rack (see page 45). Place the fillets skin-side down on the grill. Grill, uncovered, until the skin shrinks, separates from the flesh, and blackens, 2 to 3 minutes. Gently flip the fillets with a metal spatula. Grill, uncovered, until the fillets are opaque almost throughout, with translucence only at the very center, 3 to 4 minutes. Serve immediately.

Gas-Grilled Salmon Fillets

SERVES 4

If your fillets are less than 1½ inches thick, decrease the grilling time by roughly 30 seconds per side. To test fillets for doneness, either peek into the salmon with the tip of a small knife or remove the salmon from the grill and squeeze both sides of the fillet gently with your fingertips (raw salmon is squishy; medium-rare salmon is firm, but not hard).

Make sure your gas grill is very hot and perfectly clean before putting the fish on the cooking grate.

> 4   center-cut salmon fillets, each 6 to 7 ounces
>   and 1½ inches thick, pin bones removed
>   (see illustrations at left)
>   Salt and ground black pepper
>   Vegetable oil for grill rack

1. Preheat the grill with all burners set to high and the lid down until very hot, about 15 minutes. Use a wire brush to scrape clean the cooking rack. Leave all burners on high.

2. Generously sprinkle each side of the salmon fillets with salt and pepper.

3. Lightly dip a small wad of paper towels in vegetable oil; holding wad with tongs, wipe grill rack (see page 45). Place the fillets skin-side down on the grill. Grill, covered, until the skin shrinks, separates from the flesh, and blackens, 3 to 4 minutes. Gently flip the fillets with a metal spatula. Grill, covered, until the fillets

REMOVING PIN BONES FROM SALMON

1. Using the tips of your fingers, gently rub the surface of each salmon fillet to locate any pin bones, short pieces of bone left behind when the fish was filleted.

2. If you find any bones, use a pair of tweezers or needle-nose pliers to pull them out.

are opaque almost throughout, with translucence only at the very center, 4 to 5 minutes. Serve immediately.

➤ VARIATIONS

Grilled Salmon Fillets with Mustard Glaze

A spicy but sweet mustard glaze takes just minutes to assemble and adds plenty of flavor.

Mix 2 tablespoons dry mustard, 2 tablespoons sugar, and 2 teaspoons water together in a small bowl to form a thick paste. Follow the recipe for Charcoal-Grilled or Gas-Grilled Salmon Fillets, spreading the mustard paste over the flesh side of the fillets before grilling. Proceed as directed. Drizzle extra-virgin olive oil over the grilled fillets just before serving.

Grilled Salmon Fillets with Aromatic Spice Rub

Serve this spice-rubbed salmon with lime or lemon wedges.

Follow the recipe for Charcoal-Grilled or Gas-Grilled Salmon Fillets, rubbing 1 tablespoon vegetable oil into the fillets and then coating the fillets with 1 tablespoon Simple Spice Rub for Fish (page 293). Grill as directed.

Grilled Salmon Fillets with Indian Flavors and Mango Salsa

This recipe includes a simplified mango salsa.

2	tablespoons vegetable oil, plus more for grill rack
2	tablespoons grated fresh ginger
1 ½	teaspoons ground cumin
1 ½	teaspoons ground coriander
1 ½	teaspoons salt
¼	teaspoon cayenne pepper
4	center-cut salmon fillets, each 6 to 7 ounces and 1 ½ inches thick, pin bones removed (see illustrations on page 160)

MANGO SALSA

1	ripe mango, peeled, pitted, and cut into ½-inch dice
3	tablespoons lemon juice
1	tablespoon chopped fresh cilantro leaves

INGREDIENTS: Salmon

Salmon is America's most popular "dinner" fish (we consume more tuna, but most of that is canned) for good reason. The flesh is rich and flavorful, and it is relatively easy to prepare. An additional advantage lies in the fact that modern fish-farming technology all but guarantees that you can buy excellent-quality salmon any day of the year. Even at the supermarket, where other fish is often not up to our admittedly exacting standards, salmon comes in so fresh and sells out so fast that we are rarely dissatisfied.

At some high-end fish shops, you may have a choice between farmed and wild fish. This is unlikely on the East Coast, but in the West, and especially the Northwest, you may see wild salmon at certain times of year. We wondered if there are important differences between farmed and wild salmon and also wondered about any differences that might exist in salmon from various sources around the globe. The most common kind of salmon sold in the United States is Atlantic salmon farmed in pens off the coast of Maine or eastern Canada. (This species is farmed around the world, in Norway, Chile, and the Pacific Northwest.) We taste-tested salmon farmed in Chile, in Maine, and in two different areas of eastern Canada, one of these being a "Bay of Fundy Certified Quality" salmon, a brand name.

We ran pan-seared, grilled, and steamed tests of each fish. The major split developed between the fish farmed in northern versus Chilean waters. In all tests, the Chilean fish was drier even when cooked less. The steaming test brought out some subtle differences in texture and flavor that were less obvious when the fish was pan-seared or (almost completely obscured by) grilling: The nonbrand Canadian fish had a slightly mushy texture compared with the silken firm flesh of the branded and Maine fish. Steaming also showed the branded fish to have a rounder, richer flavor than its other northern counterparts.

The dryness in Chilean fish was likely due to its lower fat content. Chilean-farmed salmon is leaner than Maine, Canadian, or Norwegian salmon because it's younger. Salmon farmed in warm Chilean waters grow to market size faster than when farmed in colder northern waters. The older a salmon gets, the more fat it puts on. So, if you're buying farmed fish, steer clear of Chilean.

As for wild salmon, we found that it has a more complex, less homogenous flavor than farmed salmon. Its texture is also meatier. Because wild salmon has less fat than farmed salmon, however, it can be dry when cooked. If you happen to find some wild salmon, you may want to undercook it slightly to ensure that it remains moist.

---

1. Mix the oil, ginger, cumin, coriander, salt, and cayenne together in a small bowl. Rub the marinade over the salmon fillets. Cover and refrigerate for 30 minutes. Meanwhile, combine the mango, lemon juice, and cilantro in a small bowl and set the salsa aside.

2. Prepare the charcoal grill or gas grill according to the directions in the preceding recipes. Use a wire brush to scrape clean the cooking grate. Rub an oil-soaked wad of paper towels over the cooking grate to prevent sticking.

3. Grill the fillets according to the directions in the recipes for charcoal-grilled or gas-grilled salmon. Remove the fish from the grill and serve immediately with the mango salsa.

Grilled Salmon with Sesame-Soy Glaze

Toasted sesame seeds and oil add a nutty aroma to this salty-sweet sauce. To toast sesame seeds for this recipe, place them in a small skillet over medium heat and toast for about 6 minutes, or until they become golden and fragrant.

4	tablespoons soy sauce
I	tablespoon rice vinegar
2	tablespoon mirin (Japanese sweet rice wine)
I½	teaspoons cornstarch
I	teaspoon vegetable oil
2	teaspoons minced fresh ginger
I	tablespoon sesame seeds, toasted
I	teaspoon Asian sesame oil
I	recipe Charcoal-Grilled or Gas-Grilled Salmon Fillets

1. Mix the soy sauce, rice vinegar, mirin, and cornstarch together in a small bowl. Heat the vegetable oil in a small saucepan over medium-high heat until hot. Add the ginger and cook until fragrant, but not browned, about 30 seconds. Give the soy mixture a quick stir and pour it into the saucepan. Bring to a light boil and reduce the heat to low; cook another minute, or until the glaze is thick and transparent. Remove the pan from the heat and transfer the mixture to a heatproof bowl. Stir in the sesame seeds and sesame oil.

2. Grill the fish as directed, brushing the flesh side of the fillets generously with the soy glaze just before flipping and again just before serving.

SEA BASS FILLETS

FOR MOST SHOPPERS, SEA BASS MEANS CHILEAN sea bass. This meaty, firm-textured fish is moderately oily and quite delicious, especially when grilled. The oil in this fish keeps it from drying out on the grill. It also develops a beautiful golden brown crust, which is enhanced by brushing the fish with a little oil before grilling.

Because sea bass is so flavorful and has such a meaty texture, it's best to treat it simply. If you can find fillets with the skin on, buy them—the skin is quite delicious and makes grilling even easier. (In most markets, the fish is skinned during the filleting process.) Other varieties of sea bass, especially black sea bass from the Atlantic, can be cooked in the same fashion, although fillets may be thinner and thus require a little less time on the grill.

Charcoal-Grilled Sea Bass Fillets

SERVES 4

Sea bass grills beautifully. The golden crust on the outside contrasts texturally with the rich, buttery, full-flavored interior. This fish is best seasoned simply with salt and pepper or with other delicately flavored ingredients. As when grilling all other fish, be sure to use a clean, hot grill that has been well oiled, and use a metal spatula for turning the fillets.

4	skinless sea bass fillets, each 6½ to 7 ounces and ¾ to I inch thick
2	tablespoons extra-virgin olive oil
	Salt and ground black pepper
	Vegetable oil for grill rack

1. Light a large chimney filled with hardwood charcoal (about 2½ pounds) and allow to burn until all the charcoal is covered with a layer of fine gray ash. Build a single-level fire by spreading the coals evenly over the bottom of the grill. Set the cooking rack in place, cover the grill with the lid, and let the rack heat up, about 5 minutes. Use a wire brush to scrape clean the cooking rack. The grill is ready when the coals are medium-hot. (See how to gauge heat level on page 19.)

2. Brush the sea bass with olive oil and season with salt and pepper to taste.

3. Lightly dip a small wad of paper towels in vegetable oil; holding wad with tongs, wipe grill rack (see page 45). Grill the fish, uncovered, turning once (using a metal spatula), until opaque through to the center of the fish, 6 to 7 minutes. Serve immediately.

Gas-Grilled Sea Bass Fillets

SERVES 4

As when grilling all other fish, be sure to use a clean, hot grill that has been well oiled, and use a metal spatula for turning the fillets.

4   skinless sea bass fillets, each 6½ to 7 ounces
     and ¾ to 1 inch thick
2   tablespoons extra-virgin olive oil
     Salt and ground black pepper
     Vegetable oil for grill rack

1. Preheat grill with all burners set to high and the lid down until very hot, about 15 minutes. Use a wire brush to scrape clean the cooking rack. Leave all burners on high.

2. Brush the sea bass with olive oil and season with salt and pepper to taste.

3. Lightly dip a small wad of paper towels in vegetable oil; holding wad with tongs, wipe grill rack (see page 45). Grill the fish, covered, turning once (using a metal spatula), until opaque through to the center of the fish, 7 to 8 minutes. Serve immediately.

> VARIATION

Grilled Sea Bass Fillets in Japanese-Style Broth

This light and delicate consommé-like broth is the perfect accompaniment to grilled sea bass. Dried hondashi (sometimes called dashi), a dehydrated soup base made from dried bonito and seaweed, lends an authentic touch to the broth. You can find it at most Asian specialty food shops. Serve with plain steamed rice.

1½   teaspoons dehydrated hondashi
     (Japanese soup base)
2½   tablespoons soy sauce
6   medium shiitake mushrooms,
     stemmed and quartered
½   inch fresh ginger, cut into rounds and lightly
     smashed with the back of a knife
½   small carrot, cut into very thin strips, about 1½
     inches long
1   recipe Charcoal-Grilled or Gas-Grilled Sea Bass
1   scallion, cut into thin rounds

1. Stir together the hondashi, soy sauce, and 1½ cups water in a medium saucepan. Add the mushrooms, ginger, and carrot. Set the pan aside.

2. Grill the sea bass as directed.

3. While the fish is on the grill, bring the soy sauce mixture to a boil over medium-high heat. Remove the pan from the heat, then remove the ginger with a slotted spoon. Stir in the scallion.

4. Cut each grilled fillet crosswise into two equal pieces. Place 2 halves of sea bass stacked one atop the other in the center of a soup plate. Ladle the broth and vegetables over and around the bass and serve immediately.

SWORDFISH STEAKS

THICK SWORDFISH STEAKS ARE A FAVORITE on the grill. Their dense, meaty flesh keeps the steaks from falling apart on the grill, and their smooth surface reduces the risk of sticking.

After testing various steaks, we found that thicker steaks (close to 1¼ inches) were best because they can remain on the grill long enough to pick up some smoky flavor without drying out. Thinner steaks were either poorly seared or overcooked in the middle. Thicker pieces also retained moisture better and were easier to handle on the grill.

When grilling all fish (but especially swordfish), leave it in place long enough so that it develops good grill marks before moving it. Unlike salmon and tuna, we find that swordfish should be cooked until medium—no more, no less. A two-level fire is necessary; the fish sears over a hot fire and then cooks through on the cooler part of the grill.

Charcoal-Grilled Swordfish Steaks

SERVES 4

Because of the shape and size of swordfish, individual steaks are quite large. This recipe serves four—or more, if you are willing to cut the steaks into smaller pieces.

2   swordfish steaks, each about 1 pound and
    1 to 1¼ inches thick
2   tablespoons extra-virgin olive oil
    Salt and ground black pepper
    Vegetable oil for grill rack
    Lemon wedges

1. Light a large chimney starter filled with hardwood charcoal (about 2½ pounds) and allow to burn until all the charcoal is covered with a layer of fine gray ash. Build a two-level fire by stacking most of the coals on one side of the grill and arranging the remaining coals in a single layer on the other side of the grill. Set the cooking rack in place, cover the grill with the lid, and let the rack heat up, about 5 minutes. Use a wire brush to scrape clean the cooking rack. The grill is ready when the heat level of the stacked coals is medium-hot and that of the remaining coals is medium-low. (See how to gauge heat level on page 19.)

2. Cut the swordfish steaks in half to make four equal pieces. Brush the fish with olive oil and generously sprinkle with salt and pepper.

3. Lightly dip a small wad of paper towels in vegetable oil; holding wad with tongs, wipe grill rack (see page 45). Grill the swordfish, uncovered, turning once (using a metal spatula), over the hotter part of the grill until the steaks are covered with dark grill marks, 6 to 7 minutes. Move fish to the cooler part of the grill and cook, uncovered, turning once, until the center is no longer translucent, 3 to 5 minutes. Serve immediately with lemon wedges.

Gas-Grilled Swordfish Steaks

SERVES 4

Grill the swordfish over high heat until seared and then lower the heat to medium to cook the steaks through. Because of the shape and size of swordfish, individual steaks are quite large. This recipe serves four—or more, if you are willing to cut the steaks into smaller pieces.

2   swordfish steaks, each about 1 pound and
    1 to 1¼ inches thick
2   tablespoons extra-virgin olive oil
    Salt and ground black pepper
    Vegetable oil for grill rack
    Lemon wedges

1. Preheat the grill with all burners set to high and the lid down until very hot, about 15 minutes. Use a wire brush to scrape clean the cooking rack. Leave the burners on high.

2. Cut the swordfish steaks in half to make four equal pieces. Brush the fish with olive oil and generously sprinkle with salt and pepper.

3. Lightly dip a small wad of paper towels in vegetable oil; holding wad with tongs, wipe grill rack (see page 45). Grill the swordfish, covered, turning once (using a metal spatula), over high heat until the steaks are covered with dark grill marks, 7 to 9 minutes. Turn the heat down to medium and cook, covered, turning once, until the center is no longer translucent, 4 to 6 minutes. Serve immediately with lemon wedges.

➤ VARIATION

Grilled Swordfish Steaks with Lemon-Parsley Sauce

Garlic is a pleasant addition to this dish. If desired, add one medium clove of finely minced garlic and 1 teaspoon lemon zest to oil that is to be brushed on steaks before grilling.

¼   cup extra-virgin olive oil
1½ tablespoons lemon juice
2   tablespoons minced fresh parsley leaves
    Salt and ground black pepper
1   recipe Charcoal-Grilled or Gas-Grilled
    Swordfish

1. Combine the oil, lemon juice, parsley, and salt and pepper to taste in a small bowl. Set the sauce aside.

2. Follow the recipe for Charcoal-Grilled or Gas-Grilled Swordfish, brushing the fish with optional lemon-garlic oil instead of plain olive oil, if desired. Spoon the lemon-parsley sauce over the grilled fish just before serving.

Grilled Swordfish Steaks with Salsa Verde

This Italian sauce—with capers, olives, anchovies, and herbs—is perfect with swordfish.

Follow the recipe for Charcoal-Grilled or Gas-Grilled Swordfish, topping each portion of grilled fish with a generous tablespoon of Salsa Verde (page 295).

TUNA STEAKS

GRILLED TUNA HAS BECOME SUCH A FAMILIAR dish on the American home-cooking scene that it never occurred to us that it might also be a bear to cook. We had assumed that we could get a perfect tuna steak—beautifully seared on the outside, moist and tender on the inside—the same way we get a perfect beef or salmon steak: a quick sear over direct heat to brown and then, if the steak is really thick, a final few minutes over indirect heat to finish it. We knew that tuna, lacking the fat of salmon, would be particularly susceptible to overcooking, so we would probably need to undercook it.

But a few days of testing proved tuna to be a tougher customer than we'd imagined. No matter what thickness we sliced it or how we cooked it—medium-rare or rare, direct or indirect heat—we were startled to find that steak after steak was almost inedible. Each one was tough and dry and tasted off-puttingly strong and fishy. Clearly, more experimenting was in order.

For purposes of experimentation, we decided to work with steaks three-quarters to one inch thick, as these are the cuts usually available at supermarket fish counters. First we tried grilling over direct heat, starting with an oiled and salted steak, for 3½ minutes on each side over a medium fire. The outside of the tuna was paler than we liked and the inside was overcooked. In successive tests we determined that a hotter fire seared better, particularly since the tuna needed to cook only 3 minutes total for medium

and 4 minutes for well-done.

While the hotter fire was an improvement, the fish was still drier than we liked, particularly when it was cooked past medium-rare. So we experimented with a two-level fire that would give us a source of indirect heat. We tried searing the tuna 1½ minutes on each side over direct heat, then moving it to the other side of the grill to finish cooking over indirect heat. The tuna came off the grill with the same texture it had when grilled entirely over direct heat, but it was less well seared, so we gave up on the two-level heat approach.

We thought it was time to test steaks of different thicknesses over direct heat and learned that if we wanted the tuna both well seared and rare, it would have to be cut thicker than the standard supermarket steak, about 1½ inches instead of three-quarters to one inch. Thinner steaks had already cooked to at least medium-rare after the initial searing on both sides. But while we preferred the moistness of thick, rare steaks, we were concerned that some folks would not like to eat their tuna rare. In addition, we knew that many consumers would have difficulty locating thick steaks.

Clearly, the problem wasn't going to be solved in the actual cooking. Something had to be done to the tuna before it hit the grill. Our next inspiration was to test a marinade.

We talked to several restaurant chefs (after all, grilled tuna has become a restaurant classic), and they suggested marinating the tuna in olive oil and herbs. We marinated one 1½-inch-thick steak and one ½-inch-thick steak in an herb-flavored oil for three hours, turning every now and then. We then grilled the thick steak to rare, and the thin steak to medium. The results were amazing. Both steaks were subtly flavored with olive oil and herbs, and their texture was moist and luscious. Perhaps most surprising, we liked the well-cooked tuna as much as the rare.

We next ran tests to determine whether the type of oil made a difference. Comparing extra-virgin and pure olive oils with canola oil, we found that after one hour, only the extra-virgin olive oil made a noticeable difference in the tuna. The pure olive oil seemed to catch up after another hour, but it didn't flavor the tuna appreciably until after three hours. The canola oil never affected the taste or the texture of the tuna.

We learned that an oil marinade tenderizes tuna in much the same way that marbling tenderizes beef. The oil coats the strands of protein, allowing a tuna steak to feel moist in the mouth even after most of the moisture has been cooked out of it. The extra-virgin olive oil penetrates the fish more quickly than the other two oils because it is much richer in emulsifiers. Emulsifiers (mono- and diglycerides) have a water-soluble molecule at one end and a fat-soluble molecule at the other; this double solubility increases their mobility and hence their ability to penetrate protein. Because the filtering process extracts emulsifiers, pure olive oil takes much longer than extra-virgin olive oil to coat the protein strands.

Finally, we learned that the 1½-inch-thick steak, when cooked to rare or medium-rare, needed only brushing with the oil; soaking it in the oil actually made it a bit too moist. We liked the herbs in the marinade but found that the oil alone was still quite good. The basic recipes have just extra-virgin olive oil, salt, pepper, and tuna; see the herb variation if you are interested in something a bit different.

Charcoal-Grilled Tuna Steaks

SERVES 4

If you like your tuna rare, you must buy steaks cut about 1½ inches thick. This will allow you to sear them well without overcooking the inside. To serve four people you'll need two steaks (they run about 1 pound each). Cut each in half before grilling. If you prefer more well-done tuna, see the recipe for thin-cut tuna at right.

2   tuna steaks, each about 1 pound and
    1½ inches thick
2   tablespoons extra-virgin olive oil
    Salt and ground black pepper
    Vegetable oil for grill rack

1. Light a large chimney starter filled with hardwood charcoal (about 2½ pounds) and allow to burn until all the charcoal is covered with a layer of fine gray ash. Build a single-level fire by spreading the coals evenly over the bottom of the grill. Set the cooking rack in place, cover the grill with the lid, and let the rack heat up, about 5 minutes. Use a wire brush to scrape clean the cooking rack. The grill is ready when the coals are medium-hot. (See how to gauge heat level on page 19.)

2. Cut the tuna steaks in half to make four equal pieces. Brush the tuna with olive oil and generously sprinkle with salt and pepper.

3. Lightly dip a small wad of paper towels in vegetable oil; holding wad with tongs, wipe grill rack (see page 45). Grill the tuna, uncovered, turning once (using a metal spatula), to the desired doneness, 4 to 5 minutes for rare or 6 to 7 minutes for medium-rare. Serve immediately.

Gas-Grilled Tuna Steaks

SERVES 4

If you like your tuna rare, you must buy steaks cut about 1½ inches thick. This will allow you to sear them well without overcooking the inside. To serve four people you'll need two steaks (they run about 1 pound each). Cut each in half before grilling. If you prefer more well-done tuna, see the recipe for thin-cut tuna below. Work quickly when turning the tuna to keep the heat from dissipating.

2   tuna steaks, each about 1 pound and
    1½ inches thick
2   tablespoons extra-virgin olive oil
    Salt and ground black pepper
    Vegetable oil for grill rack

1. Preheat the grill with all burners set to high and the lid down until very hot, about 15 minutes. Use a wire brush to scrape clean the cooking rack. Leave the burners on high.

2. Cut the tuna steaks in half to make four equal pieces. Brush the tuna with olive oil and generously sprinkle with salt and pepper.

3. Lightly dip a small wad of paper towels in vegetable oil; holding wad with tongs, wipe grill rack (see page 45). Grill the tuna, covered, turning once (using a metal spatula), to the desired doneness, 5 to 6 minutes for rare or 7 to 8 minutes for medium-rare. Serve immediately.

➤ VARIATIONS
Thin-Cut Grilled Tuna Steaks

This recipe is for those who like their tuna cooked medium to well-done but still moist inside. The steaks are cut thinner for quicker cooking and are marinated in extra-virgin olive oil, both of which prevent dryness. If using a gas grill, cook over high heat, keep the lid down, and increase the cooking times by a minute or so.

> 4 tuna steaks, each about 8 ounces and
> ³⁄₄ inch thick
> 4 tablespoons extra-virgin olive oil
> Salt and ground black pepper
> Vegetable oil for grill rack

1. Combine the tuna steaks and olive oil in a gallon-sized zipper-lock plastic bag. Marinate in the refrigerator, turning several times, for at least 2 hours or overnight.

2. Prepare grill as in recipe for Charcoal- or Gas-Grilled Tuna Steaks through step 1.

3. Remove tuna from the bag and sprinkle with salt and pepper to taste.

4. Lightly dip a small wad of paper towels in vegetable oil; holding wad with tongs, wipe grill rack (see page 45). Grill the tuna, uncovered, turning once (using a metal spatula), to the desired doneness, about 3 minutes total for rare or 4 minutes total for well-done. Serve immediately.

Grilled Tuna Steaks with Herb-Infused Oil
If cooking thin-cut tuna, use the herb oil as a marinade.

> ¼ cup extra-virgin olive oil
> 1½ teaspoons grated lemon zest
> 1½ teaspoons chopped fresh
> thyme leaves
> 1 medium garlic clove, minced
> ¼ teaspoon hot red pepper flakes
> 1 recipe Charcoal-Grilled or Gas-Grilled Tuna
> (without the olive oil)

1. Heat the oil, lemon zest, thyme, garlic, and hot red pepper flakes in a small saucepan until hot. Remove the pan from the heat and cool the oil mixture to room temperature.

2. Follow the recipe for the tuna, brushing the fish with the herb oil instead of the plain extra-virgin olive oil. Season the fish with salt and pepper and proceed as directed.

Grilled Tuna Steaks with Peppercorn Crust
You can buy a whole peppercorn mix in well-stocked grocery stores or at specialty markets. These mixes may include white, black, green, pink, and/or red peppercorns. Although somewhat less complex in flavor, whole black peppercorns will do in place of the mix. Season fish with kosher salt if possible. Serve as is or with Tarragon-Lime Butter or Tapenade Butter (page 30).

> 1 tablespoon whole peppercorn mix
> 1 recipe Charcoal-Grilled or Gas-Grilled Tuna
> (without ground pepper)

1. Place whole peppercorn mix in the hopper of a spice grinder or coffee mill and pulse until peppercorns are coarsely ground, about six 1-second pulses.

2. Follow the recipe for the tuna, pressing the peppercorn mixture into the tuna after it has been brushed with oil and sprinkled with salt. Proceed as directed.

Grilled Rare Tuna Steaks with Soy, Ginger, and Wasabi
SERVES 4 AS A MAIN COURSE,
OR 8 AS AN APPETIZER

Since this tuna is served very rare, use only the freshest, highest-quality tuna you can find. It is served with a soy and pickled ginger sauce and wasabi paste. Wasabi, Japanese horseradish, is the pungent green condiment served with sushi and sashimi. Use the paste sparingly; it packs a spicy punch.

> 6 tablespoons soy sauce
> 4 teaspoons lime juice
> 2 teaspoons Asian sesame oil
> 2 tablespoons minced pickled ginger
> 2 medium scallions, thinly sliced
> 4 teaspoons wasabi powder
> 1 recipe Charcoal-Grilled or
> Gas-Grilled Tuna

1. Mix the soy sauce, lime juice, sesame oil, pickled ginger, and scallions together in a small bowl. Set aside. Mix the wasabi and 2 teaspoons of water together in a small bowl to form a thick paste. Cover and set aside.

2. Follow the recipe for the tuna, grilling the fish just until rare. Cut the tuna into ¼-inch-thick slices and fan the tuna out over individual plates. Drizzle a little soy mixture over each plate, then place a dollop of wasabi paste on each plate. Serve immediately.

Grilled Tuna Steaks with Watercress, Parsley, and Spiced Vinaigrette

The hot tuna wilts the watercress and parsley slightly, while the spiced vinaigrette adds tons of flavor and moisture.

2½	tablespoons lemon juice
2	small garlic cloves, minced
½	teaspoon salt
½	teaspoon ground cumin
¼	teaspoon sweet paprika
⅛	teaspoon cayenne pepper
2	tablespoons chopped fresh cilantro leaves
½	cup extra-virgin olive oil

	Ground black pepper
I	recipe Charcoal-Grilled or Gas-Grilled Tuna
I	bunch watercress, washed, dried well, and trimmed of tough stems
I	bunch flat-leaf parsley, washed and dried well

1. Whisk the lemon juice, garlic, salt, cumin, paprika, cayenne, and cilantro together in a small bowl. Add the oil in a slow, steady stream, whisking constantly until smooth; season with pepper to taste. Set the dressing aside.

2. While the tuna is on the grill, place the watercress and parsley in a medium bowl. Drizzle half the dressing over the greens and toss well. Divide the greens among 4 individual plates.

3. Place one grilled tuna steak on each plate over the salad greens. Drizzle the remaining dressing over the fish and serve immediately.

Substituting Different Types of Fish Fillets for Flavor Variations

The following table contains suggestions for substituting various kinds of fish fillets and steaks with the flavor variations included in this chapter. Always grill the substituted fish according to its respective charcoal or gas recipe directions. For example, if you substitute salmon fillets for bluefish fillets when making Cumin-Crusted Bluefish with Avocado Corn Relish, prepare the salmon as you would the bluefish in the variation, but grill it according to the recipe for either Charcoal-Grilled or Gas-Grilled Salmon Fillets.

RECIPE	OTHER FISH THAT GO WITH THESE FLAVORS
Bluefish Fillets, Cumin-Crusted, with Avocado-Corn Relish	Mahi-Mahi, Red Snapper, Salmon, Swordfish, Tuna
Halibut Steaks with Chipotle-Lime Butter	Bluefish, Mahi-Mahi, Red Snapper, Swordfish, Tuna
Mahi-Mahi Fillets with Shallots, Lime, and Cilantro	Bluefish (do not brine)
Red Snapper Fillets with Spicy Yellow Pepper and Tomato Salsa	Mahi-Mahi, Red Snapper, Salmon, Swordfish
Salmon Fillets with Mustard Glaze	Bluefish, Mahi-Mahi
Salmon Fillets with Aromatic Spice Rub	Bluefish, Mahi-Mahi, Sea Bass
Salmon Fillets with Indian Flavors and Mango Salsa	Bluefish, Mahi-Mahi
Salmon Fillets with Sesame-Soy Glaze	Bluefish, Mahi-Mahi, Sea Bass, Swordfish, Tuna
Sea Bass Fillets with Japanese-Style Broth	Red Snapper
Swordfish Steaks with Lemon-Parsley Sauce	Bluefish, Mahi-Mahi, Red Snapper, Sea Bass, Tuna
Swordfish Steaks with Salsa Verde	Halibut, Mahi-Mahi, Tuna
Tuna Steaks with Herb-Infused Oil	Mahi-Mahi, Red Snapper, Sea Bass, Swordfish
Tuna Steaks with Peppercorn Crust	Swordfish
Tuna Steaks with Tarragon-Lime Butter	Bluefish, Mahi-Mahi, Red Snapper, Swordfish
Tuna Steaks with Tapenade Butter	Mahi-Mahi, Salmon, Swordfish
Tuna Steaks with Watercress, Parsley, and Spiced Vinaigrette	Mahi-Mahi, Red Snapper, Swordfish

Grilled Tuna Steaks with Tarragon-Lime Butter or Tapenade Butter

Like beef, a tuna steak can be embellished with a slice of compound butter. The zesty flavors in these butters work well with the richness of the tuna.

Follow the recipe for Charcoal-Grilled or Gas-Grilled Tuna Steaks, topping each grilled tuna steak with a slice of Tarragon-Lime Butter or Tapenade Butter (page 30).

WHOLE FISH

GRILLING A WHOLE FISH IS ONE OF THOSE dazzling acts that looks harder than it really is. Most cooks don't want to bother with whole fish, but the rewards are ample. When cooked on the bone, the flesh is especially flavorful and juicy. This method also makes sense when you have caught the fish yourself.

In our testing, we discovered a number of general techniques that make grilling whole fish much easier. Sticking is the greatest challenge. Make sure your cooking rack is very hot before placing the fish on the grill. If using charcoal, we found it best to heat the cooking rack for 10 minutes rather than the standard 5 minutes. We found that oiling the fish as well as the rack also helped prevent sticking.

Most cooks encounter trouble when it comes time to turn the fish. Try to position the fish on the grill initially so it can be turned by rolling. Lifting a whole fish off the grill is risky—the fish can snap in half—so do so only when you must, that is, when the fish is done. When turning the fish, lift it gently at first to make sure that it is not sticking to the grill. If the fish is sticking, gently pull it from the cooking rack, working the sticking skin off the grill grates. The skin may still break, but at least you won't split the fish in half. To remove the whole fish from the grill once it's done, we found that two metal spatulas give the proper support and greatly reduce the risk of breaking the fish in half on the way to a platter. Ask someone to hold the platter right next to the grill for an easy transfer.

Many whole fish are fairly oily, making flare-ups a major concern. Any oil rubbed into the skin to keep it from sticking only makes matters worse. Be prepared to move the fish to another part of the grill if flare-ups occur. Better yet, keep a spray bottle filled with water nearby. Whole fish can tear and fall apart if moved too much on the grill. Dousing the flames with a spritz of water makes more sense.

WHOLE BLUEFISH

BLUEFISH IS GREAT FOR GRILLING WHOLE because its oils keep it nice and moist; it won't dry out as quickly as red snapper or striped bass. We did notice that bluefish took slightly longer to cook through than red snapper at exactly the same weight, perhaps because of the oiliness. We marinated the bluefish in lemon juice to help cut the oiliness of the fish and to balance its strong flavor.

Ideally, whole bluefish for grilling should be about 1½ pounds before gutting and scaling. Any larger and it's better to fillet the fish and cook the fillets individually on the grill (see the recipes on page 153). Larger fish will char before cooking through on the grill, not to mention the fact that they are very hard to maneuver.

As a precaution against charring this oily fish, we found it best to build a moderate fire, with the chimney only three-quarters full with charcoal.

Charcoal-Grilled Whole Bluefish

SERVES 4

Because bluefish is somewhat fatty, flare-ups occur when grilling. Be ready to spray the flames with water or to move the fish to another part of the grill when this happens.

3	tablespoons extra-virgin olive oil
3	tablespoons lemon juice
¾	teaspoon salt
	Ground black pepper
2	whole bluefish (1½ pounds each), gutted, scaled, and skin slashed on both sides (see illustrations on pages 170 and 171)
	Vegetable oil for grill rack
	Lemon wedges

1. Light a large chimney filled ¾ full with hardwood charcoal (about 2 pounds) and allow to burn until all the charcoal is covered in a layer of fine gray ash. Build a single-level fire by spreading the coals

evenly over the bottom of the grill. Set the cooking rack in place, cover the grill with the lid, and let the rack heat up, about 10 minutes. Use a wire brush to scrape clean the cooking rack. The grill is ready when the heat level of the coals is medium. (See how to gauge heat level on page 19.)

2. Meanwhile, mix the olive oil, lemon juice, salt, and pepper to taste together in a small bowl. Place the bluefish in a large shallow baking dish and pour the lemon juice mixture over it. Turn the bluefish to ensure that the lemon juice mixture coats both sides as well as the inside of each fish. Cover and refrigerate until ready to grill.

3. Lightly dip a small wad of paper towels in vegetable oil; holding wad with tongs, wipe grill rack (see page 45). Remove the fish from the marinade and place them on the grill over the coals. Grill, uncovered, until the side of the fish facing the charcoal is browned and crisp, about 7 minutes. Gently turn the fish over using two spatulas and cook until the flesh is no longer translucent at the center and the skin on both sides of each fish is blistered and crisp, 7 to 8 minutes more. (To check for doneness, peek into slashed flesh or into the interior through the opened bottom area of the fish to see that the flesh is no longer translucent.) Use two metal spatulas to transfer the fish to a platter (see illustration on page 172).

4. Fillet the fish according to the illustrations on page 173 and serve with lemon wedges.

Gas-Grilled Whole Bluefish
SERVES 4

Since the cover is down, be vigilant for signs of flare-ups, such as excessive smoking. Be ready to spray the flames with water or to move the fish to a cooler part of the grill when these occur.

3 tablespoons extra-virgin olive oil
3 tablespoons lemon juice
¾ teaspoon salt
   Ground black pepper
2 whole bluefish (1½ pounds each), gutted, scaled, and skin slashed on both sides (see illustrations below and on page 171)
   Vegetable oil for grill rack
   Lemon wedges

1. Preheat the grill with all burners set to high and the lid down until very hot, about 15 minutes. Use a wire brush to scrape clean the cooking rack. Turn all burners down to medium-high.

2. Meanwhile, mix the olive oil, lemon juice, salt, and pepper to taste together in a small bowl. Place

SCALING AND GUTTING A WHOLE FISH

We recommend asking your fishmonger to scale and gut fish. If you have caught your own fish, here's how to do this at home. Scaling is a messy job—try to do it outside or in a large, deep sink. It's also a good idea to wear rubber gloves.

1. Hold onto the fish by the tail with a kitchen towel. Using the back of a knife, a metal spoon, or a scaler, move from the tail toward the head, making short, firm strokes, until all scales are removed. You can tell if any scales remain by running your fingers along the fish in the same direction as you scale.

2. Using a very sharp knife, make an incision at the anal opening and continue cutting up the belly of the fish toward the head until the knife is just below the gills.

3. Using your fingers, pull out the innards of the fish, being sure to remove all viscera from the cavity; rinse with water. Use a spoon to scrape out any remaining innards.

the bluefish in a large shallow baking dish and pour the lemon juice mixture over it. Turn the bluefish to ensure that the lemon juice mixture coats both sides as well as the inside of each fish. Cover and refrigerate until ready to grill.

3. Lightly dip a small wad of paper towels in vegetable oil; holding wad with tongs, wipe grill rack (see page 45). Remove the fish from the marinade and place them on the grill. Grill, covered, until the side of the fish facing the fire is browned and crisp, 7 to 8 minutes. Gently turn the fish over using two spatulas and cook until the flesh is no longer translucent at the center and the skin on both sides of each fish is blistered and crisp, 7 to 8 minutes more. (To check for doneness, peek into slashed flesh or into the interior through the opened bottom area of the fish to see that the flesh is no longer translucent.) Use two metal spatulas to transfer the fish to a platter (see illustration on page 172).

4. Fillet the fish according to the illustrations on page 173 and serve with lemon wedges.

WHOLE MACKEREL

THERE ARE MANY TYPES OF MACKEREL, BUT common mackerel is usually under two pounds and has silvery blue-green skin with an attractive vertical pattern on the top of the fish. Mackerel are lean and long in appearance but are actually extremely oily fish that are well paired with the smoky flavor of the grill and with acidic or strongly flavored sauces. Mackerel do not need scaling, just gutting, which is easily done at home. These fish are also easy to grill.

SLASHING THE SKIN

Once a fish is scaled and gutted, use a sharp knife to make shallow diagonal slashes every 2 inches along both sides of the fish from top to bottom, beginning just behind the dorsal fin. This helps to ensure even cooking and also allows the cook to peek into the flesh to see if it is done.

Charcoal-Grilled Whole Mackerel

SERVES 2 TO 4

Most whole mackerel weigh between 1 and 1¼ pounds, more than enough for one person but not enough for two. If you can find larger mackerel (closer to two pounds), you can squeeze two servings out of one whole fish. Mackerel is high in fat; briefly marinating the fish in lemon juice tames some of this richness.

2	tablespoons extra-virgin olive oil
2	tablespoons lemon juice
½	teaspoon salt
	Ground black pepper
2	whole mackerel (1 to 2 pounds each), gutted and skin slashed on both sides (see illustrations on page 170 and below)
	Vegetable oil for grill rack
	Lemon wedges

1. Light a large chimney filled with hardwood charcoal (about 2½ pounds) and allow to burn until all the charcoal is covered with a layer of fine gray ash. Build a single-level fire by spreading the coals evenly over the bottom of the grill. Set the cooking rack in place, cover the grill with the lid, and let the rack heat up, about 10 minutes. Use a wire brush to scrape clean the cooking rack. The grill is ready when the coals are medium-hot. (See how to gauge heat level on page 19.)

2. Meanwhile, mix the olive oil, lemon juice, salt, and pepper to taste together in a small bowl. Place the mackerel in a large shallow baking dish and pour the lemon juice mixture over the fish. Turn the mackerel to ensure that the lemon juice mixture coats both sides as well as the inside of each fish. Cover and refrigerate until ready to grill.

3. Lightly dip a small wad of paper towels in vegetable oil; holding wad with tongs, wipe grill rack (see page 45). Remove the fish from the marinade and place them on the grill over the coals. Grill, uncovered, until the side of the fish facing the charcoal is browned and crisp, 5 to 6 minutes. Gently turn the fish over using two spatulas and cook until the flesh is no longer translucent at the center and the skin on both sides of the fish is blistered and

crisp, 5 to 6 minutes more. (To check for doneness, peek into slashed flesh or into the interior through the opened bottom area of the fish to see that the flesh is no longer translucent.) Use two metal spatulas to transfer the fish to a platter (see illustration below).

4. Fillet the fish according to illustrations on page 173 and serve with lemon wedges.

Gas-Grilled Whole Mackerel

SERVES 2 TO 4

If you have larger fish (close to 2 pound each), you can squeeze four servings out of this recipe.

2	tablespoons extra-virgin olive oil
2	tablespoons lemon juice
1/2	teaspoon salt
	Ground black pepper
2	whole mackerel (1 to 2 pounds each), gutted and skin slashed on both sides (see illustrations on pages 170 and 171)
	Vegetable oil for grill rack
	Lemon wedges

1. Preheat grill with all burners set to high and the lid down until very hot, about 15 minutes. Use a wire brush to scrape clean the cooking rack. Leave all burners on high.

2. Meanwhile, mix the olive oil, lemon juice, salt, and pepper to taste together in a small bowl. Place the mackerel in a large shallow baking dish and pour the lemon juice mixture over the fish. Turn the mackerel to ensure that the lemon juice mixture coats both sides as well as the inside of each fish. Cover and refrigerate until ready to grill.

3. Lightly dip a small wad of paper towels in vegetable oil; holding wad with tongs, wipe grill rack (see page 45). Remove the fish from the marinade and place them on the grill. Grill, covered, until the side of the fish facing the fire is browned and crisp, about 6 minutes. Gently turn the fish over using two spatulas and cook until the flesh is no longer translucent at the center and the skin on both sides of the fish is blistered and crisp, 6 to 7 minutes more. (To check for doneness, peek into slashed flesh or into the interior through the opened bottom area of the fish to see that the flesh is no longer translucent.) Use two metal spatulas to transfer the fish to a platter (see illustration below left).

4. Fillet the fish according to illustrations on page 173 and serve with lemon wedges.

➤ VARIATION

Spicy Grilled Mackerel with Garlic, Ginger, and Sesame Oil

Mackerel is a strong-flavored fish that can stand up to pungent flavors. Here it is matched with garlic, chiles, ginger, soy sauce, and sesame oil. Serve with plain steamed rice, which will act as a neutral foil for the intensely flavored fish. Have all the ingredients ready for the sauce so that it can be made quickly right after the fish come off the grill.

1	recipe Charcoal-Grilled or Gas-Grilled Mackerel
2	tablespoons vegetable or peanut oil
1	medium scallion, minced
1/2	medium jalapeño chile, stemmed, seeded, and minced
1/2	teaspoon finely grated fresh ginger
2	medium garlic cloves, minced
1	teaspoon Asian sesame oil
1	tablespoon soy sauce
	Lemon wedges

1. Grill the fish as directed, tenting foil over the platter with the grilled fish to keep them warm.

2. Heat the oil in a small skillet over medium-high heat until it shimmers. Add the scallion and jalapeño and cook until softened, about 30 seconds.

MOVING GRILLED WHOLE FISH

Once the fish is done, slide two metal spatulas under the belly, lifting gently to make sure the skin is not sticking to the grill. Quickly lift the fish and place on a nearby platter.

Add the ginger and garlic and cook until fragrant, about 30 seconds longer. Remove the pan from the heat and stir in the sesame oil and soy sauce. Spoon the sauce over the fish and serve immediately with the lemon wedges.

WHOLE POMPANO

POMPANO IS A THIN, SILVERY FISH. IT HAS rich, full-flavored, slightly oily flesh. Because the flesh is somewhat oily, flare-ups are a real concern. We found it helpful to reduce the amount of charcoal (from the standard full chimney to ¾ chimney). Still, be prepared to move the fish to another part of the grill or to douse the flames with a spray bottle if flare-ups occur.

When grilling whole pompano, be sure to buy fish caught in waters off the Gulf Coast and Florida. This variety is much larger than Pacific pompano (also called butterfish) and is better suited to grilling whole.

Charcoal-Grilled Whole Pompano

SERVES 4

This thin, silver fish has fine, rich flesh. Because some of its oil drips down into the coals during grilling, flare-ups do occur. When this happens, carefully move the fish to a cooler part of the grill or spray the flames with water to prevent the skin from charring.

2   **whole pompano (about 1½ pounds each), scaled, gutted, and skin slashed on both sides (see illustrations on pages 170 and 171)**

2   **tablespoons extra-virgin olive oil**
    Salt and ground black pepper
    Vegetable oil for grill rack
    Lemon wedges

1. Light a large chimney filled ¾ full with hardwood charcoal (about 2 pounds) and allow to burn until all the charcoal is covered with a layer of fine gray ash. Build a single layer fire by spreading the coals evenly over the bottom of the grill for a medium fire. Set the cooking rack in place, cover the grill with the lid, and let the rack heat up, about 10 minutes. Use a wire brush to scrape clean the cooking rack.

2. Rub the fish with olive oil and season generously with salt and pepper on the outside as well as inside the cavity of each fish.

3. Lightly dip a small wad of paper towels in vegetable oil; holding wad with tongs, wipe grill rack (see page 45). Place the fish on the grill over the coals. Grill, uncovered, until the side of each fish facing the charcoal is browned and crisp, 6 to 7 minutes. Gently turn the fish over using two spatulas and cook until the flesh is no longer translucent at the center and the skin on both sides of each fish is blistered and crisp, 6 to 7 minutes more. (To check for doneness, peek into the slashed flesh or into the interior through the opened bottom area of each fish to see that the flesh is no longer translucent.) Use two metal spatulas to transfer the fish to a platter (see illustration on page 172).

4. Fillet the fish according to the illustrations below and serve with lemon wedges.

FILLETING GRILLED WHOLE FISH

1. Using a sharp knife, make a vertical cut just behind the head from the top of the fish to the belly. Make another cut along the top of the fish from the head to the tail.

2. Use a metal spatula to lift the meat from the bones, starting at the head end and running the spatula over the bones to lift out the fillet. Repeat on the other side of the fish. Discard the fish head and skeleton.

Gas-Grilled Whole Pompano

SERVES 4

Be sure to keep an eye on the grill while the pompano cooks. If large amounts of smoke are coming from the grill, flare-ups are probably occurring under the closed lid. When this happens, carefully move the fish to a cooler part of the grill or spray the flames with water to prevent the skin from charring.

2 whole pompano (about 1½ pounds each), scaled, gutted, and skin slashed on both sides (see illustrations on pages 170 and 171)

2 tablespoons extra-virgin olive oil
 Salt and ground black pepper
 Vegetable oil for grill rack
 Lemon wedges

1. Preheat the grill with all burners set to high and the lid down until very hot, about 15 minutes. Use a wire brush to scrape clean the cooking rack. Turn all burners down to medium-high.

2. Rub the fish with olive oil and season generously with salt and pepper on the outside as well as inside the cavity of each fish.

3. Lightly dip a small wad of paper towels in vegetable oil; holding wad with tongs, wipe grill rack (see page 45). Place the fish on the grill. Grill, covered, until the side of each fish facing the fire is browned and crisp, about 7 minutes. Gently turn the fish over using two spatulas and cook until the flesh is no longer translucent at the center and the skin on both sides of each fish is blistered and crisp, about 7 minutes more. (To check for doneness, peek into the slashed flesh or into the interior through the opened bottom area of each fish to see that the flesh is no longer translucent.) Use two metal spatulas to transfer the fish to a platter (see illustration on page 172).

4. Fillet the fish according to illustrations on page 173 and serve with lemon wedges.

➤ VARIATION

Grilled Whole Pompano with Tarragon Butter Sauce

Pompano is a refined fish that takes well to refined sauces. Here, it is paired with a butter sauce flavored with white wine and tarragon.

1 cup dry white wine
1 tablespoon white wine vinegar
2 large shallots, minced (about ¼ cup)
¼ cup heavy cream
1 recipe Charcoal-Grilled or Gas-Grilled Whole Pompano
4 tablespoons cold unsalted butter, cut into 4 pieces
1 teaspoon chopped fresh tarragon leaves
 Salt and ground black pepper

1. Combine the wine, vinegar, and shallots in a small saucepan. Bring to a boil over high heat; reduce the heat to medium-high and simmer until almost all the liquid has evaporated, 9 to 10 minutes. Add the heavy cream and bring to a boil. Cook for 1 minute. Remove the pan from the heat and set it aside.

2. Grill the fish as directed, tenting foil over the platter with the grilled fish to keep it warm.

3. Bring the white wine/cream mixture back to a boil over medium heat. Reduce the heat to low and whisk in the butter, one piece at a time, until all pieces are incorporated into the sauce. Add the tarragon and season with salt and pepper to taste.

4. Place one fillet onto each serving plate, and spoon some of the butter sauce over the top. Serve immediately.

WHOLE RED SNAPPER, SEA BASS, AND STRIPED BASS

WE HAVE GROUPED THESE FISH TOGETHER because they are all fairly lean, white-fleshed fish that grill beautifully using the same level of heat for the same amount of time. They can also be served with the same sauces.

Red snapper is white-fleshed, firm, and lean, and when purchased it should be bright silvery red. Its flavor is mild and clean, and its skin crisps up nicely. We found that fish weighing from 1½ to 1¾ pounds are best for grilling. Fish any larger than 2 pounds are hard to grill because they are difficult to turn and to remove from the grill. Larger fish take a long time to cook through, and the skin is more likely to char. A 1½-pound red snapper will feed two people. (The same is true for sea bass and striped bass.) If you have to scale the fish yourself, be careful of the sharp spines on the fins (they can easily prick your hands). The scales are rather large and tough, so we recommend that you have a fishmonger remove them.

Sea bass is almost completely black. Once scaled, it has a black and white houndstooth sort of look to it. It is firm-fleshed, making it very suitable for grilling whole. Its flavor is quite mild.

Most small striped bass are from fish farms and are actually hybrid striped bass. They are a cross between wild striped bass (which lives in both fresh and salt water) and white bass (a freshwater variety). Striped bass is more full-flavored than red snapper, but it has the same firm texture and is fairly lean. Striped bass is grayish in color with long horizontal black stripes running along each side. Like snapper and sea bass, striped bass needs to be scaled.

Charcoal-Grilled Whole Red Snapper, Sea Bass, or Striped Bass

SERVES 4

If your fish are a little larger (between 1½ and 2 pounds), simply grill them a minute or two longer on each side. Fish weighing more than 2 pounds will be hard to maneuver on the grill and should be avoided.

> 2   whole red snapper, sea bass, or striped bass (about 1½ pounds each), scaled, gutted, and skin slashed on both sides (see illustrations on pages 170 and 171)
> 3   tablespoons extra-virgin olive oil
>   Salt and ground black pepper
>   Vegetable oil for grill rack
>   Lemon wedges

1. Light a large chimney filled with hardwood charcoal (about 2½ pounds) and allow to burn until all the charcoal is covered with a layer of fine gray ash. Build a single-level fire by spreading the coals evenly over the bottom of the grill. Set the cooking rack in place, cover the grill with the lid, and let the rack heat up, about 10 minutes. Use a wire brush to scrape clean the cooking rack. The grill is ready when the coals are medium-hot. (See how to gauge heat level on page 19.)

2. Rub the fish with olive oil and season generously with salt and pepper on the outside as well as the inside of each fish.

3. Lightly dip a small wad of paper towels in vegetable oil; holding wad with tongs, wipe grill rack (see page 45). Place the fish on the grill. Grill, uncovered, until the side of the fish facing the charcoal is browned and crisp, 6 to 7 minutes. Gently turn the fish over using two spatulas and cook until the flesh is no longer translucent at the center and the skin on both sides of each fish is blistered and crisp, 6 to 8 minutes more. (To check for doneness, peek into slashed flesh or into the interior through the opened bottom area of each fish to see that the flesh is no longer translucent.) Use two metal spatulas to transfer the fish to a platter (see illustration on page 172).

4. Fillet the fish according to the illustrations on page 173 and serve with lemon wedges.

Gas-Grilled Whole Red Snapper, Sea Bass, or Striped Bass

SERVES 4

Make sure the grill is as hot and clean as possible.

> 2   whole red snapper, sea bass, or striped bass (about 1½ pounds each), scaled, gutted, and skin slashed on both sides (see illustrations on pages 170 and 171)
> 3   tablespoons extra-virgin olive oil
>   Salt and ground black pepper
>   Vegetable oil for grill rack
>   Lemon wedges

1. Preheat the grill with all burners set to high and the lid down until very hot, about 15 minutes. Use a wire brush to scrape clean the cooking rack. Leave all burners on high.

2. Rub the fish with olive oil and season generously with salt and pepper on the outside as well as the inside of each fish.

3. Lightly dip a small wad of paper towels in vegetable oil; holding wad with tongs, wipe grill rack (see page 45). Place the fish on the grill. Grill, covered, until the side of the fish facing the fire is browned and crisp, 7 to 8 minutes. Gently turn the fish over using two spatulas and cook until the flesh is no longer translucent at the center and the skin on both sides of each fish is blistered and crisp, 6 to 8

minutes more. (To check for doneness, peek into slashed flesh or into the interior through the opened bottom area of each fish to see that the flesh is no longer translucent.) Use two metal spatulas to transfer the fish to a platter (see illustration on page 172).

4. Fillet the fish according to the illustrations on page 173 and serve with lemon wedges.

➤ VARIATIONS

Grilled Whole Red Snapper, Sea Bass, or Striped Bass with Orange, Lime, and Cilantro Vinaigrette

This vinaigrette lends a light acidic counterpoint to the smoky grilled fish.

¼	cup orange juice
1	tablespoon lime juice
1	medium clove garlic, minced
2	teaspoons sugar
½	teaspoon salt

	Ground black pepper
6	tablespoons vegetable oil
1	tablespoon chopped fresh cilantro leaves
1	recipe Charcoal-Grilled or Gas-Grilled Whole Red Snapper, Sea Bass, or Striped Bass (without lemon wedges)
	Lime wedges

1. Whisk the juices, garlic, sugar, salt, and pepper to taste together in a medium bowl. Whisk in the oil until the dressing is smooth. Whisk in the cilantro and adjust the seasonings.

2. Grill the fish as directed. Drizzle the filleted fish with the vinaigrette and serve with lime wedges.

Grilled Whole Red Snapper, Sea Bass, or Striped Bass with Lemon-Parsley Butter

Flavored butters are an easy and convenient way to flavor grilled whole fish.

WHAT ABOUT WHOLE SALMON?

A whole salmon is too large to grill over direct heat (the skin burns before the fish is cooked through), but we thought we would be able to devise a method for grill-roasting this favorite fish. (See page xiii for definitions of grill-roasting and barbecuing.) Despite visions of crispy, crackling skin and smoky, juicy, flavorful flesh, our attempts to make a well-seasoned, smoky, whole grill-roasted salmon proved unsuccessful. In fact, after several efforts, we concluded instead that barbecuing an entire side (see page 275) produces better results with less hassle and effort.

While flavorful on its own, salmon benefits greatly from being properly seasoned and browned. When cooked whole, it is especially hard to season the meat of the fish. We tried seasoning the outside of the fish, as well as the interior cavity, but to no avail; except for the skin and the small area of flesh that surrounds the cavity of the fish, the fish remained largely unseasoned and bland. Brining also seemed out of the question with such a large fish (the smallest salmon available during testing was 7 pounds) in such an odd elongated shape. There simply was no practical container in which to brine it.

Because a side of salmon contains no bones, it can be bent to fit into a large, round container for brining. Alternatively, the meat can be seasoned directly with salt and pepper, unlike the meat of the whole salmon, which is surrounded with skin. The meat on a side of salmon gains additional flavor through browning and caramelization. Unfortunately, because virtually no meat on a whole salmon is exposed during cooking, only the surrounding skin gets browned and crisp; the flavor is more like smoky poached salmon, not the roasted, rich flavor one expects.

We were surprised to find that the texture of the whole grill-roasted fish, while moist, was also unpleasantly mushy and spongy. The barbecued side of salmon, on the other hand, remained moist, but it also developed an appealing firmness and structure that the whole grill-roasted salmon lacked. Another bonus of the side of salmon was the crust that developed on the surface of the meat, making for a nice contrast with the softer texture of the interior.

Finally, we find that a whole salmon is a lot of fish to be moving on and off a grill; it has a high risk of being broken or dropped. It takes two people and a lot of effort to remove this large a fish from the grill intact, and the results are less than worth the effort. While it also takes a bit of effort to lift a side of salmon off the grill without having it stick or break, we believe that in this case it is worth the extra effort.

Follow the recipe for Charcoal-Grilled or Gas-Grilled Whole Red Snapper, Sea Bass, or Striped Bass. Cut Parsley-Lemon Butter (page 30) into four slices and top each fillet with one piece of butter. Serve immediately with lemon wedges.

Grilled Whole Red Snapper, Sea Bass, or Striped Bass with Fresh Tomato-Basil Relish

Fresh relishes are good on grilled fish. Use this recipe in the summer when tomato season is at its peak.

I   pound fresh ripe tomatoes, cored, seeded, and
     cut into ¼-inch dice
I   medium shallot, minced (about 2 tablespoons)
I   medium garlic clove, minced
2   tablespoons extra-virgin olive oil
I   teaspoon red wine vinegar
2   tablespoons chopped fresh basil leaves
     Salt and ground black pepper
I   recipe Charcoal-Grilled or Gas-Grilled Whole
     Red Snapper, Sea Bass, or Striped Bass (without
     lemon wedges)

1. Mix the tomatoes, shallot, garlic, oil, vinegar, basil, and salt and pepper to taste together in a medium bowl. (The relish can be covered and refrigerated for a day or two.)

2. Grill the fish as directed; serve the filleted fish with the relish.

WHOLE TROUT

AT THREE-QUARTERS OF A POUND, FRESH-water trout is an ideal fish for grilling. (Steelhead trout spend part of their life cycle in the ocean and taste and look more like salmon.) Freshwater trout have thin, delicate skin and fine flesh that is pinkish when raw and white when cooked.

We did not make any slits in the sides of this fish because each fish is small enough to cook through evenly without the slits and we didn't want to encourage any tearing of the trout's thin skin. Trout is not terribly oily, so flare-ups are not really a concern. The small size of the trout means that the flesh will cook through without any charring of the skin. Because each person is served a whole fish, there's no need to fillet the fish after grilling.

Charcoal-Grilled Whole Freshwater Trout

SERVES 4

This recipe is designed for freshwater trout, such as rainbow, golden, lake, or brook trout. If you find steelhead trout or arctic char, refer to the section on grilled salmon fillets. Freshwater trout is delicious grilled; the skin becomes thin and crispy, and the fine flesh is full-flavored but not fishy. If you find the presence of heads on the fish on a serving platter or dinner plate to be disturbing, simply cut the heads off before grilling or have your fishmonger do it.

4   whole freshwater trout (each about ¾ pound),
     scaled and gutted (see illustrations on page 170)
3   tablespoons extra-virgin olive oil
     Salt and ground black pepper
     Vegetable oil for grill rack
     Lemon wedges

1. Light a large chimney filled with hardwood charcoal (about 2½ pounds) and allow to burn until all the charcoal is covered in a layer of fine gray ash. Build a single-level fire by spreading the coals evenly over the bottom of the grill. Set the cooking rack in place, cover the grill with the lid, and let the rack heat up, about 10 minutes. Use a wire brush to scrape clean the cooking rack. The grill is ready when the coals are medium-hot. (See how to gauge heat level on page 19.)

2. Rub the fish with olive oil and season generously with salt and pepper on the outside as well as the inside of each fish.

3. Lightly dip a small wad of paper towels in vegetable oil; holding wad with tongs, wipe grill rack (see page 45). Place the fish on the grill. Grill, uncovered, until the side of the fish facing the charcoal is browned and crisp, about 4 minutes. Gently turn the fish over using two spatulas and cook until the flesh is no longer translucent at the center and the skin on both sides of each fish is blistered and crisp, 4 to 5 minutes more. (To check for doneness, peek into the interior through the opened bottom area of each fish to see that the flesh is no longer translucent.) Use two metal spatulas to transfer the fish to a platter (see illustration on page 172). Serve immediately with lemon wedges.

Gas-Grilled Whole Freshwater Trout

SERVES 4

This recipe is designed for freshwater trout, such as rainbow, golden, lake, or brook trout. If you find steelhead trout or arctic char, refer to the section on grilled salmon fillets. Freshwater trout is delicious grilled; the skin becomes thin and crispy, and the fine flesh is full-flavored but not fishy. If you find the presence of heads on the fish on a serving platter or dinner plate to be disturbing, simply cut the heads off before grilling or have your fishmonger do it.

4   whole freshwater trout (each about ¾ pound), scaled and gutted (see illustrations on page 170)

3   tablespoons extra-virgin olive oil

    Salt and ground black pepper

    Vegetable oil for grill rack

    Lemon wedges

1. Preheat the grill with all burners set to high and the lid down until very hot, about 15 minutes. Use a wire brush to scrape clean the cooking rack. Leave all burners on high.

2. Rub the fish with olive oil and season generously with salt and pepper on the outside as well as the inside of each fish.

3. Lightly dip a small wad of paper towels in vegetable oil; holding wad with tongs, wipe grill rack (see page 45). Place the fish on the grill. Grill, covered, until the side of the fish facing the fire is browned and crisp, about 5 minutes. Gently turn the fish over using two spatulas and cook until the flesh is no longer translucent at the center and the skin on both sides of each fish is blistered and crisp, 4 to 5 minutes more. (To check for doneness, peek into the interior through the opened bottom area of each fish to see that the flesh is no longer translucent.) Use two metal spatulas to transfer the fish to a platter (see illustration on page 172). Serve immediately with lemon wedges.

➤ VARIATION

Grilled Whole Freshwater Trout with Bacon and Horseradish-Peppercorn Sauce

You will need a large fish basket for this recipe to keep the bacon from falling off the trout during grilling. Make sure to oil the basket well and remove the fish promptly after grilling so they don't stick. If you do not have a fish basket, you can always grill the trout according to the directions in the preceding recipes and cook the bacon separately, crumbling and sprinkling it over the grilled fish just before serving.

SAUCE

¾   cup sour cream

3   tablespoons milk

2   teaspoons prepared horseradish

¾   teaspoon coarsely ground black peppercorns

1   teaspoon lemon juice

½   teaspoon salt

3   tablespoons minced chives

4   whole freshwater trout (each about ¾ pound), scaled and gutted (see illustrations on page 170)

3   tablespoons vegetable oil

8   strips bacon

    Ground black pepper

    Nonstick cooking spray for oiling fish basket

1. Mix the sour cream, milk, horseradish, peppercorns, lemon juice, salt, and chives together in a medium bowl. Cover and refrigerate the sauce for up to 1 day.

2. Rub the fish with oil and season generously with pepper on the outside as well as the inside of each fish. Lay one strip of bacon over the length of each side of each fish and place all trout in an oiled fish basket.

3. Grill the trout as directed in the recipe for Charcoal-Grilled or Gas-Grilled Whole Freshwater Trout. Remove the basket from the grill and carefully transfer the fish to four plates. Serve immediately, passing the sauce separately.

12

VEGETABLES AND FRUITS

VEGETABLES AND FRUITS ARE EASILY grilled. Once most vegetables and fruits are streaked with grill marks, they are done. Vegetables and fruits will pick up any off flavors from the grill, so make sure the cooking grate is clean. Small items may fall through the grate, so use a grill grid (see page 12) or skewers.

Since vegetables and fruits are usually grilled along with something else, we have not given separate charcoal and gas variations in this chapter. Most likely you will be lighting a fire to grill fish, chicken, or meat, and the vegetables and fruit will need to work within the constraints of that fire. In any case, the timing for grilling vegetables and fruits is the same on both charcoal and gas; just remember to keep the lid down when cooking over gas and up when cooking over charcoal.

VEGETABLES

GRILLING VEGETABLES SHOULD BE EASY. You've made a fire to grill a couple of steaks, some swordfish, or maybe a few pieces of chicken. There are some vegetables in the fridge, and you want to turn them into a side dish without having to heat up your kitchen. It sounds simple, but a number of questions immediately arise. Do you have to precook the vegetables? How thick should each vegetable be sliced? What's the best temperature for grilling them?

We decided at the outset that we wanted to develop guidelines for grilling as many kinds of vegetables as possible without precooking them. Blanching, baking, or microwaving is not hard, but each does add an extra step and time to what should be a simple process. In addition, blanching and baking heat up the kitchen. We wanted to blanch only when absolutely necessary.

Vegetables don't respond well to blazing fires—incineration is a real possibility. We found that most vegetables are best cooked over a medium or medium-hot fire. We played around with wood chips (both hickory and mesquite) and found no perceptible change in flavor. Vegetables do not cook long enough to pick up any wood flavor. If you happen to have chips on the grill to cook something else, they won't do any harm, but don't expect them to add great flavor to the vegetables.

A better way to season vegetables is to brush them with flavored oil just before grilling. (Marinating is not advised because the acids will make vegetables soggy; portobello mushrooms are the one exception.) Make sure to use a good-quality olive or peanut oil. (We found that vegetables brushed with canola, corn, or other bland oils were boring.) Try adding fresh herbs, garlic, and/or grated citrus zest to the oil, or purchase one that is already flavored. Seasoning with salt and pepper both before and after grilling is another way to maximize flavor.

A lot of equipment exists out there for grilling; much of it is designed for vegetables. We tried grilling vegetables in a hinged metal basket and felt that this tool was not very practical. One part of the grill is always hotter or colder than another and invariably some vegetables are ready to be turned before others. Large vegetables (everything from asparagus spears to sliced zucchini) are best cooked right on the grill grate.

You can skewer smaller items (like cherry tomatoes and white mushrooms) to prevent them from falling through the cooking grate. Wooden skewers are generally quite thin (which is good) but they can burn. Metal skewers are a better option. Just make sure they are thin. Thick metal skewers are fine for meat but will tear mushrooms and cherry tomatoes.

The other option is to grill small vegetables on a grill grid (see page 12). This gadget prevents the vegetables from falling through the grate but allows you to turn each piece of food individually when it has browned sufficiently.

ASPARAGUS

ASPARAGUS PRESENTS ONLY ONE PREPARATION issue: should the spears be peeled, or is it better to discard the tough, fibrous ends entirely? In our tests, we found that peeled asparagus have a silkier texture, but we preferred the contrast between the crisp peel and tender inner flesh of the unpeeled asparagus. Peeling is also a lot of work. We prefer to simply snap off the tough ends and proceed with cooking.

The intense dry heat of the grill concentrates the flavor of the asparagus, and the exterior caramelization makes the spears especially sweet. The result is asparagus with a heightened and, we think, delicious flavor.

Grilled Asparagus

SERVES 4

Thick spears will burn on the surface before they cook through. Use spears no thicker than ⅝ inch.

1½	pounds asparagus, tough ends snapped off (see illustration, below right)
1	tablespoon extra-virgin olive oil
	Salt and ground black pepper

1. Toss the asparagus with oil in a medium bowl or on a rimmed baking sheet.

2. Grill the asparagus over a medium-hot fire (see how to gauge heat level on page 19), turning once, until tender and streaked with light grill marks, 5 to 7 minutes.

3. Transfer the grilled asparagus to a platter. Season with salt and pepper to taste and serve hot, warm, or at room temperature.

> VARIATIONS

Grilled Asparagus with Peanut Sauce

The aggressive flavors in this Thai-style sauce work well with grilled asparagus.

1	tablespoon smooth peanut butter
1	tablespoon Asian sesame oil
1½	teaspoons soy sauce
1½	teaspoons rice vinegar
1	medium garlic clove, minced
1½	teaspoons minced fresh ginger
	Salt and ground black pepper
1½	pounds asparagus, tough ends snapped off (see illustration at right)
1	tablespoon minced fresh cilantro leaves

1. Whisk the peanut butter, oil, 1 tablespoon water, soy sauce, vinegar, garlic, ginger, and salt and pepper to taste together in a small bowl. Toss the asparagus with half the peanut dressing in a medium bowl or on a rimmed baking sheet. Whisk the cilantro into the remaining dressing and set it aside.

2. Grill the asparagus over a medium-hot fire (see how to gauge heat level on page 19), turning once, until tender and streaked with light grill marks, 5 to 7 minutes.

3. Transfer the grilled asparagus to a platter. Toss the asparagus with the remaining dressing. Adjust the seasonings and serve hot, warm, or at room temperature.

Grilled Asparagus with Rosemary and Goat Cheese

The woodsy flavor of rosemary highlights the grilled flavor of the asparagus.

2	tablespoons extra-virgin olive oil
1	tablespoon lemon juice
1	medium garlic clove, minced
½	teaspoon minced fresh rosemary
	Salt and ground black pepper
1½	pounds asparagus, tough ends snapped off (see illustration below)
1	ounce goat cheese, crumbled

1. Whisk the oil, lemon juice, garlic, rosemary, and salt and pepper to taste together in a small bowl. Toss the asparagus with 1 tablespoon of the dressing in a medium bowl or on a rimmed baking sheet.

2. Grill the asparagus over a medium-hot fire (see how to gauge heat level on page 19), turning once, until tender and streaked with light grill marks, 5 to 7 minutes.

3. Transfer the grilled asparagus to a platter. Toss the asparagus with the remaining dressing. Adjust the seasonings, sprinkle with the cheese, and serve hot, warm, or at room temperature.

SNAPPING OFF TOUGH ENDS FROM ASPARAGUS

In our tests, we found that the tough, woody part of the stem will break off in just the right place if you hold the spear the right way. Hold the asparagus about halfway down the stalk. With the other hand, hold the cut end between your thumb and index finger about an inch or so up from the bottom; bend the stalk until it snaps.

Grilled Asparagus with Blue Cheese and Anchovy Dressing

A little blue cheese goes a long way in this dish. If you prefer, use feta cheese instead.

2	tablespoons extra-virgin olive oil
I	tablespoon lemon juice
2	anchovy fillets, minced
I	medium garlic clove, minced
	Salt and ground black pepper
I ½	pounds asparagus, tough ends snapped off (see illustration on page 181)
I	ounce blue cheese, crumbled

1. Whisk the oil, lemon juice, anchovies, garlic, and salt and pepper to taste together in a small bowl. Toss the asparagus with 1 tablespoon of the dressing in a medium bowl or on a rimmed baking sheet.

2. Grill the asparagus over a medium-hot fire (see how to gauge heat level on page 19), turning once, until tender and streaked with light grill marks, 5 to 7 minutes.

3. Transfer the grilled asparagus to a platter. Toss the asparagus with the remaining dressing. Adjust the seasonings, sprinkle with the cheese, and serve hot, warm, or at room temperature.

Grilled Asparagus with Almonds, Green Olives, and Sherry Vinaigrette

Spanish flavors make this dish an excellent addition to an antipasto spread.

2	tablespoons extra-virgin olive oil
I	tablespoon sherry vinegar
2	tablespoons minced fresh onion
I	medium garlic clove, minced
½	teaspoon ground cumin
	Salt and ground black pepper
I ½	pounds asparagus, tough ends snapped off (see illustration on page 181)
¼	cup sliced almonds, toasted
2	tablespoons pitted and chopped green olives

1. Whisk the oil, vinegar, onion, garlic, cumin, and salt and pepper to taste together in a small bowl. Toss the asparagus with 2 tablespoons of the dressing in a medium bowl or on a rimmed baking sheet.

2. Grill the asparagus over a medium-hot fire (see how to gauge heat level on page 19), turning once, until tender and streaked with light grill marks, 5 to 7 minutes.

3. Transfer the grilled asparagus to a platter. Toss the asparagus with the remaining dressing. Adjust the seasonings, sprinkle with the almonds and olives, and serve hot, warm, or at room temperature.

CORN

DESPITE FARMSTAND SIGNS ACROSS THE country announcing "Butter and Sugar" corn for sale, no one actually grows old-time Butter and Sugar corn anymore. Nor does anybody grow most of the other old-fashioned nonhybrid varieties. Bygone varieties of corn have mostly disappeared for a reason. Their sugar converted to starch so rapidly that people literally fired up their kettles before going out to pick the corn. Corn has since been crossbred to make for sweeter ears that have a longer hold on their fresh flavor and tender texture.

Basically, there are three hybrid types: normal sugary, sugar-enhanced, and supersweet. Each contains dozens of varieties, with fancy names such as Kandy Korn, Double Gem, and Mystique. Normal sugary types, such as Silver Queen, are moderately sweet with traditional corn flavor. Their sugars convert to starches rapidly after being picked. The sugar-enhanced types are more tender and somewhat sweeter, with a slower conversion of sugar to starch. Supersweet corn has heightened sweetness, a crisp texture, and a remarkably slow conversion of sugar to starch after it is picked. It is a popular type for growers who supply distant markets and so require a product with longer shelf life. So it is most likely that any corn sold in your supermarket during the off-season is a variety of supersweet.

Beyond the above generalization, it's impossible to tell which kind of corn you have until you taste it. With that in mind, we developed a grilling method that would work with all three kinds of corn hybrids.

Grilled corn should match the juiciness of boiled without sacrificing the toasty caramelization and smoke-infused graces of the grill. We started our tests with the bare ear cooked directly over a medium-high fire. The outcome seemed too good to be true. The lightly caramelized corn was still juicy, with a toasty hit of grilled flavor and a sweet essence to chase it down.

In fact, it *was* too good to be true. The variety of corn we used was fittingly called Fantasy, which is a supersweet. When we tried grilling a normal sugary corn variety with the husk off, the outcome was a flavorless, dry, gummy turn-off. The end result was no better with sugar-enhanced corn. The direct heat was just too much for the fleeting flavor and tender texture of the normal sugary and sugar-enhanced corn types.

We went on to test another popular grilling technique; we threw the whole ear on the grill, husk and all, as is. We tried this with all three corn types at various heat levels. Half of the ears of corn were soaked in water beforehand; the other half were not. The husk-on method made for a great-tasting ear of corn—a particularly crisp, juicy one. But if it were not for the sticky charred husks you would think you were eating boiled corn. The presoaked corn in particular just steams in the husk and picks up absolutely no grilled flavor.

Since grilling with the husk off was too aggressive for nonsupersweet varieties and grilling with the husk on was no different from boiling corn, we turned to a compromise approach. We peeled off all of the husk except for the innermost layer wrapped around the ear. This layer is much more moist and delicate than the outer layers—so much so that you can practically see the kernels through the husk. When the corn was cooked over a medium-high fire, this fine husk gave the corn a jacket heavy enough to prevent dehydration yet light enough to allow a gentle toasting of the kernels. After about eight minutes (rolling the corn one-quarter turn every two minutes), we could be

certain that the corn was cooked just right because the husk picked up the dark silhouette of the kernels and began to pull back from the tip of the ear.

Grilled Corn
SERVES 4 TO 8

If you are certain that you have a supersweet variety of corn, remove the husk entirely, then follow the instructions below, grilling until the kernels are light caramel brown, 5 to 7 minutes.

> 8 ears fresh corn, prepared according to
> illustrations on page 184
> Salt and ground black pepper
> Butter (optional)

1. Grill the corn over a medium-hot fire (see how to gauge heat level on page 19), turning the ears every 1½ to 2 minutes, until the kernels have left dark outlines in the husk and the husk is charred and beginning to peel away from the tip to expose some kernels (see illustration at lower left), 8 to 10 minutes.

2. Transfer the corn to a platter; carefully remove and discard the charred husk and silk. Season the corn with salt and pepper to taste and butter, if desired. Serve immediately.

SCIENCE: STORING CORN

While the general rule of thumb is to buy and eat corn the same day it has been harvested, many of us have to break that rule pretty often. So we decided to test a variety of methods for overnight storage. We chose Silver Queen corn, one of the more perishable varieties, for our tests.

We found that the worst thing you can do to corn is to leave it sitting out on the counter. Throwing it into the refrigerator without any wrapping is nearly as bad. Storing it in an airtight bag helps, but the winning method entailed wrapping the corn (husks left on) in a wet paper bag and then in a plastic bag and refrigerating it. After 24 hours of storage, we found that the corn was still juicy, sweet, and fresh tasting while not starchy.

We spoke with several food scientists, and they told us that refrigeration slows the rate at which the corn's natural sugars are converted to starches. Wrapping the ears in a wet paper bag slows the rate of moisture loss and helps keep the kernels juicy.

JUDGING WHEN CORN IS DONE

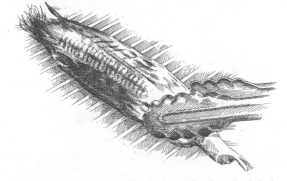

When the corn is properly grilled, the husk will pick up the dark silhouette of the kernels and begin to pull away from the tip of the ear.

➤ VARIATIONS

Grilled Corn with Herb Butter

Brush with herb butter just before serving.

6	tablespoons unsalted butter
3	tablespoons minced fresh parsley, thyme, cilantro, basil, and/or other fresh herbs
	Salt and ground black pepper
8	ears fresh corn, prepared according to illustrations below

1. Melt butter in a small saucepan. Add the herbs and salt and pepper to taste; keep the butter warm.

2. Grill the corn over a medium-hot fire (see how to gauge heat level on page 19), turning the ears every 1½ to 2 minutes, until the kernels have left dark outlines in the husk and the husk is charred and beginning to peel away from the tip to expose some kernels (see illustration on page 183), 8 to 10 minutes.

3. Transfer the corn to a platter; carefully remove and discard the charred husk and silk. Brush the herb butter over the corn and serve immediately.

Grilled Corn with Chile Butter

Toast dried ancho or chipotle chiles over the grill before grinding them in a spice grinder for the best flavor. You can substitute ½ teaspoon preground chili powder if you like.

2	ancho or 3 medium chipotle chiles
6	tablespoons unsalted butter
	Salt
8	ears fresh corn, prepared according to illustrations below

1. Grill the chiles, turning once, until puffed, 30 to 60 seconds. Cool slightly. Remove stems and seeds from the chiles and grind to a powder in a clean spice or coffee grinder.

2. Melt butter in a small saucepan. Add the chili powder and salt to taste; keep the butter warm.

3. Grill the corn over a medium-hot fire (see how to gauge heat level on page 19), turning the ears every 1½ to 2 minutes, until the kernels have left dark outlines in the husk and the husk is charred and beginning to peel away from the tip to expose some kernels (see illustration on page 183), 8 to 10 minutes.

4. Transfer the corn to a platter; carefully remove and discard the charred husk and silk. Brush the chile butter over the corn and serve immediately.

Grilled Corn with Garlic Butter and Cheese

The buttery, nutty flavor of Parmesan cheese works surprisingly well with the flavor of grilled corn.

6	tablespoons unsalted butter
1	medium garlic clove, minced
¼	teaspoon salt
8	ears fresh corn, prepared according to illustrations below
¼	cup grated Parmesan cheese, or more if desired

1. Melt butter in a small saucepan over medium heat until bubbling. Add the garlic and cook until fragrant, about 30 seconds. Remove the pan from the heat and stir in the salt. Cover and set the pan aside.

2. Grill the corn over a medium-hot fire (see how

PREPARING CORN FOR THE GRILL

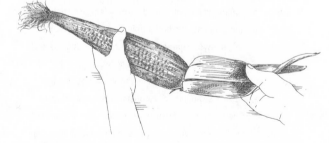

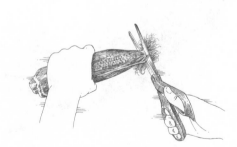

1. Remove all but the innermost layer of the husk. The kernels should be covered by, but visible through, the last husk layer.

2. Use scissors to snip off the tassel, or long silk ends, from the tip of the ear.

to gauge heat level on page 19), turning the ears every 1½ to 2 minutes, until the kernels have left dark outlines in the husk and the husk is charred and beginning to peel away from the tip to expose some kernels (see illustration on page 183), 8 to 10 minutes.

3. Transfer the corn to a platter; carefully remove and discard the charred husk and silk. Brush the garlic butter over the corn. Sprinkle with the cheese and serve immediately.

EGGPLANT

THE BIGGEST CHALLENGE THAT CONFRONTS the cook when preparing eggplant is excess moisture. That's why grilling is such an ideal method for cooking eggplant. Under the broiler or in a hot pan, the eggplant steams in its own juices and becomes mushy. Eggplant is often salted before being cooked to draw out these juices.

On the grill, there's no need to draw out moisture from eggplant slices before grilling. The moisture will fall harmlessly through the cooking grate. The eggplant browns beautifully and becomes crisp in spots. In our tests, we found that thinner slices can fall apart on the cooking grate. Thicker pieces, ideally ¾-inch rounds, can withstand grilling.

Grilled Eggplant

SERVES 4

There's no need to salt eggplant destined for the grill. The intense grill heat will vaporize excess moisture.

3	tablespoons extra-virgin olive oil
2	medium garlic cloves, minced
2	teaspoons minced fresh thyme or oregano leaves
	Salt and ground black pepper
1	large eggplant (about 1½ pounds), ends trimmed and cut crosswise into ¾-inch rounds

1. Combine the oil, garlic, herbs, and salt and pepper to taste in a small bowl. Place the eggplant on a platter and brush both sides with the oil mixture.

2. Grill the eggplant over a medium-hot fire (see how to gauge heat level on page 19), turning once, until streaked with dark grill marks, 8 to 10 minutes.

3. Transfer the grilled eggplant to a platter. Adjust the seasonings and serve hot, warm, or at room temperature.

➤ VARIATIONS
Grilled Eggplant with Ginger and Soy
Honey gives the sauce a thick texture and gentle sweetness.

2	tablespoons soy sauce
1½	tablespoons honey
1	tablespoon rice vinegar
1	teaspoon Asian sesame oil
3	tablespoons peanut oil
1	tablespoon minced fresh ginger
	Ground black pepper
1	large eggplant (about 1½ pounds), ends trimmed and cut crosswise into ¾-inch rounds
2	medium scallions, sliced thin

1. Combine the soy sauce, honey, vinegar, and 1 tablespoon water in a small skillet. Bring to a boil over medium-high heat and simmer until slightly thickened, about 2 minutes. Remove the pan from the heat and stir in the sesame oil. Set this sauce aside.

2. Combine the peanut oil, ginger, and pepper to taste in a small bowl. Place the eggplant on a platter and brush both sides with the peanut oil mixture.

3. Grill the eggplant over a medium-hot fire (see how to gauge heat level on page 19), turning once, until streaked with dark grill marks, 8 to 10 minutes.

4. Transfer the grilled eggplant to a platter. Drizzle the thickened soy mixture over the eggplant and sprinkle with scallions. Serve hot, warm, or at room temperature.

Grilled Eggplant with Sweet Miso Glaze
Miso, fermented soybean paste, is both salty and sweet. You can find it in Asian specialty food shops, natural food stores, and some supermarkets. In Japan, eggplant is traditionally grilled and then doused with this sweet glaze.

¼	cup white miso
7	tablespoons sugar
2	tablespoons mirin (sweet Japanese rice wine)
3	tablespoons peanut or vegetable oil
2	medium garlic cloves, minced

Salt and ground black pepper

1 large eggplant (about 1½ pounds), ends trimmed and cut crosswise into ¾-inch rounds

2½ tablespoons toasted sesame seeds

1. Mix the miso, sugar, mirin, and 3 tablespoons water together in a medium bowl. Set aside.

2. Combine the oil, garlic, and salt and pepper to taste in a small bowl. Place the eggplant on a platter and brush both sides with the oil mixture.

3. Grill the eggplant over a medium-hot fire (see how to gauge heat level on page 19), turning once, until streaked with grill marks, 6 to 8 minutes. Brush both sides with the miso glaze and grill until glaze is hot and eggplant is tender throughout, about 1 minute longer on each side.

4. Transfer the grilled eggplant to a platter. Adjust the seasonings and sprinkle with sesame seeds. Serve hot, warm, or at room temperature.

Grilled Curried Eggplant

Grilled eggplant takes very well to the flavors of yogurt and spices. Serve with basmati rice.

½ cup plain yogurt

1 teaspoon curry powder

2 teaspoons sugar

5 tablespoons vegetable oil

2 medium garlic cloves, minced

Salt and ground black pepper

1 large eggplant (about 1½ pounds), ends trimmed and cut crosswise into ¾-inch rounds

1. Mix the yogurt, curry powder, sugar, and 2 tablespoons of the oil together in a medium bowl. Set aside.

2. Combine the remaining 3 tablespoons of oil, garlic, and salt and pepper to taste in a small bowl. Place the eggplant on a platter and brush both sides with the garlic and oil mixture.

3. Grill the eggplant over a medium-hot fire (see how to gauge heat level on page 19), turning once, until streaked with grill marks, 6 to 8 minutes. Brush both sides with the yogurt-curry mixture and grill until glaze is hot and eggplant is tender throughout, about 1 minute longer on each side.

4. Transfer the grilled eggplant to a platter. Adjust the seasonings and serve hot, warm, or at room temperature.

ENDIVE

ALTHOUGH WE GENERALLY THINK OF CRISP and crunchy Belgian endive in terms of salads, it grills beautifully. The texture softens, but the vegetable holds its shape. Best of all, the bitter flavor softens a bit when exposed to intense heat.

We tried grilling endive whole, but it charred on the outside before the interior cooked through. We had far better results when we sliced each head in half lengthwise. With a piece of the core still attached, the layers of leaves stay together. Since the core is exposed, it softens quickly and is crisp-tender by the time the exterior is streaked with dark grill marks.

PREPARING ENDIVE

1. With a knife, shave off the discolored end of the endive. Cut the thinnest slice possible.

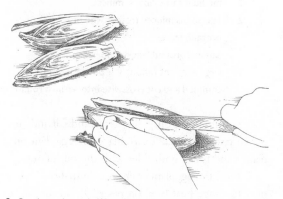

2. Cut the endive in half lengthwise through the core end. Cut this way, the halves stay intact for easy grilling.

Grilled Belgian Endive

SERVES 4 TO 8

Belgian endive is in the same family as chicory and is a slightly bitter, small, long, tightly packed head of yellow and white leaves. For grilling, the core of the endive is left intact, so that the leaves stay together for easy turning. Depending on what else is being served, plan on either one or two heads of endive per person.

8	medium heads Belgian endive, prepared according to illustrations on page 186
3	tablespoons extra-virgin olive oil
	Salt and ground black pepper

1. Toss the endive halves in a large bowl with oil and season with salt and pepper to taste.

2. Grill the endive over a medium-hot fire (see how to gauge heat level on page 19), turning once, until dark grill marks appear and the center of each is crisp-tender, 5 to 7 minutes. Serve hot or at room temperature.

➤ VARIATIONS

Grilled Belgian Endive with Mustard Dressing and Parmesan

Mustard, anchovies, garlic, and capers join together to complement the bitter flavor of Belgian endive.

1	tablespoon Dijon mustard
1	teaspoon red wine vinegar
1	medium garlic clove, minced
2	anchovy fillets, minced
1	teaspoon drained capers, chopped
1/3	cup extra-virgin olive oil
8	medium heads Belgian endive, prepared according to illustrations on page 186
	Grated Parmesan cheese

1. Whisk the mustard, vinegar, garlic, anchovies, and capers together in a large mixing bowl. Gradually whisk in the oil. Add the endive and toss to coat each piece.

2. Grill the endive over a medium-hot fire (see how to gauge heat level on page 19), turning once, until dark grill marks appear and the center of each is crisp-tender, 5 to 7 minutes.

3. Transfer the grilled endive to a platter and sprinkle with cheese to taste. Serve hot.

Grilled Belgian Endive with Balsamic Dressing

Serve with grilled bread and an assortment of Italian cheeses for a great first course.

1/4	cup balsamic vinegar
1	tablespoon honey
1	medium garlic clove, minced
1/3	cup extra-virgin olive oil
2	teaspoons chopped fresh thyme leaves
	Salt and ground black pepper
8	medium heads Belgian endive, prepared according to illustrations on page 186

1. Whisk the vinegar, honey, and garlic together in a large bowl. Gradually whisk in the oil. Stir in the thyme and salt and pepper to taste. Add the endive and toss to coat each piece.

2. Grill the endive over a medium-hot fire (see how to gauge heat level on page 19), turning once, until dark grill marks appear and the center of each is crisp-tender, 5 to 7 minutes. Serve hot or at room temperature.

FENNEL

GRILLING CAUSES THE NATURAL SUGARS IN fennel to caramelize, thereby enhancing its flavor. Like endive, fennel holds its shape well on the grill and softens to a creamy texture.

The biggest challenge when grilling fennel is slicing the bulb so that the pieces pick up as much flavor as possible without falling through the grill grate. Thin strips of fennel must be cooked on a grill grid (see page 12). We had better luck when we sliced the bulb through the core end into fan-shaped pieces. With a piece of the core still attached, the various layers remained intact as a single piece. With two flat sides, fan-shaped pieces also have plenty of surface area, so they pick up a lot of grill flavor.

Grilled Fennel

SERVES 4

Fennel grills beautifully. Its anise flavor is complemented by the caramelization of natural sugars on the surface of the vegetable.

2	medium fennel bulbs (about 2 pounds), prepared according to illustrations below
3	tablespoons extra-virgin olive oil
	Salt and ground black pepper

1. Toss the fennel and oil together in a large mixing bowl. Season with salt and pepper to taste.

2. Grill the fennel over a medium-hot fire (see how to gauge heat level on page 19), turning once, until tender and streaked with dark grill marks, 7 to 9 minutes. Serve hot, warm, or at room temperature.

➤ VARIATIONS

Grilled Fennel with Tarragon and Shallots

Tarragon gives a boost to the mild licorice flavor of fennel. Vinegar and shallots temper the sweetness of the vegetable.

1	medium shallot, minced
2	tablespoons red wine vinegar
1	teaspoon honey
	Salt and ground black pepper
1/4	cup extra-virgin olive oil
1 1/2	tablespoons minced fresh tarragon leaves
2	medium fennel bulbs (about 2 pounds), prepared according to illustrations below

1. Mix the shallot, vinegar, honey, and salt and pepper to taste together in a small bowl. Gradually whisk in the oil. Add the tarragon and fennel and toss to coat.

2. Grill the fennel over a medium-hot fire (see how to gauge heat level on page 19), turning once, until tender and streaked with dark grill marks, 7 to 9 minutes. Serve hot, warm, or at room temperature.

Grilled Fennel with Citrus

A light dressing of citrus juices lends a subtle twist to grilled fennel. Serve with a mild, white-fleshed fish such as snapper.

1	medium shallot, minced
1	medium garlic clove, minced
1/4	cup orange juice
1	tablespoon lemon juice
	Salt and ground black pepper
1/4	cup extra-virgin olive oil
2	teaspoons minced fresh thyme leaves
2	medium fennel bulbs (about 2 pounds), prepared according to illustrations below

1. Whisk the shallot, garlic, orange juice, lemon juice, and salt and pepper to taste together in large bowl. Gradually whisk in the oil. Add the thyme and fennel and toss to coat.

2. Grill the fennel over a medium-hot fire (see how to gauge heat level on page 19), turning once, until tender and streaked with dark grill marks, 7 to 9 minutes. Serve hot, warm, or at room temperature.

PREPARING FENNEL

  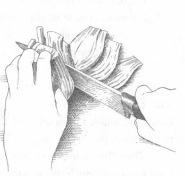

1. Cut off the stems and feathery fronds. (The fronds can be minced and used for garnishing.)

2. Trim a very thin slice from the base and remove any tough or blemished outer layers from the bulb.

3. Slice the bulb vertically through the base into 1/4-inch-thick pieces that resemble fans.

GARLIC

IT IS POSSIBLE TO ROAST GARLIC ON THE grill if you adapt the classic oven-roasting technique, which involves cutting off the top of the head of garlic to expose the cloves, oiling the garlic, and then wrapping it in foil. We found that this method worked fine as long as we didn't grill the garlic over a hot fire. Even when wrapped in a double layer of foil, garlic grilled over a hot fire scorched before the cloves had softened to a creamy consistency. Garlic must be grilled over a fairly cool fire. You have several options.

If you are grill-roasting (see page 230 for a definition of grill-roasting) or grilling over a two-level fire, simply place the garlic packet on the cool side of the grill and cook, turning once, until the garlic gives a bit when gently squeezed. If you are grilling over a single-level fire, you must wait until the fire has died down. Only when the fire has cooled to medium can you place the garlic on the grill. To trap the remaining heat, grill the garlic with the grill

GRILL-ROASTING GARLIC

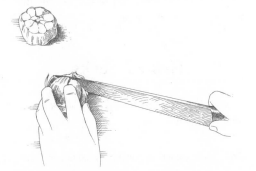

1. Before grilling, slice the top third (the side opposite the root) off the head of garlic, so that all cloves are exposed. Discard the top.

2. Once grilled, push from the root end down to squeeze the cloves from their papery skins.

cover on, whether you are using a gas or a charcoal grill. The foil protects the garlic from picking up any off flavors.

Grill-Roasted Garlic

MAKES ¹/₂ CUP

Roasted garlic can be used simply as a spread on grilled bread or to flavor any number of foods, from mashed potatoes to salads and sauces. Mash herbs into the roasted garlic for a more interesting spread; chopped fresh thyme or a small amount of chopped fresh rosemary work especially well this way.

3	medium heads of garlic, prepared according to illustration at left
1 ½	tablespoons extra-virgin olive oil
	Salt and ground black pepper

1. Cut two 12-inch squares of aluminum foil. Lay one on top of the other to form a double layer of foil. Toss the cut heads of garlic with oil in a medium bowl and season generously with salt and pepper to taste. Place the garlic in the center of the foil and wrap so that both sides of the packet are flat (you must cook both sides of the garlic on the grill).

2. If using a single- or two-level fire, grill over medium heat (see how to gauge heat level on page 19), covered, for 25 minutes, turning once. If grill-roasting, cook for 35 to 45 minutes, turning once. When done, the garlic will give a bit when lightly squeezed.

3. Remove the packet from the grill; let garlic rest, still wrapped, for 15 minutes, or until cool enough to handle. Remove the garlic from the foil and squeeze the cloves out of their papery skins (see illustration at left). The cloves should be soft enough to mash. (The garlic can be refrigerated in an airtight container overnight.)

GREEN BEANS

ALTHOUGH WE PROBABLY WOULDN'T GRILL thin, just-picked green beans, this cooking method works well with thicker, older beans. Tender beans are best boiled or steamed to preserve their delicate flavor, but thicker beans are often bland when prepared those ways. When grilled, they pick up a lightly caramelized flavor.

When simply oiled before being grilled, the green beans were a bit tough. We found that if we rinsed the beans first, then tossed them in oil without drying them, the beans were crisp-tender after about six minutes on the grill. The extra moisture clinging to the beans evaporated during the first minute or two of cooking and helped to "steam" them a bit.

Grilled Green Beans

SERVES 4

Green beans will not dry out on the grill if you rinse them and leave the excess water on the beans. They cook quickly and retain a good crunch. Add a minced clove of garlic to the oil for more flavor, or serve with crumbled goat cheese.

1½	pounds green beans, rinsed (do not pat dry)
1½	tablespoons extra-virgin olive oil
	Salt and ground black pepper

1. Toss the moist beans with oil in a large bowl. Season with salt and pepper to taste.

GRILLING GREEN BEANS

Place the beans perpendicular to the grill grate rods so they won't fall through the grate. If you prefer, use a grill grid, but the beans won't caramelize as well.

2. Grill the beans over a medium-hot fire (see how to gauge heat level on page 19), with the green beans placed perpendicular to the grill grate rods (see illustration, below left). Grill until the beans are lightly browned and crisp-tender, about 6 minutes. Serve hot, warm, or at room temperature.

LEEKS

THE UNIQUE, ONIONLIKE SWEETNESS OF leeks makes them a delicious vegetable side dish. Leeks must be precooked before grilling. When we tried grilling them without precooking, the inner layers were tough and chewy while the outer layers were dry and charred. Most sources suggest boiling leeks before grilling them, but we wondered if that was the best way to preserve and enhance their flavor.

We found that boiling as well as braising tend to wash away some of the leek flavor. However, we did like the silky, smooth texture of boiled or braised leeks. Steamed leeks had the same supple texture as leeks that were boiled or braised, but they also retained a stronger and sweeter onionlike flavor. Once steamed, the leeks can be put on the grill to pick up some smoky flavor.

Grilled Leeks

SERVES 4

Once the leeks have been steamed, they can be grilled and seasoned (see the variations).

4	leeks (preferably small to medium-sized), trimmed, soaked, and rinsed thoroughly (see illustrations on page 191)
3	tablespoons extra-virgin olive oil
	Salt and ground black pepper

1. Arrange the leeks in a single layer in a steamer basket or insert. Carefully place the basket over a pot of vigorously boiling water; cover and steam until the tip of a knife inserted in the thickest part of a leek meets no resistance, about 8 minutes for leeks ¾ inch thick or about 10 minutes for leeks 1¼ inches thick. Remove the leeks from the steamer. (The leeks can be covered and set aside for several hours.)

2. Brush the leeks with oil and season with salt and pepper to taste. Grill the leeks over a medium-hot fire (see how to gauge heat level on page 19), turning once, until streaked with light grill marks, 3 to 4 minutes. Serve hot, warm, or at room temperature.

➤ VARIATIONS

Grilled Leeks with Orange-Chive Butter

If you like, substitute lemon juice and zest for the orange, and other herbs (such as basil, cilantro, or mint) for the chives.

2	tablespoons unsalted butter, softened
1½	teaspoons grated orange zest
1	teaspoon orange juice
2	teaspoons snipped fresh chives
	Salt and ground black pepper
1	recipe Grilled Leeks

1. Combine the butter, orange zest and juice, chives, and salt and pepper to taste in a small bowl.

2. Prepare the leeks as directed. When they come off the grill, arrange the leeks on a platter and evenly distribute bits of the flavored butter over them. Serve immediately.

Grilled Leeks with Anchovies and Garlic

Serve these leeks with oily fish such as salmon or mackerel. Their intense flavors go well together.

1	recipe Grilled Leeks (without oil)
2	medium garlic cloves, minced
3	anchovy fillets, minced
2	tablespoons lemon juice
6	tablespoons extra-virgin olive oil

1. While the leeks are steaming, combine the garlic, anchovies, lemon juice, and oil in a small bowl.

2. Brush the anchovy-garlic mixture over the steamed leeks and grill as directed. Serve hot, warm, or at room temperature.

TRIMMING AND CLEANING LEEKS

1. Trim leeks about 2 inches beyond the point where the leaves start to darken.

2. Trim the root end, keeping the base intact.

3. Slit the leek lengthwise upward through the leaves, keeping the base intact.

4. By trimming only the dark green parts of each half, you can save more of the leek.

5. Soak the trimmed leeks in a sinkful of cold water to loosen excess dirt, then rinse them in cold running water, pulling apart the layers with your fingers to expose any clinging dirt.

MUSHROOMS

THE PORTOBELLO IS THE KING OF THE mushroom world. When grilled, it has the taste and texture of meat. It can be used as a sandwich filling, vegetable side dish, or even as a vegetarian entrée.

There's not much to grilling portobellos—just cook over a hot fire until nicely browned. They need to be well oiled before being grilled so they won't dry out. The other option is to marinate them before cooking. Portobellos are quite porous and will soak up a lot of liquid (and flavor) in a relatively short period of time.

In contrast, white button mushrooms have a lousy reputation. Cooks who ooh and aah over portobellos and other exotic mushrooms often consider the white mushroom, also called the button, to be beneath their consideration. But button mushrooms are inexpensive and almost always available (they are the only choice in some markets), which gives them at least some appeal. We figured there must be a way of grilling them that would bring out the deep, rich, earthy flavors for which their tonier cousins are so highly prized.

We found that there are two secrets to great grilled button mushrooms. First, the mushrooms must be skewered so they won't fall through the grill grate. Second, they must be cooked thoroughly to expel as much moisture as possible and to concentrate their flavor. We found that turning the mushrooms three times (so they spend time on all sides) was also important. Grilled this way, button mushrooms develop a rich brown crust and meaty flavor.

SKEWERING BUTTON OR CREMINI MUSHROOMS

Once these small mushrooms have been cleaned and any dry ends trimmed from the stems, they should be skewered so they won't fall through the grill grate. Make sure to skewer each mushroom through the cap and stem so it is less likely to rotate when turned on the grill.

Cremini mushrooms, light brown mushrooms that are roughly the same shape and size as white button mushrooms, can be cooked the same way as buttons. Since cremini are actually diminutive portobellos, they have a fair amount of flavor to start out with. Once grilled, they are delicious.

Grilled Button or Cremini Mushrooms

SERVES 4

Grilling improves the humble button mushroom, intensifying the earthy flavor and lending smokiness to this otherwise bland mushroom.

1	pound medium-to-large button or cremini mushrooms, cleaned and stem ends trimmed
2	tablespoons extra-virgin olive oil
	Salt and ground black pepper

1. Toss the mushrooms with oil and season with salt and pepper to taste. Thread the mushrooms onto skewers through the stems and caps (see illustration at lower left).

2. Grill the mushrooms over a medium-hot fire (see how to gauge heat level on page 19), turning once every 3 minutes, until dark brown grill marks appear on all sides and the mushrooms begin to release their liquid, about 12 minutes total. Serve immediately.

➤ VARIATION

Grilled Button or Cremini Mushrooms with Asian Flavors

Serve these mushrooms with any Asian-style grilled meat and plain steamed rice.

2	tablespoons soy sauce
1	tablespoon vegetable oil
2	teaspoons rice vinegar
2	medium garlic cloves, minced
1	teaspoon sugar
1	pound medium-to-large button or cremini mushrooms, cleaned and stem ends trimmed

1. Mix the soy sauce, oil, vinegar, garlic, and sugar together in a large bowl. Add the mushrooms

and toss to coat. Thread the mushrooms onto skewers through the stems and caps (see illustration on page 192).

2. Grill the mushrooms over a medium-hot fire (see how to gauge heat level on page 19), turning once every 3 minutes, until dark brown grill marks appear on all sides and the mushrooms begin to release their liquid, about 12 minutes total. Serve immediately.

Grilled Portobello Mushrooms

SERVES 4

Portobello mushrooms are a great alternative to meat because of their steaklike texture and large size. Use in sandwiches or in pastas in place of meat or poultry.

- **4** medium portobello mushrooms (about 4 inches in diameter), stems removed
- **3** tablespoons extra-virgin olive oil
  Salt and ground black pepper

1. On both sides of each mushroom cap, brush with oil and season with salt and pepper to taste.

2. Grill the mushrooms over a medium-hot fire (see how to gauge heat level on page 19), turning once, until tender and lightly browned, 8 to 10 minutes.

3. Slice the grilled mushrooms into wide strips (or leave whole) and serve hot.

➤ VARIATIONS

Grilled Portobello Mushrooms with Garlic, Rosemary, and Balsamic Vinegar

Mushrooms are great for marinating and grilling because they are so porous; they soak up vinaigrette readily for maximum flavor.

- **2** medium garlic cloves, minced
- **2** teaspoons minced fresh rosemary leaves
  Salt
  Ground black pepper
- **2** tablespoons balsamic vinegar
- **¼** cup extra-virgin olive oil
- **4** medium portobello mushrooms (about 4 inches in diameter), stems removed

1. Whisk the garlic, rosemary, ¼ teaspoon salt, pepper to taste, vinegar, and oil together in small bowl. On both sides of each mushroom cap, brush with the oil mixture and season with salt and pepper.

2. Grill the mushrooms over a medium-hot fire (see how to gauge heat level on page 19), turning once, until tender and lightly browned, 8 to 10 minutes.

SCIENCE: To Wash or Not to Wash Mushrooms

Common culinary wisdom dictates that mushrooms should never, ever be washed. Put these spongy fungi under the faucet or in a bowl with water, the dictum goes, and they will soak up the water like a sponge.

Like most cooks, we had always blindly followed this precept. But when we learned that mushrooms consist of more than 80 percent water, we began to question their ability to absorb yet more liquid. As we so often do in situations like this, we consulted the work of food scientist and author Harold McGee. Sure enough, in his book *The Curious Cook* (North Point Press, 1990) we found an experiment he had devised to test this very piece of accepted mushroom lore. We decided to duplicate McGee's work in our test kitchen.

We weighed out six ounces of white mushrooms and put them into a bowl, then added water to cover and let them sit. After five minutes we shook off the surface water and weighed

the mushrooms again. Our results replicated McGee's—the total weight gain for all the mushrooms together was one-quarter ounce, which translates to about 1½ teaspoons of water.

We suspected that this gain represented mostly surface moisture rather than absorption, so we repeated the experiment with six ounces of broccoli, which no one would claim is an absorbent vegetable. The weight gain after a five-minute soak was almost identical—one-fifth of an ounce—suggesting that most of the moisture was clinging to the surface of the vegetables rather than being absorbed by them.

So, as it turns out, mushrooms can be cleaned in the same way that other vegetables are cleaned—rinsed under cold water. However, it's best to rinse them just before cooking and to avoid rinsing altogether if you are using them uncooked, since the surfaces of wet mushrooms turn dark and slimy when they're exposed to air for more than four or five minutes.

3. Slice the grilled mushrooms into wide strips (or leave whole) and serve hot.

Grilled Portobello Sandwiches with Boursin Cheese and Tomatoes

SERVES 4 AS A LIGHT LUNCH

Portobello mushrooms are delicious in sandwiches. Here they are paired with Boursin cheese (a soft cheese flavored with herbs and garlic) and tomatoes. If you cannot find Boursin cheese, simply mix ¼ cup cream cheese with ½ teaspoon thyme and ½ clove minced garlic, and season with salt and pepper. Use 1 tablespoon of the cream cheese spread on each sandwich.

4	medium portobello mushrooms (about 4 inches in diameter), stems removed
6	tablespoons extra-virgin olive oil
	Salt and ground black pepper
8	slices country bread, about 4 inches in diameter and ½ inch thick
8	teaspoons Boursin cheese
2	medium tomatoes, cored and cut crosswise into ¼-inch slices
4	cups mesclun mix

1. On both sides of each mushroom cap, brush with 3 tablespoons oil and season with salt and pepper.

2. Grill the mushrooms over a medium-hot fire (see how to gauge heat level on page 19), turning once, until tender and lightly browned, 8 to 10 minutes. Cut the grilled mushrooms into ½-inch-thick slices.

3. Brush the remaining 3 tablespoons oil over both sides of each bread slice. Grill, turning once, until both sides of each slice are toasty and have dark grill marks, 1 to 2 minutes. Transfer the bread slices to a cutting board.

4. Spread 2 teaspoons Boursin cheese onto 4 slices of bread. On the remaining slices, build the sandwich: place mushroom slices on each of the 4 pieces of bread; cover with tomato slices and some mesclun mix. Place the bread with the cheese on top of the sandwich and serve immediately.

ONIONS

ONIONS CARAMELIZE ON THE GRILL AND become crisp in spots. Slices expose the greatest surface area and make the most sense. To keep the slices from falling apart, it is necessary to skewer each crosswise (from side to side) so that it can rest flat on the grill and be easily turned.

Grilled Onions

SERVES 4

These onions are wonderful on burgers or served with just about any grilled meat, game, or poultry. The onions sweeten and caramelize as they cook on the grill. If you prefer, you can grill the onions on a grill grid (page 12), but they won't brown quite as well.

2	large onions (about 1¼ pounds), papery skins removed and cut crosswise into ½-inch-thick rounds
2	tablespoons extra-virgin olive oil
	Salt and ground black pepper

1. Place the onion slices on a baking sheet and brush with oil; season with salt and pepper to taste

PREPARING ONIONS

1. Cut thick slices from large onions, then skewer them all the way through with a slender bamboo skewer that is about the same thickness as a toothpick or with a thin metal skewer.

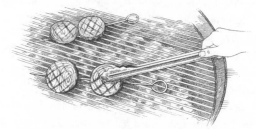

2. The skewered onion slices remain intact as they are grilled, and, best of all, they can be flipped easily with tongs.

on both sides of each slice. Thread the onions onto skewers (see illustrations on page 194).

2. Grill the onions over a medium-hot fire (see how to gauge heat level on page 19), turning once, until streaked with dark grill marks, 10 to 12 minutes. Serve hot, warm, or at room temperature.

➤ VARIATIONS

Grilled Onions with Garlic and Thyme

Garlic and thyme add an extra flavor dimension to grilled onions. Other herbs, such as chives, parsley, tarragon, oregano, or rosemary, may be substituted for the thyme. If using rosemary, reduce the amount to ½ teaspoon.

I   teaspoon chopped fresh thyme leaves

I   medium garlic clove, minced

I   teaspoon white wine vinegar

I ½   tablespoons extra-virgin olive oil

2   large onions (about I ¼ pounds), papery skins removed and cut crosswise into ½-inch-thick rounds

    Salt and ground black pepper

1. Mix the thyme, garlic, vinegar, and oil together in a small bowl. Place the onion slices on a baking sheet and brush both sides of each slice with the oil mixture. Season with salt and pepper to taste. Thread the onions onto skewers (see illustrations on page 194).

2. Grill the onions over a medium-hot fire (see how to gauge heat level on page 19), turning once, until streaked with dark grill marks, 10 to 12 minutes. Serve hot, warm, or at room temperature.

Grilled Red Onion and Tomato Salad

The sweetness of grilled onions is an excellent foil for the acidity of tomatoes. Try to use a high-quality, aged balsamic vinegar for this salad. Serve with steaks or burgers.

2   large red onions (about I ¼ pounds), peeled and cut crosswise into ½-inch-thick rounds

3   tablespoons extra-virgin olive oil

    Salt and ground black pepper

3   small, ripe tomatoes (about I pound), cored and cut into ¾-inch-thick wedges

10   large fresh basil leaves, coarsely chopped

2   teaspoons balsamic vinegar

1. Place the onions on a baking sheet and brush both sides of each slice with 2 tablespoons oil. Sprinkle generously with salt and pepper to taste. Thread the onions onto skewers (see illustrations on page 194).

2. Grill the onions over a medium-hot fire (see how to gauge heat level on page 19), turning once, until streaked with dark grill marks, 10 to 12 minutes.

3. Transfer the onions to a cutting board and cool slightly. Remove the skewers. Cut the onion slices in half, then place them in a serving bowl and toss gently to separate the layers.

4. Add the tomatoes, basil, and salt and pepper to taste to the bowl with the onions. Drizzle the remaining 1 tablespoon oil and the vinegar over the salad; toss gently. (The salad can be covered and set aside at room temperature for 1 hour.)

PEPPERS

THE ROASTING OF BELL PEPPERS HAS BECOME very popular, and for very good reasons. When roasted, sweet red bell peppers assume a complex, smoky flavor. They can be used on sandwiches or in sauces, or they can be served as part of an antipasto. Although the broiler is the best place to roast peppers, if you are grilling it is easy enough to roast peppers on the grill.

We found that you must take care not to overroast the peppers. When the skin of a pepper puffs up and turns black, it has reached the point at which flavor is maximized and the texture of the flesh is soft but not mushy. After this point, continued exposure to heat results in darkened flesh that is thinner, flabbier-textured, and slightly bitter.

Unless your fingers are made of asbestos, roasted peppers need time to cool before being handled; steaming during this time makes it a bit easier to peel off the charred skin. The ideal steaming time is 15 minutes—any less and the peppers are still too hot to work with comfortably. The best method is to use a heat-resistant bowl (glass, ceramic, or metal) with a piece of plastic wrap secured over the top to trap the steam.

Don't be tempted to rinse the seeds away as you peel the peppers. Notice the rich oils that accumulate on your fingers as you work. It seems silly to rinse away those oils rather than savor them later with your meal.

The way peppers are treated after they are peeled

will determine how long they keep. Simply wrapped in plastic wrap, peppers will keep their full, meaty texture for only about two days in the refrigerator. Drizzled with a generous amount of olive oil and placed in an airtight container, peppers will keep about one week without losing texture or flavor.

Although we love the silky texture of skinned roasted peppers, grilled bell peppers can be served with their skin on. In that case, you need to oil the peppers quite well and to cook them less—just until lightly colored. The skins should wrinkle but not blister. Grilled peppers can be seasoned in numerous ways and make an excellent side dish.

Roasted Bell Peppers on the Grill

Although peppers are usually roasted under a broiler or over an open gas burner in the kitchen, we find it practical and easy to do this job while grilling other foods.

3   large bell peppers (about 1½ pounds),
    preferably red, yellow, or orange
    Extra-virgin olive oil

1. Grill whole peppers over a medium-hot fire (see how to gauge heat level on page 19), turning as the skin on each side blisters and chars (every 3 to 4 minutes), for a total of about 15 minutes.

2. Remove the peppers from the grill and transfer to a large bowl. Cover with plastic wrap and allow to

steam for 15 minutes. With your fingers, scrape off the blackened skin from the peppers. Remove and discard the core and seeds. Place the peppers in an airtight container, drizzle with olive oil, and refrigerate for up to 1 week.

Grilled Bell Peppers

SERVES 4

Sweet bell peppers, especially red and yellow peppers, are especially tasty when grilled. Serve them as a side dish or as part of an antipasto platter with cold cuts, olives, marinated mushrooms, and marinated artichoke hearts.

3   large bell peppers (about 1½ pounds),
    prepared according to illustrations below
2   tablespoons extra-virgin olive oil
    Salt and ground black pepper

1. Toss the peppers and oil in a large heat-resistant bowl. Season to taste with salt and pepper. (Reserve the bowl with the residual oil for the grilled peppers).

2. Grill the peppers over a medium-hot fire (see how to gauge heat level on page 19), turning every 2 minutes, until dark grill marks appear, the skins begin to wrinkle, and the peppers are crisp-tender, 8 to 10 minutes total.

3. Place the peppers back in the bowl and toss to coat with the residual oil. Allow the peppers to cool, then cut into thinner strips. Serve warm or at room temperature.

PREPARING PEPPERS

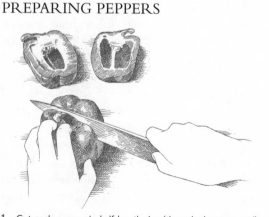

1. Cut each pepper in half lengthwise (through the stem end). Remove the core and seeds.

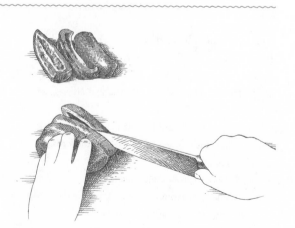

2. Cut each cleaned half in thirds lengthwise.

Spanish-Style Grilled Peppers with Green Olives and Sherry Vinegar

Sherry vinegar adds a tangy, acidic edge to this dish. We suggest using red peppers in this recipe. Serve with other tapas (small dishes) for a full Spanish-style appetizer.

I	recipe Grilled Bell Peppers
¼	cup pitted Spanish green olives, sliced
I½	tablespoons sherry vinegar
I	teaspoon chopped capers
I	tablespoon chopped fresh parsley leaves

1. Grill the peppers as directed.

2. Once the grilled peppers have cooled and been cut into thin strips, toss them with the olives, vinegar, capers, and parsley. Serve warm or at room temperature.

Grilled Bell Peppers with Black Olives and Basil

Serve these peppers as a side dish with grilled fish or chicken, or use them as a sandwich filling with slices of fresh mozzarella.

I	recipe Grilled Bell Peppers
¼	cup pitted black olives, sliced
I½	tablespoons lemon juice
I	small garlic clove, minced
I½	tablespoons thinly sliced fresh basil leaves

1. Grill the peppers as directed.

2. Once the grilled peppers have cooled and been cut into thin strips, toss them with the olives, lemon juice, garlic, and basil. Serve warm or at room temperature.

POTATOES

LIGHTLY PRECOOKED POTATO SLICES CAN be finished on the grill to give them a smoky flavor. We found that red potatoes are the best choice for this technique since they hold their shape better than starchy russets or Yukon Golds.

There are two other important points to remember. First, we found it imperative not to overcook the potato slices. If simmered too long, the potatoes will start to break apart and become "ungrillable."

Simmer the potato slices just until almost tender, about six minutes.

The other key finding in our testing was the need to coat each potato slice with oil before grilling. If left uncoated, the starches in the potato cause it to adhere to the grill. Once the potato slices have been boiled, drained, and cooled, drizzle oil over them and toss gently to coat each slice thoroughly.

Grilled Red Potatoes
SERVES 4

These potatoes are delicious served simply with ketchup and hot sauce, or you can use them in a grilled potato salad (recipes follow). Precooking the potatoes in salted simmering water helps them to retain moisture, yielding more tender and appealing spuds.

2	pounds medium red-skinned potatoes, scrubbed and cut crosswise into ½-inch-thick rounds
	Salt
3	tablespoons extra-virgin olive oil
	Ground black pepper

1. Place the sliced potatoes in a large pot. Cover with 1½ quarts of cold water. Add 1 teaspoon salt and bring to a boil over high heat. Reduce the heat to medium and simmer until the potatoes are barely tender, about 6 minutes. Strain though a colander, being careful not to break up the potatoes. Transfer the potatoes to a large bowl and drizzle oil over them. Season with salt and pepper to taste; gently turn the potatoes over to coat each slice with oil.

2. Grill the potatoes over a medium-hot fire (see how to gauge heat level on page 19), turning once, until grill marks appear and the potato slices are cooked through, about 8 minutes. Serve immediately.

Grilled Potato Salad with Mustard Vinaigrette

Serve this tangy potato salad with grilled sausages and sauerkraut.

I	recipe Grilled Red Potatoes
2	teaspoons Dijon mustard

1 tablespoon minced red onion

2 teaspoons white wine vinegar

2 tablespoons extra-virgin olive oil

2 teaspoons minced fresh tarragon leaves

1. Grill the potatoes as directed. Place in a bowl and cool to room temperature.

2. Whisk the mustard, onion, vinegar, oil, and tarragon together in small bowl until well blended. Pour the dressing over the grilled potato slices and serve at room temperature or refrigerate until cold.

Curried Grilled Potato Salad

The mustard seeds in this recipe add texture and a nutty and pleasantly bitter mustard flavor to the potato salad. The salad is delicious even without the seeds, though, so don't worry if you can't get find them.

1 recipe Grilled Red Potatoes, made with vegetable oil instead of olive oil

2 tablespoons vegetable oil

1 medium garlic clove, minced

1 teaspoon curry powder

¼ teaspoon salt

1 teaspoon sugar

2 teaspoons white wine vinegar

2 medium scallions, sliced into thin rounds

2 teaspoons mustard seeds, toasted in a covered dry skillet until they pop

1. Grill the potatoes as directed. Place in a bowl and cool to room temperature.

2. While the potatoes are cooling, heat oil in a small skillet set over medium heat. When the oil is hot, add the garlic and curry powder and cook until fragrant, 30 to 45 seconds. (The garlic should not brown.) Transfer the garlic-curry oil to a heatproof bowl and stir in the salt, sugar, and vinegar.

3. Pour the dressing over the cooled potatoes and add the scallions and mustard seeds. Toss to coat. Taste the potatoes and adjust the seasonings, if necessary. Let sit for at least 1 hour for flavors to meld. This salad is best served at room temperature.

RADICCHIO

LIKE ENDIVE, RADICCHIO IS USUALLY thought of as a salad green. Also like endive, it is delicious when grilled, as the purple leaves become lightly crisp and smoky-tasting. To keep the layers from falling apart, cut the radicchio heads through the core into thick wedges. To prevent radicchio from burning, it is necessary to brush the pieces with a fair amount of olive oil. For maximum grill flavor, turn each wedge of radicchio twice so that each side spends some time facing the fire.

Grilled Radicchio

SERVES 4

This slightly bitter vegetable is delicious with any grilled meat or poultry. The heads of radicchio are cut into wedges and lightly grilled, bringing out the sweetness of the vegetable while also letting it retain a pleasantly crisp texture.

3 medium heads radicchio, cut into quarters with core intact (see illustration below)

4 tablespoons extra-virgin olive oil
  Salt and ground black pepper

1. Place radicchio wedges on a large baking sheet and brush all sides with oil. Season with salt and pepper to taste.

2. Grill the radicchio over a medium-hot fire (see

PREPARING RADICCHIO

Remove any brown outer leaves. Cut the radicchio in half through the core. Cut each half again through the core so that you end up with four wedges.

how to gauge heat level on page 19), turning every 1½ minutes, until edges are browned and wilted but centers remain slightly firm, about 4½ minutes total. Serve immediately.

> VARIATION

Grilled Radicchio with Sweet Balsamic Vinaigrette

The small amount of sugar in the vinaigrette promotes browning and works well with the bitter flavor of the radicchio.

1½	tablespoons balsamic vinegar
1	teaspoon sugar
1	medium garlic clove, minced
4	tablespoons extra-virgin olive oil
3	medium heads of radicchio, cut into quarters with core intact (see illustration on page 198)
	Salt and ground black pepper

1. Mix the vinegar, sugar, garlic, and oil together in a small bowl.

2. Place radicchio wedges on a large baking sheet and brush all sides with the vinaigrette. Season with salt and pepper to taste.

3. Grill the radicchio over a medium-hot fire (see how to gauge heat level on page 19), turning every 1½ minutes, until edges are browned and wilted but centers remain slightly firm, about 4½ minutes total. Serve immediately.

SWEET POTATOES

BECAUSE OF THEIR CRUMBLY, STICKY texture, we find that sweet potatoes do not grill well as slices, as do red potatoes. If you don't precook the slices, they don't cook through. If you do precook the slices, they become soft almost instantly and tend to stick to the grill grate.

However, it is possible to grill-roast whole sweet potatoes over indirect heat. (See page 230 for a definition of grill-roasting.) We found it best to lightly oil the skin for maximum crispness. When cooked alongside a whole chicken, the sweet potatoes absorb a fair amount of smoke flavor. For the best results, stick with medium-sized sweet potatoes. Mammoth sweet potatoes, which weigh a pound each, are too big for single servings and will char before they cook through properly.

Grill-roasted sweet potatoes can be served with butter and salt, but they are just as delicious with salsa, hot sauce, lime wedges, or even a soy-sesame sauce.

Grill-Roasted Sweet Potatoes

SERVES 4

Sweet potatoes cooked whole on the grill are simple and phenomenally delicious. The skin crisps up and the flesh steams itself to fluffy perfection, ready to be eaten with butter and salt. We like to cook sweet potatoes this way when grill-roasting something else, such as a bird or some ribs.

4	medium sweet potatoes (10 ounces each), scrubbed and blotted dry
	Vegetable oil for rubbing on potato skin
	Salt
	Butter for passing at the table

1. Rub the sweet potatoes with a small amount of vegetable oil to barely coat the skin.

2. Grill the sweet potatoes, covered, over the cooler side of a 2-level fire, turning every 10 to 12 minutes, until the sweet potatoes are tender, 45 minutes to 1 hour. (To check for doneness, stick the tip of a paring knife into the potato. It should offer no resistance, and the skin should be dark brown and crisp.) Remove the sweet potatoes from the grill.

3. Cut a slit along the top of each sweet potato and carefully squeeze to push up the flesh. Serve hot, in the style of baked potatoes, with salt and butter.

> VARIATION

Grill-Roasted Sweet Potatoes with Sweet Sesame and Soy Sauce

Soy sauce adds a salty contrast to the sweetness of the sweet potato and the added sugar. If you don't have black sesame seeds on hand, white sesame seeds are just as tasty.

1	recipe Grilled-Roasted Sweet Potatoes, prepared through step 2
3	tablespoons soy sauce
¼	cup sugar
4	teaspoons sake (Japanese rice wine)
1	tablespoon Asian sesame oil
2	teaspoons toasted black sesame seeds

1. Grill the sweet potatoes as directed.

2. While the sweet potatoes are cooking, combine the soy sauce, sugar, sake, and oil in a small saucepan set over medium heat. Cook, stirring often, just until the sugar has dissolved. Transfer the mixture to a small bowl.

3. When the potatoes are done, cut a slit along the top of each sweet potato and carefully squeeze to push up the flesh. Drizzle a little of the soy-sesame mixture over each potato, then sprinkle with sesame seeds. Serve immediately.

TOMATOES

ROUND, PLUM, AND CHERRY TOMATOES can all be grilled very briefly. Round and plum tomatoes should be halved and seeded, leaving behind just the meaty flesh. Cherry tomatoes should be skewered and grilled whole.

We found it best to grill the tomato halves skin-side up first, then skin-side down. Cooking the tomatoes skin-side up exposes their flesh to intense grill heat and caramelizes them lightly. Then, before the tomatoes become too soft, they are flipped so that they can continue grilling with their delicate flesh protected.

Grilled Round or Plum Tomatoes

SERVES 4

Grilling concentrates the flavor of tomatoes and intensifies their sweetness. Be sure to remove the seeds from the tomatoes before grilling; they can be quite bitter and watery. Serve the tomatoes as a side dish or use them as the basis for a smoky salsa or tomato sauce.

4	small round tomatoes (about 4 ounces), cored, halved, and seeded, or 4 large plum tomatoes (about 3 ½ ounces each), cored, halved, and seeded (see illustrations at right and on page 201)
2	tablespoons extra-virgin olive oil
	Salt and ground black pepper

1. Brush both sides of each tomato half with oil and season with salt and pepper to taste.

2. Grill the tomato halves, skin-side up, over a medium-hot fire (see how to gauge heat level on page 19), until the flesh has rich grill marks, about 4 minutes. Turn the tomato halves over and cook, skin-side down, until the skins have blistered and begun to pull away from the flesh, about 2 minutes. Serve the grilled tomatoes hot, warm, or at room temperature.

Grilled Cherry Tomatoes

SERVES 4

Cherry tomatoes are great for grilling. They cook up in minutes and make a tasty addition to pasta dishes or are great served on their own as a late-summer side dish. Fresh, thinly sliced basil goes especially well with the tomatoes.

I	pound cherry tomatoes, stems removed
2	tablespoons extra-virgin olive oil
I	medium garlic clove, minced
	Salt and ground black pepper

1. Toss the tomatoes, oil, and garlic together in a medium bowl. Season with salt and pepper to taste. Thread the tomatoes onto skewers through the stem ends.

2. Grill the tomatoes over a medium-hot fire (see how to gauge heat level on page 19), turning once or twice, until dark grill marks appear and the skins begin to blister and wrinkle, about 3 minutes.

CORING TOMATOES

Tomatoes are almost always cored—that is, the tough stem end is removed and discarded.

Place the tomato on its side on the work surface. Holding the tomato stable with one hand, insert the tip of a paring knife into the tomato at an angle just outside the core. Use the paring knife to cut with a sawing motion; at the same time, rotate the tomato toward you until the core is cut free.

3. Remove the skewers from the grill and allow the tomatoes to cool slightly. Remove the tomatoes from the skewers (using a clean kitchen towel to hold the skewers) and serve immediately.

➤ VARIATION

Grilled Cherry Tomatoes, Greek Style

This marinade also works well with grilled plum or round tomatoes.

2	teaspoons red wine vinegar
¼	teaspoon sugar
I	medium garlic clove, minced
I	teaspoon chopped fresh oregano leaves
2	tablespoons extra-virgin olive oil
I	pound cherry tomatoes, stems removed
	Salt and ground black pepper

SEEDING TOMATOES

Seeding rids tomatoes of excess liquid and is an essential step before grilling them.

ROUND TOMATOES
Halve the cored tomato along the equator. If it is ripe and juicy, gently give it a squeeze and shake out the seeds and gelatinous material. If not, scoop them out with your finger or a small spoon.

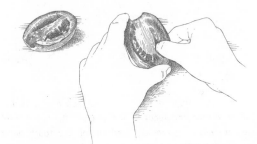

PLUM TOMATOES
Halve the cored tomato lengthwise. Cut through the inner membrane with a paring knife or break through it with your finger and scoop out the seeds and gelatinous material.

1. Mix the vinegar, sugar, garlic, oregano, and oil together in a medium bowl. Add the tomatoes and toss to coat. Season with salt and pepper to taste. Thread the tomatoes onto skewers through the stem ends.

2. Grill the tomatoes over a medium-hot fire (see how to gauge heat level on page 19), turning once or twice, until dark grill marks appear and the skins begin to blister and wrinkle, about 3 minutes.

3. Remove the skewers from the grill and allow the tomatoes to cool slightly. Remove the tomatoes from the skewers (using a clean kitchen towel to hold the skewers) and serve immediately.

WINTER SQUASH

WINTER SQUASH MAY NOT BE THE MOST obvious choice for grilling. However, in early fall, when grilling is still possible and squash fills markets, this dish makes good sense. Like potatoes, winter squash must be parboiled before being grilled. We find that butternut squash has the best texture and flavor among common squash varieties. Its smooth skin is also fairly easy to peel away.

Grilled Butternut Squash

SERVES 4 TO 6

This recipe calls for a lot of squash slices. Depending on the space between the bars on your grill grate, you might want to cook them on a grill grid (see page 12) to prevent any slices from dropping down onto the fire.

I	small butternut squash (about 2 pounds), peeled, seeded, and cut into ½-inch-thick slices (see illustrations on page 202)
	Salt
3	tablespoons extra-virgin olive oil
	Ground black pepper

1. Place the squash slices in a large pot. Cover with 2 quarts of cold water. Add 1 teaspoon salt and bring to a boil over high heat. Reduce the heat to medium and simmer until the squash is barely tender, about 3 minutes. Strain through a colander, being careful not to break up the squash slices. Transfer the squash to a large bowl; drizzle oil over the top. Season with salt and pepper to taste, and gently turn the squash over to coat both sides of each slice with oil.

2. Grill the squash over a medium-hot fire (see how to gauge heat level on page 19), turning once, until dark brown caramelization occurs and the flesh becomes very tender, 8 to 10 minutes. Serve hot, warm, or at room temperature

➤ VARIATION

Spicy Grilled Butternut Squash with Garlic and Rosemary

Serve this squash in autumn with grilled meat.

I	small butternut squash (about 2 pounds), peeled, seeded, and cut into ½-inch-thick slices (see illustrations below)
	Salt
4	tablespoons extra-virgin olive oil
2	tablespoons brown sugar
I	teaspoon chopped fresh rosemary
½	teaspoon hot red pepper flakes
I	medium garlic clove, minced

1. Place the squash slices in a large pot. Cover with 2 quarts of cold water. Add 1 teaspoon salt and bring to a boil over high heat. Reduce the heat to medium and simmer until the squash is barely tender, about 3 minutes. Strain through a colander, being careful not to break up the slices. Transfer to a large bowl and drizzle oil over the top. Sprinkle with brown sugar, rosemary, hot red pepper flakes, garlic, and salt to taste. Gently turn the squash over to coat each slice with oil and seasonings.

2. Grill the squash over a medium-hot fire (see how to gauge heat level on page 19), turning once, until dark brown caramelization occurs and the flesh becomes very tender, 8 to 10 minutes. Serve hot, warm, or at room temperature

ZUCCHINI AND SUMMER SQUASH

THE BIGGEST PROBLEM THAT CONFRONTS the cook when preparing zucchini and yellow summer squash is their wateriness. Both are about 95 percent water and will become soupy if just thrown into a hot pan. If they cook in their own juices, they won't brown. And since both are fairly bland, they really benefit from some browning.

That's why grilling is the easiest way to cook summer squash and zucchini. Cooked indoors, the squash must be shredded and squeezed dry or salted. Neither step is necessary when grilling. Simply cut the squash lengthwise into thick strips that are large enough to stay put on top of the grill rack.

PREPARING BUTTERNUT SQUASH

1. Lay squash on cutting board. Cut off about ½ inch from both ends and discard. Cut the squash crosswise just above the bulbous base to create a long narrow section and a rounded section.

2. Stand the round end up on its flat bottom. Use a sharp knife to cut down the sides of the squash, removing the tough outer skin.

3. Cut the squash straight down in half to expose the seeds. Scrape out seeds using a metal spoon. Set each half, seed-side down, on the board, and cut into ½-inch-thick half circles.

4. Stand the longer section of the squash on the cutting board and cut off the tough outer skin using the same technique described in step 2 (if this section is too tall, cut it in half crosswise first). Cut the peeled squash crosswise into ½-inch-thick rounds.

The intense heat of the grill quickly expels excess moisture from the vegetables, and that moisture drips down harmlessly onto the fire rather than sitting in a pan on to the stovetop.

Grilled Zucchini or Summer Squash

SERVES 4

Excess moisture in zucchini and summer squash evaporates over the fire, making salting before cooking unnecessary.

4   medium zucchini or summer squash (about 1 1/2 pounds), trimmed and sliced lengthwise into 1/2-inch-thick strips (see illustrations below)

2   tablespoons extra-virgin olive oil
    Salt and ground black pepper

SLICING ZUCCHINI OR SUMMER SQUASH

1. Cut a thin slice from each end of the zucchini or summer squash. Slice the trimmed zucchini or summer squash lengthwise into 1/2-inch-thick strips.

2. For aesthetic reasons, you may want to trim the peel from the outer slices so they match the others. You can do the same thing with outer eggplant slices. Besides allowing for more attractive grill marks, the flesh cooks better when directly exposed to the heat.

1. Lay the zucchini or squash on a large baking sheet and brush both sides of each slice with oil. Sprinkle generously with salt and pepper.

2. Grill the zucchini or squash over a medium-hot fire (see how to gauge heat level on page 19), turning once, until streaked with dark grill marks, 8 to 10 minutes.

3. Transfer the zucchini or squash to a platter. Adjust the seasonings and serve hot, warm, or at room temperature.

VARIATIONS

Grilled Zucchini or Summer Squash with Tomatoes and Basil

SERVES 4 TO 6

Grilled squash can also be marinated in a vinaigrette made with red wine vinegar. Substitute parsley, mint, cilantro, or tarragon for the basil if desired.

1   tablespoon balsamic vinegar
    Salt and ground black pepper

2   tablespoons extra-virgin olive oil

1   large ripe tomato, cored and cut into thin wedges

2   tablespoons minced fresh basil leaves

1   recipe Grilled Zucchini or Summer Squash

1. Whisk the vinegar and salt and pepper to taste together in a large serving bowl. Whisk in the oil. Add the tomato and basil, toss gently, and set aside to marinate for at least 30 minutes and up to 1 hour.

2. Grill the zucchini or squash as directed. Cool the grilled zucchini or squash and cut into 1-inch pieces.

3. Add the zucchini or squash to the bowl with the tomatoes, toss gently, and adjust the seasonings. Serve warm or at room temperature.

Grilled Zucchini or Summer Squash with Capers and Oregano

Capers are pretty salty, so season the zucchini sparingly.

1   tablespoon red wine vinegar

1   tablespoon chopped capers

1   medium garlic clove, minced

2   tablespoons extra-virgin olive oil
    Salt and ground black pepper

1   recipe Grilled Zucchini or Summer Squash

1   tablespoon minced fresh oregano leaves

1. Whisk the vinegar, capers, and garlic together in a large serving bowl. Whisk in the oil and add salt and pepper to taste. Set the dressing aside.

2. Grill the zucchini or squash as directed. Cool the grilled zucchini or squash and cut into 1-inch pieces.

3. Add the zucchini or squash to the bowl with the dressing and toss gently. Add the oregano and adjust the seasonings. Serve warm or at room temperature.

Grilled Zucchini or Summer Squash with Lemon and Black Olives

Use a meaty, brine-packed olive, such as kalamata, for this dish. Serve with grilled chicken or fish.

1   tablespoon extra-virgin olive oil

1   tablespoon lemon juice

1   teaspoon minced fresh oregano or thyme leaves

     Salt and ground black pepper

1   recipe Grilled Zucchini or Summer Squash

1/3   cup black olives (about 2 ounces), pitted and chopped

1. Whisk the oil, lemon juice, oregano, and salt and pepper to taste together in a small bowl (add salt sparingly as olives are salty). Set the dressing aside.

2. Grill the zucchini or squash as directed.

3. Transfer the grilled zucchini or squash to a platter. Drizzle the dressing over the zucchini or squash, then sprinkle with the olives. Serve warm or at room temperature.

Grilled Zucchini or Summer Squash, Spanish Style

To toast the almonds, place them in a small skillet over medium-high heat and toast, tossing often, until golden brown and fragrant, 4 to 5 minutes.

1   tablespoon sherry vinegar

1   medium garlic clove, minced

2   tablespoons extra-virgin olive oil

4   medium zucchini or summer squash (about 1 1/2 pounds), trimmed and sliced lengthwise into 1/2-inch-thick strips (see illustrations on page 203)

     Salt and ground black pepper

1/4   cup sliced, pitted green olives (about 6 large)

3   tablespoons sliced almonds, toasted

1   tablespoon chopped fresh chives

1. Mix the vinegar, garlic, and oil together in a small bowl. Lay the zucchini or squash on a large baking sheet and brush both sides of each slice with the oil mixture. Sprinkle with salt and pepper to taste.

2. Grill the zucchini or squash over a medium-hot fire (see how to gauge heat level on page 19), turning once, until streaked with dark grill marks, 8 to 10 minutes.

3. Transfer the grilled zucchini or squash to a platter. Sprinkle the olives, almonds, and chives over the zucchini or squash. Serve hot, warm, or at room temperature.

MIXED VEGETABLE DISHES

WHEN GRILLING MORE THAN ONE VEGETABLE at once, be prepared to take each off the grill at a different time. Serving mixed vegetable dishes warm or at room temperature makes complicated timing and sequencing unnecessary.

Grilled Italian Vegetables with Thyme and Garlic

SERVES 6

Drizzle the vegetables with balsamic vinegar at the table if desired.

1/2   cup extra-virgin olive oil

3   medium garlic cloves, minced

1   tablespoon minced fresh thyme leaves, plus several sprigs for garnish

     Salt and ground black pepper

3   medium zucchini (about 1 pound), ends trimmed and cut lengthwise into 1/2-inch-thick strips (see illustrations on page 203)

3   small eggplant (about 1 pound), ends trimmed and cut lengthwise into 1/2-inch-thick strips

2   large red onions (about 1 1/4 pounds), papery skins removed and cut crosswise into 1/2-inch-thick rounds and skewered (see illustrations on page 194)

1   large red bell pepper, prepared according to
     illustrations on page 196

1. Combine the oil, garlic, minced thyme, and salt
and pepper to taste in a small bowl. Lay the vegetables on a large baking sheet or platter and brush both
sides of each piece with the flavored oil.

2. Grill the vegetables over a medium-hot fire
(see how to gauge heat level on page 19), turning
once, until everything is streaked with dark grill
marks, 8 to 12 minutes.

3. As each vegetable looks done, transfer it to a
large platter. Garnish the platter with thyme sprigs
and serve warm or at room temperature.

Grilled Portobello Mushrooms, Red Pepper, and Garlic Croutons
SERVES 4

*This grilled bread salad can be served as a side dish or,
better still, as a first course for an outdoor grilled meal. The
grilled croutons will become soggy fairly quickly; if you prepare this dish in advance, do not add them until just before
serving.*

5   tablespoons extra-virgin olive oil
2   medium garlic cloves, minced
1   teaspoon grated lemon zest
     Salt and ground black pepper
1   large red bell pepper, prepared according to the
     illustrations on page 196
2   large portobello mushrooms, stems removed
4   slices Italian bread, each 1 inch thick
1   tablespoon lemon juice
3   tablespoons minced fresh parsley leaves

1. Combine 4 tablespoons oil with the garlic,
lemon zest, and salt and pepper to taste in a small
bowl. Place the red pepper, mushrooms, and bread
slices on a large platter. Brush both sides of the vegetables and bread with the flavored oil.

2. Place the vegetables and bread over a medium-
hot fire (see how to gauge heat level on page 19),
turning once, until everything is streaked with dark
grill marks, about 2 minutes for the bread and 8 to
10 minutes for the pepper and mushrooms.

3. Transfer the grilled vegetables and bread to a cutting board. Cut the pepper into ¼-inch-wide strips.
Halve the mushrooms, then cut them into ½-inch-
wide strips. Cut the bread into 1-inch croutons.

4. Toss the vegetables in a large serving bowl with
the remaining 1 tablespoon oil, lemon juice, and
parsley. Adjust the seasonings. (The vegetables can
be covered and kept at room temperature for 1
hour.) Stir in the croutons and serve immediately.

Grilled Caponata
SERVES 4 TO 6

*Caponata is a Sicilian eggplant relish. This dish usually
calls for sautéing and stewing the eggplant, peppers, and
tomatoes on top of the stove. Cooking the vegetables on the
grill is easier and requires less oil. This dish gets better over
time, so for the best flavor, make it a day ahead and refrigerate overnight to allow for complete marriage of flavors.
(Caponata can be refrigerated for up to 5 days.) Serve at
room temperature, as a topping for crostini (grilled bread), or
as a "salsa" with grilled chicken or fish.*

1   medium eggplant (about 1 pound), ends
     trimmed and cut crosswise into ¾-inch rounds
1   large red pepper (about 8 ounces), prepared
     according to the illustrations on page 196
2   medium plum tomatoes (about 3 ounces each),
     cored and seeded (see illustrations on pages
     200 and 201)
4   tablespoons extra-virgin olive oil
     Salt and ground black pepper
1   medium garlic clove, minced
1   tablespoon red wine vinegar
1½   tablespoons chopped capers
2   teaspoons sugar
¼   cup chopped fresh parsley leaves

1. Lay the vegetables on a baking sheet. Brush all
sides of each vegetable with 3 tablespoons of the oil
and season to taste with salt and pepper.

2. Grill the vegetables over a medium-hot fire
(see how to gauge heat level on page 19). The eggplant and red pepper should be cooked, turning
once, until dark grill marks appear, 8 to 10 minutes.
The tomatoes should be cooked for 4 minutes skin-
side up and about 2 minutes skin-side down, or until

the skins char and begin to pull away from the flesh. Transfer all vegetables back to the baking sheet. Cool to room temperature.

3. Cut the eggplant and red pepper into bite-sized pieces. Roughly chop the tomatoes. Place all vegetables in a large bowl.

4. Drizzle the remaining ingredients over the vegetables and toss to coat. Adjust the seasonings. Serve at room temperature.

FRUIT

GRILLED FRUIT MAKES A SIMPLE SUMMERTIME dessert or can be used as an accompaniment to grilled pork, chicken, or fish. Grilling intensifies the sweetness of the fruit through caramelization.

We have included those fruits that we believe do best on the grill. Use smaller plums, peaches, apples, and pears when grilling, since larger fruit may burn on the outside before heating through to the center. All fruit to be grilled should be ripe, but still firm. Grill delicate fruits with their skins intact, as the skins keep the fruit from falling apart on the grill.

Grill over a medium-hot fire (see how to gauge heat level on page 19). Brush all prepared fruit lightly with vegetable oil before grilling. Fruit is done when it is marked on the exterior and just barely softened and heated through at the center.

PREPARING A PINEAPPLE

When preparing pineapple for grilling, you need to cut pieces large enough so that they won't fall through the grill rack.

1. Cut off ½ inch from the top and bottom of the pineapple, removing the leaves at the same time. Discard top and bottom.

2. Set the flat bottom of the pineapple on the cutting board. Using a sharp knife, cut the outer ½ inch off the pineapple, running from the top to the bottom of the pineapple. Discard the outer portion.

3. Cut the peeled pineapple lengthwise through the center.

4. Cut each piece in half crosswise to yield a total of 4 equal pieces.

5. Use a chef's knife to remove the core of each piece, cutting at an angle to one side of the core and then cutting at an angle to the other side to meet the first cut, forming a V-cut. Remove core and discard.

6. Cut each cored quarter crosswise into ½-inch-thick slices. Each piece should resemble half a pineapple ring.

GLAZES AND SAUCES FOR GRILLED FRUIT

THE FOLLOWING GLAZES CAN BE BRUSHED on fruit during the last minute or so of cooking. Keep the extra for drizzling onto fruit after grilling. (The caramel sauce is too sugary to use on the grill.)

For a delicious dessert, top ice cream with grilled fruit and caramel sauce (see page 208), rum-molasses glaze, or sour orange glaze. Sprinkle with toasted nuts of your choice.

Rum-Molasses Glaze

MAKES ABOUT 1/2 CUP

This glaze goes very well with bananas, pineapple, mango, pears, peaches, and apples. Use half of the mixture to brush onto fruit during the last minute or two of cooking and the other half to drizzle over the fruit before serving. This recipe glazes four servings of fruit, with extra sauce to drizzle over the top of each serving.

- 1/4   cup plus 1/2 teaspoon dark rum
- 1   tablespoon plus 1 teaspoon lime juice
- 6   tablespoons molasses
- 3   tablespoons cold unsalted butter, cut into 1/4-inch pieces

1. Combine 1/4 cup rum, 1 tablespoon lime juice, and the molasses in a small, heavy-bottomed saucepan and bring to a boil over high heat. Reduce the heat to medium-high and cook until reduced to 1/3 cup, about 5 minutes.

2. Remove the pan from the heat and whisk in the butter until melted and incorporated. Stir in the remaining 1/2 teaspoon rum and 1 teaspoon lime juice. Use warm or at room temperature.

Sour Orange Glaze

MAKES ABOUT 1/2 CUP

As with the Rum-Molasses Glaze, this glaze can be brushed onto fruit during the last minutes of cooking and the excess can be drizzled over the fruit before serving. This glaze goes well with all the fruit included in the chart.

- 1/2   cup orange juice
- 3   tablespoons lime juice
- 1/4   cup brown sugar
- 3   tablespoons cold unsalted butter, cut into 1/4-inch pieces.

1. Combine the orange juice, 2½ tablespoons lime juice, and the brown sugar in a small saucepan and bring to a boil over high heat. Reduce the heat to medium-high and cook until reduced to 1/3 cup, about 7 minutes.

2. Remove the pan from the heat and whisk in the butter until melted and incorporated. Stir in the remaining 1/2 tablespoon lime juice. Use warm or at room temperature.

PREPARING A MANGO

1. A sharp paring knife makes it easy to peel a mango. Start by removing a thin slice from one end of the mango so that it sits flat on a work surface.

2. Hold the mango, cut side down, and remove the skin in thin strips with a paring knife, working from top to bottom.

3. Once the peel has been completely removed, cut down along the side of the flat pit to remove the flesh from one side of the mango. Do the same thing on the other side of the pit.

4. Trim around the pit to remove any remaining flesh. The flesh can be chopped as needed for recipes.

Simplified Caramel Sauce

MAKES ½ CUP

Use this sauce over ice cream and grilled fruit. This recipe makes enough for four desserts. Caramel sauce is especially good with grilled bananas, pears, apples, and peaches.

½ cup sugar
⅓ cup heavy cream
I tablespoon rum or brandy

1. Combine the sugar and 2½ tablespoons of water in a medium, heavy-bottomed saucepan over medium-low heat. Stir until the sugar dissolves. Increase the heat to high and cook, swirling pan occasionally but not stirring, until the caramel is uniformly golden amber in color, about 4 minutes.

2. Wearing oven mitts to protect your hands, remove the pan from the heat and slowly whisk in the cream, one tablespoon at a time, making sure to keep the bubbling caramel away from your arms; stir until smooth. Stir in the rum. Set the caramel sauce aside to thicken and cool.

Sweet and Spicy Hoisin Glaze

MAKES GENEROUS ¼ CUP

Fruit served with this glaze should be used as a side dish for the main meal. Use this glaze on stone fruit such as peaches and plums; it also goes well with grilled pineapple and mangoes. This recipe makes enough glaze to coat 4 servings of fruit.

2 tablespoons hoisin sauce
I tablespoon soy sauce
I tablespoon rice vinegar
I tablespoon honey
½ teaspoon hot red pepper flakes

Mix all ingredients together in a small bowl.

Grilling Fruit

FRUIT	PREPARATION	GRILLING DIRECTIONS
Apple (small)	Cut in half through core. Remove core with a melon baller or sturdy teaspoon measure. Use a paring knife to cut out stem.	Grill, skin-side up, for 5 to 6 minutes; turn and grill, skin-side down, for 5 to 6 minutes.
Banana	Leave skins on; cut in half lengthwise using a sharp paring knife.	Grill, skin-side up, for 2 minutes; turn and grill, skin-side down, for another 2 minutes.
Mango	Peel, pit, and cut into 4 pieces (see illustrations on page 207).	Grill larger pieces for 5 minutes, smaller pieces for 4 minutes, turning all pieces once.
Peach (small)	Cut in half and remove pit.	Grill, skin-side up, for 4 minutes; turn and grill, skin-side down, for 3 to 4 minutes.
Pear (small)	Cut in half lengthwise. Remove core with a melon baller or sturdy teaspoon measure. Use a paring knife to cut out the stem.	Grill, skin-side up, for 5 minutes; turn and grill, skin-side down, for 5 minutes.
Pineapple	Cut into half circles (see illustrations on page 206.)	Grill for 6 minutes, turning once halfway through cooking time.
Plum (small)	Cut in half and remove pit.	Grill, skin-side up, for 4 minutes; turn and grill, skin-side down, for another 2 minutes.

13

PIZZA AND BRUSCHETTA

GRILLED PIZZA IS AN UNEXPECTED TREAT. The fire imparts a light smoky flavor to the crust and makes it as interesting to eat as the toppings. Grilling is our favorite way to prepare pizza in the summer, especially as an appetizer before a grilled meal. If you think grilled pizza sounds like one of those silly chef-inspired creations, think again. Grilled flatbreads have a long history in Italy and elsewhere. Our goal when developing these recipes was to stay faithful to the concept but to streamline the process for American cooks.

Bruschetta is authentic Italian garlic bread. Because it starts with a purchased loaf of bread, it is much simpler to prepare than pizza. In fact, making bruschetta is an excellent way to recycle day-old bread. Thick slices of crusty country bread are grilled, rubbed with garlic, then brushed with quality olive oil. Toppings can be as simple as salt or minced fresh herbs or slightly more elaborate, such as grilled vegetables or diced fresh tomatoes.

As with vegetables and fruits, we often find ourselves grilling pizza and bruschetta as part of an entire meal from the grill. Since we generally like to eat grilled pizza and bruschetta as appetizers, we suggest grilling them first, then cooking the main course.

Bruschetta cooks so quickly that the fire will still be plenty hot for grilling. In the case of pizza, you may need to add more coals to grill the main course, if using a charcoal grill. (See page 219 for tips on grilling pizza.)

PIZZA DOUGH

PREPARING THE DOUGH IS PROBABLY THE trickiest part of making pizza at home. While pizza dough is nothing more than bread dough with oil added for softness and suppleness, we found in our testing that minor changes in the ingredient list can yield dramatically different results.

Our goal in testing was threefold: we wanted to develop a recipe that was simple to put together; the dough had to be easy to shape and stretch; and the crust needed to cook up crisp and chewy, not tough and leathery.

After some initial tests, it was clear that bread flour delivers the best texture. Bread flour makes pizza crust that is chewy and crisp. Unbleached all-purpose flour can be used in a pinch, but the resulting crust is less crisp. (See "Ingredients: Bread Flour" on page 212 for more information on the advantages of using bread flour in pizza dough.)

The second key to perfect crust is water. We found that using more water makes the dough softer and more elastic. It stretches more easily than a stiffer, harder dough made with less water.

We like to jump-start the yeast in a little warm water for five minutes. We then add more room-temperature water and oil.

When it comes to combining the dry ingredients (flour and salt) with the wet ingredients, the food processor is our first choice. The liquid gets evenly incorporated into the dry ingredients, and the blade kneads the dough in just 30 seconds. Of course, the dough can also be kneaded by hand or with a standing mixer. If making the dough by hand, resist the temptation to add a lot of flour as you knead.

When left to rise, the dough should be placed in an oiled container or bowl and covered with plastic wrap. We found that the tight seal offered by plastic wrap keeps the dough moist and protects it from drafts better than the standard damp cloth. We reserve the traditional damp cloth for use when the dough has been divided into balls and is waiting to be stretched out.

To stretch dough to its maximum diameter, let it rest one or two times during the shaping process. Once you feel some resistance from the dough, cover it with a damp cloth and wait five minutes before going at it again. Fingertips and hands generally do a better job of stretching dough than a rolling pin, which presses out air from the risen dough and makes it tough. Our low-tech method is also superior to frivolous techniques such as flipping dough in the air, which may work in a pizza parlor but can lead to disaster at home.

It is possible to change the rising time by using less yeast and/or refrigerating the dough. This way, dough can be made the night before or in the morning and be ready when you need it for dinner. Even if grilling only a few individual pizzas, make a full dough recipe. After the dough has risen and been divided, place the extra dough in an airtight container and freeze it for up to several weeks. Defrost and stretch the dough when you're ready to use it.

INGREDIENTS: Yeast

Although pizza dough does not rise dramatically, yeast is essential for chew and proper texture. There are several kinds of yeast available to home cooks. All yeast begins as a small, cultured, purified sample that feeds and multiplies continuously in a liquid medium until it reaches the desired volume and stage of development. This liquid yeast is sold by the tankerful to commercial food manufacturers. For bakeries, yeast companies remove some of the moisture from liquid yeast to create a product called "crumbled yeast," which is sold in 50-pound bags. The next processing step extrudes the yeast to make a product that remains fully hydrated yet is fine enough to press into the small cakes you see for sale on supermarket shelves labeled "cake yeast." Further processing yields dried, powdered yeast, called active dry yeast. (The same process is used to make other dry yeasts, including rapid-rise and instant yeasts, although these products start with different strains of yeast. See box below for more information.)

We use active dry yeast in our recipes since this product is the most widely available. If you want to use cake yeast, also called fresh-active, or compressed, yeast, you'll need twice as much yeast as recommended in the recipe. Note that cake yeast is highly perishable and must be refrigerated.

On rare occasions you may find that dough does not rise properly. Check to make sure that the expiration date on your yeast has not passed. Another possible reason is that the water was too hot and thereby killed the yeast. (Water used to make pizza dough should be no hotter than 115 degrees.) Poor rising may also occur if you have added too much flour or placed the dough in a cool, drafty spot. To prevent the latter situation from occurring, heat your oven for 10 minutes at 200 degrees, then turn it off; the oven can then be used as a proofing box. (The term *proofing*, as explained in "Ingredients: Rapid-Rise Yeast," below, has two meanings when used in reference to yeasted doughs. One refers to the process of dissolving yeast in water as a test to see if it is active. The other is used interchangeably with the simple term *rising*. The old-fashioned term *proofing box* refers to a place where the dough is encouraged to rise—not where yeast is proofed.)

A microwave oven can also be used as a proofing box. To do so, nearly fill a two-cup Pyrex measure with water, place it in the microwave, and bring the water to a boil. Place the dough (which should be in a bowl covered with plastic wrap) in the microwave oven with the measuring cup. The preheated water will keep the microwave oven at the proper temperature for rising.

We like to let dough rise in a straight-sided plastic container. Dough needs to be contained while it ferments, not spread out in a big bowl. (You may use a bowl—just don't use one that is too large.) A container or bowl two to three times the size of the dough is perfect. If you use a container, mark the outside of it to indicate the original volume of the dough; this makes it easy to gauge the point at which the dough has doubled.

INGREDIENTS: Rapid-Rise Yeast

Yeast is a plant, not a bacterium, and different varieties have quite different qualities, as do different varieties of, say, roses. Rapid-rise yeast has been genetically engineered to reproduce the best characteristics of yeasts from around the world. Although genetic engineering often results in loss of flavor, our blind taste tests confirmed that in this case it produced an excellent product.

As for why the yeast works faster, there are two primary reasons. Besides more rapid enzyme activity, rapid-rise yeast also has an open, porous structure, which means that it absorbs liquid instantly. When rapid-rise yeast was introduced to consumers, they had difficulty with it because they continued to follow habit rather than the manufacturer's directions—that is, they "proofed" the yeast in water rather than mixing it directly into the flour. Because of its efficiency, the rapid-rise yeast dissolved in water quickly ran out of food (starch) and died before the rising process was complete.

To correct this problem, scientists went back and added more starch to the mix, providing enough food for the yeast to survive proofing. Today, however, most yeast does not have to be proofed. Proofing used to serve two functions. First, it was an indicator of the health of the yeast. Today, yeast is both refrigerated and marked with an expiration date for freshness. (Note that these expiration dates should be taken seriously. We tried baking a loaf with yeast that was one month past its expiration date, and the rising times were double those experienced with fresh yeast. The resulting loaf was more dense, with a smaller rise.) The second function proofing served was to hydrate the yeast cells. Although most yeast consists of dead cells encapsulating live cells, the dead cells need to dissolve before the live cells can start working. While this hydration process occurs quickly when yeast and water are mixed together, it also occurs in short order in the dough mixture during kneading.

Although proofing is no longer necessary, keep in mind that the temperature of the water is still crucial when using rapid-rise yeast. Water hotter than 115 degrees can kill the yeast and is not recommended.

Garlic-Herb Pizza Dough

MAKES ENOUGH FOR 8 INDIVIDUAL PIZZAS

The food processor is our favorite tool for making pizza dough because it works so quickly. However, you can knead this dough by hand or in a standing mixer (see the directions below). This dough requires about 2 hours of rising time. You could omit the garlic and herbs from this recipe to make a plain dough, but with grilled pizzas, which are so lightly topped, the crust should be as flavorful as possible. In fact, when brushed with oil and grilled, this dough is good enough to eat on its own as an accompaniment to meals.

2	tablespoons extra-virgin olive oil
4	medium garlic cloves, minced

INGREDIENTS: Bread Flour

When milling flour, a flour company must make a number of choices that influence the way its product performs in recipes. For starters, there is the essence of the flour, the wheat itself. Bread flour is typically made from hard red winter wheat, which has a protein content of about 13 percent. In comparison, all-purpose flour is a blend of hard and soft wheats and has a protein content of 10 or 11 percent. You can actually feel this difference with your fingers; hard wheat flours tend to have a subtle granular feel, while soft wheat flours feel fine but starchy, much like cornstarch.

High-protein bread flours are generally recommended for yeasted products and other baked goods that require a lot of structural support. The reason is that the higher the protein level in a flour, the greater the potential for the formation of gluten, which is what supports the "lift" in yeasted baked products. Gluten forms sheets that are elastic enough to move with the gas released by yeast but are also sturdy enough to prevent that gas from escaping, so the dough doesn't deflate. Lower-protein flours, on the other hand, are recommended for chemically leavened baked goods such as cakes. This is because baking powder and baking soda are quick leaveners. They lack the power and endurance of yeast, which is able to force the naturally resistant gluten sheets to expand. Gluten can overpower quick leaveners, causing the final baked product to fall flat.

Because pizza is made with yeast, it came as little surprise to us that bread flour made better pizza than all-purpose flour. The crust was crispier. All-purpose flour makes a softer, chewier pizza crust.

1	teaspoon minced fresh thyme, oregano, or rosemary leaves
½	cup warm water, at about 105 degrees
1	envelope (2¼ teaspoons) active dry yeast
1¼	cups water, at room temperature
4	cups bread flour, plus extra for dusting hands and work surfaces
1½	teaspoons salt
	Vegetable oil or spray for oiling container or bowl

1. Heat oil in a small skillet over medium heat. Add the garlic and herbs and sauté until the garlic is golden, 2 to 3 minutes. Remove the pan from the heat and cool the mixture to room temperature.

2. Measure the warm water into a 2-cup measuring cup. Sprinkle in the yeast; let stand until the yeast dissolves and swells, about 5 minutes. Add the room-temperature water and garlic-herb mixture; stir to combine.

3. Pulse the flour and salt to combine in the workbowl of a large food processor fitted with the steel blade. Continue pulsing while pouring the liquid ingredients (holding back a few tablespoons) through the feed tube. If the dough does not readily form into a ball, add the remaining liquid and continue to pulse until a ball forms. Process until the dough is smooth and elastic, about 30 seconds longer.

4. The dough will be a bit tacky, so use a rubber spatula to turn it out onto a lightly floured work surface; knead by hand a few strokes to form a smooth, round ball. Put the dough into an oiled, straight-sided plastic container or deep, oiled bowl and cover with plastic wrap. Let rise until doubled in size, about 2 hours. Punch the dough down with your fist and turn it out onto a lightly floured work surface. Divide and shape the dough as directed on page 216.

➤ VARIATIONS

Hand-Kneaded Pizza Dough

Follow steps 1 and 2 of the recipe for Garlic-Herb Pizza Dough. Omit step 3 and instead combine the salt and half of the flour in a deep bowl. Add the liquid ingredients and use a wooden spoon to combine. Add the remaining flour, stirring until a cohesive mass forms. Turn the dough out onto a lightly floured work surface and knead until smooth and elastic, 7 to 8 minutes. Use as little dusting flour as possible while kneading. Form the dough into a ball, put it into an oiled, straight-sided plastic container or deep, oiled bowl, cover it with plastic wrap, and proceed with the recipe.

Pizza Dough Kneaded in a Standing Mixer

Follow steps 1 and 2 of the recipe for Garlic-Herb Pizza Dough. Omit step 3 and instead place the flour and salt in the deep bowl of a standing mixer. With the paddle attachment, briefly combine the dry ingredients on low speed. Slowly add the liquid ingredients and continue to mix on low speed until a cohesive

mass forms. Stop the mixer and replace the paddle with the dough hook. Knead until the dough is smooth and elastic, about 5 minutes. Form the dough into a ball, place it in an oiled, straight-sided plastic container or deep, oiled bowl, cover it with plastic wrap, and proceed with the recipe.

Twenty-Four-Hour Pizza Dough

If you decrease the yeast, the dough can be made a day in advance, refrigerated overnight (to retard rising), and then allowed to rise during the day at room temperature. This strategy is ideal for weeknight pizzas, since the dough rises while you are at work.

Follow the recipe for Garlic-Herb Pizza Dough, decreasing the yeast to ½ teaspoon. Let the covered dough rise in the refrigerator for up to 16 hours.

EQUIPMENT: Standing Mixer

Years ago, free-standing mixers were a kitchen staple. Your grandmother likely had a "mixmaster," which is a generic term for a free-standing mixer, though it is actually a brand name for units manufactured by Sunbeam. For a while, these large machines went out of favor with the introduction of new food processors and more powerful hand mixers, which were better suited for many of the tasks of standing mixers. If all you want to do is whip egg whites or cream, or if you only make cakes from a mix, you don't really need a heavy-duty standing mixer. But if you like to bake, a standing mixer provides maximum flexibility. Models with the most options, such as a whisk, paddle, and dough hook, will open up the most possibilities for baking everything from cakes and cookies to breads.

One of the best uses for standing mixers is mixing and kneading bread or pizza dough. Standing mixers knead perfectly in about one-third of the time required for hand kneading. (Handheld mixers lack the stability and power to do a good job.) Food processors can knead bread dough, but you must use a large-capacity model.

Unfortunately, not all brands of standing mixers are helpful kitchen allies. In the process of testing seven of the top-selling standing mixers, we found that some models are simply too difficult and frustrating to work with to make them worthwhile purchases. Outdated engineering and poorly designed beaters and bowls made it a challenge, rather than a pleasure, to prepare baked goods in several of the models we tried.

On the other hand, three of the seven models were outstanding, and making cakes, cookies, and bread with them was enjoyable and gratifying. The Rival Select was exceptional, performing every task flawlessly. The two KitchenAid models we tested were outstanding as well, although the Rival's dough hook is better designed and kneaded bread dough more quickly. These three models are also the most expensive of the group, costing $300 to $400. Are they worth it? Plainly and simply, yes. Each is designed for endurance, so it makes sense to spend the money up front, since you will derive years of use and pleasure from these models.

The Rival Select and the two KitchenAid mixers operate by "planetary action," in which a wide, flat beater (called the paddle) moves around in a stationary bowl. This proved to be the most effective way of blending ingredients, since the paddle reaches the sides as well as the center of the bowl and gathers particles quickly. As a result, there is little need to stop the machine and scrape down the sides of the bowl.

Another critical point of comparison among the mixers was stability. The Rival and KitchenAid models are heavy and barely vibrate even when put to the test of mixing stiff cookie and bread dough. A standing mixer that you have to hold down with one or two hands is not a labor-saving device.

The Rival and the KitchenAids were the best at kneading bread and pizza dough, performing the task quickly, smoothly, and efficiently, with the motors showing not the slightest sign of strain, and spilling not a speck of flour. All three models had the weight, stability, and power needed to make smooth, elastic, tender dough.

⤝✦

Fastest Pizza Dough

MAKES ENOUGH FOR 8 INDIVIDUAL PIZZAS

Although this quick dough does not have quite the same texture as our Garlic-Herb Pizza Dough, it can be prepared after coming home from work. Rapid-rise yeast makes it possible to serve pizza in little more than an hour after walking into the kitchen. Sugar also speeds up the rising process, as does putting the dough into a warm oven. Although we prefer bread flour because it delivers a crisper crust, all-purpose flour can also be used. To streamline the process, we have omitted the garlic and herbs used in the master recipe, but you can add them if you like.

1½ cups warm water, at about 105 degrees

1 envelope (2¼ teaspoons) rapid-rise dry yeast

1 tablespoon sugar

2 tablespoons extra-virgin olive oil

4 cups bread or all-purpose flour, plus extra for dusting hands and work surfaces

1½ teaspoons salt

Vegetable oil or spray for oiling container or bowl

1. Set the oven to 200 degrees for 10 minutes, then turn the oven off.

2. Meanwhile, pour the water into the workbowl of a large food processor. Sprinkle the yeast and sugar over the water and pulse twice. Add the oil, flour, and salt, and process until the mixture forms a cohesive mass. The dough should be soft and just a bit tacky. (If it is very sticky, add 2 tablespoons flour and pulse briefly. If it is stiff and tight, add 1 tablespoon water and pulse briefly.) Process another 30 seconds.

3. Use a rubber spatula to turn out the dough onto a lightly floured work surface; knead by hand a few strokes to form a smooth, round ball.

4. Put the dough into an oiled, straight-sided plastic container or deep, oiled bowl and cover it with plastic wrap. Place the bowl in the warm oven. Let the dough rise for 40 minutes or until doubled. Remove the bowl from the oven, punch the dough down, and turn it out onto a lightly floured work surface. Divide and shape the dough as directed on page 216.

EQUIPMENT: Food Processor

Spending several hundred dollars on a standing mixer is not an option for many cooks. They would rather use a food processor for grating, chopping, and shredding, as well as for kneading dough. (An inexpensive hand-held mixer can handle [if not as well] most of the other tasks usually reserved for a standing mixer, including whipping cream and beating cake batter.)

So how to go about buying a food processor that can handle pesto as well as pizza dough? We evaluated seven food processors based on the results in five general categories: chopping and grinding, slicing, grating, pureeing, and kneading.

We found that most food processors chop, grind, slice, grate, and puree at least minimally well. Of course, there are differences in the performance of models, but they were not as dramatic as in the results of our kneading tests.

A food processor doesn't really knead bread fully, but it does bring the dry and wet ingredients together beautifully to form the dough. If a recipe calls for a smooth, satiny ball of dough, you will have to knead the dough by hand on the counter after processing; however, the kneading time should be just a few minutes. With pizza, hand kneading is not necessary because a satiny ball of dough is not really needed.

We found that successful kneading in a food processor was linked directly to large bowl size as well as to the weight of the base. The 11-cup machines performed best because they provided ample space for the ball of dough to move around. A heavy base provides stability, and the nods went to KitchenAid and Cuisinart, with their substantial, 10-pound-plus bases. These machines also did the best job on other basic food processor tests.

Remove the dough from the refrigerator and allow it to rise at room temperature until it has doubled in size, 6 to 8 hours.

Eight-Hour Pizza Dough

If you reduce the amount of yeast, you can also make the dough in the morning and let it rise on the counter all day.

Follow the recipe for Garlic-Herb Pizza Dough, decreasing the yeast to ½ teaspoon. Let the covered dough rise at cool room temperature (about 68 degrees) until it has doubled in size, about 8 hours.

GRILLED PIZZA

GETTING THE TOPPING HOT IS THE HARDEST challenge when grilling pizza. Toppings have only a few minutes to heat through (any longer and the bottom crust will burn), so they must be kept fairly light.

We found that heavy toppings or liquidy sauces make grilled pizza very soggy and should thus be avoided. In our tests, raw ingredients that need only be heated through (fresh tomatoes, cheese, sliced shrimp) and cooked ingredients that are fairly dry (sautéed onions, grilled mushrooms, eggplant) worked best as toppings for grilled pizzas.

Because grilled pizzas are flipped (the bottom of the dough round eventually becomes the top of the pizza), we do not dust peels or baking sheets with sandy semolina or cornmeal, as is done for oven-baked pizza. Flour keeps the dough from sticking yet does not make the crust gritty, as did the semolina and cornmeal in our tests.

We found that oil helps keep grilled pizza dough moist, prevents sticking to the grill, and promotes even browning. Keep a brush and a small bowl of olive oil nearby when grilling pizzas. We brush some oil on the dough before it is grilled and then again when it is flipped.

Although we prefer to top grilled pizzas on a baking sheet and not on the grill, you will still spend a fair amount of time near the fire. To keep your hands as far away from the grill as possible, use tongs with long, heat-resistant handles to maneuver the dough.

Once the dough has been flipped, it's time to add the toppings. We recommend that you use small disposable aluminum pie plates to concentrate heat and to get the toppings hot by the time the bottom crust is nicely browned. If the toppings are not ready and the bottom crust is done, you can slide the pizzas onto a baking sheet and place them under the broiler.

In our testing, we found that large crusts are hard to flip, so we recommend making only small pizzas on the grill. This necessitates working in batches, so consider grilling pizzas for an informal meal when everyone is gathered in the backyard. Serve each pizza immediately as it comes off the grill. An extra pair of hands to top crusts while you tend the grill is helpful.

If you prefer not to be grilling pizzas to order, the crusts can be grilled until nicely browned on both sides and then slid onto a baking sheet, cooled, covered, and kept at room temperature for several hours. When you are ready to serve the pizzas, brush the tops of the grilled pizza rounds with a little oil, add the toppings, and slide the crusts under a preheated broiler for several minutes. While the smoky grill flavor will not be as intense, this do-ahead method is much easier than the "grill, then top, then grill" method.

Most of the following grilled pizza recipes will serve four as a light summer meal (two small pizzas per person) or eight as a first course. We particularly like to serve grilled pizzas as a first course or hors d'oeuvre with drinks and then follow with something else from the grill.

Grilled Pizza with Olive Oil and Salt

MAKES 8 INDIVIDUAL PIZZAS

This basic pizza is flavored only with good olive oil and salt. Serve it with drinks or as an accompaniment to meals. The variations add toppings and are slightly more complicated.

1	recipe Garlic-Herb Pizza Dough (page 212)
¼	cup extra-virgin olive oil
	Salt, preferably kosher

1. Prepare and shape the dough as directed. Light the grill. (See "Firing the Grill for Pizza," on page 217, for more instructions.)

2. When the grill is medium-hot, brush some oil over each stretched dough round and sprinkle with salt to taste.

3. Slide your hand under several dough rounds and

gently flip them onto the grill, oiled-side down. Grill until dark brown grill marks appear, 1 to 2 minutes. Prick any bubbles that develop on the top surface with a fork. Brush the tops with more oil and flip the dough rounds. Grill until the pizza bottoms are crisp and browned, 2 to 3 minutes. Serve immediately and repeat the process with the remaining dough rounds.

➤ VARIATIONS

Grilled Pizza with Fresh Tomatoes and Basil

When tomatoes are at their best and all your cooking is outside on the grill, think of this light pizza, which makes a good lunch for four or a first course for eight.

| 1 | recipe Garlic-Herb Pizza Dough (page 212) |
| 1/4 | cup extra-virgin olive oil |

    Salt

3	medium ripe tomatoes (about 1 pound), cored and sliced crosswise into thin rounds
1/2	cup grated Parmesan cheese (optional)
1	cup lightly packed chopped fresh basil leaves
	Ground black pepper
1/4	cup pitted and quartered oil-cured black olives (optional)

1. Prepare and shape the dough as directed. Light the grill. (See "Firing the Grill for Pizza," on page 217, for more instructions.)

2. When the grill is medium-hot, brush some oil over each stretched dough round and sprinkle with salt to taste.

3. Slide your hand under several dough rounds and gently flip them onto the grill, oiled-side down.

SHAPING PIZZA DOUGH

1. Use a chef's knife or dough scraper to divide the risen and punched-down dough into eight pieces. A single dough recipe will make eight 8-inch pies.

2. Form each piece of dough into a smooth, round ball and cover them with a damp cloth. Let the dough relax for at least 5 minutes but no more than 30 minutes.

3. Working with one ball of dough at a time and keeping the others covered, flatten the dough ball into a disk using the palms of your hands.

4. Starting at the center of the disk and working outward, use your fingertips to press the dough into a round about 1/2 inch thick.

5. Use one hand to hold the dough in place and the other to stretch the dough outward. Rotate the dough a quarter turn and stretch it again. Continue turning and stretching until the dough will not stretch any further. Let the dough relax for 5 minutes, then continue stretching until it reaches a diameter of 7 to 8 inches. The dough should be about 1/4 inch thick.

6. Use your palm to press down and flatten the thick edge of the dough. Transfer the dough rounds to baking sheets or metal peels that have been lightly dusted with flour.

FIRING THE GRILL FOR PIZZA

Pizzas should be cooked over a medium-hot, single-level fire (see page 219 for more details and illustrations). If working with a charcoal grill, light a chimney filled with hardwood charcoal, then spread the lit coals in a single layer over the bottom of the grill. Set the cooking rack in place, place the cover on the grill, and let it heat up for 5 minutes. Use a wire brush to scrape clean the cooking grate. When the fire is medium-hot (see page 19 for instructions on gauging heat level), you are ready to grill the pizzas.

We like to serve grilled pizza as an appetizer. If cooking fish or steak for the main course, you will need to add more coals to the fire once the pizzas are done. With long-handled tongs, lift up the cooking grate and throw a handful or two of unlit coals onto the pile. Wait 10 minutes to make sure the coals are lit, then check for the appropriate heat level before grilling the main course.

On a gas grill, the whole operation is quite simple. Simply preheat the grill, then turn the burners down to medium-high. Once you are done grilling the pizzas, you can adjust the burners as desired to create whatever kind of fire is needed.

The lid will be open (on both charcoal and gas) as you move pizzas on and off the grill, so you must heat toppings through by covering the pizzas with disposable pie plates. You will need to grill the pizzas in batches.

Grill until dark brown grill marks appear, 1 to 2 minutes. Prick any bubbles that develop on the top surface with a fork. Brush the tops with more oil and flip the dough rounds onto a clean baking sheet or peel, grilled-side up.

4. Brush the grilled dough surfaces with more oil. Arrange a portion of the tomatoes over each dough round, leaving a ½-inch border around the edges uncovered. Sprinkle with the Parmesan (if using), basil, and salt and pepper to taste. Drizzle with the remaining oil and dot with olives, if using.

5. Slide the pizzas back onto the grill and cover each with a disposable aluminum pie plate. Grill until the pizza bottoms are crisp and browned, the tomatoes are hot, and the cheese (if using) melts, 2 to 3 minutes. Serve immediately and repeat the process with the remaining dough rounds.

Grilled Pizza with Shrimp and Feta Cheese

This pizza is more moist than some of the others and works well as a dinner for four when served with a salad.

1	recipe Garlic-Herb Pizza Dough (page 212)
¼	cup extra-virgin olive oil, plus extra for brushing on stretched dough
6	medium garlic cloves, minced
4	teaspoons minced fresh oregano leaves
	Salt and ground black pepper
1	pound medium shrimp, peeled and halved lengthwise
8	ounces feta cheese, crumbled (2 cups)

1. Prepare and shape the dough as directed. Light the grill. (See "Firing the Grill for Pizza," above, for more instructions.) Combine ¼ cup oil, garlic, 2 teaspoons oregano, and salt and pepper to taste in a small bowl.

2. When the grill is medium-hot, brush some plain olive oil over each stretched dough round and sprinkle with salt to taste.

3. Slide your hand under several dough rounds and gently flip them onto the grill, oiled-side down. Grill until dark brown grill marks appear, 1 to 2 minutes. Prick any bubbles that develop on the top surface with a fork. Brush the tops with more plain olive oil and flip the dough rounds onto a clean baking sheet or peel, grilled-side up.

4. Arrange a portion of the shrimp over each dough round, leaving a ½-inch border around the edges uncovered. Brush some herb oil over each pizza, making sure the shrimp are lightly brushed with oil as well. Sprinkle cheese and the remaining 2 teaspoons oregano over the shrimp.

5. Slide the pizzas back onto the grill and cover each with a disposable aluminum pie plate. Grill until the pizza bottoms are crisp and browned, the shrimp are pink, and the cheese melts, 2 to 3 minutes. Serve immediately and repeat the process with the remaining dough rounds.

Grilled Pizza with Portobello Mushrooms and Onions

You can sauté the onions well in advance, but because you grill the mushrooms, it makes sense to cook them right before grilling the pizzas. These pizzas are fairly substantial; two for each diner make a nice main course.

1	recipe Garlic-Herb Pizza Dough (page 212)
¼	cup extra-virgin olive oil, plus extra for brushing on stretched dough
2	medium onions, halved and sliced thin
2	tablespoons balsamic vinegar
1	teaspoon minced fresh oregano or thyme leaves
	Salt and ground black pepper
4	medium portobello mushrooms (about 1 pound), stems discarded
½	cup grated Parmesan cheese

1. Prepare the dough as directed. Light the grill. (See "Firing the Grill for Pizza," on page 217, for more instructions.)

2. While preparing the dough, heat 2 tablespoons of the oil in a large skillet. Add the onions and sauté over medium heat until golden, about 8 minutes. Stir in the vinegar and cook until the liquid has evaporated, about 1 minute. Stir in the oregano and salt and pepper to taste. Set the onions aside.

3. Brush the mushrooms with 2 tablespoons of the oil and season with salt and pepper to taste. Grill over a medium-hot fire (see how to gauge heat level on page 19), turning once, until caps are streaked with dark grill marks, 8 to 10 minutes. Remove mushrooms from grill and cut into ¼-inch strips. Set the mushrooms aside.

4. Stretch the dough as directed in the illustrations on page 216. Check to make sure the grill is medium-hot. Brush some oil over each stretched dough round and sprinkle with salt to taste.

5. Slide your hand under several dough rounds and gently flip them onto the grill, oiled-side down. Grill until dark brown grill marks appear, 1 to 2 minutes. Prick any bubbles that develop on the top surface with a fork. Brush the tops with more oil and flip the dough rounds onto a clean baking sheet or peel, grilled-side up.

6. Arrange a portion of the onions and mushrooms over each dough round, leaving a ½-inch border around the edges uncovered. Sprinkle with cheese.

7. Slide the pizzas back onto the grill and cover each pizza with a disposable aluminum pie plate. Grill until the pizza bottoms are crisp and browned, the vegetables are hot, and the cheese melts, 2 to 3 minutes. Serve immediately and repeat the process with the remaining dough rounds.

Grilled Pizza with Grilled Eggplant and Goat Cheese

Thin rounds of eggplant are brushed with a garlicky basil oil, grilled, then layered over grilled crusts and sprinkled with goat cheese. Serves four as a main course or eight as an appetizer.

1	recipe Garlic-Herb Pizza Dough (page 212)
¼	cup extra-virgin olive oil, plus extra for brushing on stretched dough
6	medium garlic cloves, minced
4	tablespoons minced fresh basil leaves
	Salt and ground black pepper
1	large eggplant (about 1 pound), cut crosswise into ¼-inch-thick rounds
8	ounces goat cheese, crumbled (about 2 cups)

1. Prepare the dough as directed. Light the grill. (See "Firing the Grill for Pizza," on page 217, for more instructions.)

2. While preparing the dough, combine ¼ cup oil, garlic, 2 tablespoons basil, and salt and pepper to taste in small bowl. Set the herb oil aside.

3. Brush both sides of eggplant slices with half of the herb oil. Grill over a medium-hot fire (see how to gauge heat level on page 19), turning once, until the flesh is darkly colored, 8 to 10 minutes. Set the eggplant aside.

4. Stretch the dough as directed in the illustrations on page 216. Check to make sure the grill is medium-hot. Brush some plain olive oil over each stretched dough round and sprinkle with salt to taste.

5. Slide your hand under several dough rounds and gently flip them onto the grill, oiled-side down. Grill until dark brown grill marks appear, 1 to 2 minutes. Prick any bubbles that develop on the top surface with a fork. Brush the tops with more plain olive oil and flip the dough rounds onto a clean baking sheet or peel, grilled-side up.

6. Brush the grilled dough surfaces with the remaining herb oil. Arrange a portion of the eggplant slices over each dough round, leaving a ½-inch border around the edges uncovered. Sprinkle with some of the cheese and the remaining 2 tablespoons basil.

7. Slide the pizzas back onto the grill and cover each pizza with a disposable aluminum pie plate. Grill until the pizza bottoms are crisp and browned, the eggplant is hot, and the cheese melts, 2 to 3 minutes. Serve immediately and repeat the process with the remaining dough rounds.

MAKING GRILLED PIZZAS

1. Carefully lift the dough rounds and transfer them to a rimless metal baking sheet or pizza peel dusted with flour.

2. When the fire is ready, brush the tops of the dough rounds with oil and sprinkle them with salt. Slide your hand under each dough round and gently flip the dough onto the grill, oiled-side down. Cook them until dark grill marks appear, 1 to 2 minutes.

3. Use a fork to prick any bubbles that develop on the top surface of the dough rounds.

4. Brush the tops with more oil, then use long-handled tongs to flip the dough, grilled-side up, onto the (clean) baking sheet or pizza peel. (We find that topping the pizzas right on the grill can be difficult given the intense heat and thus prefer this method.)

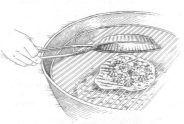

5. Brush the grilled surfaces with more oil.

6. Quickly arrange the toppings over the grilled surfaces, leaving a ½-inch border around the edges uncovered.

7. Slide the pizzas back onto the grill. Cover the pizzas with disposable aluminum pie plates and grill until the pizza bottoms are crisp and browned, 2 to 3 minutes.

Grilled Pizza with Fennel, Sun-Dried Tomato, and Asiago

The sautéed fennel and onion topping can be prepared a day in advance of grilling the pizza. Bring to room temperature before using to top pizza.

I	recipe Garlic-Herb Pizza Dough (page 212)
3	tablespoons extra-virgin olive oil, plus extra for brushing on stretched dough
I	large Spanish onion (about I pound), halved and sliced thin
I	medium fennel bulb (about ¾ pound), stems and fronds discarded; bulb halved, cored, and sliced very thin
4	large garlic cloves, minced
I	tablespoon fresh thyme leaves
I	teaspoon fennel seeds
¼	teaspoon hot red pepper flakes
	Salt
½	cup drained and slivered sun-dried tomatoes
½	cup grated Asiago cheese

1. Prepare and shape the dough as directed. Light the grill. (See "Firing the Grill for Pizza," on page 217, for more instructions.)

2. While preparing the dough, heat 3 tablespoons oil in a large skillet over medium-high heat. Add the onion and fennel and cook, stirring often, until the vegetables soften, about 8 minutes. Add the garlic and continue cooking for 2 minutes. Stir in the thyme, fennel seeds, and hot pepper flakes. Season with salt to taste. Set the onion-fennel mixture aside.

3. Check to make sure the grill is medium-hot. (See how to gauge heat level on page 19.) Brush some oil over each stretched dough round and sprinkle with salt to taste.

5. Slide your hand under several dough rounds and gently flip them onto the grill, oiled-side down. Grill until dark brown grill marks appear, 1 to 2 minutes. Prick any bubbles that develop on the top surface with a fork. Brush the tops with more oil and flip the dough rounds onto a clean baking sheet or peel, grilled-side up.

6. Brush the grilled dough surfaces with more oil. Arrange a portion of the onion-fennel mixture over each dough round, leaving a ½-inch border around the edges uncovered. Sprinkle some tomatoes and cheese over the vegetables.

7. Slide the pizzas back onto the grill and cover each pizza with a disposable aluminum pie plate. Grill until the pizza bottoms are crisp and browned, the vegetables are hot, and the cheese melts, 2 to 3 minutes. Serve immediately and repeat the process with the remaining dough rounds.

Grilled Pizza with Prosciutto, Arugula, and Gorgonzola Cheese

Cheese pizzas are layered with prosciutto and arugula salad when they come off the grill. The residual heat from the pizzas softens the prosciutto and wilts the greens. Don't dress the arugula until you are ready to start grilling. If you prefer, replace the gorgonzola with the same amount of fresh goat cheese or fresh mozzarella. This pizza makes a delicious first course for eight.

I	recipe Garlic-Herb Pizza Dough (page 212)
4	cups lightly packed stemmed arugula, washed and thoroughly dried
	Extra-virgin olive oil for brushing on stretched dough, plus 2 tablespoons for dressing arugula
	Salt and ground black pepper
4	ounces Gorgonzola cheese, crumbled
½	cup grated Parmesan cheese
¼	pound thinly sliced prosciutto

1. Prepare and shape the dough as directed. Light the grill. (See "Firing the Grill for Pizza," on page 217, for more instructions.)

2. While preparing the dough, place the arugula in a medium bowl. Drizzle 2 tablespoons oil over the arugula and sprinkle with salt and pepper to taste. Toss and set the salad aside.

3. When the grill is medium-hot (see how to gauge heat level on page 19), brush some oil over each stretched dough round and sprinkle with salt to taste.

4. Slide your hand under several dough rounds and gently flip them onto the grill, oiled-side down. Grill until dark brown grill marks appear, 1 to 2 minutes. Prick any bubbles that develop on the top surface with a fork. Brush the tops with more oil and flip the dough rounds onto a clean baking sheet or peel, grilled-side up.

5. Brush the grilled dough surfaces with more oil. Dot each round with Gorgonzola and some Parmesan, leaving a ½-inch border around the edges uncovered.

6. Slide the pizzas back onto the grill and cover each pizza with a disposable aluminum pie plate. Grill until the pizza bottoms are crisp and browned and the cheeses melt, 2 to 3 minutes.

7. When the pizzas come off the grill, cover each with a layer of prosciutto and some arugula. Serve immediately and repeat the process with the remaining dough rounds.

Grilled Pizza with Asparagus, Caramelized Onions, Black Olives, and Thyme

To save preparation time the day that you grill the pizzas, prepare the onions the day before and bring them to room temperature before topping the pizzas. These pizzas make an excellent main course for four.

I	recipe Garlic-Herb Pizza Dough (page 212)
3	tablespoons extra-virgin olive oil, plus extra for brushing on stretched dough
2	medium yellow onions, halved and sliced thin
	Salt
I	teaspoon fresh thyme leaves
	Ground black pepper
I	pound asparagus, tough ends removed
½	cup pitted and quartered kalamata olives
½	cup grated Parmesan cheese

1. Prepare and shape the dough as directed. Light the grill. (See "Firing the Grill for Pizza," on page 217, for more instructions.)

2. While preparing the dough, heat 2 tablespoons oil in a large skillet set over medium-high heat. Add the onions and sprinkle with ¼ teaspoon salt. Sauté until softened, about 5 to 7 minutes. Reduce the heat to medium-low and continue cooking until the onions are very soft and caramelized, 12 to 15 minutes longer. Stir in the thyme and season with pepper to taste.

3. Toss the asparagus with the remaining tablespoon of oil and salt and pepper to taste in a medium bowl. Grill over a medium-hot fire (see how to gauge heat level on page 19), turning once, until browned and barely tender, about 6 minutes. Remove the asparagus from the grill and cut each piece in half. Set the asparagus aside.

4. Check to make sure the grill is medium-hot. Brush some oil over each stretched dough round and sprinkle with salt to taste.

5. Slide your hand under several dough rounds and gently flip them onto the grill, oiled-side down. Grill until dark brown grill marks appear, 1 to 2 minutes. Prick any bubbles that develop on the top surface with a fork. Brush the tops with more oil and flip the dough rounds onto a clean baking sheet or peel, grilled-side up.

6. Brush the grilled dough surfaces with more oil. Arrange a portion of the onion mixture and the asparagus over each dough round, leaving a ½-inch border around the edges uncovered. Sprinkle some olives and cheese over the vegetables.

7. Slide the pizzas back onto the grill and cover each pizza with a disposable aluminum pie plate. Grill until the pizza bottoms are crisp and browned, the vegetables are hot, and the cheese melts, 2 to 3 minutes. Serve immediately and repeat the process with the remaining dough rounds.

EQUIPMENT: Rimless Baking Sheets

For grilled pizzas, we like to put the stretched dough rounds on a baking sheet or aluminum pizza peel that has been dusted with flour. To slide the dough off the sheet, there must be at least one side without a rim. For that reason, a rimmed jelly roll pan won't work, although you can turn it upside down and use it that way in a pinch. You can also use a metal peel if you have one. (We're not comfortable placing a wooden peel so close to an open fire.)

You will need the rimless baking sheet or metal peel to get the dough onto the grill. We also recommend that you flip the grilled dough rounds back onto the baking sheet or peel and then top them (as opposed to topping them right on the grill); this method keeps your hands far away from the intense heat of the grill.

Grilled Pizza with Bacon, Corn, and Cilantro

This southwestern-style pizza is delicious, if unusual. It's a perfect start to a meal from the grill.

1	recipe Garlic-Herb Pizza Dough (page 212)
12	ounces sliced bacon, cut crosswise into ¼-inch pieces
	Extra-virgin olive oil for brushing on stretched dough
	Salt
2	ears corn, husks and silk removed, kernels cut off the cob
8	ounces pepperjack cheese, shredded (2 cups)
½	cup minced fresh cilantro leaves

1. Prepare and shape the dough as directed. Light the grill. (See "Firing the Grill for Pizza," on page 217, for more instructions.)

2. While preparing the dough, place the bacon in a large skillet over medium heat. Cook until crisp and brown, about 8 minutes. Use a slotted spoon to transfer the bacon to a paper towel–lined plate.

3. When the grill is medium-hot (see how to gauge heat level on page 19), brush some oil over each stretched dough round and sprinkle with salt to taste.

4. Slide your hand under several dough rounds and gently flip them onto the grill, oiled-side down. Grill until dark brown grill marks appear, 1 to 2 minutes. Prick any bubbles that develop on the top surface with a fork. Brush the tops with more oil and flip the dough rounds onto a clean baking sheet or peel, grilled-side up.

5. Brush the grilled dough surfaces with more oil. Arrange a portion of the bacon, corn, and cheese over each dough round, leaving a ½-inch border around the edges uncovered.

6. Slide the pizzas back onto the grill and cover each pizza with a disposable aluminum pie plate. Grill until the pizza bottoms are crisp and browned, the corn is hot, and the cheese melts, 2 to 3 minutes. Sprinkle each pizza with a little cilantro and serve immediately. Repeat the process with the remaining dough rounds.

BRUSCHETTA

AUTHENTIC ITALIAN GARLIC BREAD, CALLED bruschetta, is never squishy or soft. Crisp, toasted slices of country bread are rubbed with raw garlic, brushed with extra-virgin olive oil (never butter), and then slathered with various ingredients. Toppings can be as simple as salt and pepper or fresh herbs. Ripe tomatoes, grilled mushrooms, or sautéed onions make more substantial toppings.

We found that narrow loaves of Italian bread are not suitable for bruschetta. Crusty country loaves that yield larger slices are preferable. Oblong loaves that measure about five inches across are best, but round loaves will work. As for thickness, we found that about one inch provides enough heft to support weighty toppings and gives a good chew.

Toasting the bread, which can be done over a grill or under the broiler, creates little jagged edges that pull off tiny bits of garlic when the raw clove is rubbed over the bread. For more garlic flavor, rub vigorously.

Oil can be drizzled over the garlicky toast or brushed on for more even coverage. One large piece of toast is enough for a single appetizer serving. Two or three slices make a good lunch when accompanied by a salad.

Bruschetta is always served as an appetizer, usually with something from the grill to follow. Because bread toasts so quickly on the grill (it takes just a minute or two), it's easy enough to grill bruschetta before making the main course. Although bread is best grilled over a medium fire, you can toast it over a hot fire as long as you are supervigilant. For instance, this may be necessary if you want to serve bruschetta before grilling steak, since the latter requires a hot fire.

Bruschetta

MAKES 8 LARGE SLICES

Garlic bread, Italian style. Serve this simple grilled bread as an accompaniment to meals or use as part of an hors d'oeuvre spread with cheese, meats, and vegetables.

3	tablespoons extra-virgin olive oil
	Salt and ground black pepper
1	12 by 5-inch loaf country bread, sliced crosswise into 1-inch-thick pieces, ends removed
1	large garlic clove, peeled

1. Mix the oil and salt and pepper to taste together in a small bowl. Set aside.

2. Grill the bread over a medium fire (see how to gauge heat level on page 19), turning once, until golden brown on both sides, 1 to 1½ minutes.

3. Place the toast slices on a large platter, rub the garlic over the tops, brush with the seasoned oil, and serve immediately.

Bruschetta with Tomatoes and Basil

MAKES 8 LARGE SLICES

This is the classic bruschetta, although you can substitute other herbs. Decrease the quantity of stronger herbs, such as thyme or oregano.

4	medium ripe tomatoes (about 1⅔ pounds), cored and cut into ½-inch dice
⅓	cup shredded fresh basil leaves
	Salt and ground black pepper
1	12 by 5-inch loaf country bread, sliced crosswise into 1-inch-thick pieces, ends removed
1	large garlic clove, peeled
3	tablespoons extra-virgin olive oil

1. Mix the tomatoes, basil, and salt and pepper to taste together in a medium bowl. Set aside.

2. Grill the bread over a medium fire (see how to gauge heat level on page 19) until golden brown on both sides, 1 to 1½ minutes.

3. Place the toast slices on a large platter, rub the garlic over the tops, then brush with the oil. Use a slotted spoon to divide the tomato mixture among the toast slices. Serve immediately.

Bruschetta with Fresh Herbs

MAKES 8 LARGE SLICES

Ideal as an accompaniment to meals.

5	tablespoons extra-virgin olive oil
1½	tablespoons minced fresh parsley leaves
1	tablespoon minced fresh oregano or thyme leaves
1	tablespoon minced fresh sage leaves
	Salt and ground black pepper

1	12 by 5-inch loaf country bread, sliced crosswise into 1-inch-thick pieces, ends removed
1	large garlic clove, peeled

1. Mix the oil, herbs, and salt and pepper to taste together in a small bowl. Set aside.

2. Grill the bread over a medium fire (see how to gauge heat level on page 19) until golden brown on both sides, 1 to 1½ minutes.

3. Place the toast slices on a large platter, rub the garlic over the tops, brush with the herb oil, and serve immediately.

Bruschetta with Red Onions, Herbs, and Parmesan

MAKES 8 LARGE SLICES

The sautéed onions may be prepared in advance and the toasts assembled at the last minute. Be sure to bring the prepared onions to room temperature before serving, if made ahead.

6	tablespoons extra-virgin olive oil
4	medium red onions (about 1½ pounds), halved lengthwise and sliced thin
4	teaspoons sugar
1½	tablespoons minced fresh mint leaves
2	tablespoons balsamic vinegar
	Salt and ground black pepper
1	12 by 5-inch loaf country bread, sliced crosswise into 1-inch-thick pieces, ends removed
1	large garlic clove, peeled
3	tablespoons grated Parmesan cheese

1. Heat 3½ tablespoons oil in a large skillet set over medium-high heat. Add the onions and sugar and sauté, stirring often, until softened, 7 to 8 minutes. Reduce the heat to medium-low. Continue to cook, stirring often, until the onions are sweet and tender, 7 to 8 minutes longer. Stir in the mint and vinegar and season to taste with salt and pepper. Set the onion mixture aside. (Can be covered and refrigerated for several days.)

2. Grill the bread over a medium fire (see how to gauge heat level on page 19) until golden brown on both sides, 1 to 1½ minutes.

3. Place the toast slices on a large platter, rub the garlic over the tops, then brush with the remaining 2½

tablespoons oil. Divide the onion mixture among the slices and sprinkle with the cheese. Serve immediately

---

Bruschetta with Grilled Portobello Mushrooms

MAKES 8 LARGE SLICES

For serving, the mushrooms are flipped onto the bread so their juices seep down into the toast.

4   large portobello mushrooms (about 1⅓ pounds), stemmed

6   tablespoons extra-virgin olive oil

1   tablespoon minced fresh rosemary leaves
    Salt and ground black pepper

1   12 by 5-inch loaf country bread, sliced crosswise into 1-inch-thick pieces, ends removed

1   large garlic clove, peeled

1. Place the mushroom caps on a large baking sheet. Mix 3½ tablespoons oil with the rosemary and salt and pepper to taste in a small bowl. Brush the oil mixture over both sides of the mushrooms.

2. Grill the mushrooms over a medium fire (see how to gauge heat level on page 19), turning once, until caps are cooked through and marked with dark grill stripes, 8 to 10 minutes. Transfer to a cutting board when done.

3. Meanwhile, grill the bread, turning once, until golden brown on both sides, 1 to 1½ minutes.

4. Place the toast slices on a large platter, rub the garlic over the tops, and brush with the remaining 2½ tablespoons oil.

5. Halve the grilled mushrooms. Place one half, gill-side down, over each toast. Serve immediately.

Bruschetta with Sweet Peppers and Fresh Mozzarella

MAKES 8 LARGE SLICES

The sautéed peppers in this recipe can be served warm or at room temperature. They can be made a day ahead if desired, refrigerated, then brought back to room temperature before serving.

4   tablespoons extra-virgin olive oil

3   medium red, yellow, and/or orange bell peppers, cored, seeded, and cut lengthwise into ¼-inch-wide strips

1   medium garlic clove, minced, plus 1 large clove, peeled
    Salt and ground black pepper

½   teaspoon balsamic vinegar

1   12 by 5-inch loaf country bread, sliced crosswise into 1-inch-thick pieces, ends removed

8   ounces fresh mozzarella, sliced into ¼-inch rounds

¼   cup sliced fresh basil leaves

1. Heat 1 tablespoon oil in a large skillet over medium-high heat until shimmering. Add the pepper strips and sauté until slightly browned at the edges and beginning to soften, about 5 minutes. Reduce the heat to medium-low, stir in the minced garlic, cover, and continue cooking until soft, about 8 minutes longer, stirring occasionally. Season with salt and pepper to taste; remove from heat and stir in the vinegar.

2. Grill the bread over a medium fire (see how to gauge heat level on page 19), turning once, until golden brown on both sides, 1 to 1½ minutes.

3. Place the toast slices on a large platter, rub the peeled garlic over the tops, and brush with the remaining 3 tablespoons oil.

4. Place a few slices of mozzarella cheese on each toast. Cover with a portion of the sautéed peppers, then top with a sprinkling of basil. Serve immediately.

Bruschetta with Sautéed Spicy Shrimp

MAKES 8 LARGE SLICES

The cream in this recipe is optional. If you have it on hand, it adds a little extra richness to the shrimp. Be sure to serve the shrimp mixture warm on the grilled bread; once the mixture cools down, it loses its appeal.

2   tablespoons unsalted butter

1   medium garlic clove, minced, plus 1 large clove, peeled

½   teaspoon hot red pepper flakes

1¼   pounds shrimp, peeled and cut into ¼- to ⅜-inch pieces

2   tablespoons heavy cream (optional)
    Salt and ground black pepper

1½   teaspoons lemon juice

2 tablespoons minced fresh parsley leaves

1 12 by 5-inch loaf country bread, sliced crosswise into 1-inch-thick pieces, ends removed

3 tablespoons extra-virgin olive oil

1. Melt the butter over medium-high heat in a large skillet. Once the foam begins to subside, add the minced garlic and hot red pepper flakes and sauté until fragrant but not brown, about 30 seconds. Add the shrimp and cook until pink, about 1 minute. Add the heavy cream (if using), season with salt and pepper to taste, and cook until the shrimp are bright pink and opaque at the center, 1 minute longer. Stir in lemon juice and parsley. Cover and keep warm.

2. Grill the bread over a medium fire (see how to gauge heat level on page 19), turning once, until golden brown on both sides, 1 to 1½ minutes.

3. Place the toast slices on a large platter, rub the peeled garlic over the tops, and brush with the oil.

4. Top each slice with a portion of the warm shrimp mixture and serve immediately.

Bruschetta with Tapenade and Goat Cheese

MAKES 8 LARGE SLICES

Tapenade is an intensely flavored olive spread that goes beautifully with bruschetta and goat cheese. It can be made up to one week in advance and refrigerated until needed.

1 cup kalamata olives, pitted and halved (about 20 large)

2 medium garlic cloves, roughly chopped, plus 1 large clove, peeled

4 anchovy fillets, roughly chopped

2 teaspoons drained capers

6 tablespoons extra-virgin olive oil

1 12 by 5-inch loaf country bread, sliced crosswise into 1-inch-thick pieces, ends removed

4 ounces fresh goat cheese, crumbled

1. Place the olives, chopped garlic, anchovies, capers, and oil in the workbowl of a food processor fitted with its steel blade. Process until the mixture becomes a slightly chunky paste (do not over-process). Set aside.

2. Grill the bread over a medium fire (see how to gauge heat level on page 19), turning once, until golden brown on both sides, 1 to 1½ minutes.

3. Place the toast slices on a large platter and rub the peeled garlic over the tops.

4. Spread about 2 tablespoons of the olive mixture over each slice of grilled bread. Sprinkle with some cheese and serve immediately.

Bruschetta with Grilled Eggplant, Rosemary, and Feta Cheese

MAKES 8 LARGE SLICES

If desired, the eggplant can be grilled ahead of time, refrigerated, then brought back to room temperature before serving on bruschetta. You can substitute an equal amount of ricotta salata (a firm, salted cheese) for the feta cheese if you choose.

1½ tablespoons balsamic vinegar

1 medium garlic clove, minced, plus 1 large clove, peeled

1 teaspoon chopped fresh rosemary leaves

7 tablespoons extra-virgin olive oil

1 large eggplant (about 1½ pounds), ends trimmed and cut crosswise into ¾-inch slices
  Salt and ground black pepper

1 12 by 5-inch loaf country bread, sliced crosswise into 1-inch-thick pieces, ends removed

3 ounces feta cheese, crumbled

1. Mix the vinegar, minced garlic, rosemary, and 4 tablespoons oil together in a small bowl. Lay the eggplant slices on a baking sheet and brush both sides of each slice with the vinegar/oil mixture. Sprinkle with salt and pepper to taste.

2. Grill the eggplant over a medium-hot fire (see how to gauge heat level on page 19), turning once, until streaked with dark grill marks, about 8 to 10 minutes. Remove the eggplant from the grill and cut crosswise into 1-inch strips.

3. Grill the bread over a medium fire, turning once, until golden brown on both sides, 1 to 1½ minutes.

4. Place the toast slices on a large platter, rub the peeled garlic over the tops, and brush with the remaining 3 tablespoons oil.

5. Top each toast with a portion of the eggplant slices and crumbled cheese. Serve immediately.

PART 3

GRILL-ROASTING AND BARBECUING

14

BASIC PRINCIPLES OF GRILL-ROASTING AND BARBECUING

MOST COOKS INTUITIVELY UNDERSTAND how to grill. You build the biggest fire possible and place the food—meat, seafood, chicken, vegetables, or fruit—right over the fire. Once the food is nicely seared on both sides, it's done. In most cases, steaks, chops, and other relatively thin foods can be treated this way because the interior will be cooked by the time the exterior is nicely browned.

But what about a thick pork roast or brisket? If grilled directly over a hot fire, the exterior will be charred and ashen well before the interior of such a large piece of meat has a chance to cook through. The same thing goes for a whole chicken. The solution is indirect cooking. While grilling calls for loading the grill with charcoal or lighting all the gas burners, indirect cooking on the grill relies on a smaller fire. The lit coals are banked on one side of the grill, or one (or more) of the gas burners is turned off. Foods cooked by indirect heat are placed over the "cool" part of the grill. With the lid on to trap heat, both the exterior and interior of the food cook slowly and evenly, just as they do in an oven.

Why bother with indirect cooking on the grill when you can roast in the oven? The smoky flavor we associate with ribs or pulled pork comes only from the grill. Even foods that we don't normally consider cooking on the grill—like a whole turkey or side of salmon—taste better when wood flavor is added.

Two kinds of indirect cooking are possible in a covered grill. Barbecuing is the traditional low- and slow-cooking method used with ribs, pulled pork (shredded Boston butt), and brisket. Because the goal is to impart as much smoke flavor as possible, a long cooking time over a relatively low fire is required. Barbecuing also provides ample time for fatty, tough cuts to become more tender.

Although there is much debate among experts as to the proper cooking temperature for barbecuing, we found in our testing, as mentioned earlier in the book, that it should take place between 250 and 300 degrees. While some chefs and pit masters might argue that ribs are best barbecued at 180 degrees, we found it very difficult to maintain such a low fire. Also, such low temperatures allow bacteria to multiply and increase the risk of food-borne illnesses.

Once the sustained (or average) temperature during the cooking period exceeds 300 degrees, we believe (and most experts concur) that the process becomes grill-roasting, the other method of indirect cooking. The grill setup is the same—there's just more heat. Grill-roasting is best for foods that are already tender and that don't require low and slow cooking. Birds are especially well suited to grill-roasting (at the lower temperatures of barbecuing the skin remains soft and flabby), as are tender cuts of meat (like beef tenderloin) that need to develop a crisp crust during their relatively short cooking time. Grill-roasting occurs at temperatures between 300 and 400 degrees. (It's hard to sustain much higher temperatures by means of indirect cooking; in comparison, true grilling occurs at temperatures in excess of 500 degrees.)

Our preference when grilling (that is, cooking over direct heat) is to use charcoal. We like the high heat generated and the flavor that food absorbs from hardwood charcoal (our favorite fuel for most recipes). However, when doing indirect cooking—barbecuing or grill-roasting—the differences in flavor between foods cooked over gas and charcoal diminish a bit.

Hardwood charcoal, also called natural or lump charcoal, tends to burn quickly. It's too hot to be practical when cooking with indirect heat. We like the intense fire this charcoal makes when searing steaks, but when using it to barbecue brisket, you have to open the grill and add charcoal much more often than you'd like. Also, because the fire can run hotter at the outset, there is a greater risk of burning the edges of large foods (such as turkey and ribs) that may be close to the coals. For indirect cooking, we prefer regular charcoal briquettes, which burn cooler and more slowly.

Briquettes don't have as much flavor as hardwood charcoal, but they do give foods a smokier flavor than gas. Whether cooking indirectly over briquettes or gas, wood chunks or chips must do the real flavoring work. In our testing, we consistently found that foods cooked over charcoal had a smokier flavor than those cooked over gas. That's because a charcoal fire does a better job of getting the wood (which is sitting right in the fire) to smolder and smoke. Although we eventually devised a method for maximizing the smoke from chips used in a gas grill, the smoke flavor is still not as strong as it is in foods cooked over charcoal. If you like really smoky foods and are using a gas grill, consider using more chips at the outset when grill-roasting or adding more chips to the foil tray partway through the cooking time when barbecuing.

Intense smoky flavor aside, gas grills do have some advantages over charcoal when cooking by indirect heat. It's easier to regulate the heat on a gas grill. Just turn the dial and the temperature immediately responds. Also, there is no need to add charcoal during the long cooking process, so there is less hassle and mess. Gas grills are also more convenient to use during rainy weather.

We have also found that foods cooked over gas are juicier than foods cooked over charcoal. The reason for this is simple: smoke makes foods taste great but causes them to dehydrate. Since gas grilling generates less smoke, foods retain more moisture. That's why we found that brining birds and other foods that tend to dry out is especially important when cooking over charcoal. Brining adds flavor to foods that will be cooked over gas, but it has a less noticeable effect on texture.

In the end, we found that excellent, if somewhat different, results are possible when cooking with either charcoal or gas. Each recipe in the chapters that follow includes directions for barbecuing or grill-roasting over both charcoal and gas.

One final note about barbecuing: Despite the name (barbecue), food is generally flavored with a spice rub, not barbecue sauce, as it cooks. Barbecue sauce applied to ribs before cooking will burn. If you want to use barbecue sauce, apply it during the last minutes of cooking or pass some at the table.

WOOD CHIPS AND CHUNKS

ONE OF THE BEST REASONS TO BARBECUE or grill-roast is to flavor foods with smoke. Charcoal itself has some flavor (gas adds none), but the real smoky flavor of good ribs or brisket comes from wood chunks or chips. Chips will work on either a charcoal or gas grill, but chunks are suited to charcoal fires only, since to work they must rest in a pile of lit coals. (If placed on the bottom of a gas grill they will not get hot enough to smoke.)

Chips and chunks come from the same source—trees. The only difference between them is size. Chunks are usually the size of lemons or small oranges; chips are thinner shards, more like the fine wood chips you might spread over a garden bed. (That said, it's also the case that pieces from the same bag of chips or chunks can vary greatly in size.)

Wood chips and chunks are made from hardwoods because they burn more slowly than softer woods. The most common choices are hickory, mesquite, and alder, although some stores may carry cherry or oak. Resinous woods, like pine, are not used for grilling because they give foods an off flavor.

Will Wood Chunks Make Your Fire Too Hot?

We wondered if adding wood chunks to the fire would increase the internal temperature of a charcoal grill when barbecuing or grill-roasting, making it necessary to reduce the amount of briquettes. We tested this possibility by grilling-roasting chickens, first using only briquettes as fuel, then using both briquettes. For both tests we used 50 briquettes, and for the second test we used eight ounces of wood chunks, monitoring the internal temperature of the grill every 15 minutes for 1 hour (see chart below).

We assumed that the addition of extra fuel, in the form of wood chunks, would increase the intensity of the fire, resulting in a significantly higher internal grill temperature. That did not happen: the temperature was only marginally higher at 30 minutes and at 60 minutes. We can only speculate that the moisture in the soaked wood helped to dampen the coals, compensating for the additional fuel. To conclude, you don't have to worry about increasing the internal temperature of the grill when adding soaked wood chunks for smoky flavor.

FUEL USED	TIME ELAPSED/TEMPERATURE			
	15 minutes	30 minutes	45 minutes	1 hour
50 charcoal briquettes	410 degrees	400 degrees	400 degrees	390 degrees
50 charcoal briquettes plus 8 ounces wood chunks (soaked for 1 hour)	400 degrees	410 degrees	400 degrees	400 degrees

Hickory is the most traditional wood used for out-door cooking, but mesquite and oak have their advo-cates. In our tests, we found that any hardwood chunks or chips can be used. Frankly, the differences in flavor are minimal, especially if the food has been coated with spices. The difference between hickory and mesquite, for instance, is hard to taste on spice-rubbed ribs but will be more perceptible on a chick-en that has been rubbed only with butter, salt, and pepper. We note some traditional pairings of wood type and food throughout this section of the book (such as ribs with hickory or salmon with alder), but you should feel free to use whatever wood is available.

Using wood chunks is the easiest way to add smoke flavor when cooking over charcoal. You don't want the wood to catch fire and give up all its smoke

USING A CHARCOAL GRILL FOR INDIRECT COOKING

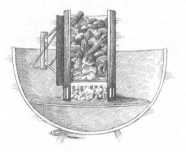  

1. Light a chimney starter: Fill the bottom section of the chimney starter with crumpled newspaper, set the starter on the bottom grate of a kettle grill, fill the main compartment with as much charcoal as directed in individual recipe, and light the newspaper.

2. Arrange the coals in the grill: When the coals are well lit and covered with a layer of gray ash, dump them onto the charcoal grate, piling the coals up on one half of the grill and leaving the other half free of coals. If necessary, use long-handled tongs to move the briquettes into place.

3. Complete the grill setup: Place soaked and drained wood chunks or a foil packet filled with wood chips on top of the coals. Set the top grate in position, heat briefly, then scrape the grate clean with a wire brush. You are now ready to cook over the cool part of the fire. Put the food on the grill and set the lid in place. Open the air vents as directed in individual recipes.

4. Monitor the heat level: We like to have some idea of what the temperature is inside a kettle grill as foods cook. A grill thermometer (see page 13) inserted through the vents on the lid can tell you if the fire is too hot or if it is getting too cool and you need to add more charcoal. You will get different readings depending on where the lid vents and thus the thermometer are in relation to the coals. Because you want to know what the temperature is where the food is being cooked, rotate the lid so that the thermometer is close to the food. Make sure, however, that the thermometer stem does not touch the food (this can be an issue when grill-roasting big cuts, like turkey).

5. Adjust the heat level: You can control the heat level to some extent by adjusting the vents on the lid and base of the grill. Opening the vents gives the fire more oxygen and causes the coals to burn hotter at first, but then the fire cools down more quickly as the coals peter out. Closing the vents partially (don't close the vents all the way or the fire will die) lowers the heat but keeps the coals from burning up too fast and helps the fire last longer.

USING WOOD CHIPS ON A CHARCOAL GRILL

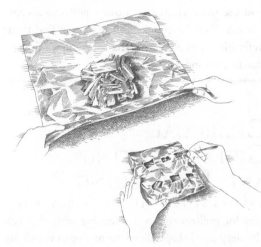

1. Place the amount of wood chips called for in the recipe in the center of an 18-inch square of heavy-duty aluminum foil. Fold in all four sides of the foil to encase the chips.

2. Turn the foil packet over. Tear about six large holes (each the size of a quarter) through the top of the foil packet with a fork to allow smoke to escape. Place the packet, with holes facing up, directly on a pile of lit charcoal.

at once. Ideally, the chunks should smolder slowly, releasing smoke for as long as possible. We found that soaking wood chunks in water adds enough moisture to prevent the wood from catching fire as soon as it is placed on the charcoal. Soak as many three-inch chunks (each the size of a tennis ball) as directed in each recipe in cold water to cover for one hour. Drain the chunks and place them directly on the lit pile of charcoal.

As might be expected, the amount of wood added to the fire will also affect the smoke flavor. For maximum wood flavor, add several chunks at the outset (just before heating up the cooking grate) and then again at the halfway point in the grill-roasting or barbecuing process.

If you can't find wood chunks, small wood chips may be used. We tried soaking the chips and throwing them directly onto the coals, but they caught fire immediately. The same thing happened when we placed the chips in an open foil tray on top of the coals; the tray does not provide enough protection for the chips and can tip over if placed on an uneven pile of charcoal. To keep the chips from burning up too quickly, we found it best to wrap them in a foil packet (see illustrations at left). There's no need to soak the chips; the foil protects them from catching fire too quickly.

Chips are the only choice for gas grills, since chunks are hard to position properly over a lit burner and may not get hot enough to smoke. Therefore, foods grill-roasted or barbecued over gas will never taste as smoky as foods cooked over charcoal. Still, we wanted to maximize the amount of smoke the chips would give off in a gas grill. We tried various methods for adding chips before we hit upon the best solution.

Both soaked and unsoaked chips thrown directly into the bottom of a gas grill burned much too quickly, giving up their smoke all at once or failing to smoke at all because they fell below the burners. We tried wrapping the chips in a foil packet, which had worked for us with charcoal, but found that in this case the packet was actually too effective a shield; not enough smoke was being released.

When cooking with a gas grill, we prefer to place the chips in an open foil tray. (See illustrations on page 234 for information on constructing a tray from heavy-duty aluminum foil.) The tray shields

PROTECTING WOOD CHIPS

Wood chips must be protected in some fashion before using them on a charcoal or gas grill. (Chunks need only be soaked in water for an hour or so.) To keep the chips from burning up too quickly, we devised the following strategies.

On a charcoal grill, we found it best to wrap the chips in a foil packet. (There's no need to soak the chips; the foil protects them from catching fire too quickly.)

On a gas grill, we found it best to place chips in an open foil tray. You can use a disposable aluminum pan or make a tray out of aluminum foil. Soak the chips in cold water for at least 15 minutes before adding them to the tray; this ensures that they smolder and don't burn out right away.

the chips from direct contact with the burner but is open on top to allow the smoke to flow freely. The tray also makes it possible to spread out the chips so that they are not piled on top of each other, as they are inside a smaller foil packet. When we placed unsoaked chips in the tray, they caught fire immediately. Soaking the chips for 15 minutes prevents them from igniting and allows them to smolder slowly and produce a lot of smoke.

Is there a difference in the results you get when using wood chunks versus wood chips? To find out, we tested the same amount by weight (eight ounces) of wood chips and wood chunks under the same conditions in a charcoal fire to see if one performed better than the other when barbecuing Boston butt to make pulled pork.

The wood chips were placed in a heavy-duty foil packet cut with holes that allow the smoke to escape and fill the grill, while the wood chunks were soaked for an hour and then drained. Each was then placed in a separate grill directly on top of 40 ignited coals. On each grill the lid was closed, the lid vents were opened halfway, and all other vents were left completely opened. The chips smoked for 30 to 35 minutes, while the chunks smoked twice as long, for one hour. As it turned out, the exposure to smoke for more than twice the amount of time had given the pork barbecued with wood chunks a greater concentration of smoky, grilled flavor than the pork made using the wood chips.

If you have a choice between wood chips and wood chunks, use the wood chunks. They deliver more smoky flavor. If you don't have a choice and must use wood chips, they make a perfectly acceptable substitute for chunks. You may even find them preferable if you prefer a lighter smoke flavor in your grill-roasted and barbecued food.

CHARCOAL GRILL-ROASTING AND BARBECUING

A KETTLE-STYLE GRILL WITH A COVER IS A must for grill-roasting or barbecuing with charcoal. The deep bowl shape allows air to circulate, and the high lid accommodates tall foods, such as turkey. A large grill, with a cooking surface that measures 22 inches across, is best for indirect cooking. On smaller grills, the "cool" part of the grill may be too small to hold large cuts of meat.

Before starting, empty the grill of any old ashes, which may block air circulation and prolong cooking times. Some experts recommend banking the coals on either side of the grill and leaving the center open for indirect cooking. They believe that having the coals on both sides of the grill promotes even cooking. When we tried this method, we found that

USING WOOD CHIPS ON A GAS GRILL

1. Start with a 12 by 18-inch piece of heavy-duty foil. Make a one-inch fold on one long side. Repeat three more times, then turn the fold up to create a sturdy side that measures about one inch high. Repeat the process on the other long side.

2. With a short side facing you, fold in both corners as if wrapping a gift.

3. Turn up the inside inch or so of each triangular fold to match the rim on the long sides of the foil tray.

4. Lift the pointed end of the triangle over the rim of foil and fold down to seal. Repeat the process on the other short side.

the edges of large pieces of food, like ribs and brisket, can burn.

In most cases, we prefer to bank all the coals on one side of the grill, leaving half of the grill free of coals and providing a large space for foods to cook without danger of burning. Because the lid is on, the heat is pretty well distributed. However, the side of the food closest to the fire will cook more quickly. For this reason, we found it necessary to flip foods (that is, turn them over) as well as rotate them (turn the side initially facing the lit coals 180 degrees on the grill so that it faces away from the lit coals). The one exception to this rule is a whole chicken, which is small enough to fit between piles of lit coals on either side of the grill. With heat attacking the bird from each side, there's no need to rotate.

GAS GRILL-ROASTING AND BARBECUING

AS WITH A CHARCOAL GRILL, SIZE MATTERS when trying to grill-roast or barbecue many foods on a gas grill. For instance, the lid must be tall enough to accommodate a turkey. (A lid that rises less than eight inches above the cooking grate will be a problem.) Likewise, the size of the cooking grate is important when preparing wide, flat cuts like brisket or ribs. Unless the cooking surface is at least 400 square inches, you might have trouble with such large cuts.

In addition to size, the number of burners is critical. It's not possible to cook indirectly on a grill with only one burner because the burner is usually positioned in the center of the grill and the "cool" parts of the grill are too small to fit most foods. You must use a grill with at least two burners. With one burner on and one burner off, at least half of the grill will be cool enough for indirect cooking.

It is just as important to buy a gas grill with a thermometer. You can stick an oven thermometer on the cooking grate near the food, but then you have to open the lid to find out what the temperature is. Opening the lid causes heat to dissipate and prolongs the total cooking time. A gas gauge also comes in handy when grill-roasting or barbecuing. Many recipes require several hours of cooking, and there's

nothing worse than running out of gas halfway through unexpectedly.

In our tests, we found it slightly easier to cook on a grill with left and right burners rather than front and back burners. The cooking grate on most gas grills is rectangular. When the grill is divided into front and back cooking zones, the cool part of the grill will be a long, relatively narrow band. Although this shape is well suited to ribs and tenderloin, it can be a challenge when cooking a turkey, especially on a moderately sized grill. When the grill is divided into left and right cooking zones, each side is roughly a square, which we find to be a better shape for cooking birds. Foods that are long and thin, like beef tenderloin, can easily be curled into a C-shape over the cool side of the grill.

To set up a gas grill for indirect cooking, remove all warming shelves attached to the hood or the back of the grill. (Leave the racks in place when making ribs on a small grill.) Position the wood chips over the primary burner. With some gas grills, one burner must be turned on first. This is the primary burner. With other grills, you may designate a primary burner yourself.

USING A GAS GRILL FOR INDIRECT COOKING

Remove part or all of the cooking grate. Place a foil tray with soaked wood chips on top of the primary burner. Make sure the tray is resting securely on the burner so it will not tip. Replace the grill rack. Light all burners and cover the grill. When you see a lot of smoke (after about 20 minutes), turn off the burner (or burners) without chips and place the food over it (or them). If the chips start to flame, douse the fire with water from a squirt bottle. Cover the grill.

15

GRILL-ROASTED BEEF AND PORK

CUTS OF BEEF AND PORK THAT ARE TOO large to grill over direct heat can be grill-roasted in a covered grill. Since grill-roasting involves fairly high temperatures and occurs fairly quickly (relative to barbecuing, that is—see page 230 for definitions of grill-roasting and barbecuing), tender cuts are a must. This means roasts taken from the rib or loin area of the animal. On the cow, this translates to the rib roast (also known as prime rib) or the tenderloin. On the pig, the loin roast is the best choice.

A prime rib is a massive cut with bones. It requires nearly two hours on the grill to cook through. Beef tenderloin and pork loin are easier to prepare and take less time to cook. These long cuts are not terribly thick and can be done in as little as 30 minutes.

Prime Rib

A PRIME RIB IS A LITTLE LIKE A TURKEY: You probably cook only one a year, usually for an important occasion, almost always for a crowd. Although you know there are alternatives to straightforward roasting at 350 degrees for "X" minutes per pound that may deliver a more interesting result, they're too risky. You don't want to be remembered as the cook who carved slices of almost raw standing rib or the host who delayed dinner for hours waiting for the roast to get done. A roast cooked according to standard procedures will at the least not embarrass you.

Well, we think it's worth considering the grill when cooking prime rib. Rather than tying up your oven for hours on end (and thus making the preparation of side dishes a real hassle), let the meat cook outside. Besides convenience, a grilled prime rib has two advantages over a roasted prime rib—a better crust and some smoky flavor. But whether you are cooking prime rib in an oven or on the grill, we think the goal is the same: Slices should be rosy pink from the surface to the center, and the meat should be juicy and tender.

We started our testing by examining the issues of trimming fat and tying the roast. We found that it is best to leave about one-quarter inch of fat on the roast to prevent it from drying out on the grill. Most of this fat drips off of the rib roast as it cooks, basting

the meat. Tying the meat before grilling is essential. Two pieces of twine keep the surrounding muscles from separating from the main part of the roast and thus improve the appearance of the grilled roast. In addition, these smaller, thin pieces of meat will overcook if they detach from the main muscle during grill-roasting.

We wondered just how few coals we could get away with. From our work in the past with prime rib cooked in the oven, we knew that a low oven temperature is kinder to prime rib, helping the meat to retain its juices and promoting even cooking. We figured the same would be true on the grill.

After much testing, we found 45 briquettes to be optimum. This was the least amount of coals we could use to make it possible to cook the whole roast

INGREDIENTS: PRIME RIB

A whole rib roast consists of ribs 6 through 12. Butchers tend to cut the roast in two, and the more desirable of the two cuts consists of ribs 10 through 12 (left). Sometimes called the loin end because of its proximity to the loin, this cut is also referred to as the small end or the first cut. Whatever it is called, it is more desirable because it contains the large, single rib-eye muscle and is less fatty. The less desirable cut, which is still an excellent roast, consists of ribs 6 to 9. This cut is closer to the chuck end and is sometimes called the second cut (right). The closer to the chuck, the more muscled the roast becomes. Since muscles are surrounded by fat, this also means a fattier roast. While some cooks may prefer the fattier, chuck end of the rib roast because the fat adds flavor, in general, the more tender and regularly formed loin end is considered the best.

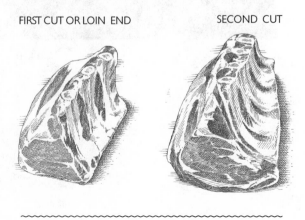

FIRST CUT OR LOIN END   SECOND CUT

properly without adding more briquettes. With 45 briquettes, the fire reaches an initial temperature of about 375 degrees and eventually burns down to about 300 degrees by the time the roast is finished (the last 45 minutes or so). Using the indirect method, you still get a lovely surface caramelization, while the interior is almost entirely pink, except for the outer half inch or so.

We wanted to add some wood to the fire to flavor the meat, but not enough to overpower its own delicious flavor. You don't want prime rib to taste like ribs. Adding two cups of chips or two larger wood chunks to the fire creates a rib roast with a nice contrast between the smoky caramelized exterior and savory, beefy interior meat.

The next issue to examine was at what internal temperature the roast should be removed from the grill. We knew that the temperature inside the roast would continue to rise as the meat rested before carving. For the perfect medium-rare, we found it best to take the meat off the grill when it hit an internal temperature of 125 degrees. When taken out at 125 degrees and then allowed to rest for 20 minutes, the temperature jumped another 12 to 13 degrees. As with rack of lamb, it is imperative with prime rib to use an instant-read thermometer. There is no really good way of telling how cooked the meat is at the very center of a rib roast without one, and if you

TYING UP PRIME RIB

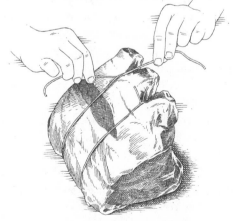

It is imperative to tie prime rib before roasting. If left untied, the outer layer of meat will pull away from the rib-eye muscle and overcook. To prevent this problem, tie the roast at both ends, running the strings parallel to the bone.

spent about $50 for a seven-pound roast, you don't want to mess up by over- or undercooking. Also, using a thermometer to determine doneness will keep you from cutting into the meat to check doneness before it's had a chance to rest; if you cut into the meat too soon (before it's rested off the grill for 20 minutes), you will lose a good amount of the juices. (During the rest period, the juices evenly redistribute themselves throughout the meat.)

Grill-Roasted Prime Rib on a Charcoal Grill

SERVES 6 TO 8

You may or may not have to trim some fat off your rib roast, depending on how well it was butchered at the store. Just be sure to leave at least ¼ inch of fat on the side opposite the bones to keep the meat from drying out; the fat will slowly render, basting the meat as it melts. Even if you don't purchase the roast a week ahead of time, as suggested in "Science: Aging Beef" (page 240), it will see some benefit from just a day or two of aging.

1	(3- or 4-rib) standing rib roast (about 7 pounds), aged up to 1 week (if desired), and tied with kitchen twine at both ends, twine running parallel to bone (see illustration at left)
2	(3-inch) wood chunks or 2 cups wood chips and heavy-duty aluminum foil
1	tablespoon vegetable oil
	Salt and ground black pepper

1. An hour before cooking, remove the roast from the refrigerator to bring it to room temperature.

2. Meanwhile, soak the wood chunks in cold water to cover for 1 hour and drain, or place the wood chips on an 18-inch square of aluminum foil, seal to make a packet, and use a fork to create about six holes to allow smoke to escape (see illustrations on page 233).

3. Light a large chimney starter filled halfway with charcoal briquettes (about 2¾ pounds, or 45 coals) and allow to burn until covered with a thin layer of gray ash. Transfer the coals from the chimney to one side of the grill, piling them up in a mound two or three briquettes high. Keep the bottom vents completely open. Lay the wood chunks or the wood

chip packet on top of the charcoal. Put the cooking grate in place, open the grill lid vents completely, and cover, turning the lid so that the vents are opposite the wood chunks or chips to draw smoke through the grill. Let the grate heat for 5 minutes. Clean the grate with a wire brush.

4. Rub the rib roast with oil. Season generously with salt and pepper.

5. Position the rib roast, bone-side down, on the grate opposite the fire, with the meaty eye of the roast closest to the fire. Cover the grill, turning the lid so that the vents are opposite the fire to draw smoke through the grill. Grill-roast without removing the lid for 1 hour. (The initial temperature will be about 375 degrees.) Remove the lid and turn the roast so that the bone side of the roast is facing up.

Replace the lid and continue grill-roasting until an instant-read thermometer inserted into the center of the roast registers 125 degrees (for medium-rare), 30 to 60 minutes. (The temperature inside the grill will gradually fall to about 300 degrees by the time the roast is done.)

6. Transfer the roast to a cutting board. Let stand at least 20 minutes to allow the juices to redistribute themselves evenly throughout the roast.

7. To carve (see illustrations on page 241), remove the twine and set the roast on a cutting board with the rib bones perpendicular to the board. Using a carving fork to hold the roast in place, cut along the rib bones to sever the meat from the bones. Set the roast cut-side down; carve the meat across the grain into thick slices. Serve immediately.

SCIENCE: Aging Beef

Meat is aged to develop its flavor and improve its texture. This process depends on certain enzymes, whose function while the animal is alive is to digest proteins. After the animal is slaughtered, the cells that contain these enzymes start to break down, releasing the enzymes into the meat, where they attack the cell proteins and break them down into amino acids, which have more flavor. In addition, the enzymes start to break down the muscles, so the tissue becomes softer. This process can take from one to several weeks. (To age meat for more than a week, however, it must be done under carefully controlled conditions—it should not be done at home.)

Traditionally, butchers have hung carcasses in meat lockers to age beef, in a process called dry aging. Today, some beef is still aged on hooks, but for the most part beef is wet-aged in sealed Cryovac packets. We wondered if it would be worthwhile for the home cook to seek out dry-aged beef and ordered both a dry-aged and wet-aged prime rib roast from a restaurant supplier in Manhattan. The differences between the two roasts were clear-cut.

Like a good, young red wine, wet-aged beef tasted pleasant and fresh on its own. When we compared it with the dry-aged beef, though, we realized its flavors were less concentrated. The wet-aged meat now tasted washed out, while the dry-aged beef truly engaged the palate. It was stronger, richer, and gamier tasting, with a pleasant tang. The dry-aged and wet-aged beef were equally tender, but the dry-aged beef had an added buttery quality. We had worried that dry aging might make meat dry—something that often happens when meat is barbecued or grill-

roasted. Thankfully, this was not the case. In sum, then, we wholeheartedly urge you to buy a dry-aged roast if you can.

Unfortunately, most butchers don't dry-age beef anymore because hanging quarters of beef take up too much refrigerator space for too much time. During the aging process, dry-aged beef does dehydrate (which means weight loss), and it requires trimming (which means more weight loss). That weight loss means less beef costs more money. Wet-aged beef loses virtually no weight during the aging process, and it comes prebutchered, packaged, and ready to sell. Since beef is expensive to begin with, most customers opt for the less expensive wet-aged beef. Why does dry aging produce a superior result? The answer is simple: oxygen. Enclosed in Cryovac, wet-aged beef is shut off from the oxygen in the air, and oxygen is the key to flavor development and concentration.

Since availability and price pose problems, you may want to try aging beef yourself. It's just a matter of making room in the refrigerator and remembering to buy the roast ahead of time, up to one week before you plan on roasting it. When you get the roast home, pat it dry and place it on a wire rack set over a paper towel–lined cake pan or plate. Set the racked roast in the refrigerator and let it age until you are ready to roast it, up to seven days. (Aging begins to have a dramatic effect on the roast after three or four days, but we detected some improvement in flavor and texture after just one day of aging.) Before roasting, shave off any exterior meat that has become completely dehydrated. Between the trimming and dehydration, count on a seven-pound roast losing a pound or so during a week's aging.

Grill-Roasted Prime Rib on a Gas Grill

SERVES 6 TO 8

You may or may not have to trim some fat off your rib roast, depending on how well it was butchered at the store. Just be sure to leave at least ¼ inch of fat on the side opposite the bones to keep the meat from drying out; the fat will slowly render, basting the meat as it melts. Even if you don't purchase the roast a week ahead of time, as suggested in "Science: Aging Beef" (see page 240), it will see some benefit from just a day or two of aging.

The gas grill variation mimics the temperatures of the charcoal grill. To make sure the wood chips begin to smoke, the grill is quite hot—550 degrees—when you first put the meat on the fire. Once you turn off all but the primary burner (which is left on medium-high), the temperature of the grill averages out to about 350 degrees. The roast cooks at this heat level for 1 hour. The primary burner is then turned down once again to medium heat, and the average temperature of the grill hovers around 300 degrees for the rest of the cooking time, which should be between 1 hour and 1 hour and 15 minutes, until the internal temperature of the roast is 125 degrees. Be sure not to open the lid of the gas grill too often during cooking; the temperature of the grill will drop significantly each time you open it, and then take some time to come back up to temperature.

If you prefer a roast with a less smoky flavor, gas grilling is the right option (as opposed to charcoal grilling). In fact, if you are simply cooking on the grill to save oven space and don't care to taste the smoky flavor of the grill, omit the use of wood chips altogether.

1 (3- or 4-rib) standing rib roast (about 7 pounds), aged up to 1 week (if desired), and tied with kitchen twine at both ends, twine running parallel to bone (see illustration on page 239)
2 cups wood chips and heavy-duty aluminum foil
1 tablespoon vegetable oil
Salt and ground black pepper

1. An hour before cooking, remove the roast from the refrigerator to bring it to room temperature.

2. Soak the wood chips for 15 minutes in a bowl of water to cover. Place the wood chips in a foil tray (see illustrations on page 234). Place the foil tray with the soaked wood chips on top of the primary burner (see illustration on page 235) and replace cooking grates. Turn all burners to high and preheat with the lid down until the chips are smoking heavily, about 20 minutes.

3. Rub the rib roast with oil. Season generously with salt and pepper.

4. Open the grill and turn the primary burner down to medium-high; turn all other burners off. Place the rib roast over the cooler side of the grill, bone-side down. Cover and cook until an instant-read thermometer inserted through to the center of the roast reads between 80 and 85 degrees, about 1 hour. (During this hour the temperature inside the grill will initially be very hot at 550 degrees and then

CARVING PRIME RIB

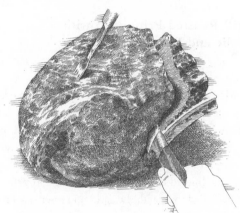

1. Using a carving fork to hold the roast in place, cut along the rib bones to sever the meat from the bones.

2. Set the roast cut-side down; carve the meat across the grain into thick slices. Serve immediately.

241

drop off to about 350 degrees.) Turn the primary burner down to medium and continue cooking, covered, until an instant-read thermometer inserted through to the center of the roast reads 125 degrees (for medium-rare), about 60 to 75 minutes longer. (During this period of time, keep the average temperature of the grill at about 300 degrees.)

5. Transfer the roast to a cutting board. Let stand at least 20 minutes to allow the juices to redistribute themselves evenly throughout the roast.

6. To carve (see illustration on page 241), remove the twine and set the roast on the cutting board with the rib bones perpendicular to the board. Using a carving fork to hold the roast in place, cut along the rib bones to sever the meat from the bones. Set the roast cut-side down; carve the meat across the grain into thick slices. Serve immediately.

➤ VARIATIONS

Grill-Roasted Prime Rib with Garlic and Rosemary Crust

Rosemary and garlic are a simple embellishment for the roast and won't overwhelm the beefy flavor of the meat.

Mix together 6 medium garlic cloves, minced, 2 tablespoons chopped fresh rosemary leaves, 2 teaspoons ground black pepper, and 1 teaspoon salt in a small bowl. Follow the recipe for Grill-Roasted Prime Rib (charcoal or gas), oiling the roast as directed. Instead of sprinkling with salt and pepper, rub the oiled roast with the garlic and rosemary mixture. Proceed as directed.

Grill-Roasted Prime Rib with Horseradish Cream Sauce

Follow the recipe for Grill-Roasted Prime Rib (charcoal or gas), serving the sliced meat with 1 cup Horseradish Cream Sauce (page 302), passed separately at the table.

BEEF TENDERLOIN

BEEF TENDERLOIN IS A TENDER CUT of meat that can be grill-roasted at a high temperature. This roast cooks quickly, and its rich, buttery slices are fork-tender. The challenge is to create a good crust on the meat while not overcooking the interior.

Despite its many virtues, beef tenderloin is not without its liabilities. Price, of course, is the biggest. Even at a local warehouse-style supermarket, the going rate for a whole beef tenderloin is $7.99 a pound, putting the average sticker price for a whole cut at about $50.

There is good reason for the tenderloin's hefty price. Because it sits up under the spine of the cow, it gets no exercise at all and is therefore the most tender piece of meat on the animal. Because it is one of the two muscles in the ultrapremium steaks known as the porterhouse and T-bone, the tenderloin is sold at ultrapremium prices when removed from the cow as a whole muscle. We purchased 11 roasts for testing and rang up a $550 bill.

A whole beef tenderloin can be purchased "unpeeled," with an incredibly thick layer of exterior fat left attached, but it's usually sold "peeled," or stripped of its fat. Because of our many bad experiences with today's overly lean pork and beef, we purchased six of the 11 roasts unpeeled, determined to leave on as much fat as possible. However, it quickly became clear that this was too much fat to leave on the roast. We found that the fat prevented the formation of a thick brown crust, one of the hallmarks of perfectly cooked tenderloin.

We then tried peeling the roasts in the test kitchen. In the end, we removed three pounds of waste from an eight-pound unpeeled roast, which had cost us $56. Since we could buy a five-pound peeled roast for just $40, the unpeeled roasts were actually more expensive per pound of edible meat and required a lot more effort. In fact, we found it best to leave the peeled roast alone, letting the scattered patches of fat on the exterior flavor the meat as it cooked.

The tenderloin's sleek, boneless form makes for quick grill-roasting, but its torpedo-like shape—thick and chunky at one end, gradually tapering at the other end—causes it to cook unevenly. For those looking for a range of doneness, this is not a bad thing, but for cooks who want a more evenly cooked roast, something must be done.

Folding the tip end of the roast under and tying it bulks up the tenderloin center to almost the same thickness as the more substantial butt tender. This ensures that the tenderloin cooks more evenly. (Even so, the tip end is always a little more well-done than the butt end.) Tying the roast at approximately 1½-inch intervals further guarantees a more uniformly shaped roast and consequently more even slices of beef. Snipping the silver skin (the translucent sheath that encases certain cuts of beef) at several points also prevents the meat from bowing during cooking. Bowing occurs when the silver skin shrinks more than the meat to which it is attached.

As for the actual cooking process, we found that a beef tenderloin cooks well over indirect heat. To build a nice thick crust on the meat, the initial charcoal fire should be fairly hot—400 to 425 degrees is ideal. We also found that searing the meat briefly over the hot coals and then moving it to the cool side of the grill improved the crust. We tried turning the roast as it cooked over indirect heat but found that opening the lid caused the fire to lose heat and that the roast was browning evenly anyway. Keep the lid on and don't check the roast until you think it is done.

Once the roast reaches an internal temperature of 125 degrees, it should be pulled off the grill and allowed to rest. The internal temperature will rise another five degrees, ensuring meat that is perfectly medium-rare. If you want rare meat, remove the roast earlier (at 120 degrees); for meat that is closer to medium, remove the roast at 130 to 135 degrees. It seems a shame to cook this meat any further since it begins to dry out once it reaches higher internal temperatures.

All roasts should rest 15 to 20 minutes after cooking to allow the juices to redistribute themselves evenly throughout the meat. We found that beef tenderloin improves dramatically if left uncarved even longer. If cut too soon, its slices are soft and flabby. A longer rest—we decided on 30 minutes—allows the meat to firm up into a texture we found much more appealing. Before carving, we preferred removing the big pockets of excess fat, which become more obvious at warm and room temperatures.

Grill-Roasted Beef Tenderloin on a Charcoal Grill
SERVES 10 TO 12

If you can't find a whole tenderloin with the tip end attached (see illustration, below left), use a smaller tenderloin and omit the tucking step. The cooking time will be about the same for the smaller roast because it is just as thick.

1   whole peeled beef tenderloin (about 5 pounds), thoroughly patted dry, silver skin cut, tip end tucked under, and tied (see illustrations on page 245)
2   (3-inch) wood chunks, or 2 cups wood chips and heavy-duty aluminum foil
2   tablespoons olive oil
2   teaspoons salt
2   tablespoons coarsely ground black pepper

1. An hour before cooking, remove the roast from the refrigerator and bring it to room temperature.

2. Meanwhile, soak the wood chunks in cold water to cover for 1 hour and drain, or place the wood chips on an 18-inch square of aluminum foil, seal to make a packet, and use a fork to create about six holes to allow smoke to escape (see illustrations on page 233).

3. Set the roast on a sheet of plastic wrap and rub all over with oil. Sprinkle with salt and pepper and then lift the wrap to press the excess seasoning into the meat (see illustration on page 245).

4. Meanwhile, light a large chimney starter filled with charcoal briquettes (about 5½ pounds or 90 coals) and allow to burn until all the charcoal is covered with a layer of fine gray ash. Transfer the hot coals to one side of the grill, piling them up in a mound three briquettes high. Keep the bottom vents completely open. Lay the wood chunks or the wood chip packet on top of the charcoal. Put the cooking

ANATOMY OF A BEEF TENDERLOIN

BUTT TENDER   TENDERLOIN TIPS

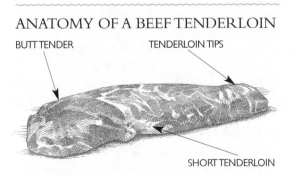

SHORT TENDERLOIN

A whole beef tenderloin is composed of three sections: The thicker end of the roast is called the butt tender; the middle portion—which is virtually an even thickness—is called the short tenderloin; and the tapering tip end is sold as part of the whole tenderloin or removed and sold as tenderloin tips.

grate in place, open the grill lid vents completely, and cover, turning the lid so that the vents are opposite the wood chunks or chips to draw smoke through the grill. Let the grate heat for 5 minutes. Clean the grate with a wire brush.

5. Roll the tenderloin off the plastic onto the grate directly over the hot coals so that the long side of the loin is perpendicular to the grill rods. Sear the meat for 2½ minutes on the first side, then give the roast one-quarter turn and sear another 2½ minutes. Repeat two more times to sear all four sides of the tenderloin directly over the coals. Move the roast to the side of the grill opposite the fire and cover the grill, turning the lid so that the vents are opposite the fire to draw smoke through the grill, and so that the long side of the loin is perpendicular to the grill rods. (The initial temperature inside the grill should be

SCIENCE: What Makes Some Cuts Tender?

Like value in real estate, tenderness in meat is largely about one thing: location. Muscles located in areas that see little movement or use, such as the tenderloin, which lies along the back of the cow, are the most tender. Those muscles located in areas that ask a lot from the animal, such as the shoulder, which is in constant use, develop a good deal of connective tissue and become tough over time. To dissolve this connective tissue, these cuts must be cooked for a long time. Tough cuts are often braised or barbecued and are usually served well-done. Cuts like the tenderloin contain very little connective tissue and are tender even when the meat is cooked just until rare.

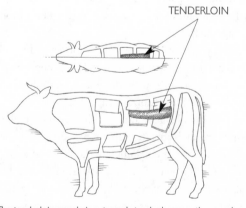

TENDERLOIN

The tenderloin muscle is extremely tender because the cow doesn't give it much exercise.

about 425 degrees.) Grill-roast the tenderloin, covered, until an instant-read thermometer inserted into the thickest part registers about 125 degrees (for medium-rare), 25 to 30 minutes longer.

6. Transfer the roast to a cutting board. Let the meat rest for 30 minutes. (The whole tenderloin can be wrapped in plastic, refrigerated up to 2 days, and served chilled.) Cut the roast into ½-inch-thick slices and serve.

Grill-Roasted Beef Tenderloin on a Gas Grill

SERVES 10 TO 12

If you can't find a whole tenderloin with the tip end attached (see illustration on page 243), use a smaller tenderloin and omit the tucking step. The cooking time will be about the same for the smaller roast because it is just as thick. Beware of the smoke given off by the wood chips when you initially open the gas grill to sear the meat.

1	whole peeled beef tenderloin (about 5 pounds), thoroughly patted dry, silver skin cut, tip end tucked under, and tied (see illustrations on page 245)
2	cups wood chips and heavy-duty aluminum foil
2	tablespoons olive oil
2	teaspoons salt
2	tablespoons coarsely ground black pepper

1. An hour before cooking, remove the roast from the refrigerator and bring it to room temperature.

2. Meanwhile, soak the wood chips in a bowl of cold water for 15 minutes. Drain the chips and place them in a foil tray (see illustrations on page 234). Place the foil tray with the soaked wood chips on top of the primary burner (see illustration on page 235), and replace the cooking grates. Turn all burners to high and preheat with the lid down until very hot, about 15 minutes.

3. Set the roast on a sheet of plastic wrap and rub all over with oil. Sprinkle with salt and pepper and then lift the wrap to press the excess seasoning into the meat (see illustration on page 245).

4. Carefully open the preheated grill (there may be some smoke), scrape clean with a wire brush, and place the roast on the side opposite the primary burner. Sear

the tenderloin for 3 minutes on the first side, then give the roast one-quarter turn and sear that side. Repeat, searing all four sides for 3 minutes each, or until dark grill marks appear. Leave the primary burner on high but turn off all other burners. Cover with the lid and grill-roast until an instant-read thermometer inserted into thickest part of roast registers about 125 degrees (for medium-rare), 25 to 30 minutes longer. (The temperature inside the grill should average between 375 and 400 degrees; adjust the lit burner as necessary.)

5. Transfer the roast to a cutting board and let it rest for 30 minutes. (The whole tenderloin can be wrapped in plastic, refrigerated up to 2 days, and served chilled.) Cut the roast into ½-inch-thick slices and serve.

➤ VARIATIONS

Grill-Roasted Beef Tenderloin with Mixed Peppercorn Crust

Buy a mixture of peppercorns at the supermarket or create your own mixture at home. Black and white peppercorns are much stronger than the pink and green varieties, so adjust the blend to suit your personal taste.

Coarsely crush 6 tablespoons black, white, pink, and green peppercorns with a mortar and pestle or with a heavy-bottomed saucepan or skillet. Follow the recipe for Grill-Roasted Beef Tenderloin (charcoal or gas), replacing the black pepper with the peppercorn mixture. Proceed as directed.

Grill-Roasted Beef Tenderloin with Garlic and Rosemary

Studding the tenderloin with slivered garlic and fresh rosemary gives it an Italian flavor.

Follow the recipe for Grill-Roasted Beef Tenderloin (charcoal or gas), making the following changes: After tying the roast, use a paring knife to make several dozen shallow incisions around the surface of the roast. Stuff a few fresh rosemary needles and 1 thin sliver of garlic into each incision. (Use a total of 1 tablespoon rosemary and 3 large garlic cloves, slivered.) Oil the roast as directed. Sprinkle with salt, pepper, and an additional 2 tablespoons minced fresh rosemary. Proceed as directed.

Grill-Roasted Beef Tenderloin with Parsley, Cornichons, and Caper Sauce

This piquant sauce is a classic with beef.

1	recipe Grill-Roasted Beef Tenderloin (charcoal or gas)
¾	cup minced fresh parsley leaves
12	cornichons, minced (6 tablespoons), plus 1 teaspoon cornichon juice
2	medium scallions, white and light green parts, minced
	Pinch salt
¼	teaspoon ground black pepper
½	cup extra-virgin olive oil

PREPARING A BEEF TENDERLOIN

1. To keep the meat from bowing as it cooks, slide a knife under the silver skin and flick the blade upward to cut through the silver skin at five or six spots along the length of the roast.

2. To ensure that the tenderloin roasts more evenly, fold the thin tip end of the roast under about 6 inches.

3. For more even cooking and evenly sized slices, use 12-inch lengths of kitchen twine to tie the roast every 1½ inches.

4. Set the meat on a sheet of plastic wrap and rub it all over with oil. Sprinkle with salt and pepper, then lift the plastic wrap up and around the meat to press any excess seasoning into the meat. This method guarantees even coverage and can be used with the recipe variation calling for a mixed peppercorn crust as well as the master recipe.

1. Grill the roast as directed.

2. While the roast is resting, combine the parsley, cornichons and their juice, scallions, salt, pepper, and oil in a medium bowl. Serve the sliced roast, passing the sauce separately at the table.

Grill-Roasted Beef Tenderloin with Horseradish Cream Sauce

Beef and horseradish are a classic pairing. You will need to double the sauce recipe.

Follow the recipe for Grill-Roasted Beef Tenderloin (charcoal or gas), serving the sliced meat with 2 cups Horseradish Cream Sauce (page 302), passed separately at the table.

PORK LOIN

A BONELESS PORK LOIN IS AN IDEAL candidate for grill-roasting. As opposed to barbecued pulled pork (see chapter 17), which starts out with a very fatty cut from the shoulder or leg, lean loin roasts are the best choice for relatively quick grill-roasting since they are already tender. However, unlike a thin pork tenderloin, the loin is too thick to cook over direct heat. The exterior chars long before the interior comes up to temperature.

The pork loin runs along one side of the backbone of the pig, starting at the shoulder, or blade bone, and ending at the hip bone. For roasting (whether on the grill or in the oven), we found that the meat from the center of the loin, called the center loin roast or center-cut loin roast, is best. This piece of meat contains a single muscle, so the grain is tender and easy to carve. The center loin roast is a fairly pale piece of meat and has a relatively mild flavor.

We cooked the two other boneless roasts from the loin before deciding to go with the center loin roast. The blade roast, also called the blade loin roast or loin roast, contains small parts of various shoulder muscles that are redder and more fibrous than the center loin. The meat at the other end of the loin, which is called the rib end, hip end, or sirloin roast, is also more fibrous and tougher than the center loin.

Unlike a beef tenderloin, a pork center loin has a fairly even thickness from end to end, so there is no need to tuck up one side or the other. To make the meat perfectly even and ensure proper cooking, we found it helpful to tie the roast at regular intervals.

A pork loin can be grill-roasted much like a beef tenderloin, although it does not need an initial searing period over direct heat. (The meat stays on the grill longer because it must be cooked to a higher internal temperature, so there's plenty of time for a nice crust to form when the roast is cooked strictly over indirect heat.)

The biggest challenge when grill-roasting pork loin is keeping the meat moist. Beef tenderloin can be pulled from the grill at 125 degrees and eaten medium-rare. Pork must be cooked to a higher temperature to make the meat palatable (rare pork has an unappealing texture) and to kill any possible parasites.

Using the kettle grill, we tried a couple of different setups for indirect cooking. We tried putting the roast in the center of the grill, with two piles of charcoal on opposite sides. This worked reasonably well, but the crust was a bit weak. Banking a full chimney of coals on one side of the grill and placing the roast over the other side worked better. To get the best crust, put the roast close to, but not directly over, the coals.

After testing various temperatures, we found that center loin roasts should be taken off the grill when the internal temperature registers 140 degrees on an instant-read thermometer. After the meat rests for 15 minutes, the temperature will rise to about 155 degrees. The meat will have a slight pink tinge, but it will be far juicier than roasts cooked to an internal temperature that is just 10 degrees higher. (A temperature of 155 degrees is high enough to kill the parasite that causes trichinosis. However, the U.S. Department of Agriculture recommends cooking all meat to an internal temperature of 160 degrees to kill bacteria such as salmonella. If safety is your primary concern, follow the USDA's guidelines.) Because the diameter of a pork loin can vary from one roast to another, allow a window of 30 to 45 minutes to cook the roast through.

While we had little trouble getting the meat properly cooked on the grill, we found pork loin to be a bit bland and not as moist as we might have liked. Both problems stem from the fact that most of the internal fat has been bred out of the pig in recent years. We hit upon two strategies for making the meat taste better and juicier when cooked.

Like poultry, lean pork responds well to brining. A brined pork roast will cook up juicier and more flavorful than a regular roast. Aggressive seasoning is also a good idea. A potent spice rub or a heady mixture of garlic and rosemary will improve the flavor of the meat. A rich mustard-maple glaze, applied when the roast is nearly cooked through, is another option.

Grill-Roasted Pork Loin on a Charcoal Grill

SERVES 4 TO 6

Make sure to buy a boneless center-cut pork loin. If the packaging is vaguely labeled "pork loin," ask the butcher if it is a center-cut roast. This roast should consist of a single pink muscle that runs all the way from one end of the roast to the other. To make sure the roast doesn't dry out during cooking, look for one covered with a layer of fat on one side that is at least ⅛ inch thick. Because the diameter of pork loins varies significantly from one to another, check the internal temperature of the loin with an instant-read thermometer at 30 minutes, then every 5 minutes or so thereafter, to make sure that your pork cooks to the optimum temperature of 140 degrees. Do not overcook the pork, since it dries out easily. Let the roast rest for at least 15 minutes to give it a chance to rise to a safe temperature (150 to 155 degrees). Use leftover meat for sandwiches.

¾	cup kosher salt or 6 tablespoons table salt
I	boneless center-cut pork loin roast (2½ to 3 pounds), tied with twine at 1½-inch intervals
2	(3-inch) wood chunks, or 2 cups wood chips and heavy-duty aluminum foil
2	tablespoons olive oil
1½	tablespoon coarsely ground black pepper

1. At least 8 hours before grill-roasting the pork loin, dissolve the salt in 3 quarts of cold water in a large container. Place the pork loin in the saltwater mixture, cover, and refrigerate for at least 8 hours or overnight.

2. An hour before cooking, remove the roast from the brine, rinse, and pat dry, leaving it out to let it come up to room temperature.

3. Soak the wood chunks in cold water to cover for 1 hour and drain, or place wood chips on an 18-inch square of aluminum foil, seal to make a packet, and use a fork to create about six holes to allow smoke to escape (see illustrations on page 233).

4. Set the roast on a sheet of plastic wrap and rub all over with oil. Sprinkle with pepper and then lift the wrap to press the excess into the meat (see illustration on page 245).

5. Meanwhile, light a large chimney filled with charcoal briquettes (about 5½ pounds, or 90 coals) and allow to burn until all the charcoal is covered with a thin layer of gray ash. Transfer the hot coals from the chimney to one side of the grill, piling them up in a mound three briquettes high. Keep the bottom vents completely open. Place the soaked wood chunks or the packet with the chips on top of the charcoal. Put the cooking grate in place and open the grill lid vents halfway. Let the grate heat for 5 minutes. Clean the grate with a wire brush.

6. Roll the pork loin off the plastic and onto the grate opposite, but close to the fire; the long side of the loin should be perpendicular to the grill rods. Cover with the lid, turning the lid so the vents are opposite the fire to draw smoke through the grill. (The initial temperature inside the grill will be about 425 degrees.) Grill-roast the pork loin, covered, until an instant-read thermometer inserted into the thickest part of the roast registers about 140 degrees, 30 to 45 minutes, depending on the thickness of the loin.

7. Transfer the loin to a cutting board. Tent loosely with foil and let stand for about 15 minutes. (The internal temperature should rise to between 150 and 155 degrees.) Cut the roast into ½-inch-thick slices and serve.

INGREDIENTS: Bone-In Pork Loin

We generally like bone-in roasts because bones add flavor to the meat while it cooks. When we tested several bone-in center-cut loins on the grill, however, we were disappointed every time. Besides being harder to carve, a bone-in roast has less surface area and therefore less room for caramelization of the crust. The crust that did form tended to burn in spots, while the bone-in roast also took longer to cook through than a boneless roast. In sum, we suggest that you stick with a boneless roast when cooking this cut on the grill.

Grill-Roasted Pork Loin on a Gas Grill

SERVES 4 TO 6

When using the gas grill for this recipe, the meat must be seared over direct heat. This is because the gas grill's maximum temperature using indirect heat is about 400 degrees, which is not quite hot enough to give the loin a deep crust in the amount of time it takes to cook through over indirect heat. Beware of the smoke given off by the wood chips when you initially open the gas grill to sear the meat.

³⁄₄	cup kosher salt or 6 tablespoons table salt
1	boneless center-cut pork loin roast (2¹⁄₂ to 3 pounds), tied with twine at 1¹⁄₂-inch intervals
2	cups wood chips and heavy-duty aluminum foil
2	tablespoons olive oil
1¹⁄₂	tablespoon coarsely ground black pepper

1. At least 8 hours before grill-roasting the pork loin, dissolve the salt in 3 quarts of cold water in a large container. Place the pork loin in the saltwater mixture, cover, and refrigerate for at least 8 hours or overnight.

2. An hour before cooking, remove the roast from the brine, rinse, and pat dry, leaving it out to let it come up to room temperature.

3. Soak the wood chips in a bowl of cold water for 15 minutes. Drain the chips and place them in a foil tray (see illustrations on page 234). Place the foil tray with the soaked wood chips on top of the primary burner (see illustration on page 235) and replace the cooking grates. Turn all burners to high and preheat with lid down until very hot, about 15 minutes.

4. Set the roast on a sheet of plastic wrap and rub all over with oil. Sprinkle with pepper and then lift the wrap to press the excess into the meat (see illustration on page 245).

5. Carefully open the preheated grill (there may be some smoke), scrape clean with a wire brush, and place the roast, fat-side down, on the side opposite the primary burner. Cover and grill until the meat is grill marked, about 4 minutes. Turn the roast over, cover again, and grill for another 4 minutes. Leave the primary burner on high, but turn off all other burners. Cover with the lid and grill-roast until an instant-read thermometer reads 140 degrees at the thickest part of the roast, 30 to 45 minutes. (The temperature inside the grill should average between 375 and 400 degrees; adjust the lit burner as necessary).

6. Transfer the loin to a cutting board. Tent loosely with foil and let stand for about 15 minutes. (The internal temperature should rise to between 150 and 155 degrees.) Cut the roast into ¹⁄₂-inch-thick slices and serve.

➤ VARIATIONS

Grill-Roasted Pork Loin with Garlic and Rosemary

Other fresh herbs, especially sage or thyme, can be used in place of the rosemary.

Follow the recipe for Grill-Roasted Pork Loin (charcoal or gas), making the following changes: After tying the roast, use a paring knife to make several dozen shallow incisions in the surface of the roast. Stuff a few fresh rosemary needles and 1 thin sliver of garlic into each incision. (Use a total of 1 tablespoon rosemary and 3 large garlic cloves, slivered.) Oil the roast as directed. Sprinkle with pepper and an additional 2 tablespoons minced fresh rosemary. Proceed as directed.

Grill-Roasted Pork Loin with Barbecue Rub and Fruit Salsa

Because of its mild flavor, pork loin benefits greatly from spice rubs. Fruit salsa adds both moisture and a sweetness that is naturally compatible with pork.

Follow the recipe for Grill-Roasted Pork Loin (charcoal or gas), replacing the pepper with 2 tablespoons Dry Rub for Barbecue (page 292). Proceed as directed, serving sliced meat with Simple Peach Salsa (page 75) or Fresh Mango Salsa (page 302).

Grill-Roasted Pork Loin with Maple-Mustard Glaze

This glaze can be prepared in seconds—literally!

Mix together ¹⁄₂ cup maple syrup, ¹⁄₂ cup whole grain mustard, and 1 teaspoon soy sauce in a medium bowl. Reserve one-half of the glaze in a separate bowl. Follow the recipe for Grill-Roasted Pork Loin (charcoal or gas), brushing half of the glaze over the loin about 5 minutes before it reaches the proper internal temperature. Serve sliced meat with reserved sauce at the table.

16

GRILL-ROASTED POULTRY

WHOLE BIRDS ARE IDEAL CANDIDATES FOR grill-roasting, with the temperature inside the grill hot enough to crisp the skin but not so hot that the skin burns before the meat is cooked through to the bone. The addition of smoke flavor improves all birds. This chapter explains how to cook whole chickens, Cornish hens, turkeys, and ducks on the grill, as well as a whole bone-in turkey breast. (For a definition of grill-roasting versus grilling and barbecuing, see page 230.)

WHOLE CHICKEN

EVERY YEAR MILLIONS OF COOKS GRILL ALL manner of chicken parts, from breasts and wings to thighs and drumsticks. If you're one of them, you can follow the recipes in chapter 8. There's only one problem with this scenario: Chicken parts don't spend enough time on the grill to pick up much smoke flavor. Since the smoky taste is one of the main reasons we at *Cook's* like to grill, we often grill a whole chicken rather than parts. When grilled over indirect heat (coals banked to the side, with the chicken over the cool part of a covered grill), the bird cooks in about an hour, which gives it plenty of time to pick up a good hit of smoke.

Grill-roasting a whole chicken turns out to be a fairly straightforward matter. On reading through various recipes while researching this topic, however, we did notice some variations in technique. Wanting to determine the very best technique, we decided to test the important variables, including how to arrange the coals, whether or not to use a V-rack, when and how to turn the bird, and how to flavor it.

When grill-roasting large birds (such as turkeys) or big cuts of meat (such as prime rib), the standard setup is to fill half of a kettle grill with charcoal and to leave the other half empty. The food is placed on the cool side of the grill, and the kettle is covered. Because one side of the food faces the lit coals, the bird or meat will cook unevenly unless it is rotated at least once. (In later testing, we found that a turkey must be rotated twice for even cooking.) Rotating is simple enough, but the heat dissipates when the lid is removed, and you often have to add more coals, which is a pain.

Since a chicken is so much smaller than a turkey or prime rib, we wondered if the lit coals could be banked on either side of the kettle grill and the chicken cooked in the middle. After several tests, we concluded that this arrangement works fine, with some caveats.

First, the coals must be piled fairly high on either side to form relatively tall but narrow piles. We split the coals between either side of the grill and ended up piling the lit briquettes three or four levels high. If the coals are arranged in wider, shorter piles, the cool spot in the middle of the grill won't be large enough to protect the bird from direct heat.

Second, don't use too much charcoal. When we divided 70 briquettes into two piles, we burned the chicken. Reducing the number of coals to just 50 kept the temperature inside the grill between 325 and 375 degrees, the ideal range for grill-roasting.

Third, use a relatively small chicken. We found that the skin on a large roaster scorches long before the meat cooks through. A broiler/fryer (see "Broilers, Fryers, Roasters, Capons, and Hens" on page 253) is a must.

Last, keep the vents in the lid halfway open so the fire burns at a fairly even pace. If the vents are open all the way, the fire burns too hot at the outset—thereby scorching the bird's skin—and then peters out before the chicken has cooked through.

With the heat attacking the chicken from two sides, the bird cooks evenly, so there's no need to rotate it. (On gas grills, where just one lit burner is used to cook by indirect heat, you will need to rotate the bird.) After our initial tests, however, we did conclude that it was necessary to flip the bird over once during the hour-long cooking process. The skin on top of the bird cooks faster than the skin touching the rack. (Although this seems counterintuitive, repeated tests confirmed this observation.) Because the side of the bird that finishes right-side up tends to look better (grill marks fade and the skin bronzes more evenly), we decided to start the chicken breast-side down.

When we cook a turkey on the grill, we always cradle it in a V-rack, which keeps the skin from scorching and promotes even cooking. We prepared several chickens with and without V-racks and found that those placed right on the grill rack browned better and cooked just fine. Again, because a chicken is small, the bird spends much less time on the grill than a turkey and the skin is less likely to burn.

With our technique perfected, we focused on the flavoring options. As expected, we found that brining the chicken in a saltwater solution helps it retain moisture while cooking and is recommended. The one exception is a kosher bird, which is salted during processing and cooks up moist—and perfectly seasoned—without brining.

During the course of our testing, we tried brushing the chicken with melted butter and olive oil before and during grilling. Although a buttered bird browned marginally better than an oiled one, we don't recommend using either. Birds coated with a spice rub cooked up more crisply and were better looking than greased birds.

Grill-Roasted Whole Chicken on a Charcoal Grill

SERVES 4

If you choose not to brine, skip that part of step 1 and season the bird generously with salt inside and out before rubbing with spices. Or, better yet, use a kosher chicken (which is salted during processing). For greatest accuracy, place a grill thermometer in the lid vents as the chicken cooks. The temperature inside the grill should be about 375 degrees at the outset and will fall to about 325 by the time the chicken is done.

I   cup kosher salt or ½ cup table salt

I   whole chicken (about 3½ pounds)

3   tablespoons spice rub (see recipes on
    page 252)

4   (3-inch) wood chunks, or 4 cups wood chips
    and heavy-duty aluminum foil

1. Dissolve the salt in 2 quarts of cold water in a large container. Immerse the chicken in the salted water and refrigerate until fully seasoned, about 1 hour. Remove the chicken from the brine and rinse inside and out with cool running water; pat dry with paper towels. Massage the spice rub all over the chicken, inside and out. Lift up the skin over the breast and rub the spice mixture directly onto the meat (see illustration at right).

2. Soak the wood chunks in cold water to cover for 1 hour and drain, or divide the wood chips between two 18-inch squares of aluminum foil, seal to make two packets, and use a fork to create about six holes in each packet to allow smoke to escape (see illustrations on page 233).

3. Light a large chimney starter filled a little more than halfway with charcoal briquettes (about 3 pounds, or 50 coals) and allow to burn until covered with a thin layer of gray ash. Empty the coals into the grill. Divide the coals in half to form two piles on either side of the grill; use long-handled tongs to move any stray coals into piles. Nestle 2 soaked wood chunks or one foil packet with chips on top of each pile. Position the grill rack over the coals and cover the grill. Heat the rack for 5 minutes, then scrape it clean with a wire brush.

4. Position the bird, breast-side down, in the middle of the rack, over that portion of the grill without any coals. Cover, opening the grill lid vents halfway. Turn the lid so that the vents are between the two piles of coals. Grill-roast for 30 minutes.

5. Working quickly to prevent excessive heat loss, remove the lid and, using 2 large wads of paper towels, turn the chicken breast-side up. Cover and grill-roast until an instant-read thermometer inserted into thickest part of thigh registers 170 to 175 degrees, 25 to 35 minutes longer.

6. Transfer the chicken to a cutting board, tent loosely with foil, and let rest 15 minutes. Carve and serve.

APPLYING THE SPICE RUB

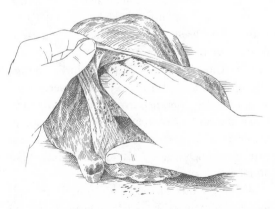

Rub the spice mixture into the skin, then carefully lift up the skin over the breast and massage some rub directly onto the meat.

Grill-Roasted Whole Chicken on a Gas Grill

SERVES 4

If you choose not to brine, skip that part of step 1 and season the bird generously with salt inside and out before rubbing with spices. Or, better yet, use a kosher chicken (which is salted during processing). While grill-roasting, adjust the lit burner as necessary to maintain a temperature of 350 to 375 degrees inside the grill.

I   cup kosher salt or ½ cup table salt

I   whole chicken (about 3½ pounds)

3   tablespoons spice rub (see recipes at right)

4   cups wood chips and heavy-duty aluminum foil

1. Dissolve the salt in 2 quarts of cold water in a large container. Immerse the chicken in the salted water and refrigerate until fully seasoned, about 1 hour. Remove the chicken from the brine and rinse inside and out with cool running water; pat dry with paper towels. Massage the spice rub all over the chicken, inside and out. Lift up the skin over the breast and rub the spice mixture directly onto the meat (see illustration on page 251).

2. Soak the wood chips for 15 minutes in a bowl of water to cover. Place the wood chips in a foil tray (see illustrations on page 234). Place the foil tray with the soaked wood chips on top of primary burner (see illustration on page 235). Turn all burners to high and preheat with the lid down until chips are smoking heavily, about 20 minutes.

3. Open the grill and turn off all but one burner. (Leave the primary burner on high.) Clean the grate with a wire brush. Place the chicken, breast-side down, over the cooler part of the grill. Cover and grill-roast for 35 minutes. Turn the chicken breast-side up so that the leg and wing that were facing away from the lit burner are now facing toward it. Close the lid and continue grill-roasting until an instant-read thermometer inserted into the thickest part of the thigh registers 170 to 175 degrees, 30 to 40 minutes longer.

4. Transfer the chicken to a cutting board, tent loosely with foil, and let rest 15 minutes. Carve and serve.

➤ VARIATION

Grill-Roasted Whole Chicken with Barbecue Sauce

If you like, barbecue sauce can be used along with the Simple Dry Spice Rub for Poultry. Wait until the bird is almost done to brush on the barbecue sauce, so that it does not scorch.

TWO RUBS FOR CHICKEN

Simple Dry Spice Rub for Poultry

MAKES ABOUT ½ CUP

This rub is aromatic but not hot.

2   tablespoons ground cumin

2   tablespoons curry powder

2   tablespoons chili powder

I   tablespoon ground allspice

I   tablespoon ground black pepper

I   teaspoon ground cinnamon

Combine all the ingredients in a small bowl. (Extra rub can be stored in an airtight container for several weeks.)

Citrus-Cilantro Wet Spice Rub for Poultry

MAKES ABOUT 3 TABLESPOONS

For extra spiciness, add up to ½ teaspoon cayenne pepper.

½   teaspoon ground cumin

½   teaspoon chili powder

½   teaspoon sweet paprika

½   teaspoon ground coriander

I   tablespoon orange juice

I½   teaspoons lime juice

I½   teaspoons extra-virgin olive oil

I   small garlic clove, minced very fine

I   tablespoon minced fresh cilantro leaves

Combine all the ingredients in a small bowl. Use immediately.

Follow the recipe for Grill-Roasted Whole Chicken (charcoal or gas), making the following changes: After rotating the chicken breast-side up, roast only until an instant-read thermometer inserted into thickest part of thigh registers 160 degrees, 15 to 30 minutes longer. Working quickly to prevent excessive heat loss, brush the outside and inside of the chicken with ½ cup any tomato-based barbecue sauce (see chapter 19). Cover and continue grill-roasting until an instant-read thermometer inserted into thickest part of thigh registers 170 to 175 degrees, 10 to 15 minutes longer. Tent and carve as directed.

Beer Can Chicken

AS WE WERE DEVELOPING OUR GRILL-roasted chicken recipes, a friend who spends many weekends at barbecue cook-offs raved to us about beer can chicken. On the barbecue circuit, she said, this is how beer can chicken is done: The bird is rubbed with spices, and then an open, partially filled beer can is inserted into the main cavity of the chicken. The chicken is grill-roasted as it "sits" on the can, which functions as a vertical roaster.

We decided to try this wacky idea, convinced we would have something silly to write about. We culled a half-dozen recipes for beer can chicken (sometimes called drunken chicken) from the Internet, and they all followed the same basic formula, with some variation in the spice rub and the liquid inside the can. We decided to stick with our favorite dry rub and a can of cheap beer for our first test.

We should have had more confidence in our friend's opinion. The bird came off the grill looking beautiful, with a deeply tanned, crisp skin. And the flavor was fantastic. Although we had a hard time tasting the beer, the spices had penetrated deep into the meat.

Beer can chicken has a number of things going for it. The beer in the open can creates steam as the chicken roasts. This steam keeps the meat incredibly juicy. The moist heat also gives the meat an unctuous, rich quality. If you have ever steamed or braised a chicken, you know what we mean. Some people may not like this texture (the meat is a bit slippery), but we found this moist meat preferable to the dry, shredded quality of chicken cooked by dry heat.

The beer can chicken also tasted better seasoned with spices—almost right down to the bone—than any chicken we have ever eaten. For the best flavor, we found it imperative to rub the spices inside the cavity (where the steam is generated) and under the breast skin.

Because our first test was such a success, we wondered about some of the variables we had uncovered in our research. We focused on the liquid in the can first, adding some barbecue sauce to the beer in one test, adding chopped aromatic vegetables to the beer

---

INGREDIENTS: Broilers, Fryers, Roasters, Capons, and Hens

Chickens were first domesticated in India about 4,000 years ago. Most of the birds raised for meat in the United States today are descended from the Cornish (a British breed) and the White Rock (a breed developed in New England). Broiler/fryers, roasters, Rock Cornish game hens, capons, and stewing/baking hens are all chickens. Each has been bred to "plump out" (an industry term indicating that the breast meat is thick and plump) upon reaching a certain age and weight.

BROILER/FRYERS, the birds we recommend for grill-roasting, are slaughtered between six and eight weeks of age, when they weigh 2½ to 4½ pounds. These young chickens (another term you might see on labels) are ideal for frying and broiling (parts from older birds are too thick to cook evenly by these methods), hence the term broiler/fryer.

ROASTERS are slaughtered between 9 and 13 weeks of age and weigh 5 to 8 pounds.

ROCK CORNISH GAME HENS have been bred to "plump out" very quickly. Cornish hens are dressed out at four to five weeks of age and weigh between 1 and 2 pounds.

CAPONS are male chickens that have been castrated. They are slaughtered between the ages of four and eight months, when the birds weigh 4 to 8 pounds, and are preferred for roasting by some cooks because of their high fat content.

STEWING/BAKING HENS are mature laying hens slaughtered between the ages of 10 and 18 months. These spent hens, weighing 5 to 6 pounds, are generally used by food processors and are not sold at the retail level.

in another, and using Guinness, a rich, dark beer, in a third test. In all cases, we couldn't detect much difference from the first bird steamed over a can of cheap beer without any additions.

We then replaced the beer with lemonade in one test and white wine in another. Tasters were able to detect a lightly sweet, lemon flavor in the bird cooked over lemonade. With the white wine, we rubbed a garlic, rosemary, and olive oil paste into the bird. This bird was a dud. The skin was not nearly as crisp and the flavor of the garlic and rosemary was confined to the surface. Furthermore, tasters thought the wine had not done much for the bird.

For one last test, we emptied a soda can and filled it with water, then rubbed the bird with spices as before. Although the differences were not dramatic, the flavor was a bit washed out and less appealing. Evidently, the beer was contributing something to the bird in addition to steam.

One last note: Chickens that weigh about 3½ pounds are ideal for this recipe. The cavity in smaller birds is too narrow to hold a beer can, and larger birds won't fit upright in most grills.

Grill-Roasted Beer Can Chicken

SERVES 4

If you prefer, use lemonade instead of beer. Fill an empty 12-ounce soda or beer can with 10 ounces (1¼ cups) of lemonade and proceed as directed.

I	cup kosher salt or ½ cup table salt
I	whole chicken (about 3½ pounds)
3	tablespoons spice rub (see recipes on page 252)
4	(3-inch) wood chunks, or 4 cups wood chips and heavy-duty aluminum foil
I	(12-ounce) can beer

1. Follow the recipe for Grill-Roasted Whole Chicken (charcoal or gas), brining chicken and applying spice rub as directed. Light charcoal or gas grill as directed.

2. Open the beer can and pour out (or drink) about ¼ cup. With a church key can opener, punch two more large holes in the top of the can (for a total of three). Slide the chicken over the can so that the drumsticks reach down to the bottom of the can and the chicken stands upright (see illustration below).

3. Place the chicken and beer can on the cool part of the grill, using the ends of the drumsticks to help steady the bird. Cover and grill-roast, rotating the bird and can 180 degrees at the halfway mark to ensure even cooking, until an instant-read thermometer inserted into the thickest part of the thigh registers 170 to 175 degrees, 70 to 90 minutes.

4. With a large wad of paper towels in each hand, transfer the chicken and can to a platter or tray, making sure to keep the can upright. Let rest for 15 minutes. Using wads of paper towel, carefully lift the chicken off the can and onto a platter or cutting board. Discard the remaining beer and can. Carve the chicken and serve.

SETTING UP BEER CAN CHICKEN

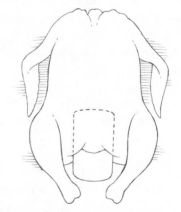

With the legs pointing down, slide the chicken over the open beer can. The two legs and the beer can form a tripod that steadies the chicken on the grill.

CORNISH HENS

CORNISH HENS ARE ANOTHER ALTERNATIVE for grill-roasting. The technique is pretty much the same as for chicken. In fact, we found that cooking time for two Cornish hens is almost the same as the cooking time for one chicken. How can it be that two 1½-pound hens take 50 to 60 minutes to grill-roast, while a 3½-pound chicken is done in 55 to 65 minutes?

One reason is that the hens are best trussed before grilling. Cornish hens have a looser frame than chickens, and the legs dangle from the bird. If not trussed, the hens emerge from the grill looking unsightly. Even worse, we occasionally had a leg fall off as we tried to remove the finished bird from the grill. A quick truss—just tie the two legs together with a length of twine—keeps the legs in place and yields a better-looking hen.

With the legs tucked against the body, the thighs cook more slowly. In addition, a hen isn't all that much thinner than a chicken. The thickness of the bird—rather than its weight—is the main factor affecting cooking time. Finally, two hens cool down the grill as much as a single chicken. If you grill-roast just a single Cornish hen (to serve two), the cooking time will be 5 or 10 minutes shorter because there's less food to absorb the heat of the grill.

In addition to trussing the legs, we found it best to tuck the wings behind the hen. These small appendages tended to flop down between the bars of the grill rack and burn. One final note: The juices in a hen can build up between the breast meat and skin, causing the skin to balloon and then burst. To prevent this problem, prick the skin carefully with the tip of a knife before cooking.

With our grill-roasting technique perfected, we moved on to flavor issues. After a few rounds of roasting, we realized that these birds didn't taste superb. Because most Cornish hens are mass-produced and not of premium quality, we were faced with the added challenge of trying to deepen their flavor. Having roasted the first few birds without brining, we wondered if they tasted good enough to even bother writing about. Although our local grocery store sells premium-quality poussins (baby chickens), all of its Cornish hens are mass-produced (see boxes below and on page 253 for more information.) We found brining to be essential—it transforms mediocre-tasting birds into something worth eating. A spice rub (use either of the rubs on page 252) adds another layer of flavor.

INGREDIENTS: Cornish Hens and Poussins

These days, it is becoming more and more difficult to find small Cornish hens. Not long ago, these dwarfed birds hovered at around a pound, but for economic reasons, producers have started growing them bigger. Now the consumer is lucky to find one under 1½ pounds.

This larger size is perfect for two people, but for individual presentation, seek out the smaller hens, or look for poussins, baby chickens sold at many butcher shops. Though a little more expensive, these baby chickens usually weigh about one pound and are perfect for one person. Poussins are likely to come from a smaller farm and generally taste better than mass-produced hens.

PREPARING HENS FOR THE GRILL

 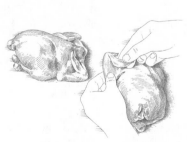

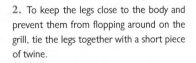

1. To prevent the skin from ballooning when juices build up, carefully prick the skin (but not the meat) on the breast and leg of each Cornish hen with the tip of a knife.

2. To keep the legs close to the body and prevent them from flopping around on the grill, tie the legs together with a short piece of twine.

3. To keep the wings close to the body and prevent them from burning or falling off, tuck the wing tips behind the back.

Grill-Roasted Cornish Hens on a Charcoal Grill

SERVES 4

If you choose not to brine, skip that part of step 1 and season the birds generously with salt inside and out before rubbing with spices. (We highly recommend you take the time to brine, since most Cornish hens are quite bland tasting.) The temperature inside the grill should be about 375 degrees at the outset and will fall to about 325 degrees by the time the hens are done.

1	cup kosher salt or ½ cup table salt
2	Cornish hens (each about 1½ pounds), trimmed of extra fat, giblets removed, and rinsed well
3	tablespoons spice rub (see page 252)
4	(3-inch) wood chunks, or 4 cups wood chips and heavy-duty aluminum foil

1. Dissolve the salt in 2 quarts of cold water in a large container. Immerse the hens in the salted water and refrigerate until fully seasoned, about 1 hour. Remove the hens from the brine and rinse inside and out with cool running water; pat dry with paper towels. Massage the spice rub all over the hens, inside and out. Lift up the skin over the breast and rub the spice mixture directly onto the meat (see illustration on page 251).

2. Soak the wood chunks in cold water to cover for 1 hour and drain, or divide the wood chips between two 18-inch squares of aluminum foil, seal to make two packets, and use a fork to create about six holes in each packet to allow smoke to escape (see illustrations on page 233).

3. Light a large chimney starter filled a little more than halfway with charcoal briquettes (about 3 pounds, or 50 coals) and allow to burn until covered with a thin layer of gray ash. Empty the coals into the grill. Divide the coals in half to form two piles on either side of the grill; use long-handled tongs to move any stray coals into piles. Nestle 2 soaked wood chunks or one foil packet with chips on top of each pile. Position the grill rack over the coals and cover the grill. Heat the rack for 5 minutes, then scrape it clean with a wire brush.

4. Position the birds, breast-side down, in the middle of the rack, over that portion of the grill without any coals. Cover, opening the grill lid vents halfway. Turn the lid so that the vents are between the two piles of coals. Grill-roast for 25 minutes.

5. Working quickly to prevent excessive heat loss, remove the lid and, using 2 large wads of paper towels, turn the hens breast-side up. Cover and grill-roast until an instant-read thermometer inserted into the thickest part of the thigh registers 170 to 175 degrees, 25 to 35 minutes longer.

6. Transfer the hens to a cutting board, tent loosely with foil, and let rest 15 minutes. Carve and serve.

Grill-Roasted Cornish Hens on a Gas Grill

SERVES 4

If you choose not to brine, skip that part of step 1 and season the birds generously with salt inside and out before rubbing with spices. (We highly recommend you take the time to brine, since most Cornish hens are quite bland tasting.) While grill-roasting, adjust the lit burner as necessary to maintain a temperature of 350 to 375 degrees inside the grill.

1	cup kosher salt or ½ cup table salt
2	Cornish hens (each about 1½ pounds), trimmed of extra fat, giblets removed, and rinsed well
3	tablespoons spice rub (see page 252)
4	cups wood chips and heavy-duty aluminum foil

1. Dissolve the salt in 2 quarts of cold water in a large container. Immerse the hens in the salted water and refrigerate until fully seasoned, about 1 hour. Remove the hens from the brine and rinse inside and out with cool running water; pat dry with paper towels. Massage the spice rub all over the hens, inside and out. Lift up the skin over the breast and rub the spice mixture directly onto the meat (see illustration on page 251).

2. Soak the wood chips for 15 minutes in a bowl of water to cover. Place the wood chips in a foil tray (see illustrations on page 234). Place the foil tray with the soaked wood chips on top of the primary burner (see illustration on page 235). Turn all burners to high and preheat with lid down until chips are

smoking heavily, about 20 minutes.

3. Open the grill and turn off all but one burner. Leave the primary burner on high. Clean the grate with a wire brush. Place the hens, breast-side down, over the cooler part of the grill. Cover and grill-roast for 30 minutes. Turn the hens breast-side up so that the leg and wing that were facing away from the lit burner are now facing toward it. Close the lid and continue grill-roasting until an instant-read thermometer inserted into the thickest part of the thigh registers 170 to 175 degrees, 20 to 30 minutes longer.

4. Transfer the hens to a cutting board, tent loosely with foil, and let rest 15 minutes. Carve and serve.

WHOLE TURKEY

WE CAN STILL REMEMBER THE FIRST TIME we cooked a whole turkey in a covered grill. We lit the charcoal, banked the coals to one side, added some wood chips, and placed a small turkey over the cool part of the grill. Two hours later, we had the best-looking and best-tasting turkey ever—the crispiest skin imaginable coupled with moist meat that had been perfumed with smoke.

Unfortunately, we can also remember the second time we tried this feat. We must have built the fire a little too hot; when we checked the bird after the first hour, the skin had burned. We nonetheless continued grilling, and, before serving, removed the charred skin from the blackened bird. We also served some juicy mango salsa to camouflage the dryness of the overcooked breast.

We have continued to grill-roast turkeys over the years, not only because the bird sometimes turns out to be fantastic but also because using the grill for the turkey frees up the oven for all the other components of a holiday meal. But the results have been consistently inconsistent.

Part of the problem is the inherent unpredictability of grill-roasting over charcoal. Sometimes the fire can be too hot, other times it can be too cool. If the day is particularly windy, the fire will cool down faster than on a hot, sultry night. Because you are cooking with the cover down to conserve fuel (frequent peeking will cause the fire to die down and is a no-no), it's hard to know what's happening inside the grill.

We decided to get serious and figure out what the variables are when grill-roasting a turkey and then devise a method for controlling these variables. Our goal was simple: We wanted a bird with crisp, browned skin, moist meat, and a good smoky flavor—every time.

Because gas grilling involves fewer variables than charcoal grilling, we decided to start with gas. We quickly learned that a small turkey (fewer than 14 pounds) works best when grill-roasting. Even on a really large gas grill, we found that the skin on a large bird burns by the time the meat comes up to temperature. For the same reason, you can't cook a stuffed turkey on the grill. A stuffed bird takes longer to cook through, and this added time almost guarantees that the skin will blacken.

Following the lead of previous turkey recipes developed for the magazine, we also confirmed that brining the turkey is a must for a tender, juicy bird. Grilling is even more punishing on delicate breast meat than oven roasting. The bird's proximity to the

HURRY-UP BRINING

If refrigerator space is at a premium, you may want to brine the bird as quickly as possible in a cool spot. This method, which uses a concentrated brine and ice packs, also allows you to brine and grill the bird on the same day.

Line a 16-quart stockpot or large, clean bucket with a turkey-sized oven bag. Dissolve 4 cups kosher salt or 2 cups table salt in 2 gallons of cold water in the bag. Add the turkey along with 4 or 5 large, clean frozen gel packs. Tie the bag shut, cover the pot or bucket, and place it in a cool spot for 4 hours. Remove the turkey from the brine and rinse well as directed; discard the gel packs.

heat source, coupled with all that smoke (which tends to dehydrate foods), makes a good case for brining to keep the meat moist. If you can't be bothered with brining, season the bird liberally with salt just before grilling and be prepared to serve the white meat with plenty of gravy or chutney.

Next we turned to the question of trussing. Our test kitchen generally ties the legs of the turkey together to keep them from splaying open as they roast. When we tried this, we noticed that the inner thigh cooked more slowly than the rest of the bird. Trussed birds needed an extra 10 to 15 minutes on the grill to get the shielded portion of the thigh up to the correct internal temperature. While this may not sound like much extra time, it translated into overcooked breast meat. Even worse, the skin burned. When we abandoned any trussing or tying of the legs, the temperature in the thighs and breasts was equalized and the skin came out extremely crisp and dark brown, but not black.

Our next set of experiments centered on turning the bird. As with oven roasting, we found it best to start the bird breast-side down. After an hour, we flipped the bird breast-side up for the remainder of the cooking time. We noticed that the side (wing and leg) closest to the fire was cooking faster than the other side. To eliminate this problem, we found it necessary to rotate the bird twice—once when it is turned breast-side up, and once when the cooking is almost completed. Each time, we turned the bird so that the opposite wing and leg faced the heat source.

We next focused on whether to cook the bird right on the grill grate or on a rack. We found that the turkey placed in a nonadjustable V-rack cooked more evenly and with less scorching of the skin than the bird placed right on the grate. But a rack with a sturdy metal base is essential. If the V-rack rests on just two little legs, those legs can slip between the grill grates and the turkey can topple over.

Our last area of investigation on the gas grill was its temperature. Clearly, we needed to grill-roast the bird over indirect heat, with one burner lit and the other burner(s) turned off. Our question was how high to keep the heat on the lit burner. We tested this recipe on three grills—two models with two burners and one model with three burners. We found it best to leave the lit burner turned to high in each case. At lower settings,

there was not enough heat to cook the bird properly. The temperature gauges on the three grills we worked with ranged from 300 to 350 degrees during the entire cooking time. Total cooking time for a bird weighing 12 to 14 pounds varied from 2 to 2½ hours. (Count on the longer time if the weather is cool or windy.)

Turkey cooked on a gas grill is delicious. The recipe is foolproof, and the skin becomes especially crisp and richly colored. But getting smoke flavor into a gas-grilled bird is not so easy. While adding wood chips before lighting the grill helps some, the resulting smoke flavor is mild. A mildly smoked bird may be fine for some meals, but we think that if you are going to bother with grilling, you might as well get the added benefit of a stronger smoke flavor. The problem with gas grills is that there's no way to add chips once the fire is going. We concluded that removing the turkey, trying to lift off the hot, heavy cooking grate, and then placing another tray of chips over the lit burner was much too dangerous.

Charcoal is another matter. We quickly realized that because we had to add fuel to the fire at the halfway point anyway, we could add more wood at the same time. We came to this conclusion after producing yet another blackened bird. We foolishly thought we could build a really big fire on one side of the grill, put the turkey on the cool side, throw on the cover, and come back two hours later. While it's possible to get the meat up to temperature with this method, the intense initial heat (upward of 425 degrees) causes the skin to burn.

PROTECTING THE WINGS

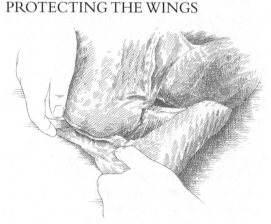

Tucking the wings under the bird will prevent them from burning.

We found it far better to build a moderate fire, bank the coals to one side of the grill, and cook the turkey breast-side down for one hour, just as we had on the gas grill. After an hour, the temperature inside the grill drops from a high of 350 to 375 degrees to somewhere around 275 degrees. At this point, the grill needs more fuel to finish cooking the turkey. Since we were removing the cooking grate anyway, we decided to add more wood along with a dozen unlit briquettes. (Unlike the very heavy gas grate, you can lift a charcoal grate with heavy-duty tongs. You can also simply toss wood into a pile of charcoal; for gas, you must position the foil tray over the burner, an impossible task when the grill is hot.)

At about this point we began experimenting with chunks of wood versus wood chips. We found that chunks, although not suitable for use with a gas grill, were far superior (they gave off a lot more smoke) and easy to use with a charcoal grill.

So would we cook our next turkey over gas or charcoal? Gas is certainly more convenient and more reliable if the weather is especially cold or windy. However, the extra smoky flavor that only charcoal and wood chunks can deliver makes the kettle grill our first choice for grill-roasting a turkey.

Grill-Roasted Turkey on a Charcoal Grill

SERVES 10 TO 12

Charcoal gives you the opportunity to add wood twice—at the outset of grilling and when the bird is turned breast-side up at the one-hour mark—for a stronger smoke flavor. Hickory and mesquite are widely available in chunk and chip form; both work well in this recipe. Hardwood charcoal burns faster and hotter than briquettes, so be sure to use briquettes when grill-roasting turkey. The total cooking time is 2 to 2½ hours, depending on the size of the bird, the ambient conditions (the bird will require more time on a cool, windy day), and the intensity of the fire. Check the internal temperature in the thigh when rotating the bird at the 1-hour-and-45-minute mark. If the thigh is nearly up to temperature (the final temperature should be 175 to 180 degrees), check the temperature again after about 15 minutes. If the thigh is still well below temperature (145 degrees or cooler), don't bother checking the bird again for at least another 30 minutes.

2	cups kosher or I cup table salt
I	turkey (12 to 14 pounds), giblets and tail removed, rinsed thoroughly, and wings tucked (see illustration on page 258)
6	(3-inch) wood chunks, or 6 cups wood chips and heavy-duty aluminum foil
	Nonstick vegetable cooking spray
2	tablespoons unsalted butter, melted

1. Dissolve salt in 2 gallons of cold water in a large (at least 16-quart) stockpot or clean bucket. Add the turkey and refrigerate, or set in a very cool spot (between 32 and 40 degrees), 12 hours or overnight. (Or try the shorter, more intense brine described on page 257.)

2. Toward the end of the brining time, soak the wood chunks in cold water to cover for 1 hour and drain, or divide the wood chips between two 18-inch squares of aluminum foil, seal to make two packets, and use a fork to create about six holes in each packet to allow smoke to escape (see illustrations on page 233).

3. Light a large chimney starter three-quarters filled with charcoal briquettes (about 4 pounds, or 70 coals) and allow to burn until covered with a thin layer of gray ash.

4. Meanwhile, spray a V-rack with nonstick cooking spray. Remove the turkey from the brine and rinse inside and out under cool running water to remove all traces of salt. Pat the turkey dry with paper towels; brush both sides with the melted butter. Set the turkey, breast-side down, in the V-rack.

5. Empty the coals into the grill and pile onto one side. Place 3 soaked wood chunks or 1 wood chip packet on top of the coals. Position the grill rack over the coals, and place the V-rack with the turkey over the cool part of the grill; open the grill lid vents halfway and cover, positioning the vents over the turkey. Cover and grill-roast for 1 hour.

6. Remove the lid from the grill. Using thick potholders, transfer the V-rack with the turkey to a rimmed cookie sheet or roasting pan. Remove the grill rack and place 12 new briquettes and the 3 remaining soaked wood chunks or remaining wood chip packet on top of the coals; replace the grill rack. With a wad of paper towels in each hand, flip the turkey breast-side up in the rack. Return the V-rack with the turkey to the cool part of the grill so that

leg and wing that were facing coals are now facing away. Cover and grill-roast for 45 minutes.

7. Using thick potholders, carefully turn the V-rack with the turkey (the breast remains up) so that the leg and wing that were facing coals are now facing away from the coals. Insert an instant-read thermometer into each thigh to check the temperature and gauge how much longer turkey must cook (see note above).

8. Cover and continue grill-roasting until a thermometer inserted into the thigh registers 175 to 180 degrees, 15 to 45 minutes more.

9. Remove the turkey from the grill, cover loosely with foil, and let rest 20 to 30 minutes. Carve and serve.

Grill-Roasted Turkey on a Gas Grill

SERVES 10 TO 12

Because it's not possible to add more wood during the cooking process, a turkey grill-roasted over a gas fire will not taste as smoky as one roasted over charcoal. The total cooking time is 2 to 2½ hours, depending on the size of the bird, the ambient conditions (the bird will require more time on a cool, windy day), and the intensity of the fire. Check the internal temperature in the thigh when rotating the bird at the 1-hour-and-45-minute mark. If the thigh is nearly up to temperature (the final temperature should be 175 to 180 degrees), check the temperature again after about 15 minutes. If the thigh is still well below temperature (145 degrees or cooler), don't bother checking the bird again for at least another 30 minutes.

2	cups kosher or 1 cup table salt
1	turkey (12 to 14 pounds), giblets and tail removed, rinsed thoroughly, and wings tucked (see illustration on page 258)
3	cups wood chips and heavy-duty aluminum foil Nonstick vegetable cooking spray
2	tablespoons unsalted butter, melted

1. Dissolve the salt in 2 gallons of cold water in a large (at least 16-quart) stockpot or clean bucket. Add the turkey and refrigerate or set in a very cool spot (between 32 and 40 degrees) 12 hours or overnight. (Or, use the shorter, more intense brine described on page 257.)

2. Toward the end of the brining time, soak the wood chips for 15 minutes in a bowl of water to cover. Place the wood chips in a foil tray (see illustrations on page 234). Place the foil tray with the soaked wood chips on top of the primary burner (see illustration on page 235). Turn all burners to high and preheat with the lid down until the chips are smoking heavily, about 20 minutes.

3. Meanwhile, spray a V-rack with nonstick vegetable cooking spray. Remove the turkey from the brine and rinse inside and out under cool running water to remove all traces of salt. Pat the turkey dry with paper towels; brush both sides with the melted butter. Set the turkey, breast-side down, in the V-rack.

4. Turn off all burners but one. Leave the primary burner on high. Place the V-rack with the turkey over the cool part of grill. Cover and grill-roast, regulating the lit burner as necessary to maintain a temperature between 300 and 350 degrees, for 1 hour.

5. Open the lid. With a wad of paper towels in each hand, flip the turkey breast-side up. The leg and wing that were facing the lit burner should now be facing away from it. Close the lid and continue grill-roasting for 45 minutes.

6. Using thick potholders, carefully turn the rack with the turkey (breast remains up) so that the leg and wing that were facing the lit burner are now facing away from it. Insert an instant-read thermometer into each thigh to check the temperature and gauge how much longer the turkey must cook. (See note above.)

7. Close the lid and continue grill-roasting until a thermometer inserted into the thigh registers 175 to 180 degrees, 15 to 45 minutes more.

8. Remove the turkey from the grill, cover loosely with foil, and let rest for 20 to 30 minutes. Carve and serve.

➤ VARIATIONS

Grill-Roasted Turkey with Cranberry–Red Pepper Relish

This relish works best with the spice-rub turkey on page 261.

4	medium red bell peppers, cored, seeded, and cut into small dice
4	cups cranberries, picked through and coarsely chopped

2	medium onions, chopped fine
I	cup cider vinegar
I ½	cups sugar
2	medium jalapeño chiles, stemmed, seeded, and minced
½	teaspoon salt
½	teaspoon hot red pepper flakes
I	recipe Grill-Roasted Turkey (charcoal or gas)

1. While the turkey is brining or grilling, mix the peppers, cranberries, onions, vinegar, sugar, chiles, salt, and hot red pepper flakes together in a medium saucepan. Bring to a boil, reduce the heat, and simmer, stirring occasionally, until the mixture thickens to a jamlike consistency, about 30 minutes. Cool to room temperature. (The relish can be refrigerated in an airtight container for 2 weeks.)

2. Prepare the turkey as directed. Serve the carved turkey with the relish passed separately at the table.

Grill-Roasted with Spice Rub

Adding a spice rub makes turkey more appropriate for summer barbecue meals, with salsas and salads, than a traditional Thanksgiving dinner.

Follow the recipe for Grill-Roasted Turkey (charcoal or gas), replacing the butter with ½ cup Simple Dry Spice Rub for Poultry (page 252), rubbing the spices inside and out as well as under the skin on the breast. Proceed as directed.

Turkey Breast

GRILL-ROASTING A WHOLE, BONE-IN TURKEY breast has plenty of appeal. Many families prefer white meat to dark meat. In addition, a whole turkey is just too much food for a small gathering. We figured that the cooking method would be similar to that used to grill-roast a whole turkey. This proved to be the case, with a couple of adjustments.

As long as you don't buy a huge turkey breast, it can be cooked through without having to add more coals to the fire at the halfway point. A full chimney will cook a breast that weighs less than 7 pounds in less than two hours. Larger breasts will need more charcoal after one hour, and, given the hassle associated with removing the bird from the grill and lifting up the cooking grate, we strongly recommend that you shop for a breast that weighs between 5½ and 7 pounds.

As with a whole turkey, brining is essential. In fact, because white meat is especially prone to drying out, brining is even more important when grill-roasting a breast. As an added precaution, make sure to remove the breast from the grill once the internal temperature reaches 165 degrees. While dark meat needs to reach a higher temperature to become palatable, white meat is fully cooked (and safe) at this temperature. Cooked any more, the breast dries out and begins to taste like sawdust.

Unlike a whole bird, which has wings and legs that can dangle dangerously close to the fire, a breast is a single piece of meat. It can be cooked right on the grill grate, without the use of a V-rack.

PREPARING TURKEY BREAST FOR THE GRILL

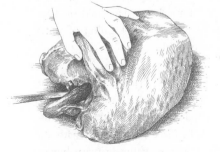

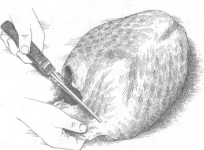

1. Use a boning knife to cut out the remaining portion of the neck. (You can reserve this piece to make stock.)

2. To facilitate carving, scrape the meat away from the wishbone with a boning knife to expose it. Pull the wishbone out with your hands.

3. Cut off any extra skin that hangs off the neck end.

Grill-Roasted Turkey Breast on a Charcoal Grill

SERVES 6 TO 8

When brining, be sure to use a container that rises at least 4 inches above the turkey once the breast is placed inside. This way, the brine can completely cover the turkey. If you are buying a frozen turkey breast, be sure to buy the turkey 3 days ahead; it takes 2 days to defrost in the refrigerator and should be brined overnight before grill-roasting.

- 1   cup kosher salt or ½ cup table salt
- 1   whole, bone-in turkey breast (5½ to 7 pounds), prepared according to illustrations on page 261 and rinsed
- 3   (3-inch) wood chunks, or 3 cups wood chips and heavy-duty aluminum foil
- 2   tablespoons unsalted butter, melted

1. Dissolve the salt in 1 gallon of cold water in a large stockpot or clean bucket. Add the turkey breast and refrigerate, or set in a very cool spot (between 32 and 40 degrees), 12 hours or overnight. (Or try the shorter, more intense brine described on page 257, but for this recipe use just 1 gallon of water with either 2 cups of kosher salt or 1 cup of table salt.)

2. Toward the end of the brining time, soak the wood chunks in cold water to cover for 1 hour and drain, or divide the wood chips between two 18-inch squares of aluminum foil, seal to make two packets, and use a fork to create about six holes in each packet to allow smoke to escape (see illustrations on page 233).

3. Light a large chimney starter three-quarters filled with charcoal briquettes (about 4 pounds or 70 coals) and allow to burn until covered with a thin layer of gray ash.

4. Meanwhile, remove the turkey breast from the brine and rinse inside and out under cool running water to remove all traces of salt. Pat the turkey dry with paper towels; brush with the melted butter.

5. Empty the coals into the grill and pile onto one side. Place the soaked wood chunks or the wood chip packet on top of the coals. Position the grill rack over the coals and place the turkey breast, meaty side down, over the cool part of the grill. Open the grill

lid vents halfway and cover, positioning the vents over the turkey. Cover and grill-roast for 1 hour.

6. Remove the lid from the grill. Using a wad of paper towels in each hand, flip the turkey breast-side up, with the side that was facing the coals now facing away from the coals. Cover and grill-roast until an instant-read thermometer inserted into the thickest part of the breast registers 165 degrees, 40 to 60 minutes more.

7. Remove the turkey breast from the grill, cover loosely with foil, and let rest 20 minutes. Carve and serve.

Grill-Roasted Turkey Breast on a Gas Grill

SERVES 6 TO 8

When brining, be sure to use a container that rises at least 4 inches above the turkey once the breast is placed inside. This way, the brine can completely cover the turkey. If you are buying a frozen turkey breast, be sure to buy the turkey 3 days ahead; it takes 2 days to defrost in the refrigerator and should be brined overnight before grill-roasting.

- 1   cup kosher salt or ½ cup table salt
- 1   whole, bone-in turkey breast (5½ to 7 pounds), prepared according to illustrations on page 261 and rinsed
- 3   cups wood chips and heavy-duty aluminum foil
- 2   tablespoons unsalted butter, melted

1. Dissolve the salt in 1 gallon of cold water in a large stockpot or clean bucket. Add the turkey breast and refrigerate, or set in a very cool spot (between 32 and 40 degrees), 12 hours or overnight. (Or try the shorter, more intense brine described on page 257, but for this recipe use just 1 gallon of water with either 2 cups of kosher salt or 1 cup of table salt.)

2. Toward the end of the brining time, soak the wood chips for 15 minutes in a bowl of water to cover. Place the wood chips in a foil tray (see illustrations on page 234). Place the foil tray with the soaked wood chips on top of the primary burner (see illustration on page 235). Turn all burners to high and preheat with the lid down until the chips are smoking heavily, about 20 minutes.

3. Meanwhile, remove the turkey breast from the brine and rinse inside and out under cool running water to remove all traces of salt. Pat the turkey dry with paper towels; brush with the melted butter.

4. Turn off the burner(s) without chips. Leave the primary burner on high. Clean the grate with a wire brush. Place the turkey breast, meaty side down, over the cool part of the grill. Cover and grill-roast, regulating the lit burner as necessary to maintain temperature between 325 and 350 degrees, for 1 hour.

5. Open the lid. Using a wad of paper towels in each hand, flip the turkey breast-side up so the side that was facing the fire is now facing away from the lit burner. Cover and grill-roast until an instant-read thermometer inserted into the thickest part of the breast registers 165 degrees, about 40 minutes more.

6. Remove the turkey breast from the grill, cover loosely with foil, and let rest 20 minutes. Carve and serve.

INGREDIENTS: Turkey Breast

Supermarkets generally offer two slightly different cuts of turkey breast. Regular, or "true cut," is the most readily available, either fresh or frozen. It is a whole turkey breast, bone in, with skin and usually with ribs, a portion of wing meat, and a portion of back and neck skin. The best ones are U.S. Department of Agriculture Grade A and are minimally processed. Although a true cut breast is excellent carved at the table, it lacks the wings, neck, and giblets, which you will want if you plan to make gravy or stock. If this is the case, try to buy a hotel or country-style turkey breast, which usually comes with wings, neck, and giblets. These breasts, which are more expensive than true cut breasts, are usually sold fresh but not frozen.

Try to avoid turkey breasts that have been injected with a saline solution, often called "self-basters," as the solution masks the natural flavor of the turkey. (If these are the only turkey breasts available, omit the brining step; these birds are already quite salty.) Also best avoided are those turkey breasts sold with a pop-up timer; it won't pop until the turkey breast is overcooked. If removed before cooking, it breaks the skin and juices can escape during cooking. If you have no choice but to purchase a pop-up, leave the timer in place until the turkey breast is fully cooked—according to internal temperature, not the timer—and pull it out just before carving the breast.

➤ VARIATION

Grill-Roasted Turkey Breast with Cumin Spice Rub

Serve slices of this cumin-flavored turkey breast with any fruit salsa (see chapter 19). The smoky and spicy flavors of the turkey go well with the sweetness of the fruit.

Mix together 1 tablespoon ground cumin, 1 tablespoon curry powder, 1 tablespoon chili powder, 1½ teaspoons ground black pepper, ½ teaspoon ground allspice, and ½ teaspoon ground cinnamon. Follow the recipe for Grill-Roasted Turkey Breast (charcoal or gas), rubbing the brined bird with spice mixture instead of melted butter. Proceed as directed.

DUCK

THE MAJOR PROBLEM THAT WE USUALLY encounter when cooking duck is the excessive amount of fat that must be rendered to attain crisp, thin, crackling-like skin. We found that grill-roasting is a great way to remedy this problem. Because the duck is cooked outdoors, we don't have to worry about smoke from dripping fat filling the kitchen. The fat drips away bit by bit, falling harmlessly into an aluminum pan set in the bottom of the grill.

We started our tests by examining two basic methods for grill-roasting duck. Some sources suggest grill-roasting a duck as we would a chicken or turkey—season and then cook over indirect heat until done. Other sources suggest steaming the duck first to render as much fat as possible and to partially cook the duck (which is how we treat duck we plan to roast in the oven). The steamed duck is then seasoned and grilled just to finish the cooking process and crisp up the skin.

We tried the first method, hoping to make this simpler process succeed. We pricked the skin with a fork before cooking to help the fat escape during cooking. We had decent results with this method but were frustrated by two aspects of the procedure. First, the skin was not as crisp as we liked, especially on the breast. Second, we found it necessary to add more coals to the fire to get the duck up to temperature. We tried salting and air-drying the duck overnight in the refrigerator and then grill-roasting. The duck was improved but not great. In addition, the cooking time was about 2½ hours, and we had to add more coals.

We then switched gears and tried steaming. Although not without problems, our first attempt at steaming then grill-roasting yielded a duck with skin that was much more thin and crisp. The meat, however, was dried out and stringy. Clearly, we had steamed the bird too long in order to get rid of all the fat. We would have to cut back on the steaming time and then let the heat of the grill render the remaining fat.

We cut the steaming time from 60 to 30 minutes and then grill-roasted the bird for one hour. This duck was the best of all, with very thin, crackling-like skin and meat that was still moist.

In addition to steaming the duck before grill-roasting, we found it important to prick the skin to help render the fat and thereby produce the wonderful, crispy skin that we desired. Although most recipes recommended using a fork, we found it hard to puncture the skin with the dull tines. We ended up using the tip of a sharp paring knife to make small holes in the skin (but without cutting into the flesh). We also found it important to make sure that we pricked the underside of the duck between the legs and breast to avoid trapping the melting fat.

After several tests, we concluded that grill-roasting a duck is best done between two piles of coals on opposite sides of the grill. The duck is placed in the center for a few reasons. First of all, a drip pan is necessary to catch the excess fat that drips from the duck; if placed in the center of a kettle grill, the pan will not block the air vents at the bottom of the grill. Without a drip pan, the rendered fat can cause a grease fire. If you do not have a disposable aluminum pan, you can fashion a grease pan out of heavy-duty aluminum foil. In addition to preventing a grease fire, placement of the duck between two piles of coals allows it to cook more evenly. With the heat attacking the bird from both sides, it is unnecessary to rotate the bird at all during cooking.

Because the duck has been steamed, it is possible to grill-roast at the relatively high temperature of 425 degrees. This level of heat is easily attained on the charcoal grill by using a full chimney of charcoal (about 90 briquettes). Because this level of heat can't be reached on a gas grill, we thought the cooking time would be longer. We found, however, that longer cooking with the indirect heat of grill-roasting just dried out the duck and did a poor job of browning it. To get the temperature inside the grill over 400 degrees (and thus to brown and crisp the skin), we would need to use a combination of direct and indirect cooking.

In the end, we steamed the bird for 30 minutes, then grill-roasted it on the gas grill with the primary burner on high and the secondary burner(s) turned off for another 30 minutes. (More fat renders during this time on the grill.) Once all of the fat was gone, we turned the secondary burner(s)—just below the

---

INGREDIENTS: Types of Duck

The ducks sold in supermarkets are Pekin or Long Island ducks. Once raised on Long Island, these birds are now grown on farms around the country, and the largest producer is located in Indiana, not New York. These birds weigh about 4½ pounds, perhaps 5 pounds at the most. Don't be fooled into thinking that one can serve five or six people. A smaller chicken feeds more people. Ducks have a larger, heavier bone structure, and they contain a lot more fat, much of which melts away during cooking. A 4½-pound duck feeds three or maybe four people if you have a lot of side dishes. Duck are almost always sold frozen.

Other duck species are available if you are willing to order by mail or can shop at a specialty butcher. The Muscovy is a South American bird that is less fatty than the Pekin and has a stronger game flavor. The Moulard is the sterile offspring of a Muscovy and a Pekin duck and is popular in France. These birds are often bred for the production of foie gras. Both the Muscovy and Moulard ducks weigh more than Pekins, often as much as 8 pounds. Because these birds are so much leaner, they require a different cooking method. Since the Pekin duck is the breed found in supermarkets, we decided to stick with this variety when developing our recipe for grill-roasted whole duck.

Although whole Muscovy and Moulard ducks are hard to find, their breasts are often sold separately at better supermarkets and butcher shops. This meat is usually quite plump and lean. Most duck breasts are sold whole, with the skin on but without the bones. They can be split nicely into two halves, each weighing about 6 ounces. For information on grilling boneless duck breasts, see page 125.

duck—to low to boost the temperature inside the grill above 400 degrees. We cooked the bird for another 40 to 50 minutes at this temperature to brown and crisp the skin. Although we were afraid that the bottom of the bird would dry out from the direct heat at the end of cooking, we found that the meat was still moist. Best of all, the skin was crisp and brown.

We also learned that a sweet glaze elevates the flavor of the duck. To get the glaze to caramelize a bit, apply it during the last few minutes of cooking. If applied any earlier, the glaze will burn. The sweetness not only complements the richness of the duck but also gives the skin a nice color and finish.

Grill-Roasted Duck on a Charcoal Grill

SERVES 3 TO 4

Use a sharp knife to trim away any skin that is not directly above meat or bone. Pull back any remaining skin in the neck cavity and cut away pieces of fat on the underside of the skin to expose the back of the wing joints. The excessive amount of fat under the skin of the duck is rendered through two cooking processes: steaming and then grill-roasting. This method produces very thin, crisp skin and meat that is cooked through but still moist. If you don't have an aluminum pan to catch the dripping fat on the grill, fashion one out of heavy-duty aluminum foil.

2	(3-inch) wood chunks, or 2 cups wood chips and heavy-duty aluminum foil
I	whole Pekin duck (about 4½ pounds), neck and giblets discarded, excess skin and fat removed
	Salt and ground black pepper
	Small disposable aluminum drip pan
I	cup orange juice
2	tablespoons fresh lime juice
2	tablespoons honey

1. Soak the wood chunks in cold water to cover for 1 hour and drain, or place the wood chips on an 18-inch square of aluminum foil, seal to make a packet, and use a fork to create about 6 holes to allow smoke to escape (see illustrations on page 233).

2. Meanwhile, using the tip of a paring knife, make several pricks in the skin over the entire body of the duck, making sure not to cut into the meat. Set a V-rack inside a large roasting pan (you can also set a round rack inside a wok large enough to contain the entire duck). Place the duck, breast-side up, onto the rack. Place the roasting pan over two burners (or one burner if using a wok) and add enough water to come just below the bottom of the duck. Bring the water to a boil over high heat, cover tightly with aluminum foil (or pan cover, if available), and adjust the heat to medium. Steam, adding more hot water to maintain the water level, if necessary, until the fat beads on the pores of the duck and the bird is partially cooked through, 30 minutes. Lift the duck from the rack, pat the skin gently, so as not to break it, with paper towels to remove excess fat and moisture. Season the bird with salt and pepper to taste.

3. Light a large chimney filled with charcoal briquettes (about 5½ pounds, or 90 coals) and allow to burn until covered with a layer of fine gray ash. Pour the charcoal out onto the bottom of the grill and separate into two piles on opposite sides of the grill using long-handled tongs. Place a drip pan in the center between the two piles. Add one soaked wood chunk to each of the piles, or place the chip packet on one of the piles. Replace the cooking grate, open the grill lid vents halfway, and place the lid on the grill. Let the grate heat for 5 minutes; clean with wire brush.

4. Position the duck, breast-side up, in the middle of the cooking grate between the two piles of charcoal. Cover the grill, turning the lid so that the vents are between the two piles of coals. Grill-roast until the skin is crisp, thin, and richly browned, about 1 hour. (The initial temperature inside the grill should be about 425 degrees. It will drop to about 375 degrees by the time the duck is done.)

5. Meanwhile, bring the orange juice, lime juice, and honey to a boil in a small saucepan. Reduce the heat to medium-low and simmer until slightly thickened and reduced to ¼ cup, 25 to 30 minutes.

6. Brush the duck generously with the orange glaze. Cover the grill and cook until the glaze heats through, 3 to 5 minutes. (Be careful to make sure the glaze does not burn.)

7. Transfer the duck to a cutting board and let rest for 10 minutes. Carve and serve.

Grill-Roasted Duck
on a Gas Grill

SERVES 3 TO 4

Use a sharp knife to trim away any skin that is not direct-ly above meat or bone. Pull back any remaining skin in the neck cavity and cut away pieces of fat on the underside of the skin to expose the back of the wing joints. The meat on a duck that is grill-roasted on the gas grill will be more moist than the meat on a bird cooked on the charcoal grill, but the skin on the gas grill–roasted bird will be a touch less crisp. Make sure that you use a drip pan under the bird to pre-vent a grease fire in the grill, as an excessive amount of fat will render from the duck. If you don't have an aluminum pan to catch the dripping fat, fashion one out of heavy-duty aluminum foil.

1	whole Pekin duck (about 4½ pounds), neck and giblets discarded, excess skin and fat removed
	Salt and ground black pepper
2	cups wood chips and heavy-duty aluminum foil
	Small disposable aluminum drip pan
1	cup orange juice
2	tablespoons fresh lime juice
2	tablespoons honey

1. Use the tip of a paring knife to make several pricks into the skin over the entire body of the duck, making sure not to cut into the meat. Set a V-rack inside a large roasting pan (you can also set a round rack inside a wok large enough to contain the entire duck). Place the duck, breast-side up, onto the rack. Place the roasting pan over two burners (or one burner if using a wok) and add enough water to come just below the bottom of the duck. Bring the water to a boil over high heat, cover tightly with alu-minum foil (or pan cover, if available), and adjust the heat to medium. Steam, adding more hot water to maintain the water level if necessary, until the fat beads on the pores of the duck and the bird is par-tially cooked through, 30 minutes. Remove the duck from the rack, pat the skin gently, so as not to break the skin, with paper towels to remove excess fat and moisture. Season the bird with salt and pepper.

2. Meanwhile, soak the wood chips for 15 min-utes in a bowl of water to cover. Place the wood chips in a foil tray (see illustrations on page 234). Place the foil tray with the soaked wood chips on top of the primary burner (see illustration on page 235). Place the drip pan over the secondary burn-er(s). Turn all burners to high and preheat with the lid down until the chips are smoking heavily, about 20 minutes.

3. Open the grill and turn off all but the pri-mary burner, which should be left on high. Clean the grate with a wire brush. Position the duck, breast-side up, directly over the drip pan. Cover and grill-roast, allowing the fat to render, until the duck just begins to brown, about 30 minutes. The average temperature should be between 325 and 350 degrees. Turn the secondary burner(s) to low and grill-roast until the skin is dark brown and crisp, 40 to 50 minutes. (The average temperature will be between 425 and 450 degrees during this period).

4. Meanwhile, bring the orange juice, lime juice, and honey to a boil in a small saucepan. Reduce the heat to medium-low and simmer until slightly thick-ened and reduced to ¼ cup, 25 to 30 minutes.

5. Brush the duck generously with the orange glaze. Cover the grill and cook until the glaze heats through, 3 to 5 minutes. (Be careful to make sure the glaze does not burn.)

➤ VARIATION

Grill-Roasted Five-Spice Duck with Soy Glaze

Mix 1½ tablespoons soy sauce, 2 teaspoons five-spice powder, and 1 teaspoon Asian sesame oil together in a small bowl. Follow the recipe for Grill-Roasted Duck (charcoal or gas) but do not season with salt and pepper. Instead, brush the five-spice mixture onto all sides of the duck, being careful not to tear the skin. Place 3 large scallions, ends trimmed off and cut into thirds, and 1½ inches of unpeeled ginger, cut into thin coins, into the cavity of the duck. Grill as directed. Replace the orange glaze with an un-cooked mixture of 2 tablespoons honey, 2 table-spoons rice vinegar, and 1 tablespoon soy sauce.

17

BARBECUED BEEF BRISKET, PULLED PORK, AND SALMON

THIS CHAPTER IS DEVOTED TO THREE large boneless cuts that are well suited to the slow, low cooking of barbecue. (See page 230 for the culinary definition of barbecue.) Brisket and pulled pork are cuts that are so tough they can take all day to become tender on the grill. In both cases, we have resorted to a compromise method that calls for infusing the meat with smoke on the grill for several hours and then transferring the meat to a low oven to finish cooking through. Although not strictly authentic, this regimen obviates the need to tend the grill all day and add more coals every few hours. A large side of salmon certainly does not require prolonged cooking to become tender. However, we like to barbecue this fish to infuse it with plenty of smoke flavor. The result is somewhere between grilled salmon and smoked salmon.

Brisket

OUR FAVORITE WAY TO COOK BRISKET IS on the barbecue. When prepared correctly, the meat picks up a great smoky flavor and becomes fork-tender. Unfortunately, many a barbecued brisket ends up burnt, tough, or chewy. This is because brisket is so tough to begin with. Unless it is fully cooked, the meat is very chewy and practically inedible. Because brisket is so large (a full cut can weigh 13 pounds), getting the meat "fully cooked" can take many hours. Our goal was to make the meat as tender as possible as quickly as possible.

What does "fully cooked" mean when talking about brisket? To find out, we roasted four small pieces to various internal temperatures. The pieces cooked to 160 and 180 degrees were dry and quite tough. A piece cooked to 200 degrees was slightly less tough, although quite dry. A final piece cooked to 210 degrees had the most appealing texture and the most pleasant chew, despite the fact that it was the driest.

So what's going on here? Heat causes muscle proteins to uncoil and then bond together, which drives out juices in the same way that wringing removes moisture from a wet cloth. This process starts in earnest at around 140 degrees, and by the time the meat reaches 180 degrees, most of its juices have been expelled. This explains why a medium-rare steak (cooked to 130 degrees) is much juicier than a well-done steak (cooked to 160 degrees).

With tender cuts, like steak, the lower the internal temperature of the meat, the juicier and less tough the meat will be. However, with cuts that start out tough, like brisket, another process is also at work. Brisket is loaded with waxy-looking connective tissue called collagen, which makes the meat chewy and tough. Only when the collagen has been transformed into gelatin will the meat be tender. Collagen begins to convert to gelatin at 130 to 140 degrees, but the conversion process occurs most rapidly at temperatures above 180 degrees.

When cooking brisket, the gelatinization of collagen must be the priority. Thus, the meat should be cooked as fully as possible, or to an internal temperature of 210 degrees. The muscle juices will be long gone (that's why the sliced meat is served with barbecue sauce), but the meat will be extremely tender because all the collagen will have been converted to gelatin.

It is important to point out that moist-heat cooking methods (such as braising) are appropriate for

LOCATING THE BRISKET

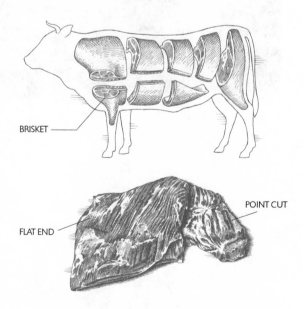

Butchers sometimes separate the whole brisket into two parts, the flat end (left portion) and the point cut (right portion). The point cut is a bit thicker and contains more fat. It is more tender than the flat end when barbecued.

cooking meats to such high internal temperatures because water is a more efficient conductor of heat than air. Meats cooked in a moist environment heat up faster and can be held at high internal temperatures without burning or drying out.

Given the fact that brisket must be fully cooked and that it can be so big, the meat needs 10 or 12 hours of barbecuing to reach the fork-tender stage. Even when butchers separate the brisket into smaller pieces, as is often the case, the cooking time is astronomical. Most cooks are not prepared to keep a fire going that long.

To get around this tending-the-fire-all-day-long problem, we found it necessary to commit barbecue heresy. After much testing, we decided to start the meat on the grill but finish it in the oven, where it could be left to cook unattended. We wondered how long the meat would have to stay on the grill to pick up enough smoke flavor. In our testing, we found that two hours allowed the meat to absorb plenty of smoke flavor and created a dark brown, crusty exterior.

At this point, the meat is ready for the oven. We found it best to wrap the meat in foil to create a moist environment. (Unwrapped briskets cooked up drier, and the exterior was prone to burning.) After barbecuing, a whole brisket requires three hours or so in a 300-degree oven to become fork-tender. Barbecue purists might object to our use of the oven, but this method works, and it doesn't require a tremendous commitment of hands-on cooking time.

Some further notes about our testing. Although many experts recommend basting a brisket regularly as it cooks on the grill to ensure moistness, we disagree. Taking the lid off wreaked havoc with our charcoal fire, and the meat didn't taste any different despite frequent basting with sauce. Likewise, we

FINAL STEPS FOR BARBECUED BRISKET

1. After barbecuing, place the brisket on two 4-foot sections of heavy-duty aluminum foil that have been sealed together to make a 4 by 3-foot rectangle. Bring the short ends of the foil up over the brisket and crimp tightly to seal.

2. Seal the long sides of the foil packet tightly up against the sides of the meat. Put the brisket on a jelly roll pan and in the oven.

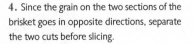

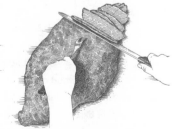

3. After the brisket comes out of the oven, use oven mitts to lift the jelly roll pan and carefully pour the juices into a bowl. Reserve the juices and defat if you like. They make a delicious addition to the barbecue sauce.

4. Since the grain on the two sections of the brisket goes in opposite directions, separate the two cuts before slicing.

5. Carve the brisket into long, thin slices, cutting against the grain on the diagonal.

don't recommend placing a pan filled with water (we also tried beer) on the grill. Some barbecue masters believe that the liquid adds moisture and flavor to the meat, but we couldn't tell any difference between brisket cooked with and without the pan of liquid.

Brisket comes with a thick layer of fat on one side. We tried turning the brisket at it cooks, thinking this might promote even cooking, but we had better results when we barbecued the brisket fat-side up the entire time. This way, the fat slowly melts, lubricating the meat below.

Barbecued Beef Brisket on a Charcoal Grill

SERVES 18 TO 24

Cooking a whole brisket, which weighs at least 10 pounds, may seem like overkill. However, the process is easy, and the leftovers keep well in the refrigerator for up to four days. (Leave leftover brisket unsliced, and reheat the foil-wrapped meat in a 300-degree oven until warm.) Don't worry if your brisket is a little larger or smaller; split-second cooking times are not critical since the meat is eaten very well-done. Still, if you don't want to bother with a big piece of meat, barbecuing brisket for less than a crowd is easy to do. Simply ask your butcher for either the point or flat portion of the brisket (we prefer the point cut; see page 268), each of which weighs about half as much as a whole brisket. Then follow this recipe, reducing the spice rub by half and barbecuing for just 1½ hours. Wrap the meat tightly in foil and reduce the time in the oven to 2 hours. No matter how large or small a piece you cook, it's a good idea to save the juices the meat gives off while in the oven to enrich the barbecue sauce. Hickory and mesquite are both traditional wood choices with brisket.

¾	cup Dry Rub for Barbecue (page 292)
1	whole beef brisket (9 to 11 pounds), fat trimmed to ¼-inch thickness
2	(3-inch) wood chunks or 2 cups wood chips Heavy-duty aluminum foil
2	cups barbecue sauce (see chapter 19)

1. Apply the rub liberally to all sides of the meat, pressing down to make sure the spices adhere and completely obscure the meat. Wrap the brisket tightly in plastic wrap and refrigerate for 2 hours. (For stronger flavor, you can refrigerate the brisket for up to 2 days.)

2. About 1 hour prior to cooking, remove the brisket from the refrigerator, unwrap, and let it come up to room temperature. Soak the wood chunks in cold water to cover for 1 hour and drain, or place the wood chips on an 18-inch square of aluminum foil, seal to make a packet, and use a fork to create about six holes to allow smoke to escape (see illustrations on page 233).

3. Meanwhile, light a large chimney filled a bit less than halfway with charcoal briquettes (about 2½ pounds or 40 coals) and allow to burn until covered with a thin layer of gray ash. Empty the coals into one side of the grill, piling them up in a mound two or three briquettes high. Keep the bottom vents completely open. Place the wood chunks or the packet with the chips on top of the charcoal. Put the cooking grate in place, open the grill lid vents completely, and cover, turning the lid so that the vents are opposite the wood chunks or chips to draw smoke through the grill. Let the grate heat for 5 minutes and clean it with a wire brush.

4. Position the brisket, fat-side up, on the side of the grill opposite the fire. Barbecue, without removing lid, for 2 hours. (The initial temperature will be about 350 degrees and will drop to 250 degrees after 2 hours.)

5. Adjust an oven rack to the middle position and preheat the oven to 300 degrees. Attach two pieces of heavy-duty foil, 48 inches long, by folding the long edges together two or three times, crimping tightly to seal well, to form an approximate 48 by 36-inch rectangle. Position the brisket lengthwise in the center of the foil. Bring the short edges over the brisket and fold down, crimping tightly to seal. Repeat with the long sides of the foil to seal the brisket completely. (See illustrations on page 269.) Place the brisket on a jelly roll pan. Bake until the meat is fork-tender, 3 to 3½ hours.

6. Remove the brisket from the oven, loosen the foil at one end to release steam, and let rest for 30 minutes. If you like, drain the juices into a bowl (see illustration on page 269) and defat the juices in a gravy skimmer.

7. Unwrap the brisket and place it on a cutting board. Separate the meat into two sections and carve

it against the grain on the diagonal into long, thin slices (see illustrations on page 269). Serve with plain barbecue sauce or with barbecue sauce that has been flavored with up to 1 cup of defatted brisket juices.

Barbecued Beef Brisket on a Gas Grill

SERVES 18 TO 24

You will need a pretty large grill to cook a whole brisket. If your grill has less than 400 square inches of cooking space, barbecue either the point or flat end, each of which weighs about half as much as a whole brisket. Then follow this recipe, reducing the spice rub by half and barbecuing for just 1½ hours. Wrap the meat tightly in foil and reduce the time in the oven to 2 hours. No matter how large or small a piece you cook, it's a good idea to save the juices the meat gives off while in the oven to enrich the barbecue sauce.

¾	cup Dry Rub for Barbecue (page 292)
1	whole beef brisket (9 to 11 pounds), fat trimmed to ¼-inch thickness
2	cups wood chips
	Heavy-duty aluminum foil
2	cups barbecue sauce (see chapter 19)

1. Apply the rub liberally to all sides of the meat, pressing down to make sure the spices adhere and completely obscure the meat. Wrap the brisket tightly in plastic wrap and refrigerate for 2 hours. (For stronger flavor, refrigerate the brisket for up to 2 days.)

2. About 1 hour prior to cooking, remove the brisket from the refrigerator, unwrap, and let come to room temperature.

3. Soak the wood chips for 15 minutes in a bowl of water to cover. Place the wood chips in a foil tray (see illustrations on page 234). Place the foil tray with the soaked wood chips on top of primary burner (see illustration on page 235). Turn all burners to high and preheat with lid down until chips are smoking heavily, about 20 minutes.

4. Scrape the grate clean with a wire brush. Turn the primary burner down to medium and turn off the other burner(s). Position the brisket, fat-side up, over the cool part of the grill. Cover and barbecue for 2 hours. (The temperature inside grill should be a con-stant 275 degrees; adjust the lit burner as necessary).

5. Adjust an oven rack to the middle position and preheat the oven to 300 degrees. Attach two 48-inch pieces of heavy-duty foil by folding the long edges together two or three times, crimping tightly to seal well, to form a rectangle of about 36 by 48 inches. Position the brisket lengthwise in the center of the foil. Bring the short edges over the brisket and fold down, crimping tightly to seal. Repeat with the long sides of the foil to seal the brisket completely. (See illustrations on page 269.) Place the brisket on a jelly roll pan. Bake until the meat is fork-tender, 3 to 3½ hours.

6. Remove the brisket from the oven, loosen the foil at one end to release steam, and let rest for 30 minutes. If you like, drain the juices into a bowl (see illustration on page 269) and defat the juices in a gravy skimmer.

7. Unwrap the brisket and place it on a cutting board. Separate the meat into two sections and carve it against the grain on the diagonal into long, thin slices (see illustrations on page 269). Serve with plain barbecue sauce or with barbecue sauce that has been flavored with up to 1 cup of defatted brisket juices.

PULLED PORK

PULLED PORK, ALSO CALLED PULLED PIG or sometimes just plain barbecue, is slow-cooked pork roast that is shredded, seasoned, and then served on a hamburger bun (or sliced white bread) with just enough of your favorite barbecue sauce, a couple of dill pickle chips, and a topping of coleslaw.

Our goal was to devise a procedure for cooking this classic southern dish that was at once both doable and delicious. The meat should be tender, not tough, and moist but not too fatty. Most barbecue joints use a special smoker. We wanted to adapt the technique for the grill. We also set out to reduce the hands-on cooking time, which in some recipes can stretch to eight hours of constant fire tending.

There are two pork roasts commonly associated with pulled pork sandwiches: the shoulder roast and the fresh ham. In their whole state, both are massive roasts, anywhere from 14 to 20 pounds. Because they are so large, most butchers and supermarket meat departments cut both the front and back leg roasts into more manageable sizes. The part of the front leg containing the shoulder blade is usually sold as either a pork shoulder roast or a Boston butt and runs from 6 to 8 pounds. The meat from the upper portion of the front leg is marketed as a picnic roast and runs about the same size. The meat from the rear leg is often segmented into three or four separate boneless roasts called a fresh ham or boneless fresh ham roast.

For barbecue, we find it best to choose a cut of meat with a fair amount of fat, which helps keep the meat moist and succulent during long cooking and adds considerably to the flavor. For this reason, we think the pork shoulder roast, or Boston butt, is the best choice. We found that picnic roasts and fresh hams will also produce excellent results, but they are our second choice.

To set our benchmark for quality, we first cooked a Boston butt using the traditional low-and-slow barbecue method. Using a standard 22-inch kettle grill, we lit about 30 coals and cooked the roast over

indirect heat, adding about eight coals every half-hour or so. It took seven hours to cook a seven-pound roast. While the meat was delicious, tending a grill fire for seven hours is not something many people want to do.

In our next test we tried a much bigger initial fire, with about five pounds of charcoal. After the coals were lit, we placed the pork in a small pan and set it on the grate. The trick to this more intense method is not to remove the lid for any reason until the fire is out three hours later. Because you start with so many coals, it is not necessary to add charcoal during the cooking time. Unfortunately, the high initial heat charred the exterior of the roast, while the interior was still tough and not nearly "fork-tender" when we took it off the grill.

Next we tried a combination approach: a moderate amount of charcoal (more than in the low-and-slow method but less than in the no-peek procedure), cooking the pork roast for three hours on the grill and adding more coal four times. We then finished the roast in a 325-degree oven for two hours. This method produced almost the same results as the traditional barbecue, but in considerably less time and with nine fewer additions of charcoal.

We find it helpful to let the finished roast rest in a sealed paper bag for an hour to allow the meat to reabsorb the flavorful juices. In addition, the sealed bag produces a steaming effect that helps break down any remaining tough collagen. The result is a much more savory and succulent roast. Don't omit this step; it's the difference between good pulled pork and great pulled pork.

As with most barbecue, pork roast benefits from being rubbed with a ground spice mixture. However, because the roast is so thick, we find it best to let the rubbed roast "marinate" in the refrigerator for at least three hours and preferably overnight. The salt in the rub is slowly absorbed by the meat and carries some of the spices with it. The result is a more evenly flavored piece of meat.

THREE PORK ROASTS

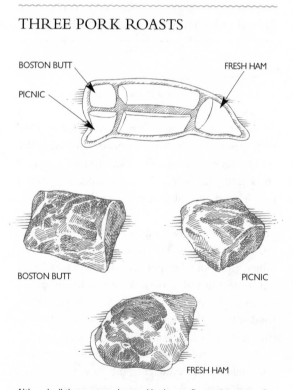

Although all three cuts make good barbecue, Boston butt is our first choice because it has enough fat to keep the meat moist and succulent throughout the long cooking process.

Barbecued Pulled Pork on a Charcoal Grill

SERVES 8

Preparing pulled pork requires little effort but lots of time. Plan on nine hours from start to finish: three hours with the spice rub, three hours on the grill, two hours in the oven, and one hour to rest. Hickory is the traditional choice with pork, although mesquite may be used if desired. Serve the pulled pork on plain white bread or warmed buns with the classic accompaniments of dill pickle chips and coleslaw.

I	bone-in pork roast, preferably Boston butt (see illustration on page 272), 6 to 8 pounds
¾	cup Dry Rub for Barbecue (page 292)
4	(3-inch) wood chunks or 4 cups wood chips
	Heavy-duty aluminum foil
	Disposable aluminum roasting pan (about 8 by 10 inches)
	Brown paper grocery bag
2	cups barbecue sauce (see chapter 19)

1. If using a fresh ham or picnic roast, remove the skin (see illustration below). Massage the dry rub into the meat. Wrap the meat tightly in a double layer of plastic wrap and refrigerate for at least 3 hours. (For stronger flavor, the roast can be refrigerated for up to 3 days.)

2. At least 1 hour prior to cooking, remove the roast from the refrigerator, unwrap, and let it come up to room temperature. Soak the wood chunks in cold water to cover for 1 hour and drain, or place the wood chips on an 18-inch square of aluminum foil, seal to make a packet, and use a fork to create about six holes to allow smoke to escape (see illustrations on page 233).

3. Meanwhile, light a large chimney filled a bit less than halfway with charcoal briquettes (about 2½ pounds or 40 coals) and allow to burn until covered with a thin layer of gray ash. Empty the coals into one side of the grill, piling them up in a mound two or three briquettes high. Keep the bottom vents completely open. Place the wood chunks or the packet with the chips on top of the charcoal.

4. Set the unwrapped roast in the disposable pan and place it on the grate opposite the fire (see illustration below). Open the grill lid vents three-quarters of the way and cover, turning the lid so that the vents are opposite the wood chunks or chips to draw smoke through the grill. Cook, adding about 8 briquettes every hour or so to maintain an average temperature of 275 degrees, for 3 hours.

5. Adjust an oven rack to the middle position and preheat the oven to 325 degrees. Wrap the pan holding the roast with heavy-duty foil to cover completely. Place the pan in the oven and bake until meat is fork-tender, about 2 hours.

6. Slide the foil-wrapped pan with the roast into

KEY STEPS FOR PULLED PORK

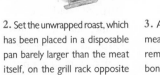
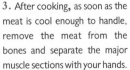

1. If using fresh ham or a picnic roast (seen here), cut through the skin with the tip of a chef's knife. Slide the knife blade just under the skin and work around to loosen the skin while pulling it off with your other hand. Boston butt does not need to be trimmed.

2. Set the unwrapped roast, which has been placed in a disposable pan barely larger than the meat itself, on the grill rack opposite the coals and the wood.

3. After cooking, as soon as the meat is cool enough to handle, remove the meat from the bones and separate the major muscle sections with your hands.

4. Remove as much fat as desired and tear the meat into thin strips.

a brown paper bag. Crimp the top shut. Let the roast rest for 1 hour.

7. Transfer the roast to a cutting board and unwrap. When cool enough to handle, "pull" the pork by separating the roast into muscle sections, removing fat if desired, and tearing the meat into thin shreds with fingers (see illustrations on page 273). Place the shredded meat in a large bowl. Toss with 1 cup barbecue sauce, adding more to taste. Serve, with the remaining sauce passed separately.

Barbecued Pulled Pork on a Gas Grill

SERVES 8

Preparing pulled pork requires little effort but lots of time. Plan on nine hours from start to finish: three hours with the spice rub, three hours on the grill, two hours in the oven, and one hour to rest. The key to using the gas grill is maintaining the proper temperature so that the pork cooks slowly. Adjust the lit burner as necessary. Serve the pulled pork on plain white bread or warmed buns with the classic accompaniments of dill pickle chips and coleslaw.

I	bone-in pork roast, preferably Boston butt (see illustration on page 272), 6 to 8 pounds
¾	cup Dry Rub for Barbecue (page 292)
4	cups wood chips
	Heavy-duty aluminum foil
	Disposable aluminum roasting pan (about 8 by 10 inches)
	Brown paper grocery bag
2	cups barbecue sauce (see chapter 19)

1. If using a fresh ham or picnic roast, remove the skin (see illustration on page 273). Massage the dry rub into the meat. Wrap the meat tightly in a double layer of plastic wrap and refrigerate for at least 3 hours. (For stronger flavor, the roast can be refrigerated for up to 3 days.)

2. At least 1 hour prior to cooking, remove the roast from the refrigerator, unwrap, and let it come up to room temperature.

3. Soak the wood chips for 15 minutes in a bowl of water to cover. Place the wood chips in a foil tray (see illustrations on page 234). Place the foil tray with the soaked wood chips on top of the primary burner (see illustration on page 235). Turn all burners to high and preheat with the lid down until the chips are smoking heavily, about 20 minutes.

4. Turn the primary burner down to medium and turn off the other burner(s). Set the unwrapped roast in the disposable pan and position the pan over the cool part of the grill. Barbecue for 3 hours. (The temperature inside the grill should be a constant 275 degrees; adjust the lit burner as necessary.)

5. Adjust an oven rack to the middle position and preheat the oven to 325 degrees. Wrap the pan holding the roast with heavy-duty foil to cover completely. Place the pan in the oven and bake until meat is fork-tender, about 2 hours.

6. Slide the foil-wrapped pan with the roast into a brown paper bag. Crimp the top shut. Let the roast rest for 1 hour.

7. Transfer the roast to a cutting board and unwrap. When cool enough to handle, "pull" the pork by separating the roast into muscle sections, removing fat if desired, and tearing the meat into thin shreds with fingers (see illustrations on page 273). Place the shredded meat in a large bowl. Toss with 1 cup barbecue sauce, adding more to taste. Serve, with the remaining sauce passed separately.

➤ VARIATION

Cuban-Style Barbecued Pork with Mojo Sauce

This pork is delicious served with rice and black beans. Wood is not traditional in this dish and can be omitted if you prefer to keep the emphasis on the pork and seasonings.

Mix together 9 medium garlic cloves, minced (about 3 tablespoons), 1 tablespoon ground cumin, 1 tablespoon dried oregano, 1 tablespoon salt, 1½ teaspoons ground black pepper, 2 teaspoons brown sugar, and 3 tablespoons extra-virgin olive oil in a small bowl. Follow the recipe for Barbecued Pulled Pork (charcoal or gas) replacing the Dry Rub for Barbecue with the garlic mixture. Proceed with the recipe, but do not toss pulled pork with barbecue sauce. To serve, pass Mojo Sauce (page 302) separately with the pulled pork.

SALMON

IS IT POSSIBLE TO MAKE SMOKED SALMON
at home without a smoker? We thought it was worth
a try and started off by attempting to make a covered
grill act like a cold smoker, which cooks foods in a
range of 75 to 110 degrees. We used very few coals,
adding them as we went along, often putting out the
fire with handfuls of wet smoking chips. The results
were disappointing; the salmon was lacking in flavor,
and the texture was a bit too wet.

Patience is supposed to be a virtue, but in this case
impatience turned out to be the key to success. We
simply got tired of messing with the process of cold
smoking. In fact, at this point we realized that cold
smoking, which is used by commercial smokers to
make smoked salmon, is simply not practical for
home cooks. It takes a very long time, requires both
skill and patience, and, because of the low cooking
temperatures involved, can be disastrous if health
precautions are not followed carefully. We decided to
use more briquettes in the initial fire. This eliminated the need to add more coals during the smoking
process, and the larger fire was less likely to go out
when we added wet wood chunks. This time the
results were gratifying. The hotter fire cooked the
fish more, giving it a more pleasing and flaky texture.

We continued to refine this method over many
months of trial and error. Eventually, we perfected a
procedure that yields a salmon that has many of the
attributes of good smoked salmon but that is crustier
and a whole lot easier to make. In fact, the technique

is similar to traditional barbecue. The difference
between barbecued salmon and cold-smoked salmon
is largely one of texture: the cold-smoked salmon is
more silky, like lox, whereas barbecued salmon will
actually flake.

But the drawback of this method—and the reason
why salmon is usually cold-smoked—is that it dries
out the fish. We figured that brining might help the
fish hold onto moisture as it cooked and experimented with various brining times, eventually settling on
three to four hours for a fillet weighing 2½ to 3
pounds. Any longer and the flavor of the brine was
too intense; any shorter and it didn't produce the
desired results as far as texture was concerned. This
brined, barbecued salmon definitely had the moistness
and texture we had been longing for, but we were still
looking for more flavor to complement its smokiness.

To improve the flavor we added some sugar to
the brine. We also experimented with various
salt/sugar/water ratios; with different brining times
for these new mixtures (from 2 to 24 hours); and
with all manner of smoking woods (alder, apple,
hickory, and oak). We eventually settled on the recipe
below, which calls for three hours of brining in a
solution of 1 cup each of sugar and salt to 7 cups of
water. It also favors alder wood chips for the distinctive flavor they give the fish. The salmon this recipe
produces has a moist but flaky texture and is just
smoky enough, with the natural flavors of the
salmon getting a boost from the brining process.

Barbecued salmon can be served warm off the

KEY STEPS FOR BARBECUED SALMON

1. Slide the salmon off the foil
and onto the grill. To make it easier to remove the salmon from
the grill once it is done, position
the fillet so that the long side is
perpendicular to the grill rods.

2. Use two spatulas to transfer
the cooked fish from the grill to
a jelly roll pan or cutting board.

3. To serve, cut through the
pink flesh, but not the skin, to
divide into individual portions.

4. Slide a spatula between the
fillet and the skin to remove
individual pieces, leaving the skin
behind.

grill as well as chilled, and it works as both a traditional hors d'oeuvre and, somewhat surprisingly, an entrée. For hors d'oeuvres, it is absolutely delicious as is or accompanied with melba toast (or any other flat bread or cracker), finely chopped white onion, capers, and lemon wedges. If you serve the salmon as an entrée, simple wedges of lemon will suffice, or you might try sour cream flavored with fresh dill.

INGREDIENTS: Alder Wood

For years, alder wood has been the top choice for smoking salmon, a tradition begun eons ago with the American Indians of the Pacific Northwest. Apple wood is often recommended as a close second. (If you use apple wood from your own trees, make sure no chemical pesticides or fungicides have been applied to them.) We wondered if you could really taste any difference from the effects of the various woods. In a blind tasting, we found that alder wood does taste a bit better on salmon than other woods. Otherwise, we think it's darned near impossible to tell the difference between mesquite, hickory, apple, or any other hardwood chips or chunks. Even the difference with alder was slight, so feel free to use whichever wood is most readily available.

Barbecued Salmon on a Charcoal Grill

SERVES 4 TO 6 AS A MAIN COURSE

Alder wood (see above) is best for this recipe, but hickory or mesquite is also fine. The grill rack must be hot and thoroughly clean before you place the salmon on it; otherwise the fish might stick.

1	cup kosher salt or ½ cup table salt
1	cup sugar
1	skin-on salmon fillet (about 2½ pounds), pin bones removed (see illustrations on page 160)
2	(3-inch) wood chunks or 2 cups wood chips Heavy-duty aluminum foil
2	tablespoons vegetable oil
1½	teaspoons sweet paprika
1	teaspoon ground white pepper

1. Dissolve the salt and sugar in 2 cups of hot water in a gallon-sized zipper-lock plastic bag. Add 5 cups cold water and the salmon, seal the bag, and refrigerate until the fish is fully brined, about 3 hours.

2. Meanwhile, soak the wood chunks in cold water to cover for 1 hour and drain, or place the wood chips on an 18-inch square of aluminum foil, seal to make a packet, and use a fork to create about six holes to allow smoke to escape (see illustrations on page 233).

3. Remove the salmon from the brine and blot dry completely with paper towels. Place the fillet, skin-side down, on a 30-inch sheet of heavy-duty foil. Rub both sides of the fillet, especially the skin side, with the oil. Dust the flesh side of the fillet with the paprika and pepper.

4. Meanwhile, light a large chimney starter filled halfway with charcoal briquettes (about 2¾ pounds or 45 coals) and allow to burn until covered with a thin layer of gray ash. Empty the coals into one side of the grill, piling them up in a mound two or three briquettes high. Keep the bottom vents completely open. Place the wood chunks or the packet with the chips on top of the charcoal. Put the cooking grate in place, open the grill lid vents completely, and cover, turning the lid so that the vents are opposite the wood chunks or chips to draw smoke through the grill. Let the grate heat for 5 minutes and clean it with a wire brush.

5. Following the illustration on page 275, slide the salmon off the foil and onto the grill rack opposite the fire so that the long side of the fillet is perpendicular to the grill rods. Barbecue until cooked through and heavily flavored with smoke, 1½ hours. (The initial temperature will be about 350 degrees but will drop to about 250 degrees by the time the salmon is done.)

6. Following the illustration on page 275, use two spatulas to remove the salmon from the grill. Serve either hot or at room temperature, cutting through the flesh but not the skin to divide the salmon into portions and sliding a spatula between the flesh and skin to remove the individual pieces, leaving the skin behind (see illustrations on page 275).

Barbecued Salmon on a Gas Grill

SERVES 4 TO 6 AS A MAIN COURSE

Alder wood (see page 276) is best for this recipe, but hickory or mesquite is also fine. The grill rack must be hot and thoroughly clean before you place the salmon on it; otherwise the fish might stick. Keep a close eye on the grill thermometer to make sure that the temperature remains around 275 degrees.

1	cup kosher salt or ½ cup table salt
1	cup sugar
1	skin-on salmon fillet (about 2½ pounds), pin bones removed (see illustrations on page 160)
2	cups wood chips
	Heavy-duty aluminum foil
2	tablespoons vegetable oil
1½	teaspoons sweet paprika
1	teaspoon ground white pepper

1. Dissolve the salt and sugar in 2 cups of hot water in a gallon-sized zipper-lock plastic bag. Add 5 cups cold water and the salmon, seal the bag, and refrigerate until the fish is fully brined, about 3 hours.

2. Remove the salmon from the brine and blot dry completely with paper towels. Place the fillet, skin-side down, on 30-inch sheet of heavy-duty foil. Rub both sides of the fillet, especially the skin side, with the oil. Dust the flesh side of the fillet with the paprika and pepper.

3. Meanwhile, soak the wood chips for 15 minutes in a bowl of water to cover. Place the wood chips in a foil tray (see illustrations on page 234). Place the foil tray with the soaked wood chips on top of the primary burner (see illustration on page 235). Turn all burners to high and preheat with lid down until chips are smoking heavily, about 20 minutes. Scrape the grate clean with a wire brush. Turn the primary burner down to medium and turn off the other burner(s).

4. Following the illustration on page 275, slide the salmon off the foil and onto the rack opposite the fire so that the long side of the fillet is perpendicular to the grill rods. Barbecue until cooked through and heavily flavored with smoke, 1½ hours. (The temperature inside the grill should be a constant 275 degrees; adjust the lit burner as necessary.)

5. Following the illustration on page 275, use two spatulas to remove the salmon from the grill. Serve either hot or at room temperature, cutting through the flesh but not the skin to divide the salmon into portions and sliding a spatula between the flesh and skin to remove the individual pieces, leaving the skin behind (see illustrations on page 275).

➤ VARIATIONS

Barbecued Salmon with Horseradish Cream Sauce

Horseradish and crème fraîche are natural partners to the smoky salmon. They also make the fish seem a bit more moist, as does the sauce in the next variation.

Follow the recipe for Barbecued Salmon (charcoal or gas), serving the fish with Horseradish Cream Sauce (page 302).

Barbecued Salmon with Mustard-Dill Sauce

Use Dijon, honey, or grainy mustard as desired. Depending on your choice of mustard, this sauce can be fairly hot.

Combine 1 cup mustard with ¼ cup minced fresh dill in a small bowl. (The sauce can be covered and refrigerated overnight.) Follow the recipe for Barbecued Salmon (charcoal or gas), serving the fish with the mustard-dill sauce.

18

BARBECUED RIBS

THIS CHAPTER COVERS THREE KINDS OF ribs: pork ribs (which include spareribs, baby back ribs, and country-style ribs), beef ribs, and (beef) short ribs. Pork ribs and regular beef ribs are best barbecued until the meat is fall-off-the-bone tender and smoky tasting. The process for barbecuing both kinds of ribs is fairly similar, with only minor differences in timing and seasoning.

Short ribs are another matter and are included in this chapter only because they are ribs. They come from the cow, but because of their diminutive size they are not ideal candidates for barbecue; they would shrink up to nothing after two hours on the grill. Instead, we found that these delicious ribs are best grilled quickly over a hot fire.

All three kinds of ribs covered in this chapter do have one thing in common—they make excellent eating.

PORK RIBS

WHEN PEOPLE USE THE WORDS "RIBS" AND "barbecue" in the same sentence, they are usually talking about pork spareribs. We wanted to know whether it is possible to produce authentic "ribs" (the kind you get at a barbecue joint) at home.

We started our tests by cooking one slab of ribs over indirect heat, parboiling and then grilling another over direct heat, and cooking a third on our grill's rotisserie attachment (although reluctant to use this unusual bit of equipment, we thought, in the name of science, that we should give it a shot). All three tests were conducted over charcoal with hickory chips in a covered grill.

The ribs cooked over indirect heat were the hands-down favorite. Those cooked on the rotisserie were not nearly as tender, and the parboiled ribs retained the unappealing flavor of boiled meat. While the indirect method needed some refinement, we became convinced that it is the best way to cook ribs at home. It also comes closest to replicating the method used by barbecue pit masters.

We tested a number of popular techniques for barbecuing ribs. Some experts swear by placing a source of moisture in the grill, most often an aluminum pan filled with water or beer. We filled a pan

with water and put it next to the coals to create some steam. We couldn't taste the difference between the ribs cooked with and without the water.

Next, we tested turning and basting. We found that for the even melting of the fat, it is best to turn the ribs every half-hour. Turning also ensures even cooking. When turning, work as quickly as possible to conserve heat in the grill; don't leave the lid off and wander away to find a pair of tongs. Basting proved to be a bust. Tomato-based sauces burned over the long cooking time, and we didn't find the meat any more moist than without basting.

Under normal weather conditions, we found the ribs were done in two to three hours. Signs of doneness include the meat starting to pull away from the ribs (if you grab one end of an individual rib bone and twist it, the bone will actually turn a bit and separate from the meat) and a distinct rosy glow on the exterior. Since the ribs require a relatively short cooking time, there is no need to replenish the coals. A fire that starts out at 350 degrees will drop back to around 250 degrees at the end of two hours.

At this point in our testing, we had produced good ribs, but they were not quite as moist and tender as some restaurant ribs. We spoke with several pit masters, and they suggested wrapping the ribs when

THREE KINDS OF PORK RIBS

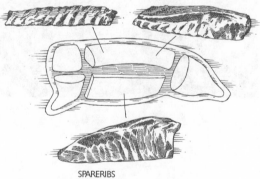

BABY BACK RIBS · COUNTRY-STYLE RIBS · SPARERIBS

Spareribs come from the side or underbelly of the pig and have the most fat, making them the best choice for barbecuing. Baby back ribs (sometimes called back ribs or loin back ribs) come from the loin, or back, of the pig, where the bones are shorter. Country-style ribs are cut from farther along the back (closer to the legs). These ribs are quite large and meaty.

they come off the grill. We wrapped the ribs in foil and then placed them in a brown paper bag to trap any escaping steam. After an hour, we unwrapped the ribs and couldn't believe the difference. The flavor, which was great straight off the grill, was the same, but the texture was markedly improved. The wrapped ribs literally fell off the bone.

We spoke with several food scientists, who explained that as the ribs rest, the juices redistribute throughout the meat, making the ribs more moist and tender. In fact, our ribs are so flavorful and tender that we consider sauce optional.

As indicated above, several kinds of pork ribs are available in most markets. Spareribs come from the underbelly, or lower rib cage, of the pig. A full slab contains 13 ribs and weighs about three pounds. Baby back ribs don't come from a young pig. Rather, they are from the upper, front end of the rib cage and are smaller than spareribs. Country-style ribs come from the upper rear end of the rib cage (opposite the lean tenderloin).

We prefer regular spareribs to either baby back ribs or country-style ribs. The latter ribs are leaner, but the extra fat on spareribs helps keep the meat tender and moist during the long cooking process. Baby back ribs are especially prone to drying out, as are country-style ribs, though to a lesser extent.

Barbecued Spareribs on a Charcoal Grill

SERVES 4

Hickory is the traditional wood choice with ribs, but some of our tasters liked mesquite as well. If you like, serve the ribs with barbecue sauce, but they are delicious as is.

- 2   full slabs pork spareribs (about 6 pounds total)
- ¾   cup Dry Rub for Barbecue (page 292)
- 2   (3-inch) wood chunks or 2 cups wood chips
     Heavy-duty aluminum foil
     Brown paper grocery bag
- 2   cups barbecue sauce (see chapter 19), optional

1. Rub both sides of the ribs with the dry rub and let stand at room temperature for 1 hour. (For stronger flavor, wrap the rubbed ribs in a double layer of plastic and refrigerate for up to 1 day.)

2. Soak the wood chunks in cold water to cover for 1 hour and drain, or place the wood chips on an 18-inch square of aluminum foil, seal to make a packet, and use a fork to create about six holes to allow smoke to escape (see illustrations on page 233).

3. Meanwhile, light a large chimney filled a bit less than halfway with charcoal briquettes (about 2½ pounds or 40 coals) and allow to burn until covered with a thin layer of gray ash. Empty the coals into one side of the grill, piling them up in a mound two or three briquettes high. Keep the bottom vents completely open. Place the wood chunks or the packet with the chips on top of the charcoal. Put the cooking grate in place, open the grill lid vents completely, and cover, turning the lid so that the vents are opposite the wood chunks or chips to draw smoke through the grill. Let the grate heat for 5 minutes and clean it with a wire brush.

4. Position the ribs over the cool part of the grill. Barbecue, turning the ribs every 30 minutes, until the meat starts to pull away from the bones and has a rosy glow on the exterior, 2 to 3 hours. (The initial temperature inside the grill will be about 350 degrees; it will drop to 250 degrees after 2 hours.)

5. Remove the ribs from the grill and completely wrap each slab in foil. Put the foil-wrapped slabs in a brown paper bag and crimp the top of the bag to seal tightly. Allow to rest at room temperature for 1 hour.

6. Unwrap the ribs and brush with barbecue sauce if desired, or serve with sauce on the side.

Barbecued Spareribs on a Gas Grill

SERVES 4

If working with a small grill, cook the second slab of ribs on the warming rack.

- 2   full slabs pork spareribs (about 6 pounds total)
- ¾   cup Dry Rub for Barbecue (page 292)
- 2   cups wood chips
     Heavy-duty aluminum foil
     Brown paper grocery bag
- 2   cups barbecue sauce (see chapter 19), optional

1. Rub both sides of the ribs with the dry rub and let stand at room temperature for 1 hour. (For

stronger flavor, wrap the rubbed ribs in a double layer of plastic and refrigerate for up to 1 day.)

2. Soak the wood chips for 15 minutes in a bowl of water to cover. Place the wood chips in a foil tray (see illustrations on page 234). Place the foil tray with the soaked wood chips on top of the primary burner (see illustration on page 235). Turn all burners to high and preheat with lid down until chips are smoking heavily, about 20 minutes.

3. Scrape the grate clean with a wire brush. Turn the primary burner down to medium and turn off the other burner(s). Position the ribs over the cool part of the grill. Barbecue, turning the ribs every 30 minutes, until the meat starts to pull away from the bones and has a rosy glow on the exterior, 2 to 3 hours. (The temperature inside the grill should be a constant 275 degrees; adjust the lit burner as necessary.)

4. Remove the ribs from the grill and completely wrap each slab in foil. Put the foil-wrapped slabs in a brown paper bag and crimp the top of the bag to seal tightly. Allow to rest at room temperature for 1 hour.

5. Unwrap the ribs and brush with barbecue sauce if desired, or serve with sauce on the side.

➤ VARIATIONS

Barbecued Spareribs with Hoisin, Honey, and Ginger Glaze

A combination of ground Szechuan peppercorns, coriander, and white peppercorns gives these ribs a complex peppery flavor. Use a spice grinder or coffee grinder to grind the peppercorns.

Mix 1½ tablespoons ground Szechuan peppercorns, 4 teaspoons ground white peppercorns, and 1½ teaspoons ground coriander together in a small bowl. Follow the recipe for Barbecued Spareribs (charcoal or gas), replacing the Dry Rub for Barbecue with the Szechuan peppercorn mixture. Grill as directed. When the meat starts to pull away from the bones, brush the ribs with ½ cup Hoisin, Honey, and Ginger Glaze (page 299) and barbecue for another 15 minutes. Wrap the ribs as directed and serve with more Hoisin, Honey, and Ginger Glaze, passed separately at the table. (Omit the barbecue sauce.)

Barbecued Spareribs with Mexican Flavors

Barbecue Sauce with Mexican Flavors (page 296) is ideal in this recipe, although any barbecue sauce will taste fine.

Mix 2 tablespoons chili powder, 2 tablespoons ground cumin, 2 tablespoons dried oregano, 4 teaspoons ground coriander, 1 tablespoon salt, 2 teaspoons ground cinnamon, 2 teaspoons brown sugar, 2 teaspoons ground black pepper, and ¼ teaspoon ground cloves together in a medium bowl. Follow the recipe for Barbecued Spareribs (charcoal or gas), replacing the Dry Rub for Barbecue with the chili powder mixture. Proceed as directed.

BEEF RIBS

BARBECUING BEEF RIBS IS BASICALLY THE same as barbecuing pork ribs. The goal is to get tender, smoky, red-tinged meat that almost falls off the bone. Because beef ribs are the bones included in prime rib, they are already tender and flavorful, so they require less cooking time than pork ribs. However, you don't want to cut the cooking time too much, because you still need to render excess fat and infuse the ribs with smoke flavor.

Butchers generally cut beef rib bones from the prime rib to make either boneless rib roasts or ribeye steaks. If you don't see beef ribs in the meat case, ask your butcher if there are some in the back that are not packaged.

Prime rib has seven bones. Sometimes we found an entire slab of beef ribs with 7 bones, but often we saw just a couple of ribs packaged together. As long as there are at least 4 ribs in a row, it's fine to barbecue them. These bones are quite large, so just a few make a serving. We think that 12 bones (in either two or three partial slabs) are enough to feed four. When shopping, get the meatiest bones you can. We found that even the leanest ribs have more than enough fat to keep them moist during barbecuing. If you can only find ribs that are really fatty, trim away some surface fat before cooking them.

You will need a large kettle or gas grill to cook 12 beef ribs. It's fine if the ribs overlap slightly at the outset; we found that the meat quickly shrinks and that the ribs will fit in a single layer within 30 minutes or so. Don't try to cook more than 12 ribs at once; they just don't brown properly when stacked on top of each other.

Although some sources say that beef ribs can be quick-cooked on the grill, we thought ribs cooked this way were bland. Yes, they were tender, but we wanted more smoke as well as that red tinge you get from slow cooking on the grill. We ended up using the same method that worked with pork, with some modifications.

At first, we lit the same amount of coal that we had used for the spareribs (pork), but we found that the beef ribs were getting too dark too quickly and that the ends were getting a touch burnt and dried out. So we reduced the number of briquettes from 40 to 30, with great results. The ribs were able to cook longer without burning, and some of the interior layers of fat now had time to render and drip off the ribs. When we let the ribs cook for only 1 hour and 15 minutes, we found them to be a little too fatty still. Barbecuing for 1 hour and 45 minutes to 2 hours produced better results.

As we had done with spareribs, we tested wrapping the beef ribs in foil and a paper bag for an hour; this method worked for us again. The wrapped beef ribs were more tender and moist throughout. When the

BEEF RIBS

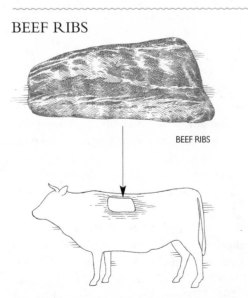

BEEF RIBS

Conventional beef ribs are cut from the rib roast along the back of the animal. These bones are sold in partial or full slabs (a full slab has seven bones) about eight inches long.

ribs were taken straight off the grill and eaten, they were still delicious, but some of the meat on the ends of the ribs was a little bit dry and tough. Letting them rest in the foil and paper bag redistributed the moisture throughout the ribs, making them more appealing.

Barbecued Beef Ribs on a Charcoal Grill

SERVES 4

Beef rib bones are quite large, so you may need to carefully arrange them on the grill to make them fit. (You will need a large kettle grill for this recipe.) Don't worry if the ribs overlap a bit—they will shrink while cooking to fit comfortably in the grill. While a classic barbecue sauce can be used with beef ribs, tasters felt that a more acidic sauce better complemented the richness of the beef.

12	beef ribs in 2 or 3 slabs (about 5 pounds total), trimmed of excess fat if necessary
½	cup plus 2 tablespoons Dry Rub for Barbecue (page 292)
2	(3-inch) wood chunks or 2 cups wood chips Heavy-duty aluminum foil Brown paper grocery bag
2	cups Sweet-Sour-Spicy Barbecue Sauce (page 298)

1. Rub both sides of the ribs with the dry rub and let stand at room temperature for 1 hour. (For stronger flavor, wrap the rubbed ribs in a double layer of plastic and refrigerate for up to 1 day.)

2. Soak the wood chunks in cold water to cover for 1 hour and drain, or place the wood chips on an 18-inch square of aluminum foil, seal to make a packet, and use a fork to create about six holes to allow the smoke to escape (see illustrations on page 233).

3. Meanwhile, light a large chimney filled one-third with charcoal briquettes (about 1¾ pounds or 30 coals) and allow to burn until covered with a thin layer of gray ash. Empty the coals into one side of the grill, piling them up in a mound two briquettes high. Keep the bottom vents completely open. Place the wood chunks or the packet with the chips on top of the charcoal. Put the cooking grate in place, open the grill lid vents completely, and cover, turning the lid so that the vents are opposite the wood chunks or chips

to draw smoke through the grill. Let the grate heat for 5 minutes and then clean it with a wire brush.

4. Position the ribs over the cool part of the grill. Barbecue, turning the ribs every 30 minutes, until the meat starts to pull away from the bones and has a rosy glow on the exterior, 1¾ to 2 hours. (The initial temperature inside the grill will be about 325 degrees and will drop to 250 degrees after 2 hours.)

5. Remove the ribs from the grill and completely wrap each slab in foil. Put the foil-wrapped slabs in a brown paper bag and crimp the top of the bag to seal tightly. Allow to rest at room temperature for 1 hour.

6. Unwrap the ribs and brush with some sauce. Serve, passing extra sauce at the table.

Barbecued Beef Ribs on a Gas Grill

SERVES 4

Beef rib bones are quite large, so you may need to carefully arrange them on the grill to make them fit. (You will need a large grill for this recipe.) Don't worry if the ribs overlap a bit—they will shrink while cooking to fit comfortably in the grill. Keep an eye on the grill thermometer and adjust the lit burner as necessary to prevent the ribs from browning too quickly. While a classic barbecue sauce can be used with beef ribs, tasters felt that a more acidic sauce better complemented the richness of the beef.

12	beef ribs in 2 or 3 slabs (about 5 pounds total), trimmed of excess fat if necessary
½	cup plus 2 tablespoons Dry Rub for Barbecue (page 292)
2	cups wood chips
	Heavy-duty aluminum foil
	Brown paper grocery bag
2	cups Sweet-Sour-Spicy Barbecue Sauce (page 298)

1. Rub both sides of the ribs with the dry rub and let stand at room temperature for 1 hour. (For stronger flavor, wrap the rubbed ribs in a double layer of plastic and refrigerate for up to 1 day.)

2. Soak the wood chips for 15 minutes in a bowl of water to cover. Place the wood chips in a foil tray (see illustrations on page 234). Place the foil tray with the soaked wood chips on top of the primary burner (see illustration on page 235). Turn all burners to high and preheat with lid down until chips are smoking heavily, about 20 minutes.

3. Scrape the grate clean with a wire brush. Turn the primary burner down to medium and turn off the other burner(s). Position the ribs over the cool part of the grill. Barbecue, turning the ribs every 30 minutes, until the meat starts to pull away from the bones and has a rosy glow on the exterior, 2 to 2½ hours. (The temperature inside the grill should be a constant 275 degrees; adjust the lit burner as necessary.)

4. Remove the ribs from the grill and completely wrap each slab in foil. Put the foil-wrapped slabs in a brown paper bag and crimp the top of the bag to seal tightly. Allow to rest at room temperature for 1 hour.

5. Unwrap the ribs and brush with some sauce. Serve, passing extra sauce at the table.

➤ VARIATION

Barbecued Beef Ribs, Chinese Style

Mix 1 tablespoon five-spice powder, 2 teaspoons garlic powder, 1 teaspoon ground white pepper, 1 teaspoon ground ginger, 1 teaspoon brown sugar, and ¾ teaspoon salt together in a small bowl. Follow the recipe for Barbecued Beef Ribs (charcoal or gas), replacing the Dry Rub for Barbecue with a five-spice powder mixture. Proceed as directed, brushing the ribs with Sweetened Soy Glaze (page 298).

SHORT RIBS

SHORT RIBS ARE JUST WHAT THEIR NAME says they are: "short ribs" cut from any location along the length of the cow's ribs. They can come from the lower belly section or higher up toward the back, from the shoulder (or chuck) area or the forward midsection. There is no way to know, either by appearance or labeling, from where short ribs have been cut.

No matter what part of the rib section they come from, short ribs can be butchered in one of two ways. In most supermarkets, you will see English-style short ribs, in which each rib bone has been separated, with the thick chunk of meat attached, and the bone and the meat cut into manageable, rectangular chunks. In the other style of butchering, called flanken-style, the short ribs are cut into thin cross sections that contain two or three pieces of bone surrounded by pieces of meat.

Both styles of short ribs are fairly fatty, making them ideal candidates for the grill. Most cooks braise this cheap cut, which turns yielding and tender in a stew. However, the cook must jump through several hoops—trimming the excess fat before cooking, draining off fat from the browned ribs, degreasing the stew liquid before serving—to keep the braise from tasting greasy. On the grill, the fat melts harmlessly into the fire and is not really an issue.

Although short ribs are similar to beef ribs in that each contains meat and bone, our research indicates that most cooks prefer to grill short ribs rather quickly. Given their diminutive size, this makes sense. If you gave a short rib enough time on the grill to truly barbecue it, it would shrink up to a tiny speck of meat.

Since English-style short ribs are more available, we started our tests with them. Our first efforts produced terrible results. At first, we burned the exterior before the thick middle portion of the meat was cooked through. We lowered the temperature and still found the interior to be tough by the time the exterior was charred. We figured maybe all the experts were wrong and that we should grill-roast English-style short ribs in a kind of compromise between barbecuing and grilling (see page 230 for a definition of grill-roasting). Although this method worked better, the meat became dry and stringy after half an hour of grill-roasting. Worse, there were several layers of unrendered fat throughout each rib that were flabby and unappealing.

Next, we tried simmering the ribs on the stovetop and finishing them on the grill. This method is tedious. First, you have to make a flavorful liquid for the meat to stew in, and then you have to cook the ribs down in the liquid for a few hours to make them tender. Finally, you have to finish by grilling the ribs until crisped and browned, which takes only eight minutes or so—not enough time to give them much smoke flavor. We'd rather spend all that time making braised short ribs, where you end up not only with tender meat but a great, satisfying, rich sauce that becomes a complete meal with mashed potatoes or noodles. It seemed like a waste to have to fire up the grill just to brown the ribs, after you'd spent three hours braising them. It made more sense to brown the ribs on the stovetop before braising them.

At this point, we decided to follow some Asian recipes in which short ribs are butchered further before being cooked. In effect, the meat is slit crosswise several times and opened up like a book until it is quite thin (between ¼ and ½ inch thick), which makes it eligible for straightfoward grilling. (See illustrations on page 286.) While this method worked well—the meat cooked quickly, it became tender, and the fat was easily rendered—there was a drawback: the need to butcher each short rib at home.

You can avoid this hassle by asking the butcher for flanken-style ribs. Because the meat is already cut thin and across the grain, flanken-style ribs are much easier to cook on the grill. While these ribs are not supertender (you have to work a little at eating them), they are juicy, rich, and packed with beefy flavor, especially near the bones, which are great to gnaw on. Furthermore, these ribs have a large surface area for caramelization, which makes for better

TWO KINDS OF SHORT RIBS

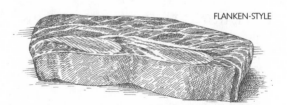

FLANKEN-STYLE

Flanken-style short ribs are cut across the rib bones. Because they are thin and the meat is cut across the grain, flanken-style short ribs are suitable for quick, high-heat grilling.

ENGLISH-STYLE

The tips of the ribs can be sectioned between the bones to render cube-shaped short ribs, called English-style short ribs. This cut contains a single, long bone and a fat block of meat. It must be butchered at home before being grilled (see illustrations on page 286).

flavor. When marinated, the ribs are infused with lots of good flavor because the meat is so thin.

When purchasing the ribs, try to get thinly sliced flanken-style ribs, which should be, on average, about one-quarter inch thick. If you end up having to buy English-style, be sure that you get meaty ribs. We've seen ribs that are mostly bone. The meat should extend at least one inch above the rib bones. Also, in addition to butchering the ribs Asian-style, you will need to trim off the silver skin and fat on the surface of the ribs.

Grilling the ribs is extremely easy. It's pretty hard to mess it up as long as your fire is hot enough to sear the meat. Because the meat is so thin, it cooks extremely quickly. In this case, it's impossible to go for medium-rare or even medium. You just want to have good caramelization to add a layer of sweet flavor on the surface of the ribs. We found that a medium-hot fire (a full chimney of hardwood charcoal) sears the meat in about five minutes. Because the ribs are so high in fat, be sure to have a spray bottle on hand to extinguish any fires that might occur.

Charcoal-Grilled Beef Short Ribs
SERVES 4

If you are using English-style ribs, purchase only ribs with a good amount of meat on the bones; there should be at least 1 inch of meat above the bone. Keep a spray bottle handy to douse any flare-ups caused by this fatty cut of meat. Short ribs are delicious enough to eat when seasoned with just salt and pepper. The variations offer more complex flavors.

2½   pounds flanken-style short ribs, about ¼ inch thick, or 3 pounds English-style short ribs, prepared according to illustrations below
Salt and ground black pepper

1. Light a large chimney full of hardwood charcoal (about 2½ pounds) and allow to burn until covered with a thin layer of gray ash, about 15 minutes. Build a single-level fire by spreading the coals evenly over the bottom of the grill. Set the cooking rack in place, cover the grill with the lid, and let the rack heat up, about 5 minutes. Use a wire brush to scrape clean the grill. The fire is ready when the coals are medium-hot. (See how to gauge heat level on page 19.)

PREPARING ENGLISH-STYLE RIBS

Flanken-style short ribs are thin enough to marinate and cook as is. Thicker English-style short ribs must be opened up into a flatter piece of meat before being marinated, as shown here.

1. With a paring or boning knife, trim off the surface fat and silver skin from each rib.

2. Right above the bone, make a cut into the meat. Continue cutting almost all the way, but not quite through, the meat.

3. Open the meat and bone onto a cutting board, as you would open a book. Make another cut into the meat, parallel to the board; make the lower half of the meat that you are slicing about ¼ inch thick, cutting almost, but not all the way through, to the end of the meat. Open the meat again, like a book.

4. Repeat step 3 one to two more times, until the meat is about ¼ inch thick throughout. You should have a bone connected to a long strip of meat, about ¼ inch thick.

2. Season the ribs with salt and pepper to taste. Grill half of the ribs, uncovered and turning once, until richly browned on both sides, about 4½ minutes total. Transfer the ribs to a serving platter and cover with foil. Repeat with the second batch of ribs. Serve immediately.

Gas-Grilled Beef Short Ribs
SERVES 4

If you are using English-style ribs, purchase only ribs with a good amount of meat on the bones; there should be at least 1 inch of meat above the bone. Be sure the gas grill is as hot as can be before cooking these ribs; the hotter the grill, the better the caramelization. Keep a spray bottle handy to douse any flames.

2½	pounds flanken-style short ribs, about ¼ inch thick, or 3 pounds English-style short ribs, prepared according to illustrations on page 286
	Salt and ground black pepper

1. Preheat the grill with all burners turned to high and the lid down until very hot, about 15 minutes. Scrape the grill clean with a wire brush.

2. Season the ribs with salt and pepper to taste. Grill half of the ribs, covered and turning once, until richly browned on both sides, 5 to 5½ minutes total. Transfer the ribs to a serving platter and cover with foil. Repeat with the second batch of ribs. Serve immediately.

➤ VARIATIONS

Grilled Beef Short Ribs, Korean Style

This recipe is based on kalbi, a standard barbecued short rib dish from Korea. The sweet, salty marinade promotes excellent browning on the grill. Be sure to marinate the ribs for at least 4 hours or, preferably, overnight. If you like, add ½ teaspoon or more of hot red pepper flakes to the marinade. Serve with steamed rice and kimchee (spicy Korean pickled vegetables, available in Asian markets).

1	medium, ripe pear, halved, cored, peeled, and cut into ½-inch pieces
6	medium garlic cloves, chopped
2	teaspoons chopped fresh ginger
½	cup soy sauce
2	tablespoons Asian sesame oil
6	tablespoons sugar
3	medium scallions, ends removed, green and white parts thinly sliced
1	tablespoon rice vinegar
1	recipe Charcoal-Grilled or Gas-Grilled Beef Short Ribs (omit salt and pepper)

1. Place the pear, garlic, ginger, and soy sauce in the workbowl of a food processor fitted with a steel blade. Pulse until smooth, scraping down the sides of the bowl as necessary. Transfer the mixture to a medium bowl and stir in the sesame oil, sugar, scallions, and vinegar.

2. Place the ribs in a gallon-sized, zipper-lock plastic bag and pour the soy sauce mixture over them. Seal the bag. Place the bag in the refrigerator and marinate the ribs for at least 4 hours or overnight.

3. Remove the ribs from the marinade and grill as directed.

Grilled Beef Short Ribs with Chipotle and Citrus Marinade

This marinade has some heat, smoky flavor, and acidity.

2	canned chipotle chiles packed in adobo sauce, minced, with 1½ teaspoons adobo sauce
3	tablespoons lime juice
6	tablespoons olive oil
1	tablespoon honey
6	tablespoons chopped fresh cilantro leaves
1½	teaspoons chili powder
1½	teaspoons ground cumin
4	medium garlic cloves, minced
1½	teaspoons salt
1½	teaspoons ground black pepper
1	recipe Charcoal-Grilled or Gas-Grilled Beef Short Ribs (omit salt and pepper)
	Lime wedges

1. Mix the chiles and adobo sauce, lime juice, olive oil, honey, cilantro, chili powder, cumin, garlic, salt, and pepper together in a medium bowl.

2. Place the ribs in a gallon-sized, zipper-lock plastic bag and pour the chile mixture over them. Seal the bag. Place the bag in the refrigerator and marinate the ribs for at least 4 hours or overnight.

3. Grill the ribs as directed, serving them with lime wedges.

PART 4

FLAVORINGS

19

RUBS, BARBECUE SAUCES, AND SALSAS

SPICE RUBS, BARBECUE SAUCES, AND SALSAS add flavor (and in some cases moisture) to grilled foods. Rubs, sauces, and salsas each have a different function and are used at different times in the cooking process.

RUBS AND PASTES

RUBS (MIXTURES OF DRY SPICES) AND pastes (spices and herbs moistened with oil and/or other liquids) are often used to coat foods before grilling. Rubs and pastes encourage the formation of a deeply browned crust filled with complex, concentrated flavors. Like marinades, spice rubs and pastes add flavor to food before it is cooked, but we think rubs and pastes have several advantages over marinades.

Because rubs and pastes are composed almost solely of spices and herbs, they impart stronger flavors than marinades. (Marinades are mostly oil and an acidic liquid, such as lemon juice or vinegar.) Rubs and pastes also stick better to foods than marinades (after all, they are massaged directly into foods before grilling). Better sticking means better flavor. Finally, marinades almost always contain a lot of oil, which can cause flare-ups. Spice rubs and herb pastes can be left on foods for several hours without causing fires.

Spice rubs and herb pastes can be used with virtually any type of food, and, in general, you can mix and match rubs and pastes with different foods with abandon. There are, though, a couple of guidelines worth following. You should consider matching the strength of the rub or paste with the nature of the food being cooked. For example, earthier spices are better with meat, lighter spices and herbs with fish and chicken. Also keep in mind that spices like cumin and paprika are good "bulk" spices, while aromatic spices like cinnamon and cloves should be used lightly.

We find that bare hands—not brushes—are the best tools for applying rubs and pastes. Use a bit of pressure to make sure the spices actually adhere to the food. Although rubs and pastes can be applied right before cooking, we've found that the flavor of the spices penetrates deeper into the food if given some time. In general, we like to refrigerate rubbed meats for a few hours to allow the flavor to develop.

Dry Rub for Barbecue
MAKES ABOUT 1 CUP

You can adjust the proportions of spices in this all-purpose rub or add or subtract a spice as you wish. For instance, if you don't like spicy foods, reduce or eliminate the cayenne. Also, if you are using hot chili powder, you may want to eliminate the cayenne. This rub works well with ribs and brisket and with Boston butt if you want to make pulled pork.

4	tablespoons sweet paprika
2	tablespoons chili powder
2	tablespoons ground cumin
2	tablespoons dark brown sugar
2	tablespoons salt
1	tablespoon dried oregano
1	tablespoon granulated sugar
1	tablespoon ground black pepper
1	tablespoon ground white pepper
1 to 2	teaspoons cayenne pepper

Mix all ingredients together in a small bowl. (The rub can be stored in an airtight container at room temperature for several weeks.)

Simple Barbecue Rub
MAKES ABOUT 1 CUP

This rub is even simpler than the previous recipe. It's less peppery and not as sweet. A hint of cloves makes this basic rub interesting.

1/2	cup sweet paprika
2	tablespoons ground cumin
2	tablespoons mild chili powder
2	tablespoons ground black pepper
1	teaspoon cayenne pepper
1/2	teaspoon ground cloves

Mix all ingredients together in a small bowl. (The rub can be stored in an airtight container at room temperature for several weeks.)

Simple Spice Rub for Beef or Lamb

MAKES SCANT $^1/_4$ CUP

This fragrant rub is good on most cuts of beef and lamb, especially flank steak, shoulder steak, lamb shoulder chops, and butterflied leg of lamb.

I	tablespoon black peppercorns
I	tablespoon white peppercorns
I $^1/_2$	teaspoons coriander seeds
I $^1/_2$	teaspoons cumin seeds
$^1/_2$	teaspoon hot red pepper flakes
$^1/_2$	teaspoon ground cinnamon

1. Toast the peppercorns, coriander, and cumin in a small skillet over medium heat, shaking the pan occasionally to prevent burning, until the first wisps of smoke appear, 3 to 5 minutes. Remove the pan from the heat, cool the spices to room temperature, then mix with the pepper flakes and cinnamon.

2. Grind the spice mixture to a powder in a spice grinder or coffee mill. (The rub can be stored in an airtight container at room temperature for several weeks.)

Simple Spice Rub for Pork

MAKES ABOUT $^1/_4$ CUP

If you want some heat, add cayenne pepper or hot red pepper flakes to the mix. This rub is great with pork shoulder or loin.

I $^1/_2$	tablespoons fennel seeds
I $^1/_2$	tablespoons cumin seeds
I $^1/_2$	tablespoons coriander seeds
I	teaspoon ground cinnamon
2	teaspoons dry mustard
2	teaspoons brown sugar

1. Toast the fennel, cumin, and coriander seeds in a small skillet over medium heat, shaking the pan occasionally to prevent burning, until the first wisps of smoke appear, 3 to 5 minutes. Remove the pan from the heat, cool the spices to room temperature, then mix with the cinnamon, mustard, and brown sugar.

2. Grind the spice mixture to a powder in a spice grinder or coffee mill. (The rub can be stored in an airtight container at room temperature for several weeks.)

Simple Spice Rub for Fish

MAKES ABOUT $^1/_4$ CUP

Use this aromatic mixture on oily fish such as salmon, mackerel, or bluefish. It's delicious on our Barbecued Salmon (page 275), when used in place of the white pepper and paprika.

I $^1/_2$	tablespoons fennel seeds
I $^1/_2$	tablespoons coriander seeds
I $^1/_2$	tablespoons white peppercorns
3	whole cloves
2	whole star anise

1. Toast the fennel, coriander, peppercorns, cloves, and star anise in a small skillet over medium heat, shaking the pan occasionally to prevent burning, until the first wisps of smoke appear, 3 to 5 minutes. Remove the pan from the heat and cool the spices to room temperature.

2. Grind the spice mixture to a powder in a spice grinder or coffee mill. (The rub can be stored in an airtight container at room temperature for several weeks.)

SCIENCE: Toasting Spices

Many of our spice rub recipes call for toasting whole spices in a warm pan and then grinding them in a coffee mill or spice grinder. Why not just start with ground spices? In some cases, ground spices are just fine. However, when we want a particularly fragrant or aromatic rub, toasting whole spices produces better results. When whole spices are toasted, heat releases oils and chemicals in the spice that break down and reform into new tastes and aromas. You want to heat the spices long enough to release as much flavor as possible. However, you don't want to burn the spices. At the first signs of smoke, remove the pan from the heat. Also, make sure to toast the spices over medium heat; higher heat can cause the spices to burn.

EQUIPMENT: Spice Grinder

You can buy a specialized tool designed just for grinding spices. However, most cooks will find it easier to invest in a cheap coffee mill that they use exclusively for grinding spices. (Don't try to grind coffee beans in a mill that has been used for spices. Mills are impossible to clean thoroughly, and cumin-flavored coffee isn't the best way to start your day.) Don't use an expensive burr coffee grinder; spices can be ground perfectly well in a blade-type grinder with the small hopper on top. To get an even grind, see the illustration below.

Hold the coffee mill in one hand and place the other hand over the hopper on top. Lift the whole unit off the counter and grind, shaking the unit gently to move the spices around the blade and grind them evenly and finely.

Aromatic Rub for Poultry

MAKES ABOUT ¹/₂ CUP

This rub (and the one that follows) is less potent and peppery than the Dry Rub for Barbecue (page 292), making it well suited to poultry. A single recipe will coat a turkey, two chickens, two ducks, or four Cornish hens.

1 ½	tablespoons ground cardamom
1 ½	tablespoons ground ginger
1 ½	tablespoons ground black pepper
1	tablespoon ground turmeric
1	tablespoon ground cumin
1	tablespoon ground coriander
1 ½	teaspoons ground allspice
½	teaspoon ground cloves

Mix all the ingredients together in a small bowl. (The rub can be stored in an airtight container at room temperature for several weeks.)

Indian Spice Rub for Poultry

MAKES ABOUT ¹/₂ CUP

This rub gets a lot of flavor from four flavorful spices. A single recipe will coat a turkey, two chickens, two ducks, or four Cornish hens.

3	tablespoons curry powder
3	tablespoons chili powder
1 ½	tablespoons ground allspice
1 ½	teaspoons ground cinnamon

Mix all the ingredients together in a small bowl. (The rub can be stored in an airtight container at room temperature for several weeks.)

Classic Pesto

MAKES ABOUT ³/₄ CUP

Pesto can be rubbed under the skin of chicken parts before grilling, or you can dollop some pesto over pieces of grilled fish. Basil usually darkens in homemade pesto, but you can boost the green color by adding the optional parsley. For sharper flavor, substitute 1 tablespoon finely grated pecorino cheese for 1 tablespoon of the Parmesan.

¹/₄	cup pine nuts, walnuts, or almonds
3	medium garlic cloves, unpeeled
2	cups packed fresh basil leaves
2	tablespoons fresh flat-leaf parsley leaves (optional)
7	tablespoons extra-virgin olive oil
	Salt
¹/₄	cup finely grated Parmesan cheese

1. Toast the nuts in a small, heavy skillet over medium heat, stirring frequently, until just golden and fragrant, 4 to 5 minutes. Transfer the nuts to a plate.

2. Add the garlic to the empty pan. Toast, shaking the pan occasionally, until fragrant and the color of the cloves deepens slightly, about 7 minutes. Transfer the garlic to a plate, cool, peel, and chop.

3. Place the basil and parsley (if using) in a heavy-duty, quart-sized, zipper-lock bag. Pound the bag with the flat side of a meat pounder until all the leaves are bruised (see illustration on page 295).

4. Place the nuts, garlic, mixed herbs, oil, and ½ teaspoon salt in the workbowl of a food processor. Process until smooth, stopping as necessary to scrape down the sides of the bowl. Transfer the mixture to a small bowl, stir in the cheese, and adjust the salt. (The surface of the pesto can be covered with a sheet of plastic wrap or a thin film of oil and refrigerated for up to 3 days.)

Salsa Verde

MAKES ABOUT ½ CUP

Not to be mistaken for the Mexican salsa made from tomatillos, this Italian sauce is similar to pesto (both sauces are raw) but combines fresh parsley and basil with piquant capers, olives, and anchovies.

2	tablespoons minced fresh parsley leaves
1	tablespoon minced fresh basil leaves
1	tablespoon pitted and minced green olives
1½	teaspoons drained and minced capers
1	medium garlic clove, minced
1	anchovy fillet, minced
2	tablespoons extra-virgin olive oil
1	tablespoon lemon juice
	Ground black pepper

Combine all the ingredients, including pepper to taste, in a small bowl. (The surface of the salsa verde can be covered with a sheet of plastic wrap or a thin film of oil and refrigerated for up to 3 days.)

MAKING PESTO

Bruising herb leaves in a zipper-lock plastic bag with the flat side of a meat pounder (or rolling pin) is a quick but effective substitute for hand-pounding with a mortar and pestle, and it helps to release their flavor.

Mediterranean Herb and Garlic Paste

MAKES ⅓ CUP

You may omit one or two of the herbs in this recipe, but be sure to compensate with the other herbs so that the total amount equals a scant quarter cup. This all-purpose paste is great rubbed onto steaks and chops (beef, pork, or lamb) before grilling. Be sure to season them with salt and pepper as well (unless brined).

1	tablespoon chopped fresh parsley leaves
2	teaspoons chopped fresh sage leaves
2	teaspoons chopped fresh thyme leaves
2	teaspoons chopped fresh rosemary leaves
2	teaspoons chopped fresh oregano leaves
3	medium garlic cloves, minced
¼	cup extra virgin olive oil

Mix all ingredients together in a small bowl. Rub the paste onto meat before grilling, making sure to season the meat with salt and pepper to taste.

BARBECUE SAUCES AND GLAZES

BARBECUE SAUCE IS THE MOST COMMON sauce used for grilling. However, other sauces, such as a sweetened soy glaze or a hoisin and ginger glaze, can also be used to flavor grilled foods. Almost all sauces and glazes contain ingredients, such as tomatoes or a sweetener, that will cause them to burn if left on grilled foods for any length of time. For this reason, it is usually best to brush these sauces on grilled foods during the last few minutes of cooking and then serve at the table as well.

Classic barbecue sauce is relatively easy to make. We found that the combination of tomato sauce and whole tomatoes in juice cooks down to a thick, glossy texture. Vinegar, brown sugar, and molasses add the sour and sweet notes, while spices (paprika, chili powder, black pepper, and salt) round out the flavors. For some brightness, we like to add a little fresh orange juice as well.

This basic sauce can be left as is or flavored with Mexican, Asian, or Caribbean ingredients. The only

295

problem with this sauce is that it takes at least two hours of gentle simmering for the flavors to come together and for the tomatoes to break down into a sauce of the proper consistency.

We wondered if there was a way to shortcut the process. The first thing we had to do was get rid of the canned whole tomatoes—they took too long to cook down into a thick sauce. We had better luck with ketchup, which is already sweet, tart, and thick.

The only other major obstacle we encountered when developing our quick barbecue sauce was the onion. After two hours of simmering in the sauce, the onions became very soft and lost their texture. In a quick-cooked sauce, they remained crunchy. We tried pureeing the sauce after it had cooked, but this quick barbecue sauce lost its glossy texture when pureed and instead became grainy. One of our test cooks suggested using onion juice—made by pureeing raw onion with water—to give the sauce some onion flavor. This worked liked a charm.

At this point, it was only a matter of adding more flavor. Worcestershire sauce and Dijon mustard added depth to the quick-cooked sauce. The usual spices—chili powder, cayenne, black pepper—provided more flavor and heat.

INGREDIENTS: Liquid Smoke

What gives homemade or bottled barbecue sauce its smoky flavor? It's a compound called liquid smoke. Many home cooks avoid this product because they assume it's full of unhealthful compounds. Actually, liquid smoke is an all-natural product made by burning hickory hardwood, condensing the smoke, and then filtering it to remove impurities. Look for liquid smoke in supermarkets and other stores that sell grilling paraphernalia.

SCIENCE: Food Safety

Never use the same brush to apply sauces to raw and cooked foods. Also, never apply sauce from the same source to foods that are raw and cooked. The reason is simple: bacterial contamination. If you brush a sauce onto raw chicken parts, you must assume that both the brush and the marinade are contaminated. To avoid this problem, reserve some of the sauce in a separate bowl. Use the reserved sauce for basting. To use the brush again, wash it in hot, soapy water or in the dishwasher.

Classic Barbecue Sauce

MAKES 3 CUPS

Barbecue sauces should be applied only in the last few minutes of grilling; otherwise, the sweeteners in most sauces will cause the skin to burn. Serve additional sauce on the side as an accompaniment to the cooked chicken, ribs, brisket, or pulled pork. Refrigerate or freeze extra sauce.

2	tablespoons vegetable oil
I	medium onion, minced
I	can (8 ounces) tomato sauce
I	can (28 ounces) whole tomatoes with juice
¾	cup distilled white vinegar
¼	cup firmly packed dark brown sugar
2	tablespoons molasses
I	tablespoon sweet paprika
I	tablespoon chili powder
2	teaspoons liquid smoke (optional)
I	teaspoon salt
2	teaspoons ground black pepper
¼	cup orange juice

1. Heat the oil in a large, heavy-bottomed saucepan over medium heat until hot and shimmering (but not smoking). Add the onion and sauté until golden brown, 7 to 10 minutes, stirring frequently. Add the remaining ingredients. Bring to a boil, then reduce the heat to the lowest possible setting and simmer, uncovered, until thickened, 2 to 2½ hours.

2. Puree the sauce, in batches if necessary, in a blender or the workbowl of a food processor. Transfer to a bowl and use immediately or cover in an airtight container. (The sauce can be refrigerated for up to 2 weeks or frozen for several months.)

➤ VARIATIONS

Barbecue Sauce with Mexican Flavors

A few ingredients added to basic barbecue sauce give this recipe a south-of-the-border flavor.

Follow the recipe for Classic Barbecue Sauce, stirring 1½ teaspoons ground cumin, 1½ teaspoons chili powder, 6 tablespoons lime juice, and 3 tablespoons chopped fresh cilantro leaves into the finished sauce.

Barbecue Sauce with Asian Flavors

Soy sauce, ginger, and sesame oil give this tomato-based sauce an Asian flavor.

Follow the recipe for Classic Barbecue Sauce, stirring 1 tablespoon minced fresh ginger, 6 tablespoons soy sauce, 6 tablespoons rice vinegar, 3 tablespoons sugar, and 1½ tablespoons Asian sesame oil into the finished sauce.

Barbecue Sauce with Caribbean Flavors

Serve Black Bean and Mango Salsa (page 300) on the side when you're brushing foods with this sauce.

Follow the recipe for Classic Barbecue Sauce, stirring 2 tablespoons pineapple juice, 2 tablespoons dark rum, 1 tablespoon Caribbean hot sauce, 2 teaspoons sugar, and pinch ground allspice into the finished sauce.

Quick Barbecue Sauce

MAKES ABOUT 1½ CUPS

Classic barbecue sauce must simmer for a long time to break down the tomatoes. However, we found that if you start with ketchup, you can shortcut the process. Use this sauce as you would any other barbecue sauce—brushed on foods during the last minutes of grilling and served at the table as a dipping sauce.

1	medium onion, peeled and quartered
1	cup ketchup
2	tablespoons cider vinegar
2	tablespoons Worcestershire sauce
2	tablespoons Dijon mustard
5	tablespoons molasses
1	teaspoon hot pepper sauce, such as Tabasco
¼	teaspoon ground black pepper
1½	teaspoons liquid smoke (optional)
2	tablespoons vegetable oil
1	medium garlic clove, minced
1	teaspoon chili powder
¼	teaspoon cayenne pepper

1. Process the onion and ¼ cup water in the workbowl of a food processor fitted with the steel blade until pureed and the mixture resembles slush, about 30 seconds. Pass the mixture through a fine-mesh strainer into a liquid measuring cup, pressing on the solids with a rubber spatula to obtain ½ cup juice. Discard the solids in the strainer.

2. Whisk the onion juice, ketchup, vinegar, Worcestershire, mustard, molasses, hot pepper sauce, black pepper, and liquid smoke (if using) together in a medium bowl.

3. Heat the oil in a large nonreactive saucepan over medium heat until shimmering but not smoking. Add the garlic, chili powder, and cayenne pepper; cook until fragrant, about 30 seconds. Whisk in the ketchup mixture and bring to a boil; reduce the heat to medium-low and simmer gently, uncovered, until the flavors meld and the sauce is thickened, about 25 minutes. Cool the sauce to room temperature before using. (The sauce can be refrigerated in airtight container for up to 1 week.)

INGREDIENTS: Bottled Barbecue Sauces

Despite the best of intentions, there's not always time to make barbecue sauce. Even our quick recipe requires 10 minutes of prep time and a half hour of cooking time. It's no surprise that many cooks turn to bottled sauces.

We wondered if some brands of bottled barbecue sauce were much better than others. Are the "gourmet" brands worth the extra money, or will a supermarket brand suffice? We tasted 11 samples to find out.

Our panel preferred the more expensive sauces because they were the spiciest and had the strongest flavors. Tasters loved Mad Dog, Gates, and Stubb's, three boutique brands with distinctive flavors. All had good hits of vinegar and spice.

Sweet, ketchupy sauces landed at the bottom of the ranking. Most of the supermarket brands were in this group. The one exception was Bull's-Eye, which was sweet, but not overly so. It also had a fair amount of smoke. Heinz, KC Masterpiece, and Kraft rated much lower. When we checked the ingredient labels after the tasting, we found that most of the low-rated sauces contained corn syrup and starch. These ingredients were associated with gooey, syrupy sweet sauces.

As with our homemade recipes, bottled sauces are finishing sauces, not basting sauces. They all contain sugar and tomatoes, which will cause foods to burn within minutes after application. Don't marinate food destined for the grill in barbecue sauce. The food will burn and taste awful. Just brush on a little sauce during the last two or three minutes of cooking and then brush again just before serving.

Sweet-Sour-Spicy Barbecue Sauce

MAKES ABOUT ¾ CUP

We developed this highly acidic sauce for beef ribs. It is quite strong, so brush only a little bit of the sauce onto the ribs to begin with. If you like your sauce especially spicy, add another ¼ teaspoon of cayenne pepper.

½	cup distilled white vinegar
2	tablespoons tomato paste
1	tablespoon salt
¼	cup sugar
1	tablespoon sweet paprika
1	teaspoon dried mustard
1	teaspoon ground black pepper
¼	teaspoon cayenne pepper
¼	teaspoon onion powder
¼	teaspoon garlic powder
¼	teaspoon chili powder
2	tablespoons vegetable oil

1. Mix the vinegar, tomato paste, salt, and sugar together in a medium bowl. In another bowl, combine the paprika, dried mustard, black pepper, cayenne pepper, onion powder, garlic powder, and chili powder.

2. Heat the oil in a small saucepan over medium heat. Add the spice mixture and cook until sizzling and fragrant, 30 to 45 seconds. Stir in the vinegar mixture and increase the heat to high. Bring to a boil, reduce the heat to low, and simmer for 5 minutes. Remove the pan from the heat and cool to room temperature. (The sauce can be refrigerated in an airtight container for up to 1 week.)

Eastern North Carolina–Style Barbecue Sauce

MAKES ABOUT 2 CUPS

This sauce contains no tomato but is rich with heat and vinegar. It is traditionally served with pulled pork (page 273) but can also be brushed onto ribs or brisket.

1	cup distilled white vinegar
1	cup cider vinegar
1	tablespoon sugar

1	tablespoon hot red pepper flakes
1	tablespoon hot red pepper sauce, such as Tabasco
	Salt and ground black pepper

Mix all ingredients, including salt and pepper to taste, together in a medium bowl. (The sauce can be refrigerated in an airtight container for several days.)

Mid–South Carolina Mustard Sauce

MAKES 2½ CUPS

Another classic sauce for pulled pork that works well with most any cut of grilled pork.

1	cup cider vinegar
6	tablespoons Dijon mustard
2	tablespoons maple syrup or honey
4	teaspoons Worcestershire sauce
1	teaspoon hot red pepper sauce, such as Tabasco
1	cup vegetable oil
2	teaspoons salt
	Ground black pepper

Mix all ingredients, including pepper to taste, in a medium bowl. (The sauce can be refrigerated in an airtight container for several days.)

Sweetened Soy Glaze

MAKES 1 GENEROUS CUP

This Asian barbecue sauce is more traditional than the recipe for Barbecue Sauce with Asian Flavors on page 297 because it does not contain any tomato products. It is great on beef ribs.

½	cup soy sauce
¼	cup water
¼	cup sugar
1	tablespoon rice vinegar
2	teaspoons minced fresh ginger
1	medium garlic clove, minced
2	teaspoons cornstarch dissolved in 1 tablespoon cold water
1	teaspoon Asian sesame oil
1	medium scallion, trimmed and sliced into thin rings

1. Mix the soy sauce, water, sugar, vinegar, ginger, and garlic together in a medium saucepan. Bring to a boil. Whisk in the cornstarch and cook for 1 minute.

2. Remove the pan from the heat and whisk in the sesame oil and scallion. (The glaze can be refrigerated in an airtight container for a day or two.)

Hoisin, Honey, and Ginger Glaze

MAKES ABOUT 1 1/2 CUPS

This glaze is great on ribs or any cut of pork.

1/2	cup soy sauce
1/4	cup ketchup
1/4	cup honey
2	tablespoons brown sugar
2	tablespoons lemon juice
1 1/2	tablespoons hoisin sauce
2	teaspoons vegetable oil
1	teaspoon minced fresh ginger
2	medium garlic cloves, minced

1. Mix the soy sauce, ketchup, honey, brown sugar, lemon juice, and hoisin sauce together in a medium bowl.

2. Heat the oil in a small saucepan over medium-high heat. Add the ginger and garlic and cook until fragrant but not browned, about 30 seconds. Add the soy mixture and bring to a boil. Cook for 1 minute and remove the pan from the heat. Cool to room temperature. (The glaze may be refrigerated in an airtight container for up to 1 week.)

Salsas, Salads, Relishes, Chutneys, and Slaws

THE CONDIMENT-LIKE SALADS IN THIS section are served at the table with grilled foods. Many are made with raw ingredients; the rest are lightly cooked. Most can be made in advance and refrigerated for several days. Bring all salsas and related salads (except those with dairy) to room temperature before serving.

The terms *salsa, salad,* and *relish* can be used interchangeably, although salsas are usually made with Latino ingredients or flavors. The term *slaw* is usually reserved for salads with cabbage and other shredded vegetables. *Chutney* usually refers to a cooked sauce with a jamlike consistency.

Classic Red Table Salsa

MAKES ABOUT 5 CUPS

Our Mexican-style salsa is equally good with fajitas, fish, or tortilla chips. To reduce the heat in the salsa, seed the chile.

3	large, very ripe tomatoes (about 2 pounds), cored and diced small
1/2	cup tomato juice
1	small jalapeño or other fresh chile, stemmed, seeded if desired, and minced
1	medium red onion, diced small
1	medium garlic clove, minced
1/2	cup chopped fresh cilantro leaves
1/2	cup lime juice
	Salt

Mix all ingredients, including salt to taste, together in a medium bowl. Refrigerate the salsa in an airtight container to blend flavors, at least 1 hour and up to 5 days.

Avocado-Corn Relish

MAKES ABOUT 2 CUPS

Serve this chunky salsa with fish or chicken.

1	ear corn, husked and cut in half
1	ripe but firm avocado, peeled, pitted, and diced large (see illustrations on page 300)
1/2	small red onion, diced small
1/2	small red bell pepper, cored, seeded, and diced small
2	tablespoons extra-virgin olive oil
1 1/2	tablespoons red wine vinegar
1	medium garlic clove, minced
	Dash hot red pepper sauce, or to taste
1	teaspoon ground cumin
1/4	teaspoon chili powder
1 1/2	tablespoons chopped fresh oregano leaves
2 1/2	tablespoons lime juice
	Salt and ground black pepper

1. Bring about 1 quart of water to a boil in a medium saucepan. Add the corn and boil until just cooked, 3 to 5 minutes. Drain and rinse the corn under cold, running water. Cut the kernels from each half of the cob.

2. Mix the corn with remaining ingredients, including salt and pepper to taste, in a medium bowl. (The relish can be refrigerated in an airtight container for 1 day.)

Chunky Guacamole

MAKES 2 1/2 TO 3 CUPS

Guacamole is an essential companion to fajitas with grilled flank steak. To minimize the risk of discoloration, prepare the minced ingredients first so they are ready to mix with the avocados as soon as they are cut. Ripe avocados are essential here. To test for ripeness, flick the small stem off the end of the avocado. If it comes off easily and you can see green underneath it, the avocado is ripe. If it does not come off or if you see brown underneath, the avocado is not ripe.

PREPARING AN AVOCADO

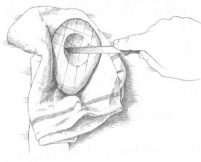

1. Use a dish towel to hold the avocado steady. Make 1/2-inch crosshatch incisions in the flesh of each avocado half with a dinner knife, cutting down to but not through the skin.

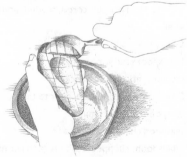

2. Separate the diced flesh from the skin using a spoon inserted between the skin and flesh, gently scooping out the avocado cubes.

3	medium, ripe avocados (preferably pebbly-skinned Haas)
2	tablespoons minced onion
I	medium garlic clove, minced
I	small jalapeño chile, stemmed and minced
1/4	cup minced fresh cilantro leaves
1/4	teaspoon salt
1/2	teaspoon ground cumin (optional)
2	tablespoons lime juice

1. Halve one avocado, remove the pit, and scoop the flesh into a medium bowl. Mash the flesh lightly with the onion, garlic, chile, cilantro, salt, and cumin (if using) with the tines of a fork until just combined.

2. Halve and pit the remaining two avocados. Make 1/2-inch crosshatch incisions in the flesh of each avocado half with a dinner knife, cutting down to but not through the skin (see illustration 1, at left). Separate the diced flesh from the skin using a spoon inserted between the skin and flesh, gently scooping out the avocado cubes (see illustration 2). Add the cubes to the bowl with the mashed avocado mixture.

3. Sprinkle lime juice over the diced avocado and mix the entire contents of the bowl lightly with a fork until combined but still chunky. Adjust the seasonings with salt, if necessary, and serve. (The guacamole can be covered with plastic wrap, pressed directly onto the surface of the mixture, and refrigerated up to 1 day. Return the guacamole to room temperature, removing the plastic wrap just before serving.)

Black Bean and Mango Salsa

MAKES 2 1/2 CUPS

This Caribbean-inspired mixture is great with grilled fish, pork, or chicken. It's also very tasty as a snack with tortilla chips. See page 207 for instructions on removing the skin and pit from a mango.

1/2	cup cooked black beans
I	mango, peeled, pitted, and diced small
1/4	medium red bell pepper, cored, seeded, and diced small
1/4	medium green bell pepper, cored, seeded, and diced small
1/4	medium red onion, diced small

6	tablespoons pineapple juice
¼	cup lime juice
¼	cup chopped fresh cilantro leaves
1	tablespoon ground cumin
½	small jalapeño or other fresh chile, stemmed, seeded, and minced
	Salt and ground black pepper

Mix all ingredients, including salt and pepper to taste, together in a medium bowl. Refrigerate the salsa in an airtight container to blend the flavors, at least 1 hour or up to 4 days.

Red Pepper–Jícama Slaw

MAKES ABOUT 3 ½ CUPS

This crunchy, refreshing slaw is mildly sweet, making it a good foil to spicy foods.

1 ½	tablespoons lime juice
¼	teaspoon ground cumin
¼	teaspoon chili powder
2	teaspoons honey
¼	teaspoon salt
3	tablespoons vegetable oil
	Ground black pepper
1	medium red pepper, cored, seeded, and cut into thin strips
½	small jícama (8 ounces), tough outer skin removed and cut into thin matchsticks (see illustrations below)
1	medium Granny Smith apple, quartered, cored, and cut into ¼-inch dice
2	small scallions, thinly sliced

1. Whisk lime juice, cumin, chili powder, honey, salt, oil, and pepper to taste together in a small bowl.

2. Place the red pepper, jícama, apple, and scallions in a large bowl and pour the dressing over the top; toss to coat. Adjust the seasonings. (The slaw can be refrigerated in an airtight container for several hours.)

Spicy Yellow Pepper and Tomato Salsa

MAKES ABOUT 2 CUPS

Depending on how hot you like your salsa, you can add or omit the seeds and ribs from the jalapeño chile. This salsa is perfect with grilled fish.

2	small tomatoes (about ½ pound), cored and cut into ¼-inch dice
½	medium yellow bell pepper, cored, seeded, and cut into ¼-inch dice (about ½ cup)
¼	cup finely chopped red onion
½	medium jalapeño chile, stemmed, seeded if desired, and minced (see note above)
1	tablespoon lime juice
1	tablespoon chopped fresh cilantro leaves
½	teaspoon bottled hot sauce (optional)
1	medium garlic clove, minced
½	teaspoon salt
¼	teaspoon sugar

Mix all the ingredients together in a medium bowl. Cover and refrigerate to blend flavors, at least 1 hour and preferably overnight. (The salsa can be refrigerated in an airtight container for several days.)

PREPARING JÍCAMA

1. Slice the jícama in half through its equator.

2. Use a paring knife to peel the brown outer skin.

3. Place each half flat-side down on the cutting board and slice into half circles ⅛ inch thick.

4. Stack the half-circles and slice lengthwise into thin matchsticks.

Grilled Corn Salsa

MAKES ABOUT 2 CUPS

A great use for leftover grilled corn that has not been buttered. Serve this salsa with tortilla chips or, better yet, as a condiment for grilled seafood or chicken.

2	ears grilled corn (see recipe on page 183), kernels cut from cobs (about 1 cup)
1	medium red bell pepper, cored, seeded, and diced small
1	medium scallion, sliced thin
1	small garlic clove, minced
1/2	medium jalapeño chile, stemmed, seeded, and minced
1 1/2	tablespoons corn or vegetable oil
1 1/2	tablespoons lime juice
1	teaspoon ground cumin
1	tablespoon chopped fresh cilantro leaves
	Salt

Place all ingredients, including salt to taste, in a medium bowl. Toss and adjust the seasonings. (The salsa can be refrigerated in an airtight container for 1 day.)

Fresh Mango Salsa

MAKES 2 CUPS

This salsa goes especially well with pork, duck, and grilled fish. See page 207 for tips on preparing the mangoes.

2	medium mangoes (3/4 pound each), peeled, pitted, and cut into 1/4-inch dice (about 1 1/2 cups total)
1/2	medium red onion, minced
2	scallions, sliced thin
1/2	medium jalapeño chile, stemmed, seeded if desired, and minced
1	tablespoon lime juice
2	tablespoons minced fresh cilantro leaves
	Salt and ground black pepper

Mix all ingredients, including salt and pepper to taste, together in a medium bowl. (The salsa can be refrigerated in an airtight container for several days.)

Horseradish Cream Sauce

MAKES ABOUT 1 CUP

This sauce is a classic with beef as well as salmon. The sauce will be looser and creamier if made with crème fraîche but is also delicious with sour cream.

1	cup crème fraîche or sour cream
2	tablespoons prepared horseradish, or more to taste
2	tablespoons minced fresh chives
	Pinch salt

Combine all ingredients in a small bowl. (The sauce can be refrigerated in an airtight container overnight.)

Mojo Sauce

MAKES 1 GENEROUS CUP

This Cuban citrus sauce is delicious with pork, fish, or chicken.

1/2	cup extra-virgin olive oil
6	medium garlic cloves, minced (about 2 tablespoons)
1/2	teaspoon ground cumin
1/2	cup orange juice
1/4	cup lime juice
1	teaspoon salt
1/2	teaspoon ground black pepper

1. Heat the oil in a small, deep saucepan over medium heat. Add the garlic and cumin and cook until fragrant but not browned, about 30 to 45 seconds.

2. Remove the pan from the heat and add the orange juice, lime juice, salt, and pepper. Place the pan back over the heat and bring to a simmer, cooking for another minute. Remove the pan from the heat and cool the sauce to room temperature. (The sauce can be refrigerated in an airtight container for up to 3 days.)

Quick Onion and Parsley Relish

MAKES GENEROUS ¾ CUP

Serve with lamb or beef.

½	medium red onion, diced small
½	cup chopped fresh parsley leaves
¼	cup extra-virgin olive oil
¼	cup lemon juice
	Salt and ground black pepper

Mix the onion, parsley, olive oil, and lemon juice together in a small bowl. Season to taste with salt and pepper. (The relish can be covered and set aside at room temperature for several hours.)

Cucumber Salad with Yogurt and Mint

MAKES ABOUT 3½ CUPS

Creamy yogurt salads like this one are known as raita in India, where they are served as a cooling contrast with curry dishes.

1	cup plain low-fat yogurt
2	tablespoons extra-virgin olive oil
¼	cup minced fresh mint leaves
2	small garlic cloves, minced
	Salt and ground black pepper
3	medium cucumbers, sliced, salted, and drained (see illustrations below)

Whisk the yogurt, oil, mint, garlic, and salt and pepper to taste together in a medium bowl. Add the cucumbers and toss to coat. Adjust the seasonings. (The salad can be refrigerated in an airtight container for several hours.)

Curried Fruit Chutney with Lime and Ginger

MAKES ABOUT 4 CUPS

Beef is a good choice with curried fruits. Unlike most chutneys, this one is only lightly cooked, so the fruits remain distinct.

1	tablespoon olive oil
1	small onion, halved and sliced very thin
1	tablespoon minced fresh ginger
1	large garlic clove, minced
1½	teaspoons ground coriander
1	teaspoon curry powder
½	teaspoon ground cinnamon
½	teaspoon hot red pepper flakes
½	medium mango, peeled, pitted, and cut into ¼-inch dice (see page 207)
1	medium peach, peeled, pitted, and quartered
1	medium plum, pitted and quartered
1	medium apricot, peeled, pitted, and quartered
1	medium nectarine, peeled, pitted, and quartered
1	tablespoon orange juice
2	tablespoons lime juice
	Salt and ground black pepper

SALTING CUCUMBERS

1. Peel and halve each cucumber lengthwise. Use a small spoon to remove the seeds and surrounding liquid from each cucumber half.

2. Lay the cucumber halves flat-side down on a work surface and slice them on the diagonal into ¼-inch-thick pieces.

3. Toss the cucumbers and salt (1 teaspoon for each cucumber) in a colander set in a bowl. Place a gallon-sized plastic bag filled with water on top of the cucumbers to weigh them down and force out the liquid. Drain for at least 1 hour and up to 3 hours.

1. Heat the oil in a large saucepan over medium-high heat until shimmering. Add the onion and sauté until lightly browned, 4 to 5 minutes. Add the ginger and garlic and sauté until fragrant, about 1 minute.

2. Lower the heat to medium and add the remaining ingredients, including salt and pepper to taste. Cook until the fruits start to soften but have not fallen apart, about 5 minutes. Adjust the seasonings. (The chutney can be refrigerated in an airtight container for several days.)

Dried Peach and Apple Salad with Almonds and Cumin

MAKES ABOUT 4 CUPS

Dried apricots, plums, or nectarines can be substituted for the dried peaches in this North African–style salad. Although this salad would seldom be eaten with pork in North Africa, its ingredients are a perfect match for this meat. Any mild-flavored fish, such as snapper or mahi-mahi, also works well with this salad. Toast the almonds in a dry skillet over medium heat until fragrant, about 5 minutes.

6	ounces dried peaches, cut into ¼-inch strips (about 2 cups)
¼	cup dry red wine
¼	cup warm water
1½	teaspoons minced fresh ginger
2	small tart apples, quartered, cored, and sliced thin
¼	cup blanched, slivered almonds, toasted
2	tablespoons brown sugar
½	teaspoon ground coriander
½	teaspoon ground cumin
¼	teaspoon cayenne pepper
2	tablespoons lime juice
2	tablespoons orange juice
2	tablespoons minced fresh cilantro leaves
	Salt and ground black pepper

1. Soak the peaches in a medium bowl with the wine and water until tender, about 15 minutes.

2. Mix the ginger, apples, almonds, sugar, coriander, cumin, and cayenne together in a medium bowl. Stir in the peaches and their liquid, along with the lime juice, orange juice, cilantro, and salt and pepper to taste. (The salad can be refrigerated in an airtight container for several hours.)

Pureed Red Pepper Sauce with Basil

MAKES ABOUT 1 CUP

Most pureed bell pepper sauces call for roasted, peeled peppers. In this recipe, diced raw peppers are sweated in a covered pan until very tender and then pureed to create a rich, thick sauce. Serve with pork, chicken, or white-fleshed fish such as snapper.

1½	tablespoons extra-virgin olive oil
1	small onion, chopped
1	large red bell pepper, cored, seeded, and diced
½	cup canned low-sodium chicken broth
1	medium garlic clove, minced
2	tablespoons minced fresh basil leaves
1–2	teaspoons balsamic vinegar
	Salt and ground black pepper

1. Heat the oil in a small saucepan over medium heat. Add the onion and sauté until softened, about 3 minutes. Reduce the heat to low. Add the red pepper, cover, and cook, stirring frequently, until very tender, 15 to 20 minutes.

2. Transfer the mixture to a blender or food processor. Add the broth and process until smooth.

3. Return the mixture to a clean saucepan. Add the garlic and simmer to blend flavors, about 5 minutes. (The sauce can be refrigerated in an airtight container for several days. When ready to serve, reheat the sauce gently.) Stir in the basil and season with vinegar, salt, and pepper to taste. Serve immediately.

Warm Cucumber and Red Onion Relish with Mint

MAKES ABOUT 2 CUPS

This relish is perfect with salmon but works with most fish.

5	tablespoons extra-virgin olive oil
2	medium cucumbers, halved, seeded, and sliced thin
1	medium red onion, halved and sliced thin
	Salt and ground black pepper
2	tablespoons red wine vinegar
2	tablespoons chopped fresh mint leaves

1. Heat 2 tablespoons of oil in a large skillet. Add the cucumbers and sauté over medium-high heat until lightly colored, about 2 minutes. Add the onion and salt and pepper to taste. Cook just until the vegetables turn translucent, about 2 minutes longer.

2. Turn the cucumber mixture into a medium bowl. Stir in the vinegar, mint, and remaining 3 tablespoons of oil. Adjust the seasonings. Serve warm.

Tomatillo-Chile Sauce

MAKES ABOUT 1 CUP

Serve this tart, fragrant sauce with seafood, beef, or even chicken. Vary the amount of chiles as desired.

1/2	pound fresh tomatillos, husked and washed
1–2	medium jalapeño or serrano chiles, stemmed and seeded
2	tablespoons chopped fresh cilantro leaves
1/2	small onion, chopped
1	small garlic clove, chopped
1 1/2	teaspoons vegetable oil
1/2	cup canned low-sodium chicken broth
	Salt

1. Place the tomatillos and chiles in a medium saucepan and add water to cover. Bring to a boil, cover, and simmer until barely tender, about 8 minutes. Drain and transfer the tomatillos and chiles to a blender or food processor. Add the cilantro, onion, and garlic and pulse to a coarse puree.

2. Heat the oil in a medium skillet over medium-high heat until shimmering. Add the tomatillo puree all at once and cook, stirring often, until the mixture darkens and thickens, about 5 minutes. Add the broth and simmer, stirring occasionally, over medium heat until the mixture thickens, 10 to 15 minutes. Season with salt to taste. (The sauce can be refrigerated in an airtight container for 2 days.)

Onion, Black Olive, and Caper Relish

MAKES ABOUT 2 CUPS

This intensely flavored, highly acidic relish complements fish, especially bluefish and tuna.

1/2	cup extra-virgin olive oil
2	medium onions, halved and sliced thin
6	medium garlic cloves, sliced thin
1/2	cup black olives, such as kalamatas, pitted and chopped coarse
1/4	cup drained capers
2	anchovy fillets, minced
1/4	cup balsamic vinegar
1	teaspoon minced fresh marjoram or oregano leaves
2	tablespoons minced fresh parsley leaves
	Salt and ground black pepper

1. Heat 2 tablespoons of oil in a large skillet. Add the onions and sauté over medium heat until softened, about 5 minutes. Add the garlic and sauté until fragrant, about 1 minute longer.

2. Turn the onion mixture into a medium bowl. Stir in the remaining ingredients, including salt (use sparingly) and pepper to taste. Serve warm or at room temperature. (The relish can be covered and set aside at room temperature for several hours.)

INDEX